PROGRAMMING BUSINESS SYSTEMS WITH BASIC

David R. Adams
Associate Professor of Information Systems
Department of Business Administration
Northern Kentucky University
Highland Heights, Kentucky

William E. Leigh
Associate Professor
Department of Computer and Information Science
School of Science at Indianapolis
Purdue University
Indianapolis, Indiana

Published by

J98   **SOUTH-WESTERN PUBLISHING CO.**

CINCINNATI   WEST CHICAGO, ILL.   DALLAS   PELHAM MANOR, N.Y.   PALO ALTO, CALIF.

Copyright © 1984
by South-Western Publishing Co.
Cincinnati, Ohio

ISBN: 0-538-10980-7

Library of Congress Catalog Card Number: 83-51622

1 2 3 4 5 6 7 8 D 7 6 5 4

Printed in the United States of America

CONTENTS

JIM GERBER

PART II. APPLICATION DEVELOPMENT

PREFACE

COMPUTER PROGRAMS AND PROGRAMMING

Computers are a fact of life. Wherever you go, whatever you do, you will encounter a computer or computer-produced goods and services—every day. Although computers affect people in ways that were unimaginable only a few decades ago, people themselves still retain final control over computers. People are the designers, builders, and operators of computers. People employ computers and bring them into service to fulfill human needs. Thus, the need for people to understand and use computers has become almost as important as the need for people to read and write.

One of the main ways in which people control computers is through computer *programs*. Programs are sets of instructions that operate computers and control their processing activities. Programs tell the computer the steps to follow in carrying out the work required. Computer programs, or *software*, control the operations of devices as complex as satellites, as mundane as home appliances, and as entertaining as video games.

Computer programming, or the process of developing computer programs, is an industry in itself. Today, you can purchase computer software to design buildings, to conduct geological surveys, to maintain complete sets of accounting records for a business, to diagnose illnesses, to play games with you, and even to teach you how to program a computer. Computer programming has become an important and rapidly growing occupational area as well as a popular pastime for the hundreds of thousands of people who own personal computers.

COMPUTER INFORMATION SYSTEMS

This book is about computer programs, programming, and the effective use of computers in business-type organizations. More specifically, the text explains the development of computer software as the basis for a *computer information system (CIS)*. Computer information systems provide administrative and management information required for the successful operation of businesses. A CIS facilitates the flow of work through a company and provides decision-making information for managers and top-level executives. Thus, the kinds of programs and programming activities discussed in this text are applicable to computer-based systems in business, government, education, and most manufacturing and service organizations.

This book presents a programming approach based on the most current research and practices in software design and development. Programming is treated as a rigorous, systematic process worthy of a disciplined approach similar to that used in the engineering disciplines. However, this approach does not discount that programming can be rewarding and enjoyable.

THE BASIC LANGUAGE

Computer programs are written in special *programming languages* that computers can understand and execute. BASIC is one of the most popular of these languages and is the language used throughout this book. BASIC (an acronym for Beginner's All-purpose Symbolic Instruction Code) was developed by professors John Kemeny and Thomas Kurtz at Dartmouth College as a vehicle for teaching computer programming.

Although the BASIC language is easy to learn, its commands are powerful and versatile. Thus, BASIC has become the most popular language used on most minicomputers and microcomputers. With the rising popularity of these types of small computer systems in business, BASIC also has become an important business applications programming language. In fact, virtually all microcomputers now being delivered and installed for business applications are supported by some variety of BASIC.

ORGANIZATION OF THIS BOOK

Chapter 1 contains a brief review of computer software and hardware components. Also discussed are the types of files encountered by programmers and the elements of information systems that require programs or *systems of programs*.

In Chapter 2, a framework for program development is presented. This five-step development process is provided as a guide for you to follow in working through every program and programming assignment in this book. The discussion of these steps stresses the importance of programming as a mental, problem-solving process that you work through independent of computer languages and hardware considerations.

In Chapters 3 through 8, you use the five-step process described in Chapter 2 to design, write, and operate programs that are integrated to implement a computer system. These chapters present programming techniques and programs that are used to create and operate a hypothetical business system. *Master* and *transaction* files are discussed as the bases of most computer information systems.

Chapter 3 explains procedures for creating master files, which serve as the foundation upon which all other computer files are built.

Chapters 4 and 5 discuss the production of computer-generated reports used by business managers to guide a company's operations effectively and efficiently. Information contained in computer files is provided to management primarily through the printing of reports that either detail or summarize file content.

Chapters 6, 7, and 8 explain the creation of transaction files and ways in which these files are used to keep master file information accurate and up-to-date.

Chapters 9, 10, and 11 augment the first two sections of the book with presentations on file processing techniques used in actual businesses. Due to the large sizes of computer files within a business system and the special, tailored needs of businesses themselves, real-world systems design requires programmers to challenge their creative abilities and technical skills in solving unique problems.

Appendixes A and B contain the case study material that you use to create your own information system.

ACKNOWLEDGMENT

An important contribution toward assurance of the quality of this book was made by Kamiran S. Badrkhan, Assistant Dean, Computer Science and Electronics, at Los Angeles Trade Technical College, Los Angeles, CA, who reviewed the manuscript and provided important support and suggestions.

I
PROGRAMMING STRATEGIES AND TECHNIQUES

Part I of this text has two chapters that lay a foundation upon which computer programming skills can be built. Topics covered include basic strategies for analyzing problems and developing computer-based solutions, as well as techniques for implementing these solutions as computer programs.

The first chapter serves as a review, an introduction, or both—depending upon your own situation. This chapter includes a brief survey of computer devices and their functions. Programs are explained within a context of systems. That is, programs do not exist for their own sake, but implement systems. Systems, in turn, solve problems or meet needs.

Because programs do not exist on their own as independent entities, care and thought must go into their development. Chapter 2 outlines a process, or set of orderly procedures, that will help you to use your own time efficiently and will help you to develop programs of high quality that are produced at a reasonable cost.

1
COMPUTERS, PROGRAMS, AND SYSTEMS

OVERVIEW AND OBJECTIVES

This chapter reviews the basic concepts and components of computers and computer systems. Three types of computer information systems and their common features are discussed. Also, the chapter presents an overview of the principal types of programs that are developed to implement computer information systems and of the general context within which systems of computer programs are developed for business.

When you complete your work in this chapter, you should be able to:

☐ Describe what a computer is.

☐ List and describe the main components of computer systems.

☐ Identify the three types of computer information systems used in business and describe the general functions of each.

☐ Name the two types of files that support most computer information systems and describe the functions of each type.

☐ Name and describe the basic types of programs from which most computer information systems are built.

COMPUTER PROCESSING

In concept, a computer is a very simple device. Basically, a computer performs arithmetic and logical operations. Whenever it is provided with *data*, or facts and figures, a computer can process them by applying addition, subtraction, multiplication, division, or other kinds of arithmetic. The computer also can perform logical operations on the data and compare two values to determine whether one is greater than, equal to, or less than the second. Apart from some additional computer operations necessary to get data into and out of the computer and to move them internally, there is little more that a computer can do at an operational level—regardless of its size or its cost.

The simplistic nature of these capabilities is highlighted by the fact that such functions are referred to as *primitives.* These primitive functions represent the total capabilities available on any computer. These limitations, in turn, mean that a computer requires the intelligence of people to select and organize those operations in meaningful ways that cause the computer to carry out demanding tasks.

COMPUTER PROGRAMS

A computer can perform its data processing tasks without human intervention by following the instructions provided to it in a *computer program.* A program is a listing of the operations that the computer carries out to process data. It is a set of detailed instructions establishing the sequence in which processing activities must be performed to produce the desired results. Once this set of instructions has been placed inside the computer, the equipment can execute automatically the processing called for. Computer programs, or *software,* are the primary tools that people use to bring computers into their service.

Computer programs are written by people. The computer is capable of doing no more, nor any less, than it is instructed to do. The people who write these programs and solve the problems are called *computer programmers.* Programmers determine the sequence of separate computer operations required to solve a specific problem.

To use a computer, therefore, people must supply two requirements—programs and data. A program is prepared and placed inside the computer. Then, control is turned over to the computer, which follows the instructions in the program. Under program control, the computer accesses the data that are provided and processes them according to the instructions.

COMPUTER SYSTEM

The computer itself, along with other devices for getting programs and data into and out of the computer, is called the *computer system.* Most computer systems include four types of *hardware,* or pieces of equipment. These are:

- The *processor unit,* which has two parts—computer *memory,* where programs and data reside temporarily during processing, and the *central processing unit (CPU),* where the arithmetic and logical operations take place.
- *Input units,* which are used to enter programs and data into memory.
- *Output units,* which print or display programs and the results of processing.
- *Storage units,* which are used as files for long-term retention of programs and data within the computer system.

These four units, represented in Figure 1-1, are present in all computer systems—regardless of size and cost. The major differences among computers are in their processing speeds, their memory capacities, and in the varieties of input, output, and storage devices available.

COMPUTERS AND PROBLEM SOLVING

Computers are general-purpose data processing devices. That is, a computer can perform any type of work and solve any type of problem as long as it is provided with the instructions for performing the task and the needed data. These instructions must be drawn from the limited repertoire of input, arithmetic, logical, output, and storage operations available for any given computer. If people can devise solutions to problems and describe those solutions in terms of basic computer operations, the range of problems to which the computer can be applied is virtually limitless.

In essence, then, computer programming is a mental, problem-solving process. It is the process through which people apply intelligence to problems to evolve computer solutions.

COMPUTERS IN BUSINESS

Most people will encounter computers or work with computers in the business world. As employees or customers of business, government, education, or other kinds of production and service industries, people either will use computers in their jobs or will be affected by computers in some way. Business computer applications are the most pervasive in today's society.

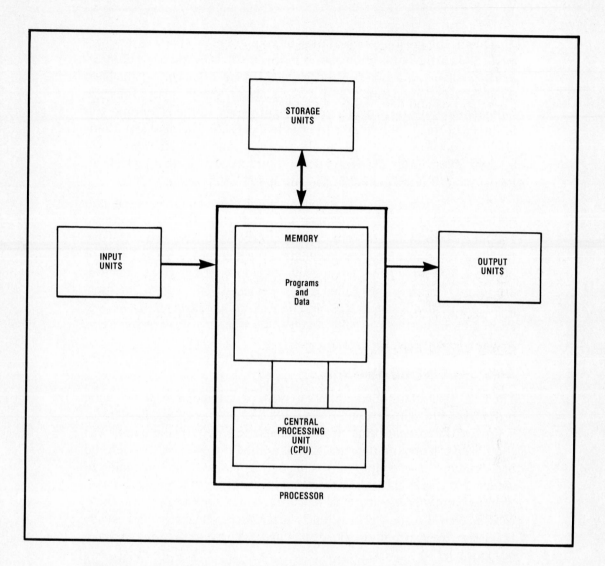

Figure 1-1. A computer system consists of four types of hardware: input units, a processor unit, output units, and storage units.

Computers have been used in business only since the early 1950s. Yet, during this time, the computer has been a vital force in the production and distribution of goods and services. From the time a new product or service is conceived until it is delivered to the consumer, it is likely that a computer was involved in the process.

One of the most important uses of computers in business, and the application area that is emphasized in this book, is as the basis of *information systems*. Information is the life-blood of any organization, the basis on which decisions are made in managing a business enterprise. The right information must be provided to the right people at the right time and in the right form. Only then can effective decisions be made. Without effective decisions, the organization cannot survive. Therefore, the systems of hardware, software, people, and procedures that provide information are fundamental to the success of using organizations.

Today, the computer is playing a vital role in management and decision making. Through *computer information systems (CIS)*, accurate and timely information is being captured, processed, and made available for planning, controlling, and facilitating the administrative activities of business. The three general categories of computer-based systems that are found in business are called *data processing systems (DPS), management information systems (MIS)*, and *decision support systems (DSS)*. Programming in business usually involves producing software for these kinds of systems.

Data Processing Systems

The first applications of computers in business were of a record-keeping or bookkeeping nature. Computers were used to record business transactions and to prepare reports on business activity. The computer was used primarily to automate and facilitate the flow of work through the organization, to account for business transactions, and to maintain company records. These data processing systems are still the workhorses of most computer installations, since the computer can perform these clerical, record-keeping chores much faster, more accurately, and usually at far less expense than people. A data processing system is diagrammed in Figure 1-2.

Management Information Systems

The next step in using computers in business was in assisting managers in making routine decisions. In the 1960s, computers became the basis for management information systems. In an MIS, as shown in Figure 1-3, the computer prepares summary reports to management on business activity. These summaries consist of totals for groups of data items and provide information on trends in operations and on business operations that have veered off course from plans and expected outcomes.

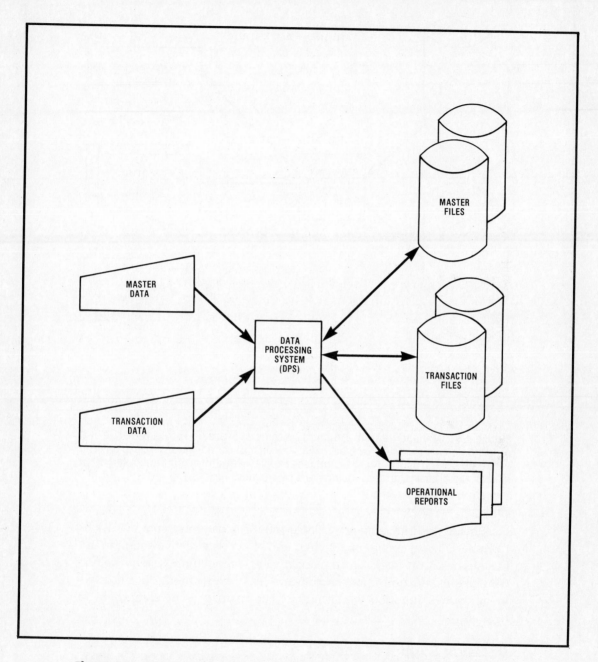

Figure 1-2. Data processing systems (DPS) are used to create and maintain the files of master and transaction data. Such data represent the day-to-day business activities of an organization. A DPS also is used to produce operational reports and other documents that facilitate the daily flow of work through a company.

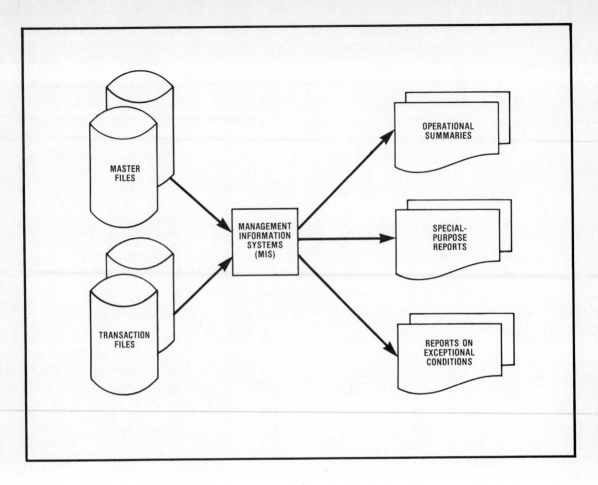

Figure 1-3. Management information systems (MIS) are used to summarize and report on business activity so that managers can correct deviations from plans and expected performance. An MIS produces reports from information contained in master and transaction files maintained by the data processing system.

Having this information available allows managers to spot deviations from the normal course of activities and to take corrective action to put business back on track. Thus, management information systems help to control business operations once plans are implemented. This management control function is still one of the main uses of computers in business.

Decision Support Systems

Today the computer is being used to support the planning functions of top-level managers and executives. Decision support systems like those illustrated in Figure 1-4 can project the results of decisions before they

8

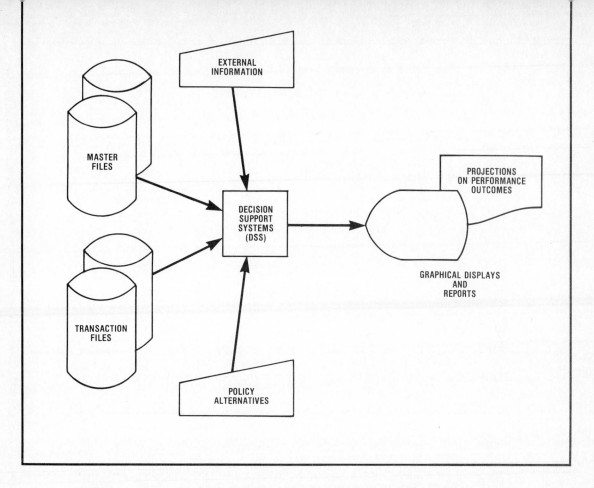

Figure 1-4. Decision support systems (DSS) analyze the current status of a business and project the results of various policies under consideration. Input data for a DSS include master and transaction data maintained by the company and information regarding the economy, government policies, competitors, and other entities that affect the organization.

are made to allow managers to evaluate the consequences of decisions before committing company resources to them. It is not uncommon nowadays to find computer terminals located in the executive offices and boardrooms. Such computers are helping to formulate policies and plans for the long-term growth and success of business enterprises.

These three general types of information systems operate at three levels of a business organization. As shown in Figure 1-5, at the *operational level*, data processing systems use computers to facilitate the flow of work through the company and to record and maintain information on day-to-day business activity. At the middle-management level, or *control level*,

9

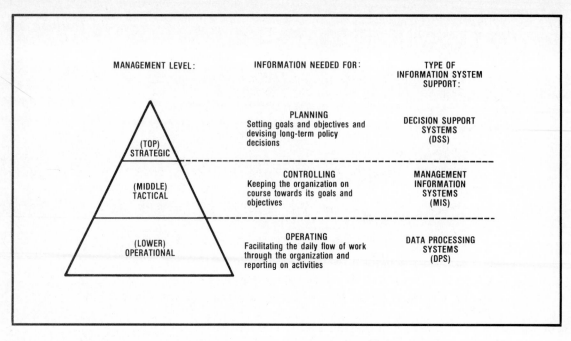

MANAGEMENT LEVEL:	INFORMATION NEEDED FOR:	TYPE OF INFORMATION SYSTEM SUPPORT:
(TOP) STRATEGIC	PLANNING Setting goals and objectives and devising long-term policy decisions	DECISION SUPPORT SYSTEMS (DSS)
(MIDDLE) TACTICAL	CONTROLLING Keeping the organization on course towards its goals and objectives	MANAGEMENT INFORMATION SYSTEMS (MIS)
(LOWER) OPERATIONAL	OPERATING Facilitating the daily flow of work through the organization and reporting on activities	DATA PROCESSING SYSTEMS (DPS)

Figure 1-5. Each of the three main types of computer information systems provides information for a particular level of management.

management information systems use computers to report on operational trends and deviations from plans so that corrective or sustaining action can be taken. Finally, at the executive level, or *planning level*, decision support systems use computers to project results of policies and plans so that top-level managers can evaluate consequences before implementing those plans.

COMPUTER FILES

Data processing, management information, and decision support systems all share common processing features. The main shared feature is that, fundamentally, all computer information systems are file processing systems.

A *file* is a repository for data and information. It is a storage area within the computer system in which information is kept so that it can be located and retrieved conveniently as needed. Usually, storage devices such as magnetic tape and magnetic disk are used for maintaining files.

A business organization generally maintains many different kinds of files: Personnel files contain information on company employees; billing files contain information on sales transactions; and inventory files contain information related to manufactured products and/or raw materials and supplies in stock. These and many other files are maintained to provide complete, up-to-date information on the operations and status of the business.

The word file is connected traditionally with an image of a filing cabinet filled with cardboard folders. The folders, or *records,* contain pieces of paper with items, or *fields,* of data pertaining to some person, object, or event. Usually, the file folders are set up to facilitate reference by printing an identifier (a *record key* in information system terms) on the tab of the file folder.

In computer files, information also is organized into fields and records. A field is a single item of data. A record is a collection of fields pertaining to a person, object, or event. Figure 1-6 shows a format, or layout, illustrating the inclusion of fields within a record. One or more

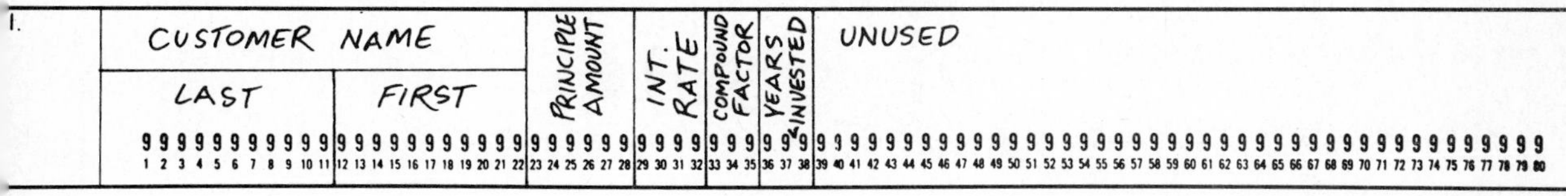

Figure 1-6. Format of fields for an investment input record.

records written together constitute a file. Normally, each record in a file is identified by and accessed through a record key. In computer files, which usually are kept on storage devices such as magnetic tapes or magnetic disks, the data are recorded electronically as series of magnetic spots. Otherwise, the methods of organizing the data are the same. Figure 1-7 diagrams the arrangement of records according to record keys on tape and disk files.

COMPUTER FILE PROCESSING

In terms of their functions, there are two main types of files used in computer information systems. These are *master files* and *transaction files.*

Master Files

Master files contain permanent or semipermanent information that represents the current status of a business. For example, an inventory file contains records showing, among other things, such data items as

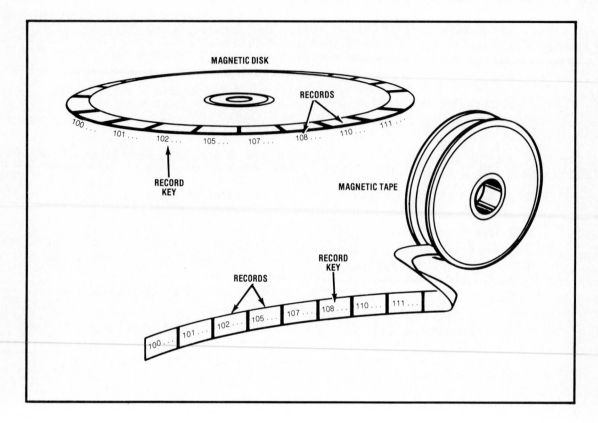

Figure 1-7. Records in a magnetic disk or tape file normally are arranged according to record keys, which facilitate access.

the product number, product name, manufacturing cost, and current stock of each item in inventory. An inventory-control manager might access this file to find out what quantity of stocked items were on hand to decide whether to purchase new supplies.

The master record for each inventory item, therefore, must be kept current. Whenever items are withdrawn from stock or new items are added, the inventory record should reflect those transactions. That is, the quantity-on-hand field should be *updated* by adding the number of items replaced or by subtracting the number of items withdrawn. Following updating, the file reflects the current status of the business and is the source of information used to manage, control, and plan for the company's inventory of products.

Transaction Files

Data contained in master files are updated regularly to reflect ongoing business activity. Therefore, in addition to master files, businesses maintain transaction files. These files are used for recording day-to-day business activity and for updating master files with this new information.

To continue the example, whenever items are withdrawn from inventory or are placed in inventory, a record of that event is created and written to a transaction file. Periodically—daily, hourly, or even at the time the transaction takes place—these transaction records are used to change the information in the master file to bring it up-to-date.

Master and transaction files are fundamental to most computer information systems. The creation of these files and the subsequent updating of master files with transaction data are the main functions of data processing systems. Accessing these files and reporting their content are the main functions of management information systems. Using these files to make projections based on their content are the main purposes of decision support systems. The programmer who works with computer-based information systems must be able to design and write file processing software. These types of programs are at the heart of every computer information system.

FILE PROCESSING SYSTEMS

As noted above, computer information systems are basically file processing systems. DPS, MIS, and DSS applications rely on files as their primary input. Because files and file processing techniques are a common denominator of all three types of information systems, there are common software components of these systems, as well. Further, regardless of the application area, file processing systems are built from only a few different types of programs. These generic program types, illustrated in Figure 1-8, are:

- File creation programs
- File updating programs
- Report writing programs
- File inquiry programs.

Virtually all computer information systems are built from these basic program types.

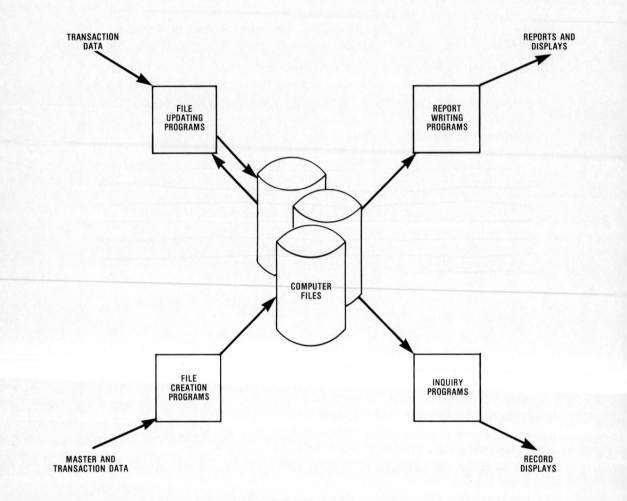

Figure 1-8. Computer information systems are basically file processing systems. The four main types of file processing programs are file creation, file updating, report writing, and file inquiry. These programs and files can be combined in various ways to build data processing, management information, and decision support systems.

File Creation Programs

File creation programs are necessary to build the master files and to create the transaction files that result from business activity. Master and transaction data normally are entered into the computer by a terminal operator who types the information on a keyboard. The computer processes these data by *formatting*, or arranging, the fields of data into standard record formats and then writing the records to the file. After the files are built, they can be used for additional processing applications.

File Updating Programs

File updating programs are used to keep the information in master files current. There are two general types of updating programs.

Posting programs update master files with transactions that result from normal, day-to-day business operations. For example, within a checking account file at a bank, a customer's master record will contain a field of data representing the account balance. Whenever the customer makes deposits or withdrawals, transaction records are created. Periodically, the balance field is updated to current status through posting of the transactions to the master file.

Maintenance programs keep master and transaction files correct and complete. Maintenance functions add new records to a file, delete old records from a file, or replace information that has changed or is in error with correct information. For instance, file maintenance at a bank would take place when a new customer opens an account, when a customer closes a bank account, or when an account balance has been discovered to be in error and the master record field must be changed.

Report Writing Programs

The main reason for keeping information in files is for access by people who need to know something about the business. Therefore, all information systems contain *report writing programs.* Two levels of reports are found in most systems.

Detail reports present all or most of the content of a file. Such reports show detailed information contained in file records and are used to provide a readable copy of the file. This kind of report can be used for verification of file content or as a data file itself within the manual, nonautomated portions of a system. Detail reports are useful to people at the operational level of a company, where there is a need for detailed information on day-to-day operations of the business.

Summary reports present the highlights of file content. These reports summarize information and, therefore, are useful to managers who do not have the time or the need to sift through all the data in detail reports.

Report writing can take place on a periodic basis, on demand, or on an exception basis.

Scheduled reports are issued at regular intervals. Some types of reports are prepared yearly, some quarterly, some monthly, some daily, and some even more frequently. The reporting period depends on the nature of the report.

On-demand, or *ad hoc, reports* are not regularly scheduled. Such reports are produced as needed to fulfill some special need that is not met by periodic, scheduled reports.

Exception reports are produced by the system whenever business operations are not proceeding according to plan. An exception report can be triggered by the computer whenever data in its files are not considered normal according to some given management criteria.

Reports can be presented in many different formats on many different output devices. Reports can be printed on paper as *hard-copy* output or displayed on video display screens. Reports also can be presented as charts and graphs on plotting devices or graphic terminals, and such graphic output can be displayed in a multitude of colors. All of these methods of reporting file content fall into the category of report writing.

Inquiry Programs

Often, output requirements involve immediate access to just one record in a file. For example, a bank teller might need to verify the status of a customer's account before cashing that person's check. The teller needs one particular record—immediately. For situations such as these, *inquiry programs* are used. These programs allow immediate, *on-line* access to files. Usually, file access is through computer terminals so that information can be printed back or displayed on the terminal printer or screen.

Virtually all computer information systems provide one or more of these types of outputs. Therefore, people who work as business application programmers will usually be responsible for developing file creation, file updating, report writing, and inquiry processing programs. The remaining chapters in this book discuss how to design and write these types of programs and how programs are integrated to produce computer information systems.

PROGRAMMING LANGUAGES

Computer programs are written in special *programming languages* that are understandable by the computer. More than 200 different kinds of programming languages have been developed, although only a dozen or so are in common use. One of the most popular of these languages is BASIC. It is used in the discussions, illustrations, and example programs that are presented in this book.

BASIC (an acronym for Beginner's All-purpose Symbolic Instruction Code) was developed originally as a vehicle for teaching computer programming. It is relatively easy to learn, has fairly powerful commands, and is well suited for introducing programming to novice computer users. Since its introduction in the mid-1960s, BASIC has enjoyed widespread acceptance and has become the most popular language on microcomputers and minicomputers. With the rising popularity of these types of small computer systems in business, BASIC has become an important business applications programming language.

PROGRAMMING AND CODING

Throughout this book, you will learn how to code computer programs using the BASIC language. More important, however, you will learn to develop computer programs. Also, you will come to recognize the differences between program design and program code.

As noted earlier, computer programming—involving design and development—is a problem-solving process. Such programming is a way of thinking about problems and of formulating computer-based solutions. Thus, computer programming is primarily a thought process that takes place without regard to the specific computer or programming language used. In this sense, a program is a *logical solution* to a problem.

Writing the solution to a problem, whether it be in BASIC or in any other programming language, is called *coding.* Computer code is the *physical implementation* of a program in a language understandable by the computer. It is the version of the program that can be executed by the computer to solve the problem. In effect, then, coding is the clerical process that takes place after the program is written. In this book, you will learn both computer programming and BASIC coding.

COMPUTERS COME IN MANY shapes and sizes. Equipment and features of computer systems are set up for special user jobs. At top left, an IBM Personal Computer presents a display of a typing keyboard as a learning aid for computer users. At bottom, left, is an Apple Lisa system that provides program selection and function control through the use of a "mouse" (foreground). In the photo above, operators change disk packs on a large-scale, random-access storage device. The photo above, right, demonstrates graphic output on a microcomputer system. The display on the computer at bottom, right, illustrates a display of a menu from which a user can select needed services.

COMPUTERS ARE THE FOCUS OF ATTENTION for many types of users. The photo above, left, shows a graphic display generated with the aid of a "mouse" (right, foreground) on an Apple Macintosh microcomputer. Operator in photo at bottom, left, uses a graphics program to cause data to create a display on an IBM Personal Computer. Below, an audience in a classroom built into a display at a major trade show (the Office Automation Conference) focuses attention on the presenter explaining features of a microcomputer system.

COLLECTIONS OF ELECTRONIC DEVICES are connected to form computer systems. At top, a large-scale, or mainframe, computer consists of interconnected devices to store data, print reports, and control operations. At right, above, is a desk-top computer that includes separate diskette drives for data storage, a monitor to display data, and a printer. The computer itself is housed in the same unit as the keyboard. In the photo below, right, a diskette is being inserted into a micro-computer that has all devices—keyboard, display, processor, and storage units—built into a single housing.

SYSTEMS OF PROGRAMS

In business organizations, there may be hundreds, or even thousands, of programs. Most often, however, these are not isolated programs, independent of or unrelated to one another. Rather, programs usually are organized into *systems of programs* that work together to perform major processing jobs.

For example, several programs may be required to implement an automated order processing and billing system for a retail store. Another set of programs may be required for the inventory control system. Still other groups of programs may be necessary to automate the payroll system, the accounting system, the purchasing system, and any number of other typical business application systems. The point is that programmers seldom prepare individual, isolated programs; they develop systems of programs that implement major processing applications.

The person who wishes to become an effective computer programmer needs to develop this systems perspective. This awareness will affect directly the quality of programming that is done because a systems perspective provides an understanding of how programs work together, in concert with other programs, with people, and with the noncomputerized portions of information systems.

This book takes a systems perspective in discussing computer programming. It treats programs in an integrated fashion. All of the examples present this viewpoint and all of the programming exercises require development of systems of programs that are based on typical computer information systems in business.

YOU, THE PROGRAMMER

When you have completed this study, you will have acquired a solid foundation for becoming a computer programmer. Although one book or one course will not prepare you to be a professional programmer, the material presented here will put you on the right path. Even if you do not intend to make computer programming your profession, you will become a more effective personal-use programmer by applying the processes and practices discussed here.

Chapter Summary

1. A computer is an electronic device that performs arithmetic and logical operations without human intervention.

2. A program is a set of detailed instructions establishing the sequence in which processing activities must be performed by a computer to produce the desired results.

3. To use a computer, people must provide two things: programs and data. A program is prepared and placed inside the computer. Under program control, data are entered into the computer and processed to produce specified results.

4. A computer system consists of a group of connected devices known collectively as hardware. Hardware includes input units, the processor unit, output units, and storage units.

5. The processor is at the heart of the computer system. It includes main memory, in which programs and data are retained during processing, and the central processing unit, in which actual computer processing operations are carried out.

6. Input units are used to enter programs and data into memory. Output units are used to communicate the results of processing to people. Storage units are used for long-term retention of programs and data.

7. Computers are general problem-solving devices. They are capable of performing any work that can be described in a set of computer operating instructions.

8. The types of computer applications found in business are known collectively as computer information systems (CIS). These systems include data processing systems, management information systems, and decision support systems.

9. Master files and transaction files are the two main types of files processed by computers. Master files contain information that is to be retained over a long period of time.

Transaction files contain data representing current business activity. The data in transaction files are used to update master files to keep them current.

10. All computer information systems use certain common types of programs. These program types include file creation programs, file updating programs, report writing programs, and file inquiry programs.

11. File creation programs are used to build the master files and to create the transaction files that result from business activity.

12. File updating programs are used to post transaction data to master files and to maintain the accuracy and completeness of master files.

13. Report writing programs are used to supply detailed or summary information to people who need information contained in computer files. Business reports can be produced on a regularly scheduled basis, on demand, or to indicate exception conditions in which business activity is not proceeding according to plan.

14. Inquiry programs are used to gain access to only one record in a file at a time and to have the content of that record displayed immediately.

15. Computer programs are written in special languages understandable by computers. One of the most popular of these languages is BASIC.

16. Programming is primarily a mental, problem-solving process. It requires careful thought in developing a logical solution to a problem. Coding, on the other hand, is the process of translating a problem solution into a set of processing commands understandable by the computer.

17. For the most part, programs do not exist in isolation. They are organized into systems of programs to perform major business processing tasks.

Review Questions

1. What is a computer program?

2. What are the four types of hardware required by a computer, and how does each device function within the system?

3. What do the words *data* and *information* mean in terms of CIS requirements?

4. What are the three main types of business CIS, and how is each system used by business organizations?

5. How are the words *field, record,* and *file* defined in terms of computer function?

6. What are the two types of files used by computer information systems, and how do these files function within the system?

7. What are the four basic types of programs used within a file processing system, and what processing task (or tasks) does each program perform?

8. When are report writing programs implemented?

Key Terms

1. data
2. primitive
3. computer program
4. computer programmer
5. computer system
6. hardware
7. processor unit
8. memory
9. central processing unit (CPU)
10. input unit
11. output unit
12. storage unit
13. information system
14. computer information system (CIS)
15. data processing system (DPS)
16. management information system (MIS)
17. decision support system (DSS)
18. operational level
19. control level
20. planning level
21. file
22. record
23. field
24. record key
25. master file
26. transaction file
27. update
28. file creation program
29. formatting
30. file updating program
31. posting program
32. maintenance program
33. report writing program
34. detail report
35. summary report
36. scheduled report
37. on-demand report
38. ad hoc report
39. exception report
40. hard copy
41. inquiry program
42. on-line
43. programming language
44. logical solution
45. coding
46. physical implementation
47. system of programs

2
THE PROGRAM DEVELOPMENT PROCESS

OVERVIEW AND OBJECTIVES

This chapter discusses and illustrates a process for controlling development and assuring quality of programs. The process presented consists of a series of ordered steps, under which the programmer analyzes a problem for computer solution, designs the program that will solve the problem, and implements the program on a computer.

When you complete your work in this chapter, you should be able to:

☐ List and describe the five steps in the program development process.

☐ Perform data flow analysis for a simple programming problem.

☐ Identify and describe the three logical control structures that govern processing activities in a program.

☐ Illustrate, through use of a structure chart, the basic computer information systems program model, and describe generally the processing that takes place in each program module.

☐ Create a structural design for a simple program.

☐ Develop pseudocode for a simple program.

PROGRAMMING AND PROBLEM SOLVING

Computer program development is a problem-solving process. Primarily, the process is mental, involving analysis of problems and development of computer-based solutions. The process does involve certain routine, computer-related tasks. These tasks include coding the program in a computer language, entering the program into the computer through a computer terminal, and testing the program to verify that it works properly. However, most of the programming effort—the original, creative work involved in designing the procedures to be followed—is completed by the time the programmer is ready to undertake these activities.

Because writing actual instructions for a program and running these instructions on a computer is an intriguing challenge, there is a temptation to skip the initial design and planning steps and get right into the business of running the computer. Invariably, however, front-end short-cuts lead to later grief. The real challenge—and thrill—of computer programming is to produce a sound and workable design. A well-designed program will run properly the first time it is executed. On the other hand, a programmer who rushes to coding before careful analysis of the problem can expect to spend more time correcting mistakes than actually writing the program.

Programming is problem solving. Problem solving is an exercise requiring *analysis* and *synthesis.* Often, a problem is too complex to be dealt with as a whole. Analysis is applied to *partition* the problem into its component parts—a series of well-defined, easily solved subproblems. Then the programmer synthesizes the identified parts of the problem—that is, organizes and combines the solutions of the subproblems into an integrated whole that can be implemented on a computer. A major part of the programming effort is devoted to these partitioning and organizing tasks, regardless of the programming language or computer hardware to be used.

PROGRAMMING SPECIFICATIONS

Programmers normally work from a set of *programming specifications.* These specifications describe the input, processing, output, and storage requirements for the program. Specifications are prepared by a person called a *systems analyst.*

Systems analysts are professionals responsible for identifying needs to be met by a computer information system and for designing systems to meet those needs. The systems analyst works closely with *users,* the people who need and will use the information produced by a system. The analyst identifies problems and specifies solutions that include computer programs. The programming specifications are then implemented by the programming staff.

CIS departments in most medium- and large-sized organizations employ full-time systems analysts. In smaller organizations, there may not be enough demand to support full-time analysts. Individuals called *programmer/analysts* may both design systems and write the programs to implement them.

In any case, detailed specifications should exist as a starting point for program development. These specifications should be complete and precise. The programmer has little, if any, discretion in modifying those specifications. The program should be written to perform exactly the processing called for—neither more, nor less—even if the programmer believes modifications would lead to improvement. If the programmer feels strongly about modifying a program requirement, the suggestion should be discussed with the responsible systems analyst. Changes in specifications should come only through the analyst, with concurrence of the user. A program that does not meet written specifications is as defective as a program that contains processing errors. The programming assignments in this book are described by programming specifications. You will be expected to follow them to the letter, just as would be expected in a job situation.

STEPS IN THE PROGRAM DEVELOPMENT PROCESS

The process of programming encompasses several well-defined, orderly steps during which specifications are evolved into programs of assured quality. The five steps in computer programming are:

1. *Analyze the problem.* The programmer reviews the specifications for the program under development. This review stresses analysis of input, processing, output, and storage requirements. The result should be a clear understanding of the nature of the problem and of the problem components, or processing tasks, required to solve the problem.

2. *Design the program.* The programmer defines the program components that will perform the processing tasks identified during program analysis. These program components then are combined and organized into a program structure that embodies a computer program solution for the stated problem.

3. *Specify program processing.* Having devised the overall structure of processing tasks necessary to solve the problem, the programmer

determines and lists the actual computer operations that will be required within each portion of the program. For each program component, the required sequence of fundamental, primitive computer operations is specified. Recall that program primitives are the simple tasks of which computers are capable—the actual input, arithmetic, logical, output, and storage operations that process the data and produce desired output. This step produces a complete, detailed specification of the program in a series of stylized English statements known as *pseudocode*. As its name implies, pseudocode is a representation of the actual instructions that will form the final computer program. Use of pseudocode separates the design of processing procedures from the task of writing actual program code. Pseudocoding makes possible detailed analysis of processing design before code is written. Also, use of pseudocode renders program design independent from program coding.

4. *Code the program.* At this point, the pseudocoded specifications are translated into a computer language. The coded program is composed of sets of commands that direct the computer to carry out the processing operations. Coded instructions are drawn from the available set of input, arithmetic, logical, output, and storage commands of a particular programming language. In this book, programs will be translated into the BASIC language.

5. *Test and debug the program.* Program errors, or *bugs*, are improperly written commands that produce incorrect or unexpected outputs from the computer. Bugs must be located and corrected. There are two types of errors that can occur in a program. Errors in *syntax* occur when the programmer violates the rules of grammar for the programming language. For example, misspelling the name of a command would produce a syntactical error. Errors in logic, on the other hand, occur when the program fails to produce expected results, even though the program itself may be syntactically perfect. Logical errors are caused by the incorrect use of a command, which results in the computer processing the wrong data or applying the wrong processing to the data. Program *testing*, or running the program with example data, locates logical errors. The process of correcting errors, then, is referred to as *debugging*.

This program development process is shown graphically in Figure 2-1. The remainder of this chapter presents a further discussion of these steps and illustrates the process by developing an example program.

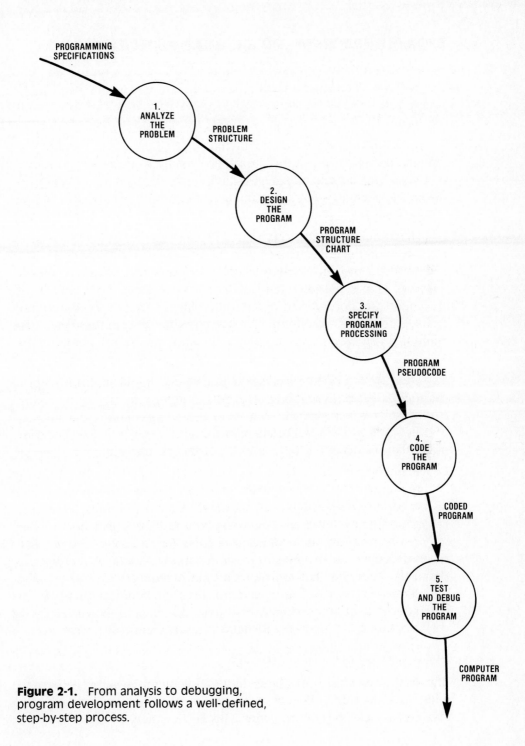

Figure 2-1. From analysis to debugging, program development follows a well-defined, step-by-step process.

EXAMPLE PROGRAM—PROGRAMMING SPECIFICATIONS

Figure 2-2 presents the programming specifications for a sample program that will report and classify ticket sales for the Capri movie theater. The program output will list all ticket sales by category and price. In accounting terms, this output is a sales journal listing income transactions.

Note that the specifications include descriptions and graphic representations of the program's input, processing, and output. As shown in the output specifications, the computer will begin processing by displaying headings identifying the program. Then, a set of instructions will be displayed to tell the terminal operator how to use the program.

The computer terminal operator will enter data, through the terminal keyboard, on the quantity and type (adult or child) of tickets sold. The computer will provide *prompts* to lead the operator through the processing steps. That is, the computer will display the message "QTY,TYPE . . . ?" to remind the operator to enter these values into the keyboard and transmit them to the computer. As the operator keys in these data, the computer will *echo* them, or display the entered values, alongside the prompt.

After the computer receives the two values, it will continue its processing. Calculations will be performed to determine the total amount to charge. This processing is done through multiplication of the quantity of tickets sold by the appropriate price for adult or child tickets. The computer then displays the total amount of the purchase on the terminal screen or printer.

Any number of ticket requests can be processed. The computer will keep asking for input data, calculating the amount and displaying the results as long as ticket sales data are entered by the operator. To terminate the program, the operator will enter the values, 0,0 (zero, zero) when the computer prompts for quantity and type data. This entry will signal the program that there are no more requests for tickets. The double-zero entry serves as an end-of-processing indicator that tells the computer to stop processing. At that point, the computer will display a confirmation ("*** END OF SESSION ***") and will halt processing.

Step 1: Analyze the Problem

The programming specifications define a problem. To solve a programming problem, remember, the first step is to partition the overall problem into a series of subproblems. This is the analysis step. Then, the

Figure 2-2. Programming specifications for ticket order processing.

<u>PROGRAMMING SPECIFICATIONS</u>

System: TICKET SALES   Date: 03/05/XX
Program: TICKET ORDER PROCESSING   Program I.D.: TKTORD Analyst: B. LEIGH

Design and write a program to compute ticket costs for the Capri Movie Theatre.
The quantities and types of tickets desired are the program input. Output
will be a listing of these quantities and types and the total cost of the
tickets. The total cost is calculated by multiplying the quantity purchased
times the individual ticket price. Input data are entered through a terminal
keyboard. Output will be displayed on the terminal screen or printer. The
program will be coded in BASIC. Figure 2-2.1 shows the system flowchart for
this application.

Figure 2-2.1

<u>INPUT</u>

Customers' ticket requests are the program input. Two types of input data are
provided by the terminal operator: the number of tickets desired and the type
of tickets to be purchased. A code is entered for each of the two types of
tickets. The codes are A for adult tickets and C for child tickets. The
following set of data values is used to test this program:

QUANTITY	TYPE
3	A
3	C
1	A
1	C
2	A
5	C
10	A

<u>PROCESSING</u>

For each ticket request, the computer calculates the total purchase amount.
The quantity is multiplied times the ticket price. The adult ticket price is
$3.25 and the child ticket price is $1.75.

<u>OUTPUT</u>

Output from this program will be a listing of the ticket transactions in the
format shown in Figure 2-2.2.

```
        CAPRI MOVIE THEATRE
            TICKET SALES

    ENTER THE QUANTITY AND TYPE OF
    TICKETS ORDERED, SEPARATED BY
    A COMMA.  END THE SESSION BY
    TYPING THE VALUES '0,0'.

    QTY,TYPE.....? 3,A
    TOTAL AMOUNT:  9.75

    QTY,TYPE.....? 3,C
    TOTAL AMOUNT:  5.25

    QTY,TYPE.....? 1,A
    TOTAL AMOUNT:  3.25

    QTY,TYPE.....? 1,C
    TOTAL AMOUNT:  1.75

    QTY,TYPE.....? 2,A
    TOTAL AMOUNT:  6.50

    QTY,TYPE.....? 5,C
    TOTAL AMOUNT:  8.75

    QTY,TYPE.....? 10,A
    TOTAL AMOUNT: 32.50

    QTY,TYPE.....? 0,0
    *** END OF SESSION ***
```

Fig. 2-2.2

Program development should include data flow analysis, structure charts, pseudocode, and thorough documentation.

Figure 2-2. Concluded.

solutions to the subproblems are combined (synthesized) and organized into an integrated whole. The immediate task, then, is to partition the problem.

Data flow analysis. A convenient and effective way to gain an understanding of necessary processing tasks is through the technique of *data flow analysis*. As the name implies, data flow analysis traces the movement of data from the point of input, through the processing steps, or *transformations*, to outputs. Transformations, in effect, are any functions that process data to create information. Data flow analysis is a way of visualizing the continuity of processing from the viewpoint of the computer.

Data flow for the example problem is illustrated in Figure 2-3. This diagram shows the movement of data into, within, and out of computer

36

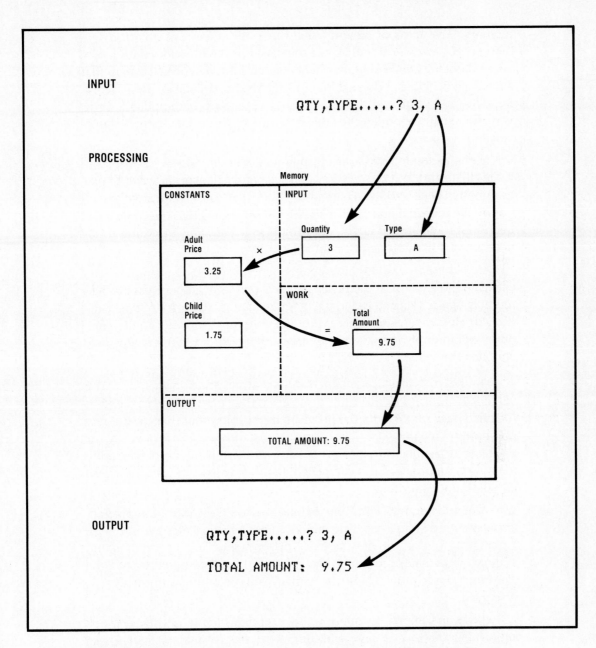

INPUT

QTY,TYPE.....? 3, A

PROCESSING

Memory

CONSTANTS | INPUT

Adult Price × Quantity | Type

3.25 | 3 | A

WORK

Child Price | Total Amount

1.75 | = | 9.75

OUTPUT

TOTAL AMOUNT: 9.75

OUTPUT

QTY,TYPE.....? 3, A

TOTAL AMOUNT: 9.75

Figure 2-3. Data flow analysis traces data from point of input, through processing, and to output. The flow of data is analyzed to identify processing operations and the items of data that will be involved in the processing. Data flow analysis is used in conjunction with programming specifications to gain an understanding of the processing operations required to solve the problem.

memory. The areas of memory that must be set aside to hold the data being input are identified, as are the areas that will hold data that are created during processing. In effect, Figure 2-3 is a processing map that shows memory being divided into four areas, for constants, input, working data, and output. Although memory actually is not subdivided this way, the illustration identifies the different kinds of data that will be involved in processing.

In the example, two areas in memory have been reserved for the values that represent the quantity and type of tickets purchased. The programming specifications, remember, state that these values will be input by the terminal operator. The illustration shows that the value 3 has been input and stored as the quantity purchased, and the value A has been input for the type of ticket sold.

After these two values have been input and stored, the computer can calculate the amount of the purchase. This processing operation involves multiplying the value stored in the quantity area by the price of the ticket. If, as in Figure 2-3, the ticket-type field contains the value A, the computer will multiply the quantity by the adult price. If the ticket-type field contains the value C, the child price is the multiplier.

The ticket prices are retained in two other areas in memory. The value 3.25 appears in the adult price area; the value 1.75 is retained as the child price. Note from the program description that these values are not input by the operator. The values are established as *constants* by the program at the beginning of processing and will remain unchanged in memory until processing is completed. In other words, the program itself will define these values.

After the computer has performed the multiplication, the product (answer) is placed in a separate memory area labeled Total Amount. (See Figure 2-3.) Within the output area, this sales amount is *formatted* into a line of information in which the sales total is placed next to a "Total Amount:" descriptor. Then, the entire content of this output area is displayed.

These operations complete the processing of one purchase transaction. For the second and subsequent ticket sales transactions, these same processing operations are repeated: The operator enters the two values, the calculations are made, and the results are displayed. Even though new data are input continually and new amounts are calculated, no additional areas in memory are required. The same constants, input, work, and output areas are used, with the new data simply replacing the old data for each subsequent transaction entry.

This processing will continue until the operator enters the values 0,0 for quantity and type. Then, the program will display its end-of-session message and processing will be halted.

Problem partitioning.   The programming specifications, together with the analysis of data flow, serve as a basis for identifying the separate functions necessary to make this program work. At this point, the following list of processing functions can be identified:

- Print program headings and operator instructions.
- Define program constants and output formats.
- Input ticket quantities and type codes.
- Calculate ticket amounts.
- Display formatted ticket amounts.
- Display end-of-session message.
- Halt processing.

Although these activities are not listed necessarily in the order in which they will be carried out by the computer, they have, nonetheless, been identified as the major processing functions required to solve the problem. The next step is to organize these activities into a properly sequenced computer program.

Step 2: Design the Program

Problem analysis involves identifying the input, processing, and output functions that must be performed. The next step is to determine how to structure those activities into a computer program. A program's structure defines the relationships among processing activities and the order in which the functions will be carried out by the computer.

Most well-designed problem solutions modeled for computer processing focus on the three major sections that are found in virtually all business-oriented computer programs. The following processing activities take place in each of these three sections:

1. *Begin processing activities* occur one time only—at the beginning of processing.

2. *Main processing activities* occur repeatedly, usually once for each set of input data.

3. *End processing activities* occur one time only—at the completion of processing.

This three-part structure provides a basic model for organizing processing activities into computer programs.

Program structure.   When this model is applied to the ticket processing problem, it produces the *program structure* presented in outline form in Figure 2-4. Note that the indented outline form clarifies the relationships among the program functions.

The outline in Figure 2-4 describes the processing activities to be performed by the program and shows the order in which they will be carried out. It models the general structure of the ticket sales program.

Note that the processing activities are organized into a *hierarchy*. The program is broken down into the three major categories of processing activity—begin processing, main processing, and end processing. Each of these major activities serves as a partition, or branch, of the program. The branches, in turn, are broken down into major processing functions. Those functions, in turn, are broken down even further into more detailed processing tasks, as appropriate. Thus, the program itself is partitioned into smaller and smaller sections. Partitioning follows this *hierarchical*, or *top-down*, design path until, at the lowest level, single, easily identified processing tasks have been isolated for ease of program design, coding, and testing.

Structure charts.   A convenient way to describe the structure of a program—as compared with preparation of a list like the one in Figure 2-4—is with a *structure chart*, or *hierarchy chart*. A structure chart is a formal method of describing the organization of, and relationships among, parts of a program. Structure charts also show the order in which program functions will be performed. Figure 2-5 presents the structure chart for the ticket processing program.

The boxes in the structure chart represent program *modules*. A module is a program function. It represents a specific processing task that will be performed by the computer. Each box contains the name of the function and a number representing its relationship to other modules in the program.

The modules are organized into a hierarchy. The top-level module represents the function of the program as a whole. At the next level, the program is divided into the three basic categories of functions: begin processing activities, main processing activities, and end processing activities. At succeeding, lower levels, the modules that will perform the actual processing functions of the program are represented.

Structure charts resemble business organization charts. Just as an organization chart shows the hierarchical relationship of managers in

```
0.0 PROGRAM: PROCESS TICKET ORDERS
    1.0 BEGIN PROCESSING
        1.1 DEFINE CONSTANTS
            Before the computer begins processing ticket requests, the
            adult and child ticket prices will be placed in memory as
            constants.  Also, the format for the total amount line will
            be defined.
        1.2 PRINT HEADINGS
            The computer will display heading lines that identify the
            program and provide operator instructions.
        1.3 INPUT FIRST ORDER
            The first set of quantity and type data is requested from
            the operator and is placed in memory.  At this point, the
            computer has the requisite data to begin main processing
            activities.
    2.0 MAIN PROCESSING
        2.1 COMPUTE TICKET AMOUNT
            One of the following functions will be selected depending
            whether the request is for adult or child tickets.
                2.1.1 COMPUTE ADULT AMOUNT
                    The value in the quantity field is multiplied by
                    the adult price constant and the result is placed
                    in a separate memory area.
                2.1.2 COMPUTE CHILD AMOUNT
                    The value in the quantity field is multiplied by
                    the child price constant and the result is placed
                    in a separate memory area.
        2.2 PRINT TOTAL AMOUNT
            The value in the total amount area is formatted and displayed
            on the output line.
        2.3 INPUT NEXT ORDER
            The next set of input data is requested from the operator
            and placed in memory so that data are available when main
            processing is repeated.
    3.0 END PROCESSING
        3.1 DISPLAY TERMINATION MESSAGE
            After main processing is complete, the computer will
            display an end-of-session message to indicate that no
            more ticket requests are to be processed.
        3.2 STOP PROCESSING
            When processing has terminated, the computer is
            instructed to halt execution of the program.
```

Figure 2-4. Outline showing the ticket sales program structure and order of processing activities.

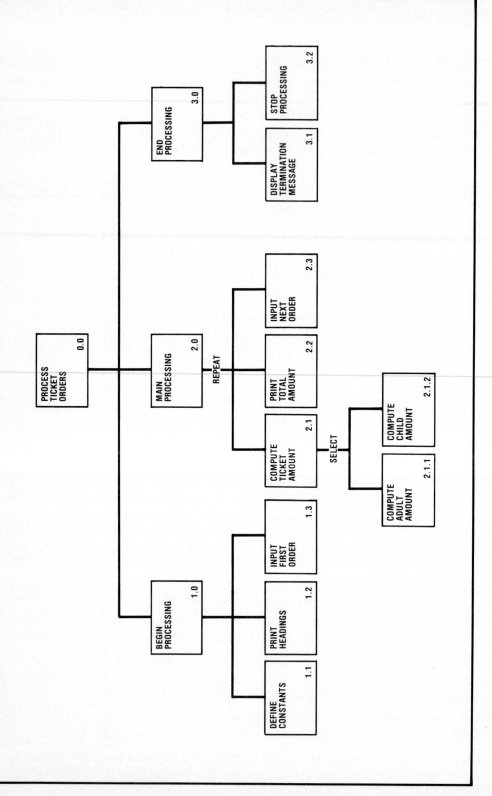

Figure 2-5. The structure chart for the ticket processing program presents the organization of processing functions (modules) that will be performed by the program. The chart documents the structural and logical organization of modules.

a business, a program structure chart shows the functional organization of program processing modules.

A structure chart also includes notations that identify the program's *logical control structure.* A program's control structure reflects the order in which the processing functions are carried out and the number of times the modules are activated.

The normal sequence of execution is implied by the top-to-bottom, left-to-right order of the modules. Thus, the begin processing activities occur first, followed by the main processing activities, and then the end processing activities. Within each of these three sections of the program, the detailed processing modules will be activated in this general left-to-right order.

Unless indicated otherwise on the structure chart, each module will be activated one time only. Note, however, that the modules subordinate to the MAIN PROCESSING module are to be activated more than once. The notation REPEAT indicates that this set of program functions will be performed repeatedly (in this case, until a data input with a value of 0,0 is encountered).

The SELECT notation on the structure chart indicates that only one of the two available modules is activated. Subordinate to the COMPUTE TICKET AMOUNT module are two alternate processing modules. Either the COMPUTE ADULT AMOUNT or COMPUTE CHILD AMOUNT module will be activated, depending on whether the data entry is for adult or child tickets. During processing, the program will select one or the other of these processing alternatives, but not both.

A structure chart, then, describes the *architectural structure* of a program. A structure chart specifies the modules, or functions, that complete the program and shows how the modules are related to one another by program control logic.

Logical control structures.   The processing modules in a program are related to one another in specific, clearly defined ways. There are three such logical control structures:

- *Sequences* are the normal order in which modules are presented to the computer and activated. The usual sequence followed in processing conforms to the physical order in which modules are placed within a program. Within a structure chart, sequences are determined by top-to-bottom, left-to-right placement of program modules.

- *Repetitions*, also called *iterations* or *loops*, are repeated activations of program modules. In a program, a module or sequence of modules may be repeated for each successive set of data that is presented for processing. The repetitions continue until some processing condition or signal occurs that causes the program to exit from the loop and continue in sequence to the next module.

- *Selections* occur whenever one of two or more modules should be activated. The value contained in a data field determines which module is selected for processing. The select control structure is also known as the *case construct*.

Figure 2-6 shows the general formats for denoting these logical control structures on a structure chart.

A CIS program model.   The top levels of the structure chart for the ticket processing program can serve as a model for the design of a wide variety of CIS programs. Even though there may be differences in the detailed processing functions that are required, virtually all business-related processing programs incorporate begin processing, main processing, and end processing activities. In addition, most programs embody some common and similarly structured detailed processing requirements. For instance, the begin processing module usually includes an initial input function that enters the first set of data to be processed into memory. Also, the final module in the main processing section of the program usually is the input function for the second and subsequent sets of data to be processed.

Figure 2-7 presents the computer information systems program model that is the basis for all programs discussed in this book. This single structure can be adapted as the underlying design for virtually any business-related computer program. Thus, the solution for each new programming problem you will encounter can be constructed as a variation of this single, general model.

As noted in the previous chapter, virtually all computer information systems consist of similar types of file creation, file updating, report writing, and inquiry programs. The general CIS program model can be elaborated into a generalized model for each kind of program. For example, all report writing programs are similar in general structural organization and use similar processing modules. Thus, a general model for a report writing program can be developed so that each new program is simply an adaptation of the model.

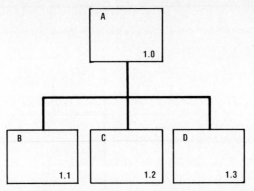

In a *sequence* control structure, program functions are carried out one after another to conform to the physical order in which the modules appear in the program.

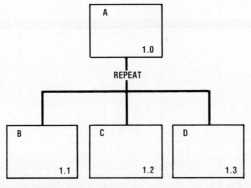

In a *repetition* control structure, one or more modules are activated repeatedly until some processing condition occurs to terminate the loop.

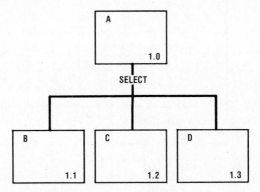

In a *selection* control structure, one of two or more modules is activated, depending on the value contained in a data field.

Figure 2-6. Program modules are related logically to each other through a limited set of program control structures: sequences, repetitions, and selections.

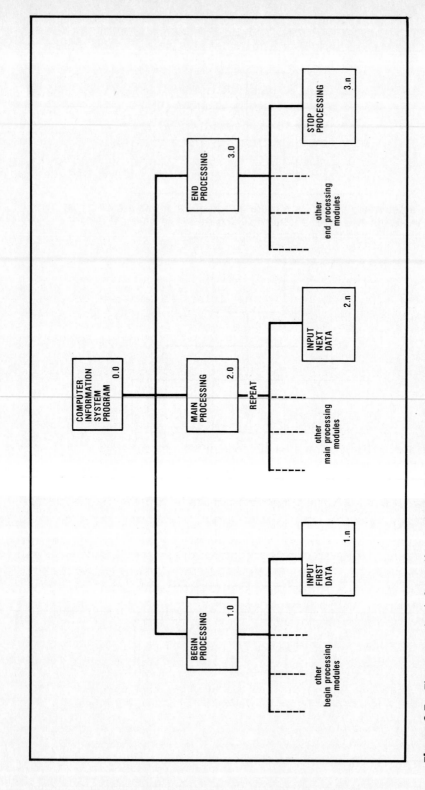

Figure 2-7. The computer information systems program model can be used to design virtually all programs, especially those that perform business-type processing. At the bottom, detail levels, processing varies from program to program.

By using a standardized, general computer software model and generic program modules for basic CIS programs, the programmer can save time in the design, coding, and testing and debugging phases of software development. Then, the major portion of a programmer's time and effort can be devoted to the analysis and the design of solutions—keys to quality programming.

Step 3: Specify Program Processing

Recall that a structure chart reflects the architectural design of a program. Putting it another way, a structure chart is a plan for solving a problem through an orderly, logical set of computer functions. However, the program modules described by the structure chart are not yet in a form that a computer can execute. The modules themselves still have to be amplified into sets of primitive computer operations.

Pseudocode.   As indicated previously, module processing is specified through use of a notation method called pseudocode. Pseudocode consists of sets of brief, precise statements in English. Each statement corresponds, usually, with one primitive computer operation. One or more of these primitive operations will be necessary to implement a module on a computer.

It would be possible to continue defining additional levels of modules on the structure chart until each module at the lowest level represents a single computer operation. However, doing so would complicate the structure chart and obscure the program structure with processing details. Besides, drawing a structure chart with hundreds of modules, each representing a single computer operation, would be an awesome task. Therefore, a structure chart describes only the structure of processing functions while pseudocode specifies detailed computer operations to implement the functions.

Figure 2-8 shows the pseudocode for the ticket sales program. Notice that the organization of the pseudocode follows that of the structure chart in Figure 2-5. The module names and numbers are used to cross-reference the pseudocode with the structure chart.

The specific computer operations required to implement a program are derived from the original specifications and the data flow analysis. These input, processing, and output activities are written in pseudocode

```
0.0 PROCESS TICKET ORDERS
    1.0 BEGIN PROCESSING
        1.1 DEFINE CONSTANTS
                Set Adult Price = 3.25
                Set Child Price = 1.75
                Define total amount line format
        1.2 PRINT HEADINGS
                Print heading lines
                Print blank line
                Print operator instructions line
        1.3 INPUT FIRST ORDER
                Print blank line
                Print operator prompt
                Input Quantity, Type
    2.0 MAIN PROCESSING
        REPEAT: until end of orders
            2.1 COMPUTE TICKET AMOUNT
                SELECT: on Type
                    2.1.1 COMPUTE ADULT AMOUNT
                            Set Total Amount = Quantity x Adult Price
                    2.1.2 COMPUTE CHILD AMOUNT
                            Set Total Amount = Quantity x Child Price
                END SELECT
            2.2 PRINT TOTAL AMOUNT
                Print Total Amount line
            2.3 INPUT NEXT ORDER
                Print blank line
                Print operator prompt
                Input Quantity, Type
        END REPEAT
    3.0 END PROCESSING
        3.1 DISPLAY TERMINATION MESSAGE
            Print end-of-session line
        3.2 STOP PROCESSING
            Stop
```

Figure 2-8. Pseudocode for the ticket processing program expands the structure chart into sets of detailed computer processing operations.

notation to provide an intermediate step that improves the quality of program design and the code that will be written from these design documents.

Pseudocoding control structures. In Figure 2-8, note how the logical control structures are specified. The general sequence of operations is read from top to bottom of the pseudocode. Unless told otherwise, the computer will carry out processing in this sequential order.

Operations within the MAIN PROCESSING module are included within the repetition control structure. The REPEAT . . . END REPEAT notation signifies that all modules and operations between these two boundaries are to be performed in a continuous loop. The "until" phrase of the REPEAT notation gives the condition for ending the repetition and proceeding to the next module.

A selection is specified in the COMPUTE TICKET AMOUNT module. The SELECT . . . END SELECT lines form the boundaries of this control structure, and imply that only one of the modules listed between the boundaries will be activated. Part of the SELECT line specifies the data item to be tested to determine which of the modules to select. Figure 2-9 shows how, in general, the logical control structures are translated from the structure chart into pseudocode.

Step 4: Coding the Program

Each line of program pseudocode can be translated on almost a one-to-one basis into BASIC language commands. In effect, the program is written completely before it is coded into a computer language. The most difficult aspect of programming—analyzing the problem and designing and specifying its solution—has been completed. The coding process is mostly clerical.

The BASIC language is relatively easy to use. The 15 elementary command types, or *statements*, listed in Figure 2-10 will enable you to write virtually all BASIC programs. Figure 2-11 gives the BASIC code for the ticket processing program. Although you have not yet been introduced formally to the language, you should be able to follow the general logic and processing implied by the program. In the next chapter, these commands are explained and you will begin using and understanding them. You should note from the illustration, however, the correspondence between the program code in Figure 2-11 and the pseudocode in Figure 2-8.

Step 5: Test and Debug the Program

As indicated previously, testing locates and debugging corrects errors in programs. Errors in syntax are misspellings of commands or other violations of language rules. These errors are discovered by the computer itself. As the coded source statements are entered into the computer, the computer translates the statements into the machine language required for computer execution of the program. As the program instructions are processed, the computer outputs messages to indicate any syntactical errors and pinpoints the line of code and the incorrectly written command. The erroneous statements are then rewritten and re-entered.

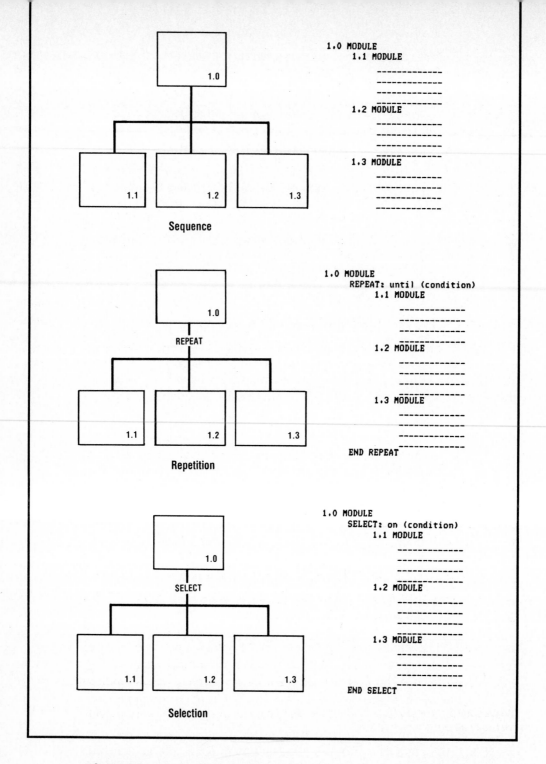

Figure 2-9. The logical control structures that appear on the structure chart are converted into pseudocode notation.

BASIC Statement Type	Usage
CLOSE	To disassociate a data file from a program
DATA	To define files that are used as constants within a program
DIM	To define and reserve areas within memory to be used as program tables
END	To identify the physical end of a program
GOSUB	To transfer control to a program subroutine
GOTO	To transfer control from one point in a program to another
IF	To test a data field for a particular value
INPUT	To accept data from an input unit and to retain values in memory
LET	To assign a value to an area in memory
OPEN	To link a data file to a program
PRINT	To transfer data from memory to an output unit
READ	To input data from a file of constant data in memory
REM	To provide documentation for a program
RETURN	To transfer control from a subroutine back to the calling module
STOP	To cause the computer to halt processing

Figure 2-10. These elementary statement types, or primitives, are used to code virtually all programs in BASIC.

```
100 REM TKTODR                        DA/WL
110 REM        TICKET ORDER PROCESSING
120 REM
130 REM THIS PROGRAM COMPUTES TICKET PRICES FOR
140 REM THE CAPRI MOVIE THEATRE.  INPUT TO THE
150 REM PROGRAM ARE QUANTITIES AND TYPES OF TICKETS
160 REM REQUESTED.  OUTPUT IS A LISTING OF THE
170 REM TOTAL SALES AMOUNT OF THE TICKETS ORDERED.
180 REM PROCESSING INVOLVES COMPUTING THE TICKET
190 REM AMOUNT BY MULTIPLYING THE QUANTITY ORDERED
200 REM TIMES THE PRICE PER TICKET.  ANY NUMBER OF
210 REM REQUESTS CAN BE PROCESSED.
220 REM
230 REM              VARIABLE NAMES
240 REM CONSTANTS:
250 REM    P1...ADULT PRICE
260 REM    P2...CHILD PRICE
270 REM    F$...OUTPUT LINE FORMAT
280 REM INPUT:
290 REM    Q....QUANTITY OF TICKETS ORDERED
300 REM    T$...TYPE OF TICKET
310 REM         "A" = ADULT
320 REM         "C" = CHILD
330 REM OUTPUT:
340 REM    A....TOTAL SALES AMOUNT
350 REM
360 REM 0.0 PROCESS TICKET ORDERS
370 REM
375 REM ************************
380 REM * 1.0 BEGIN PROCESSING *
385 REM ************************
390 REM
400 REM 1.1 DEFINE CONSTANTS
410        LET P1 = 3.25
420        LET P2 = 1.75
430        LET F$ = "TOTAL AMOUNT: ##.##"
440 REM
450 REM 1.2 PRINT HEADINGS
460        PRINT "    CAPRI MOVIE THEATRE"
470        PRINT "       TICKET SALES"
480        PRINT
490        PRINT "ENTER THE QUANTITY AND TYPE OF"
500        PRINT "TICKETS ORDERED, SEPARATED BY"
510        PRINT "A COMMA.  END THE SESSION BY"
520        PRINT "TYPING THE VALUES '0,0'."
530 REM
540 REM 1.3 INPUT FIRST ORDER
550        PRINT
560        PRINT "QTY,TYPE.....";
570        INPUT Q, T$
580 REM
585 REM ************************
590 REM * 2.0 MAIN PROCESSING  *
595 REM ************************
600 REM REPEAT
610    IF Q = 0 THEN GOTO 880
620 REM
630 REM    2.1 COMPUTE TICKET AMOUNT
640 REM        SELECT
650            IF T$ = "A" THEN GOTO 690
660            IF T$ = "C" THEN GOTO 730
670                        GOTO 770
680 REM
690 REM        2.1.1 COMPUTE ADULT AMOUNT
700            LET A = Q * P1
710                        GOTO 770
720 REM
```

```
730 REM         2.1.2 COMPUTE CHILD AMOUNT
740                   LET A = Q * P2
750                         GOTO 770
760 REM
770 REM         END SELECT
780 REM
790 REM     2.2 PRINT TOTAL AMOUNT
800                 PRINT USING F$, A
810 REM
820 REM     2.3 INPUT NEXT ORDER
830                 PRINT
840                 PRINT "QTY,TYPE.....";
850                 INPUT Q, T$
860 REM
870     GOTO 600
880 REM END REPEAT
890 REM
895 REM *************************
900 REM * 3.0 END PROCESSING    *
905 REM *************************
910 REM
920 REM 3.1 DISPLAY TERMINATION MESSAGE
930         PRINT "*** END OF SESSION ***"
940 REM
950 REM 3.2 STOP PROCESSING
960         STOP
970 END
```

Figure 2-11. BASIC code for ticket processing program.

Errors in program logic are detected by running the program with test data. Test data are entered into the computer and the output results are inspected. When the output differs from the expected results, the program contains logical errors. Among the causes of logical errors are coded statements out of sequence, specification of the wrong data fields for processing, and statements missing from the program. Logical errors will produce erroneous results even if the program is syntactically perfect.

Logical errors are the most difficult to uncover and correct, since the computer itself cannot check for them. Logical errors, then, must be found and corrected by the programmer. Because the detection and correction of logical errors is time-consuming, tedious, and generally unproductive, it is best to avoid making such errors in the first place. For this reason, the programming process presented here concentrates on the "front-end" activities of problem analysis, structural design, and processing design. This emphasis will help to eliminate most of the logical errors that occur inevitably if coding is undertaken before a thorough design is developed. If the processing steps are followed with care, the programmer should be confident that the program will run correctly the first time. Such an attitude is a natural outgrowth of the systematic approach to programming presented here.

Chapter Summary

1. Computer programming is a systematic problem-solving process applied in developing computer solutions for problems.

2. Programming is a five-step process involving (1) problem analysis, (2) program design, (3) program specification, (4) program coding, and (5) program testing and debugging.

3. The most important steps in programming are problem analysis, program design, and program specification. These steps lead to the understanding necessary to develop the program that solves the problem.

4. The programmer normally works from programming specifications prepared by a systems analyst. These specifications describe the input, processing, output, and storage requirements for the program. If these specifications do not exist, they should be prepared by the programmer prior to program development.

5. Problem analysis, the first step in program development, partitions a problem into its component parts. Partitioning leads to an understanding of the structure of the problem.

6. Data flow analysis enhances understanding by tracing the movement of data from input, through the processing transformations applied to the data, until output is produced. This technique identifies the required processing functions and the data items necessary to carry out those functions.

7. During design, the program is viewed from the standpoint of a computer processing model. That is, design focuses on begin processing activities (those that occur one time only at the start of processing), main processing activities (those that occur repeatedly, once for each set of input data), and end processing activities (those that occur one time only at the completion of processing).

8. Program design involves (1) defining program modules that will solve the subproblems identified during analysis,

(2) organizing the modules into a hierarchical structure, and (3) defining the logical control structures that will govern module execution.

9. A structure chart is used to describe the architectural structure of processing modules in a program. The chart shows the modules that complete the program and the manner in which the modules are related to one another through logical control structures.

10. A set of three logical control structures is used to describe the ordering of processing activities in a program: sequences, repetitions, and selections.

11. A sequence is a logical control structure that causes the computer to perform the processing functions in the physical sequence in which the instructions are written within the program and presented to the computer.

12. A repetition is a control structure in which a module, or group of modules, is activated repeatedly, usually until some specified processing condition occurs. At that point, control returns to normal sequential order. Repetitions are known also as iterations or loops.

13. A selection is a control structure in which one of two or more modules is activated in response to a condition that arises during processing. Selections are known also as case constructs.

14. The basic program model based upon the begin processing, main processing, and end processing branches is useful as a general guide to the design of virtually all business-type programs.

15. Pseudocode is used to specify the computer operations necessary to implement program modules. Pseudocode statements that use English terminology represent a further level of partitioning—following the preparation of structure charts—that occurs during the program specification step. Each pseudocoded statement will be translated, usually, into one command in a programming language. With the completion of pseudocoding, the program, in essence, is written. The writing of code becomes a routine, clerical-type function.

16. Testing procedures detect errors in a program. Syntactical errors are caused by violations of the rules of a particular programming language. These errors are detected by the

computer when the program is entered for processing. Logical errors occur when the program fails to produce expected results, as indicated by the test data. Debugging is the process of correcting syntactical and logical errors.

17. The programmer always should be motivated to produce a program that will work correctly the first time and every time.

Review Questions

1. How does the role of the systems analyst differ from that of the programmer?

2. What are programming specifications?

3. Why should a programmer never change programming specifications without first consulting the systems analyst?

4. How does the technique of data flow analysis help the programmer to analyze the problem defined by program specifications?

5. What are the three major processing sections found in most business-oriented computer programs?

6. What are structure charts, or hierarchy charts, and how are they useful to program design?

7. What is the relationship of pseudocode to structure charts and to the BASIC programming language?

8. How could a program that has no syntactical errors still fail to produce the expected results?

Practice Assignment

The BASIC code for the Capri movie theatre ticket sales program is presented in Figure 2-11. As your first programming practice assignment, enter this code into your own computer and run the program.

Key Terms

1. analysis
2. synthesis
3. partition
4. programming specifications
5. systems analyst
6. programmer/analyst
7. pseudocode
8. bug
9. syntactical error
10. logical error
11. testing
12. debugging
13. prompt
14. echo
15. data flow analysis
16. transformation
17. constant
18. formatted
19. begin processing
20. main processing
21. end processing
22. program structure
23. hierarchy
24. top-down
25. structure chart
26. hierarchy chart
27. module
28. logical control structure
29. architectural structure
30. sequence
31. repetition
32. iteration
33. loop
34. selection
35. case construct
36. statement

II
APPLICATION DEVELOPMENT

In the six chapters that make up Part II, you operate within the framework of the program development process covered in Chapter 2 to master a practical set of techniques that can be used to create actual information processing programs.

In sequence, the chapters in this part of your BASIC text explain how to create computer files, develop programs to produce detail reports, create summary reports, build transaction files, use transaction files to update master files, inquire into files, and maintain files. The need for processing cycles also is explained.

In working your way through these chapters, you observe closely the development of a complete system of programs to perform processing for a hypothetical business. In parallel, you have an opportunity to develop a complete set of programs for a business situation that you devise.

3
CREATING COMPUTER FILES

OVERVIEW AND OBJECTIVES

Files are the bases of most computer information systems. Programs within these systems create files, update files, produce reports derived from file content, or inquire into files. This chapter discusses programs that create sequential files.

When you complete your work in this chapter, you should be able to:

☐ Describe how computer files are organized to allow sequential access to records.

☐ Perform data flow analysis for simple file creation programs.

☐ Draw structure charts for file creation programs.

☐ Develop pseudocode specifications for file creation programs.

☐ Write file creation programs using BASIC.

☐ Describe the operation of program subroutines.

☐ Explain the formats and operations of BASIC statements necessary to create sequential files.

SEQUENTIAL FILE ORGANIZATION

Computer files are created and maintained on auxiliary storage devices such as magnetic disk and magnetic tape units. Once files have been written onto disk or tape media, the data will remain there until they are erased or replaced. Thus, disk and tape media provide permanent or long term storage. Whenever information contained in these files is needed, required records can be accessed conveniently by the computer and presented in human-readable form.

A file is organized into fields and records. A field is a single item of data—a basic fact represented by numbers, alphabetic characters, special characters, or any combination of these symbols. A record is a combination of fields. An individual record usually contains a group of fields that relate to a single person, object, or event.

A file is a collection of related records. Files are organized in some systematic fashion to facilitate location and retrieval of records. One common way to organize records in a file is in sequential order according to their record keys. Recall that a key is a field of data that identifies the record of which the key is a part. The key value, therefore, must be unique so that a particular record can be distinguished from all other records in the file. Records are retrieved according to either the ascending or descending sequence of the key values. This method of arranging records is called *sequential file organization.*

For example, in an accounts receivable file, customer records may be arranged alphabetically by the customer's name. In such a case, the name field serves as the record key. Alternatively, the file also might be organized by account number, in which case the ascending sequence of account numbers, from smallest to largest, would serve to organize the records.

Creating Files for Sequential Access

Computer files are created under control of a computer program. A file creation program normally accepts data fields entered by an operator at a computer terminal. Fields are grouped in the computer's memory as a record and then written to a magnetic file. This entry sequence is repeated for each record written to a file.

When a file is created, records are written in the sequence in which they are entered into the computer. Therefore, the operator must make keyboard entries in record-key sequence. After a file is created, it can be retrieved by a program, which will present records for processing in the same order in which they were written to the file originally. Thus, if a file is going to be used for *sequential access*—in which the records will be retrieved in record-key order—the records must be written in this same sequence.

File creation programs may be *interactive*. That is, they cause the computer to interact, or communicate, with the operator during data entry.

Usually, interactive programs will *prompt* the operator; they trigger requests for the entry of a field of data, then pause while the data are keyed in and transmitted. When all the fields for a single record have been assembled, they are written to the file.

EXAMPLE PROGRAM—FILE CREATION

The following example illustrates how a file creation program is developed. Figure 3-1 presents the program specifications to be used.

This program, to be developed for the American Fun Amusement Park, will create a master file of attractions. Each record in the file will contain fields with data on a particular park attraction. Multiple records are written to the file, which will be stored on a magnetic disk. The attraction-number field will be used as the record key for sequencing records as they are placed in the file. The amusement park master file will be used for further processing applications to provide information for operating and managing the park. This master file creation program is the first in a series of integrated programs designed to implement an Amusement Park Information System.

The output specifications in Figure 3-1 illustrate the format of the terminal data entry session. Because the file will be created interactively, the program will prompt repeatedly for an input field by displaying the name of the field. Following each prompt, the operator enters either numeric data, identified by the format symbol #, or alphabetic characters, identified by the X symbol. After all fields for a particular record are keyed, the operator indicates whether the captured data are correct by entering either Y (for Yes) or N (for No) in response to the verification prompt. When all the data fields have been keyed and verified, they are written to the file.

A CONCEPTUAL VIEW OF FILES

Notice that the format of the output file in Figure 3-2 resembles a *table*. That is, logically, the data are organized into *rows* and *columns*. Each row of the table represents a record written to the file; each column represents a field within every record. Physically, the data fields and records will be written *serially* (one after another) on the storage device. Fields will be separated by commas, as shown in the output section of the programming specifications. However, for programming purposes, it is convenient and proper to visualize computer files as tables.

<u>PROGRAMMING SPECIFICATIONS</u>

System: AMUSEMENT PARK   Date: 04/08/XX
Program: MASTER FILE CREATION   Program I.D.: FUN01 Analyst: B. LEIGH

Design and write a program to create a master file of attraction information
for the American Fun Amusement Park. Data for the master records are entered
interactively through a terminal. The records are written to a disk file in
attraction number sequence. The program will be coded in BASIC. Figure 3-1.1
shows the system flowchart for this application.

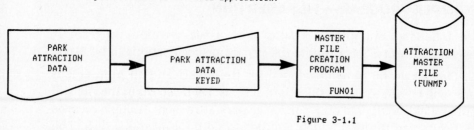

Figure 3-1.1

<u>INPUT</u>

The amusement park attraction and operation data are the program input. The
following 15 records will be written to the disk file in the order listed:

Park Location Code	Attraction Number (Key)	Attraction Type	Attraction Name	Days in Operation this Month	Attendance this Month
10	101	A	THE BLAZER	3	1,246
10	104	A	WATERSLIDE	1	311
10	105	F	KREEPY KASTLE	3	124
20	201	C	KIDDIE KAR	3	86
20	202	F	PIRATE'S COVE	2	343
20	207	F	JUNGLE SAFARI	1	819
20	210	A	DEVIL'S PIT	1	212
30	310	A	THE DUNGEON	1	113
30	312	C	MERRY MOUSE	3	1,043
30	320	F	WILD CHICKEN	3	832
40	406	A	CRASHIN' CARS	3	797
40	419	F	MUSIC SHOW	2	312
40	420	A	THE CORKSCREW	1	67
50	510	F	FRONTIER DAYS	3	118
50	515	F	SPACE PROBE	2	247

The attraction-type codes are A for adult, C for child, and F for family.

<u>PROCESSING</u>

For each record of attraction data, the following processing steps take place:

   1. The computer prompts the operator for the fields one at a time.
      Fields are entered on a keyboard. As the data are keyed, they
      are echoed by the system and displayed next to the prompt.

   2. After all fields for a single record are entered, they are veri-
      fied visually by the operator, who indicates whether the data are
      correct or incorrect.

   3. If the data are correct, they will be written to the disk file.
      If they are incorrect, the operator will be permitted to rekey
      them.

   4. After all records are written to disk, a final end-of-file (EOF)
      record is written.

Figure 3-1.2 shows the file creation session as it will appear to the operator
on the terminal screen or printer.

```
       0000000001111111111222222222233333333333
       1234567890123456789012345678901234567889
01        MASTER FILE CREATION
02        *********************
03
04 KEY THE DATA FIELDS INDICATED.
05 TO END THE PROGRAM, KEY THE FIELDS:
06 '0,0,0,END OF FILE,0,0' TO CREATE
07 AN END-OF-FILE RECORD.
08
09 LOCATION CODE........? ##
10 ATTRACTION NUMBER....? ###
11 ATTRACTION TYPE......? X
12 ATTRACTION NAME......? XXXXXXXXXXX
13 DAYS IN OPERATION....? #
14 ATTENDANCE TO DATE...? ####
15    VERIFY (Y/N)......? X
16    .
17    .
18    .
19 LOCATION CODE........? 0
20 ATTRACTION NUMBER....? 0
21 ATTRACTION TYPE......? 0
22 ATTRACTION NAME......? END OF FILE
23 DAYS IN OPERATION....? 0
24 ATTENDANCE TO DATE...? 0
25    VERIFY (Y/N)......? Y
26
27 *** END OF SESSION ***
28
29
```

Figure 3-1.2

Figure 3-1.3 shows the image of the disk file that will be created. Records
will be written in attraction number sequence. An EOF record should appear as
the final record in the file. As each field is written, it should be separated
from other fields by a comma. The name of the master file will be "FUNMF".

```
10 , 101 ,A,THE BLAZER, 3 , 1246
10 , 104 ,A,WATERSLIDE, 1 , 311
10 , 105 ,F,KREEPY KASTLE, 3 , 124
20 , 201 ,C,KIDDIE KAR, 3 , 86
20 , 202 ,F,PIRATE'S COVE, 2 , 343
20 , 207 ,F,JUNGLE SAFARI, 1 , 819
20 , 210 ,A,DEVIL'S PIT, 1 , 212
30 , 310 ,A,THE DUNGEON, 1 , 113
30 , 312 ,C,MERRY MOUSE, 3 , 1043
30 , 320 ,F,WILD CHICKEN, 3 , 832
40 , 406 ,A,CRASHIN' CARS, 3 , 797
40 , 419 ,F,MUSIC SHOW, 2 , 312
40 , 420 ,A,THE CORKSCREW, 1 , 67
50 , 510 ,F,FRONTIER DAYS, 3 , 118
50 , 515 ,F,SPACE PROBE, 2 , 247
0 , 0 ,0,END OF FILE, 0 , 0
```

Figure 3-1.3

Figure 3-1. Programming specifications for master file creation program (FUN01).

63

10	101	A	THE BLAZER	3	1246
10	104	A	WATERSLIDE	1	311
10	105	F	KREEPY KASTLE	3	124
20	201	C	KIDDIE KAR	3	86
20	202	F	PIRATE'S COVE	2	343
20	207	F	JUNGLE SAFARI	1	819
20	210	A	DEVIL'S PIT	1	212
30	310	A	THE DUNGEON	1	113
30	312	C	MERRY MOUSE	3	1043
30	320	F	WILD CHICKEN	3	832
40	406	A	CRASHIN' CARS	3	797
40	419	F	MUSIC SHOW	2	312
40	420	A	THE CORKSCREW	1	67
50	510	F	FRONTIER DAYS	3	118
50	515	F	SPACE PROBE	2	247
0	0	0	END OF FILE	0	0

Figure 3-2. Data in a file are viewed collectively as a table. Each row of the table represents a record, and each column represents a data field within the record. Although fields and records are written to disk serially, for programming purposes it is correct to visualize a file as a table.

PROBLEM ANALYSIS

Figure 3-3 presents the data flow analysis for the problem to be solved. The diagram identifies the areas in memory that will be required to carry out the processing and the general flow of data into and out of memory.

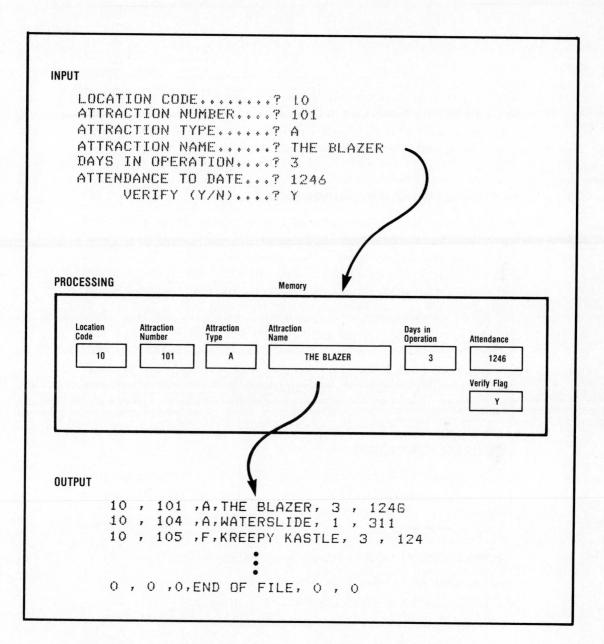

INPUT

```
LOCATION CODE.........? 10
ATTRACTION NUMBER.....? 101
ATTRACTION TYPE.......? A
ATTRACTION NAME.......? THE BLAZER
DAYS IN OPERATION.....? 3
ATTENDANCE TO DATE...? 1246
      VERIFY (Y/N)....? Y
```

PROCESSING

Memory

Location Code	Attraction Number	Attraction Type	Attraction Name	Days in Operation	Attendance
10	101	A	THE BLAZER	3	1246

Verify Flag

Y

OUTPUT

```
10 , 101 ,A,THE BLAZER, 3 , 1246
10 , 104 ,A,WATERSLIDE, 1 , 311
10 , 105 ,F,KREEPY KASTLE, 3 , 124
            •
            •
            •
0 , 0 ,0,END OF FILE, 0 , 0
```

Figure 3-3. Data flow analysis for master file creation program (FUN01).

The terminal operator begins by entering—one field at a time—the record with the lowest attraction-number key. Entered data are placed in memory and echoed on the terminal so that the operator can verify the entry visually. When all the fields of one record have been entered and verified, they are written to the disk file as an attraction record. This sequential entry of input fields and writing of records continues—in attraction-number key order—for each record in the file.

Handling End-Of-File Conditions

After all master records have been entered into the computer and written to the disk file, an *end-of-file (EOF)* record is created. This record contains zeros in all the fields except the attraction-name field, in which the value END OF FILE appears. An EOF record is created so that programs accessing the file subsequently can determine when all the records have been input.

Some computer systems that use BASIC do not require an EOF record. Such systems produce EOF indicators automatically. On other systems, however, a processing error can occur if an EOF record is omitted. System differences can be neutralized by writing a special EOF record to the file every time, since this technique will work on all systems.

PROGRAM FUNCTIONS

After performing problem analysis and reviewing the programming specifications, the following list of major processing functions can be identified:

1. Display program identification and operator instructions.
2. Prepare the disk file to receive master records.
3. Enter master record fields into memory.
4. Format and write the master records to the file.
5. Write the end-of-file record to the disk file.
6. Disassociate the disk file from the program.
7. Display end-of-session message.
8. Stop processing.

These functions must now be organized into a computer program.

PROGRAM DESIGN

The structural design for the following program is based on the general computer information systems program model introduced in the last chapter. Recall that this model has three major sections that appear in virtually all programs. A begin processing section includes those activities that occur one time only at the beginning of processing. A main processing section includes those activities that occur repeatedly, usually once for each input record to be processed. End processing activities occur one time only at the completion of processing. The appropriate detailed processing functions are then allocated to each of these sections. By adopting this three-section program model, the programmer automatically completes a major portion of the program design.

Figure 3-4 presents the structure chart for this program. The begin processing activities include displaying the program heading and operator instructions, preparing the disk file to receive the master records, and inputting the first record into memory. Main processing activities include writing a master record to the file and inputting the next set of master data. These two functions are repeated until there are no more master records to input. End processing activities include writing an EOF record, disassociating the program from the file, and halting processing.

OPENING AND CLOSING FILES

Records cannot be written to or accessed from a file unless a link is established between the file and the program that processes the file. To establish this link, a file must be identified by a name to which the program can refer. It may also be necessary to indicate to the computer system whether the file is an input or an output file. And, in the case of a new disk file, space must be reserved on the storage device to hold the records that will be written. All of these activities are referred to as *opening* a file. A file must be opened before processing can begin. Thus, in the current program, the file opening function is one of the begin processing activities.

After file processing is completed, the file must be *closed*. This action disassociates, or unlinks, the file from the program, disallowing further access. In the current program, the file closing function takes place only one time at the completion of processing. Therefore, the program module used to close the file is located in the end processing section, after the module that writes the EOF record.

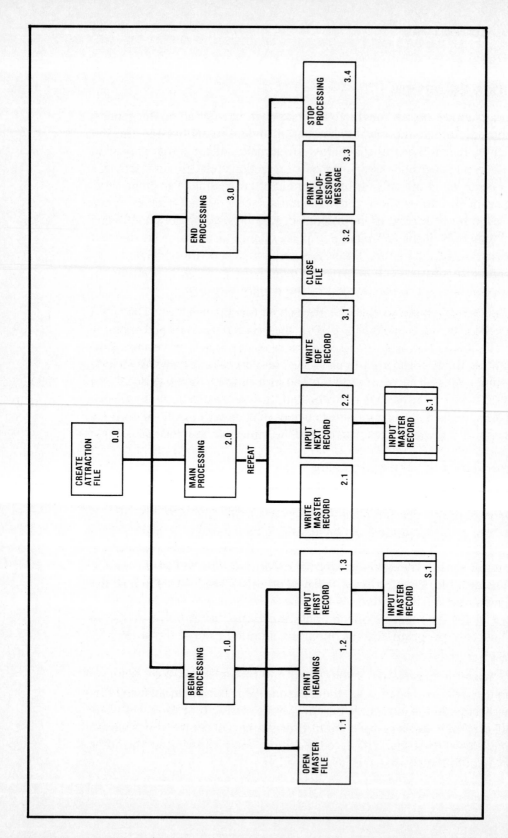

Figure 3-4. Structure chart for master file creation program (FUN01).

Indicating End of Input Data

The main processing functions—WRITE MASTER RECORD and INPUT NEXT RECORD—are repeated until all master records have been written. The main processing loop will continue until the operator types the EOF data. That is, the attraction-name field contains the value END OF FILE and all other input fields contain zero values. The program then will end the repeat control structure and proceed to its end processing activities, at which time these EOF fields are written as part of the last record in the master file.

Program Subroutines

The two input modules—INPUT FIRST RECORD and INPUT NEXT RECORD—implement a *look-ahead* input technique. That is, the first record to be processed is input within the begin processing section of the program. All subsequent records are input as part of the activities in the main processing section of the program. Both modules are, in fact, identical. Although some programs do not require look-ahead inputting, *double reading* works in all programs and *single reading*, in which case a single input module appears at the beginning of the main processing loop, does not. Therefore, using the double-reading technique in all programs is more convenient than trying to determine which programs accept single-reading.

With programs requiring only a few input commands, it is relatively easy to duplicate the commands in the second input module. Such duplicate statements appear in the example program in Chapter 2.

In other programs, however, several computer instructions are involved in the input function. For example, in the current program, the computer prompts and operator responses necessary to input a single record require 15 separate computer instructions. These same operations are required in both the INPUT FIRST RECORD and INPUT NEXT RECORD modules. In such a case, duplicating the code to the INPUT NEXT RECORD module is inconvenient.

By using a *subroutine*, an operator can avoid duplicate coding. A subroutine is a program module that can perform its processing whenever needed. A subroutine can be called, or activated, from any point in a program at any time. An activated subroutine carries out its processing and then returns control to the module in which the subroutine was called.

The INPUT MASTER RECORD module appearing on the structure chart in Figure 3-4 is an example of a subroutine. This module contains the instructions necessary to input all the fields for a master record. When it is time to input the first master record, this subroutine will be called. When it is time to input each subsequent master record, this same subroutine will be called. Thus, the input instructions need to be specified only once. Subsequent input instructions can be performed whenever needed simply by activating the subroutine. The structure chart presents the graphic technique used for documenting subroutines.

PROCESSING SPECIFICATIONS

Figure 3-5 presents the pseudocode specifications for the *mainline* program, which contains the overall processing logic, apart from any subroutines that are used. Each structure chart module has been specified as one or more computer operations required to implement the

```
0.0 CREATE ATTRACTION FILE
    1.0 BEGIN PROCESSING
        1.1 OPEN MASTER FILE
            Open "FUNMF" for output
        1.2 PRINT HEADINGS
            Print program indentification heading lines
            Print blank line
            Print operator instructions lines
        1.3 INPUT FIRST RECORD
            Perform S.1 INPUT MASTER RECORD
    2.0 MAIN PROCESSING
        REPEAT: until end of Master data
            2.1 WRITE MASTER RECORD
                Write Location Code, Attraction Number, Attraction Type,
                    Attraction Name, Days in Operation, Attendance to Date
            2.2 INPUT NEXT RECORD
                Perform S.1 INPUT MASTER RECORD
        END REPEAT
    3.0 END PROCESSING
        3.1 WRITE EOF RECORD
            Write Location Code, Attraction Number, Attraction Type,
                Attraction Name, Days in Operation, Attendance to Date
        3.2 CLOSE FILE
            Close "FUNMF"
        3.3 PRINT END-OF-SESSION MESSAGE
            Print blank line
            Print end-of-session line
        3.4 STOP PROCESSING
            Stop
```

Figure 3-5. Pseudocode for mainline master file creation program.

function. The operations are listed in the general sequence in which they will be performed by the computer.

The required operations have been determined by studying the data flow within the computer to identify the data items involved in the processing. The input and output formats for the data have been determined by studying the programming specifications. Note especially how the logical control structures have been written in pseudocode and how the EOF test is specified.

DESIGN OF INPUT SUBROUTINE

Notice in Figure 3-5 how the calls to the program subroutine have been pseudocoded. Within the INPUT FIRST RECORD and INPUT NEXT RECORD modules, a single *subroutine call* operation—Perform S1.0 INPUT MASTER RECORD—is specified. Perform S1.0 INPUT MASTER RECORD indicates that a subroutine will be called upon to perform the processing at this point. Figure 3-6 presents the structure chart and pseudocode for the input subroutine. At the beginning of the subroutine, a record verification *flag*, or indicator, defines the storage area in which the operator's response to the verification prompt will be placed. On entry to the subroutine, a blank character is placed in this storage area to erase the Y or N stored during the previous activation of the subroutine. At this point, the storage area is prepared to receive the new value.

Next, a program loop is set up to control the input function. Within this loop, the program will lead the operator through the data entry operations necessary to input the master record fields. After all fields are entered, the program prompts for the verification flag. The operator checks the displayed data visually and enters either a Y or an N in the verify-flag storage area. The program then tests this flag.

If the flag contains a Y, the program exits from the subroutine and returns to the mainline program, in which the data are written as a master record. If the flag contains an N, the input loop is repeated, allowing the operator to re-key the data. Re-keying continues until the data are signaled as being correct.

PROGRAM CODE

There is a clear distinction between programming and coding. In many computer installations, for example, programmers develop programs up through program specifications in pseudocode. With completion of

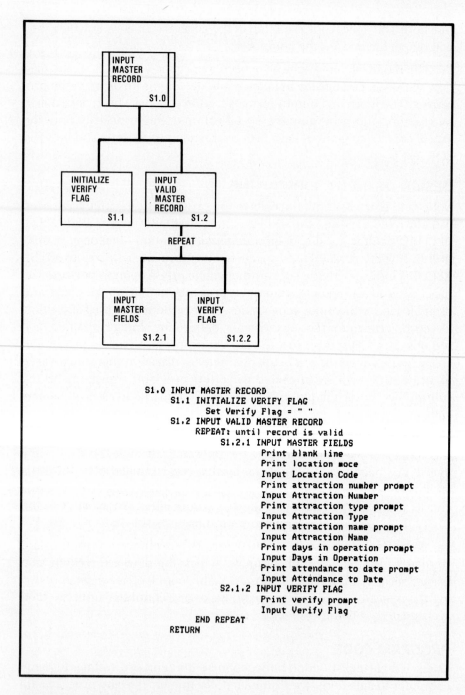

```
                    S1.0 INPUT MASTER RECORD
                       S1.1 INITIALIZE VERIFY FLAG
                              Set Verify Flag = " "
                       S1.2 INPUT VALID MASTER RECORD
                           REPEAT: until record is valid
                              S1.2.1 INPUT MASTER FIELDS
                                     Print blank line
                                     Print location moce
                                     Input Location Code
                                     Print attraction number prompt
                                     Input Attraction Number
                                     Print attraction type prompt
                                     Input Attraction Type
                                     Print attraction name prompt
                                     Input Attraction Name
                                     Print days in operation prompt
                                     Input Days in Operation
                                     Print attendance to date prompt
                                     Input Attendance to Date
                              S2.1.2 INPUT VERIFY FLAG
                                     Print verify prompt
                                     Input Verify Flag
                           END REPEAT
                       RETURN
```

Figure 3-6. Design for Input Master Record subroutine.

pseudocoding, the solution to the programming problem has been developed and written. In effect, the most difficult tasks of programming have been completed. Thereafter, people called *coders* translate the programs into programming languages. The complete BASIC code for the example program is presented in Figure 3-7. The following sections discuss BASIC code and coding conventions.

Statements and Line Numbers

The computer operations specified during pseudocoding are translated into BASIC code. Normally, a single line of pseudocode can be converted into a single line of BASIC code. That is, there is a one-to-one correspondence between the pseudocoded operations and the BASIC commands. Each line, or statement, in BASIC represents one computer operation. The statements are numbered in an ascending sequence that corresponds generally with the execution sequence of the statements.

Each line in a BASIC program must have a *line number.* Normally, line numbers are incremented in tens when they are first assigned. Thus, additional lines can be inserted between existing lines without disrupting the original numbering scheme. Also, as an aid in aligning statements and improving the readability of the program, all line numbers should contain the same number of digits.

BASIC Statement Types

Most BASIC programs include four general types of statements:

- *Documentation* statements help the reader to understand what the program does and how it works. Documentation statements are useful during the program development testing and debugging steps, and when program changes are made. Documentation statements are not executable. That is, the computer ignores them during program processing.

- *Processing* statements instruct the computer to perform data manipulation operations. The input, arithmetic, and output commands used to perform the main processing tasks are included within this group.

- *Control* statements establish the logical sequence of processing operations. Normally, statements are executed in the order in which they are presented to the computer. Special logical control statements are

```
1000 REM FUN01                                        WEL/DRA
1010 REM                MASTER FILE CREATION
1020 REM
1030 REM THIS PROGRAM CREATES A MASTER FILE NAMED "FUNMF"
1040 REM WHICH CONTAINS INFORMATION ON PARK ATTRACTIONS FOR
1050 REM THE AMERICAN FUN AMUSEMENT PARK.  RECORDS FOR THE
1060 REM FILE WILL BE ENTERED INTERACTIVELY THROUGH A
1070 REM COMPUTER TERMINAL.  THE RECORDS WILL BE ORGANIZED
1080 REM FOR SEQUENTIAL ACCESS USING THE ATTRACTION NUMBER
1090 REM AS THE RECORD KEY.
1100 REM
1110 REM VARIABLE NAMES
1120 REM
1130 REM    L.....PARK LOCATION CODE
1140 REM    N.....ATTRACTION NUMBER
1150 REM    T$...ATTRACTION TYPE
1160 REM    N$...ATTRACTION NAME
1170 REM    D.....DAYS IN OPERATION (THIS MONTH)
1180 REM    A.....ATTENDANCE TO DATE (THIS MONTH)
1190 REM    V$...VERIFY FLAG
1200 REM
1210 REM 0.0 CREATE ATTRACTION FILE
1220 REM
1230 REM ***************************
1240 REM * 1.0 BEGIN PROCESSING *
1250 REM ***************************
1260 REM
1270 REM 1.1 OPEN MASTER FILE
1280          OPEN "FUNMF" FOR OUTPUT AS FILE #1
1290 REM
1300 REM 1.2 PRINT HEADINGS
1310          PRINT "    MASTER FILE CREATION"
1320          PRINT "    *********************"
1330          PRINT
1340          PRINT "TYPE THE DATA FIELDS INDICATED."
1350          PRINT "TO END THE PROGRAM, TYPE THE FIELDS:"
1360          PRINT "'0,0,0,END OF FILE,0,0' TO CREATE"
1370          PRINT "AN END-OF-FILE RECORD."
1380 REM
1390 REM 1.3 INPUT FIRST RECORD
1400          GOSUB 2000
1410 REM
1420 REM ***************************
1430 REM * 2.0 MAIN PROCESSING  *
1440 REM ***************************
1450 REM REPEAT
1460      IF N$ = "END OF FILE" THEN GOTO 1550
1470 REM
1480 REM    2.1 WRITE MASTER RECORD
1490             PRINT #1, L;",";N;",";T$;",";N$;",";D;",";A
1500 REM
1510 REM    2.2 INPUT NEXT RECORD
1520             GOSUB 2000
1530 REM
1540      GOTO 1450
1550 REM END REPEAT
1560 REM
1570 REM ***************************
1580 REM * 3.0 END PROCESSING   *
1590 REM ***************************
1600 REM
1610 REM 3.1 WRITE EOF RECORD
1620          PRINT #1, L;",";N;",";T$;",";N$;",";D;",";A
1630 REM
1640 REM 3.2 CLOSE FILE
1650          CLOSE #1
1660 REM
1670 REM 3.3 PRINT END-OF-SESSION MESSAGE
1680          PRINT
1690          PRINT "*** END OF SESSION ***"
```

```
1700 REM
1710 REM 3.4 STOP PROCESSING
1720          STOP
1730 REM
1740 REM
2000 REM *****************************
2010 REM * S1.0 INPUT MASTER RECORD *
2020 REM *****************************
2030 REM
2040 REM S1.1 INITIALIZE VERIFY FLAG
2050          LET V$ = " "
2060 REM
2070 REM S1.2 INPUT VALID MASTER RECORD
2080 REM      REPEAT
2090          IF V$ = "Y" THEN GOTO 2310
2100 REM
2110 REM         S1.2.1 INPUT MASTER FIELDS
2120                    PRINT
2130                    PRINT "LOCATION CODE........";
2140                    INPUT L
2150                    PRINT "ATTRACTION NUMBER....";
2160                    INPUT N
2170                    PRINT "ATTRACTION TYPE......";
2180                    INPUT T$
2190                    PRINT "ATTRACTION NAME......";
2200                    INPUT N$
2210                    PRINT "DAYS IN OPERATION....";
2220                    INPUT D
2230                    PRINT "ATTENDANCE TO DATE...";
2240                    INPUT A
2250 REM
2260 REM         S1.2.2 INPUT VERIFY FLAG
2270                    PRINT "     VERIFY (Y/N)....";
2280                    INPUT V$
2290 REM
2300             GOTO 2080
2310 REM      END REPEAT
2320 REM
2330      RETURN
9990 END
```

Figure 3-7. BASIC code for master file creation program.

used to alter this sequence for implementation of the repeat and select constructs.

- *Data definition* statements identify data files to be processed. File opening and closing statements are included within this group.

Program Documentation—The REM Statement

Documentation is important to any program. Documentation refers to any explanatory notes that will assist the program reader's understanding of what the program does, what its logical structure is, and how the program works. It can be difficult, even for the programmer, to understand a program by examining its code. Therefore, a program may contain more lines of documentation than actual processing code.

In BASIC, documentation is provided in *remarks* statements. The keyword REM is coded, followed by any words, sentences, or other combinations of printable characters, including blank (space) characters. REM statements, since they are ignored by the computer during processing, can appear anywhere in the program.

In the sample program, REM statements appear at the beginning of the code (lines 1000 through 1190). This particular type of documentation identifies the program, explains its purpose, and defines the names assigned to memory areas. (These names are explained below.) Documentation lines also appear throughout the program to identify program modules and, in general, to improve the readability of the code. Note that remarks statements are used to cross-reference the module names to the pseudocoded program. Also, REM statements are used to insert blank lines within the program listing to facilitate reading. Figure 3-8 presents the general format for the REM statement.

Opening Files—The OPEN Statement

Recall that a record cannot be written to or accessed from a file unless the file has been opened. The file opening operation links the program with the file and makes the file available for processing.

Files are opened through an OPEN statement. Figure 3-9 presents the formats for the OPEN statements required by several types of popular computer systems. The example programs in this book use the format

---

General Format:
    line number REM comments

Example:

```
1030 REM THIS PROGRAM CREATES A MASTER FILE
```

The keyword REM is followed by any combination of printable characters, including the blank (space) character. On some computer systems, an exclamation mark (!) or apostrophe (') can be used in place of the word REM. (See program code used in Chapters 9 through 11.)

Figure 3-8. Format for the REM statement.

Figure 3-9. Formats for the OPEN statement.

Digital Equipment Corporation (DEC) System

General Format:
line number OPEN "file name" $\begin{Bmatrix} \text{FOR INPUT} \\ \text{FOR OUTPUT} \end{Bmatrix}$ AS FILE #file num.

Example:

```
1280 OPEN "FUNMF" FOR OUTPUT AS FILE #1
```

The file name is supplied by the programmer, who keys from one to six alphabetic and numeric characters. The first character must be alphabetic. The file name must be enclosed in quotation marks. The optional phrases FOR INPUT or FOR OUTPUT may be coded. If neither phrase is used, the system will attempt to open the file for input. However, if the file does not exist yet, the system will open a new file to receive output. The phrase AS FILE # is followed by a file reference number. Any integer from 1 to 12 may be used.

Radio Shack TRS-80 System

General Format:

line number OPEN $\begin{Bmatrix} \text{"I"} \\ \text{"O"} \end{Bmatrix}$, buffer number, "file name"

Example:

```
1280 OPEN "O", 1, "FUNMF"
```

The mode "I", for input, or "O", for output, is used to open the file. The buffer number is used in a manner similar to the file reference number for the DEC system. The file name may contain one to eight characters. The first character must be a letter of the alphabet. The file name must be enclosed in quotation marks.

IBM/Microsoft System

General Format:
line number OPEN "file name" $\begin{Bmatrix} \text{FOR INPUT} \\ \text{FOR OUTPUT} \end{Bmatrix}$ AS FILE #file num.

Example:

```
1280 OPEN "FUNMF" FOR OUTPUT AS #1
```

The file name may contain one to eight characters and must be enclosed in quotation marks. The file reference number associates the named file with a particular input or output statement.

Apple II System

General Format:
line number PRINT CHR$(4); "OPEN file name"

Example:

```
1280 PRINT CHR$(4); "OPEN FUNMF"
```

This statement is used to open a file for either input or output. If a file does not exist for input, the system will open a new file for output. The file name may contain up to 30 characters. The first character must be alphabetic.

Figure 3-9. Concluded.

---

for DEC (Digital Equipment Corporation) systems. However, you will have to use the format that applies to your particular computer. The OPEN statement used for the DEC system can be found in line 1280 of the example program. This line can be substituted with other appropriate OPEN statement formats.

NOTE: Different kinds of computer systems use different methods for specifying and working with files. File input and output operations tend to be *machine-dependent*. Therefore, it is necessary to know the specific OPEN statement for the system on which you are programming.

Closing Files—The CLOSE Statement

A file must be closed after processing has been completed. This action unlinks the program from the file and disallows further access.

The CLOSE statement for the amusement park master file can be found in line 1650 of the sample program. Figure 3-10 presents the general formats for CLOSE statements used by the computer systems identified above.

Printing Strings—The PRINT Statement

The statements used to print or display a program identification heading and operator instructions can be found in lines 1310 through 1370. This printing or display is performed by a PRINT statement.

DEC, TRS-80, IBM/Microsoft Systems

General Format:
  line number CLOSE #file number

Example:

```
1650 CLOSE #1
```

The keyword CLOSE is followed by the file reference number (or buffer number) that appeared in the OPEN statement.

Apple II System

General Format:
  line number PRINT CHRS$(4); "CLOSE file name"

Example:

```
1650 PRINT CHR$(4); "CLOSE FUNMF"
```

The file name that appeared in the OPEN statement is repeated in the CLOSE statement.

Figure 3-10. Formats for the CLOSE statement.

When used to print or display heading lines, the PRINT statement specifies the exact string of characters for a single line appearing on the CRT screen or printer. The character *string*, enclosed by quotation marks, may include any number of printable characters, including the blank (space) character. Normally, each PRINT statement specifies the printing that will appear on a single line. Thus, the number of PRINT statements required will be the same as the number of lines to be printed. Notice, in line 1330, that a PRINT statement without a string specification is used to print a blank line.

The same type of PRINT statement is used in the module to display the end-of-session message. In line 1680, a blank line is printed, followed by the printing of the string "*** END OF SESSION ***" in line 1690. Figure 3-11 presents the general PRINT statement formats used to print character strings. These formats apply to all versions of BASIC.

General Formats:
  line number PRINT
  line number PRINT "string"

Examples:

```
1330 PRINT
1340 PRINT "KEY THE DATA FIELDS INDICATED."
```

The keyword PRINT is followed by either (1) no additional
specifications, which causes a blank line to be displayed, or
(2) a string of printable characters enclosed in quotation marks.
The string represents the literal value to be displayed.

Figure 3-11. Formats for the PRINT statement used to display or print blank lines
or character strings.

Calling Subroutines—The GOSUB . . . RETURN Statements

A GOSUB statement transfers program control to a subroutine. Control
is sent to the statement referenced by the line number that follows the
keyword GOSUB. Thus, in line 1400 of the example program, the statement GOSUB 2000 transfers control, or *branches*, to line 2000. Starting
in line 2000, the subroutine inputs the data fields of a master record.
Processing then continues sequentially for the statements in the subroutine. The RETURN statement in line 2330 transfers control back to
the statement that follows the GOSUB statement, and normal sequential
processing continues.

Note that the statement GOSUB 2000 appears twice in the program.
In line 1400, the subroutine is called to input the first master record. In
line 1520, the subroutine is called to input the second and subsequent
records. Figure 3-12 presents the general format used to call and return
control from subroutines.

Inputting Data—The PRINT and INPUT Statements

The program subroutine coded in lines 2000 through 2330 contains the
statements for inputting the fields of a master record. The PRINT
statements in the INPUT MASTER FIELDS module provide prompts to

General Formats:
    line number GOSUB line number
    line number RETURN

Examples:

```
1400 GOSUB 2000
    •
    •
    •
2330 RETURN
```

The line number that follows the keyword GOSUB is used for
the first statement of a subroutine. Control branches to that
statement to execute the statements within the subroutine.
When the program reaches the RETURN statement (the last line
of a subroutine), control branches back to the statement immediately following the GOSUB statement to continue the
normal sequential execution of statements. The action of a
subroutine call and return is represented in the following lines
of code:

```
                •
                •
                •
  ┌────────1400 GOSUB 2000
  │ ┌──►1410
  │ │      •
  │ │      •
  │ │      •
  └─┼──►2000 REM S.1 INPUT MASTER RECORD
    │      •
    │      •
    │      •
    └─── 2330 RETURN
```

Figure 3-12. Formats and logic flow for GOSUB and RETURN statements.

the terminal operator. The operator then keys in data values, which the INPUT statements store in memory. The general format that was used to print headings is used also for the PRINT statements here. That is, a character string enclosed in quotation marks follows the key word PRINT. The character strings represent operator prompts, reminding the terminal operator which data field values should be entered. The only difference in these PRINT statements is the semicolon (;) used to end a statement.

Recall that one line of printing results for each PRINT command coded in the format described previously. Thus, each time the computer executes a PRINT statement, the display on the terminal screen or the printing mechanism on the printer advances to the next line.

According to the programming specifications, however, the data values, when keyed, should be echoed by the computer for display on the same line as the prompt. That is, the display *cursor* or printing mechanism should not be advanced after the PRINT statement is executed. Therefore, the semicolon is used to override the normal advance to the next line during the subsequent input operation.

Data fields are accepted by the computer and placed in memory with the INPUT statement. This statement uses the keyword INPUT, followed by one or more *variables*, or *variable names*. These names, assigned by the programmer, represent areas within memory used to retain data values. Once retained, data values can be referenced and processed under their variable names. For example, in line 2140, the INPUT L statement assigns the name L to a memory area, accepts location code data from the terminal keyboard, and places the input value in the named area. During subsequent processing, the value for the location code can be referenced through the variable L.

After printing an operator prompt, the computer pauses while the operator keys the data value. Execution of the INPUT statement causes the computer to display a question mark (?) prompt following the operator prompt. The operator then keys the value, which is echoed by the computer and appears next to the prompt. At this point, the operator transmits the keyed value for placement within the named memory area.

The same memory areas are reused for each set of data fields to be input. When the data for the second and subsequent master records are input, the values previously entered under the variable names are replaced. Thus, the six memory areas required to hold the six data values for each input record will contain different values for each new record that is input. Figure 3-13 presents the general INPUT statement format used to accept data from a terminal keyboard.

NAMING PROGRAM VARIABLES

Variable names must be assigned to the memory areas that will hold entered data. Specific rules must be followed in naming variables. The rules differ depending on the type of data to be retained:

- For retaining *numeric* data—which include the decimal digits 0–9, the decimal point (.), and the optional sign symbols (+, –)—the name can be a single alphabetic (A–Z) character, or a combination of a single alphabetic character followed by a single numeric (0–9) digit.

- For retaining *alphanumeric* data—which include alphabetic characters, special symbols ($, #, %, &, etc.), and numeric digits that will not be involved in arithmetic operations—the name can be a single alphabetic character followed by a dollar sign ($), or a single alphabetic character followed by a single numeric digit followed by a dollar sign.

General Format:
    line number INPUT variable name {, variable name . . .}

Examples:

```
2140 INPUT L
3000 INPUT A, B, C$, N1
```

The keyword INPUT is followed by one or more variable names. Variables are separated from each other by commas. For each INPUT statement, the computer prints a question mark prompt and pauses while the operator enters and transmits the expected number of data values. The transmitted data are retained in memory under the variable names. The values must be keyed in the order implied by the list of names. Also, the expected data type (numeric or alphanumeric) is implied by the names.

Figure 3-13. Format for the INPUT statement used to accept data from a terminal keyboard.

In the example program, the variable name L is assigned to the numeric location code area. The name N is assigned to the numeric variable used to hold the attraction number. The variable T$ is used to hold the attraction type, represented by one of the alphabetic characters A, C, or F. The variable N$ represents the attraction name. The variable D represents the numeric value for days in operation. The name A is used for numeric attendance values.

Notice that the documentation at the beginning of the example program defines these variable names. The REM statements, which are nonexecutable, do not assign variable names. The remarks only remind the program reader of the meanings of the variable names. The names are assigned to the memory areas when the INPUT statements are executed the first time. During subsequent statement executions, the variable names simply identify existing memory locations in which incoming data are to be placed.

In some versions of BASIC, *extended* variable names can be used, which provide for better name descriptions than versions without the extended variable name capability. For example, in the current program, the extended variable name ATTRACTION . NAME$ could be used instead of N$. Such names can contain 30 or more alphabetic and numeric characters.

Coding Repetitions—The IF . . . GOTO Statements

The MAIN PROCESSING module is implemented by lines 1450 through 1550 of the sample program. Recall that the MAIN PROCESSING module contains a repetition control structure. Within this module are two subordinate modules. These two modules will be activated repeatedly until the operator enters the EOF record.

A repetition control structure is coded with an IF statement and a GOTO statement. These two statements form the boundaries of the repetition, or loop. In general, the IF statement tests whether the condition for ending the repetition has occurred. In the example program, a test is made in line 1460 to determine if the variable N$ contains (=) the END OF FILE value. If not, program processing continues within the loop, in sequence, statement by statement, until the GOTO statement is encountered in line 1540. The GOTO statement transfers control to the beginning of the loop, and the *condition test* is repeated.

This repeated processing continues as long as the test—N$ = "END OF FILE"—is false. That is, if the variable N$ does not contain this value, the computer will continue writing a master record and inputting the next record. Eventually, however, the operator will enter the EOF record. Then, when control returns to the top of the loop, the condition test will be evaluated as true. With this evaluation, control branches directly to line 1550, bypassing the loop and continuing normal sequential execution.

This test to check for the end of input data could have been conducted for any of the data fields. For example, the program could have checked for L = 0, N = 0, T$ = "0", D = 0, or A = 0. Any of these tests would have indicated that the EOF record had been entered. However, the N$ = "END OF FILE" test was chosen because the code itself indicates clearly the type of condition being tested. For example, if the test L = 0 had appeared in the program, the actual situation for ending the loop

General Formats:
    line number IF condition test THEN GOTO line number
    line number GOTO line number

Example:

```
---►1450 REM REPEAT
    1460 REM IF N$ = "END OF FILE" THEN GOTO 1550---
        .
        .
        .
----1540       GOTO 1450
    1550 REM END REPEAT◄-----------------------------
```

The keyword IF is followed by a condition test. If the test result is false, the program continues to process statements, in sequence, until the GOTO statement is encountered. The GOTO statement transfers control to the top of the loop, where the test is repeated. This looping continues until the test result is true. Then, control branches out of the loop. If the test involves alphanumeric data, the string must be enclosed in quotation marks.

Figure 3-14. Formats for the IF and GOTO statements used to implement the repetition control structure.

would have been less clear. Figure 3-14 presents the general IF and GOTO statement formats used to implement a repetition control structure.

Note in lines 1450 and 1550 that REM statements have been used to document the REPEAT . . . END REPEAT boundaries of the loop. These statements, although nonexecutable, have been included to make the program more understandable. As repetition boundaries, the REM statements serve also as targets for the GOTO statements. When control is transferred to a REM statement, computer processing will continue with the next executable statement in sequence.

A repeat loop also is included within the input subroutine. In the example program, master field and verification flag inputting continue until the verify flag contains the value "Y" entered by the operator. At this point in the subroutine, control branches from the loop to the RETURN statement.

Assigning Data to Variables—The LET Statement

In line 2050 of the subroutine, the verify flag (V$) is cleared initially to prepare for operator input. The flag is cleared by assigning a blank space to the variable. The blank space replaces the "Y" entered by the operator during the previous call to the subroutine. If the flag is not cleared before the input loop is entered, the test in the IF statement (V$ = "Y") would be true. The program, then, would exit from the subroutine and bypass the input function. Therefore, the flag must be cleared each time the subroutine is entered.

A LET statement is an *assignment* statement that places a data value into a named memory area. In line 2050 of the subroutine, the value " " (blank space) is assigned (=) to the variable V$. This LET statement retains a value generated by the program itself, rather than a value that was input. Figure 3-15 presents the general LET statement format used to assign program-generated values to variables.

Writing Records to Files—The PRINT Statement

The PRINT statement, when used to write records to files, must reference a file and identify the variables that are to be written. Line 1490 of the example program, shows a file reference number (#1) following the word PRINT. This number is identical to the number used in the associated OPEN statement. Thus, a connection is made between the PRINT statement and a particular disk file.

General Format:
    line number LET variable name = $\left\{\begin{array}{l}\text{numeric data value}\\\text{string value}\end{array}\right\}$

Examples:

```
2050 LET V$ = "   "
3120 LET A = 5.75
3130 LET Z$ = "THIS IS A STRING"
```

The keyword LET is followed by the name of an area within memory where either a numeric or alphanumeric (string) data value will be placed. The variable name is followed by an equal sign and the particular value to be retained in memory. To retain alphanumeric data, the string must be enclosed in quotation marks.

Figure 3-15. General format for the LET statement used to assign data values to areas in memory.

Following the reference number are the names of the storage areas for data values to be written to the file. The names are listed in the order in which they are to appear as fields within the output record. In the example, the location code (L) will be written first, followed by the attraction number (N), the attraction type (T$), the attraction name (N$), the days in operation (D), and, finally, the attendance (A).

The above six data values must be written to a disk as separate fields. In BASIC, the computer separates the fields with commas. Therefore, the string "," is written to the disk between each of the variables. This string serves as a field *delimiter*. When the first master record is written to the file, for example, it will appear in the following form:

10, 101, A, THE BLAZER, 3, 1246

The comma delimiters will enable the computer to distinguish the data fields when this file is input to a subsequent program.

Each of the variable names and comma strings in the PRINT statement is separated by a semicolon (;). A semicolon must appear between printing specifications within a PRINT statement. Figure 3-16 presents

DEC, TRS-80, IBM/Microsoft Systems

General Format:
  line number PRINT #file number, variable name {;",";variable
  name . . . }

Example:

```
1490 PRINT #1, L;",";N;",";T$;",";N$;",";D;",";A
```

The keyword PRINT is followed by the file reference number
(buffer number) that appeared in the associated OPEN statement. A comma is coded next. Thereafter, one or more variable
names are keyed in the order in which the fields are to appear
in the record. Field values are separated by commas. The
variable names and commas are separated by semicolons.

Apple II System

General Formats:
  line number PRINT CHR$(4); "WRITE file name"
  line number PRINT CHR$(4);variable name {;","; variable
    name . . . }
  line number PRINT CHR$(4)

Examples:

```
1490 PRINT CHR$(4); "WRITE FUNMF"
1491 PRINT CHR$(4); L;",";N;",";T$;",";N$;",";
     D;",";A
1492 PRINT CHR$(4)
```

Three PRINT statements are required to write a record to a file.
The first statement indicates the file to which the record will be
written. The second provides the variable names that contain
the data for the record fields. The second statement also writes
commas between the fields. The third statement tells the computer to stop writing to the file so that subsequent PRINT
statements, which may be intended to display headings or
prompts, are not activated.

Figure 3-16. Formats for the PRINT statement used to write records to a file.

the general PRINT statement formats used by the different systems to write records to files.

The same type of PRINT statement is used in line 1620 to write the EOF record. The data fields will appear in the same format as the attraction records.

Halting Processing—The STOP Statement

After all processing is completed, the STOP statement halts program execution. At this point, the computer will await further commands from the terminal operator. The STOP statement appears at the *logical* end of the program, which is not always the *physical* end of the program. For example, in the current program, the statement appears prior to the subroutine code. The program completes its processing with the writing of the EOF record, closing of the file, and printing of the end-of-session message. The program does not complete its processing following execution of the subroutine. Figure 3-17 presents the general format for the STOP statement.

The END Statement

The END statement is the final statement in a program. This statement always must appear last and must carry the highest line number. The END statement indicates the physical end of the program to the computer. It is not a processing command but simply marks the end of the code. The format for the END statement appears in Figure 3-18.

```
General Format:
  line number STOP

Example:

1720 STOP

The keyword STOP appears on a line by itself, with no other
specifications.
```

Figure 3-17. Format for the STOP statement.

```
General Format:
  line number END

Example:

9990 END

The keyword END appears by itself, with no other specifica-
tions, and always on the last line of the program.
```

Figure 3-18. Format for the END statement.

PROGRAM TESTING AND DEBUGGING

After coding in BASIC is completed, the program is entered into the computer. Each program line is keyed exactly as coded. After a line is keyed, it is transmitted to the computer by depressing the *carriage return, entry,* or *transmit* key. The entire program is loaded into memory line by line.

On many systems, as each line is keyed and transmitted, the computer checks the statement for syntactical errors. That is, the computer will make certain that the BASIC rules for style and statement format have been followed. If a syntactical error is encountered, the computer will generate an error message and allow the terminal operator to re-enter the line. When the format of the instruction is correct, interpreting proceeds to the next instruction. Thus, syntax checking takes place as a program is entered.

Once entered into memory, the program is ready to be tested for logical errors. Logical errors are those that result in incorrect processing, even though a program may be syntactically perfect. Logical errors can be caused by such oversights as coding statements out of sequence, using the wrong variable names, omitting necessary statements, or branching to the wrong line numbers.

Testing takes place when the program is executed. The command RUN is keyed and transmitted to the computer, at which point control is turned over to the program. Each BASIC instruction, in turn, is translated by the interpreter program into machine language and carried out. After completing program processing, the computer returns control to the terminal and awaits the next operator command.

Testing and debugging are important programming activities. In some cases, however, programmers spend more time locating and correcting errors than writing programs. This need not be the case. Programming is not an error-prone activity if approached in a proper, systematic manner.

You will find that the more time you spend on the problem analysis, program design, and program specification steps, the less time you will spend testing and debugging. Most serious programming errors occur when people rush into coding without giving adequate thought to the "front end" of the program development process. The analysis, design, and specification methods presented here will help focus your attention on these important programming steps.

PROGRAM CODING CONVENTIONS

The BASIC code for the file creation program illustrated in Figure 3-7 uses the REM statement extensively for program documentation. In addition to providing program explanations and defining variable names, REM statements are used to identify program modules. The modules are identified by level numbers and names for cross-referencing to the pseudocode and structure chart. These style conventions simplify reading and understanding of the program, and assist in program debugging, testing, and long-term maintenance.

This style of code is used throughout the book since it provides for easy cross-referencing among the coded program, the pseudocode, and the structure chart. In coding the programming assignments, however, it is not necessary to provide such elaborate documentation. Reference numbers and names can be omitted if the program modules are identified clearly. Also, some versions of BASIC allow for the use of alternate, abbreviated symbols for the REM statement. These symbols make it easier to key in the program.

Figure 3-19 shows another style of code that is acceptable for the example program. Note that the exclamation mark (!) can be used in place of the letters REM. In other versions, the apostrophe (') or other symbols can be used.

In this example, only the three top-level modules and the subroutine are numbered and named. For identification purposes, subordinate modules are set apart from one another with blank lines. Modules within a repeat structure are indented. Even though full documentation is not

```
1000! FUN01
1010!                    MASTER FILE CREATION                    WEL/DRA
1020!
1030! THIS PROGRAM CREATES A MASTER FILE NAMED "FUNMF" WHICH
1040! CONTAINS INFORMATION ON PARK ATTRACTIONS FOR THE
1050! AMERICAN FUN AMUSEMENT PARK.   RECORDS FOR THE FILE
1060! WILL BE ENTERED INTERACTIVELY THROUGH A COMPUTER
1070! TERMINAL.   THE RECORDS WILL BE ORGANIZED FOR
1080! SEQUENTIAL ACCESS USING THE ATTRACTION NUMBER AS
1090! THE RECORD KEY.
1100!
1110! VARIABLE NAMES
1120!
1130!    L....PARK LOCATION CODE
1140!    N....ATTRACTION NUMBER
1150!    T$...ATTRACTION TYPE
1160!    N$...ATTRACTION NAME
1170!    D....DAYS IN OPERATION (THIS MONTH)
1180!    A....ATTENDANCE TO DATE (THIS MONTH)
1190!    V$...VERIFY FLAG
1200!
1210! 0.0 CREATE ATTRACTION FILE
1220!
1230! ************************
1240! * 1.0 BEGIN PROCESSING *
1250! ************************
1260!
1270   OPEN "FUNMF" FOR OUTPUT AS FILE #1
1280!
1290   PRINT "      MASTER FILE CREATION"
1300   PRINT "      *********************"
1310   PRINT
1320   PRINT "TYPE THE DATA FIELDS INDICATED."
1330   PRINT "TO END THE PROGRAM, TYPE THE FIELDS:"
1340   PRINT "'0,0,0,END OF FILE,0,0' TO CREATE"
1350   PRINT "AN END-OF-FILE RECORD."
1360!
1370   GOSUB 2000   !INPUT FIRST RECORD
1380!
1390! ************************
1400! * 2.0 MAIN PROCESSING  *
1410! ************************
1420! REPEAT
1430   IF N$ = "END OF FILE" THEN GOTO 1500
1440!
1450      PRINT #1, L;",";N;",";T$;",";N$;",";D;",";A
1460!
1470      GOSUB 2000   !INPUT NEXT RECORD
1480!
1490   GOTO 1420
1500! END REPEAT
1510!
1520! ************************
1530! * 3.0 END PROCESSING   *
1540! ************************
1550!
1560   PRINT #1, L;",";N;",";T$;",";N$;",";D;",";A
1570!
1580   CLOSE #1
1590!
1600   PRINT
1610   PRINT "*** END OF SESSION ***"
```

```
1620!
1630    STOP
1640!
2000! ****************************
2010! * S1.0 INPUT MASTER RECORD *
2020! ****************************
2030!
2040    LET V$ = " "
2050!
2060! REPEAT
2070    IF V$ = "Y" THEN GOTO 2270
2080!
2090       PRINT
2100       PRINT "LOCATION CODE........";
2110       INPUT L
2120       PRINT "ATTRACTION NUMBER....";
2130       INPUT N
2140       PRINT "ATTRACTION TYPE......";
2150       INPUT T$
2160       PRINT "ATTRACTION NAME......";
2170       INPUT N$
2180       PRINT "DAYS IN OPERATION....";
2190       INPUT D
2200       PRINT "ATTENDANCE TO DATE...";
2210       INPUT A
2220!
2230       PRINT "     VERIFY (Y/N)....";
2240       INPUT V$
2250!
2260    GOTO 2060
2270! END REPEAT
2280!
2290    RETURN
2300!
2310    END
```

Figure 3-19. Alternate coding conventions for BASIC programs.

used, the program still is easy to read and understand, and its structure can be related back to the pseudocode and structure chart.

PROGRAMMING CASE STUDIES

For Chapters 3 through 8, programming practice assignments are provided that require you to design, write, code, and run programs that illustrate the material presented in each chapter. The assignments appear in Appendix A.

These assignments are divided into two sets, identified as CASE STUDY ONE and CASE STUDY TWO. As you work through the assignments for each case study, you will learn first-hand how a computer information system is built. You should be able to identify the interrelationships among the programs that, together, implement a business system.

Each case study, then, contains practice assignments that closely parallel the techniques and illustrations in the chapters. Since each program builds upon previous programs, it becomes important for all programs to work correctly. Otherwise, subsequent programs cannot perform their intended functions.

The system that you will build requires long-term operation across multiple business cycles, as is the case with most business information systems. Thus, upon completion of either CASE STUDY ONE or CASE STUDY TWO, you should have developed an understanding of the components of computer-based systems, and a systems perspective on the integration of hardware/software resources within computer information systems.

Chapter Summary

1. A computer file is organized into records and fields. A field is a single item of data—a basic fact represented by numbers, alphabetic characters, or special symbols. A record is a collection of fields usually relating to a single person, object, or event. A file is a collection of records.

2. Records within a file are organized according to a control field, or record key, to facilitate retrieval. Normally, records are written in ascending record key value sequence.

3. Files are created under control of a computer program. A file creation program accepts data fields from a terminal keyboard, organizes these fields into records, and then writes the records to the file.

4. For programming purposes, a file can be visualized as a table in which each row represents a record written to the file; each column represents a field within that record. Physically, however, records are written serially, one after another, on the storage device.

5. File creation programs are based on the CIS program model. Program functions can be allocated readily to the begin processing, main processing, and end processing sections of the model. A look-ahead reading technique is used.

6. Files must be opened prior to processing and closed when processing is completed.

7. A program subroutine is used to avoid duplication of code. A subroutine implements a program function that is required repeatedly by the program.

8. During program coding, each line of pseudocode specification usually is translated into one line of code.

9. A BASIC computer instruction is written as a line, or statement. Each statement must have a line number. This number is assigned in an increasing numeric sequence that should correspond to the execution sequence of the statements.

10. There are four general types of BASIC commands, or statements. Documentation statements, identified by the keyword REM, are used to help the reader's understanding of a program. Processing statements, identified by such keywords as INPUT, LET, and PRINT, instruct the computer to process data operations. Control statements, identified by the keywords GOSUB, GOTO, IF, RETURN, and STOP, establish the logical sequence in which the processing operations are to be performed. Data definition statements, using such keywords as OPEN and CLOSE, identify data files to be processed. Data definition statements also make data files available to the program.

11. The END statement signals the physical end of the program to the computer.

12. The programmer assigns names to areas in memory where input data will be retained. Different naming conventions apply to numeric data and alphanumeric data.

13. Program debugging is performed by the computer to locate syntactical errors when the program statements are keyed into memory.

14. Program testing is performed to locate logical errors. Testing is accomplished by running the program with test data.

Review Questions

1. What is sequential file organization and why is this technique used?

2. How are the data in output files formatted?

3. Why is it necessary to open a file?

4. Why must a file be closed after processing is completed?

5. What is a subroutine and why is it used?

6. What are the four general types of statements included in most computer programs and what purpose does each statement serve?

7. What is the purpose of assigning variable names to areas in memory?

8. When do most serious programming errors occur?

Programming Assignments

Programming practice assignments for Chapter 3 are located in Appendix A, CASE STUDY ONE and CASE STUDY TWO.

Key Terms

1. sequential file organization
2. sequential access
3. interactive
4. prompt
5. table
6. rows
7. columns
8. serial
9. end-of-file (EOF) record
10. look ahead
11. double reading
12. single reading
13. subroutine
14. call
15. mainline
16. subroutine call
17. flag
18. coder
19. line number
20. documentation statement
21. processing statement
22. control statement
23. data definition statement
24. documentation
25. remarks statement
26. string
27. branch
28. variable
29. variable name
30. numeric data
31. alphanumeric data
32. condition test
33. assignment statement
34. delimiter
35. logical end
36. physical end
37. carriage return key
38. entry key
39. transmit key

BASIC Library

1. OPEN
2. REM
3. CLOSE
4. PRINT
5. GOSUB
6. RETURN
7. INPUT
8. IF
9. GOTO
10. LET
11. STOP
12. END

4
PRODUCING
DETAIL REPORTS

OVERVIEW AND OBJECTIVES

One of the main reasons for creating files is to provide a collection of information that can be drawn from and reported to people with a need to know something about the organization. For instance, managers must have access to current and historical data in order to perform their control functions. They need to know what the status of the business is so that action to sustain or correct deviations from plans and objectives can be taken.

File information is provided primarily through printed reports. One of the most common types of reports is the detail report. This report lists all or selected records from a file. There are four main uses of these reports: for verification of file content, to provide management control information, for use as manual files, and to provide backup copies of computer files. Each of these uses is discussed in this chapter. Then, programs to produce detail reports are described and illustrated. Two different programs are presented. The first is a detail listing of the contents of a file; the second is an exception report to management highlighting areas that require attention.

When you complete your work in this chapter, you should be able to:

☐ List and describe the primary uses of detail reports.

☐ Design and write programs to produce formatted listings from file content.

☐ Design and write programs to produce reports listing selected records from files.

☐ Design and write program modules to perform simple arithmetic.

☐ Design and write program modules containing simple selection constructs.

THE NATURE OF DETAIL REPORTS

Detail reports are printed or displayed listings drawn from the content of data files. In most cases, these reports list all of the records in a file and all of the fields within those records. Thus, the reports present file details at the record and field levels. Detail reports are put to four main uses in business organizations:

- Verification of file content
- Operational management control
- Manual files
- Backup for computer files.

Each of these uses is described below. Then programs that produce detail reports are discussed and illustrated.

Verification of File Content

The sample program in the previous chapter builds a master file containing data on amusement park attractions. The program supports interactive creation of records through operator entry of fields of data through a terminal keyboard.

The resulting master file will become the basis for an entire system of programs. The amusement park information system will consist of programs to generate management reports, to update the file to reflect ongoing business transactions, and to allow selective inquiry about the status of particular attractions. As the central focus of the information system, the master file must represent, currently and accurately, the status of the business. There can be no erroneous data.

During file creation, data entering the master file are verified visually by the terminal operator. As data fields are keyboarded, their values are echoed by the computer system and printed or displayed on the output device. This technique for input validation is relatively standard, establishing automatic input control that can be applied for all data entries. However, file content can be verified through other methods. Some of the more common of these techniques involve the use of detail reports.

Line-by-line comparison.   The printing of a detail report listing the entire content of a file can be used to check on the accuracy of data entry.

In this case, each record in the file and each field of data are printed or displayed. Then, the records of the original *source documents*, containing the data that were keyed, are compared visually—record for record, line for line—with the detailed listing. Any identified errors are corrected.

Control totaling.   A second method for verifying file content is known as *control totaling*, or *batch balancing*. This technique is applicable for files containing numeric data fields.

Control totaling is a multi-step procedure. The first step occurs before data are entered into the computer. Adding machine or calculator totals are developed for each of the numeric fields in the records to be used for control purposes. These *control totals* are accumulated for individual fields across all records. The control tapes then accompany the source documents to the file creation step.

During file creation, the same numeric fields are accumulated as they are entered under control of the file creation program. Following processing, the computer prints or displays the totals developed during file creation. These totals are compared with those from the adding machine or calculator tapes. If the totals match, the data are assumed to have been captured with an acceptable level of accuracy. If the totals do not match, a detail report is prepared so that each record in the file can be checked against its original source record.

The generation of computer control totals also can be done after the file is created. A detail report is printed listing all records in the file as well as totals for the numeric fields. The totals are compared with the adding machine control totals and any discrepancies are resolved by checking the record listings.

Hash totaling.   Control totals can be produced for all numeric fields in a record. In most instances, these totals represent accumulations of amount fields in which the data values are amounts of money or quantities that can be counted. Yet, other kinds of numeric data can produce control totals.

A common type of control total that does not utilize an amount field is a *hash total*. A hash total is the accumulation of a numeric field such as a record key or other form of identification number. Although meaningless in an information processing sense, such totals can provide easy verification that numbers in key or identification fields have been entered correctly.

Correcting file records. Obviously, if incorrect data are found in files, they must be corrected. The integrity of any information produced from the file is only as great as the accuracy of the data in the file. Misinformation in files can destroy the reliability of a computer information system as the basis for decision making. Accuracy of file data is an absolute requirement.

Changes to existing files are made as part of normal file maintenance activities. Maintenance involves locating the record in error, correcting the error, and placing the corrected record back into the file. File maintenance is covered in later chapters. An opportunity to write programs to change file records is presented at that time.

Operation Management Control

Detail reports are tools of management. Information must be available that enables managers to evaluate and control day-to-day business operations. Managers must be able to tell the extent to which the company is meeting its objectives and if action is needed to keep the company on its course. The information that supports management evaluations and decisions comes from an organization's files.

Managers require access to file information. Further, the information must be presented in a readable, understandable, and usable form. Communication of file content to managers is accomplished chiefly through formal detail reports.

In some cases, all records within a file—including all data fields within every record—are listed on a detail report. Depending on management needs, totals for amount fields also may be presented.

In other cases, managers do not require a comprehensive file report. As long as business activity is proceeding smoothly, the manager need not be bothered with the news that operations are progressing according to plan. Rather, the manager's attention should be drawn to activities that are not proceeding according to plan and thus need corrective action. Unexpected or irregular developments in an organization's operations are known as *exceptions*. The methodology that concentrates attention on out-of-control situations is called *management by exception*. The reports used for this purpose are called *exception reports.* These are detail reports that present data on only those situations that are in need of attention. Such reports present selective information from the file rather than entire sets of records. Exception reports are primary tools of efficient, effective management.

Manual Files

Another use of detail reports is as substitutes for computer files. Access to information in files frequently is required to support the work of an organization's employees. Yet, with computer-based files, it is not always practical to allow everyone open access to those files. Besides, there simply may not be enough computer terminals to satisfy total information reference demand.

Detail reports that list the content of computer files can, in these situations, become surrogate files within the manual, nonautomated portions of information systems. These reports become reference data for carrying out processing operations for which access to the computer is not available. As file content changes, new reports are issued. Depending on the application, detail reports may be produced monthly, weekly, daily, or even more often.

Backup Files

Finally, detail reports provide emergency *backup* copies of computer files. As complete file listings, these reports can replace files temporarily in case the computer malfunctions. At least a portion of file processing can continue while computer files are inaccessible. In case of a disaster such as a fire or flood, it even may be necessary to recreate computer files by keyboarding detail listings.

DETAIL REPORT FORMATS

Regardless of the uses to which detail reports are put, these computer-produced documents are presented in fairly standard printed or displayed formats. Normally, there are three main sections of a detail report:

- At the top of a report, *heading* lines present identification information. This information includes a *report title* that describes the purpose of or information contained in the report. Following the title, *column headings* describe the content of each column of data presented.

- The report *body* contains the data extracted from the file. Usually, each *detail line* of the report presents the fields of data contained in a single file record. The fields are aligned in columns to make the information easy to read and understand. There are as many detail lines as there are records—unless only certain categories of records have been selected from the file.

- The report *footing* appears last. This section of the report contains accumulated totals for numeric fields or other types of summary information. Footing lines are specified as needed to meet the purpose for which the report is being developed.

Figure 4-1 presents the general layout of detail reports. This particular report is produced by the first program described in this chapter.

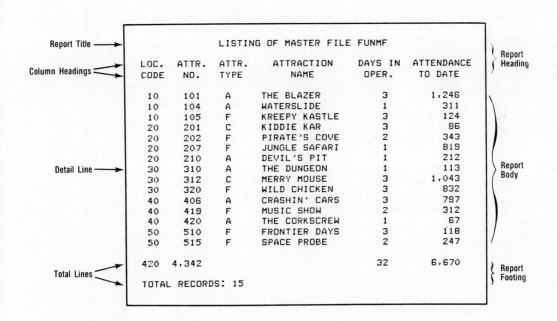

Figure 4-1. General format for printed or displayed detail reports.

PROGRAMMING SPECIFICATIONS—DETAIL REPORT

The first program to be designed and developed in this chapter produces a detailed listing of the records contained in the amusement park master file that was created in the last chapter. The report will be used to verify the content of the file before further applications programs are run.

The specifications for this program are presented in Figure 4-2. Each record in the master file (named FUNMF) will be listed as a separate line on the report. The six data fields will be printed in separate columns across the report body. After all records have been listed, control totals will be printed for each of the numeric fields, including hash totals of

```
                     PROGRAMMING SPECIFICATIONS

System:  AMUSEMENT PARK                           Date:    04/12/XX
Program: DETAIL REPORT          Program I.D.: FUN02   Analyst: B. LEIGH

Design and write a program to produce a printed detail report that lists all
records in the attraction master file (FUNMF) for the American Fun Amusement
Park.  The attraction records in this file are organized in attraction number
sequence.  The program will be coded in BASIC.  The system flowchart for this
application is shown in Figure 4-2.1.
```

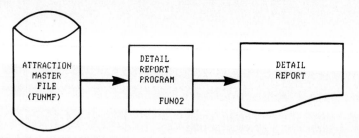

Figure 4-2.1

```
INPUT

The master file records are input to the program in the following format:

                  Field Name              Data Type
                  -------------------     -----------
                  Location Code           Numeric
                  Attraction Number       Numeric
                  Attraction Type         Alphanumeric
                  Attraction Name         Alphanumeric
                  Days in Operation       Numeric
                  Attendance to Date      Numeric

A final EOF record is written to the file.  This record contains the character
string "END OF FILE" in the attraction-name field.
```

PROCESSING

The following processing steps are performed:

1. A control total is accumulated for the days-in-operation fields and for the attendance-to-date fields.

2. A hash total is developed for the location-code fields and for the attraction-number fields.

3. The records in the file are counted and the total number is produced.

OUTPUT

The detail report will be printed in the format shown in Figure 4-2.2. As indicated, the report title should be centered over the report. Also, each column heading should be centered over its column of data. The report body is to be single-spaced with the control-total line separated from the body of the report by a single blank line. The total-records line should appear two spaces below the control-total line.

```
      0000000001111111111222222222233333333334444444444555555555
      123456789012345678901234567890123456789012345678901234567
01             LISTING OF MASTER FILE FUMMF
02
03 LOC.  ATTR. ATTR.    ATTRACTION     DAYS IN  ATTENDANCE
04 CODE  NO.   TYPE        NAME         OPER.    TO DATE
05
06 ##    ###   X      XXXXXXXXXXXXX       ##      ##,###
07 ##    ###   X      XXXXXXXXXXXXX       ##      ##,###
08
09
10
11
12
13 ### ##,###                           ###     ###,###
14
15 TOTAL RECORDS: ##
16
17.
```

Figure 4-2.2.

Figure 4-2. Programming specifications for detail report program.

the location code and attraction number columns. Finally, the total number of records in the file will be listed. Appropriate report title and column heading lines will be included to identify the information on the report.

Notice in Figure 4-2 that the input specifications list the names and content of the fields included in each record. The specifications also indicate the types of data—numeric or alphanumeric—appearing in the fields. All records appear in this same format. To write the program, therefore, it is not necessary to know the actual data values of the records in the file. Only the record formats must be known.

The output specifications present the general format of the report. These records identify the exact report and column headings that will be printed—as well as the printer or video display columns at which printing will take place. Within the body and footing of the report, only locations of data fields are shown. Again, it is not necessary to know, nor is it likely that the programmer will know, the data values that will be printed. Rather, the programmer need only be aware of the size of each field, the type of data in the field (numeric, alphabetic, or alphanumeric), and the location of the field within the report.

The conventions followed in this and subsequent programming specifications for indicating data output formats are:

- The symbol X is used to indicate an alphanumeric character. One or more of these symbols, depending on the total size of the field, is shown on the report spacing form within the columns that will contain an alphanumeric field.

- The symbol # is used to indicate a numeric character. One or more of these symbols, plus optional commas (,), decimal points (.), dollar signs ($), and other special formatting symbols, are used to show the layout of the field.

PROBLEM ANALYSIS

The general flow of data for computer processing of the detail report is shown in the processing map in Figure 4-3. In this diagram, computer memory is divided into three areas, used for input, output, and accumulation of totals. Although memory is not actually subdivided as shown, this illustration technique is an effective way to demonstrate processing requirements—and also to provide a reminder that memory space must be allocated to support the application.

Separate memory areas are defined for each of the six fields of data contained in the input records. Whenever a record is input from the master file into memory, the fields are retained separately so they can be processed individually within the computer.

Since control totals will be developed for the numeric fields, an *accumulator* is defined for each total. Amounts or values within the input records are added into the memory areas used as accumulators. A running total will be maintained for each numeric field. Thus, after all records are processed, the accumulator will contain the sums of the values for all fields. A fifth accumulator is required for totaling the

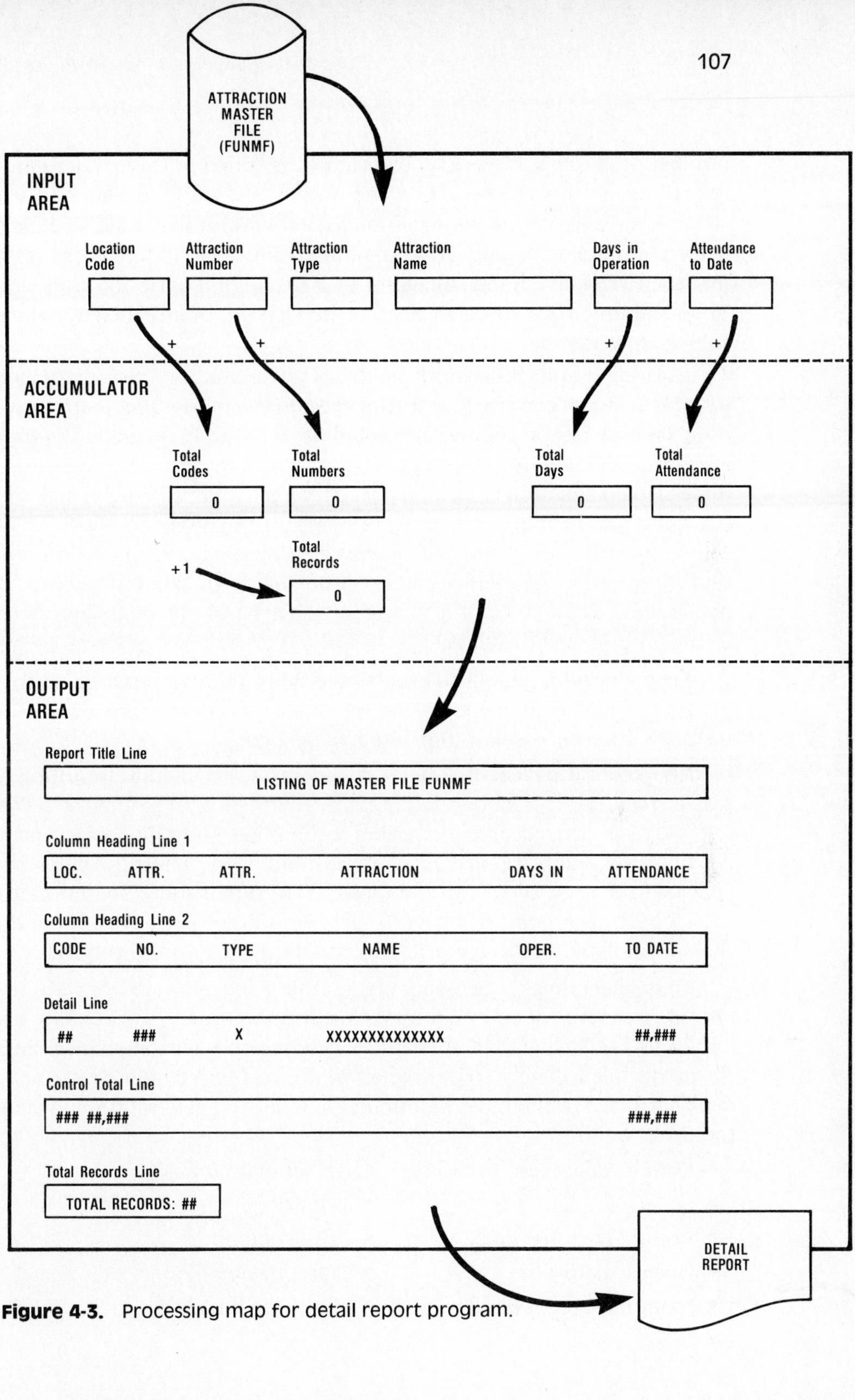

Figure 4-3. Processing map for detail report program.

number of records in the file. The value 1 is added to this accumulator for each record processed from the file.

It is necessary that all accumulators contain initial values of zero before summation begins. This operation is similar to that of depressing the "clear" key on a hand calculator before adding a series of numbers. The computer registers also need to be cleared, or initialized, before values are entered.

During printing, the input fields are arranged, or formatted, as a detail line on the report. The output area on the processing map shows how the data will be aligned into columns. Separately formatted output areas are described for the two total lines. Thus, there are three formats under which lines will be printed on the report—a detail line format and two total line formats. It is not necessary at this point to show exact columns at which printing will take place. It is only necessary to indicate that three different line formats will be required. Column alignment details will be covered in the coding for the program through reference to the output specifications.

Report heading lines also are defined within the output area. In this program, each heading line will be retained as a character string within memory, then accessed and printed as needed.

The general processing steps in this program include inputting a master record into memory, adding the values within the numeric fields into the respective accumulators, adding the value 1 into the total records accumulator, and printing a detail line on the report. These activities are repeated for each record in the master file. When there are no more master records (that is, whenever the end-of-file record is encountered), the accumulated totals are printed as footing lines on the report.

To support these processing tasks, other program functions are required. Heading, detail, and total line formats must be defined, accumulators will have to be set to zero, heading lines will be printed, and the master file will have to be opened before and closed after processing. Problem analysis, then, has identified the following general functions of the program:

- Define report line formats.
- Set accumulators to zero.
- Print report headings.
- Open master file.
- Input master record.
- Accumulate totals.
- Print detail line.
- Print total line.
- Close master file.
- Stop processing.

NOTE: The first function on the preceding list, define report line formats, applies only to DEC, IBM/Microsoft, and TRS-80 computers. The Apple II computer does not recognize this function. However, alternate formatting options appropriate to all systems are discussed later in this chapter.

Once identified, these functions must be allocated to the appropriate sections of a program and arranged in a logical order so that they will be carried out at the right time and for the correct number of times.

PROGRAM DESIGN

The design of this report writing program follows the general CIS model program introduced earlier. Recall that this model identifies three basic program sections to which processing functions are allocated—begin processing, main processing, and end processing. A structure chart illustrating this program design and showing the allocation of program functions to these sections is shown in Figure 4-4.

PROGRAM SPECIFICATION

Following structural design, program modules are elaborated to include the detailed computer operations necessary to implement their functions. The required operations can be identified by reviewing the processing map and programming specifications for details.

The pseudocode notation for specifying processing in the report program is presented in Figure 4-5. The program is now in a form that can be translated directly into BASIC code.

PROGRAM CODE

Complete BASIC code for the detail report program is given in Figure 4-6. The discussions that follow this code explain the rules covering use of certain instructions and also the reasons that certain lines of code are included.

Printing Report Lines

The discussions in this section apply to computers that allow use of PRINT USING statements. The DEC, IBM/Microsoft, and TRS-80 computers have this feature. The Apple II does not. Alternative printing

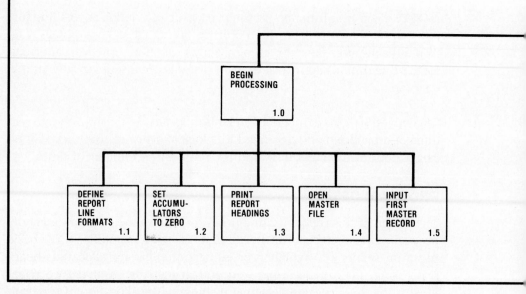

Figure 4-4. Structure chart for detail report program.

```
0.0 PRODUCE DETAIL REPORT
    1.0 BEGIN PROCESSING
        1.1 DEFINE REPORT LINE FORMATS
            Define Report Title Line
            Define Column Heading Line 1
            Define Column Heading Line 2
            Define Detail Line
            Define Control Total Line
            Define Total Records Line
        1.2 SET ACCUMULATORS TO ZERO
            Set Total Codes = 0
            Set Total Numbers = 0
            Set Total Days = 0
            Set Total Attendance = 0
            Set Total Records = 0
        1.3 PRINT REPORT HEADINGS
            Print Report Title Line
            Print blank line
            Print Column Heading Line 1
            Print Column Heading Line 2
            Print blank line
        1.4 OPEN MASTER FILE
            Open "FUNMF" for input
        1.5 INPUT FIRST MASTER RECORD
            Input Location Code, Attraction Number, Attraction Type,
                Attraction Name, Days in Operation, Attendance to Date
```

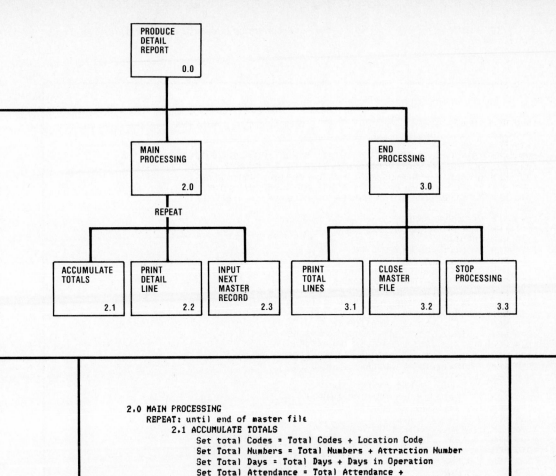

```
2.0 MAIN PROCESSING
    REPEAT: until end of master file
        2.1 ACCUMULATE TOTALS
            Set total Codes = Total Codes + Location Code
            Set Total Numbers = Total Numbers + Attraction Number
            Set Total Days = Total Days + Days in Operation
            Set Total Attendance = Total Attendance +
                Attendance to Date
            Set Total Records = Total Records + 1
        2.2 PRINT DETAIL LINE
            Print Detail Line using Location Code, Attraction Number,
                Attraction Type, Attraction Name, Days in Operation,
                    Attendance to Date
        2.3 INPUT NEXT MASTER RECORD
            Input Location Code, Attraction Number, Attraction Type,
                Attraction Name, Days in Operation, Attendance to Date
    END REPEAT
3.0 END PROCESSING
    3.1 PRINT TOTAL LINES
        Print blank line
        Print Control Total Line using Total Codes, Total Numbers,
            Total Days, Total Attendance
        Print blank line
        Print Total Records Line using Total Records
    3.2 CLOSE MASTER FILE
        Close "FUNMF"
    3.3 STOP PROCESSING
        Stop
```

Figure 4-5. Pseudocode for detail report program.

```
1000 REM FUN02                                    WEL/DRA
1010 REM           MASTER FILE DETAIL LISTING
1020 REM
1030 REM THIS PROGRAM PRINTS A DETAIL REPORT OF THE CONTENTS
1040 REM OF THE PARK ATTRACTIONS MASTER FILE (FUNMF) OF THE
1050 REM AMERICAN FUN AMUSEMENT PARK.  CONTROL TOTALS ARE
1060 REM LISTED AT THE END OF THE REPORT ALONG WITH THE
1070 REM COUNT OF THE TOTAL NUMBER OF RECORDS IN THE FILE.
1080 REM
1090 REM VARIABLE NAMES
1100 REM
1110 REM INPUT:
1120 REM     L.....LOCATION CODE
1130 REM     N.....ATTRACTION NUMBER
1140 REM     T$....ATTRACTION TYPE
1150 REM     N$....ATTRACTION NAME
1160 REM     D.....DAYS IN OPERATION (THIS MONTH)
1170 REM     A.....ATTENDANCE TO DATE (THIS MONTH)
1180 REM ACCUMULATORS:
1190 REM     T1....TOTAL LOCATION CODES
1200 REM     T2....TOTAL ATTRACTION NUMBERS
1210 REM     T3....TOTAL DAYS IN OPERATION
1220 REM     T4....TOTAL ATTENDANCE TO DATE
1230 REM     T5....TOTAL NUMBER OF RECORDS
1240 REM OUTPUT:
1250 REM     F1$...REPORT TITLE LINE
1260 REM     F2$...COLUMN HEADING LINE 1
1270 REM     F3$...COLUMN HEADING LINE 2
1280 REM     F4$...DETAIL LINE
1290 REM     F5$...CONTROL TOTAL LINE
1300 REM     F6$...TOTAL RECORDS LINE
1310 REM
1320 REM 0.0 PRODUCE DETAIL REPORT
1330 REM
1335 REM *************************
1340 REM * 1.0 BEGIN PROCESSING *
1345 REM *************************
1350 REM
1360 REM 1.1 DEFINE REPORT LINE FORMATS
1370         LET F1$ = "              LISTING OF MASTER FILE FUNMF"
1380         LET F2$ = "LOC.  ATTR.  ATTR.     ATTRACTION       DAYS IN   ATTENDANCE"
1390         LET F3$ = "CODE   NO.   TYPE        NAME            OPER.     TO DATE"
1400         LET F4$ = "  ##    ###    !     \              \     ##      ##,###"
1410         LET F5$ = "*### ##,###                               ###    ###,###"
1420         LET F6$ = "TOTAL RECORDS: ##"
1430 REM
1440 REM 1.2 SET ACCUMULATORS TO ZERO
1450         LET T1 = 0
1460         LET T2 = 0
1470         LET T3 = 0
1480         LET T4 = 0
1490         LET T5 = 0
1500 REM
1510 REM 1.3 PRINT REPORT HEADINGS
1520         PRINT F1$
1530         PRINT
1540         PRINT F2$
1550         PRINT F3$
1560         PRINT
1570 REM
1580 REM 1.4 OPEN MASTER FILE
1590         OPEN "FUNMF" FOR INPUT AS FILE #1
```

```
1600 REM
1610 REM 1.5 INPUT FIRST MASTER RECORD
1620          INPUT #1, L, N, T$, N$, D, A
1630 REM
1635 REM *************************
1640 REM * 2.0 MAIN PROCESSING   *
1645 REM *************************
1650 REM REPEAT
1660     IF N$ = "END OF FILE" THEN GOTO 1820
1670 REM
1680 REM     2.1 ACCUMULATE TOTALS
1690             LET T1 = T1 + L
1700             LET T2 = T2 + N
1710             LET T3 = T3 + D
1720             LET T4 = T4 + A
1730             LET T5 = T5 + 1
1740 REM
1750 REM     2.2 PRINT DETAIL LINE
1760             PRINT USING F4$, L, N, T$, N$, D, A
1770 REM
1780 REM     2.3 INPUT NEXT MASTER RECORD
1790             INPUT #1, L, N, T$, N$, D, A
1800 REM
1810     GOTO 1650
1820 REM END REPEAT
1830 REM
1835 REM *************************
1840 REM * 3.0 END PROCESSING    *
1845 REM *************************
1850 REM
1860 REM 3.1 PRINT TOTAL LINES
1870             PRINT
1880             PRINT USING F5$, T1, T2, T3, T4
1890             PRINT
1900             PRINT USING F6$, T5
1910 REM
1920 REM 3.2 CLOSE MASTER FILE
1930             CLOSE #1
1940 REM
1950 REM 3.3 STOP PROCESSING
1960             STOP
1970 END
```

Figure 4-6. BASIC code for detail report program.

specifications that are standard to all systems are presented in the next section, Standard Printing Specifications.

For printed data to be aligned properly within a report, the lines of printing must be described in standard formats. The computer then is presented with these printing *images,* or pictorial representations, that show where and how data values and character strings will appear on the report. During printing or display operations, output data are arranged, or formatted, according to these images. Thus, each type of output line appears in an identical format.

In BASIC, a printing format is described by a character string. This string contains special symbols to describe fields of output data, including their sizes, positions along the printed line, and other formatting instructions. These character strings, one for each line format, are retained in memory. Then, to print a formatted line, the computer references the appropriate format description and prints the output data in that image.

Figure 4-7 presents and annotates the statements required for formatted printing of the detail report. The line images are defined and retained in memory with LET statements. Recall that the LET statement is a general assignment statement used to hold values. In this case, the values are character strings representing printing formats. The general format for LET statements used to define print formats is given in Figure 4-8.

The report heading lines are described exactly as they will be printed on the report. These three lines are assigned to named memory areas— F1$, F2$, and F3$—in which a string value for each line will be placed to await printing at the beginning of the program.

The detail line is described and assigned to variable name F4$. This format string contains special symbols representing field formats: a number (pound) sign (#) represents a print position at which a numeric character will be printed. One or more of these symbols describes a field of data. An exclamation point (!) represents a position at which a single alphanumeric character will be printed. The pairs of backslashes (\ \ ) represent the beginning and ending positions within which an alphanumeric field of two or more characters will appear.

These *editing* symbols are grouped to represent fields of numeric or alphanumeric characters. The symbols are distributed within the string, separated by the appropriate number of blank spaces, to produce an image of the printed line. The length of each field is sufficient to hold the maximum expected length of data values that will be printed. Figures 4-9 and 4-10 show examples of the use of editing symbols for numeric and alphanumeric fields.

In Figure 4-7, the report total line images are stored under variable names F5$ and F6$. The totals are aligned beneath the data fields appearing in the columns. In format F6$, an identification heading, described exactly as it will appear on the report, is included along with the numeric field specification.

All of the report line formats are contained within a single module, 1.1 DEFINE REPORT LINE FORMATS, appearing at the beginning of the program. The reason for isolating the line formats here is to make them

```
LET F1$ = "            LISTING OF MASTER FILE FUNMF"
LET F2$ = "LOC.   ATTR.   ATTR.     ATTRACTION      DAYS IN   ATTENDANCE"
LET F3$ = "CODE    NO.    TYPE         NAME          OPER.     TO DATE"
LET F4$ = "  ##    ###      !    \               \     ##      ##,###"
LET F5$ = "### ##,###                                  ###    ###,###"
LET F6$ = "TOTAL RECORDS: ##"
                  .
                  .
        PRINT F1$
        PRINT                                        ⎫
        PRINT F2$                                    ⎬  Heading Lines
        PRINT F3$                                    ⎭
        PRINT
                  .
                  .
        PRINT USING F4$, L, N, T$, N$, D, A          Detail Line
                  .
                  .
        PRINT                                        ⎫
        PRINT USING F5$, T1, T2, T3, T4              ⎬  Total Lines
        PRINT                                        ⎭
        PRINT USING F6$, T5
                  .
                  .
```

```
                    LISTING OF MASTER FILE FUNMF

        LOC.   ATTR.   ATTR.     ATTRACTION      DAYS IN   ATTENDANCE
        CODE    NO.    TYPE         NAME          OPER.     TO DATE

          10    101      A     THE BLAZER           3         1,246
          10    104      A     WATERSLIDE           1           311
          10    105      F     KREEPY KASTLE        3           124
          20    201      C     KIDDIE KAR           3            86
          20    202      F     PIRATE'S COVE        2           343
          20    207      F     JUNGLE SAFARI        1           819
          20    210      A     DEVIL'S PIT          1           212
          30    310      A     THE DUNGEON          1           113
          30    312      C     MERRY MOUSE          3         1,043
          30    320      F     WILD CHICKEN         3           832
          40    406      A     CRASHIN' CARS        3           797
          40    419      F     MUSIC SHOW           2           312
          40    420      A     THE CORKSCREW        1            67
          50    510      F     FRONTIER DAYS        3           118
          50    515      F     SPACE PROBE          2           247

         420  4,342                                32         6,670

        TOTAL RECORDS: 15
```

Figure 4-7. Relationships among line format images and printing specifications for detail report program.

DEC, TRS-80, IBM/Microsoft Systems

General Format:
  line number LET variable name$ = string

Examples:

```
150 LET F1$ = "      MAIN HEADING"
170 LET F2$ = "COL.1      COL.2      COL.3"
210 LET F3$ = "###     ! \                \   ##,###.##"
340 LET F4$ = "TOTAL = $##,###.##"
```

The keyword LET is followed by the name of a string variable,
an equal sign (=), and a character string enclosed in quotation
marks. The string can include heading values and/or field
editing symbols arranged to provide an image of a printed line.
The string is assigned to (retained in) the variable and is
available for use at any time during program execution.

Apple II System

The LET statement is valid for retaining character strings in
memory. However, the strings cannot be used as printing formats because the Apple II does not recognize format images
and does not have a PRINT USING statement.

Figure 4-8. Format for the LET statement used to define printing formats.

---

easily accessible for possible future changes. If output formats have to
be changed in the future, the programmer can find and work with all
formatting instructions within a single segment of the program—without
having to search throughout the program and risk overlooking needed
changes.

Once report line images are defined and retained in memory, they
can be called up and used whenever they are needed. Printing of lines
under these formats is carried out by the PRINT and PRINT USING
statements. As shown in Figure 4-7, these statements make reference to
the variable name containing the line image. Then, if necessary, the
statements specify the names of the data items that will be printed under
that format. The variable names are listed in the order in which they will

VALUE IN MEMORY	EDITING FORMAT	EDITED OUTPUT

Whole numbers:

123	###	123
1234	####	1234
12	###	12
1234	#,###	1,234
123	##,###	123
12345	###,###	12,345

Digits are assigned to the field format from right to left. Unused format specifications are ignored. The comma will appear in the field if a significant (nonzero) digit appears to the left of the comma position.

Numbers with decimal points and signs:

1.2	#.#	1.2
12.3	###.##	12.30
123.452	###.##	123.45
1234.5	##,###.##	1,234.50
.123	##.###	0.123
−1.2	##.#	−1.2

Digits are assigned from the decimal point outward to the left and right. Unused positions to the right of the decimal point are padded with zeros. The first position to the left of the decimal point is padded with a zero. Unused digits on the right are truncated. Sufficient space must be defined for a possible minus sign.

Numbers with dollar signs:

12.34	$##.##	$12.34
1.23	$##.##	$ 1.23
123.452	$#,###.##	$ 123.45
12.34	$$#,###.##	$12.34
.12	$$##.##	$0.12
1234.562	$##,###.##	$ 1,234.56

A single dollar sign editing symbol prints the sign in a fixed location. A pair of dollar signs beginning the specification causes the sign to float to the right, up against the first significant digit.

Figure 4-9. Editing formats for numeric fields.

VALUE IN MEMORY	EDITING FORMAT	EDITED OUTPUT
A	!	A
ABC	!	A
ABCDE	\ \	ABCDE
ABCDEFG	\ \	ABCDE
ABC	\ \	ABC
AB	\ \	AB

An exclamation point (!) describes a one-character field. A pair of backslashes (\ \) describes a multiple-character field. The backslashes appear in the first and last positions of the field. Characters are left-margin justified. Unused positions are padded with blank spaces and extra characters truncated.

Figure 4-10.   Editing formats for alphanumeric fields.

appear across the report line. Because no data fields are printed in headings, only the PRINT command followed by the name of the variable containing the heading image is used. The general format for the PRINT USING statement is given in Figure 4-11.

In some versions of BASIC, the line formats are described with *image* statements rather than LET statements. As shown in Figure 4-12, an image statement is identified by a colon (:) in its first position following the line number. Also, the format specification for an alphanumeric field is different from that used in the LET statement. Otherwise, the line images are described in the same way. When this image statement is used, the PRINT USING statement refers to the line number of the image rather than to a variable name identified in a LET statement.

Standard Printing Specifications

Some computers, including the Apple II, do not support the PRINT USING feature. For these systems, a different strategy must be followed in formatting lines of printing. Although not as flexible in its approach to formatting, this alternative is standard to all versions of BASIC and can be used on any computer.

DEC, TRS-80, IBM/Microsoft Systems

General Format:
   line number PRINT USING variable name$ {, variable name . . . }

Examples:

```
1520 PRINT USING F1$
1760 PRINT USING F4$, L, N, T$, N$, D, A
```

The keywords PRINT USING are followed by the variable name that references the appropriate format string retained with the LET statement. The printing of heading lines does not require any additional specifications because the heading values are defined by the format itself. When data are printed according to the format, the variable name that references the format is followed by a comma and by one or more variable names of the areas in memory that contain the data. These variable names must be listed in the order in which they will be printed across the line.

IBM and TRS-80 Systems (with printers)

General Format:
   line number LPRINT USING variable name$ {, variable
   name . . . }

With the IBM and TRS-80 computers, the LPRINT USING statement is used to format the output to be printed. All other specifications are the same as those used with the PRINT USING statement that formats output to the CRT screen.

DEC System (alternate format)

General Format:
   line number PRINT USING line number {, variable name . . . . }

When an image statement is used to retain printing formats in memory, the PRINT USING statement includes the line number of the associated image statement (:).

Figure 4-11. Format for the PRINT USING statement.

```
General Format:
  line number: string

Examples:

1370:          LISTING OF MASTER FILE FUNMF
1400: ##    ### 'L   'LLLLLLLLLLLLL   ###   ##,###
1420: TOTAL RECORDS: ##
```

The line number is followed by a colon (:) and by the character
string that describes the image of the printed line. Alphanumeric fields are indicated by one or more L characters. The
number of L characters used depends on the size of the field.
The L string is preceded by an apostrophe ('). Numeric fields are
described the same as in the LET statement.

Figure 4-12. Format for the image statement used to define printing formats.

Within standard BASIC, a line of printing is assumed to contain
several fixed-length *print zones* within which fields of data can be aligned.
These zones normally are 14 to 16 columns wide, although width may
vary for different types of equipment. The number of zones available
across the line also will vary to match the physical width of the printing
device or CRT screen.

Figure 4-13 shows the detail report, along with the corresponding
BASIC code, printed in this standard format. Notice that all data fields
are aligned in the beginning columns of the print zones. Numeric fields,
although they appear at the left margins of the zones, are preceded by
a single blank space. This space always appears in front of numeric fields
and is reserved for any optional sign symbols (+ or −) that might be
printed.

All fields are left-justified within the zones. Although this position-
ing results in misalignment of numeric fields, it cannot be helped because
of the absence of field editing capabilities. Character strings, however,
can be adjusted within the zones by including leading blank spaces within
the strings.

Printing within zones is controlled through use of PRINT statements.
The keyword PRINT is followed by a list of character strings and/or

variable names—presented in the order in which they will be printed. Commas are used to separate the field specifications and to indicate the print zones to be used. Each comma directs the computer to advance to the next zone before printing. To skip any zone, an extra comma is entered between field specifications.

It is possible to override automatic use of print zones for those cases in which output will not appear in aligned columns. For example, consider the final total line shown in Figure 4-13. Here, the total number of

```
PRINT ,," 	LISTING OF MASTER FILE FUNMF"
PRINT
PRINT "LOC.","ATTR.","ATTR.","  ATTRACTION",,"DAYS IN","ATTENDANCE"
PRINT "CODE"," NO.","TYPE","      NAME",," OPER."," TO DATE"
PRINT
      .
      .
      .
PRINT L, N, T$, N$,, D, A
      .
      .
      .
PRINT
PRINT T1, T2,,,, T3, T4
PRINT
PRINT "TOTAL RECORDS:"; T5
      .
      .
      .
```

```
                    LISTING OF MASTER FILE FUNMF

  LOC.         ATTR.        ATTR.        ATTRACTION       DAYS IN      ATTENDANCE
  CODE          NO.          TYPE           NAME           OPER.        TO DATE

   10           101           A          THE BLAZER          3            1246
   10           104           A          WATERSLIDE          1            311
   10           105           F          KREEPY KASTLE       3            124
   20           201           C          KIDDIE KAR          3            86
   20           202           F          PIRATE'S COVE       2            343
   20           207           F          JUNGLE SAFARI       1            819
   20           210           A          DEVIL'S PIT         1            212
   30           310           A          THE DUNGEON         1            113
   30           312           C          MERRY MOUSE         3            1043
   30           320           F          WILD CHICKEN        3            832
   40           406           A          CRASHIN' CARS       3            797
   40           419           F          MUSIC SHOW          2            312
   40           420           A          THE CORKSCREW       1            67
   50           510           F          FRONTIER DAYS       3            118
   50           515           F          SPACE PROBE         2            247

  420          4342                                         32           6670

TOTAL RECORDS: 15
```

Figure 4-13. Report formatting by use of print zones.

records in the file will be printed immediately following the string "TOTAL RECORDS:". To cause the printing of a value in the next immediate column, the preceding field specification is followed by a semicolon (;). This punctuation symbol places the field that follows in the next available print space. If a numeric field is being printed, an automatic blank space will precede and follow the number. In most versions of BASIC, use of a semicolon or use of no punctuation at all between field specifications will have the same effect and can be used interchangeably.

Sometimes, the number of columns required to format a report will not fit within the dimensions of a CRT screen or sheet of paper if print zones are used. The report width becomes too great when the report is formatted into zones. In these cases, the zones must be overridden, with fewer spaces appearing between columns.

Print zones can be overridden through use of TAB specifications within the PRINT statement. As shown in Figure 4-14, the keyword TAB is followed by a column number enclosed in parentheses. This number identifies the column at which printing is to begin for the data field or string that follows. By interspersing TAB specifications with variable names and strings, columnar printing can be retained without the constraints imposed by print zones. The general format for this PRINT statement for report lines is shown in Figure 4-15.

Within programs that do not use PRINT USING techniques, line formatting takes place at the same time as line printing. Therefore, it is not possible to isolate definitions of line images within a separate program module. PRINT statements that include full printing specifications appear throughout the program, at whatever points printing is required. This technique makes it more difficult to maintain or alter programs, so the PRINT USING method should be followed whenever possible.

Computer Arithmetic—The LET Statement

To accumulate totals for the detail report, five separate accumulator areas must be defined. At the beginning of the program, these memory areas are valued, or set, to a value of zero to clear them before amounts are entered for accumulation. Then, for each input record, the numeric fields are added into the hash and control total accumulators and the total records accumulator is incremented by 1. After all records have been processed, the content of these accumulators is printed.

```
        PRINT TAB(14);"LISTING OF MASTER FILE FUNMF"
        PRINT
        PRINT "LOC.  ATTR.  ATTR.     ATTRACTION      DAYS IN   ATTENDANCE"
        PRINT "CODE   NO.   TYPE        NAME          OPER.     TO DATE"
        PRINT
                .
                .
                .
        PRINT L; TAB(6); N; TAB(15); T$; TAB(21); N$; TAB(38); D; TAB(47); A
                .
                .
        PRINT
        PRINT T1; TAB(6); T2; TAB(38); T3; TAB(47); T4
        PRINT
        PRINT "TOTAL RECORDS:"; T5
                .
                .
                .
```

```
                    LISTING OF MASTER FILE FUNMF

         LOC.   ATTR.   ATTR.     ATTRACTION     DAYS IN    ATTENDANCE
         CODE    NO.    TYPE        NAME          OPER.      TO DATE

          10     101     A       THE BLAZER         3          1246
          10     104     A       WATERSLIDE         1          311
          10     105     F       KREEPY KASTLE      3          124
          20     201     C       KIDDIE KAR         3          86
          20     202     F       PIRATE'S COVE      2          343
          20     207     F       JUNGLE SAFARI      1          819
          20     210     A       DEVIL'S PIT        1          212
          30     310     A       THE DUNGEON        1          113
          30     312     C       MERRY MOUSE        3          1043
          30     320     F       WILD CHICKEN       3          832
          40     406     A       CRASHIN' CARS      3          797
          40     419     F       MUSIC SHOW         2          312
          40     420     A       THE CORKSCREW      1          67
          50     510     F       FRONTIER DAYS      3          118
          50     515     F       SPACE PROBE        2          247

         420    4342                                32         6670

         TOTAL RECORDS: 15
```

Figure 4-14. Report formatting by use of TAB specifications.

Accumulation of totals takes advantage of the computer's capability to perform arithmetic. The computer can add, subtract, multiply, divide, and carry out other types of arithmetic computations. In general, the computer is presented with an arithmetic problem to solve. After making the described calculations, the result is assigned to a memory area. This retained value then can be used either for further calculation or for printed output.

The *arithmetic expression* to be evaluated is constructed by combining variable names and/or numeric constants with *arithmetic operators*.

General Format:

$$\text{line number PRINT} \begin{bmatrix} \text{string} \\ \text{variable name} \end{bmatrix} \left\{ \begin{matrix} , \\ ; \end{matrix} \right| \begin{bmatrix} \text{TAB(column number)} \end{bmatrix} \begin{bmatrix} \text{string} \\ \text{variable name} \end{bmatrix} \right\} \ldots$$

The keyword PRINT is followed by one or more strings and/or variable names, which are separated by the following specifications:

TAB This specification identifies the column number in which to print the variable data or string that follows the TAB.

Comma (,) This specification causes printing to begin in the next print zone.

Semicolon (;) This specification directs printing to continue in the next immediate column. In some versions of BASIC, a semicolon is not required to cause printing in the next column.

The IBM and TRS-80 systems use the LPRINT keyword instead of PRINT to direct output to an attached printer rather than to the CRT screen.

On Apple II computers, if the integer value refers to the printer interface card slot used, output is directed to an attached printer with the following command:

    line number PR #integer

Typically, slot #1 contains the printer interface card. This command must appear in the program prior to the first use of the associated PRINT statement. For example, the following statements will direct output of variables A, B, and C$ to the printer:

```
220 PR #1
230 PRINT A, B, C$
```

To return output to the CRT screen, the following command precedes a PRINT statement that directs printing to the screen:

    line number PR #0

The PR statement can direct output interchangeably between the CRT screen and printer.

Figure 4-15. General format for the PRINT statement used to print report lines.

For simple arithmetic, these operators direct addition (+), subtraction (−), multiplication (∗), and division (/) of the values represented by the variable names and constants.

Figure 4-16 presents these arithmetic operators and gives examples of how they are used to construct arithmetic expressions. Note specifically that sets of parentheses can be used to control the order in which calculations are carried out. Parentheses are needed because of the implied hierarchy (structured order) in which arithmetic operations normally are evaluated.

Under the BASIC language, a computer performs multiplication and division before addition and subtraction. For instance, in processing the expression A + B + C / 3, the computer first would divide variable C by the constant 3, then add the quotient to the sum of A + B. Thus, if the intent was to find the average of the three values A, B, and C, the wrong answer would result. To derive the average of A, B, and C, the expression should be written (A + B + C) / 3. With this instruction, the computer first would clear the parentheses by adding A + B + C. The sum then would be divided by 3, giving the average. Rather than trying to sort out the normal sequence of execution for each set of calculations, it is usually best to state problems in sets of parentheses that control the order of evaluation for arithmetic expressions.

Arithmetic Operator	Meaning	Examples
+ − ∗ /	Addition Subtraction Multiplication Division	A + B, A + 3, A + B + C A − B, A − 3, A + B − C A ∗ B, A ∗ 3, A ∗ B ∗ C A/B, A/3, A ∗ B/C A + B − (C ∗ D) (A ∗ B) + (C/D) A ∗ ((B + C)/(D − E)) + 5

Figure 4-16. Arithmetic operators and expressions.

In BASIC, arithmetic is initiated through use of the LET statement. As shown in Figure 4-17, LET is a general assignment statement in which a data value is placed in a memory area. The content of another variable, a constant, or the result of an arithmetic expression can be assigned to a named variable. The format shown in Figure 4-17 is an expansion of that shown in Figure 3-15, which illustrates the assignment of constants to variables.

Accumulation of Report Totals

To develop hash and control totals for the sample program, the computer first will have to clear the accumulator areas by assigning the value 0 to them. The five LET statements required to do this appear in module 1.2 SET ACCUMULATORS TO ZERO. This activity takes place one time at the beginning of the program.

For each record input from the master file, the computer will add the values in its numeric fields into the appropriate accumulators. These operations will maintain running totals for the location-code, attraction-number, days-in-operation, and attendance-to-date fields. In practice, the input values are added to the current accumulator values and the resulting sums are reassigned to the accumulators, replacing the existing totals with the new totals. In effect, the input values are added into the accumulators. Also, for each input record, the value 1 is added to the total records accumulator. The five LET statements required to develop these totals appear in module 2.1 ACCUMULATE TOTALS.

Accessing the Master File

Within module 1.4 OPEN MASTER FILE, the file named "FUNMF" is opened and associated with a file reference number. This is the same file that was created in the previous program. In this case, however, it will be used for input rather than for output.

In module 1.5 INPUT FIRST MASTER RECORD and 2.3 INPUT NEXT MASTER RECORD, the INPUT statement accepts a master record from the input file and places the six data fields within six separate memory areas. This statement differs from the INPUT statement used in the previous program to input data fields from a keyboard. In this case, the statement is associated with a file reference number, and multiple data fields are input. The instruction contains the names of the fields, listed in the order of their appearance within the input record. The general

General Format:

line number LET variable name = $\begin{bmatrix} \text{variable name} \\ \text{constant} \\ \text{expression} \end{bmatrix}$

The keyword LET is followed by the name of an area in memory
where a value will be assigned (=). The content of another area
in memory, a numeric or string constant, or the results of an
arithmetic calculation can be retained in the variable.

Examples:

```
120 LET A = B
130 LET A$ = B$
```

The content of the area in
memory named to the right of
the equal sign is copied into
the area named to the left of
the equal sign. Then, both
areas contain the same value.

```
210 LET A = 0
220 LET A = 3.5
230 LET A$ = "STRING"
```

The numeric or string constant
appearing to the right of the
equal sign is retained in the
area named to the left of the
equal sign.

```
310 LET A = B + C
320 LET A = B - C
330 LET A = B * C
340 LET A = B / C
350 LET A = A + 1
360 LET A = (B + C + D) / E
370 LET A = (B * (C - D)) - 5
```

The result of the arithmetic expression given to the right of
the equal sign is assigned to
the variable to the left of the
equal sign. Arithmetic expressions are formed with variable
names and/or numeric con-
stants combined with arithmetic
operators. The operators are +
(add), − (subtract), * (multiply),
and / (divide). Parentheses are
used to control the order of computation. The computer clears
parentheses from the innermost
to the outermost set.

Figure 4-17. General format for the LET statement.

format for the INPUT statement used to access records from a file is shown in Figure 4-18.

Recall from the previous program that the terminal input procedure was constructed as a subroutine. This approach avoided the need to duplicate a large amount of code in two separate places in the program. In this program, however, redundant coding of input commands presents no special problems. There is only one INPUT statement to code. Therefore, this statement appears in both input modules. There is no advantage in using a subroutine that contains only a single INPUT command.

PROGRAMMING SPECIFICATIONS—EXCEPTION REPORT

Recall that one of the uses of detail reports is to provide control information for use by operating managers. In particular, exception reports highlight special, or abnormal, conditions that require management attention.

The next program to be written generates an exception report from the data contained in the amusement park master file. Management wishes to know when any attractions have an attendance figure lower than 100 per day. To develop this information, the program will calculate the attendance per day for each attraction and then print records for only those with daily attendance below 100. The programming specifications for this report are shown in Figure 4-19.

PROBLEM ANALYSIS

Data flow analysis for this program appears in Figure 4-20. For each input record, the attendance to date is divided by the days in operation to derive average daily attendance. This number is compared with the minimum attendance constant to determine if it is less than 100. If so, a detail line is printed on the report. If the attendance is equal to or greater than the constant, no line is printed.

PROGRAM DESIGN

The structure chart for this program appears in Figure 4-21. Program design follows the general CIS model used in previous programs.

Within the main processing section, module 2.2 PROCESS ATTENDANCE STATUS compares the calculated daily attendance figure with

---

DEC, TRS-80, IBM/Microsoft Systems

General Format:
   line number INPUT #file number, variable name {, variable
      name . . . }

Example:

```
1620 INPUT #1, L, N, T$, N$, D, A
```

The keyword INPUT is followed by the file reference number
(buffer number) that appears in the associated OPEN statement.
A comma is coded next, followed by one or more variable
names in the order in which the fields appear in the input
record. The variable names are separated by commas.

Apple II System

General Formats:

   line number PRINT CHR$(4); "READ file name"
   line number INPUT variable name {, variable name . . . }

Examples:

```
1615 PRINT CHR$(4); "READ FUNMF"
1620 INPUT L, N, T$, N$, D, A
```

The PRINT statement identifies the file from which records will
be input and signifies that the subsequent INPUT statement will
read from this file. The INPUT statement lists the variable
names that will be associated with the input fields. The variable
names are listed in the order in which the fields appear.

Figure 4-18. Formats for the INPUT statement used to access a file.

---

the minimum attendance constant (100). If the daily attendance is less
than the constant, module 2.2.1 PRINT REPORT LINE is selected and the
report line identifying this particular attraction is printed. Otherwise, no
line is printed on the report. The minimum attendance constant is
established and valued in module 1.2 DEFINE PROGRAM CONSTANTS.

System: AMUSEMENT PARK   Date: 04/15/XX
Program: EXCEPTION REPORT   Program I.D.: FUN03   Analyst: B. LEIGH

Design and write a program to produce an exception report listing the attractions at the American Fun Amusement Park that draw an attendance of fewer than
100 people per day. The amusement park master file (FUNMF) is the program
input. Output will be a printed exception report. The program will be coded
in BASIC. Figure 4-19.1 shows the system flowchart for this application.

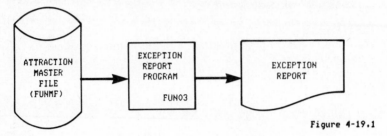

Figure 4-19.1

INPUT

The master file records are input to the program in the following format:

Field Name	Data Type
Location Code	Numeric
Attraction Number	Numeric
Attraction Type	Alphanumeric
Attraction Name	Alphanumeric
Days in Operation	Numeric
Attendance to Date	Numeric

A final EOF record is written to the file. This record contains the character
string "END OF FILE" in the attraction-name field.

PROCESSING

For each input record, the daily attendance for the attraction is calculated.
The attendance figure is derived by dividing the attendance to date by the
days in operation. If an attendance figure is fewer than 100 people per day,
that record is listed on the report.

OUTPUT

The exception report will be printed in the format shown in Figure 4-19.2.

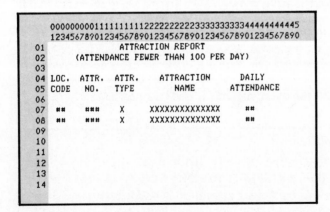

Figure 4-19.2

Figure 4-19. Programming specifications for exception report program.

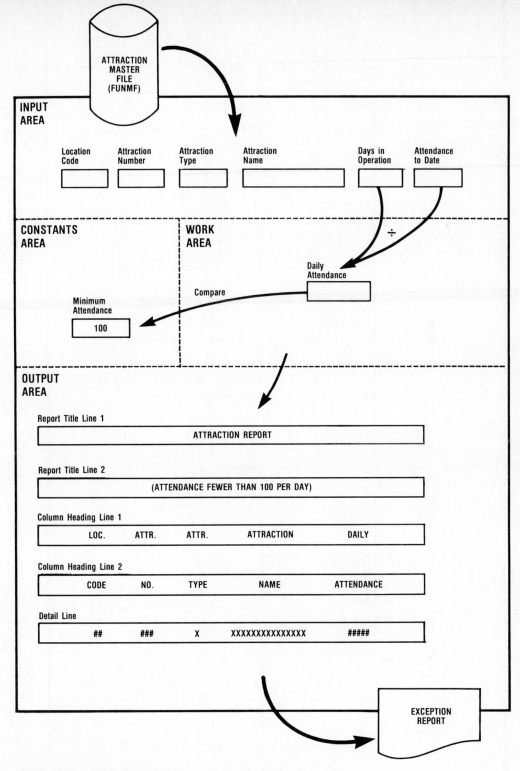

Figure 4-20. Data flow analysis for exception report program.

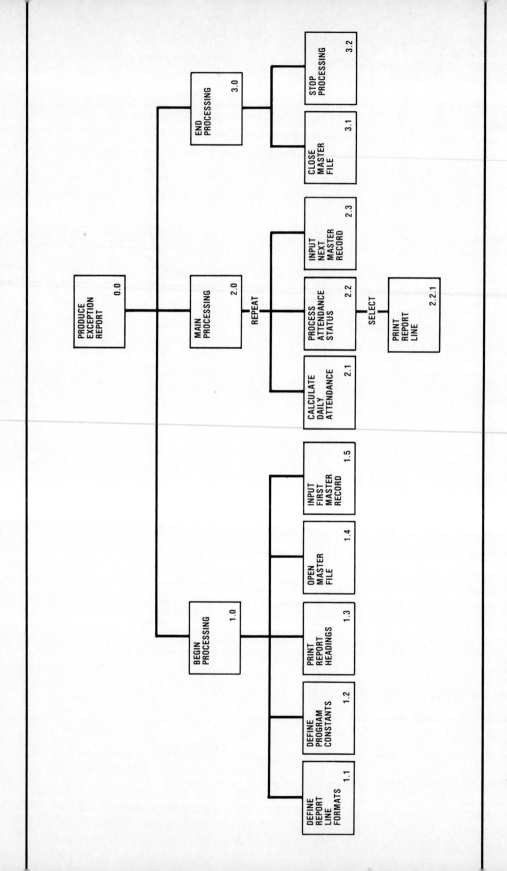

Figure 4-21. Structure chart for exception report program.

PROGRAM SPECIFICATION

Pseudocode for this program is shown in Figure 4-22. In module 1.2 DEFINE PROGRAM CONSTANTS, the minimum attendance constant is defined and the value 100 is placed in the memory area. The number remains there throughout program execution and is used as a value against which the daily attendance figure can be compared. As a general rule, all data items used as constants in a program—values that do not change during program execution—should be defined one time at the beginning

```
0.0 PRODUCE EXCEPTION REPORT
    1.0 BEGIN PROCESSING
        1.1 DEFINE REPORT LINE FORMATS
            Define Report Title Line 1
            Define Report Title Line 2
            Define Column Heading Line 1
            Define Column Heading Line 2
            Define Detail Line
        1.2 DEFINE PROGRAM CONSTANTS
            Set Minimum Attendance = 100
        1.3 PRINT REPORT HEADINGS
            Print Report Title Line 1
            Print Report Title Line 2
            Print blank line
            Print Column Heading Line 1
            Print Column Heading Line 2
            Print blank line
        1.4 OPEN MASTER FILE
            Open "FUNMF" for input
        1.5 INPUT FIRST MASTER RECORD
            Input Location Code, Attraction Number, Attraction Type,
                  Attraction Name, Days in Operation, Attendance to Date
    2.0 MAIN PROCESSING
        REPEAT: until end of master file
            2.1 CALCULATE DAILY ATTENDANCE
                Set Daily Attendance = Attendance to Date/Days in Operation
            2.2 PROCESS ATTENDANCE STATUS
                SELECT: on Daily Attendance < Minimum Attendance
                    2.2.1 PRINT REPORT LINE
                        Print Detail Line using Location Code,
                            Attraction Number, Attraction Type
                                Attraction Name, Daily Attendance
                END SELECT
            2.3 INPUT NEXT MASTER RECORD
                Input Location Code, Attraction Number, Attraction Type,
                      Attraction Name, Days in Operation, Attendance to Date
        END REPEAT
    3.0 END PROCESSING
        3.1 CLOSE MASTER FILE
            Close "FUNMF"
        3.2 STOP PROCESSING
            Stop
```

Figure 4-22. Pseudocode for exception report program.

of the program. These constants should be isolated within a single module. In this way, changes in program specification requiring alternative constant values can be handled without having to search the entire program for occurrences of the constants.

Within the main processing section, module 2.2.1 PRINT REPORT LINE is shown within a selection control structure. As suggested by the pseudocode, this module will be performed only if the daily attendance figure is less than the minimum attendance constant. The printed line includes the first four fields of the input record, along with the calculated daily attendance figure.

PROGRAM CODE

The BASIC code for the program is presented in Figure 4-23. The exception report produced by this program is given in Figure 4-24. Programming techniques introduced with this program are discussed below.

Coding Program Constants

In module 1.2 DEFINE PROGRAM CONSTANTS, a memory area named M is established as the minimum attendance constant and the value 100 is entered. The LET statement is used to assign the value to the named

```
1000 REM FUN03                                      WEL/DRA
1010 REM                   EXCEPTION REPORT
1020 REM
1030 REM THIS PROGRAM PRODUCES A REPORT LISTING THE ATTRAC-
1040 REM TIONS AT THE AMERICAN FUN AMUSEMENT PARK THAT HAVE
1050 REM FEWER THAN 100 PEOPLE IN DAILY ATTENDANCE.  THE
1060 REM INPUT FILE IS THE PARK ATTRACTION MASTER FILE
1070 REM (FUNMF).
1080 REM
1090 REM VARIABLE NAMES
1100 REM
1110 REM INPUT:
1120 REM     L......LOCATION CODE
1130 REM     N......ATTRACTION NUMBER
1140 REM     T$.....ATTRACTION TYPE
1150 REM     N$.....ATTRACTION NAME
1160 REM     D......DAYS IN OPERATION (THIS MONTH)
1170 REM     A......ATTENDANCE TO DATE (THIS MONTH)
1180 REM CONSTANTS:
1190 REM     M......MINIMUM ATTENDANCE
1200 REM WORK AREAS:
1210 REM     A1.....DAILY ATTENDANCE
1220 REM OUTPUT:
1230 REM     F1$....REPORT TITLE LINE 1
1240 REM     F2$....REPORT TITLE LINE 2
1250 REM     F3$....COLUMN HEADING LINE 1
1260 REM     F4$....COLUMN HEADING LINE 2
1270 REM     F5$....DETAIL LINE
```

```
1280 REM
1290 REM 0.0 PRODUCE EXCEPTION REPORT
1300 REM
1305 REM **************************
1310 REM * 1.0 BEGIN PROCESSING *
1315 REM **************************
1320 REM
1330 REM 1.1 DEFINE REPORT LINE FORMATS
1340        LET F1$ = "                ATTRACTION REPORT"
1350        LET F2$ = "        (ATTENDANCE FEWER THAN 100 PER DAY)"
1360        LET F3$ = "LOC.  ATTR.  ATTR.    ATTRACTION      DAILY"
1370        LET F4$ = "CODE   NO.   TYPE        NAME      ATTENDANCE"
1380        LET F5$ = "  ##    ###    !     \              \     ##"
1390 REM
1400 REM 1.2 DEFINE PROGRAM CONSTANTS
1410        LET M = 100
1420 REM
1430 REM 1.3 PRINT REPORT HEADINGS
1440        PRINT F1$
1450        PRINT F2$
1460        PRINT
1470        PRINT F3$
1480        PRINT F4$
1490        PRINT
1500 REM
1510 REM 1.4 OPEN MASTER FILE
1520        OPEN "FUNMF" FOR INPUT AS FILE #1
1530 REM
1540 REM 1.5 INPUT FIRST MASTER RECORD
1550        INPUT #1, L, N, T$, N$, D, A
1560 REM
1565 REM **************************
1570 REM * 2.0 MAIN PROCESSING   *
1575 REM **************************
1580 REM REPEAT
1590     IF N$ = "END OF FILE" THEN GOTO 1780
1600 REM
1610 REM     2.1 CALCULATE DAILY ATTENDANCE
1620            LET A1 = A / D
1630 REM
1640 REM     2.2 PROCESS ATTENDANCE STATUS
1650 REM         SELECT
1660             IF A1 < M THEN GOTO 1690
1670                        GOTO 1720
1680 REM
1690 REM         2.2.1 PRINT REPORT LINE
1700                PRINT USING F5$, L, N, T$, N$, A1
1710 REM
1720 REM         END SELECT
1730 REM
1740 REM     2.3 INPUT NEXT MASTER RECORD
1750            INPUT #1, L, N, T$, N$, D, A
1760 REM
1770     GOTO 1580
1780 REM END REPEAT
1790 REM
1795 REM **************************
1800 REM * 3.0 END PROCESSING    *
1805 REM **************************
1810 REM
1820 REM 3.1 CLOSE MASTER FILE
1830        CLOSE #1
1840 REM
1850 REM 3.2 STOP PROCESSING
1860        STOP
1870 END
```

Figure 4-23. BASIC code for exception report program.

```
                      ATTRACTION REPORT
                 (ATTENDANCE FEWER THAN 100 PER DAY)

        LOC.   ATTR.   ATTR.      ATTRACTION        DAILY
        CODE    NO.    TYPE          NAME         ATTENDANCE

         10     105     F        KREEPY KASTLE        41
         20     201     C        KIDDIE KAR           29
         40     420     A        THE CORKSCREW        67
         50     510     F        FRONTIER DAYS        39
```

Figure 4-24. Output from exception report program.

---

memory area. Once stored, the value will remain available and unchanged throughout program execution.

Coding Selections

Lines 1650 through 1720 implement the selection control structure. This structure is based upon the ability of the computer to make condition tests and to take alternative courses of action on the results of the tests.

In making a condition test, the computer compares two data values. The test determines whether one value is less than, equal to, greater than, less than or equal to, greater than or equal to, or not equal to a second value. The comparison can be made between two numeric or alphanumeric values. The test is made by relating the two values with a *relational operator.* The relational operator is a symbol that causes the program to make the desired comparison. The operators used to construct condition tests in BASIC are shown in Figure 4-25. The computer evaluates the relationship presented and determines whether the result of the test is true or false.

In BASIC, a condition test is coded within an IF statement. The general format for this statement is shown in Figure 4-26. If the tested condition is true, the computer branches to the line number given in the THEN clause. If the test is evaluated as false, the branch is ignored and processing continues with the next statement in sequence.

The processing logic for the selection control structure in this program is illustrated in Figure 4-27. The IF statement tests whether the

Relational Operator	Meaning	Example
=	equal to	N$ = ''END OF FILE''
<	less than	A < B
>	greater than	A > B
< =	less than or equal to	A < = B
> =	greater than or equal to	A > = B
< >	not equal to	A < > B

Figure 4-25. Relational operators and condition tests.

General Format:
   line number IF condition test THEN GOTO line number

Example:

```
1660 IF A1 < M THEN GOTO 1690
```

The keyword IF is followed by a condition test. The test compares two values using the relational operators < (less than), = (equal to), > (greater than), < = (less than or equal to), > = (greater than or equal to), or < > (not equal to). If the test is evaluated as true, control branches to the line number that follows the word GOTO. If the test is evaluated as false, processing continues, in sequence, starting with the statement that follows the IF statement.

Figure 4-26. General format for the IF statement.

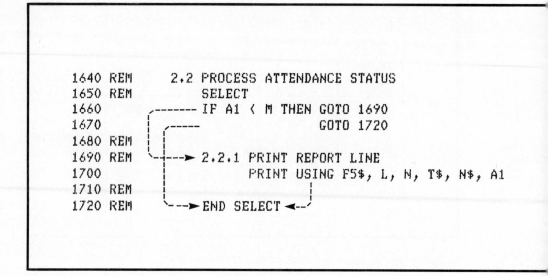

```
1640 REM     2.2 PROCESS ATTENDANCE STATUS
1650 REM         SELECT
1660         ,------- IF A1 < M THEN GOTO 1690
1670         |  ,-----               GOTO 1720
1680 REM     |  |
1690 REM     '-+---> 2.2.1 PRINT REPORT LINE
1700         |            PRINT USING F5$, L, N, T$, N$, A1
1710 REM     |
1720 REM     '---> END SELECT <--'
```

Figure 4-27.   Flow of control within selection control structure in exception report program.

calculated daily attendance (A1) is less than the minimum attendance constant (M). If the result is true, the program branches to line 1690, which causes the report line to be printed. If the result of the test is false (daily attendance is *not* less than minimum attendance), the branch is ignored, and the next statement in sequence is executed. This next statement—GOTO 1720—branches around the print module. In either case, control ends up at the END SELECT comment in line 1720. Thus, there is a common exit point from the selection control structure.

The general format for the selection, or case, construct is presented in Figure 4-28. In general, there will be an IF statement testing each of any number of expected true conditions, along with a branch to the corresponding module to be executed. Immediately following these IF statements will be a single GOTO statement that will be executed if all of the tested conditions are false. This GOTO statement branches to the end of the selection control structure in case none of the processing modules is selected. The final statement in all but the last processing module also will be a GOTO statement branching to the end of the selection structure. This statement skips over any remaining processing modules that were not selected.

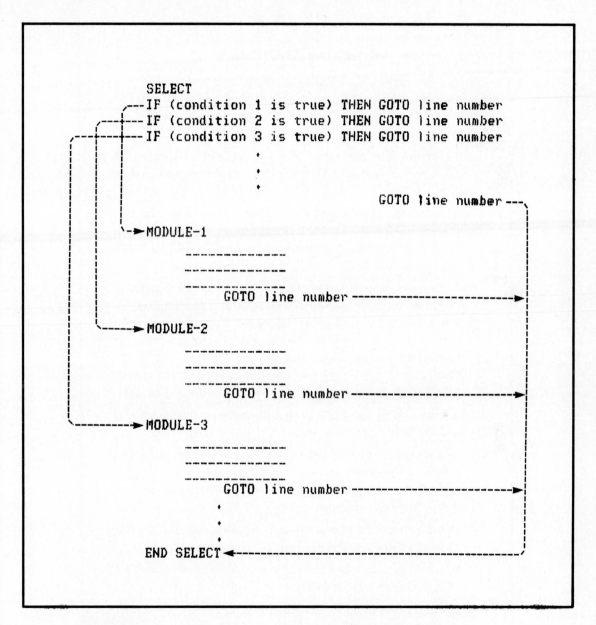

Figure 4-28. General format for coding the selection control structure.

Chapter Summary

1. A detail report is a printed or displayed listing of the content of a file. Usually, each line of the report presents all or most of the data fields of a record, and all or most of the records in a file are listed.

2. There are four main uses of detail reports: verification of file content, management control, manual files, and backup files.

3. One method of verifying the content of files is to compare the source input records with the detail report listing all records in the file. Alternatively, batch, or control, totaling can be used.

4. A control total is a summation of a numeric field across all records. Control totals are developed for the batch of input records by adding field content by hand or with a calculator. After a file is created, a detail control report is run, which also develops control totals for the same fields. Comparisons of the original control totals with the report totals uncover discrepancies caused by miskeying of data.

5. A control total that is developed for a field such as a record key or identification number is called a hash total.

6. Management control information is provided by exception reports. An exception report presents selective information from files to highlight business conditions that are not within expected ranges.

7. Detail reports can be used as reference files within the nonautomated portions of information systems.

8. Detail reports can serve as backup copies of computer files in case the regular files are inaccessible.

9. Detail reports include three sections: headings, the report body, and footing lines.

10. Program totals are developed within accumulators. An accumulator is a memory area within which numeric values are totaled. An accumulator must be valued to zero initially, before data are entered.

11. Report line formats are defined as line images through use of special editing symbols to indicate the type of data and size of field to be printed. These formats are used during printing to align data fields.

12. An alternative method of formatting lines of printing is by use of predefined print zones. These zones make possible automatic column alignment of fields; however, numeric columns are left-justified rather than aligned on the decimal point.

13. Another method of formatting lines involves use of TAB specifications to identify particular columns in which data fields are to appear.

14. The computer can be instructed to perform arithmetic by combining arithmetic operators with variable names and numeric constants. The results of the computations then are assigned to a named memory area.

15. Condition tests are made by relating variables and constants through use of relational operators. The results of the tests are evaluated as true or false. When used in program decision making, test results can cause the computer to take alternative courses of action. Condition tests are the bases for selection control structures.

Review Questions

1. What are detail reports?

2. How do business organizations use detail reports?

3. What formatting information does a programmer need before writing a detail report program?

4. What are the three main sections of a detail report?

5. What are exception reports?

6. How can file content be verified?

Programming Assignments

Programming practice assignments for Chapter 4 are located in Appendix A, CASE STUDY ONE and CASE STUDY TWO.

Key Terms

1. detail report
2. source document
3. control totaling
4. batch balancing
5. control total
6. hash total
7. exception
8. management by exception
9. exception report
10. backup
11. heading
12. report title

13. column heading
14. body
15. detail line
16. footing
17. accumulator
18. image
19. editing
20. image statement
21. print zone
22. arithmetic expression
23. arithmetic operator
24. relational operator

BASIC Library

1. PRINT USING
2. TAB

5
PRODUCING
SUMMARY REPORTS

OVERVIEW AND OBJECTIVES

Detail reports present listings of individual file records. Either the entire content of a file can be presented or selected records can be chosen for printing, depending on the purpose of the report. In some cases, total lines printed as footings summarize the content of reports. However, a basic characteristic of a detail report is that information is presented in the form of record details. Little or no information is presented to characterize groups of records, or categories of data. Organizing and totaling data content according to some characteristic is a function of summary reports.

Like detail reports, summary reports can include literal printouts of data records. However, summary reports add an extra dimension by including summaries, or subtotals, for groups or categories of data items. Summary reports thus allow managers to review both details of items within groups of records and also to gain an overall perspective through the content of printed totals that summarize groups of detail items.

The program discussed and illustrated in this chapter produces a summary report. The report lists individual file records and also presents subtotals for selected groups of records. In addition, the report is printed on multiple pages.

When you complete your work in this chapter, you should be able to:

☐ Discuss the uses of summary, or control-break, reports.

☐ Describe the general organization and format for summary reports.

☐ Describe the concept of a control break.

☐ Design, specify, and code programs that include single-level control breaks.

☐ Design, specify, and code programs that print multiple-page reports.

THE NATURE OF SUMMARY REPORTS

Reports are tools for management control over business activity. As explained in the previous chapter, a detail report is one type of output used to communicate the operational status. In particular, an exception report presents operational details that vary from expected outcomes to highlight situations that require corrective action.

In some cases, complete detailing of records from computer files may represent more information than is needed. There can be so much detail that understanding of overall situations can become virtually impossible. To gain a perspective on what is happening in a broad section of a business, managers may require summaries—rather than complete listings of content—from computer-maintained files.

For example, a marketing manager of a department store must know about sales volumes and merchandise movement for all departments. The manager will want to compare current sales with, say, last month's sales, sales of the preceding month, and, possibly, sales activity for the same month over the past several years. With this information, the manager can measure the relative success of current operations.

One obvious but less-than-satisfactory method of getting this information is to review all of the sales slips for all of the sales transactions during a given period. Alternatively, and almost as impractical, the computer could generate a listing of all sales transactions if the transactions happen to be recorded in a sales file accessible to the computer.

In this scenario, sufficient data are available, but relevant information is not. In other words, for decision-making purposes there is simply too much data presented in the wrong format. The real need is for sales totals, categorized by department or merchandise type, for each of the periods of interest. A quick comparison of these figures would lead to effective analysis.

In most cases, therefore, management reporting is accomplished with *summary reports.* In general, summary reports reduce the volume of data included on reports to a few representative facts. Report content presents summaries of file content. This representation eliminates the need for managers to search through vast amounts of data to deduce needed information. The information is presented, usually, through various levels of subtotals that summarize content of groupings of records. For instance, in the department store example, a report could be prepared that lists sales totals for each of the merchandise departments for each time period. Therefore, the information would be organized and presented concisely and directly for management consumption.

For some business needs, summary reports may contain record details. That is, all records in a file appear on the report; however, the records are interspersed with summary lines. For example, in a sales report, there might be a line showing details of each sales transaction. Then, for each merchandise category—clothing, appliances, housewares, etc.—a summary line would be printed. This subtotal line would summarize all sales for the particular line of merchandise. Also, a final total line at the foot of the report might summarize sales for all categories of merchandise. Thus, the manager could evaluate sales initially by looking at the summary figures only. Then, to gain additional information about particular items of merchandise, the detail figures could be investigated. In any case, the intent of the report would be to provide summary information to management without the need for an extensive search through unneeded or unimportant details.

THE FORMAT OF SUMMARY REPORTS

An example of a general format for a summary report is presented in Figure 5-1. This report is based on the information contained in the amusement park master file presented in Chapter 3 and used for the detail report in Chapter 4.

This type of summary report contains both detail lines and two levels of total lines. A subtotal line is printed for each group of attraction records with the same location code. Also, a final total line is printed to summarize operation and attendance data for all attractions.

Amusement park management could use this type of report to evaluate attendance for each area of the park as a basis for adjusting staffing levels to correspond with attendance patterns. Furthermore, information contained in the report could be compared with similar figures for previous periods to spot attendance trends and to uncover attention-worthy situations.

```
              ATTRACTION SUMMARY REPORT      PAGE   1
                    BY PARK LOCATION

      LOC.   ATTR.      ATTRACTION      DAYS IN    ATTENDANCE
      CODE   TYPE         NAME          OPER.      TO DATE

       10     A      THE BLAZER            3        1,246
       10     A      WATERSLIDE            1          311
       10     F      KREEPY KASTLE         3          124

             TOTALS FOR LOCATION 10        7        1,681

       20     C      KIDDIE KAR            3           86
       20     F      PIRATE'S COVE         2          343
       20     F      JUNGLE SAFARI         1          819
       20     A      DEVIL'S PIT           1          212

             TOTALS FOR LOCATION 20        7        1,460

       30     A      THE DUNGEON           1          113




              ATTRACTION SUMMARY REPORT      PAGE   2
                    BY PARK LOCATION

      LOC.   ATTR.      ATTRACTION      DAYS IN    ATTENDANCE
      CODE   TYPE         NAME          OPER.      TO DATE

       30     C      MERRY MOUSE           3        1,043
       30     F      WILD CHICKEN          3          832

             TOTALS FOR LOCATION 30        7        1,988

       40     A      CRASHIN' CARS         3          797
       40     F      MUSIC SHOW            2          312
       40     A      THE CORKSCREW         1           67

             TOTALS FOR LOCATION 40        6        1,176

       50     F      FRONTIER DAYS         3          118
       50     F      SPACE PROBE           2          247

             TOTALS FOR LOCATION 50        5          365

      PARK TOTALS                         32        6,670
```

Figure 5-1. Format for summary report.

CONTROL-BREAK PROCESSING

The report illustrated in Figure 5-1 is produced through one of the most common methods of producing summary reports, *control-break* processing. In general, a control break occurs whenever the value in a record *control field* changes and triggers some special processing. A control field is any field in an input record that is used for identification purposes.

Normally, the control field value represents some form of logical grouping, or classification scheme, for data contained in file records. For example, in the amusement park attraction file, the values in the location code field and the attraction type field represent classification values. A record can contain attraction data pertaining to one of five park locations (coded 10, 20, 30, 40, and 50). A record can also represent one of three attraction types (coded A, C, and F). The codes identify and classify records into meaningful categories.

Such classification schemes make it possible to implement special processing instructions on the basis of data categories. As suggested in the example report, records corresponding to different park locations can be identified and put through special processing to produce summaries. Whenever there is a change in the control field value, a subtotal line is printed.

As a prerequisite for control-break processing, the values in the control field usually are sequenced in ascending order—from the lowest to the highest value—with all records containing the same control value grouped together. Although it is possible to perform control-break processing with records in descending order from highest to lowest control value—or in no particular control field order—this is seldom done.

Whatever the sequential arrangement might be, it is still important that all records within a logical group appear together. Any change in a control value triggers a control break. The assumption is that the change signals the end of a *control group* and the beginning of a new group. Therefore, records within the same group cannot be scattered throughout the file; the records must appear together.

With records sequenced in control groups, a control-break report can be produced with a single processing of the file. Because of this grouping limitation, a control-break report would not be produced, for example, on the basis of the attraction type codes in the amusement park file. These values are not grouped together within A, C, and F categories.

Thus, control-break processing is not practical unless the records are rearranged and grouped within these three categories, and unless the groups appear one after another in the file.

PROGRAMMING SPECIFICATIONS—SUMMARY REPORT

The program illustrated in this chapter, designed for control-break processing, produces the summary report in Figure 5-1.

The programming specifications for this program appear in Figure 5-2. These specifications recognize that the records in the amusement park master file are ordered by and grouped according to their location code values. A control break will be signaled by a change in the value of this field. When this change occurs, a subtotal line will be printed for the group just processed. At the end of the report, a final total line summarizes all file records.

Notice that the report will be printed on multiple pages. Each page of printing is assumed to hold 20 lines of output. Therefore, more than one page will be required to hold the information on the report. The pages will be numbered within the first line of the report title; the heading lines will appear on each page of the report.

PROGRAMMING SPECIFICATIONS

System: AMUSEMENT PARK   Date: 04/18/XX
Program: SUMMARY REPORT   Program I.D.: FUN04   Analyst: B. LEIGH

Design and write a program to produce a multiple-page summary report of the American Fun Amusement Park attractions master file (FUNMF). Records are organized in attraction number sequence. The records also are grouped by location code. The report will be a printed listing of all records in the file, with subtotals printed for each location-code group. Final totals will be printed at the bottom of the report. The program will be coded in BASIC. Figure 5-2.1 shows the system flowchart for this application.

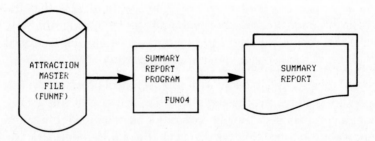

Figure 5-2.1

The master file records are input to the program in the following format:

Field Name	Data Type
Location Code	Numeric
Attraction Number	Numeric
Attraction Type	Alphanumeric
Attraction Name	Alphanumeric
Days in Operation	Numeric
Attendance to Date	Numeric

A final EOF record is written to the file. This record contains the character string "END OF FILE" in the attraction name field.

PROCESSING

1. A total is accumulated and printed for the days-in-operation fields and for the attendance-to-date fields. Group subtotals for these fields are printed whenever the location code changes. Final totals are printed at the bottom of the report.

2. A maximum of 20 lines are printed on a page. After each group of 20 lines, a page break should occur and a new set of heading lines printed. The pages should be numbered. Assume a physical page size of 25 lines.

OUTPUT

Figure 5-2.2 shows the format of the summary report. Following a page break, at least one detail line should be printed after the headings. A subtotal or final total line should not appear as the first line on any page.

```
         0000000001111111111222222222233333333334444444444 5
         1234567890123456789012345678901234567890123456789 0
01              ATTRACTION SUMMARY REPORT        PAGE ##
02                   BY PARK LOCATION
03
04 LOC.   ATTR.     ATTRACTION      DAYS IN    ATTENDANCE
05 CODE   TYPE        NAME          OPER.      TO DATE
06
07 ##      X     XXXXXXXXXXXXX       ##          #,###
08 ##      X     XXXXXXXXXXXXX       ##          #,###
09
10        TOTALS FOR LOCATION ##    ###         ##,###
11
12 ##      X     XXXXXXXXXXXXX       ##          #,###
13 ##      X     XXXXXXXXXXXXX       ##          #,###
14
15        TOTALS FOR LOCATION ##    ###         ##,###
16
17 PARK TOTALS                     #,###       ###,###
18
19
```

Figure 5-2.2

Figure 5-2. Programming specifications for summary report program.

PROBLEM ANALYSIS

Normal processing for the summary report resembles the processing for a detail report with total lines. For each input record, the days in operation and attendance to date values are added into their respective accumulators. In this case, two levels of totals are accumulated—subtotals and final totals. Also, for each input record, a detail line is printed on the report. Apart from the special processing that takes place whenever a different group of input records is encountered or whenever heading lines should be printed, the program logic is basically the same as for other types of report writing programs.

INITIALIZATION OF PROCESSING

Figure 5-3 diagrams memory status following program initialization activities. Each of the output lines has been defined and formatted, the four accumulators have been set at zero, and the first master record has been input.

Two special accumulators have been defined for use in printing report headings. The page counter, which is initially valued at zero, will be incremented by 1 and printed on the report title line whenever a page break occurs. The line counter, also set initially at zero, is used to tally the number of lines printed on a page. Whenever a detail line is printed, this counter is incremented by 1; whenever a subtotal line is printed, the counter is incremented by 3 to account for the subtotal line and the blank lines above and below. During processing, the program will check continually to see whether the line counter has reached the maximum number of lines per page (20). If so, then the program will space to the top of a new page and print the report headings before continuing with the body of the report.

The two constants appearing on the processing map in Figure 5-3 also are used to print headings. The line limit constant has been valued at 20, representing the maximum number of lines to be printed on each page. The line counter will be compared against this constant every time a detail line is formatted to determine whether a page break should occur before printing. The page size constant, containing the value 25, gives the physical page size. This constant will be used in calculating the remaining number of lines on a page at a page-break point. The use of these counters, constants, and calculations for printing of report headings is described in the discussion below on heading processing.

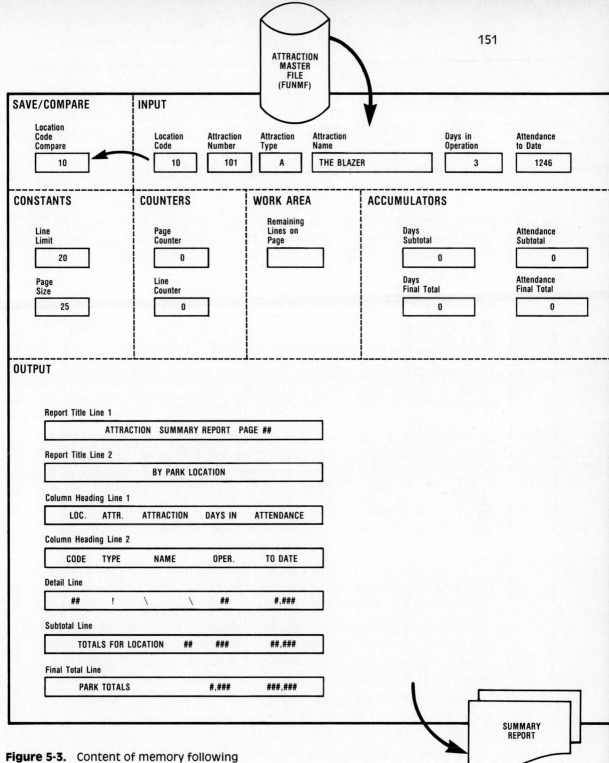

Figure 5-3. Content of memory following initialization of processing.

During program processing, a control break will be signaled by a change in the location code—that is, when the value of the code for the record that was just input is different from the code of the previous group of records. To make this comparison possible, the code for the first record of a control group must be saved in a different storage area from the input area. Then, as successive records are input from the master file, their location codes can be compared with the saved code to determine if a change has taken place in the control group field. During program initialization, therefore, the location code for the first record of the first control group is copied into a compare area where it will be available for subsequent comparisons.

CONTROL-BREAK PROCESSING

In this program, special control-break processing involves four activities.

First, the computer will print a subtotal line on the report. This line contains the current values in the two subtotal accumulators. These subtotals are printed along with the location code identifying the group. Remember, a control break is indicated when the input value for the location code differs from the value saved from the first record in the group. Therefore, the input location code represents the beginning of the next group. The location code that will be printed is the code of the previous group. This value is the one in the compare area, not in the input area.

Second, when the subtotal line is printed, the line counter must be incremented to account for the number of lines printed. In this case, the value 3 is added to the line counter. This value provides for the subtotal line plus a preceding and following blank line.

Third, after the subtotal line has been printed, the subtotal accumulators must be reset to zero. These accumulators are cleared out so that totals for the next group of records can be tallied.

The fourth and last control-break function is to save the new location code. The value representing the previous group is replaced by the value of the current group, whose first record was just input and triggered the control break. Now, the location codes for successive records can be compared with this new value to determine when the next control break occurs. These control-break activities are illustrated in Figure 5-4.

It should be noted that the final control break within the program will take place whenever processing reaches the end of the master file.

The end of this final control group, still, is signaled by a change in the location code. In this instance, the code value 0—the content of the location code field of the EOF record—is different from the code for the last control group. Therefore, the logic used to test for a control break is the same as if there were an actual file record.

PRINTING MULTIPLE PAGES

The sample summary report will require more than one page of printing. It is assumed that the physical page size used for this report has a maximum of 25 lines for printing. The standard page size is 66 lines on paper of 11 inches in length. For this program, however, a length of 25 lines is used to illustrate paging.

Printing, of course, will not take place on every possible line. Only a maximum of 20 lines will be printed on each page to allow a sufficient margin at the bottom of the page. When 20 lines have been printed, a page break will occur. The program will space to the top of a new page, write the heading lines and a page number, and then continue printing detail and total lines.

A page break should occur only prior to the printing of a detail line. In other words, a new page should never begin with a subtotal line. Neither should a final total line appear on a page by itself. At least one detail line always should be printed at the beginning of a new page. Therefore, the test for a page break and page-break processing always should occur before a detail line is scheduled to be printed. This requirement is met in the program design discussed in the next section.

It is possible that a subtotal line (and, possibly, a final total line) will be printed at the bottom of a page, before a page break occurs. For example, assume that a control break occurs and that the last detail line printed for a control group appears on the last line of printing. That is, a page break should occur; however, the subtotal line should not be printed on the next page, separated from the control group it represents. This situation requires that sufficient room be left at the bottom of any page to allow printing of total lines that happen to fall at that point. In the current program, the physical page size is 25 lines; the maximum number of lines to be printed per page (the "logical" page size) is 20. Therefore, if a subtotal line (and, possibly, a final total line) should be printed on the page, and if the last detail line appeared on line 20, there is still sufficient room to print the total lines without printing across page

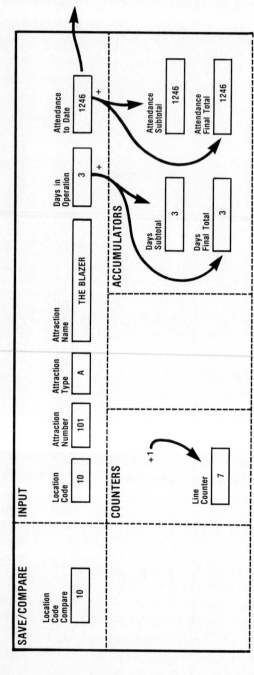

Normal processing involves adding the input values into the appropriate accumulators, printing a detail line on the report, and adding 1 to the line counter.

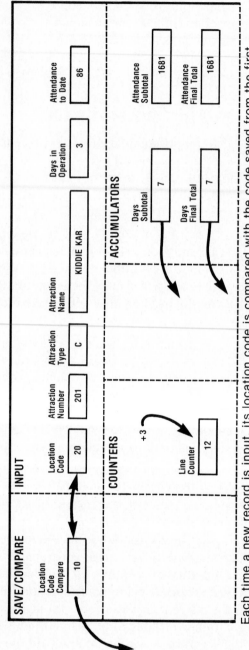

Each time a new record is input, its location code is compared with the code saved from the first record input from a group. If the two codes are different, a control break has occurred. At that point, a subtotal line is printed.

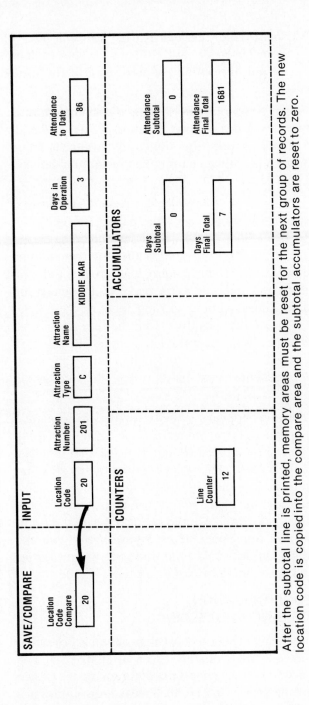

After the subtotal line is printed, memory areas must be reset for the next group of records. The new location code is copied into the compare area and the subtotal accumulators are reset to zero.

Figure 5-4. Content of memory during control-break processing.

boundaries. Thus, as a general rule, the logical page size will be the difference between the physical page size and the total number of lines required for a bottom margin plus the number of lines required for printing all levels of total lines.

Each time a detail line or a subtotal line is printed, the line counter is incremented the required number of lines. Printing of lines and adding to the line counter continues until the line counter reaches 20 or more. Note that the counter may advance up to 23 if a subtotal line appears at the bottom of a page.

When the line counter reaches 20 or more, a page break occurs. First, the program must space to the top of a new page. This operation involves printing as many blank lines as there are lines remaining on the current page. This figure is calculated by subtracting the line counter value from the page limit value. Next, the heading lines are printed. The page counter is incremented by 1 and used as the page number appearing on the first report title line. The remaining heading lines are printed, including a blank line to separate the headings from the first detail line. The final page-break operation is to reset the line counter. Because six heading lines are printed, the line counter is revalued to 6 to begin counting the lines on the new page. These page-break processing steps are illustrated in Figure 5-5.

Naturally, heading lines will appear on the first page of the report. This formatting is accomplished, however, within the main processing section of the program by testing the page counter. Recall that the page counter was valued initially at zero. This value, in effect, indicates that no pages have been printed at the time when program execution begins. During page-break processing, the page counter can be tested. If it contains the value zero, then a page break should occur to write the set of headings on the first page of the report. Thus, a page break will take place under two conditions: on printing of the first page (page counter = 0) or on reaching the logical line limit (line counter > = 20).

CONTROL-BREAK PROGRAM DESIGN, SPECIFICATION, CODE, AND PROCESSING

The structure chart for the mainline control-break program is presented in Figure 5-6. Pseudocode specifications are given in Figure 5-7. The design of the program is based on the general CIS program model. Design and pseudocode for the page-break and control-break subroutines are given in Figure 5-7.1 and Figure 5-7.2, respectively.

Within the begin processing section of the program, seven functions are required:

- The printing formats for the report lines are defined.
- The line limit and page size constants are defined and valued.
- The line and page counters are set to zero.
- The subtotal and final total accumulators are valued at zero.
- The master file is opened.
- The first master record is input into memory.
- The location code for this first record is copied into a compare area.

With the completion of these operations, the program can begin its main processing tasks.

Notice that, unlike programs reviewed previously, this program does not include the printing of report headings as a begin processing activity. Report headings should be included in begin processing activities only when the report will contain only one set of headings. In this program, however, headings will be printed multiple times and always in conjunction with the printing of a detail line. Therefore, it is appropriate to include the heading routine within the main processing section—prior to the printing of detail lines.

The main processing section of the program includes the normal processing functions:

- Accumulate totals.
- Print the detail line.
- Add to the line counter.
- Input the next master record.

In addition, page-break and control-break processing are included. Before a detail line is printed, the computer will check to see whether a page break is needed. If so, this processing is carried out prior to printing the detail line.

Note that page-break processing will be coded as a subroutine. The reason for doing this is to improve the readability of the program by removing these special processing statements from within the main logic of the program. The main processing routine will become much cleaner in appearance without this code. Yet, the logic to test for a page break still will remain obvious.

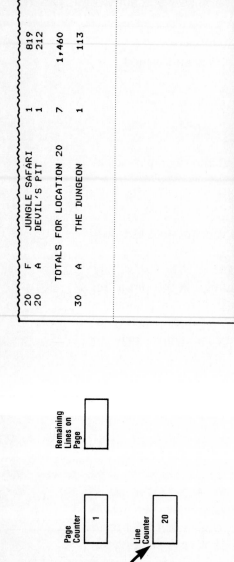

Before printing a detail line, the program compares the current value of the line counter with the maximum number of lines to be printed on a page. If the line counter is equal to or greater than the line limit, a page break should be taken.

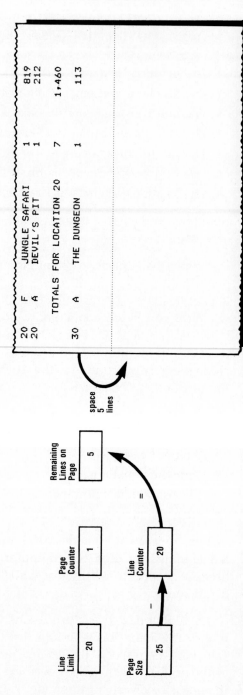

The number of lines remaining on the page is calculated by subtracting the current value of the line counter from the physical page size. The result is the number of blank lines to be printed so that the printer spaces to the top of a new page.

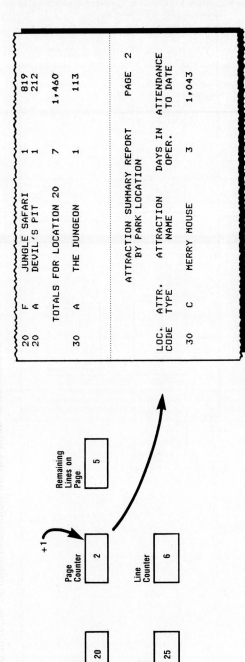

The page counter is incremented by 1 and printed as the page number within the first report title line. The remaining heading lines are printed and the line counter is reset to the number of heading lines printed. Then, processing continues with the printing of the next detail line.

Figure 5-5. Page-break processing for summary report program.

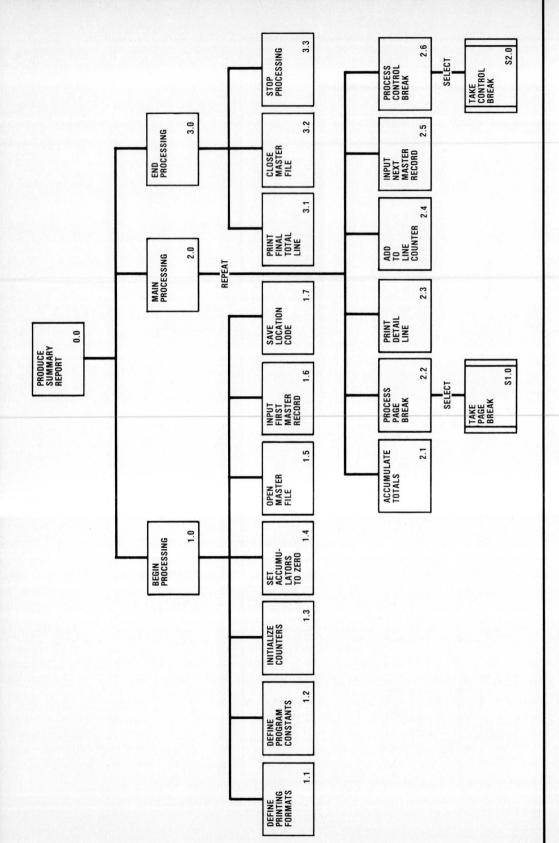

Figure 5-6. Structure chart for mainline control-break program.

```
0.0 PRODUCE SUMMARY REPORT
    1.0 BEGIN PROCESSING
        1.1 DEFINE PRINTING FORMATS
            Define Report Title Line 1
            Define Report Title Line 2
            Define Column Heading Line 1
            Define Column Heading Line 2
            Define Detail Line
            Define Subtotal Line
            Define Final Total Line
        1.2 DEFINE PROGRAM CONSTANTS
            Set Line Limit = 20
            Set Page Size = 25
        1.3 INITIALIZE COUNTERS
            Set Page Counter = 0
            Set Line Counter = 0
        1.4 SET ACCUMULATORS TO ZERO
            Set Days Subtotal = 0
            Set Attendance Subtotal = 0
            Set Days Final Total = 0
            Set Attendance Final Total = 0
        1.5 OPEN MASTER FILE
            Open "FUNMF" for input
        1.6 INPUT FIRST MASTER RECORD
            Input Location Code, Attraction Number, Attraction Type,
                Attraction Name, Days in Operation, Attendance to Date
        1.7 SAVE LOCATION CODE
            Set Saved Code = Location Code
    2.0 MAIN PROCESSING
    REPEAT: until end of master file
        2.1 ACCUMULATE TOTALS
            Set Days Subtotal = Days Subtotal + Days in Operation
            Set Attendance Subtotal = Attendance Subtotal +
                Attendance to Date
            Set Days Final Total = Days Final Total + Days in Operation
            Set Attendance Final Total = Attendance Final Total +
                Attendance to Date
        2.2 PROCESS PAGE BREAK
            SELECT: on Page Counter = 0
                    or Line Counter >= Line Limit
                2.2.1 TAKE PAGE BREAK
                        Perform S1.0 TAKE PAGE BREAK
            END SELECT
        2.3 PRINT DETAIL LINE
            Print using Detail Line Format, Location Code,
                Attraction Type, Attraction Name, Days in Operation,
                Attendance to Date
        2.4 ADD TO LINE COUNTER
            Set Line Counter = Line Counter + 1
        2.5 INPUT NEXT MASTER RECORD
            Input Location Code, Attraction Number, Attraction Type,
                Attraction Name, Days in Operation, Attendance to Date
        2.6 PROCESS CONTROL BREAK
            SELECT: on Location Code <> Saved Code
                2.6.1 TAKE CONTROL BREAK
                        Perform S2.0 TAKE CONTROL BREAK
            END SELECT
    END REPEAT
    3.0 END PROCESSING
        3.1 PRINT FINAL TOTAL LINE
            Print using Final Total Line Format, Days Total,
                Attendance Total
        3.2 CLOSE MASTER FILE
            Close "FUNMF"
        3.3 STOP PROCESSING
            Stop
```

Figure 5-7. Pseudocode for mainline control-break program.

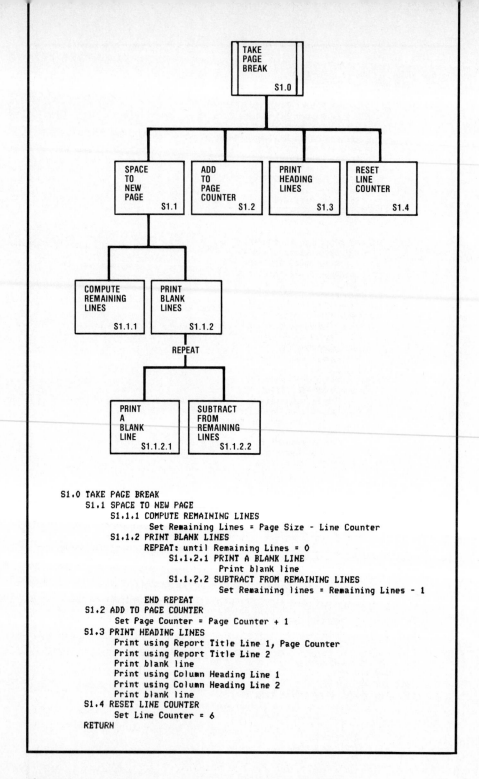

```
S1.0 TAKE PAGE BREAK
     S1.1 SPACE TO NEW PAGE
          S1.1.1 COMPUTE REMAINING LINES
                 Set Remaining Lines = Page Size - Line Counter
          S1.1.2 PRINT BLANK LINES
                 REPEAT: until Remaining Lines = 0
                      S1.1.2.1 PRINT A BLANK LINE
                               Print blank line
                      S1.1.2.2 SUBTRACT FROM REMAINING LINES
                               Set Remaining lines = Remaining Lines - 1
                 END REPEAT
     S1.2 ADD TO PAGE COUNTER
          Set Page Counter = Page Counter + 1
     S1.3 PRINT HEADING LINES
          Print using Report Title Line 1, Page Counter
          Print using Report Title Line 2
          Print blank line
          Print using Column Heading Line 1
          Print using Column Heading Line 2
          Print blank line
     S1.4 RESET LINE COUNTER
          Set Line Counter = 6
     RETURN
```

Figure 5-7.1. Design for page-break processing subroutine.

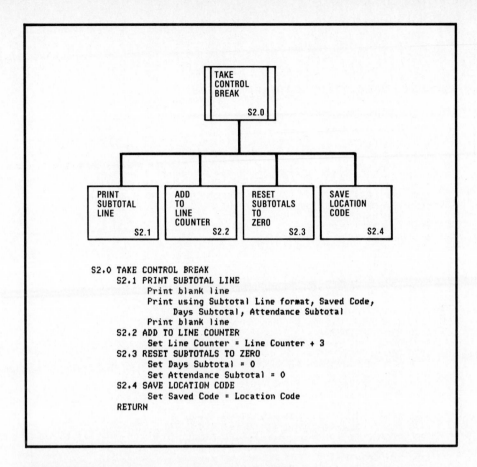

```
                    ┌──────────────┐
                    │ TAKE         │
                    │ CONTROL      │
                    │ BREAK        │
                    │        S2.0  │
                    └──────────────┘
        ┌─────────────┬──────┴──────┬─────────────┐
┌──────────┐  ┌──────────┐  ┌──────────┐  ┌──────────┐
│ PRINT    │  │ ADD      │  │ RESET    │  │ SAVE     │
│ SUBTOTAL │  │ TO       │  │ SUBTOTALS│  │ LOCATION │
│ LINE     │  │ LINE     │  │ TO       │  │ CODE     │
│          │  │ COUNTER  │  │ ZERO     │  │          │
│     S2.1 │  │     S2.2 │  │     S2.3 │  │     S2.4 │
└──────────┘  └──────────┘  └──────────┘  └──────────┘
```

```
S2.0 TAKE CONTROL BREAK
     S2.1 PRINT SUBTOTAL LINE
             Print blank line
             Print using Subtotal Line format, Saved Code,
                 Days Subtotal, Attendance Subtotal
             Print blank line
     S2.2 ADD TO LINE COUNTER
             Set Line Counter = Line Counter + 3
     S2.3 RESET SUBTOTALS TO ZERO
             Set Days Subtotal = 0
             Set Attendance Subtotal = 0
     S2.4 SAVE LOCATION CODE
             Set Saved Code = Location Code
     RETURN
```

Figure 5-7.2. Design for control-break subroutine.

The test for a control break occurs immediately after a record is input from the master file. At this point, the program tests whether the input location code is different from the saved code. If the test shows an unequal condition, control-break processing takes place. If the codes are the same, normal processing continues. Control-break processing will be coded as a subroutine, again, to make the program more readable and understandable than would be the case if all the code were to appear within the main processing module.

When there are no more master records to process, a last control break is taken before the program exits from the main processing loop. Then, the final totals are printed on the report, the master file is closed, and processing stops.

The coded program is shown in Figure 5-8. No new BASIC statements are required.

Figure 5-8. BASIC code for summary report program.

```
1000 REM FUN04                                        WEL/DRA
1010 REM                    SUMMARY REPORT
1020 REM
1030 REM THIS PROGRAM PRODUCES A REPORT SUMMARIZING THE
1040 REM DAYS IN OPERATION AND ATTENDANCE AT THE AMERICAN
1050 REM FUN AMUSEMENT PARK, CATEGORIZED BY PARK LOCATION
1060 REM OF ATTRACTIONS.  THE INPUT FILE IS THE ATTRACTION
1070 REM MASTER FILE (FUNMF).
1080 REM
1090 REM VARIABLE NAMES
1100 REM
1110 REM INPUT:
1120 REM     L.....LOCATION CODE
1130 REM     N.....ATTRACTION NUMBER
1140 REM     T$....ATTRACTION TYPE
1150 REM     N$....ATTRACTION NAME
1160 REM     D.....DAYS IN OPERATION (THIS MONTH)
1170 REM     A.....ATTENDANCE TO DATE (THIS MONTH)
1180 REM CONSTANTS:
1190 REM     P1....MAXIMUM LINES PER PAGE
1200 REM     P2....PHYSICAL PAGE SIZE
1210 REM SAVE/COMPARE AREA:
1220 REM     L1....LOCATION CODE COMPARE
1230 REM WORK AREA:
1240 REM     R.....REMAINING LINES ON PAGE
1250 REM ACCUMULATORS:
1260 REM     S1....DAYS IN OPERATION SUBTOTAL
1270 REM     S2....ATTENDANCE TO DATE SUBTOTAL
1280 REM     T1....DAYS IN OPERATION FINAL TOTAL
1290 REM     T2....ATTENDANCE TO DATE FINAL TOTAL
1300 REM COUNTERS:
1310 REM     K1....PAGE COUNTER
1320 REM     K2....LINE COUNTER
1330 REM OUTPUT:
1340 REM     F1$...REPORT TITLE LINE 1
1350 REM     F2$...REPORT TITLE LINE 2
1360 REM     F3$...COLUMN HEADING LINE 1
1370 REM     F4$...COLUMN HEADING LINE 2
1380 REM     F5$...DETAIL LINE
1390 REM     F6$...SUBTOTAL LINE
1400 REM     F7$...FINAL TOTAL LINE
1410 REM
1420 REM 0.0 PRODUCE SUMMARY REPORT
1430 REM
1435 REM ************************
1440 REM * 1.0 BEGIN PROCESSING *
1445 REM ************************
1450 REM
1460 REM 1.1 DEFINE PRINTING FORMATS
1470         LET F1$ = "          ATTRACTION SUMMARY REPORT      PAGE ##"
1480         LET F2$ = "                   BY PARK LOCATION"
1490         LET F3$ = "LOC.  ATTR.     ATTRACTION     DAYS IN   ATTENDANCE"
1500         LET F4$ = "CODE  TYPE        NAME          OPER.     TO DATE"
1510         LET F5$ = " ##    !     \            \     ##       #,###"
1520         LET F6$ = "     TOTALS FOR LOCATION ##   ###     ##,###"
1530         LET F7$ = "PARK TOTALS                  #,###   ###,###"
1540 REM
1550 REM 1.2 DEFINE PROGRAM CONSTANTS
1560         LET P1 = 20
1570         LET P2 = 25
```

```
1580 REM
1590 REM 1.3 INITIALIZE COUNTERS
1600        LET K1 = 0
1610        LET K2 = 25
1620 REM
1630 REM 1.4 SET ACCUMULATORS TO ZERO
1640        LET S1 = 0
1650        LET S2 = 0
1660        LET T1 = 0
1670        LET T2 = 0
1680 REM
1690 REM 1.5 OPEN MASTER FILE
1700        OPEN "FUNMF" FOR INPUT AS FILE #1
1710 REM
1720 REM 1.6 INPUT FIRST MASTER RECORD
1730        INPUT #1, L, N, T$, N$, D, A
1740 REM
1750 REM 1.7 SAVE LOCATION CODE
1760        LET L1 = L
1770 REM
1775 REM *************************
1780 REM * 2.0 MAIN PROCESSING  *
1785 REM *************************
1790 REM REPEAT
1800     IF N$ = "END OF FILE" THEN GOTO 2190
1810 REM
1820 REM     2.1 ACCUMULATE TOTALS
1830             LET S1 = S1 + D
1840             LET S2 = S2 + A
1850             LET T1 = T1 + D
1860             LET T2 = T2 + A
1870 REM
1880 REM     2.2 PROCESS PAGE BREAK
1890 REM         SELECT
1900         IF K1 =  0   THEN GOTO 1940
1910         IF K2 >= P1 THEN GOTO 1940
1920                         GOTO 1970
1930 REM
1940 REM         2.2.1 TAKE PAGE BREAK
1950                 GOSUB 3000
1960 REM
1970 REM         END SELECT
1980 REM
1990 REM     2.3 PRINT DETAIL LINE
2000             PRINT USING F5$, L, T$, N$, D, A
2010 REM
2020 REM     2.4 ADD TO LINE COUNTER
2030             LET K2 = K2 + 1
2040 REM
2050 REM     2.5 INPUT NEXT MASTER RECORD
2060             INPUT #1, L, N, T$, N$, D, A
2070 REM
2080 REM     2.6 PROCESS CONTROL BREAK
2090 REM         SELECT
2100         IF L <> L1 THEN GOTO 2130
2110                         GOTO 2160
2120 REM
2130 REM         2.6.1 TAKE CONTROL BREAK
2140                 GOSUB 4000
2150 REM
2160 REM         END SELECT
2170 REM
2180     GOTO 1790
2190 REM END REPEAT
2200 REM
2205 REM *************************
2210 REM * 3.0 END PROCESSING    *
2215 REM *************************
2220 REM
2230 REM 3.1 PRINT FINAL TOTAL LINE
2240        PRINT USING F7$, T1, T2
```

```
2250 REM
2260 REM 3.2 CLOSE MASTER FILE
2270        CLOSE #1
2280 REM
2290 REM 3.3 STOP PROCESSING
2300        STOP
2310 REM
2320 REM
3000 REM **************************
3005 REM * S1.0 TAKE PAGE BREAK *
3010 REM **************************
3015 REM
3020 REM S1.1 SPACE TO NEW PAGE
3030 REM
3040 REM      S1.1.1 COMPUTE REMAINING LINES
3050                 LET R = P2 - K2
3060 REM
3070 REM      S1.1.2 PRINT BLANK LINES
3080 REM             REPEAT
3090                 IF R = 0 THEN GOTO 3180
3100 REM
3110 REM             S1.1.2.1 PRINT A BLANK LINE
3120                          PRINT
3130 REM
3140 REM             S1.1.2.2 SUBTRACT FROM REMAINING LINES
3150                          LET R = R - 1
3160 REM
3170                 GOTO 3080
3180 REM             END REPEAT
3190 REM
3200 REM S1.2 ADD TO PAGE COUNTER
3210        LET K1 = K1 + 1
3220 REM
3230 REM S1.3 PRINT HEADING LINES
3240        PRINT USING F1$, K1
3250        PRINT USING F2$
3260        PRINT
3270        PRINT USING F3$
3280        PRINT USING F4$
3290        PRINT
3300 REM
3310 REM S1.4 RESET LINE COUNTER
3320        LET K2 = 6
3330 REM
3340     RETURN
3350 REM
3360 REM
4000 REM *****************************
4005 REM * S2.0 TAKE CONTROL BREAK *
4010 REM *****************************
4015 REM
4020 REM S2.1 PRINT SUBTOTAL LINE
4030        PRINT
4040        PRINT USING F6$, L1, S1, S2
4050        PRINT
4060 REM
4070 REM S2.2 ADD TO LINE COUNTER
4080        LET K2 = K2 + 3
4090 REM
4100 REM S2.3 RESET SUBTOTALS TO ZERO
4110        LET S1 = 0
4120        LET S2 = 0
4130 REM
4140 REM S2.4 SAVE LOCATION CODE
4150        LET L1 = L
4160 REM
4170     RETURN
4180 END
```

Figure 5-8. Concluded.

BUILDING A SIMPLE SYSTEM

In the previous chapters, an attraction master file is created for the American Fun Amusement Park. This file will become the basis for a simple park attractions information system. This system will maintain information concerning the attractions and will produce management and operational reports. So far, four programs have been developed to implement the first part of the system:

- A file creation program
- A detail report program
- An exception report program
- A summary report program.

The structure chart for this portion of the Amusement Park Information System (APIS) is illustrated in Figure 5-9.

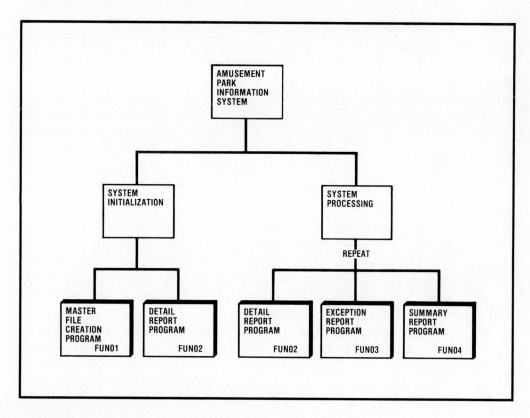

Figure 5-9. Structure of Amusement Park Information System software.

The system was initialized, or established, with the creation of the master file and verification of file content through the detail report program. These two programs are used one time in the life of the system—to create a valid master file at the time of system initialization. Once established, the master file becomes the basis for regular, repeated system processing. During each processing cycle, the master file will be updated with new information reflecting the ongoing operations of the park.

Periodically, reports are produced. The detail report program, for example, may be run each time the master file is updated with new transaction data. Depending on management needs, the exception report program and the summary report program also will be run as managers feel the need to overview operating status. These four programs are supplemented with additional programs as system building continues in subsequent chapters. By the end of the first eight chapters of the book, an entire file creation, updating, and reporting system will be in place.

The system-level structure chart in Figure 5-9 describes the organization of system programs. This chart documents the structural relationships among the programs in terms of their functions and execution cycles. Another method for documenting a system is called a *data flow diagram (DFD)*. This technique traces the flow of data through a system, identifies the files that are used, and designates the processing that takes place within system programs and within manual, nonautomated, portions of the system. Whereas a structure chart is a somewhat static picture of what the system is at a point in time, a data flow diagram is a more dynamic representation of what a system does.

Figure 5-10 presents the data flow diagram for the current status of the Amusement Park Information System. In general, the arrows represent flows of data through the system; the *bubbles* (circles) represent processing activities (programs and manual procedures) that transform the data or add to their information content. The open-ended rectangles represent files, or *data stores*, that are used within the system. The boxes show sources and/or destinations of data and information. A DFD is a convenient tool for understanding the relationships among data, processing functions, and information produced by the system.

Another type of system documentation is a *systems flowchart*, as shown in Figure 5-11. This flowchart shows the physical implementation of the system as a set of hardware and software components. Special

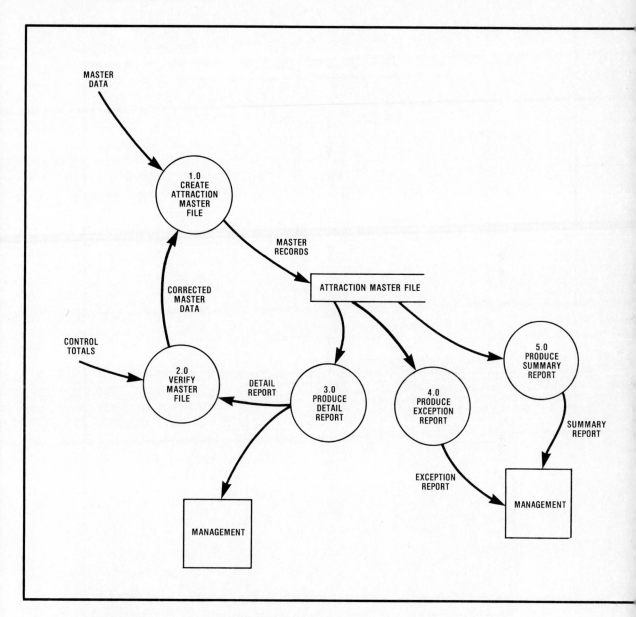

Figure 5-10. Data flow diagram showing functions of Amusement Park Information System.

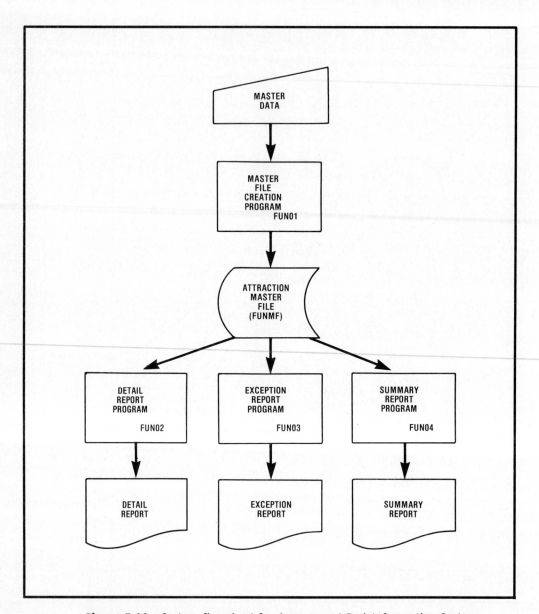

Figure 5-11. System flowchart for Amusement Park Information System.

symbols for input, output, and storage devices are used to indicate the hardware features of the system. For example, the diagram shows that data to create the master file are entered through a computer terminal and are written to magnetic disk. The reports are produced on printers. Usually, a systems flowchart is prepared as the last step in systems design. The flowchart documents how the processing functions illustrated in a data flow diagram actually are implemented within a hardware environment. The flowchart shows the flow of processing through the system rather than the flow of data as in the data flow diagram.

In general, a data flow diagram illustrates the logical functions of a system and the data involved in the processing; a systems flowchart illustrates the physical implementation of the system as processing links among hardware and software components; and a systems-level structure chart illustrates the structure of software components of the system and the cyclical nature of the processing. All three graphic diagrams present different viewpoints of the system and complement one another. All of these graphic tools are used throughout this book to describe different aspects of systems under study. The diagrams help emphasize the important fact that programs do not perform their functions in isolation, but are integrated within an entire system of programs to implement a complete computer information system.

Basic system reporting functions now have been implemented for the Amusement Park Information System. Needed information can be pulled from the master file and reported to management. The requirement now is to have the capability to keep the master file up to date to reflect the transactions involved in ongoing park operations. Therefore, beginning in the next chapter, the processing of transaction data against the master file is discussed.

Chapter Summary

1. A summary report presents representative facts that characterize the content of a file.

2. A summary report may contain detail lines but is defined by the inclusion of subtotals and final totals that summarize file content.

3. The value of a summary report is that it provides concise information to allow users the convenience of gaining knowledge about the file without the burden of excessive details.

4. Summary reports often are produced through a technique known as control-break processing. A control break occurs when any change takes place in an identification field, or control field, of a record for which special processing is required.

5. To facilitate control-break processing, file records are grouped into meaningful categories identified by their control fields. A change in the value contained in the control field signals the end of a control group and the point at which special processing should occur. Usually, the special processing involves printing of subtotal lines summarizing numeric fields for the preceding group of records.

6. The design of a summary report, or control-break, program is based on the general computer information systems program model. Within the begin processing section and following the reading of the first record from the file, the control field value is copied into a compare area. Further, following each subsequent reading of a record, the program tests for a control break, indicated by a difference between the value of the control field just input and the value in the compare area. If the two values are different, control-break processing is completed before normal processing is resumed.

7. Control-break processing usually involves printing a subtotal line, incrementing a line counter, resetting subtotal accumulators to zero, and copying the new control field value into the compare area.

8. Summary reports of multiple pages require page breaks. During page-break processing, the program spaces to the top of a new page and prints report heading lines before continuing with the body of the report.

9. In multiple-page reports, each page should begin with at least one detail line. A subtotal or final total line should not appear as the first line on a page. Therefore, tests for page breaks should always occur immediately prior to printing of a detail line.

10. In determining bottom margins of pages of multiple-page reports, sufficient space should be left for printing any total lines that might be required. The logical page length can be derived by subtracting from the physical page length the bottom margin plus the number of lines required for all levels of totals.

11. Page-break processing requires that a counter be established for tallying the number of lines printed. This accumulator is incremented each time a line is printed. Also, a page counter is defined. It is incremented each time a page break occurs and is used in printing page numbers.

12. A data flow diagram illustrates the logical processing functions of a system—including manual and computerized activities. It presents a dynamic view of the nature of the system, including sources and destinations of data and information, data flows throughout the system, files that support processing, and transformations of the data.

13. A systems flowchart shows the hardware/software environment within which the system is implemented. It illustrates the flow of processing control in the system and identifies the physical input, output, and storage devices that are used.

14. A system-level structure chart illustrates the organization of software components of an information system. It portrays the relationships among programs and their processing cycles.

Review Questions

1. What is a control field?

2. In general, when does a control break occur?

3. To implement control-break processing, why is it important that all records with the same control field value appear together, one record after another, in a file?

4. Why should the test for a page break and page-break processing always occur before a detail line is scheduled to be printed?

5. What is a data flow diagram?

6. What is a systems flowchart?

7. What is a systems-level structure chart?

Programming Assignments

Programming practice assignments for Chapter 5 are located in Appendix A, CASE STUDY ONE and CASE STUDY TWO.

Key Terms

1. control break

2. control field

3. control group

4. data flow diagram (DFD)

5. bubbles

6. data store

7. systems flowchart

6
CREATING
TRANSACTION FILES

OVERVIEW AND OBJECTIVES

Master files contain data records that are maintained over long periods of time. These files must be kept current so that reports always reflect the present status of the business.

Master files are updated to reflect current transactions. That is, in the normal conduct of a business, detailed records are kept to reflect the effects of all transactions. Periodically—weekly, daily, or as the transactions accumulate—these data are added to the information in the master files. Thus, subsequent detail, exception, and summary reports are based on current business data.

In this chapter, programs are developed to create and validate transaction records and to prepare a file of business transactions to be used in updating a master file.

When you complete your work in this chapter, you should be able to:

☐ Describe what a transaction is, how it originates, and its relationship to master file information.

☐ Discuss data editing and validation and describe the types of editing that can be performed by a computer.

☐ Describe common methods for setting up batch controls for verification of computer input.

☐ Design and write programs to create transaction files and produce edit reports.

☐ Design and write programs to implement multiple control breaks.

☐ Design and write programs that use multiple files.

☐ Design and write programs that use table searching.

☐ Use several common BASIC mathematical functions.

THE NATURE OF TRANSACTIONS

A *transaction* is, broadly, an act of doing business. Whenever merchandise is sold, whenever a bill is paid, or whenever any business activity takes place, a transaction occurs. Transactions are sources of data. Usually, a transaction is recorded in some fashion. Often, documents are used to record transactions, as occurs when a salesperson prepares an invoice, or bill, listing merchandise purchased by a customer. Recording the transaction serves as an historical record of the business activity and gives rise to data that will enter a data processing system.

Transactions represent day-to-day business activity. Over time, records of transactions are accumulated and are posted, or entered to, a company's master files on periodic schedules. Updating causes these files to reflect ongoing business transactions. For example, a company might maintain a customer account file containing information on the amounts owed by customers who purchase merchandise on credit. As sales transactions take place, the data are added to the customer master file to keep customer accounts current. At the close of each billing period, the file is used to prepare bills requesting payment of the accumulated amounts in the master file.

In general, therefore, businesses maintain master files and transaction files. Master files contain permanent or semipermanent information about entities associated with the company—customers, products, employees, materials, and other business requirements. Master files also contain summary information about business transactions affecting those entities—customer purchases, product costs and volumes, materials on hand, and so on.

Transaction files, on the other hand, contain detailed records of business transactions. These files are produced daily, as transactions occur. Data collected within transaction files then are used to update master files periodically. Following updating, master files contain current operating summaries.

Master and transaction files form the basis of the Amusement Park Information System described throughout this book. Any sale of tickets represents a business transaction. The customer purchases a book of tickets to be used as admission coupons to the attractions. Data items generated by each transaction include the attraction number, type of ticket, time of purchase, cost of ticket, and possibly other data representing the business activity of ticket sales. These data are accumulated in a file of transactions to be combined subsequently with the master file of attraction data to reflect current business status.

USING TRANSACTION FILES

So far, the Amusement Park Information System contains programs and procedures to produce a master file of attraction information and to generate detail, exception, and summary reports based on the file's content. At this point, however, there is no way to keep the file up to date with information on continuing park activities. In particular, the system requires procedures to collect data on attendance and to update the master file with this attendance information. In this chapter, therefore, programs are developed that create a transaction file of attendance data. In the chapter that follows, this file is used to update the master file.

Transaction processing in the amusement park system involves both manual and automated procedures. The initial step is the sale of tickets to customers. On entering the park, the customer purchases books of tickets. The ticket seller collects the money and prepares a receipt listing the charge. At this point, only the total amount of the sale and the number of adult and child tickets sold are recorded.

At each attraction location, an attendant collects a ticket from each customer. At the end of each shift, the attendant gathers the tickets and prepares an Attendance Summary Form. This form, illustrated in Figure 6-1, contains the date, the shift, the location code, the attraction number, and the number of adult and child tickets collected. This form is a type of *source document* containing data collected at the point of the transaction. At the end of the work shift, this form, along with the tickets, is delivered to the park office. At the amusement park office, a clerk checks the data on the form against the tickets collected to verify that the data are correct.

Attendance Summary Forms are collected from all the attractions for each of the two shifts. After the forms have been verified as correct, the data are logged on an Attendance Transmittal Form. This form, shown

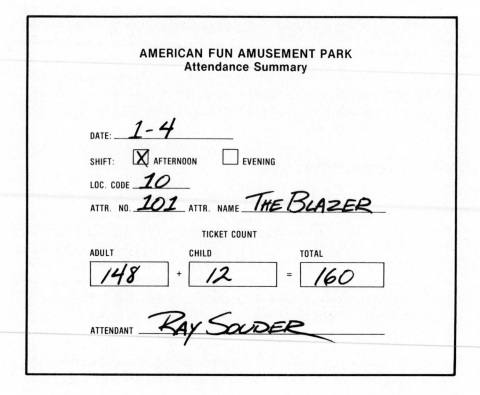

Figure 6-1. Daily Attendance Summary Form.

in Figure 6-2, summarizes the transaction data according to park location, attraction number, and shift. Attractions that were not in operation on that day are excluded from the form. The clerk then runs adding machine totals for the attendance columns and enters the totals at the bottom of the form. The transmittal form is sent to the data processing department for entry of the data into the computer system.

A data entry program similar to the one described in Chapter 3 for creation of the attraction master file is used to build the attendance transaction file. This transaction file contains records capturing the data on the transmittal form. Each line of the form becomes one record in the file. Later, this file will be used to update the master file with data on daily transactions pertaining to each of the attractions.

After the attendance transaction file has been created, an *edit report* is prepared. This report lists the content of the file and prints an error

AMERICAN FUN AMUSEMENT PARK
ATTENDANCE TRANSMITTAL FORM

DATE __1-4__

NOTE: Do not key data for which no attendance figures are given.

LOC CODE	ATTR. NO.	SHIFT CODE	ADULT TICKETS	CHILD TICKETS	TOTAL TICKETS
10	101	A	148	12	160
10	101	E	352	65	417
10	104	A	130	15	145
10	104	E	128	22	150
10	105	A	15	7	22
10	105	E	19	10	29
20	201	A			
20	201	E			
20	202	A	38	26	64
20	202	E	45	31	76
20	207	A	209	176	385
20	207	E	295	144	439
20	210	A	43	18	61
20	210	E	57	29	86
30	310	A			
30	310	E			
30	312	A	37	150	187
30	312	E	42	195	237
30	320	A	67	50	117
30	320	E	89	72	161
40	406	A	54	8	62
40	406	E	109	14	123
40	419	A	30	22	52
40	419	E	48	37	85
40	420	A	28	7	35
40	420	E	31	19	50
50	510	A	5	5	10
50	510	E	18	20	38
50	515	A	37	25	62
50	515	E	59	42	101
			2,133	1,221	3,354

CLERK __S. Duggal__

Figure 6-2. Daily Attendance Transmittal Form.

message for each field of data that is invalid or contains unreasonable data. Errors caused by miskeying of data into the computer system or by transposing or copying the wrong data onto the transmittal form are caught before the data are used to update the master file. The report is returned to the clerk, who checks the data against the transmittal form and the attendance summary forms. Corrections are returned to the data processing department and are keyed into the transaction file.

Finally, a daily Transactions Report is prepared. This report lists the attendance figures for each attraction, for each shift, and prints subtotals for each attraction and location. The report is sent to the park manager, who files it in date sequence along with the other daily reports.

Figure 6-3 shows the data flow diagram of the Amusement Park Information System expanded to include the procedures necessary to build the attendance transaction file. Three programs are required to implement the new portion of the system:

- A transaction file creation program
- A transaction file editing program
- A transaction file report program.

These three programs are discussed below.

FILE CREATION PROGRAM

The file creation program is designed to build the transaction file from the data contained on the transmittal form. This program is structurally similar to the master file creation program described in Chapter 3, with one additional processing technique added. After the terminal operator has keyed the data for a transaction record, the program will ask the operator for verification. If the operator has made a mistake in entering the data, the program will allow the record to be rekeyed before writing it to the transaction file. This approach will permit the operator to correct most key entry errors without having to rekey the entire file. The specifications for this program are given in Figure 6-4.

The structure chart for the program is presented in Figure 6-5. Note that the date will be input by the operator one time at the beginning of the program. The date field will be appended to the other input fields and written as part of each transaction record. The data that form the record are input within a subroutine. Figure 6-6 gives the pseudocode for the mainline program.

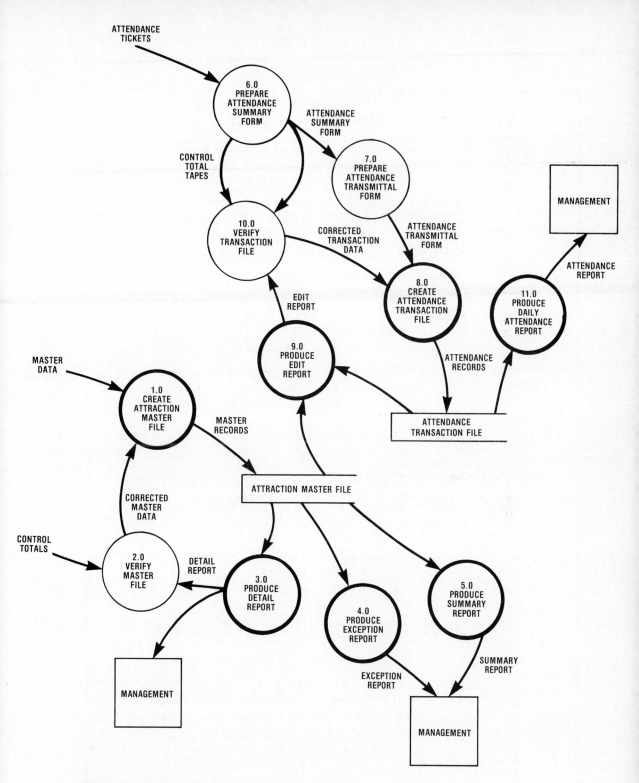

Figure 6-3. Data flow diagram for Amusement Park Information System. Automated portions of system are highlighted.

<u>PROGRAMMING SPECIFICATIONS</u>

System: AMUSEMENT PARK   Date: 04/20/XX
Program: TRANSACTION FILE CREATION   Program I.D.: FUN05   Analyst: B. LEIGH

Design and write a program to create a transaction file of daily attendance
data for the American Fun Amusement Park. Data records will be entered
interactively through a terminal and written to disk. Also, the records will
be entered in attraction number sequence. The program will be coded in BASIC.
Figure 6-4.1 shows the system flowchart for this application.

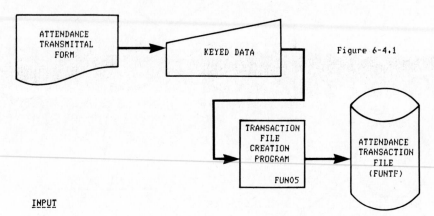

Figure 6-4.1

<u>INPUT</u>

The program input is the daily attendance data taken from the attendance
transmittal form shown in Figure 6-2. First, the operator enters the current
date, in the format MMDD. This field appears in each transaction record.
Next, each line of the transmittal form is keyed by the operator. The format
of the fields is:

Field Name	Data Type
Location Code	Numeric
Attraction Number	Numeric
Shift Code	Alphanumeric
Adult Attendance	Numeric
Child Attendance	Numeric

A final EOF record is written to the file. This record contains zero values in
all fields except the shift code field, which contains the string "END OF
FILE."

<u>PROCESSING</u>

Processing involves writing the input records to the transaction file. The
current date field and the five input fields are written to the file.

The program should allow the operator to reenter any records that are miskeyed.
For each record, the operator keys the five data fields. If a keying error is
discovered during visual verification, the operator informs the program, which
permits the operator to rekey the data. Any number of rekeying attempts can be
made. When the operator signals that the data are correct, the record is
written to the file.

Figure 6-4.2 shows the format of the data entry session.

```
       000000000011111111112222222222333333333344444444445
       12345678901234567890123456789012345678901234567890
01         TRANSACTION FILE CREATION
02         **************************
03
04 KEY THE DATA FIELDS INDICATED.  VERIFY
05 EACH RECORD AND REENTER THOSE IN ERROR.
06 TO END THE PROGRAM, KEY AN END-OF-FILE
07 RECORD: '0,0,END OF FILE,0,0'.
08
09 ENTER DATE (MMDD)....? ####
10
11 LOCATION CODE........? ##
12 ATTRACTION NUMBER....? ###
13 SHIFT CODE...........? X
14 ADULT ATTENDANCE.....? ###
15 CHILD ATTENDANCE.....? ###
16    VERIFY (Y/N)......? X
17        .
18        .
19        .
20 LOCATION CODE........? 0
21 ATTRACTION NUMBER....? 0
22 SHIFT CODE...........? END OF FILE
23 ADULT ATTENDANCE.....? 0
24 CHILD ATTENDANCE.....? 0
25    VERIFY (Y/N)......? Y
26
27 *** END OF SESSION ***
28
29
```

Figure 6-4.2

OUTPUT

Program output will be the attendance transaction file (FUNTF). Each record in this file will contain the following data fields: date, location code, attraction number, shift code, adult attendance, child attendance. The disk file will be organized in attraction number sequence.

Figure 6-4. Programming specifications for transaction file creation program.

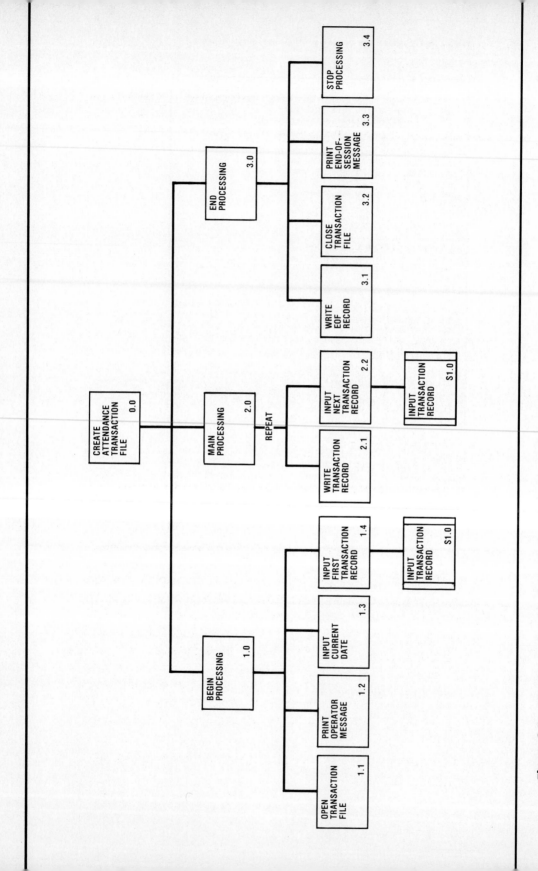

Figure 6-5. Structure chart for transaction file creation program.

```
0.0 CREATE ATTENDANCE TRANSACTION FILE
   1.0 BEGIN PROCESSING
      1.1 OPEN TRANSACTION FILE
         Open "FUNTF" for output
      1.2 PRINT OPERATOR MESSAGE
         Print message lines
         Print blank line
      1.3 INPUT CURRENT DATE
         Print blank line
         Print date prompt
         Input Date
      1.4 INPUT FIRST TRANSACTION RECORD
         Perform S1.0 INPUT TRANSACTION RECORD
   2.0 MAIN PROCESSING
      REPEAT: until end of transaction data
         2.1 WRITE TRANSACTION RECORD
            Write Date, Location Code, Attraction Number,
               Shift Code, Adult Attendance, Child Attendance
         2.2 INPUT NEXT TRANSACTION RECORD
            Perform S1.0 INPUT TRANSACTION RECORD
      END REPEAT
   3.0 END PROCESSING
      3.1 WRITE EOF RECORD
         Write Date, Location Code, Attraction Number,
            Shift Code, Adult Attendance, Child Attendance
      3.2 CLOSE TRANSACTION FILE
         Close "FUNTF"
      3.3 PRINT END-OF-SESSION MESSAGE
         Print end-of-session message
      3.4 STOP PROCESSING
         Stop
```

Figure 6-6. Pseudocode for mainline transaction file program.

The structure chart and pseudocode for the input subroutine are shown in Figure 6-7. Recall that the operator will be allowed to key the data as many times as necessary to produce an error-free transaction record. Therefore, the INPUT TRANSACTION DATA module is placed within a repeat structure. This processing will be repeated until the operator indicates that the record is correct by keying the value "Y" (for Yes) in response to the verify prompt. At that point, the record is written to the file. Notice that each time the subroutine is activated, the valid record flag (V$) is initialized to a blank space value before the input module is entered.

Figure 6-8 presents the code for this file creation program. No new statement types are required.

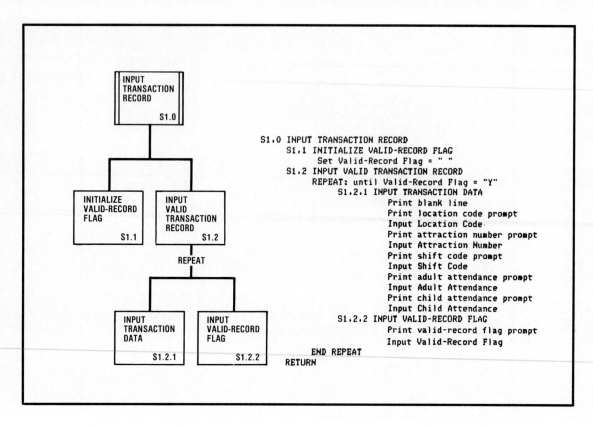

```
                              S1.0 INPUT TRANSACTION RECORD
                                 S1.1 INITIALIZE VALID-RECORD FLAG
                                      Set Valid-Record Flag = " "
                                 S1.2 INPUT VALID TRANSACTION RECORD
                                      REPEAT: until Valid-Record Flag = "Y"
                                         S1.2.1 INPUT TRANSACTION DATA
                                                Print blank line
                                                Print location code prompt
                                                Input Location Code
                                                Print attraction number prompt
                                                Input Attraction Number
                                                Print shift code prompt
                                                Input Shift Code
                                                Print adult attendance prompt
                                                Input Adult Attendance
                                                Print child attendance prompt
                                                Input Child Attendance
                                         S1.2.2 INPUT VALID-RECORD FLAG
                                                Print valid-record flag prompt
                                                Input Valid-Record Flag
                                      END REPEAT
                              RETURN
```

Figure 6-7.   Structure chart and pseudocode for transaction input subroutine.

EDIT REPORT PROGRAM

After the transaction file has been built, it is processed through an edit program to check for errors within the records. Although the file creation program permits the terminal operator to correct obvious errors, other errors might slip by. For example, the operator may not catch every keying error, or the data that are recorded on the transmittal form may be incorrect. Perhaps the clerk transposed numbers taken from the attendance summary form or simply copied the wrong data. For whatever reason, there is no assurance that the data keyed into the transaction file are correct.

It is common practice, therefore, to produce an edit report on the transaction file before the data are posted to the master file. An edit program makes additional checks on the validity of the data in the file and

Figure 6-8. BASIC code for transaction file creation program.

```
1000 REM FUN05                                        WEL/DRA
1010 REM             TRANSACTION FILE CREATION
1020 REM
1030 REM THIS PROGRAM CREATES A TRANSACTION FILE NAMED
1040 REM "FUNTF" WHICH CONTAINS DAILY ATTENDANCE DATA FOR
1050 REM THE AMERICAN FUN AMUSEMENT PARK.  DATA ARE ENTERED
1060 REM THROUGH A COMPUTER TERMINAL AND RECORDS ARE WRITTEN
1070 REM IN SEQUENCE WITHIN A DISK FILE.  THE RECORDS ARE
1080 REM ORDERED BY ATTRACTION NUMBER.  THE PROGRAM ALLOWS
1090 REM THE OPERATOR TO VERIFY AND CORRECT RECORDS BEFORE
1100 REM THEY ARE PLACED IN THE FILE.
1110 REM
1120 REM VARIABLE NAMES
1130 REM
1140 REM     D1...DATE IN MMDD FORMAT
1150 REM     L1...LOCATION CODE
1160 REM     N1...ATTRACTION NUMBER
1170 REM     S1$..SHIFT CODE
1180 REM     A1...ADULT ATTENDANCE
1190 REM     A2...CHILD ATTENDANCE
1200 REM     V$...VERIFICATION FLAG
1210 REM
1220 REM 0.0 CREATE ATTENDANCE TRANSACTION FILE
1230 REM
1240 REM *************************
1250 REM * 1.0 BEGIN PROCESSING *
1260 REM *************************
1270 REM
1280 REM 1.1 OPEN TRANSACTION FILE
1290         OPEN "FUNTF" FOR OUTPUT AS FILE #1
1300 REM
1310 REM 1.2 PRINT OPERATOR MESSAGE
1320         PRINT "     TRANSACTION FILE CREATION"
1330         PRINT "     *************************"
1340         PRINT
1350         PRINT "TYPE THE DATA FIELDS INDICATED.  VERIFY"
1360         PRINT "EACH RECORD AND REENTER THOSE IN ERROR."
1370         PRINT "TO END THE PROGRAM, TYPE AN END-OF-FILE"
1380         PRINT "RECORD:  '0,0,END OF FILE,0,0'."
1390 REM
1400 REM 1.3 INPUT CURRENT DATE
1410         PRINT
1420         PRINT "ENTER DATE (MMDD)....";
1430         INPUT D1
1440 REM
1450 REM 1.4 INPUT FIRST TRANSACTION RECORD
1460         GOSUB 2000
1470 REM
1480 REM *************************
1490 REM * 2.0 MAIN PROCESSING   *
1500 REM *************************
1510 REM REPEAT
1520     IF S1$ = "END OF FILE" THEN GOTO 1610
1530 REM
1540 REM     2.1 WRITE TRANSACTION RECORD
1550         PRINT #1, D1;",";L1;",";N1;",";S1$;",";A1;",";A2
1560 REM
1570 REM     2.2 INPUT NEXT TRANSACTION RECORD
1580         GOSUB 2000
```

```
1590 REM
1600       GOTO 1510
1610 REM END REPEAT
1620 REM
1630 REM ***************************
1640 REM * 3.0 END PROCESSING     *
1650 REM ***************************
1660 REM
1670 REM 3.1 WRITE EOF RECORD
1680       PRINT #1, D1;",";L1;",";N1;",";S1$;",";A1;",";A2
1690 REM
1700 REM 3.2 CLOSE TRANSACTION FILE
1710       CLOSE #1
1720 REM
1730 REM 3.3 PRINT END-OF-SESSION MESSAGE
1740       PRINT
1750       PRINT "*** END OF SESSION ***"
1760 REM
1770 REM 3.4 STOP PROCESSING
1780       STOP
1790 REM
1800 REM
2000 REM ***********************************
2010 REM * S1.0 INPUT TRANSACTION RECORD *
2020 REM ***********************************
2030 REM
2040 REM S1.1 INITIALIZE VALID-RECORD FLAG
2050       LET V$ = " "
2060 REM
2070 REM S1.2 INPUT VALID TRANSACTION RECORD
2080 REM      REPEAT
2090          IF V$ = "Y" THEN GOTO 2290
2100 REM
2110 REM          S1.2.1 INPUT TRANSACTION DATA
2120                  PRINT
2130                  PRINT "LOCATION CODE........";
2140                  INPUT L1
2150                  PRINT "ATTRACTION NUMBER....";
2160                  INPUT N1
2170                  PRINT "SHIFT CODE...........";
2180                  INPUT S1$
2190                  PRINT "ADULT ATTENDANCE.....";
2200                  INPUT A1
2210                  PRINT "CHILD ATTENDANCE.....";
2220                  INPUT A2
2230 REM
2240 REM          S1.2.2 INPUT VALID-RECORD FLAG
2250                  PRINT "    VERIFY (Y/N)....";
2260                  INPUT V$
2270 REM
2280          GOTO 2080
2290 REM      END REPEAT
2300 REM
2310     RETURN
2320 END
```

Figure 6-8. Concluded.

outputs a report listing the fields in error. In the amusement park system, this report is returned to the clerk who prepared the transmittal form. Thus, the file content can be compared against the transmittal form, the calculator control tapes, and the attendance summary source documents to locate and correct any errors. Corrections are returned to the data processing department for rekeying of source transactions.

Computer programs can perform certain types of editing to flag potential or actual errors. The computer can be instructed to compare values in a field with expected values retained as constants to determine if there is a match. Edit programs can determine whether the value in a field lies within a particular range of values as a test of the reasonableness of the data. Field values can also be compared with other input fields to determine the internal consistency of data values. Although the computer cannot ensure against errors in a file, it can test data against expected criteria and indicate possible errors. Therefore, edit programs play an important, but not all-inclusive, role in verifying file content. Edit routines are part of a package of programs, adding machine control tapes, batch control total methods, and other procedures that locate and correct data entry errors to protect the integrity of the system's data resources.

Programming Specifications

Figure 6-9 presents the programming specifications for the edit report program. This program inputs the attendance transaction file that was created in the previous program and performs edits on all fields except the date field. Individual date field edits are not necessary because the same value is introduced into all records by the file creation program.

The attraction numbers and location codes in the transaction records are checked against the corresponding fields in the master file. This test will verify that a matching master record exists for each of the transaction records. A programming technique known as *table lookup* will be used to perform this edit. In general, the table lookup technique involves building a reference table in memory containing the attraction numbers and location codes represented in the master file. Then, for each transaction record, the attraction number is compared with the numbers in the table to see if there is a matching value. Similarly, the transaction location codes are compared with the table values. Matching numbers and codes will indicate that the transaction values are correct.

System: AMUSEMENT PARK   Date: 04/25/XX
Program: EDIT REPORT   Program I.D.: FUN06   Analyst: B. LEIGH

Design and write a program to produce an edit report of the American Fun
Amusement Park daily attendance transaction file. A table lookup will be
conducted on information in the attraction master file. Also, validity and
reasonableness tests will be performed on the transaction data. Figure 6-9.1
shows the system flowchart for this application.

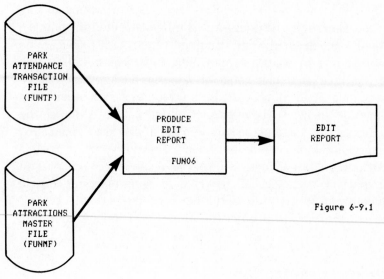

Figure 6-9.1

INPUT

The attendance transaction file is the primary program input. This file
contains the data to be edited. Also, the attraction master file is input and
used to build tables of location codes and attraction numbers for comparisons
with the transaction fields. Field formats for these two files are given in
the following tables:

Transaction Record		Master Record	
Field Name	Data Type	Field Name	Data Type
Date	Numeric	Location Code	Numeric
Location Code	Numeric	Attraction Number	Numeric
Attraction Number	Numeric	Attraction Type	Alphanumeric
Shift Code	Alphanumeric	Attraction Name	Alphanumeric
Adult Attendance	Numeric	Days in Operation	Numeric
Child Attendance	Numeric	Attendance to Date	Numeric

PROCESSING

Main program processing involves editing the fields of the transaction records
to produce a report that indicates fields in error. The following edits are
made:

> Attraction Number: This field is compared with the attraction-
> number fields in the master file to verify
> that a matching master record exists. The
> master fields are loaded into a program table

against which the search is made. A transaction attraction number should be flagged as an error if the number is not matched in the table.

Location Code:

If a valid, matching attraction number exists, the transaction location code is checked by comparing it against a table of location codes built from the master file. A nonmatching code should be indicated on the report as an error. If a valid attraction number does not exist, the location-code edit is skipped. However, the report should indicate that a valid number was not located.

Shift Code:

This field is tested to verify that either the character A (for Afternoon) or E (for Evening) is present. Any other character is invalid.

Adult Attendance:

This field is checked for reasonableness. A value of less than 0 or greater than 500 should be flagged as a potential error.

Child Attendance:

The same edits performed on the adult attendance field are made on this field; that is, the value should be no less than 0 and no greater than 500.

OUTPUT

Program output will be a multiple-page edit report in the format shown in Figure 6-9.2. Each page should have a maximum of 23 lines and a physical page size of 30 lines.

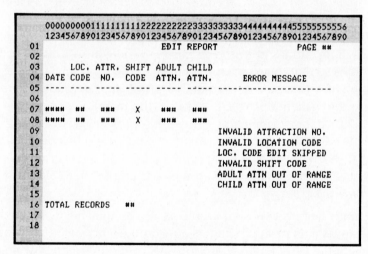

```
          000000000111111111122222222223333333333444444444455555555556
          1234567890123456789012345678901234567890123456789012345678901234567890
01                            EDIT REPORT                    PAGE ##
02
03            LOC. ATTR. SHIFT ADULT CHILD
04   DATE CODE  NO.  CODE  ATTN. ATTN.        ERROR MESSAGE
05   ---- ---- ----- ----- ----- -----   -------------------------
06
07   ####  ##  ###    X    ###   ###
08   ####  ##  ###    X    ###   ###
09                                          INVALID ATTRACTION NO.
10                                          INVALID LOCATION CODE
11                                          LOC. CODE EDIT SKIPPED
12                                          INVALID SHIFT CODE
13                                          ADULT ATTN OUT OF RANGE
14                                          CHILD ATTN OUT OF RANGE
15
16   TOTAL RECORDS    ##
17
18
```

Figure 6-9.2

Figure 6-9. Programming specifications for edit report program.

The shift code field will be tested for the presence of either the value "A" or "E". Appearance of any other character indicates the presence of invalid data.

Finally, the adult and child attendance fields will be checked for reasonableness. It is assumed that the value can be expected to range between zero and 500 people in attendance during any shift. Any negative value is obviously incorrect; any value over 500 is to be regarded as suspect and should be checked against the transmittal form or shift attendance summary form. Although the program cannot test these attendance fields for total accuracy, it can indicate values that appear to be unreasonable in light of the expected range of values.

The edit report will list the content of each transaction record. Then, for any field that fails an edit check, an error message line is printed indicating the type of error encountered.

Program Design

The structure chart for the edit report program is given in Figure 6-10. Pseudocode specifications for the mainline program appear in Figure 6-11. The overall structure of the program is similar to previous programs. Subroutines are used to perform the editing and other related functions so that the main control logic of the program is not disrupted by the appearance of these detailed processing operations embedded within the mainline program. Because the mainline program is similar in structure to previous types of detail report programs, no discussion is required on the processing functions and logic. The reader can verify from the structure chart and pseudocode that the program follows the general CIS program model. Figure 6-12 presents the BASIC code for this mainline program.

Analysis of program requirements is presented below for each of the program functions appearing as subroutines. Because this program is somewhat more complex than previous programs, data flow analysis is performed for individual processing functions rather than for the program as a whole.

Program Tables

Editing of attraction numbers and location codes involves searching through reference tables to locate values that match those in the transaction records. Therefore, at the beginning of the program, these tables

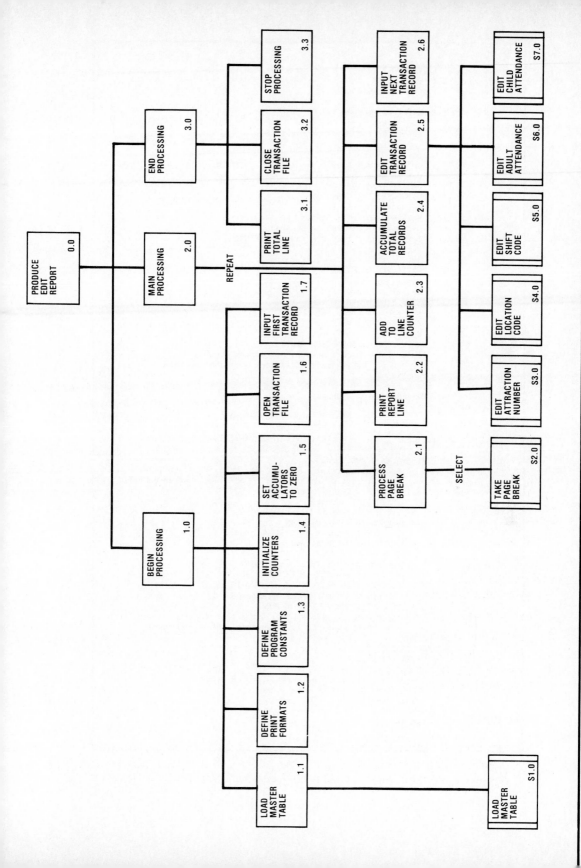

Figure 6-10. Structure chart for mainline edit report program.

```
0.0 PRODUCE EDIT REPORT
    1.0 BEGIN PROCESSING
        1.1 LOAD MASTER TABLE
            Perform S1.0 LOAD MASTER TABLE
        1.2 DEFINE PRINT FORMATS
            Define Report Title Line
            Define Column Heading Line 1
            Define Column Heading Line 2
            Define Dotted Line
            Define Detail Line
            Define Error Message Line
            Define Total Line
        1.3 DEFINE PROGRAM CONSTANTS
            Set Afternoon Shift Code = "A"
            Set Evening Shift Code = "N"
            Set Minimum Attendance Constant = 0
            Set Maximum Attendance Constant = 500
            Set Line Limit = 23
            Set Page Size = 30
        1.4 INITIALIZE COUNTERS
            Set Page Counter = 0
            Set Line Counter = 0
        1.5 SET ACCUMULATORS TO ZERO
            Set Total Records = 0
        1.6 OPEN TRANSACTION FILE
            Open "FUNTF" for input
        1.7 INPUT FIRST TRANSACTION RECORD
            Input Date, Location Code, Attraction Number,
                Shift Code, Adult Attendance, Child Attendance
    2.0 MAIN PROCESSING
        REPEAT: until end of transaction file
            2.1 PROCESS PAGE BREAK
                SELECT: on Page Counter = 0
                        or Line Counter >= Line Limit
                    2.1.1 TAKE PAGE BREAK
                        Perform S2.0 TAKE PAGE BREAK
                END SELECT
            2.2 PRINT REPORT LINE
                Print using Detail Line format, Date, Location Code,
                    Attraction Number, Shift Code, Adult Attendance,
                        Child Attendance
            2.3 ADD TO LINE COUNTER
                Set Line Counter = Line Counter + 1
            2.4 ACCUMULATE TOTAL RECORDS
                Set Total Records = Total Records + 1
            2.5 EDIT TRANSACTION RECORD
                Perform S3.0 EDIT ATTRACTION NUMBER
                Perform S4.0 EDIT LOCATION CODE
                Perform S5.0 EDIT SHIFT CODE
                Perform S6.0 EDIT ADULT ATTENDANCE
                Perform S7.0 EDIT CHILD ATTENDANCE
            2.6 INPUT NEXT TRANSACTION RECORD
                Input Date, Location Code, Attraction Number,
                    Shift Code, Adult Attendance, Child Attendance
        END REPEAT
    3.0 END PROCESSING
        3.1 PRINT TOTAL LINE
            Print blank line
            Print using Total Line format, Total Records
        3.2 CLOSE TRANSACTION FILE
            Close "FUNTF"
        3.3 STOP PROCESSING
            Stop
```

Figure 6-11. Pseudocode for mainline edit report program.

Figure 6-12. BASIC code for mainline edit transaction file program.

```
1000 REM FUN06                                      WEL/DRA
1010 REM                   EDIT REPORT
1020 REM
1030 REM THIS PROGRAM EDITS THE ATTENDANCE TRANSACTION FILE
1040 REM (FUNTF) OF THE AMERICAN FUN AMUSEMENT PARK AND
1050 REM PRODUCES AN EDIT REPORT ON FIELDS IN ERROR.  THE
1060 REM PROGRAM MAKES USE OF TABLES OF ATTRACTION NUMBERS
1070 REM AND LOCATION CODES BUILT FROM THE ATTRACTION MASTER
1080 REM FILE (FUNMF).
1090 REM
1100 REM VARIABLE NAMES
1110 REM
1120 REM TRANSACTION FILE INPUT:
1130 REM     D1....DATE
1140 REM     L1....LOCATION CODE
1150 REM     N1....ATTRACTION NUMBER
1160 REM     S1$...SHIFT CODE
1170 REM     A1....ADULT ATTENDANCE
1180 REM     A2....CHILD ATTENDANCE
1190 REM MASTER FILE INPUT:
1200 REM     L.....LOCATION CODE
1210 REM     N.....ATTRACTION NUMBER
1220 REM     T$....ATTRACTION TYPE
1230 REM     N$....ATTRACTION NAME
1240 REM     D.....DAYS IN OPERATION (THIS MONTH)
1250 REM     A.....ATTENDANCE TO DATE (THIS MONTH)
1260 REM CONSTANTS:
1270 REM     C1$...AFTERNOON SHIFT CONSTANT
1280 REM     C2$...EVENING SHIFT CONSTANT
1290 REM     C3....MINIMUM ATTENDANCE CONSTANT
1300 REM     C4....MAXIMUM ATTENDANCE CONSTANT
1310 REM     P1....MAXIMUM LINES PER PAGE
1320 REM     P2....PHYSICAL PAGE SIZE
1330 REM TABLES:
1340 REM     L9....LOCATION CODE TABLE
1350 REM     N9....ATTRACTION NUMBER TABLE
1360 REM SUBSCRIPTS:
1370 REM     S.....TABLE SUBSCRIPT
1380 REM COUNTERS:
1390 REM     K1....PAGE COUNTER
1400 REM     K2....LINE COUNTER
1410 REM ACCUMULATORS:
1420 REM     T.....TOTAL RECORDS ACCUMULATOR
1430 REM WORK AREAS:
1440 REM     R.....REMAINING LINES ON PAGE
1450 REM     Z.....TABLE SIZE
1460 REM REPORT OUTPUT:
1470 REM     F1$...REPORT TITLE LINE
1480 REM     F2$...COLUMN HEADING LINE 1
1490 REM     F3$...COLUMN HEADING LINE 2
1500 REM     F4$...DOTTED LINE
1510 REM     F5$...DETAIL LINE
1520 REM     F6$...ERROR MESSAGE LINE
1530 REM     F7$...TOTAL LINE
1540 REM
1550 REM 0.0 PRODUCE EDIT REPORT
1560 REM
1570 REM ************************
1580 REM * 1.0 BEGIN PROCESSING *
1590 REM ************************
1600 REM
1610 REM 1.1 LOAD MASTER TABLE
1620          GOSUB 3000
1630 REM
```

```
1640 REM 1.2 DEFINE PRINT FORMATS
1650         LET F1$="                        EDIT REPORT                PAGE ##"
1660         LET F2$="     LOC. ATTR. SHIFT ADULT CHILD"
1670         LET F3$="DATE CODE  NO.  CODE  ATTN. ATTN.     ERROR MESSAGE"
1680         LET F4$="---- ---- ----- ----- ----- ----- --------------------------"
1690         LET F5$="####  ##   ###    !    ###   ###"
1700         LET F6$="                                       \                    \"
1710         LET F7$="TOTAL RECORDS = ##"
1720 REM
1730 REM 1.3 DEFINE PROGRAM CONSTANTS
1740         LET C1$ = "A"
1750         LET C2$ = "E"
1760         LET C3  = 0
1770         LET C4  = 500
1780         LET P1  = 23
1790         LET P2  = 30
1800 REM
1810 REM 1.4 INITIALIZE COUNTERS
1820         LET K1 = 0
1830         LET K2 = 30
1840 REM
1850 REM 1.5 SET ACCUMULATORS TO ZERO
1860         LET T = 0
1870 REM
1880 REM 1.6 OPEN TRANSACTION FILE
1890         OPEN "FUNTF" FOR INPUT AS FILE #2
1900 REM
1910 REM 1.7 INPUT FIRST TRANSACTION RECORD
1920         INPUT #2, D1, L1, N1, S1$, A1, A2
1930 REM
1940 REM *************************
1950 REM * 2.0 MAIN PROCESSING   *
1960 REM *************************
1970 REM REPEAT
1980     IF S1$ = "END OF FILE" THEN GOTO 2310
1990 REM
2000 REM     2.1 PROCESS PAGE BREAK
2010 REM         SELECT
2020             IF K1 =  0   THEN GOTO 2060
2030             IF K2 >= P1 THEN GOTO 2060
2040                          GOTO 2090
2050 REM
2060 REM         2.1.1 TAKE PAGE BREAK
2070                 GOSUB 4000
2080 REM
2090 REM         END SELECT
2100 REM
2110 REM     2.2 PRINT REPORT LINE
2120         PRINT USING F5$, D1, L1, N1, S1$, A1, A2
2130 REM
2140 REM     2.3 ADD TO LINE COUNTER
2150         LET K2 = K2 + 1
2160 REM
2170 REM     2.4 ACCUMULATE TOTAL RECORDS
2180         LET T = T + 1
2190 REM
2200 REM     2.5 EDIT TRANSACTION RECORD
2210         GOSUB 5000
2220         GOSUB 6000
2230         GOSUB 7000
2240         GOSUB 8000
2250         GOSUB 9000
2260 REM
2270 REM     2.6 INPUT NEXT TRANSACTION RECORD
2280         INPUT #2, D1, L1, N1, S1$, A1, A2
2290 REM
2300     GOTO 1970
2310 REM END REPEAT
2320 REM
2330 REM *************************
2340 REM * 3.0 END PROCESSING    *
2350 REM *************************
```

```
2360 REM
2370 REM 3.1 PRINT TOTAL LINE
2380         PRINT
2390         PRINT USING F7$, T
2400 REM
2410 REM 3.2 CLOSE TRANSACTION FILE
2420         CLOSE #2
2430 REM
2440 REM 3.3 STOP PROCESSING
2450         STOP
2460 REM
2470 REM
```

Figure 6-12. Concluded.

must be defined and loaded with reference values. The actual values to be placed in the tables come from the attraction number and location code fields in the previously created master file. As noted on the structure chart, this table-loading function takes place at the beginning of the program and is coded as a subroutine.

A program *table* is a set of contiguous areas within memory that are referenced collectively through use of a single variable name. Data values are placed within each area, or *element*, of the table. Once the data are placed in the table, they are available throughout program execution. Often, tables are used to retain and reference program constants when it would be impractical to retain each constant in a separately named area in memory. This use of tables to reference program constants is characteristic of the edit report program. Figure 6-13 illustrates the structure and content of the attraction number and location code tables as they will appear in memory after being loaded with data from the master file.

Since the complete set of table elements is referenced by a single identifier, or table name, *subscripts* are used to identify each unique element in the table. These subscripts correspond with positions of the elements in relation to the first element of the table. That is, the first table position is referred to as element 1, the second position as element 2, the third as element 3, and so on through the last position in the table. See Figure 6-13.

The table name followed by the subscript value enclosed in parentheses is used to refer to a particular table element. Thus, in Figure 6-13, the data value 101 is stored in the element ATTRACTION NUMBER TABLE (1), the value 104 is stored in ATTRACTION NUMBER TABLE (2), and so on. Thus, individual data values can be accessed through reference to their locations within the table.

197

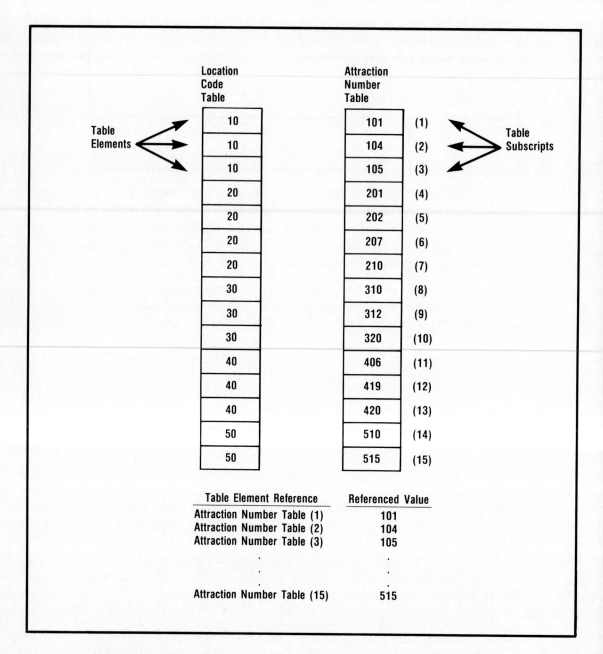

Figure 6-13. Organization of program tables and references to data values retained in tables.

Defining and Loading Tables

Program tables must be defined and *dimensioned* within memory before they can be used. That is, the program must assign names to tables and allocate enough positions within the tables to hold the data values to be placed there. In the edit report program, an Attraction Number Table and a Location Code Table will be defined and 15 positions will be allocated for each, since there are 15 different attraction numbers with 15 associated location codes.

After the tables have been defined, they can be loaded with data. The master file is opened, records are input into memory, and the attraction numbers and location codes in consecutive master records are placed into consecutive elements in the two tables. This table-building process takes place within a program loop. On each pass through the loop, the table subscript points to the next set of table elements to receive the next set of data. This process of *indexing* through the tables is accomplished by defining a program variable as a table subscript and *incrementing* the subscript value during each pass through the loop.

Figure 6-14 presents the program design and pseudocode for loading the master file data into the program tables, including techniques for defining and building tables. The structure of this subroutine is similar to that of a complete file processing program that follows the CIS program model.

At the beginning of the subroutine, the two tables are named and a sufficient number of table elements are allocated for each. These activities are implied in module 6.1.1 DEFINE TABLES. Next, the master file is opened and the first record is input into memory. Also, prior to entering the main processing loop, a table subscript is defined as a means for indexing through the tables. This subscript is given an initial value of zero.

Within the main processing loop, the subscript is incremented by 1 to point to the next available set of table elements. The first time through the loop, this subscript will be set to 1. Therefore, a program reference to the variable named Location Code Table (Subscript) is actually a reference to Location Code Table (1). Thus, the location code value from the first master record is placed in the first element of the table. The same holds true for the Attraction Number Table and the corresponding attraction number from the master record. The loop is completed with the reading of the next master record.

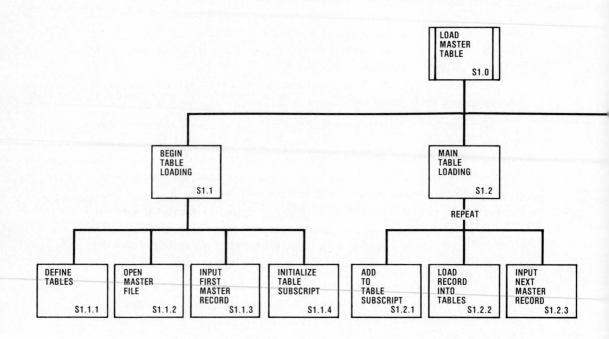

Figure 6-14. Structure chart and pseudocode for table loading subroutine.

When the loop is entered the second time, the subscript variable is incremented to 2. Data from the second master record are placed in the second set of table elements. Then, the next master record is input. This process of incrementing the subscript, assigning master data to the corresponding table elements, and inputting the next master record continues until the end of the master file is reached. This procedure is illustrated in Figure 6-15. Recall from the earlier program that the end of the file is indicated by the appearance of the string "END OF FILE" in the attraction name field.

After the file is closed, the ending value of the subscript is assigned as the size of the table. This table size variable will be used later in the

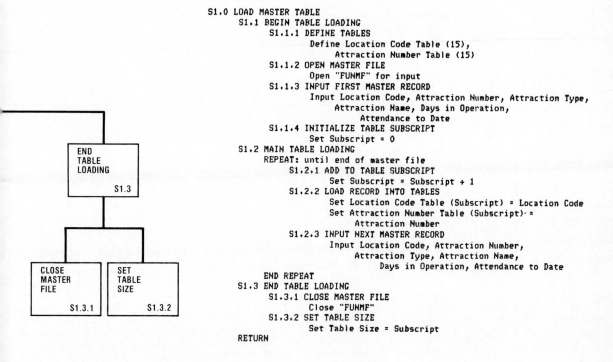

```
S1.0 LOAD MASTER TABLE
    S1.1 BEGIN TABLE LOADING
        S1.1.1 DEFINE TABLES
                Define Location Code Table (15),
                    Attraction Number Table (15)
        S1.1.2 OPEN MASTER FILE
                Open "FUNMF" for input
        S1.1.3 INPUT FIRST MASTER RECORD
                Input Location Code, Attraction Number, Attraction Type,
                    Attraction Name, Days in Operation,
                        Attendance to Date
        S1.1.4 INITIALIZE TABLE SUBSCRIPT
                Set Subscript = 0
    S1.2 MAIN TABLE LOADING
        REPEAT: until end of master file
            S1.2.1 ADD TO TABLE SUBSCRIPT
                    Set Subscript = Subscript + 1
            S1.2.2 LOAD RECORD INTO TABLES
                    Set Location Code Table (Subscript) = Location Code
                    Set Attraction Number Table (Subscript) =
                        Attraction Number
            S1.2.3 INPUT NEXT MASTER RECORD
                    Input Location Code, Attraction Number,
                        Attraction Type, Attraction Name,
                            Days in Operation, Attendance to Date
        END REPEAT
    S1.3 END TABLE LOADING
        S1.3.1 CLOSE MASTER FILE
                Close "FUNMF"
        S1.3.2 SET TABLE SIZE
                Set Table Size = Subscript
RETURN
```

program to indicate when the end of the tables has been reached during table searching.

These table building techniques are coded in BASIC as shown in Figure 6-16. The dimension (DIM) statement is used to assign names to program tables and to allocate memory areas for the positions. In line 3070, the attraction number table (N9) and location code table (L9) are both assigned 15 elements. The general format for the DIM statement is given in Figure 6-17. In line 3160, the subscript (S) is set to zero prior to execution of the main processing loop.

Within the loop, the statements LET N9(S) = N and LET L9(S) = L assign the master record values for the attraction number (N) and location code (L) to the particular table elements referenced by the subscript. Because S will have a value of 1 during the first pass through the loop,

Figure 6-15. Loading data from an input record into program tables.

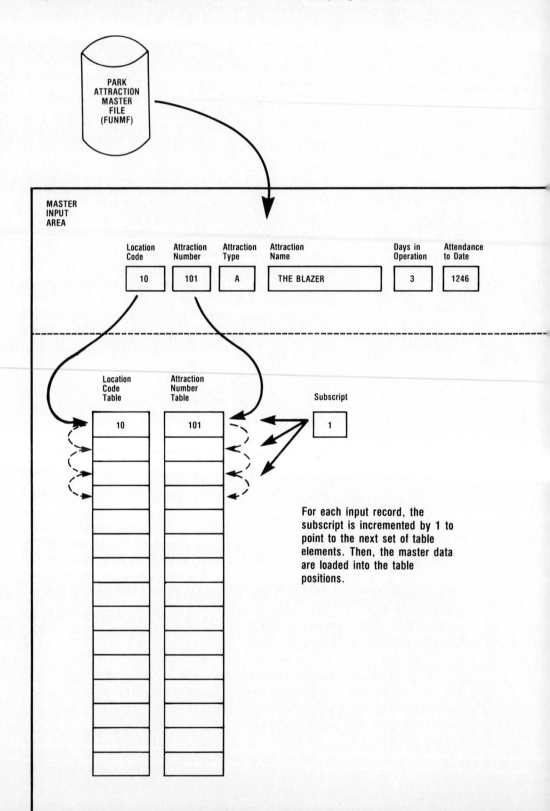

For each input record, the subscript is incremented by 1 to point to the next set of table elements. Then, the master data are loaded into the table positions.

```
3000 REM ****************************
3010 REM * S1.0 LOAD MASTER TABLE *
3020 REM ****************************
3030 REM
3040 REM S1.1 BEGIN TABLE LOADING
3050 REM
3060 REM      S1.1.1 DEFINE TABLES
3070              DIM N9(15), L9(15)
3080 REM
3090 REM      S1.1.2 OPEN MASTER FILE
3100              OPEN "FUNMF" FOR INPUT AS FILE #1
3110 REM
3120 REM      S1.1.3 INPUT FIRST MASTER RECORD
3130              INPUT #1, L, N, T$, N$, D, A
3140 REM
3150 REM      S1.1.4 INITIALIZE TABLE SUBSCRIPT
3160              LET S = 0
3170 REM
3180 REM S1.2 MAIN TABLE LOADING
3190 REM      REPEAT
3200          IF N$ = "END OF FILE" THEN GOTO 3330
3210 REM
3220 REM      S1.2.1 ADD TO TABLE SUBSCRIPT
3230              LET S = S + 1
3240 REM
3250 REM      S1.2.2 LOAD RECORD INTO TABLES
3260              LET L9(S) = L
3270              LET N9(S) = N
3280 REM
3290 REM      S1.2.3 INPUT NEXT MASTER RECORD
3300              INPUT #1, L, N, T$, N$, D 1
3310 REM
3320          GOTO 3190
3330 REM      END REPEAT
3340 REM
3350 REM S1.3 END TABLE LOADING
3360 REM
3370 REM      S1.3.1 CLOSE MASTER FILE
3380              CLOSE #1
3390 REM
3400 REM      S1.3.2 SET TABLE SIZE
3410              LET Z = S
3420 REM
3430      RETURN
3440 REM
3450 REM
```

Figure 6-16. BASIC code for table loading subroutine of edit program.

General Format:
line number DIM variable name(No. of elements) {, variable name(no. of elements) . . . }

Example:

```
3070 DIM N2(15), L2(15)
```

The keyword DIM (dimension) precedes one or more variable names to be assigned to program tables. Immediately following each name, the number of storage positions, or elements, of the table is coded within parentheses. The variables are separated by commas. Any number of DIM statements can appear in the program.

Figure 6-17. General format for the DIM statement.

the data will be assigned to the first set of elements. On subsequent executions of the loop, S will take on values of 2, 3, 4, and so on through 15, and subsequent master data will be loaded into the table elements according to these subscript values.

At the completion of the loop, the master file is closed. When control returns to the main program, reference tables will be available for use in editing the transaction data.

Table Searching

To edit the attraction number in the transaction record, the Attraction Number Table is searched to locate a matching number. The design of this table searching routine appears in Figure 6-18.

The table subscript is valued initially at 1 so that it points to the first element of the table when the search module is activated. A comparison between the number in the transaction file and the value of the table element is made at the beginning of the loop. If the values are equal, the search is terminated. If the values are not equal, the subscript is incremented by 1 and the test is repeated. The program increments the subscript and tests the two variables until either a match is found or the subscript is incremented past the end of the table, signifying failure to find a match.

If there is a match, the transaction entry for the attraction number is valid. Control returns from the subroutine to the mainline program. If, however, a match does not occur—that is, the subscript is incremented

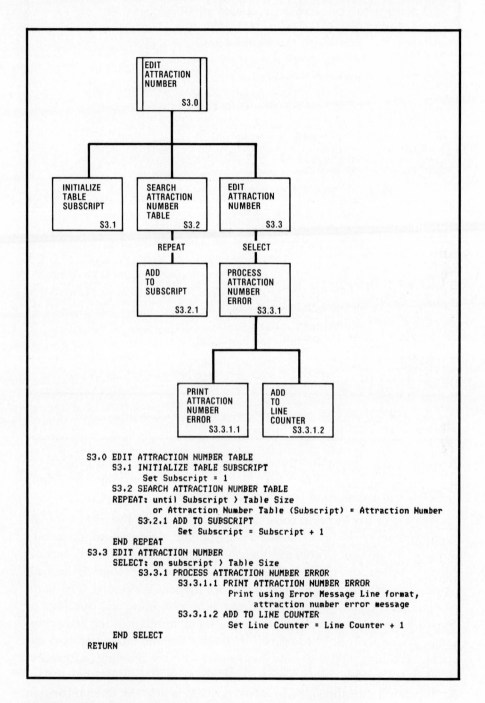

```
                              ┌──────────────┐
                              │EDIT          │
                              │ATTRACTION    │
                              │NUMBER        │
                              │              │
                              │        S3.0  │
                              └──────────────┘
                                     │
         ┌───────────────────────────┼───────────────────────┐
┌────────────────┐      ┌────────────────┐      ┌────────────────┐
│INITIALIZE      │      │SEARCH          │      │EDIT            │
│TABLE           │      │ATTRACTION      │      │ATTRACTION      │
│SUBSCRIPT       │      │NUMBER          │      │NUMBER          │
│                │      │TABLE           │      │                │
│           S3.1 │      │           S3.2 │      │           S3.3 │
└────────────────┘      └────────────────┘      └────────────────┘
                            REPEAT                   SELECT
                        ┌────────────────┐      ┌────────────────┐
                        │ADD             │      │PROCESS         │
                        │TO              │      │ATTRACTION      │
                        │SUBSCRIPT       │      │NUMBER          │
                        │                │      │ERROR           │
                        │         S3.2.1 │      │         S3.3.1 │
                        └────────────────┘      └────────────────┘
                                                       │
                                       ┌────────────────┴──────────┐
                              ┌────────────────┐      ┌────────────────┐
                              │PRINT           │      │ADD             │
                              │ATTRACTION      │      │TO              │
                              │NUMBER          │      │LINE            │
                              │ERROR           │      │COUNTER         │
                              │       S3.3.1.1 │      │       S3.3.1.2 │
                              └────────────────┘      └────────────────┘
```

```
S3.0 EDIT ATTRACTION NUMBER TABLE
     S3.1 INITIALIZE TABLE SUBSCRIPT
          Set Subscript = 1
     S3.2 SEARCH ATTRACTION NUMBER TABLE
     REPEAT: until Subscript ) Table Size
             or Attraction Number Table (Subscript) = Attraction Number
          S3.2.1 ADD TO SUBSCRIPT
               Set Subscript = Subscript + 1
     END REPEAT
S3.3 EDIT ATTRACTION NUMBER
     SELECT: on subscript ) Table Size
          S3.3.1 PROCESS ATTRACTION NUMBER ERROR
               S3.3.1.1 PRINT ATTRACTION NUMBER ERROR
                        Print using Error Message Line format,
                          attraction number error message
               S3.3.1.2 ADD TO LINE COUNTER
                        Set Line Counter = Line Counter + 1
     END SELECT
RETURN
```

Figure 6-18. Design for Edit Attraction Number subroutine.

```
5000 REM *******************************
5010 REM * S3.0 EDIT ATTRACTION NUMBER *
5020 REM *******************************
5030 REM
5040 REM S3.1 INITIALIZE TABLE SUBSCRIPT
5050          LET S = 1
5060 REM
5070 REM S3.2 SEARCH ATTRACTION NUMBER TABLE
5080 REM      REPEAT
5090          IF S      > Z   THEN GOTO 5160
5100          IF N9(S) = N1 THEN GOTO 5160
5110 REM
5120 REM      S3.2.1 ADD TO SUBSCRIPT
5130              LET S = S + 1
5140 REM
5150          GOTO 5080
5160 REM      END REPEAT
5170 REM
5180 REM S3.3 EDIT ATTRACTION NUMBER
5190 REM      SELECT
5200          IF S > Z THEN GOTO 5230
5210                     GOTO 5310
5220 REM
5230 REM      S3.3.1 PROCESS ATTRACTION NUMBER ERROR
5240 REM
5250 REM          S3.3.1.1 PRINT ATTRACTION NUMBER ERROR
5260                  PRINT USING F6$, "INVALID ATTR. NUMBER"
5270 REM
5280 REM          S3.3.1.2 ADD TO LINE COUNTER
5290                  LET K2 = K2 + 1
5300 REM
5310 REM      END SELECT
5320 REM
5330      RETURN
5340 REM
5350 REM
```

Figure 6-19. BASIC code for Edit Attraction Number subroutine.

past the end of the table—the appropriate error message is printed on the edit report before the return to the mainline program. The BASIC code for this subroutine is shown in Figure 6-19.

Editing of the location code takes place following the test of the attraction number. If there is a matching number, the corresponding code in the Location Code Table can be tested against that of the transaction record. If the attraction number is in error, however, there is no way of validating the corresponding code. So, the test is skipped. The comparison takes place between the transaction code value and the value in the code table corresponding to the matching number in the attraction table. There is no need to search through the code table, because the correct location code is the one associated with the matching attraction number. If the codes match, control returns from the subroutine; if they do not match, the appropriate error message is printed. Design for this subroutine appears in Figure 6-20.

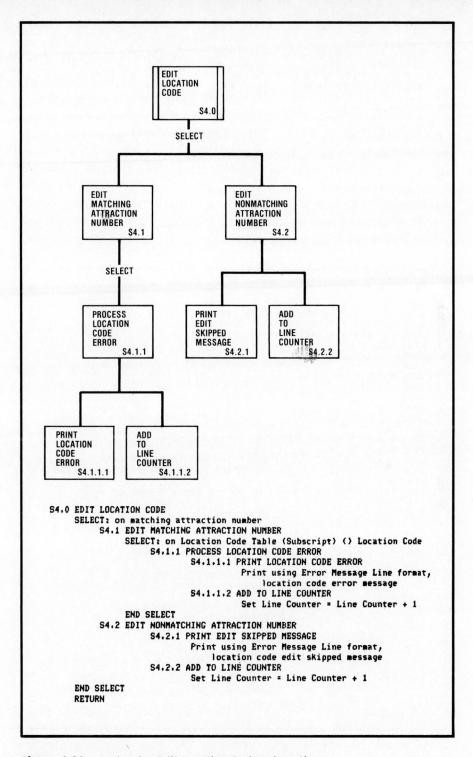

```
S4.0 EDIT LOCATION CODE
      SELECT: on matching attraction number
            S4.1 EDIT MATCHING ATTRACTION NUMBER
                  SELECT: on Location Code Table (Subscript) <> Location Code
                        S4.1.1 PROCESS LOCATION CODE ERROR
                              S4.1.1.1 PRINT LOCATION CODE ERROR
                                          Print using Error Message Line format,
                                              location code error message
                              S4.1.1.2 ADD TO LINE COUNTER
                                          Set Line Counter = Line Counter + 1
                  END SELECT
            S4.2 EDIT NONMATCHING ATTRACTION NUMBER
                  S4.2.1 PRINT EDIT SKIPPED MESSAGE
                              Print using Error Message Line format,
                                  location code edit skipped message
                  S4.2.2 ADD TO LINE COUNTER
                              Set Line Counter = Line Counter + 1
      END SELECT
      RETURN
```

Figure 6-20. Design for Edit Location Code subroutine.

207

The BASIC code is given in Figure 6-21. Notice, in the BASIC code, that the test of whether there is a matching attraction number is determined by whether the subscript has been incremented past the end of the table. Although the program, logically, should test for a matching attraction number—using, for example, the statement IF N9(S) = N1—in this case, it cannot be done. If a match does not occur within the 15 table elements, the subscript will take on the value 16 upon final entry to the search loop. The statement IF N9(S) = N1 will cause a program execution error because table element N9(16) is undefined. Therefore, the test for the match takes place indirectly through the test of the subscript.

```
6000 REM ****************************
6010 REM * S4.0 EDIT LOCATION CODE *
6020 REM ****************************
6030 REM SELECT
6040      IF S > Z THEN GOTO 6230
6050                GOTO 6070
6060 REM
6070 REM S4.1 EDIT MATCHING ATTRACTION NUMBER
6080 REM      SELECT
6090           IF L9(S) <> L1 THEN GOTO 6120
6100                     GOTO 6200
6110 REM
6120 REM      S4.1.1 PROCESS LOCATION CODE ERROR
6130 REM
6140 REM           S4.1.1.1 PRINT LOCATION CODE ERROR
6150                     PRINT USING F6$, "INVALID LOCATION CODE"
6160 REM
6170 REM           S4.1.1.2 ADD TO LINE COUNTER
6180                     LET K2 = K2 + 1
6190 REM
6200 REM      END SELECT
6210           GOTO 6310
6220 REM
6230 REM S4.2 EDIT NONMATCHING ATTRACTION NUMBER
6240 REM
6250 REM      S4.2.1 PRINT EDIT SKIPPED MESSAGE
6260                PRINT USING F6$, "LOC. CODE EDIT SKIPPED"
6270 REM
6280 REM      S4.2.2 ADD TO LINE COUNTER
6290                LET K2 = K2 + 1
6300 REM
6310 REM END SELECT
6320 REM
6330      RETURN
6340 REM
6350 REM
```

Figure 6-21. BASIC code for Edit Location Code subroutine.

Multiple Condition Tests

Separate subroutines are used to edit the shift code and the daily attendance figures. The shift code can take on either of two values—"A" or "E". Therefore, these values are set up as program constants against which the transaction shift code is compared. The design for this editing subroutine is presented in Figure 6-22. The BASIC code is given in Figure 6-23.

The relational operators introduced in Chapter 5 (=, <, >, <=, >=, and <>) are used to construct conditions that are tested in an IF

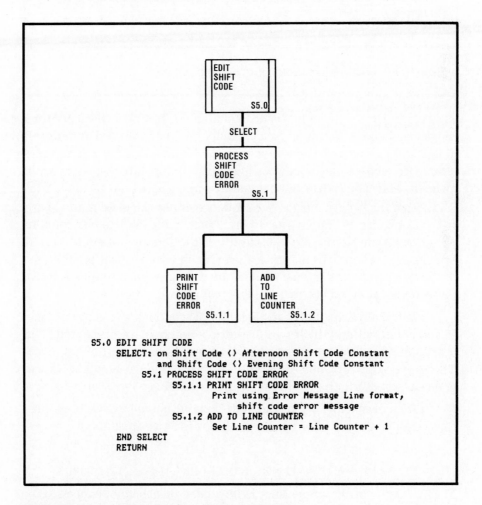

```
S5.0 EDIT SHIFT CODE
     SELECT: on Shift Code <> Afternoon Shift Code Constant
             and Shift Code <> Evening Shift Code Constant
        S5.1 PROCESS SHIFT CODE ERROR
             S5.1.1 PRINT SHIFT CODE ERROR
                    Print using Error Message Line format,
                       shift code error message
             S5.1.2 ADD TO LINE COUNTER
                    Set Line Counter = Line Counter + 1
     END SELECT
     RETURN
```

Figure 6-22. Design for Edit Shift Code subroutine.

```
7000 REM ************************
7010 REM * S5.0 EDIT SHIFT CODE *
7020 REM ************************
7030 REM SELECT
7040      IF S1$ <> C1$ THEN GOTO 7060
7050                     GOTO 7170
7060      IF S1$ <> C2$ THEN GOTO 7090
7070                     GOTO 7170
7080 REM
7090 REM S5.1 PROCESS SHIFT CODE ERROR
7100 REM
7110 REM      S5.1.1 PRINT SHIFT CODE ERROR
7120              PRINT USING F6$, "INVALID SHIFT CODE"
7130 REM
7140 REM      S5.1.2 ADD TO LINE COUNTER
7150              LET K2 = K2 + 1
7160 REM
7170 REM END SELECT
7180 REM
7190      RETURN
7200 REM
7210 REM
```

Figure 6-23. BASIC code for Edit Shift Code subroutine.

statement. Up to this point, each IF statement has been used to test a single condition. In some cases, a condition is to be evaluated as true only if it passes two or more condition tests. For instance, in the current program, the shift code must pass two tests before an editing error is printed. The code must not be equal to A *and* it must not be equal to E.

Within the program code, the sequence of tests is implemented with two consecutive IF statements. In line 7040, if the code is not equal to A, control branches to line 7060 to test if the code is not equal to E. If both of these conditions are true, the error message is printed. If either of the two conditions is false (that is, the code is equal to either A or E), the code is valid and control returns from the subroutine.

An alternative method of testing multiple conditions is to use a single IF statement within which two or more conditions are presented. The conditions are connected with *logical operators* to form multiple tests. These operators include AND, OR, and NOT. Figure 6-24 shows the general format for the IF statement that uses these types of tests.

In the current program, the shift code tests could have been performed through use of either of the following two formats:

IF S1$ < > C1$ AND S1$ < > C2$ THEN GOTO 7090

IF NOT S1$ = C1$ AND NOT S1$ = C2$ THEN GOTO 7090

In general, the programmer should be guided by clarity of expression—rather than by efficiency of coding—in forming the tests.

Logical Operator	Meaning
AND	Both conditions are true
OR	Either condition is true
NOT	The reverse of the condition is true

General Format:

line # IF {NOT} condition $\begin{Bmatrix} AND \\ OR \end{Bmatrix}$ {NOT} condition $\begin{Bmatrix} \begin{Bmatrix} AND \\ OR \end{Bmatrix} \end{Bmatrix}$ {NOT} condition . . .

THEN GOTO line number

Examples:

```
1070 IF A = B AND C = D THEN GOTO 1150
1780 IF A = B OR C = D THEN GOTO 1800
2160 IF A < B AND NOT C < D THEN GOTO 2240
2250 IF A > B AND C > D AND E <= F THEN GOTO 2300
```

Figure 6-24. Logical operators used in condition tests.

Range tests are made on the adult and child attendance figures. Each must fall within the range zero through 500 to pass the edit test. These range limit values are defined as program constants. Within individual subroutines, the transaction values are compared with these constants. The structure charts and pseudocode for the two subroutines appear in Figure 6-25. The BASIC code is shown in Figure 6-26.

Again, multiple conditions can be tested within a single IF statement. Instead of the code given in lines 8040 and 8050, for example, the following statement could have been used:

IF A1 < C3 OR A1 > C4 THEN GOTO 8080

Either format will accomplish the same purpose.

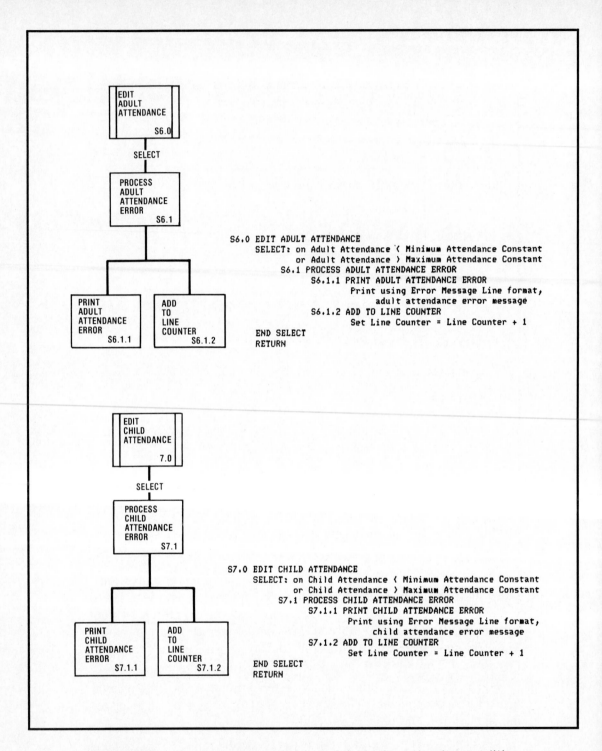

S6.0 EDIT ADULT ATTENDANCE
    SELECT: on Adult Attendance < Minimum Attendance Constant
              or Adult Attendance > Maximum Attendance Constant
    S6.1 PROCESS ADULT ATTENDANCE ERROR
        S6.1.1 PRINT ADULT ATTENDANCE ERROR
                Print using Error Message Line format,
                    adult attendance error message
        S6.1.2 ADD TO LINE COUNTER
                Set Line Counter = Line Counter + 1
END SELECT
RETURN

S7.0 EDIT CHILD ATTENDANCE
    SELECT: on Child Attendance < Minimum Attendance Constant
              or Child Attendance > Maximum Attendance Constant
    S7.1 PROCESS CHILD ATTENDANCE ERROR
        S7.1.1 PRINT CHILD ATTENDANCE ERROR
                Print using Error Message Line format,
                    child attendance error message
        S7.1.2 ADD TO LINE COUNTER
                Set Line Counter = Line Counter + 1
END SELECT
RETURN

Figure 6-25. Structure charts and pseudocode for attendance editing subroutines.

```
8000 REM ******************************
8010 REM * S6.0 EDIT ADULT ATTENDANCE *
8020 REM ******************************
8030 REM SELECT
8040     IF A1 < C3 THEN GOTO 8080
8050     IF A1 > C4 THEN GOTO 8080
8060                 GOTO 8160
8070 REM
8080 REM S6.1 PROCESS ADULT ATTENDANCE ERROR
8090 REM
8100 REM     S6.1.1 PRINT ADULT ATTENDANCE ERROR
8110             PRINT USING F6$, "ADULT ATTN OUT OF RANGE"
8120 REM
8130 REM     S6.1.2 ADD TO LINE COUNTER
8140             LET K2 = K2 + 1
8150 REM
8160 REM END SELECT
8170 REM
8180     RETURN
8190 REM
8200 REM
9000 REM ******************************
9010 REM * S7.0 EDIT CHILD ATTENDANCE *
9020 REM ******************************
9030 REM SELECT
9040     IF A2 < C3 THEN GOTO 9080
9050     IF A2 > C4 THEN GOTO 9080
9060                 GOTO 9160
9070 REM
9080 REM S7.1 PROCESS CHILD ATTENDANCE ERROR
9090 REM
9100 REM     S7.1.1 PRINT CHILD ATTENDANCE ERROR
9110             PRINT USING F6$, "CHILD ATTN OUT OF RANGE"
9120 REM
9130 REM     S7.1.2 ADD TO LINE COUNTER
9140             LET K2 = K2 + 1
9150 REM
9160 REM END SELECT
9170 REM
9180     RETURN
9190 END

Ready
```

Figure 6-26. BASIC code for attendance editing subroutines.

Page-Break Processing

Finally, the edit report will be printed on multiple pages. A page-break processing subroutine similar to the one illustrated previously has been included in the edit program. The structure chart and pseudocode for this subroutine are given in Figure 6-27. The operation of this subroutine is identical to the one included in the control-break program reviewed in Chapter 5. The only differences relate to the number of lines to be

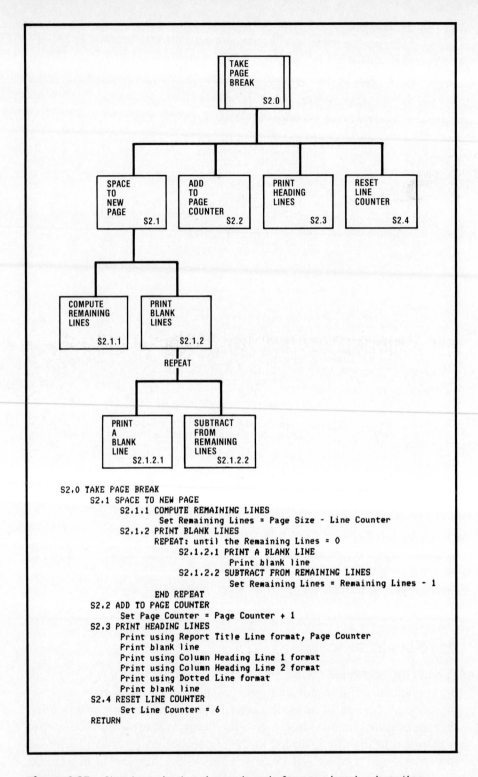

```
S2.0 TAKE PAGE BREAK
    S2.1 SPACE TO NEW PAGE
        S2.1.1 COMPUTE REMAINING LINES
                Set Remaining Lines = Page Size - Line Counter
        S2.1.2 PRINT BLANK LINES
                REPEAT: until the Remaining Lines = 0
                    S2.1.2.1 PRINT A BLANK LINE
                            Print blank line
                    S2.1.2.2 SUBTRACT FROM REMAINING LINES
                            Set Remaining Lines = Remaining Lines - 1
                END REPEAT
    S2.2 ADD TO PAGE COUNTER
            Set Page Counter = Page Counter + 1
    S2.3 PRINT HEADING LINES
            Print using Report Title Line format, Page Counter
            Print blank line
            Print using Column Heading Line 1 format
            Print using Column Heading Line 2 format
            Print using Dotted Line format
            Print blank line
    S2.4 RESET LINE COUNTER
            Set Line Counter = 6
    RETURN
```

Figure 6-27. Structure chart and pseudocode for page-break subroutine.

printed on each page and the assumed physical page size. Code for this subroutine appears in Figure 6-28.

Program Output

Figure 6-29 gives an example of the report produced by the program. Erroneous data have been included in the transaction file to illustrate the set of messages generated during editing.

Recall that this report, along with the transmittal form from which the transaction file was built, is returned to the clerk for verification and

```
4000 REM ************************
4010 REM * S2.0 TAKE PAGE BREAK *
4020 REM ************************
4030 REM
4040 REM S2.1 SPACE TO NEW PAGE
4050 REM
4060 REM        S2.1.1 COMPUTE REMAINING LINES
4070                  LET R = P2 -K2
4080 REM
4090 REM        S2.1.2 PRINT BLANK LINES
4100 REM               REPEAT
4110                   IF R = 0 THEN GOTO 4200
4120 REM
4130 REM               S2.1.2.1 PRINT A BLANK LINE
4140                             PRINT
4150 REM
4160 REM               S2.1.2.2 SUBTRACT FROM REMAINING LINES
4170                             LET R = R - 1
4180 REM
4190                   GOTO 4100
4200 REM               END REPEAT
4210 REM
4220 REM S2.2 ADD TO PAGE COUNTER
4230          LET K1 = K1 + 1
4240 REM
4250 REM S2.3 PRINT HEADING LINES
4260          PRINT USING F1$, K1
4270          PRINT
4280          PRINT F2$
4290          PRINT F3$
4300          PRINT F4$
4310          PRINT
4320 REM
4330 REM S2.4 RESET LINE COUNTER
4340          LET K2 = 6
4350 REM
4360      RETURN
4370 REM
4380 REM
```

Figure 6-28. BASIC code for page-break subroutine.

```
                            EDIT REPORT                      PAGE  1

            LOC. ATTR. SHIFT ADULT CHILD
       DATE CODE  NO.  CODE  ATTN. ATTN.      ERROR MESSAGE
       ---- ----  ----- ----- ----- -----    -------------------------

        104  10   101    A    148    12
        104  10   101    E    352   -65
                                              CHILD ATTN OUT OF RANGE
        104  10   104    A    130    15
        104  10   107    E    128    22
                                              INVALID ATTR. NUMBER
                                              LOC. CODE EDIT SKIPPED
        104  10   105    A     15     7
        104  19   105    E     19    10
                                              INVALID LOCATION CODE
        104  20   202    X     38    26
                                              INVALID SHIFT CODE
        104  20   202    E     45    31
        104  20   207    A    209   176
        104  20   208    E    595   144
                                              INVALID ATTR. NUMBER
                                              LOC. CODE EDIT SKIPPED
                                              ADULT ATTN OUT OF RANGE

       TOTAL RECORDS = 10
```

Figure 6-29. Example output from edit report program.

correction of invalid data. After the corrections are made, the marked copy of the report is returned to the data processing department, where corrections are included in the transaction file.

Only after an error-free edit report is produced will the file be used for updating the master file. Within the present system, errors in the transaction file only can be corrected by recreating the entire file by running the file creation program (FUN05) again. Obviously, this is not the most efficient way of correcting transaction files. In later chapters, therefore, file maintenance programs will be written to allow selective changes to be made in file records without the need to rekey the entire file.

MULTIPLE CONTROL-BREAK PROGRAM

The attendance transaction file is used to produce a daily attendance report. This report summarizes the total attendance at the park, by attraction and location. The specifications for this program are given in Figure 6-30.

This program is similar to the control-break program described in the previous chapter. In this case, attendance subtotals will be developed at three levels—for each attraction, for each location, and for the park as a whole. Therefore, this is an example of a multiple control-break program. Subtotals are written when there is a change in attraction number, a change in location code, and at the end of the transaction file.

Figure 6-31 shows the structure chart for this program. The main difference between this program and the previous control-break program is in the number of processing breaks required. The program must contain instructions that determine the level at which each break occurs and then carry out required processing for that level.

As transaction records are being processed, one of two levels of breaks can occur. A *minor control break* takes place whenever there is a change in the attraction number of a transaction record. This event signals the printing of the lowest, or minor, level of totals, the attraction total.

A *major control break* occurs whenever there is a change in location code. This is a higher level break because the total is, in effect, an accumulation of the minor level totals. The organization of the report thus reflects the structure of the file. That is, the report is organized with attraction totals appearing subordinate to location totals just as attraction fields are part of location records.

In general, a program may have several control-break levels. There may be one or more *intermediate control breaks*, as well as major and minor breaks. For example, consider a file containing sales records giving the amounts of sales made by representatives for a major company with several divisions. This file could be arranged so that individual sales records are categorized by department and, in turn, by division. Thus, a report produced from this file might present individual sales totals (minor) within department totals (intermediate) within division totals (major).

Within the attendance report program, a change in attraction number signals that the attraction total should be printed before processing the next detail record. As in normal control-break processing, the total is printed, the accumulator is reset to zero, and the attraction number for the next group of records is saved in a compare area. Program module S2.0 TAKE ATTRACTION CONTROL BREAK handles this processing whenever there is a minor-level break.

PROGRAMMING SPECIFICATIONS

System: AMUSEMENT PARK   Date: 04/28/XX
Program: ATTENDANCE REPORT   Program I.D.: FUN07   Analyst: B. LEIGH

Design and write a program to produce an attendance report for the American Fun
Amusement Park. The attendance transaction file (FUNTF) is the program input.
The output report will list attendance totals by attraction number and location
code. Also, a cumulative attendance total for all attractions will be produced. The program will be coded in BASIC. Figure 6-30.1 shows the system
flowchart for this application.

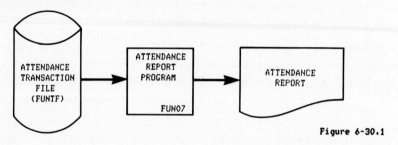

Figure 6-30.1

INPUT

The attendance transaction file (FUNTF) is the program input. The format of
records is as follows:

Field Name	Data Type
Date	Numeric
Location Code	Numeric
Attraction Number	Numeric
Shift Code	Alphanumeric
Adult Attendance	Numeric
Child Attendance	Numeric

The final EOF record contains the string "END OF FILE" in the shift code field.

PROCESSING

For each transaction record, the adult attendance is added to the child
attendance to derive the total attendance for a shift. This attendance figure
is used to derive totals for each attraction, for each location, and for all
transaction records.

The date field, in the format MMDD, must be separated into a month and a day
field to print within the report title line. The integer value of the date is
divided by 100 to derive the month portion of the field. The day portion is
calculated by subtracting the month value times 100 from the date. The
computations are: Month = Integer(Date / 100), and Day = Date - (Month * 100).

OUTPUT

Program output will be a daily attendance report in the format shown in Figure
6-30.2. The report will contain multiple pages. Each page should consist of
no more than 33 lines. The physical page size should be 40 lines.

```
          0000000000111111111122222222223333333333444444444445
          1234567890123456789012345678901234567890123456789012
01                   AMERICAN FUN AMUSEMENT PARK          PAGE ##
02                   ATTENDANCE REPORT FOR ##/##
03
04   LOC.    ATTR.   SHIFT   ADULT   CHILD   TOTAL
05   CODE    NO.     CODE    ATTN.   ATTN.   ATTN.
06
07   ##      ###     X       ###     ###     ###
08   ##      ###     X       ###     ###     ###
09
10                           ATTRACTION TOTAL     ###
11
12   ##      ###     X       ###     ###     ###
13   ##      ###     X       ###     ###     ###
14
15                           ATTRACTION TOTAL     ###
16
17                           LOCATION TOTAL    #,### (==
18                           FINAL TOTAL      ##,### (===
19
20
```
Figure 6-30.2

Figure 6-30. Programming specifications for attendance report program.

A change in location code signals a major level break. In this case, two levels of totals are printed. A change in location code also signals a change in attraction number. Therefore, both the minor level total and the major level total are printed, in that order. First, module S2.0 TAKE ATTRACTION CONTROL BREAK and then module S3.0 TAKE LOCATION CONTROL BREAK are activated. This processing logic is implied within the 2.7 PROCESS CONTROL BREAK module in the structure chart.

In general, this same logic applies regardless of the number of levels of control breaks. The program tests for control breaks beginning with the major level and continuing through the intermediate levels and the minor level. Control-break processing, however, is carried out in reverse order. That is, at any level of break, processing begins at the minor level and continues up through the level at which the break occurred. This general model for control-break processing is illustrated in the structure chart and pseudocode in Figure 6-32.

Figure 6-33 presents the pseudocode for the mainline control-break program. It is similar in structure and processing to the earlier program. Note especially how the general control-break model has been adapted to this program. The control-break processing subroutines are shown in Figures 6-34 and 6-35. There are only minor differences between these two structures, centering upon the level of control breaks.

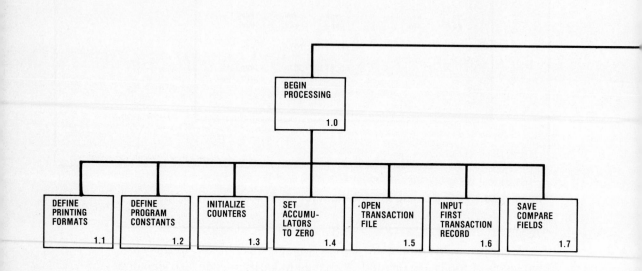

Figure 6-31. Structure chart for mainline attendance report program.

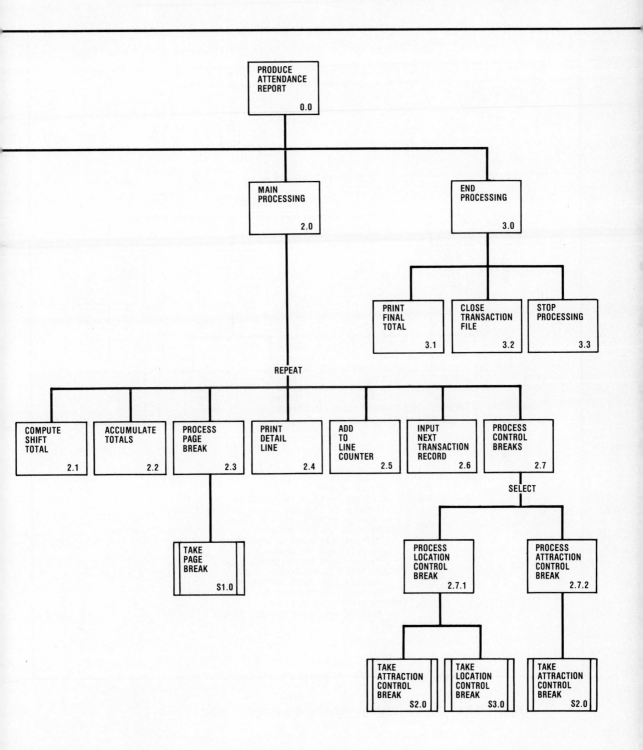

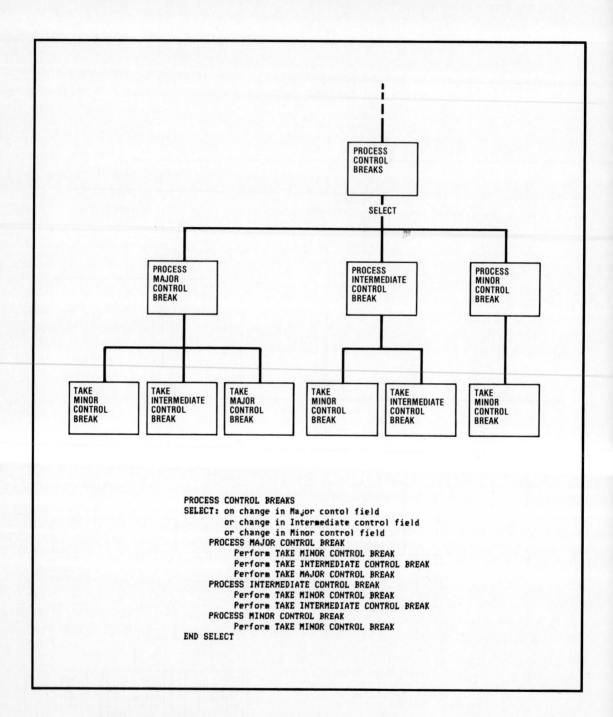

```
PROCESS CONTROL BREAKS
SELECT: on change in Major contol field
        or change in Intermediate control field
        or change in Minor control field
   PROCESS MAJOR CONTROL BREAK
       Perform TAKE MINOR CONTROL BREAK
       Perform TAKE INTERMEDIATE CONTROL BREAK
       Perform TAKE MAJOR CONTROL BREAK
   PROCESS INTERMEDIATE CONTROL BREAK
       Perform TAKE MINOR CONTROL BREAK
       Perform TAKE INTERMEDIATE CONTROL BREAK
   PROCESS MINOR CONTROL BREAK
       Perform TAKE MINOR CONTROL BREAK
END SELECT
```

Figure 6-32.   General model for control-break processing.

```
0.0 PRODUCE ATTENDANCE REPORT _
    1.0 BEGIN PROCESSING
        1.1 DEFINE PRINTING FORMATS
                Define Report Title Line 1
                Define Report Title Line 2
                Define Column Heading Line 1
                Define Column Heading LIne 2
                Define Detail Line
                Define Attraction Total Line
                Define Location Total Line
                Define Final Total Line
        1.2 DEFINE PROGRAM CONSTANTS
                Set Line Limit = 33
                Set Page Size = 40
        1.3 INITIALIZE COUNTERS
                Set Page Counter = 0
                Set Line Counter = 0
        1.4 SET ACCUMULATORS TO ZERO
                Set Attraction Total = 0
                Set Location Total = 0
                Set Final Total = 0
        1.5 OPEN TRANSACTION FILE
                Open "FUNTF" for input
        1.6 INPUT FIRST TRANSACTION RECORD
                Input Date, Location Code, Attraction Number,
                        Shift Code, Adult Attendance, Child Attendance
        1.7 SAVE COMPARE FIELDS
                Set Saved Location Code = Location Code
                Set Saved Attraction Number = Attraction Number
    2.0 MAIN PROCESSING
        REPEAT: until end of transaction file
            2.1 COMPUTE SHIFT TOTAL
                    Set Shift Total = Adult Attendance + Child Attendance
            2.2 ACCUMULATE TOTALS
                    Set Attraction Total = Attraction Total + Shift Total
                    Set Location Total = Location Total + Shift Total
                    Set Final Total = Final Total + Shift Total
            2.3 PROCESS PAGE BREAK
                SELECT: on Page Counter = 0
                        or Line Counter >= Line Limit
                    2.3.1 TAKE PAGE BREAK
                            Perform S1.0 TAKE PAGE BREAK
                END SELECT
            2.4 PRINT DETAIL LINE
                    Print using Detail Line format, Location Code,
                        Attraction Number, Shift Code, Adult Attendance,
                            Child Attendance, Shift Total
            2.5 ADD TO LINE COUNTER
                    Set Line Counter = Line Counter + 1
            2.6 INPUT NEXT TRANSACTION RECORD
                    Input Date, Location Code, Attraction Number,
                        Shift Code, Adult Attendance, Child Attendance
            2.7 PROCESS CONTROL BREAKS
                SELECT: on change in Location code
                        or change in Attraction Number
                    2.7.1 PROCESS LOCATION CONTROL BREAK
                            Perform S2.0 TAKE ATTRACTION CONTROL BREAK
                            Perform S3.0 TAKE LOCATION CONTROL BREAK
                    2.7.2 PROCESS ATTRACTION CONTROL BREAK
                            Perform S2.0 TAKE ATTRACTION CONTROL BREAK
                END SELECT
        END REPEAT
    3.0 END PROCESSING
        3.1 PRINT FINAL TOTAL
                Print using Final Total Line format, Final Total
        3.2 CLOSE TRANSACTION FILE
                Close "FUNTF"
        3.3 STOP PROCESSING
                Stop
```

Figure 6-33. Pseudocode for mainline attendance report program.

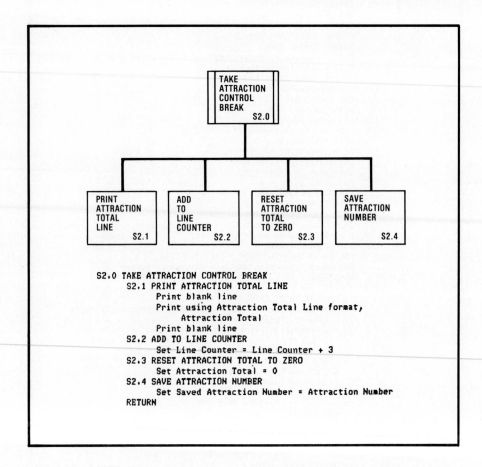

Figure 6-34. Structure chart and pseudocode for attraction control break.

The page break subroutine is given in Figure 6-36. The code for the complete program appears in Figure 6-37 and the attendance report itself is shown in Figure 6-38.

BASIC Mathematical Functions

Within the page-break subroutine presented in Figure 6-36, special processing is required to convert the date in the transaction record into a form that can be printed as part of the second report title line. The date is a single numeric field within the transaction record. The date format is MMDD. For printing purposes, this value must be separated into individual month and day values.

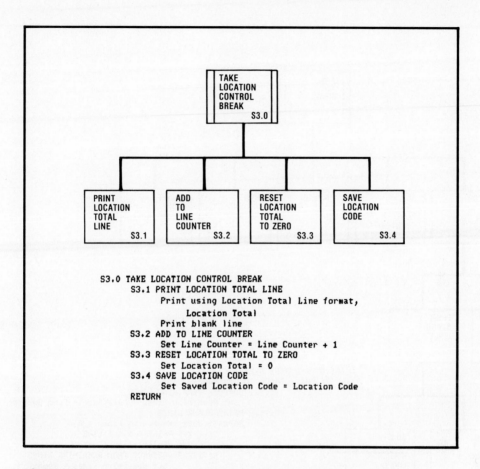

```
S3.0 TAKE LOCATION CONTROL BREAK
    S3.1 PRINT LOCATION TOTAL LINE
        Print using Location Total Line format,
            Location Total
        Print blank line
    S3.2 ADD TO LINE COUNTER
        Set Line Counter = Line Counter + 1
    S3.3 RESET LOCATION TOTAL TO ZERO
        Set Location Total = 0
    S3.4 SAVE LOCATION CODE
        Set Saved Location Code = Location Code
    RETURN
```

Figure 6-35. Structure chart and pseudocode for location control break.

The month portion of the date can be derived by dividing the date by 100 (in effect, calculating the decimal value MM.DD) and then assigning the whole, integer value MM to a separate variable. In BASIC this is done by using the INT (integer) function. This function applies the integer value of a decimal number presented in the format INT(expression). The expression can be an arithmetic variable, a constant, or a formula. Therefore, the variable Month can be stored with the value INT (Date / 100).

Once the month has been calculated, the day portion of the date can be derived. This computation involves subtracting the month multiplied by 100 from the date. In effect, the calculation is DD = MMDD − MM00.

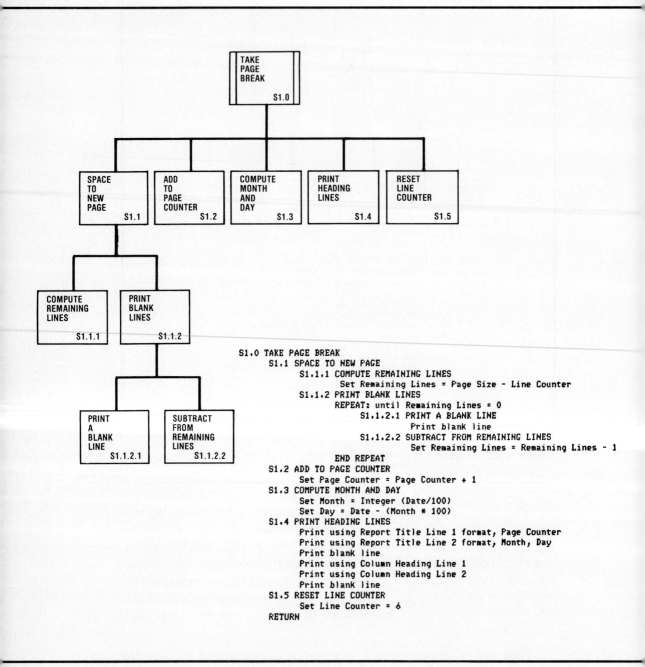

```
S1.0 TAKE PAGE BREAK
     S1.1 SPACE TO NEW PAGE
          S1.1.1 COMPUTE REMAINING LINES
                 Set Remaining Lines = Page Size - Line Counter
          S1.1.2 PRINT BLANK LINES
                 REPEAT: until Remaining Lines = 0
                      S1.1.2.1 PRINT A BLANK LINE
                               Print blank line
                      S1.1.2.2 SUBTRACT FROM REMAINING LINES
                               Set Remaining Lines = Remaining Lines - 1
                 END REPEAT
     S1.2 ADD TO PAGE COUNTER
          Set Page Counter = Page Counter + 1
     S1.3 COMPUTE MONTH AND DAY
          Set Month = Integer (Date/100)
          Set Day = Date - (Month * 100)
     S1.4 PRINT HEADING LINES
          Print using Report Title Line 1 format, Page Counter
          Print using Report Title Line 2 format, Month, Day
          Print blank line
          Print using Column Heading Line 1
          Print using Column Heading Line 2
          Print blank line
     S1.5 RESET LINE COUNTER
          Set Line Counter = 6
     RETURN
```

Figure 6-36. Structure chart and pseudocode for page-break subroutine.

Figure 6-37. BASIC code for attendance report program.

```
1000 REM FUN07                                        WEL/DRA
1010 REM                    ATTENDANCE REPORT
1020 REM
1030 REM THIS PROGRAM PRODUCES A DAILY ATTENDANCE REPORT FOR
1040 REM THE AMERICAN FUN AMUSEMENT PARK.  INPUT IS THE
1050 REM ATTENDANCE TRANSACTION FILE (FUNTF).  THE OUTPUT
1060 REM REPORT SUMMARIZES ATTENDANCE BY ATTRACTION NUMBER,
1070 REM LOCATION CODE, AND FINAL ATTENDANCE TOTAL.
1080 REM
1090 REM VARIABLE NAMES
1100 REM
1110 REM INPUT:
1120 REM     D1....DATE
1130 REM     L1....LOCATION CODE
1140 REM     N1....ATTRACTION NUMBER
1150 REM     S1$...SHIFT CODE
1160 REM     A1....ADULT ATTENDANCE
1170 REM     A2....CHILD ATTENDANCE
1180 REM CONSTANTS:
1190 REM     P1....MAXIMUM LINES PER PAGE
1200 REM     P2....PHYSICAL PAGE SIZE
1210 REM SAVE/COMPARE AREAS:
1220 REM     L2....LOCATION CODE COMPARE
1230 REM     N2....ATTRACTION NUMBER COMPARE
1240 REM WORK AREAS:
1250 REM     A3....SHIFT TOTAL ATTENDANCE
1260 REM     R.....REMAINING LINES ON PAGE
1270 REM     M.....MONTH
1280 REM     D.....DAY
1290 REM ACCUMULATORS:
1300 REM     T1....ATTRACTION TOTAL
1310 REM     T2....LOCATION TOTAL
1320 REM     T3....FINAL TOTAL
1330 REM COUNTERS:
1340 REM     K1....PAGE COUNTER
1350 REM     K2....LINE COUNTER
1360 REM OUTPUT:
1370 REM     F1$...REPORT TITLE LINE 1
1380 REM     F2$...REPORT TITLE LINE 2
1390 REM     F3$...COLUMN HEADING LINE 1
1400 REM     F4$...COLUMN HEADING LINE 2
1410 REM     F5$...DETAIL LINE
1420 REM     F6$...ATTRACTION TOTAL LINE
1430 REM     F7$...LOCATION TOTAL LINE
1440 REM     F8$...FINAL TOTAL LINE
1450 REM
1460 REM 0.0 PRODUCE ATTENDANCE REPORT
1470 REM
1480 REM *************************
1490 REM * 1.0 BEGIN PROCESSING *
1500 REM *************************
1510 REM
1520 REM 1.1 DEFINE PRINTING FORMATS
1530         LET F1$ = '          AMERICAN FUN AMUSEMENT PARK      PAGE ##'
1540         LET F2$ = '             ATTENDANCE REPORT FOR ##/##'
1550         LET F3$ = 'LOC.    ATTR.    SHIFT    ADULT    CHILD    TOTAL'
1560         LET F4$ = 'CODE     NO.     CODE     ATTN.    ATTN.    ATTN.'
1570         LET F5$ = ' ##      ###       !       ###      ###     ###'
1580         LET F6$ = '                        ATTRACTION TOTAL   ###  '
1590         LET F7$ = '                        LOCATION TOTAL    #,### <=='
1600         LET F8$ = '                           FINAL TOTAL   ##,### <==='
```

```
1610 REM
1620 REM 1.2 DEFINE PROGRAM CONSTANTS
1630         LET P1 = 33
1640         LET P2 = 40
1650 REM
1660 REM 1.3 INITIALIZE COUNTERS
1670         LET K1 = 0
1680         LET K2 = 40
1690 REM
1700 REM 1.4 SET ACCUMULATORS TO ZERO
1710         LET T1 = 0
1720         LET T2 = 0
1730         LET T3 = 0
1740 REM
1750 REM 1.5 OPEN TRANSACTION FILE
1760         OPEN "FUNTF" FOR INPUT AS FILE #1
1770 REM
1780 REM 1.6 INPUT FIRST TRANSACTION RECORD
1790         INPUT #1, D1, L1, N1, S1$, A1, A2
1800 REM
1810 REM 1.7 SAVE COMPARE FIELDS
1820         LET L2 = L1
1830         LET N2 = N1
1840 REM
1850 REM *************************
1860 REM * 2.0 MAIN PROCESSING   *
1870 REM *************************
1880 REM REPEAT
1890     IF S1$ = "END OF FILE" THEN GOTO 2360
1900 REM
1910 REM    2.1 COMPUTE SHIFT TOTAL
1920            LET A3 = A1 + A2
1930 REM
1940 REM    2.2 ACCUMULATE TOTALS
1950            LET T1 = T1 + A3
1960            LET T2 = T2 + A3
1970            LET T3 = T3 + A3
1980 REM
1990 REM    2.3 PROCESS PAGE BREAK
2000 REM        SELECT
2010            IF K1 =, 0  THEN GOTO 2050
2020            IF K2 >= P1 THEN GOTO 2050
2030                            GOTO 2080
2040 REM
2050 REM        2.3.1 TAKE PAGE BREAK
2060                GOSUB 3000
2070 REM
2080 REM        END SELECT
2090 REM
2100 REM    2.4 PRINT DETAIL LINE
2110            PRINT USING F5$, L1, N1, S1$, A1, A2, A3
2120 REM
2130 REM    2.5 ADD TO LINE COUNTER
2140            LET K2 = K2 + 1
2150 REM
2160 REM    2.6 INPUT NEXT TRANSACTION RECORD
2170            INPUT #1, D1, L1, N1, S1$, A1, A2
2180 REM
2190 REM    2.7 PROCESS CONTROL BREAK
2200 REM        SELECT
2210            IF L1 <> L2 THEN GOTO 2250
2220            IF N1 <> N2 THEN GOTO 2300
2230                            GOTO 2330
2240 REM
2250 REM        2.7.1 PROCESS LOCATION CONTROL BREAK
2260                GOSUB 4000
2270                GOSUB 5000
2280                    GOTO 2330
2290 REM
2300 REM        2.7.2 PROCESS ATTRACTION CONTROL BREAK
2310                GOSUB 4000
```

```
2320 REM
2330 REM          END SELECT
2340 REM
2350      GOTO 1880
2360 REM END REPEAT
2370 REM
2380 REM **************************
2390 REM * 3.0 END PROCESSING    *
2400 REM **************************
2410 REM
2420 REM 3.1 PRINT FINAL TOTAL
2430         PRINT USING F8$, T3
2440 REM
2450 REM 3.2 CLOSE TRANSACTION FILE
2460         CLOSE #1
2470 REM
2480 REM 3.3 STOP PROCESSING
2490         STOP
2500 REM
2510 REM
3000 REM **************************
3010 REM * S1.0 TAKE PAGE BREAK *
3020 REM **************************
3030 REM
3040 REM S1.1 SPACE TO NEW PAGE
3050 REM
3060 REM      S1.1.1 COMPUTE REMAINING LINES
3070                LET R = P2 - K2
3080 REM
3090 REM      S1.1.2 PRINT BLANK LINES
3100 REM             REPEAT
3110                 IF R = 0 THEN GOTO 3200
3120 REM
3130 REM             S1.1.2.1 PRINT A BLANK LINE
3140                           PRINT
3150 REM
3160 REM             S1.1.2.2 SUBTRACT FROM REMAINING LINES
3170                           LET R = R - 1
3180 REM
3190                 GOTO 3100
3200 REM             END REPEAT
3210 REM
3220 REM S1.2 ADD TO PAGE COUNTER
3230         LET K1 = K1 + 1
3240 REM
3250 REM S1.3 COMPUTE MONTH AND DAY
3260         LET M = INT(D1 / 100)
3270         LET D = D1 - (M * 100)
3280 REM
3290 REM S1.4 PRINT HEADING LINES
3300         PRINT F1$, K1
3310         PRINT F2$, M, D
3320         PRINT
3330         PRINT F3$
3340         PRINT F4$
3350         PRINT
3360 REM
3370 REM S1.5 RESET LINE COUNTER
3380         LET K2 = 6
3390 REM
3400      RETURN
3410 REM          .
3420 REM
4000 REM ******************************************
4010 REM * S2.0 TAKE ATTRACTION CONTROL BREAK *
4020 REM ******************************************
4030 REM
4040 REM S2.1 PRINT ATTRACTION TOTAL LINE
4050         PRINT
4060         PRINT USING F6$, T1
4070         PRINT
```

```
4080 REM
4090 REM S2.2 ADD TO LINE COUNTER
4100         LET K2 = K2 + 3
4110 REM
4120 REM S2.3 RESET ATTRACTION TOTAL TO ZERO
4130         LET T1 = 0
4140 REM
4150 REM S2.4 SAVE ATTRACTION NUMBER
4160         LET N2 = N1
4170 REM
4180     RETURN
4190 REM
4200 REM
5000 REM *************************************
5010 REM * S3.0 TAKE LOCATION CONTROL BREAK *
5020 REM *************************************
5030 REM
5040 REM S3.1 PRINT LOCATION TOTAL LINE
5050         PRINT USING F7$, T2
5060         PRINT
5070 REM
5080 REM S3.2 ADD TO LINE COUNTER
5090         LET K2 = K2 + 1
5100 REM
5110 REM S3.3 RESET LOCATION TOTAL TO ZERO
5120         LET T2 = 0
5130 REM
5140 REM S3.4 SAVE LOCATION CODE
5150         LET L2 = L1
5160 REM
5170     RETURN
5180 END
```

Figure 6-37. Concluded.

INT is one of several mathematical functions available in BASIC. These built-in functions perform common mathematical operations. Use of such functions makes it unnecessary to write detailed code for such frequently encountered jobs. A number of mathematical functions useful for business data processing applications are described in Figure 6-39.

THE CURRENT INFORMATION SYSTEM

With the addition of the transaction processing programs, the Amusement Park Information System has a software structure like that shown in Figure 6-40. Transaction and master file processing are repeated in cycles. Each day, a transaction file is created from the transmittal forms prepared in the park office. Transaction data are entered into the file and are corrected until a valid file of transaction records has been built. Then (not yet shown), the file can be used to update the attraction master file with daily operations data.

The resulting master file is available for production of management reports. Managers can choose from detail, exception, and summary

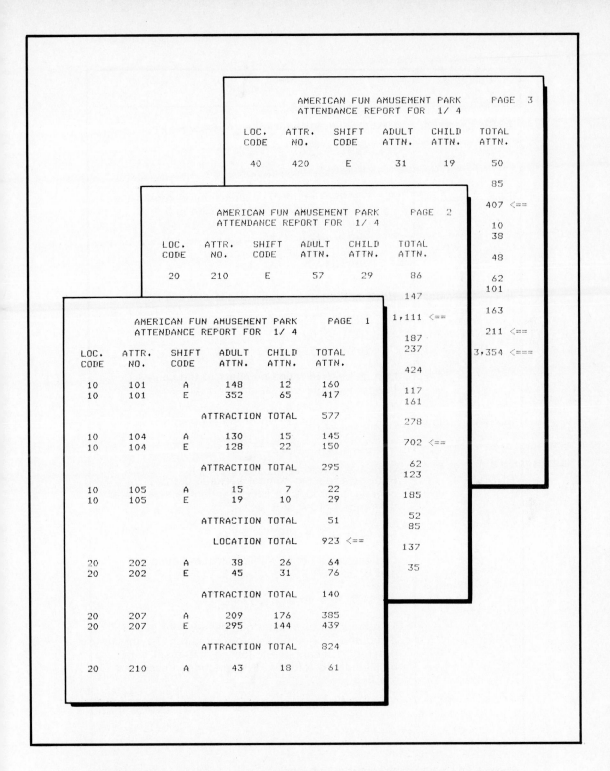

Figure 6-38. Attendance report produced from attendance report program.

231

Function Code	Meaning
ABS(expression)	Returns the absolute value of the expression. ABS(-5.27) = 5.27 ABS(+80.1) = 80.1
SGN(expression)	Returns the sign of the expression preceding the value 1 except when the expression is 0. SGN(1.45) = +1 SGN(-2.7) = -1 SGN(0) = 0
INT(expression)	Returns the integer value of the expression. INT(3.75) = 3 INT(-8.06) = -8 INT(16.5 * 2.7) = 44 Can be used to round numbers to the nearest integer with the expression INT(expression + .5)
SQR(expression)	Returns the square root of the expression. SQR(144) = 12
RND	Returns a random number between 0 and 1. In general, to produce a set of random numbers over the range from A to B, use: (B - A) * RND + A To generate a set of whole numbers between 1 and B, use: INT(B * RND + .5) The same set of random numbers will be generated each time the program is run. To obtain different numbers, the following statement must be included before the RND function is executed the first time: line number RANDOMIZE

Figure 6-39. BASIC mathematical functions.

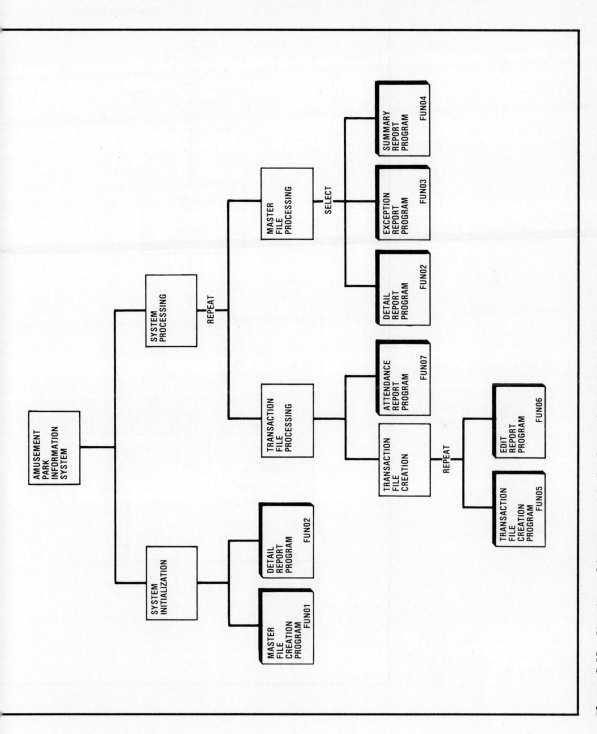

Figure 6-40. Structure of Amusement Park Information System software.

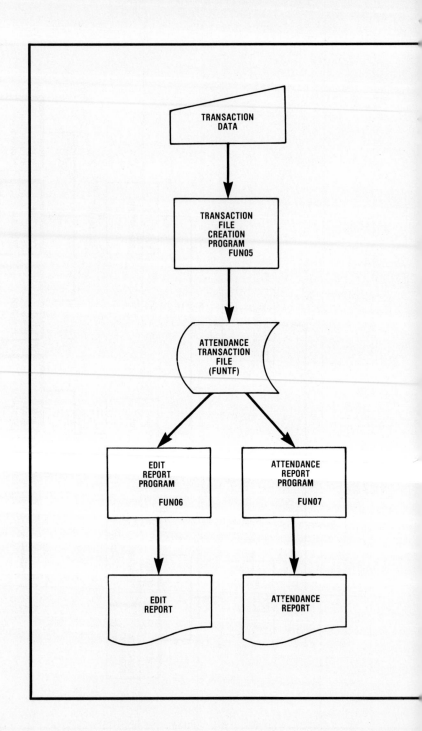

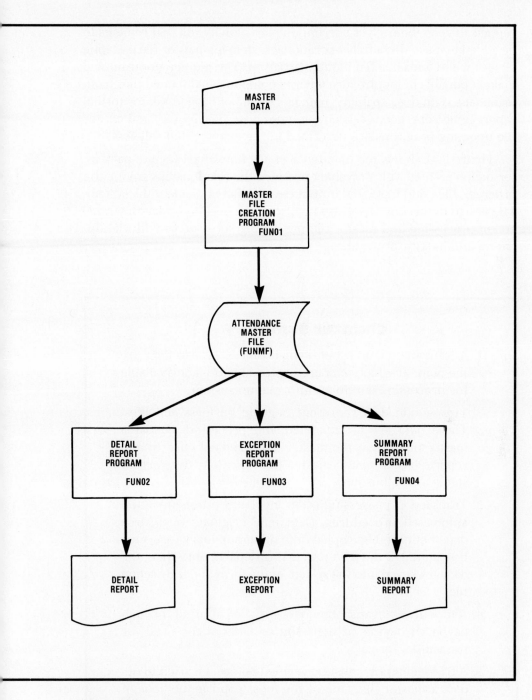

Figure 6-41. System flowchart for Amusement Park Information System.

reports to keep themselves current on park activity. All that remains to be added to make this a fully operational system is a master file updating program and a master file inquiry program. The inquiry program will make it possible to inquire directly into computer-maintained files from terminals. With this capability, managers will not have to ask for formal reports when operations-related questions arise. The inquiry and master file updating programs are described in the chapter that follows.

Figure 6-41 shows the updated systems flow chart for the park information system. This flowchart presents the relationships among the program, files, and input and output devices that implement the system. The design of this flowchart also highlights the need to bridge the transaction processing and master file processing subsystems with file updating and inquiry procedures.

Chapter Summary

1. A transaction is an act of doing business. Transactions are the point at which data are captured and made available for processing within an information system.

2. Transaction data represent ongoing business activities. These data are accumulated and processed against a master file so that the master data are kept current and reports based on the master file represent the current status of the business.

3. Transaction processing often involves both manual and automated procedures. Data may originate on source documents and be copied onto other summary forms for transmittal to the data processing department. Then, the data are keyed into the system in the form of a transaction file.

4. Alternatively, transaction data may be captured through keyboard devices at their source without the need for transmittal forms.

5. A transaction file must be verified before it is used to update a master file. One of the most popular methods of verification is to produce an edit report. An edit program

checks fields of data against known criteria and flags those containing errors. The edit report is returned to the originators of the data for correction of invalid data.

6. The edit report can be used in conjunction with batch control totals such as adding machine tapes, or other verification documents. The edit procedure is vitally important to the integrity of the data entering the system and, eventually, to the ability of managers and others to rely on system outputs.

7. Data entry programs often allow the terminal operator several chances to type the correct data. This form of visual verification and rekeying helps eliminate inclusion of erroneous data in transaction files.

8. Data edits performed by a program usually involve comparing input data with other, correct data. These correct data can be set up as program constants or can be loaded from other files into reference tables within the program. Common data validation techniques include tests for the occurrence of actual values or for values within a range of expected values.

9. A program table is a set of contiguous areas within computer memory that are collectively referenced by a single variable name. Each position within the table is called a table element. Each element is referenced through a subscript value that corresponds to the sequential position the element occupies within the table.

10. Tables are defined in DIM statements. The names of the tables and the number of elements within each table are coded.

11. Tables can be loaded with data values appearing within records in a file. For each record input into memory, the table subscript is incremented from the first through the last table element. Each subsequent input value is placed in each succeeding table position.

12. Table searching uses a similar technique. The subscript is incremented from the first through the final table element within a repeat structure. For any particular table element, processing can proceed as if a single, standard variable were involved.

13. Sometimes, data editing requires the testing of multiple conditions within an IF statement. Logical operators are

available to make combination tests using AND, OR, and NOT in conjunction with condition tests.

14. Multiple control-break programs produce subtotals whenever there is a change in a major, intermediate, and/or minor control field. In general, the program tests for the change in control field beginning with the major level. For each type of break, actual processing proceeds from the minor level up through and including the level at which the break occurred.

15. Several built-in mathematical functions are available in BASIC. The common business processing functions include ABS (to return the absolute value of an expression), INT (to return the integer value of an expression), SQR (to return the square root of an expression), and RND (to return a random number). The RANDOMIZE statement is used to generate different random numbers on each run of the program.

Review Questions

1. What is an edit report?

2. Why is an edit report program used before transaction data are posted to the master file?

3. What is a program table and how is it used?

4. How can a single IF statement be used to test for multiple conditions?

5. What is a multiple control-break program?

6. How does the order used to test for control breaks differ from the order used to carry out the actual control-break processing?

Programming Assignments

Programming practice assignments for Chapter 6 are located in Appendix A, CASE STUDY ONE and CASE STUDY TWO.

Key Terms

1. transaction
2. source document
3. edit report
4. table lookup
5. element
6. subscript
7. dimension
8. logical operators
9. minor control break
10. major control break
11. intermediate control break

Basic Library

1. DIM
2. AND
3. OR
4. NOT
5. INT

7
FILE UPDATING AND INQUIRY

OVERVIEW AND OBJECTIVES

A valuable and useful information system supplies valid, up-to-date information. A company's master files provide its main information source. By drawing information from master files, management can monitor business operations and guide the enterprise toward its goals and objectives.

Master files must reflect business operations accurately and contain current data. Therefore, periodic updating of master files with transaction data is an important CIS function. Further, updated information must be made available to managerial and operational personnel to provide current, timely information as a basis for their decisions.

This chapter discusses master file updating procedures. The chapter also discusses programs that allow for ad hoc inquiries into selected master file records.

When you complete your work in this chapter, you should be able to:

☐ Discuss file updating and backup procedures.

☐ Design and write programs that update master files to include data from transaction files.

☐ Design and write programs that allow selective inquiry into files.

☐ Design menu-driven interactive programs.

☐ Understand and explain the benefits of program designs that separate control from detail processing.

MASTER FILE UPDATING

Master files contain permanent or semipermanent information about people, objects, and events important to business operations. Master files also contain operational summaries reflecting the current status of the entities a business owns, employs, uses, or with which business is transacted. Managers reference master file information to assist in administration and planning decisions. Operational personnel use master file information to facilitate day-to-day business activities.

File *updating* procedures keep master files accurate and current. Updating, in this sense, means that transaction data are posted, or added, to master files periodically to keep the information current. Therefore, collecting and posting transaction data are important CIS tasks.

FILE BACKUP PROCEDURES

The security of master file data is extremely important. If master file data are lost or destroyed, the business itself may not survive. Reconstructing the current history of the organization from surviving documents would be extremely difficult. Effective management without information would be impossible. Most companies, therefore, implement file security procedures.

Maintaining *backup files* is one basic file security procedure. A backup file is simply a copy of an original file. Backup files are produced on a regular basis and often are stored off-site, away from the original file. Then, if the original file is lost or destroyed, the backup can be retrieved.

Backup files are often the products of scheduled file updating procedures. For example, when a transaction file is posted to a master file, an entirely new master file may be created. This new master file becomes the current file. The old master file and the transaction file are placed in storage. If the new master file is lost or damaged, the old file and the transaction file can be used to recreate the new master.

Companies may keep several *generations*, or cycles, of files. During each processing cycle, the old master file and the transaction file are retained, since old information may be needed to reconstruct files accurately. Figure 7-1 illustrates a file updating and backup procedure in which two generations of file backups are maintained. Detail reports, exception reports, and summary reports are produced by the system,

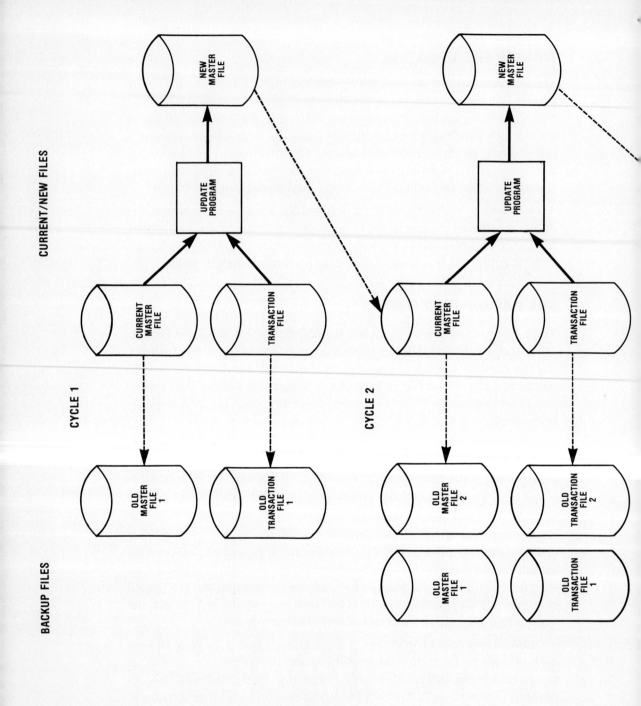

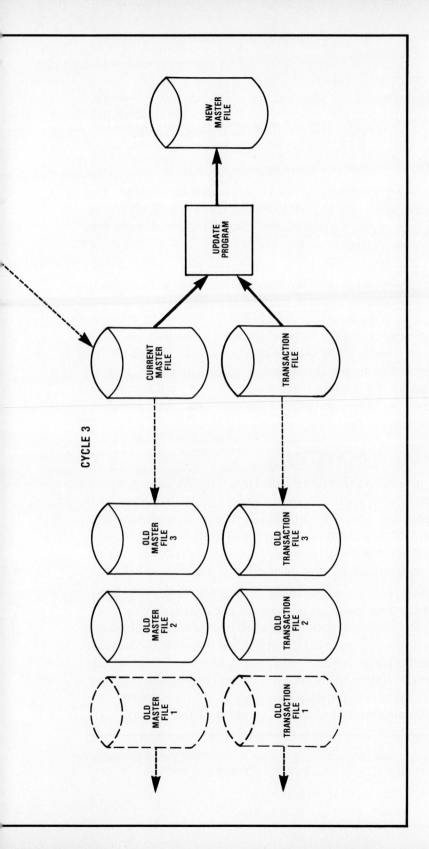

Figure 7-1. Procedure for maintaining backup files within a data processing cycle.

usually at regular intervals, and supplied to management. Since management often anticipates and plans for regularly scheduled reports, programs are written to produce these reports in a timely fashion.

FILE INQUIRY

Sometimes, however, a manager's needs cannot be anticipated. The needed information may not lend itself to inclusion in a scheduled report. To meet information needs, managers may have to inquire directly into computer files—and receive immediate replies.

File inquiry programs provide rapid information retrieval by permitting a person to locate and display file information selectively. In many cases, a record identification code is used by the system to locate and display immediately the content of that record. The record identification may be the data value of the key field or any field value that has informational meaning to the inquirer. The program searches the file for the record, or records, that match the selection criteria and then displays the content. Inquiry processing, therefore, permits rapid access to selective information when scheduled reports are impractical or nonexistent.

THE AMUSEMENT PARK SYSTEM

Two additional programs must be added to make the Amusement Park Information System fully functional. First, a master file updating program will post the transaction file's daily attendance data to the corresponding master file attendance fields. This updating program will complete the link between the two subsystems and permit ongoing processing cycles. As part of this updating procedure, backup files will be created.

Also, an inquiry program will be added to allow for display of selected master file records. This program will permit park managers to check the current status of any attraction. Inquiry will be based on three search parameters: the attraction number, the attraction name, or the location code of the attraction. The manager will provide the identification code interactively and the system will search the file and display the matching record. Figure 7-2 presents the data flow diagram for the system with these two additional programs shown in bubbles 12.0 and 13.0.

Figure 7-2. (Facing page) Data flow diagram for Amusement Park Information System with two additional programs shown in bubbles 12.0 and 13.0.

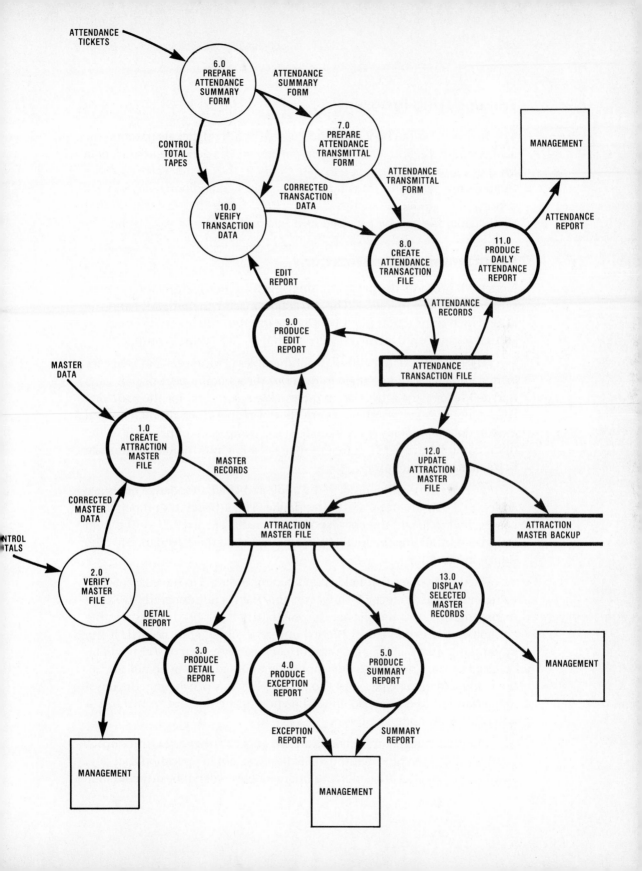

File Updating Program

The first program to be written processes the attendance transaction file against the attraction master file. In particular, the daily attendance data are posted to the attendance-to-date fields in the master records. Also, the days-in-operation field is updated to reflect an additional day of park activity. The updated master file is written to another disk file so that the original file can be retained as a backup.

Programming Specifications

Figure 7-3 presents the programming specifications for updating. Three separate files are involved. The attraction master file (FUNMF) and the attendance transaction file (FUNTF) are input to the updating program so that a new, updated attraction master file (FUNNM) is output.

Files can be updated within program tables. The master file fields are loaded into tables and retained in memory throughout updating. For each updated record, the attraction number table is searched for the matching transaction record number. Then, the corresponding attendance and days-in-operation fields are updated. At the completion of processing, the updated tables are written to a new master file and the old master file is retained as a backup.

For each transaction record, the adult and child attendance fields are added to derive the total shift attendance. The attraction number table is searched to locate the corresponding master record. Then, the field is updated by adding the total attendance figure to the attendance-to-date figure in the table.

The days-in-operation field is updated by adding 1 to the current field value in the master record. However, this field is not updated for every transaction record. Recall that, for each attraction, the transaction file contains an afternoon shift record and an evening shift record. If the days-in-operation field is updated for each record, each day also will be counted twice. Thus, the fields should be updated only once per attraction rather than once per shift. To accomplish this processing, the days-in-operation field is changed only while processing the first record pair—when the shift code value is A.

Note that transaction records do not appear for every attraction. A missing record denotes that the attraction was not in operation that day. Obviously, then, the attraction attendance fields will not be affected, nor

Figure 7-3. Programming specifications for master file update program.

PROGRAMMING SPECIFICATIONS

System: AMUSEMENT PARK   Date: 05/02/XX
Program: MASTER FILE UPDATE   Program I.D.: FUN08   Analyst: B. LEIGH

Design and write a program to update the attraction master file (FUNMF) with
transaction data in the attendance transaction file (FUNTF). A new master
file (FUNNM) will be created. The old master file will be retained as a
backup. The program will be coded in BASIC. Figure 7-3.1 shows the system
flowchart for this application.

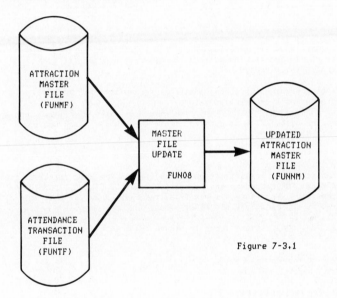

Figure 7-3.1

INPUT

The attraction master file and attendance transaction file are the program
input. The following tables show the formats of records in these two files:

Attraction Master File		Attendance Transaction File	
Field Name	Data Type	Field Name	Data Type
Location Code	Numeric	Date	Numeric
Attraction Number	Numeric	Location Code	Numeric
Attraction Type	Alphanumeric	Attraction Number	Numeric
Attraction Name	Alphanumeric	Shift Code	Alphanumeric
Days in Operation	Numeric	Adult Attendance	Numeric
Attendance to Date	Numeric	Child Attendance	Numeric

The string "END OF FILE" appears in the attraction-name field of the master file. The transaction file contains this same string in the shift-code field of the last record in the file.

PROCESSING

The attendance-to-date and days-in-operation fields of the master records are updated. Then, these fields are used to create a new, updated master file. Updating involves the following procedures:

1. Because the master file is updated in memory, the entire file is loaded into program tables at the start of processing. Transaction records are input one at a time and used to update matching master records.

2. The attendance-to-date field of the master record is updated by adding to it the total attendance figure for a particular shift. This shift attendance figure is derived by adding the adult-attendance and child-attendance values in the transaction record. The attraction-number field of the transaction record is matched with the number in the attraction-number table that locates the corresponding master data. Then, the attendance value in the corresponding attendance-to-date table is updated.

3. The days-in-operation field of the master record is updated by adding 1 to it for each attraction represented in the transaction file. The days-in-operation value that corresponds to the table location of the matching attraction number is updated for each afternoon-shift record.

4. The total number of records updated is accumulated for each afternoon-shift transaction record.

5. After the master file is updated within the tables, a new master file is written.

OUTPUT

Program output will be a new attraction master file in the same format as the old file. A final EOF record in the format 0,0,0,END OF FILE,0,0 should be written to the file. To create the new file, the updated master data in the program tables is copied to the old file.

During processing, the messages shown in Figure 7-3.2 should be displayed.

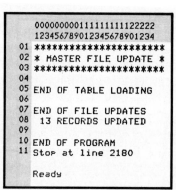

```
   0000000001111111111122222
   12345678901234567890123 4
01 ************************
02 * MASTER FILE UPDATE *
03 ************************
04
05 END OF TABLE LOADING
06
07 END OF FILE UPDATES
08  13 RECORDS UPDATED
09
10 END OF PROGRAM
11 Stop at line 2180

   Ready
```

Figure 7-3.2

Figure 7-3. Concluded.

will the days-in-operation field be updated. The master file will show that this attraction has been in operation one day less than the attractions represented in the transaction file.

The system does not display or print output automatically during file updating. Therefore, the program should be instructed to display confirmation messages at key processing points. The name of the current program is displayed at the beginning of program execution. Operator messages are displayed at the conclusion of both table loading and updating. Finally, the total number of updated records is displayed and the end of program execution is signaled. Confirmation messages help identify processing steps in which execution problems arise by allowing the operator to monitor program progress.

Program Design and Coding

Figure 7-4 presents the structure chart for the mainline file updating program. BASIC code for this mainline routine is presented in Figure 7-5. In this case, pseudocode is absent because previous programs already have detailed the structural design and code. At this point, translating directly from logical design to physical implementation is accomplished easily. However, pseudocode will be used to describe new processing routines that require an understanding of new concepts or processing techniques.

Variable Length Tables

Figure 7-6 presents the table loading subroutine design. The BASIC code appears in Figure 7-7. In this program section, the data fields of the attraction master records are placed within program tables. Six tables are defined. These tables are used to retain the six fields contained within each record. When the program is coded, each table will be allocated 20 elements, even though the file contains only 15 attraction records. The five extra positions allow for future master file expansion. Thus, it will be unnecessary to recode the program to increase table dimensions or to accommodate future file expansion.

Table loading proceeds much as in the previous program. A master record is brought into memory and the fields are assigned to designated table positions. The table subscript is incremented to the next available table element for each input record. Record inputting and table loading continue until the EOF flag is encountered.

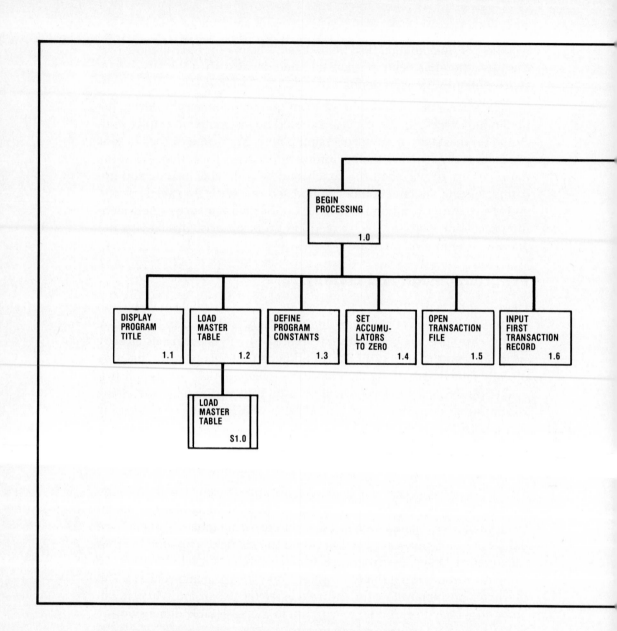

Figure 7-4. Structure chart for mainline master file updating program.

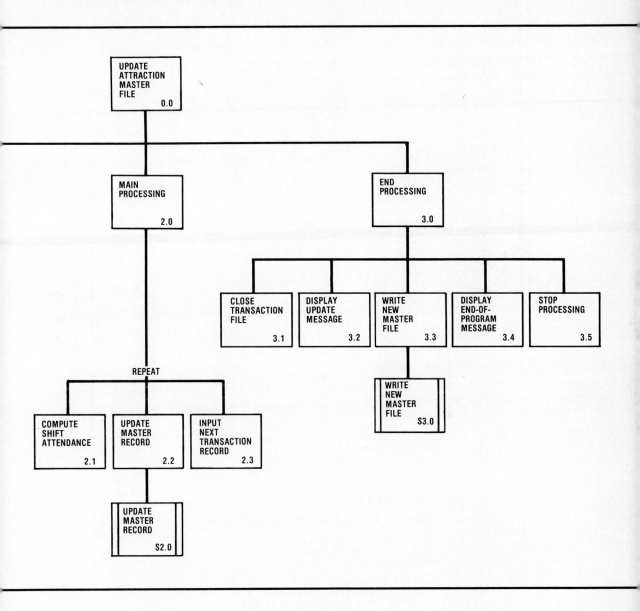

```
1000 REM FUN08                                        WEL/DRA
1010 REM                 MASTER FILE UPDATE
1020 REM
1030 REM THIS PROGRAM UPDATES THE ATTRACTION MASTER FILE
1040 REM (FUNMF) OF THE AMERICAN FUN AMUSEMENT PARK WITH
1050 REM TRANSACTIONS IN THE ATTENDANCE TRANSACTION FILE
1060 REM (FUNTF).  A NEW MASTER FILE (FUNNM) IS CREATED.
1070 REM ALL UPDATES TAKE PLACE WITHIN PROGRAM TABLES BUILT
1080 REM FROM THE OLD MASTER FILE.  FOLLOWING UPDATING,
1090 REM THE NEW FILE IS WRITTEN TO DISK FROM THE TABLES.
1100 REM
1110 REM VARIABLE NAMES
1120 REM
1130 REM MASTER FILE INPUT:
1140 REM     L.....LOCATION CODE
1150 REM     N.....ATTRACTION NUMBER
1160 REM     T$....ATTRACTION TYPE
1170 REM     N$....ATTRACTION NAME
1180 REM     D.....DAYS IN OPERATION (THIS MONTH)
1190 REM     A.....ATTENDANCE TO DATE (THIS MONTH)
1200 REM TRANSACTION FILE INPUT:
1210 REM     D1....DATE
1220 REM     L1....LOCATION CODE
1230 REM     N1....ATTRACTION NUMBER
1240 REM     S1$...SHIFT CODE
1250 REM     A1....ADULT ATTENDANCE
1260 REM     A2....CHILD ATTENDANCE
1270 REM CONSTANTS:
1280 REM     C1$...AFTERNOON SHIFT CONSTANT
1290 REM WORK AREAS:
1300 REM     A3....SHIFT ATTENDANCE
1310 REM     Z.....TABLE SIZE
1320 REM ACCUMULATORS:
1330 REM     T.....TOTAL RECORDS UPDATED
1340 REM TABLES:
1350 REM     L9....LOCATION CODE TABLE
1360 REM     N9....ATTRACTION NUMBER TABLE
1370 REM     T9$...ATTRACTION TYPE TABLE
1380 REM     N9$...ATTRACTION NAME TABLE
1390 REM     D9....DAYS IN OPERATION TABLE
1400 REM     A9....ATTENDANCE TO DATE TABLE
1410 REM SUBSCRIPTS:
1420 REM     S.....TABLE SUBSCRIPT
1430 REM
1440 REM 0.0 UPDATE ATTRACTION MASTER FILE.
1450 REM
1460 REM *************************
1470 REM * 1.0 BEGIN PROCESSING *
1480 REM *************************
1490 REM
1500 REM 1.1 DISPLAY PROGRAM TITLE
1510         PRINT "**********************"
1520         PRINT "* MASTER FILE UPDATE *"
1530         PRINT "**********************"
1540 REM
1550 REM 1.2 LOAD MASTER TABLE
1560         GOSUB 3000
1570 REM
1580 REM 1.3 DEFINE PROGRAM CONSTANTS
1590         LET C1$ = "A"
1600 REM
1610 REM 1.4 SET ACCUMULATORS TO ZERO
1620         LET T = 0
```

```
1630 REM
1640 REM 1.5 OPEN TRANSACTION FILE
1650         OPEN "FUNTF" FOR INPUT AS FILE #2
1660 REM
1670 REM 1.6 INPUT FIRST TRANSACTION RECORD
1680         INPUT #2, D1, L1, N1, S1$, A1, A2
1690 REM
1700 REM *************************
1710 REM * 2.0 MAIN PROCESSING   *
1720 REM *************************
1730 REM REPEAT
1740     IF S1$ = "END OF FILE" THEN GOTO 1860
1750 REM
1760 REM    2.1 COMPUTE SHIFT ATTENDANCE
1770            LET A3 = A1 + A2
1780 REM
1790 REM    2.2 UPDATE MASTER RECORD
1800            GOSUB 4000
1810 REM
1820 REM    2.4 INPUT NEXT TRANSACTION RECORD
1830            INPUT #2, D1, L1, N1, S1$, A1, A2
1840 REM
1850     GOTO 1730
1860 REM END REPEAT
1870 REM
1880 REM *************************
1890 REM * 3.0 END PROCESSING    *
1900 REM *************************
1910 REM
1920 REM 3.1 CLOSE TRANSACTION FILE
1930         CLOSE #2
1940 REM
1950 REM 3.2 DISPLAY UPDATE MESSAGE
1960         PRINT
1970         PRINT "END OF FILE UPDATES"
1980         PRINT T; "RECORDS UPDATED"
1990 REM
2000 REM 3.3 WRITE NEW MASTER FILE
2010         GOSUB 5000
2020 REM
2030 REM 3.4 DISPLAY END-OF-PROGRAM MESSAGE
2040         PRINT
2050         PRINT "END OF PROGRAM"
2060 REM
2070 REM 3.5 STOP PROCESSING
2080         STOP
2090 REM
2100 REM
```

Figure 7-5. Code for mainline master file updating program.

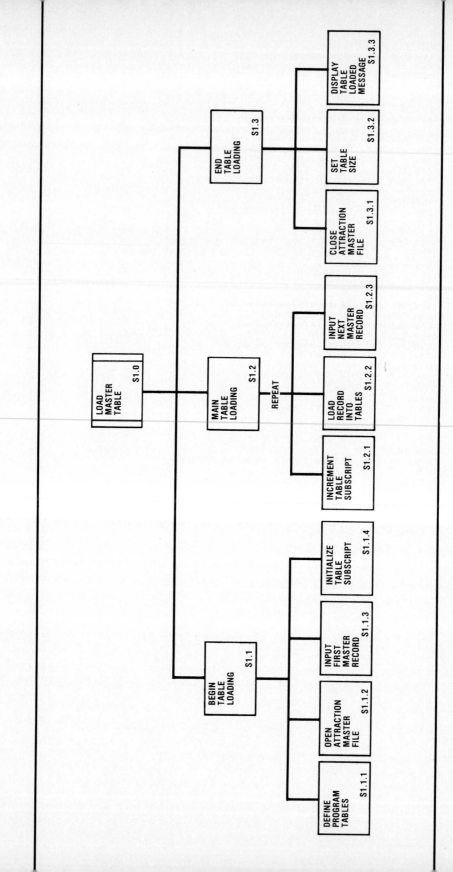

Figure 7-6. Structure chart for master file loading subroutine.

```
3000 REM ***************************
3010 REM * S1.0 LOAD MASTER TABLE *
3020 REM ***************************
3030 REM
3040 REM S1.1 BEGIN TABLE LOADING
3050 REM
3060 REM        S1.1.1 DEFINE PROGRAM TABLES
3070                   DIM L9(20), N9(20), T9$(20), N9$(20)
3080                   DIM D9(20), A9(20)
3090 REM
3100 REM        S1.1.2 OPEN ATTRACTION MASTER FILE
3110                   OPEN "FUNMF" FOR INPUT AS FILE #1
3120 REM
3130 REM        S1.1.3 INPUT FIRST MASTER RECORD
3140                   INPUT #1, L, N, T$, N$, D, A
3150 REM
3160 REM        S1.1.4 INITIALIZE TABLE SUBSCRIPT
3170                   LET S = 0
3180 REM
3190 REM S1.2 MAIN TABLE LOADING
3200 REM        REPEAT
3210            IF N$ = "END OF FILE" THEN GOTO 3380
3220 REM
3230 REM            S1.2.1 INCREMENT TABLE SUBSCRIPT
3240                       LET S = S + 1
3250 REM
3260 REM            S1.2.2 LOAD RECORD INTO TABLES
3270                       LET L9(S)  = L
3280                       LET N9(S)  = N
3290                       LET T9$(S) = T$
3300                       LET N9$(S) = N$
3310                       LET D9(S)  = D
3320                       LET A9(S)  = A
3330 REM
3340 REM            S1.2.3 INPUT NEXT MASTER RECORD
3350                       INPUT #1, L, N, T$, N$, D, A
3360 REM
3370            GOTO 3200
3380 REM        END REPEAT
3390 REM
3400 REM S1.3 END TABLE LOADING
3410 REM
3420 REM        S1.3.1 CLOSE ATTRACTION MASTER FILE
3430                   CLOSE #1
3440 REM
3450 REM        S1.3.2 SET TABLE SIZE
3460                   LET Z = S
3470 REM
3480 REM        S1.3.3 DISPLAY TABLE LOADED MESSAGE
3490                   PRINT
3500                   PRINT "END OF TABLE LOADING"
3510 REM
3520      RETURN
3530 REM
3540 REM
```

Figure 7-7. Code for Load Master Table subroutine.

At the end of the master file, records will have been loaded into the first 15 elements of the tables. The remaining five positions in the tables are unused. During subsequent processing, therefore, it will be necessary to identify this logical end of the tables—the last set of data values appearing in them—rather than the physical end of the tables. When the master file tables are searched, for instance, the program will proceed through the tables until the data are exhausted. The program will not continue to the end of the tables. The example program would search only through the first 15 elements, because there are 15 master file records. Although the programmer may not know the exact number of records to be placed in the tables, the program must be able to handle any number.

During loading, the program indexes through the tables by incrementing a subscript. Therefore, after the last data record is loaded, the subscript will point to this last set of table elements. At this point, then, the value of the subscript can be assigned as the logical table size. At the end-of-table loading in the current program, the table size is assigned as an end-of-table flag. For subsequent processing, the value can be used to indicate the last set of table values. The final subscript will indicate the logical end of the table, regardless of the number of master records.

Techniques for handling variable length tables are illustrated in the example program. These techniques are important to learn, because they can eliminate the need to recode programs when the number of data items to be placed in tables is changed. Even though the DIM statement must specify for the program an exact allocation number of physical table elements, this number need not be a programming constraint. The number can be thought of as a maximum table size within which fewer data elements may be handled.

In general, table dimensions will reflect estimates of the loaded file's volatility. That is, the programmer or analyst estimates the maximum number of records to be contained in the file and must take into consideration records that will be added or deleted. The rate and extent of change is volatility. The maximum value forecast for file size becomes the table dimension coded in the program. When the file is loaded into the tables, the subscript serves as a counter, tallying the number of records and table elements used. Following table loading, the subscript is assigned to a table size variable, which, in turn, becomes an end-of-table flag. The end-of-table flag is used in the same manner as an EOF record. Of course, in some cases, the number of records in a file never changes. For these cases, therefore, a table size variable may not be necessary. The values of the physical table dimensions can be used as end-of-table indicators.

In the table loading subroutine example, line space was insufficient to dimension all program tables in a single DIM statement. Therefore, two separate statements were required. This coding, shown in lines 3070 and 3080, is equivalent to a single DIM statement, or to one DIM statement used per table. Any number of statements can be used. Also, the order in which the tables are dimensioned can be changed.

Updating Master Records

After the master file has been loaded into the tables, the records are updated with daily operational data from the attendance transaction file. Figures 7-8 and 7-9 present the design and code for this updating routine.

For each transaction record, the attraction number table is searched for the corresponding number. A match between the transaction value and the value in the table will indicate the set of table elements for the corresponding master record. The values are searched within a repeat loop that increments the table subscript, beginning with the first table element. When a match is found, the program exits the loop. The program also will exit the loop if the end of the table is encountered without finding a match.

When the matching table value is located, the subscript points to the corresponding attendance-to-date element in the attendance table. Thus, the transaction value is added to the attendance table value. Also, the corresponding value in the days-in-operation table is updated. In this case, though, the value 1 is added to the table value only if the transaction record contains a shift code of A (afternoon). Finally, the record counter is incremented for each record pair updated. Following updating, program control returns from the subroutine to the mainline program. If no matching attraction number is found, an error message is displayed and control returns to the mainline routine.

The master file will be updated sequentially, because transaction and master files are ordered sequentially by attraction number. The first pair of transaction records updates the first master record, the second pair updates the second master record, and so on. Master record updating continues in this sequence until the end of the files is reached.

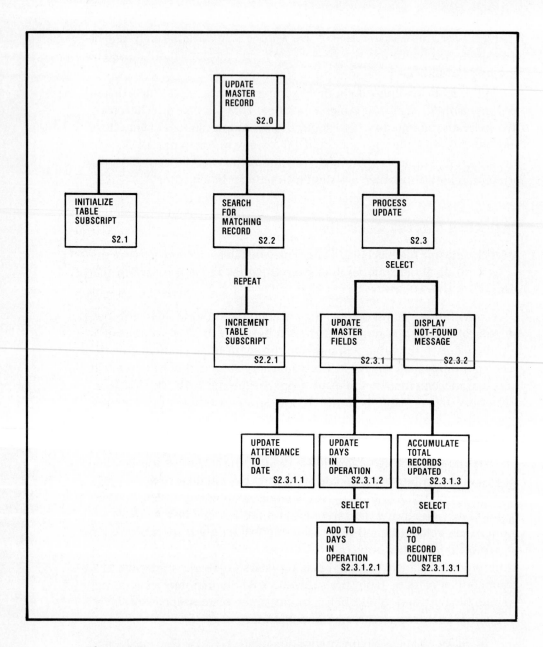

Figure 7-8.   Design for Update Master Record subroutine.

```
4000 REM *******************************
4010 REM * S2.0 UPDATE MASTER RECORD *
4020 REM *******************************
4030 REM
4040 REM S2.1 INITIALIZE TABLE SUBSCRIPT
4050         LET S = 1
4060 REM
4070 REM S2.2 SEARCH FOR MATCHING RECORD
4080 REM      REPEAT
4090         IF S > Z       THEN GOTO 4160
4100         IF N9(S) = N1 THEN GOTO 4160
4110 REM
4120 REM         S2.2.1 INCREMENT TABLE SUBSCRIPT
4130                 LET S = S + 1
4140 REM
4150         GOTO 4080
4160 REM      END REPEAT
4170 REM
4180 REM S2.3 PROCESS UPDATE
4190 REM      SELECT
4200         IF S > Z       THEN GOTO 4480
4210         IF N9(S) = N1 THEN GOTO 4230
4220 REM
4230 REM      S2.3.1 UPDATE MASTER FIELDS
4240 REM
4250 REM             S2.3.1.1 UPDATE ATTENDANCE TO DATE
4260                     LET A9(S) = A9(S) + A3
4270 REM
4280 REM             S2.3.1.2 UPDATE DAYS IN OPERATION
4290 REM                 SELECT
4300                     IF S1$ = C1$ THEN GOTO 4330
4310                                  GOTO 4360
4320 REM
4330 REM                 S2.3.1.2.1 ADD TO DAYS IN OPERATION
4340                         LET D9(S) = D9(S) + 1
4350 REM
4360 REM                 END SELECT
4370 REM
4380 REM             S2.3.1.3 ACCUMULATE TOTAL RECORDS UPDATED
4390 REM                 SELECT
4400                     IF S1$ = C1$ THEN GOTO 4430
4410                                  GOTO 4460
4420 REM
4430 REM                 S2.3.1.3.1 ADD TO RECORD COUNTER
4440                         LET T = T + 1
4450 REM
4460 REM                 END SELECT
4470                     GOTO 4520
4480 REM
4490 REM      S2.3.2 DISPLAY NOT-FOUND MESSAGE
4500             PRINT "***RECORD"; L1; "NOT FOUND***"
4510 REM
4520 REM      END SELECT
4530 REM
4540     RETURN
4550 REM
4560 REM
```

Figure 7-9. Code for Update Master Record subroutine.

Writing Updated Files

The tables of master file records now contain up-to-date summary information on park attractions. This information must be written to a new disk file. The old master file, then, will be retained as a backup. Also, the transaction file will be retained in case the new master file is damaged or destroyed. Should the new master file have to be recreated, the old master and transaction files can be reprocessed through the update program.

Figures 7-10 and 7-11 present the design and code for the new master file writing subroutine, which resembles a complete CIS program model. Basically, the subroutine indexes the tables and writes each set of corresponding table elements to the file. The elements are written in the field order that appears in the old master file. After all table entries have been written, the program writes an EOF record using the format of the original file. Note that the subscript is incremented for each table element

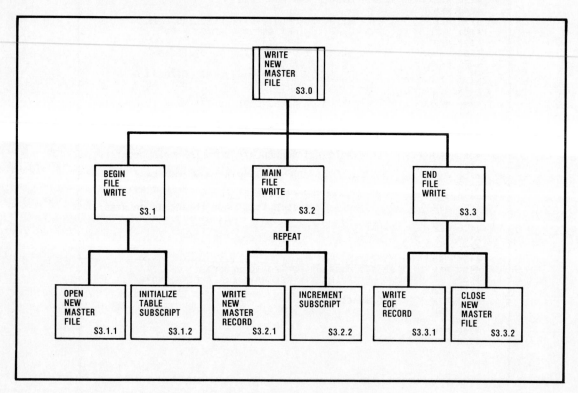

Figure 7-10. Design for Write New Master File subroutine.

until the subscript value is larger than the logical table size. This end-of-table indication branches program control out of the writing loop to the end of the subroutine. Thus, this subroutine will work without modification for any number of table elements up to and including the physical dimensions of the tables.

Several PRINT statements are used to write the new master table data to the file so that the data will remain within the margins established for coding. Notice, in lines 5170 through 5190, that a single master record is written with three PRINT statements. All but the last statement must end with a semicolon to denote continued writing of fields for a single record.

```
5000 REM ******************************
5010 REM * S3.0 WRITE NEW MASTER FILE *
5020 REM ******************************
5030 REM
5040 REM S3.1 BEGIN FILE WRITE
5050 REM
5060 REM      S3.1.1 OPEN NEW MASTER FILE
5070                OPEN "FUNNM" FOR OUTPUT AS FILE #3
5080 REM
5090 REM      S3.1.2 INITIALIZE SUBSCRIPT
5100                LET S = 1
5110 REM
5120 REM S3.2 MAIN FILE WRITE
5130 REM      REPEAT
5140          IF S > Z THEN GOTO 5250
5150 REM
5160 REM          S3.2.1 WRITE NEW MASTER RECORD
5170                  PRINT #3, L9(S); ","; N9(S); ",";
5180                  PRINT #3, T9$(S); ","; N9$(S); ",";
5190                  PRINT #3, D9(S); ","; A9(S)
5200 REM
5210 REM          S3.2.2 INCREMENT SUBSCRIPT
5220                  LET S = S + 1
5230 REM
5240          GOTO 5130
5250 REM      END REPEAT
5260 REM
5270 REM S3.3 END FILE WRITE
5280 REM
5290 REM      S3.3.1 WRITE EOF RECORD
5300                PRINT #3, "0, 0, 0, END OF FILE, 0, 0"
5310 REM
5320 REM      S3.3.2 CLOSE NEW MASTER FILE
5330                CLOSE #3
5340 REM
5350      RETURN
5360 END
```

Figure 7-11. Code for Write New Master File subroutine.

Processing Multiple Files

This program processes three different files. Therefore, each file is assigned a different reference number (#1, #2, #3). These numbers identify uniquely the old master file, the transaction file, and the new master file, respectively, and associate each with a disk device.

Program Output

Figure 7-12 shows the displayed program execution output, and Figure 7-13 shows the updated contents of the new master file produced by program FUN02.

After the master file has been updated, the new version is written to a file named FUNNM. The previous report writing programs and the file updating program, however, use file FUNMF for input reference. Thus, it is necessary to rename the two versions of the master file so that the updated version can be used with the existing program and can

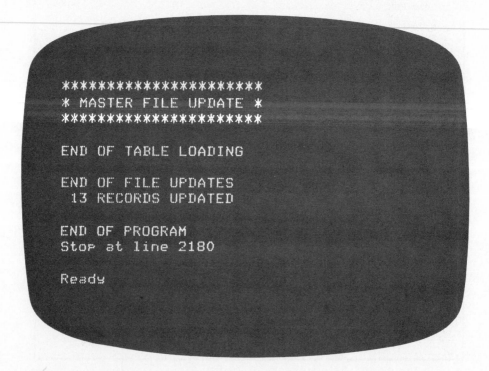

Figure 7-12. Terminal display for execution of master file update program.

```
                LISTING OF MASTER FILE FUNMF

      LOC.   ATTR.  ATTR.     ATTRACTION      DAYS IN   ATTENDANCE
      CODE    NO.   TYPE        NAME          OPER.      TO DATE

       10    101     A      THE BLAZER           4         1,823
       10    104     A      WATERSLIDE           2           606
       10    105     F      KREEPY KASTLE        4           175
       20    201     C      KIDDIE KAR           3            86
       20    202     F      PIRATE'S COVE        3           483
       20    207     F      JUNGLE SAFARI        2         1,643
       20    210     A      DEVIL'S PIT          2           359
       30    310     A      THE DUNGEON          1           113
       30    312     C      MERRY MOUSE          4         1,467
       30    320     F      WILD CHICKEN         4         1,110
       40    406     A      CRASHIN' CARS        4           982
       40    419     F      MUSIC SHOW           3           449
       40    420     A      THE CORKSCREW        2           152
       50    510     F      FRONTIER DAYS        4           166
       50    515     F      SPACE PROBE          3           410

      420   4,342                               45        10,024

      TOTAL RECORDS: 15
```

Figure 7-13. Output from program FUN02. Output lists content of attraction master file following updates.

become input to the next processing cycle. Therefore, the old master file is renamed FUNBK and the new file is given the name FUNMF. Renaming uses various system-level commands that depend on the particular type of computer in use. Typical commands are:

NAME "FUNMF" AS "FUNBK"
NAME "FUNNM" AS "FUNMF".

Acceptable alternatives are:

RENAME FUNMF, FUNBK
RENAME FUNNM, FUNMF.

The commands are keyed directly into the system and executed immediately. At this point, the new master file can be used as input to amusement park information system programs.

FILE INQUIRY PROGRAM

The master file inquiry program will allow managers and other personnel to make ad hoc requests for file information and will display selected file records on demand. These displays are supplementary to regularly scheduled reports. Figure 7-14 provides the programming specifications for the file inquiry program.

Figure 7-14. Programming specifications for master file inquiry program.

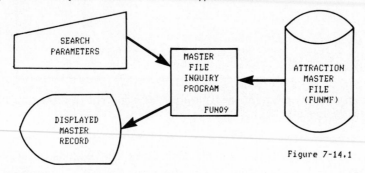

PROGRAMMING SPECIFICATIONS

System: AMUSEMENT PARK   Date: 05/08/XX
Program: MASTER FILE INQUIRY   Program I.D.: FUN09   Analyst: B. LEIGH

Design and write a program to allow selective inquiry into and display of
records from the attraction master file (FUNMF). This program will be
interactive and menu driven. The terminal operator provides the attraction
numbers, attraction names, or location codes of records to be selected from
the file and displayed. Any number of inquiries can be made. Figure 7-14.1
presents the system flowchart for this application.

Figure 7-14.1

INPUT

The attraction master file is the program input. Records are loaded into
program tables from which selected records will be displayed. The format of
master records is shown below:

Field Name	Data Type
Location Code	Numeric
Attraction Number	Numeric
Attraction Type	Alphanumeric
Attraction Name	Alphanumeric
Days in Operation	Numeric
Attendance to Date	Numeric

The string "END OF FILE" appears in the attraction-name field of the last
master record. Enough space should be provided for loading as many as 20
records into the program tables.

PROCESSING AND OUTPUT

Inquiry processing involves entering attraction numbers, attraction names, or
location codes through a terminal keyboard. Then, the computer is instructed
to search the program tables to locate and display the matching master record.

The program can handle any number of inquiries. For each inquiry, the program
displays a menu of the types of searches that can be made. The operator keys
the number that corresponds with the search parameter to be supplied. Then,
the program prompts for the value of the desired attraction number, attraction
name, or location code. The operator keys the value and the program searches
through the appropriate table to locate a matching value. When the value is

found, the corresponding record fields are displayed. Then, the menu is displayed again. This processing continues until the operator ends the session
with the appropriate menu code. Figure 7-14.2 shows the displays for the
inquiry session.

Fig. 7-14.2

```
I------------------I
I   INQUIRY MENU   I
I                  I
I  ATTR. NO.....1  I
I  ATTR. NAME...2  I
I  LOC. CODE....3  I
I  STOP.........4  I
I                  I
I------------------I

ENTER CODE...? 1

ENTER ATTRACTION NUMBER...? 320

LOCATION CODE:       30
ATTRACTION NUMBER:   320
ATTRACTION TYPE:     F
ATTRACTION NAME:     WILD CHICKEN
DAYS IN OPERATION:   4
ATTENDANCE TO DATE:  1110

I------------------I
I   INQUIRY MENU   I
I                  I
I  ATTR. NO.....1  I
I  ATTR. NAME...2  I
I  LOC. CODE....3  I
I  STOP.........4  I
I                  I
I------------------I

ENTER CODE...? 2

ENTER ATTRACTION NAME...? JUNGLE SAFARI

LOCATION CODE:       20
ATTRACTION NUMBER:   207
ATTRACTION TYPE:     F
ATTRACTION NAME:     JUNGLE SAFARI
DAYS IN OPERATION:   2
ATTENDANCE TO DATE:  1643

I------------------I
I   INQUIRY MENU   I
I                  I
I  ATTR. NO.....1  I
I  ATTR. NAME...2  I
I  LOC. CODE....3  I
I  STOP.........4  I
I                  I
I------------------I

ENTER CODE...? 3

ENTER LOCATION CODE...? 50

LOCATION CODE:       50
ATTRACTION NUMBER:   510
ATTRACTION TYPE:     F
ATTRACTION NAME:     FRONTIER DAYS
DAYS IN OPERATION:   4
ATTENDANCE TO DATE:  166

HIT <CR> TO CONTINUE...?
```

```
LOCATION CODE:        50
ATTRACTION NUMBER:    515
ATTRACTION TYPE:      F
ATTRACTION NAME:      SPACE PROBE
DAYS IN OPERATION:    3
ATTENDANCE TO DATE:   410

HIT <CR> TO CONTINUE...?
I------------------I
I   INQUIRY MENU   I
I                  I
I  ATTR. NO.....1  I
I  ATTR. NAME...2  I
I  LOC. CODE....3  I
I  STOP.........4  I
I                  I
I------------------I

ENTER CODE...? 4
```

Normally, after the program displays a master record, the inquiry menu is
displayed again. For a search on the location code, however, more than one
record is listed. After each record is displayed, the program waits until the
operator depresses the carriage return (CR) key before displaying the next
record with a matching code.

Provision should be made to check the accuracy of codes and values keyed by the
operator. Figure 7-14.3 shows how the program should respond to erroneous
entries and nonmatching values.

```
I------------------I
I   INQUIRY MENU   I
I                  I
I  ATTR. NO.....1  I
I  ATTR. NAME...2  I
I  LOC. CODE....3  I
I  STOP.........4  I
I                  I
I------------------I

ENTER CODE...? 7
*** ENTER CORRECT CODE...? 1

ENTER ATTRACTION NUMBER...? 100

NO MATCHING RECORD

I------------------I
I   INQUIRY MENU   I
I                  I
I  ATTR. NO.....1  I
I  ATTR. NAME...2  I
I  LOC. CODE....3  I
I  STOP.........4  I
I                  I
I------------------I

ENTER CODE...? 2

ENTER ATTRACTION NAME...? JUNGLE SAFARY

NO MATCHING RECORD
```

Fig. 7-14.3

Figure 7-14. Concluded.

MENU-DRIVEN PROGRAMS

The program illustrates some of the processing techniques characteristic of *menu-driven,* interactive programs. An interactive program provides immediate computer response to user inputs that are presented to the system in a give-and-take manner. That is, the user intervenes to control program processing activity while the program is running. In previous programs, the sequence of processing activities was determined by the program, with the operator responding to computer prompts. In this case, however, the computer responds to processing requests made by the operator.

A menu-driven program displays a *menu,* or list, of processing options from which the user selects. Then, the selected operations are carried out. Note in the programming specifications, for example, that the user can choose any of three processing tasks:

- File records can be selected for display based on a given attraction number, attraction name, or location code.

- The operator can indicate the type of file search to be made. The computer then asks for a value representing the search parameter.

- The operator enters the number, name, or code with which the search is to be made, and the computer locates and displays the matching record. After search and display, the menu is presented again and the next selection is made.

In general, therefore, the operator controls the type of processing that will be carried out.

DISTRIBUTION OF CONTROL IN PROGRAMS

The design for this program, shown in the *structure chart* in Figure 7-15, uses subroutines to perform all the major processing functions. In effect, this design separates the program control function from the program processing function. The mainline program uses *executive* control modules, which provide the overall control logic for the program. The subroutines are *detail* modules, which carry out the processing under control of the executive modules.

The structure chart resembles organization charts typically prepared by companies to delineate the hierarchical relationships among executives, managers, and workers in a company. The boxes near the top

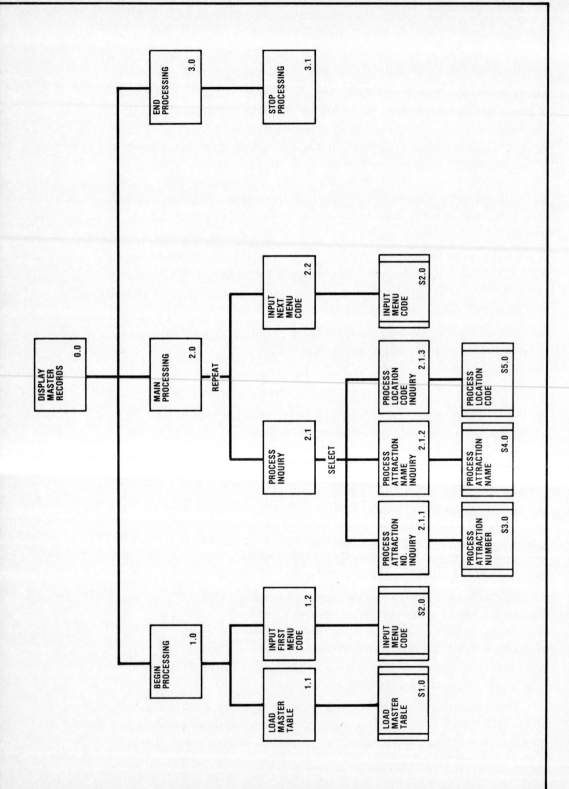

Figure 7-15. Structure chart for mainline inquiry program.

of the structure chart are analogous to managerial personnel. Management's main task is to oversee the work carried out by subordinates. Conversely, people at the bottom of the organizational hierarchy work under the supervision of management.

This characteristic *distribution of control* exists within most organizations. Organizational control resides primarily in the upper-level positions, with less and less decision-making authority given to employees at the lower levels of an organization. At the bottom of the hierarchy, there is little, if any, control responsibility—only responsibility for carrying out assigned tasks. This arrangement separates the control function from the actual work functions, and results in a formal structure of responsibility and authority that is effective in managing business complexities.

In a similar vein, a program is a collection of processing complexities that must be managed and controlled. Thus, the lessons of organizational control find application within programming. A program structure that separates control logic from detail processing is an effective way to simplify and manage program complexity.

In the current program, the executive-level modules perform no actual processing operations. These modules are arranged to correspond with the basic CIS program model and to carry out the required processing by calling upon subordinate detail modules. The CIS module itself is a program control structure that is superimposed upon all programs to simplify the overall management of processing tasks.

Processing functions are allocated to the appropriate subordinate modules once the control structure is in place. These detail modules can be designed and coded with little concern for the overall logic of the program. The programmer can concentrate on the specific processing task of the module.

Allocating program control logic and program processing to separate modules within a structural hierarchy is an important and highly practical programming concept. During the program design stage, this separation of tasks focuses the programmer's attention on the overall logic of the program rather than on irrelevant processing details. During detailed design and coding, on the other hand, the programmer can concentrate on the specific module under development. The programmer need not be concerned with the details of interfacing with other modules. Finally, during testing and debugging, tracing of errors is simplified. Within complex programs, the difficulty in writing error-free code usually lies in the confusion resulting from intermixing of control statements (primarily GOTO statements) and processing statements. Often, program logic is obscured by the large number of processing statements within which control statements are embedded. Understanding program logic is critical to program debugging and testing. Therefore, the practice of separating, and thereby highlighting, program logic eases the task of correcting program errors.

BASIC code for this mainline program is given in Figure 7-16. Notice that all statements are logic control statements. The mainline program manages processing tasks, determining the order in which processing functions are to be carried out. The mainline program calls upon subordinate subroutines to perform the actual program processing.

Detail Design and Coding

Building the tables that will contain the master data is the program's first task. The same table loading techniques used in the last program are implemented here. Figure 7-17 presents the structure chart for this subroutine and Figure 7-18 provides the BASIC code. This subroutine is

```
1000 REM FUN09                                        WEL/DRA
1010 REM                    MASTER FILE INQUIRY
1020 REM
1030 REM THIS PROGRAM ALLOWS SELECTIVE INQUIRY INTO THE
1040 REM ATTRACTION MASTER FILE (FUNMF) OF THE AMUSEMENT
1050 REM PARK INFORMATION SYSTEM.  IT IS A MENU-DRIVEN
1060 REM PROGRAM THAT PERMITS THE TERMINAL OPERATOR TO
1070 REM DISPLAY RECORDS SELECTED ON THE BASIS OF LOCATION
1080 REM CODE, ATTRACTION NUMBER, OR ATTRACTION NAME.  THE
1090 REM MASTER FILE IS LOADED INTO PROGRAM TABLES, WHICH
1100 REM ARE SEARCHED FOR RECORDS THAT MATCH INTERACTIVELY
1110 REM INPUT SEARCH PARAMETERS.
1120 REM
1130 REM VARIABLE NAMES
1140 REM
1150 REM MASTER FILE INPUT:
1160 REM      L......LOCATION CODE
1170 REM      N......ATTRACTION NUMBER
1180 REM      T$.....ATTRACTION TYPE
1190 REM      N$.....ATTRACTION NAME
1200 REM      D......DAYS IN OPERATION (THIS MONTH)
1210 REM      A......ATTENDANCE TO DATE (THIS MONTH)
1220 REM MASTER FILE TABLES:
1230 REM      L9.....LOCATION CODE TABLE
1240 REM      N9.....ATTRACTION NUMBER TABLE
1250 REM      T9$....ATTRACTION TYPE TABLE
```

```
1260 REM    N9$...ATTRACTION NAME TABLE
1270 REM    D9....DAYS IN OPERATION TABLE
1280 REM    A9....ATTENDANCE TO DATE TABLE
1290 REM SUBSCRIPTS:
1300 REM    S.....TABLE SUBSCRIPT
1310 REM WORK AREAS:
1320 REM    Z.....TABLE SIZE
1330 REM INPUT PARAMETERS:
1340 REM    C.....MENU CODE
1350 REM    L1....LOCATION CODE
1360 REM    N1....ATTRACTION NUMBER
1370 REM    N1$...ATTRACTION NAME
1380 REM    P$....CONTINUE DISPLAY FLAG
1390 REM
1400 REM 0.0 DISPLAY MASTER RECORDS
1410 REM
1420 REM ************************
1430 REM * 1.0 BEGIN PROCESSING *
1440 REM ************************
1450 REM
1460 REM 1.1 LOAD MASTER TABLE
1470        GOSUB 3000
1480 REM
1490 REM 1.2 INPUT FIRST MENU CODE
1500        GOSUB 4000
1510 REM
1520 REM ************************
1530 REM * 2.0 MAIN PROCESSING  *
1540 REM ************************
1550 REM REPEAT
1560     IF C = 4 THEN GOTO 1810
1570 REM
1580 REM    2.1 PROCESS INQUIRY
1590 REM        SELECT
1600           IF C = 1 THEN GOTO 1640
1610           IF C = 2 THEN GOTO 1680
1620           IF C = 3 THEN GOTO 1720
1630 REM
1640 REM        2.1.1 PROCESS ATTRACTION NO. INQUIRY
1650               GOSUB 5000
1660                  GOTO 1750
1670 REM
1680 REM        2.1.2 PROCESS ATTRACTION NAME INQUIRY
1690               GOSUB 6000
1700                  GOTO 1750
1710 REM
1720 REM        2.1.3 PROCESS LOCATION CODE INQUIRY
1730               GOSUB 7000
1740 REM
1750 REM        END SELECT
1760 REM
1770 REM    2.2 INPUT NEXT MENU CODE
1780        GOSUB 4000
1790 REM
1800     GOTO 1550
1810 REM END REPEAT
1820 REM
1830 REM ************************
1840 REM * 3.0 END PROCESSING   *
1850 REM ************************
1860 REM
1870 REM 3.1 STOP PROCESSING
1880        STOP
1890 REM
1900 REM
```

Figure 7-16. Code for mainline inquiry program.

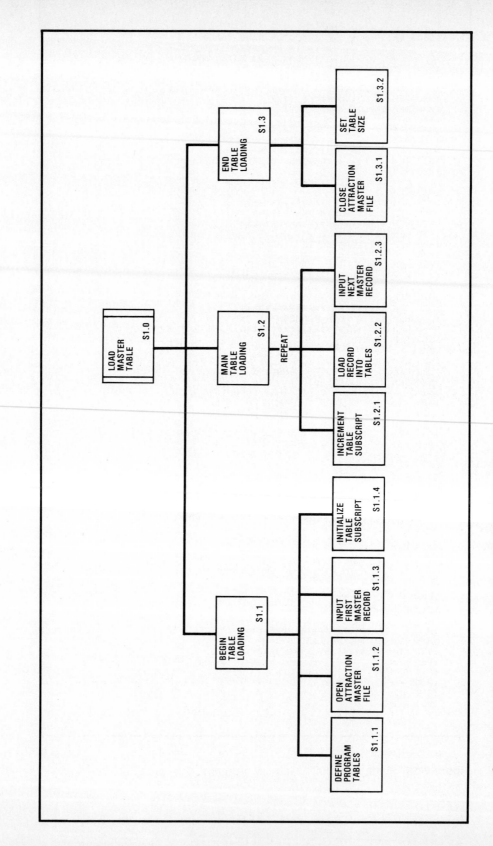

Figure 7-17. Structure chart for Load Master Table subroutine.

```
3000 REM ***************************
3010 REM * S1.0 LOAD MASTER TABLE *
3020 REM ***************************
3030 REM
3040 REM S1.1 BEGIN TABLE LOADING
3050 REM
3060 REM        S1.1.1 DEFINE PROGRAM TABLES
3070                   DIM L9(20), N9(20), T9$(20)
3080                   DIM N9$(20), D9(20), A9(20)
3090 REM
3100 REM        S1.1.2 OPEN ATTRACTION MASTER FILE
3110                   OPEN "FUNMF" FOR INPUT AS FILE #1
3120 REM
3130 REM        S1.1.3 INPUT FIRST MASTER RECORD
3140                   INPUT #1, L, N, T$, N$, D, A
3150 REM
3160 REM        S1.1.4 INITIALIZE TABLE SUBSCRIPT
3170                   LET S = 0
3180 REM
3190 REM S1.2 MAIN TABLE LOADING
3200 REM        REPEAT
3210            IF N$ = "END OF FILE" THEN GOTO 3380
3220 REM
3230 REM           S1.2.1 INCREMENT TABLE SUBSCRIPT
3240                      LET S = S + 1
3250 REM
3260 REM           S1.2.2 LOAD RECORD INTO TABLES
3270                      LET L9(S)  = L
3280                      LET N9(S)  = N
3290                      LET T9$(S) = T$
3300                      LET N9$(S) = N$
3310                      LET D9(S)  = D
3320                      LET A9(S)  = A
3330 REM
3340 REM           S1.2.3 INPUT NEXT MASTER RECORD
3350                      INPUT #1, L, N, T$, N$, D, A
3360 REM
3370            GOTO 3200
3380 REM        END REPEAT
3390 REM
3400 REM S1.3 END TABLE LOADING
3410 REM
3420 REM        S1.3.1 CLOSE ATTRACTION MASTER FILE
3430                   CLOSE #1
3440 REM
3450 REM        S1.3.2 SET TABLE SIZE
3460                   LET Z = S
3470 REM
3480        RETURN
3490 REM
3500 REM
```

Figure 7-18. Code for Load Master Table subroutine.

identical to the one in the previous program except that an operator message was displayed in the update program.

Figure 7-19 provides the design and code for the subroutine that inputs the menu options. These options represent the particular types of inquiry to be made. The menu is displayed and the program inputs the option code selected by the user. The entered value is tested to make sure the code is valid. If the code is invalid, repeated opportunities are given for the operator to key in a correct value.

On return to the mainline program, the code is checked to determine which type of inquiry is requested. Then, one of the three inquiry subroutines is called to perform the processing.

Figure 7-20 provides the design and code for processing an inquiry based on attraction number. The program asks for and inputs the number from the terminal operator. Then, a table search is performed to locate a matching value in the attraction number table. If no match is found, an appropriate message is displayed. When a match is located, another subroutine is called to display the master record. The display function is coded as a subroutine, because all three types of inquiries require display.

Figure 7-21 contains the design and code for processing an inquiry based on an attraction name. The structure and logic of this subroutine are identical to those used in the attraction number inquiry subroutine.

Figure 7-22 presents the subroutine used to process an inquiry based on location code. In this case, more than one record may be displayed. Therefore, records are searched and displayed within a program loop. The program prompts the operator after each record is listed. Printing will not continue until the user depresses the carriage return [CR] key. This carriage return operation is treated as an input operation. A variable must be defined to receive the input, even though no character will be transmitted. Rather, a *null* character, a special character whose meaning is undefined, is produced to satisfy the input requirement. The prompt provides the operator enough time to read through a displayed record before another is produced.

After a subroutine completes its processing, the mainline program calls up the menu again and the user selects the next processing code. Inquiry processing continues until the user wishes to end the program. Then, the stop code is entered in response to the menu options.

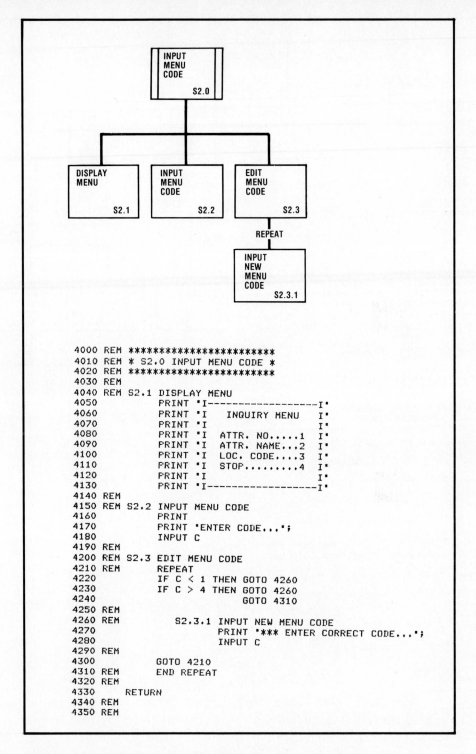

```
4000 REM ************************
4010 REM * S2.0 INPUT MENU CODE *
4020 REM ************************
4030 REM
4040 REM S2.1 DISPLAY MENU
4050          PRINT "I---------------------I"
4060          PRINT "I    INQUIRY MENU     I"
4070          PRINT "I                     I"
4080          PRINT "I   ATTR. NO.....1    I"
4090          PRINT "I   ATTR. NAME...2    I"
4100          PRINT "I   LOC. CODE....3    I"
4110          PRINT "I   STOP.........4    I"
4120          PRINT "I                     I"
4130          PRINT "I---------------------I"
4140 REM
4150 REM S2.2 INPUT MENU CODE
4160          PRINT
4170          PRINT "ENTER CODE...";
4180          INPUT C
4190 REM
4200 REM S2.3 EDIT MENU CODE
4210 REM      REPEAT
4220          IF C < 1 THEN GOTO 4260
4230          IF C > 4 THEN GOTO 4260
4240                   GOTO 4310
4250 REM
4260 REM      S2.3.1 INPUT NEW MENU CODE
4270             PRINT "*** ENTER CORRECT CODE...";
4280             INPUT C
4290 REM
4300          GOTO 4210
4310 REM      END REPEAT
4320 REM
4330      RETURN
4340 REM
4350 REM
```

Figure 7-19. Design and code for Input Menu Code subroutine.

275

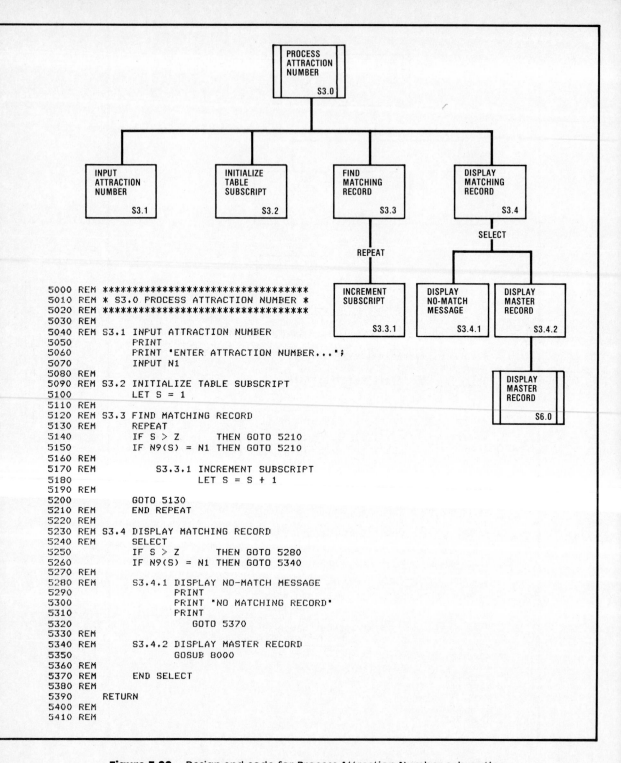

```
5000 REM *********************************
5010 REM * S3.0 PROCESS ATTRACTION NUMBER *
5020 REM *********************************
5030 REM
5040 REM S3.1 INPUT ATTRACTION NUMBER
5050          PRINT
5060          PRINT "ENTER ATTRACTION NUMBER...";
5070          INPUT N1
5080 REM
5090 REM S3.2 INITIALIZE TABLE SUBSCRIPT
5100          LET S = 1
5110 REM
5120 REM S3.3 FIND MATCHING RECORD
5130 REM      REPEAT
5140          IF S > Z       THEN GOTO 5210
5150          IF N9(S) = N1 THEN GOTO 5210
5160 REM
5170 REM          S3.3.1 INCREMENT SUBSCRIPT
5180                   LET S = S + 1
5190 REM
5200          GOTO 5130
5210 REM      END REPEAT
5220 REM
5230 REM S3.4 DISPLAY MATCHING RECORD
5240 REM      SELECT
5250          IF S > Z       THEN GOTO 5280
5260          IF N9(S) = N1 THEN GOTO 5340
5270 REM
5280 REM      S3.4.1 DISPLAY NO-MATCH MESSAGE
5290                   PRINT
5300                   PRINT "NO MATCHING RECORD"
5310                   PRINT
5320                      GOTO 5370
5330 REM
5340 REM      S3.4.2 DISPLAY MASTER RECORD
5350                   GOSUB 8000
5360 REM
5370 REM      END SELECT
5380 REM
5390      RETURN
5400 REM
5410 REM
```

Figure 7-20. Design and code for Process Attraction Number subroutine.

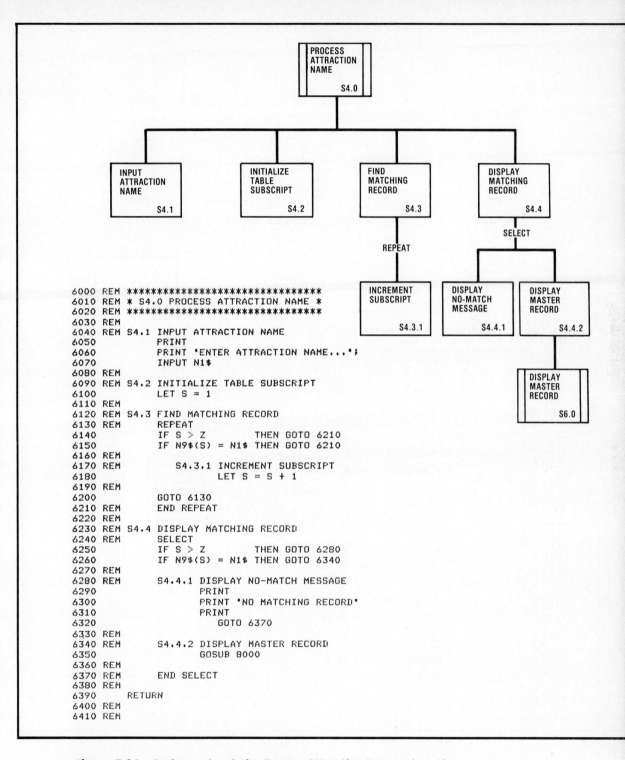

Figure 7-21. Design and code for Process Attraction Name subroutine.

277

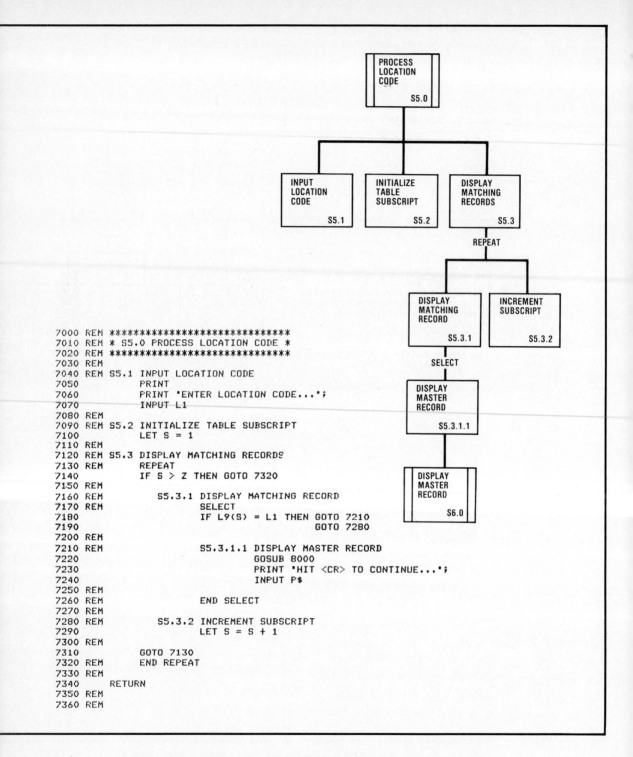

```
7000 REM *******************************
7010 REM * S5.0 PROCESS LOCATION CODE *
7020 REM *******************************
7030 REM
7040 REM S5.1 INPUT LOCATION CODE
7050          PRINT
7060          PRINT "ENTER LOCATION CODE...";
7070          INPUT L1
7080 REM
7090 REM S5.2 INITIALIZE TABLE SUBSCRIPT
7100          LET S = 1
7110 REM
7120 REM S5.3 DISPLAY MATCHING RECORDS
7130 REM      REPEAT
7140          IF S > Z THEN GOTO 7320
7150 REM
7160 REM          S5.3.1 DISPLAY MATCHING RECORD
7170 REM               SELECT
7180                    IF L9(S) = L1 THEN GOTO 7210
7190                                    GOTO 7280
7200 REM
7210                    S5.3.1.1 DISPLAY MASTER RECORD
7220                         GOSUB 8000
7230                         PRINT "HIT <CR> TO CONTINUE...";
7240                         INPUT P$
7250 REM
7260 REM               END SELECT
7270 REM
7280 REM          S5.3.2 INCREMENT SUBSCRIPT
7290                    LET S = S + 1
7300 REM
7310          GOTO 7130
7320 REM      END REPEAT
7330 REM
7340      RETURN
7350 REM
7360 REM
```

Figure 7-22. Design and code for Process Location Code subroutine.

278

Figure 7-23 provides the code for the master record display subroutine. The inquiry subroutines produce the same formatted listing by calling this display subroutine.

THE AMUSEMENT PARK INFORMATION SYSTEM

Programs and manual procedures for the Amusement Park Information System are now in place. The information system can operate across any number of daily processing cycles. In addition to maintaining operational data within master files, the system also produces management reports and inquiry displays that provide a current overview of park activities for management personnel. The software structure of this system is summarized in Figure 7-24. A systems flowchart appears in Figure 7-25.

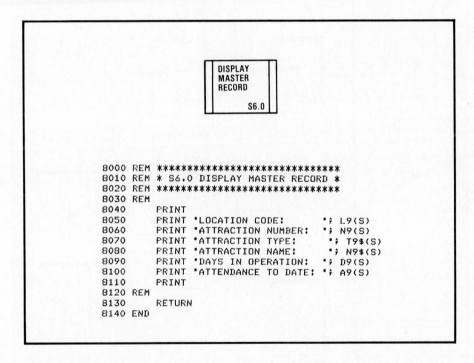

Figure 7-23. Code for Display Master Record subroutine.

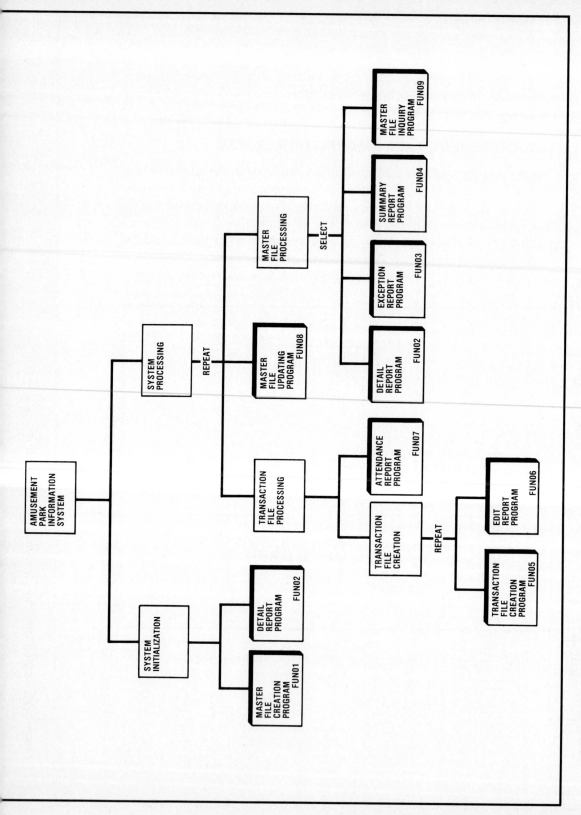

Figure 7-24. Software structure for Amusement Park Information System.

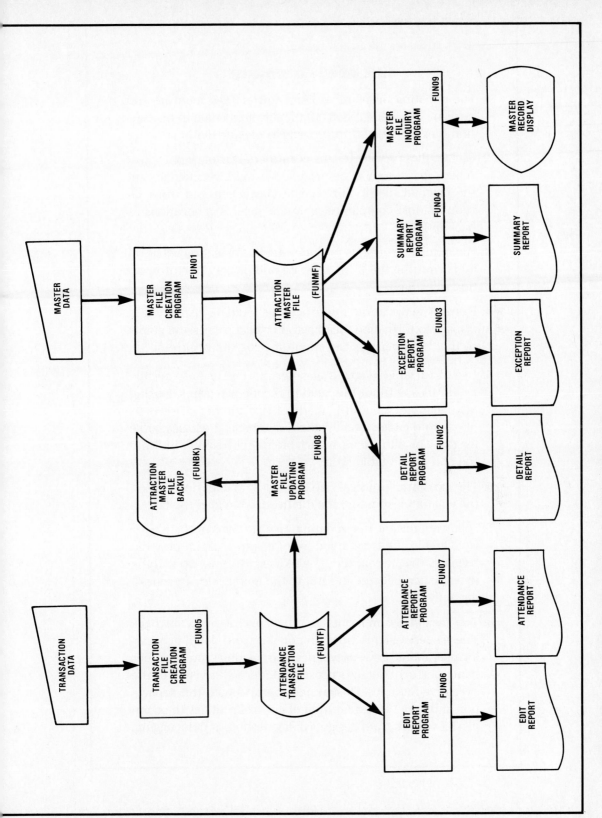

Figure 7-25. System flowchart for Amusement Park Information System.

Chapter Summary

1. File updating procedures keep master files accurate and current. Updating means that operational data in transaction files are posted to records in master files.

2. Backup files provide for the security of organizational data. A backup is a copy of an original file and is retained in case the original file is damaged or destroyed and must be rebuilt. Most companies maintain several generations of backup files.

3. File inquiry programs provide rapid information retrieval by permitting the user to locate and display file information selectively.

4. During file updating, the program should be instructed to display confirmation messages at critical processing points so that the operator can monitor program progress.

5. Use of variable length tables permits the use of variable length files without the need to recode programs. During table loading, a count is made of the number of records placed into tables. The final tally is used as the logical table length. This table length variable then is used to indicate the end of the table data.

6. The maximum physical size of program tables depends on the volatility estimated for the file used to load the tables.

7. Following master file updating, two versions of the file exist. The old file is retained as a backup and the new file becomes the current file. The files are renamed so that the new file can become input into the next cycle of processing activities.

8. Top-level program modules control overall program logic. These executive modules do not carry out detail processing operations. Lower-level program modules, on the other hand, perform detail processing under supervision of the executive modules. Designing programs with this separation and general distribution of control reduces the complexities of program design, coding, testing, and debugging.

Review Questions

1. What is file updating?
2. What is a backup file and why are such files maintained?
3. What is a file inquiry program?
4. Why are file inquiry programs used?
5. What is an interactive program?
6. What is a menu-driven program?
7. How may the distribution of control within a business relate to distribution of control within computer programs for using files?

Programming Assignments

Programming practice assignments for Chapter 7 are located in Appendix A, CASE STUDY ONE and CASE STUDY TWO.

Key Terms

1. updating
2. backup file
3. generation
4. file inquiry
5. menu
6. menu-driven
7. structure chart
8. executive control module
9. detail module
10. distribution of control
11. null character

8
FILE MAINTENANCE AND PROCESSING CYCLES

OVERVIEW AND OBJECTIVES

The two final programs of the Amusement Park Information System are discussed in this chapter. A master file maintenance program will allow for interactive changes to records within the master file. A zero-balance program will initialize fields within the master file to zero in preparation for the next processing cycle. These two programs provide processing continuity for the system. In its final form, the system will serve as a model for computer information systems found in many organizations.

When you complete your work in this chapter, you should be able to:

☐ Explain the purposes of file maintenance programs and the kinds of processing these programs allow.

☐ Explain the concept of processing cycles and the kinds of processing activities that occur within the cycles.

☐ Design maintenance programs that allow for interactive additions, changes, and deletions affecting files.

☐ Code maintenance programs that use tables to support maintenance processing.

☐ Explain the purposes of log files and how log files are used to provide an audit trail within information systems.

☐ Design and code zero-balance programs that initialize files for the beginning of processing cycles.

☐ Describe a general model of an information system with programs that meet cyclical processing requirements.

☐ Explain the benefits of a systems perspective on programming.

MASTER FILE MAINTENANCE

Master files are the main storehouses for a company's information. To maintain master files, operational data must be posted periodically to reflect the current status of a business. Posting programs similar to those described in the previous chapter are used to update master files.

Posting programs are used to accumulate balances of financial or other numeric accounts contained in master records. For example, master records typically contain year-to-date and/or month-to-date account fields that are accumulations of daily transactions. The update procedure provides current summaries of operations by posting transaction data to these fields.

In the normal course of a business, however, other types of transactions also affect the currency of information in master files. For instance, acquiring new customers means that new accounts must be created. Records containing the new customer accounts must be added to master files so that subsequent account transactions can be recorded. Also, when customers discontinue their business, the inactive accounts must be removed from master files. Further, the information in master files can become outdated. Customers and other entities associated with a business may experience changes of name, changes of address, or changes in the type of relationship maintained with the business.

All such changes must be reflected in the master files. Also, an operator may make errors inadvertently in creating or updating master files. A method must be provided to locate and correct these errors.

File *maintenance* is the process of changing or correcting information in files. In general, file maintenance encompasses the activities of adding, changing, and deleting records. Unlike posting activities, file maintenance does not involve accumulating ongoing balances. Maintenance activities are limited to making selective changes to files.

Files are maintained by processing a transaction file of additions, changes, and deletions against the master file. A new, updated master file results. The maintenance transactions can be applied in either batch or interactive mode. That is, the additions, changes, and deletions can be entered into a transaction file on some secondary storage device and processed collectively against the master. Alternatively, the transactions can be processed as they occur by keying them directly into an on-line terminal.

PROCESSING CYCLES

Posting and maintenance programs continue across any number of *processing cycles.* A processing cycle is, in general, the length of time between key events in a company's operations. The end of the business year is one such key event. At this time, yearly reports to government agencies, stockholders, employees, and other parties with an interest in the organization are due. Also, at the end of a three-month period, federal tax payments are due, thus defining the close of a quarterly business cycle. Further, a business may establish a monthly cycle, at the end of which payments from credit customers are collected, accounts owed by the company are paid, and monthly operations summaries are reported to management. Some companies may have weekly, daily, or even more frequent cycles that signal special processing from computer information systems.

Data collection, posting, maintenance, and reporting events all define cycles within a data processing system. Collection and posting activities may take place daily. Reporting on file content may take place daily, weekly, or monthly. File maintenance may occur whenever the need for master file changes is brought to the attention of the company.

Zero balancing is a common processing activity at the close of a cycle. This term refers to the practice of resetting balance fields within master records to zero so that accumulation of totals for the next cycle can begin. For example, following the issuance of W-2 tax forms at the end of a year, it is standard practice to initialize year-to-date payroll deductions fields in employee master records to zero. Then, the fields are used to accumulate wage and salary amounts for the following year. Also, sales files often contain monthly and/or quarterly summaries of sales transactions. At the end of the month and/or quarter, comparative sales reports are produced and the balances are reset to zero to allow accumulation of totals for the next cycle. Zero balancing, like file posting and maintenance, assures a continuity of processing within computer information systems.

THE AMUSEMENT PARK SYSTEM

Once the master file maintenance and zero-balance programs are added, the Amusement Park Information System will be complete. The maintenance program will allow for new records, representing new park attractions, to be added to the attraction master file. Also, the maintenance program will permit changes to any fields within any records and will provide the ability to delete any master records for attractions that have been discontinued. This program will operate interactively, allowing updates to be entered from computer terminals. The zero-balance program will be run at the end of each month to reset the days-in-operation and attendance-to-date balances to zero in preparation for the next monthly cycle of operations.

Although not a part of this system, a transaction file maintenance program also might be useful. Within the current system, errors made in creating the attendance transaction file can be corrected only by rekeying the entire file. A maintenance program for updating the transaction file before records are posted to the master file would be a sensible and prudent addition. However, the design and coding for such a program are very similar to those used for the master file maintenance program and, thus, are not discussed here.

Figure 8-1 presents a data flow diagram for the complete system. The functions shown as highlighted circles within this diagram represent the computerized portions of the system. The diagram can be used as a working model for many different kinds of computer information systems handling recurring business transactions across multiple processing cycles.

PROGRAMMING SPECIFICATIONS—MAINTENANCE PROGRAM

Figure 8-2 presents the programming specifications for the master file maintenance program. This program will allow interactive updates in the form of additions and changes to the attraction master file, as well as deletions of records from the file. As a result of maintenance, a new file named FUNUP is created. After the additions, changes, and deletions are verified, this file is renamed FUNMF and replaces the old version of the file.

PROGRAMMING TECHNIQUES

For small files, all maintenance activities are performed within program tables. That is, the master file is loaded into tables at the start of processing and remains there throughout the additions, changes, and deletions that are applied against the file. At the end of processing, the set of updated tables is written to a new disk file.

For large files that contain, say, 100 or more records with many more fields per record, the amount of storage needed to define the requisite

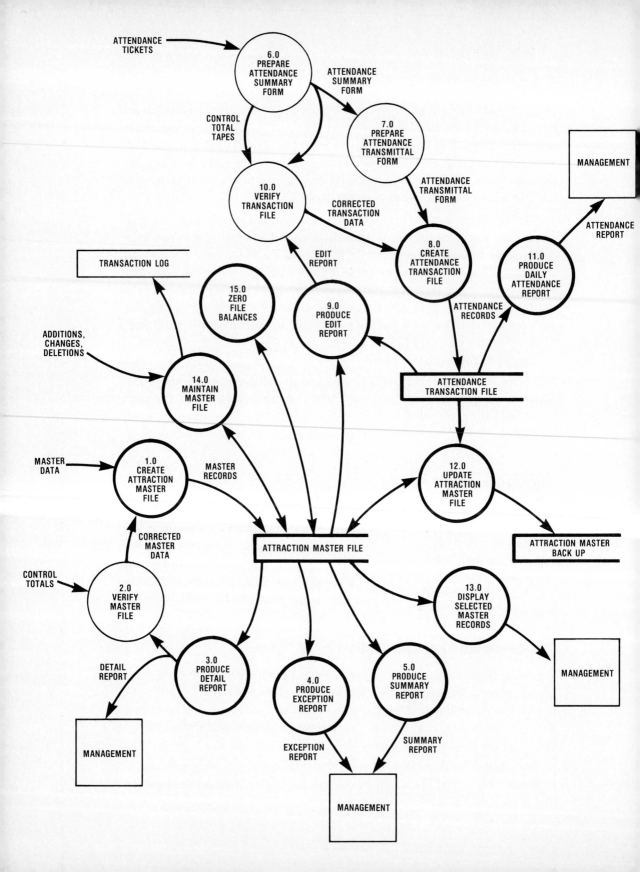

Figure 8-1. (Facing page) Data flow diagram for complete Amusement Park Information System. Automated portions of system are highlighted.

Figure 8-2. Programming specifications for master file maintenance program.

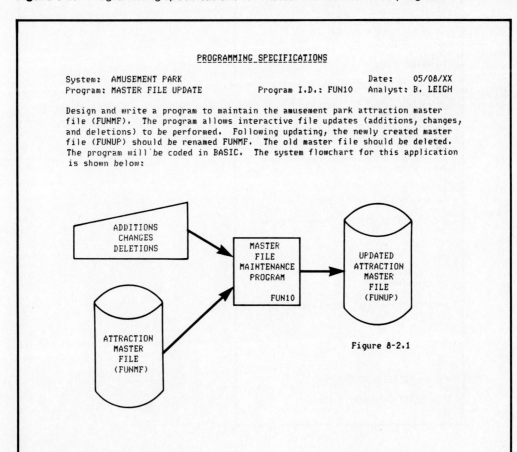

```
                    PROGRAMMING SPECIFICATIONS

   System:  AMUSEMENT PARK                           Date:     05/08/XX
   Program: MASTER FILE UPDATE        Program I.D.: FUN10   Analyst: B. LEIGH

   Design and write a program to maintain the amusement park attraction master
   file (FUNMF).  The program allows interactive file updates (additions, changes,
   and deletions) to be performed.  Following updating, the newly created master
   file (FUNUP) should be renamed FUNMF.  The old master file should be deleted.
   The program will be coded in BASIC.  The system flowchart for this application
   is shown below:
```

Figure 8-2.1

INPUT

The attraction master file and file updates keyed through computer terminals are the program input. The following table shows the format of records in the master file:

```
                  Attraction Master File
        ----------------------------------
        Field Name              Data Type
        ------------------      ------------
        Location Code           Numeric
        Attraction Number       Numeric
        Attraction Type         Alphanumeric
        Attraction Name         Alphanumeric
        Days in Operation       Numeric
        Attendance to Date      Numeric
```

The string "END OF FILE" should appear in the attraction-name field of the last file record.

Maintenance transactions are entered interactively through a terminal keyboard. The program is menu-driven and prompts for the information to be updated. Figure 8-2.2 shows the display format of interaction between the program and the operator.

```
   0000000001111111111222222222233333333333
   12345678901234567890123456789012345678
01 ******************************
02 * MASTER FILE MAINTENANCE *
03 ******************************
04
05     ADD NEW RECORD....A
06     CHANGE A RECORD...C
07     DELETE A RECORD...D
08     STOP..............S
09
10 ENTER CODE...? X
11
12 *** ADD NEW RECORD ***
13
14 LOCATION CODE........ ##
15 ATTRACTION NUMBER.... ###
16 ATTRACTION TYPE...... X
17 ATTRACTION NAME...... XXXXXXXXXXXX
18 DAYS IN OPERATION.... ##
19 ATTENDANCE TO DATE... ####
20     VERIFY (Y/N)...... X
21
22
23 *** CHANGE A RECORD ***
24
25 ATTRACTION NUMBER...? ###
26
27                              CHANGE?
28                              (Y/N)
29                              -------
30 LOCATION CODE  : ##          ? X
31 ATTRACTION NO. : ###         ? X
32 ATTRACTION TYPE: X           ? X
33 ATTRACTION NAME: XXXXXXXXXXXX ? X
34 DAYS IN OPER.  : ##          ? X
35 ATTN. TO DATE  : ####        ? X
36                ? ####
37     VERIFY (Y/N)? X
38
39
40 *** DELETE A RECORD ***
41
42 ATTRACTION NUMBER...? ###
43
```

Figure 8-2.2

PROCESSING

Master file updates take place in memory. Thus, the file is loaded into program tables at the start of processing. The tables should be dimensioned
sufficiently larger than the file itself. The additional table elements will
allow for file expansion should records need to be added later.

Adding Records: The computer promts the operator for the sequence of
                  fields contained in a master record. After all fields
                  are entered, the operator visually verifies the entries.
                  If all entries are correct, the new record is added to
                  the file in its appropriate attraction-number sequence.
                  The attraction-number table is searched to locate the
                  first record with a larger attraction number than that
                  of the record to be added. This location is the posi-
                  tion at which the new record will appear in the file.
                  To make room for the new record, all records with a
                  larger attraction number are moved down one position in
                  the tables. After the new record is inserted, the table
                  length is increased by one to signify the new logical
                  table length.

Changing Records: The operator enters the attraction number of the record
                  to be changed. Then, the attraction-number table is
                  searched to locate the matching record. The fields of
                  the current record are displayed one at a time. The
                  operator indicates whether the displayed field is to be
                  changed by keying a Y (for Yes) or an N (for No). If
                  no change is indicated, the computer displays the next
                  field. If the field value is to be replaced, a prompt
                  is displayed on the next line below the current value
                  and the new value is entered on this line.

                  After all changes or skips are completed, the operator
                  verifies the entries. If an error is found, the prompts
                  are repeated. As each replacement value is keyed, the
                  change is made to the table that corresponds to the
                  changed field.

Deleting Records: The operator keys the attraction number of the record
                  to be deleted. Then, the program searches the table to
                  locate the matching number. All records below the rec-
                  ord to be deleted are moved up one position in the
                  tables. This operation overwrites the undesired record.
                  Following deletion, the table size variable is decreased
                  by 1 to indicate the new logical table length.

Error Processing: Several different kinds of errors can occur during these
                  maintenance activities. Figure 8-2.3 shows the errors to
                  be anticipated and the system responses to these errors.

```
   00000000011111111112222222222233333333333444
   12345678901234567890123456789012345678901234567890012
01 ****************************
02 * MASTER FILE MAINTENANCE *
03 ****************************
04
05      ADD NEW RECORD....A
06      CHANGE A RECORD...C
07      DELETE A RECORD...D
08      STOP..............S
09
10 ENTER CODE...? X
11 *** ENTER CORRECT CODE ***
12 ? X
13
```

Figure 8-2.3

```
14 *** ADD NEW RECORD ***
15
16 LOCATION CODE.........? ##
17 ATTRACTION NUMBER.....? ###
18 ATTRACTION TYPE.......? X
19 ATTRACTION NAME.......? XXXXXXXXXXXXX
20 DAYS IN OPERATION.....? ##
21 ATTENDANCE TO DATE...? ####
22    VERIFY (Y/N).......? X
23 *** RECORD ALREADY EXISTS ***
24
25 *** CHANGE A RECORD ***
26
27 ATTRACTION NUMBER...? ###
28 *** RECORD NOT FOUND ***
29
30 *** DELETE A RECORD ***
31
32 ATTRACTION NUMBER...? ###
33 *** RECORD NOT FOUND ***
34
35
```

OUTPUT
After all maintenance activites are completed, the table data are written to a
new disk file named FUNUP. Records in this file have the same format as the
master file. A final EOF record should be written to the new file.

Figure 8-2. Concluded.

tables could be prohibitive on small computer systems. Thus, other updating techniques are used in such cases. These real-world constraints
are discussed in the chapter that follows. The example program,
however, uses table-driven file maintenance methods.

Figure 8-3 provides the structure chart for the mainline program. At
this level of design, the structure chart represents a general model for
maintenance programs. At the beginning of processing, the master file
is loaded into program tables. Then, the first transaction code is input.
Main, repetitive processing involves analyzing the code to determine
which maintenance operation is required and then calling the appropriate
add, change, or delete subroutine. Following transaction processing, the
next code is input and the processing loop is repeated. Finally, after all
transactions have been processed, the new, updated file is written and
the program is terminated.

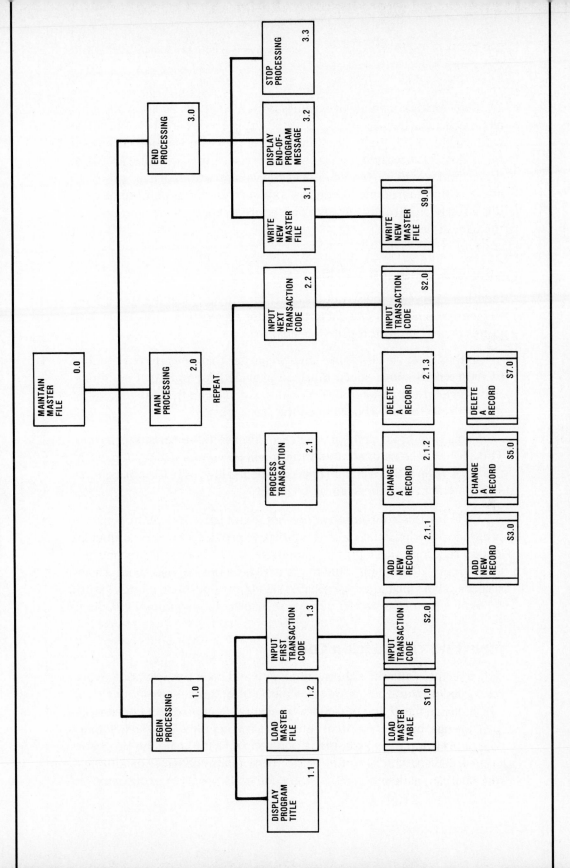

Figure 8-3. Structure chart for mainline master file maintenance program (FUN01).

Code for this mainline program is presented in Figure 8-4. Notice that all processing activities, except operator displays, are coded as subroutine calls. At this level, the overall logic of the program is emphasized and highlighted. Processing details that are irrelevant to the total software design and would introduce unnecessary complexities are disguised, in effect, within subroutines. With the code represented as subroutine calls, it is a relatively straightforward procedure to verify the correctness of the overall design.

Loading Program Tables

Figure 8-5 presents the structure chart for the table-loading subroutine. The design is nearly identical to the master file posting and inquiry programs developed in the previous chapter.

In this instance, table sizes must be larger than the current number of file records, since space must be provided for potential additions. Allowance for expansion is based on discussions with the systems analyst and with personnel who will use the file.

Table sizes of 20 elements each are defined in the current program. Thus, it has been estimated that there will be no more than 20 park attractions. Even if this estimate proves to be too low, only the table dimension statements will need to be changed.

Code for this subroutine is presented in Figure 8-6. As in previous programs, the logical size of the tables is provided by the number of loaded records. Although the dimension statements indicate physical table sizes of 20 elements, only the first 15 positions are filled with master records. Therefore, the logical table size (Z) will be 15 elements. Figure 8-7 shows the organization of master records following table loading.

Inputting Transaction Codes

Figure 8-8 presents the subroutine design and code for accepting transaction codes from the operator. A menu of options is presented from which one of the alphabetic codes is selected. The program checks that the code is valid. If so, control returns to the mainline program. Otherwise, a new entry is requested. Upon return to the mainline program, control is dispatched to one of the three maintenance subroutines—add, change, or delete—or the stop code ends program processing.

Figure 8-4. Code for mainline master file maintenance program.

```
1000 REM FUN10                                              WEL/DRA
1010 REM                 MASTER FILE MAINTENANCE
1020 REM
1030 REM THIS PROGRAM ALLOWS INTERACTIVE ADDITIONS, CHANGES,
1040 REM AND DELETIONS TO BE MADE TO THE AMUSEMENT PARK
1050 REM MASTER FILE OF ATTRACTIONS (FUNMF).  THE MASTER
1060 REM FILE IS LOADED INTO TABLES WITHIN WHICH MAINTENANCE
1070 REM TAKES PLACE.  AFTER ALL TRANSACTIONS ARE COMPLETED,
1080 REM A NEW MASTER FILE (FUNUP) IS WRITTEN.
1090 REM
1100 REM VARIABLE NAMES
1110 REM
1120 REM PROGRAM TABLES:
1130 REM     L9....LOCATION CODE TABLE
1140 REM     N9....ATTRACTION NUMBER TABLE
1150 REM     T9$...ATTRACTION TYPE TABLE
1160 REM     N9$...ATTRACTION NAME TABLE
1170 REM     D9....DAYS IN OPERATION TABLE
1180 REM     A9....ATTENDANCE TO DATE TABLE
1190 REM TABLE SUBSCRIPTS:
1200 REM     S.....SEARCH SUBSCRIPT
1210 REM     S1....MOVE FIELD SUBSCRIPT
1220 REM COUNTERS:
1230 REM     Z.....TABLE SIZE
1240 REM MASTER FILE INPUT:
1250 REM     L.....LOCATION CODE
1260 REM     N.....ATTRACTION NUMBER
1270 REM     T$....ATTRACTION TYPE
1280 REM     N$....ATTRACTION NAME
1290 REM     D.....DAYS IN OPERATION
1300 REM     A.....ATTENDANCE TO DATE
1310 REM MENU INPUT:
1320 REM     C$....TRANSACTION CODE
1330 REM PROGRAM FLAGS:
1340 REM     V$....VERIFY FLAG
1350 REM ADD TRANSACTION INPUT:
1360 REM     L1....LOCATION CODE ADD
1370 REM     N1....ATTRACTION NUMBER ADD
1380 REM     T1$...ATTRACTION TYPE ADD
1390 REM     N1$...ATTRACTION NAME ADD
1400 REM     D1....DAYS IN OPERATION ADD
1410 REM     A1....ATTENDANCE TO DATE ADD
1420 REM CHANGE TRANSACTION INPUT:
1430 REM     N2....ATTRACTION NUMBER CHANGE
1440 REM     R$....CHANGE RESPONSE
1450 REM DELETE TRANSACTION INPUT:
1460 REM     N3....ATTRACTION NUMBER DELETE
1500 REM
1510 REM
1520 REM 0.0 MAINTAIN MASTER FILE
1530 REM
1540 REM **************************
1550 REM * 1.0 BEGIN PROCESSING *
1560 REM **************************
1570 REM
1580 REM 1.1 DISPLAY PROGRAM TITLE
1590         PRINT "**************************"
1600         PRINT "* MASTER FILE MAINTENANCE *"
1610         PRINT "**************************"
1620 REM
```

```
1630 REM 1.2 LOAD MASTER FILE
1640         GOSUB 3000
1650 REM
1660 REM 1.3 INPUT FIRST TRANSACTION CODE
1670         GOSUB 4000
1680 REM
1690 REM ************************
1700 REM * 2.0 MAIN PROCESSING  *
1710 REM ************************
1720 REM REPEAT
1730     IF C$ = "S" THEN GOTO 1980
1740 REM
1750 REM    2.1 PROCESS TRANSACTION
1760 REM        SELECT
1770            IF C$ = "A" THEN GOTO 1810
1780            IF C$ = "C" THEN GOTO 1850
1790            IF C$ = "D" THEN GOTO 1890
1800 REM
1810 REM           2.1.1 ADD NEW RECORD
1820                  GOSUB 5000
1830                  GOTO  1920
1840 REM
1850 REM           2.1.2 CHANGE A RECORD
1860                  GOSUB 7000
1870                  GOTO  1920
1880 REM
1890 REM           2.1.3 DELETE A RECORD
1900                  GOSUB 9000
1910 REM
1920 REM        END SELECT
1930 REM
1940 REM    2.2 INPUT NEXT TRANSACTION CODE
1950         GOSUB 4000
1960 REM
1970     GOTO 1720
1980 REM END REPEAT
1990 REM
2000 REM ************************
2010 REM * 3.0 END PROCESSING   *
2020 REM ************************
2030 REM
2040 REM 3.1 WRITE NEW MASTER FILE
2050         GOSUB 10000
2060 REM
2070 REM 3.2 DISPLAY END-OF-PROGRAM MESSAGE
2080         PRINT
2090         PRINT "*** END OF PROCESSING ***"
2100 REM
2110 REM 3.3 STOP PROCESSING
2120         STOP
2130 REM
2140 REM
```

Figure 8-4. Concluded.

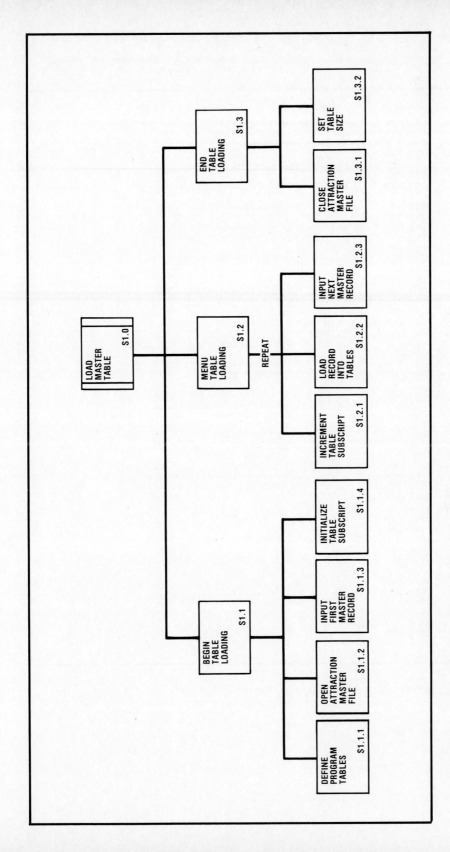

Figure 8-5. Structure chart for Load Master Table subroutine.

```
3000 REM ****************************
3010 REM * S1.0 LOAD MASTER TABLE *
3020 REM ****************************
3030 REM
3040 REM S1.1 BEGIN TABLE LOADING
3050 REM
3060 REM      S1.1.1 DEFINE PROGRAM TABLES
3070              DIM L9(20), N9(20), T9$(20), N9$(20)
3080              DIM D9(20), A9(20)
3090 REM
3100 REM      S1.1.2 OPEN ATTRACTION MASTER FILE
3110              OPEN "FUNMF" FOR INPUT AS FILE #1
3120 REM
3130 REM      S1.1.3 INPUT FIRST MASTER RECORD
3140              INPUT #1, L, N, T$, N$, D, A
3150 REM
3160 REM      S1.1.4 INITIALIZE TABLE SUBSCRIPT
3170              LET S = 0
3180 REM
3190 REM S1.2 MAIN TABLE LOADING
3200 REM      REPEAT
3210          IF N$ = "END OF FILE" THEN GOTO 3380
3220 REM
3230 REM          S1.2.1 INCREMENT TABLE SUBSCRIPT
3240                  LET S = S + 1
3250 REM
3260 REM          S1.2.2 LOAD RECORD INTO TABLES
3270                  LET L9(S)  = L
3280                  LET N9(S)  = N
3290                  LET T9$(S) = T$
3300                  LET N9$(S) = N$
3310                  LET D9(S)  = D
3320                  LET A9(S)  = A
3330 REM
3340 REM          S1.2.3 INPUT NEXT MASTER RECORD
3350                  INPUT #1, L, N, T$, N$, D, A
3360 REM
3370          GOTO 3200
3380 REM      END REPEAT
3390 REM
3400 REM S1.3 END TABLE LOADING
3410 REM
3420 REM      S1.3.1 CLOSE ATTRACTION MASTER FILE
3430              CLOSE #1
3440 REM
3450 REM      S1.3.2 SET TABLE SIZE
3460              LET Z = S
3470 REM
3480      RETURN
3490 REM
```

Figure 8-6. Code for Load Master Table subroutine.

Location Code	Attraction Number	Attraction Type	Attraction Name	Days in Operation	Attendance to Date	
10	101	A	THE BLAZER	4	1823	
10	104	A	WATERSLIDE	2	606	
10	105	F	KREEPY KASTLE	4	175	
20	201	C	KIDDIE KAR	3	86	
20	202	F	PIRATE'S COVE	3	483	
20	207	F	JUNGLE SAFARI	2	1643	
20	210	A	DEVIL'S PIT	2	359	
30	310	A	THE DUNGEON	1	113	
30	312	C	MERRY MOUSE	4	1467	
30	320	F	WILD CHICKEN	4	1110	
40	406	A	CRASHIN' CARS	4	982	
40	419	F	MUSIC SHOW	3	449	
40	420	A	THE CORKSCREW	2	152	
50	510	F	FRONTIER DAYS	4	166	
50	515	F	SPACE PROBE	3	410	Table Size Z = 15
						Table Dimension = 20
L9	N9	T9$	N9$	D9	A9	

Figure 8-7. Organization and content of program tables following table loading.

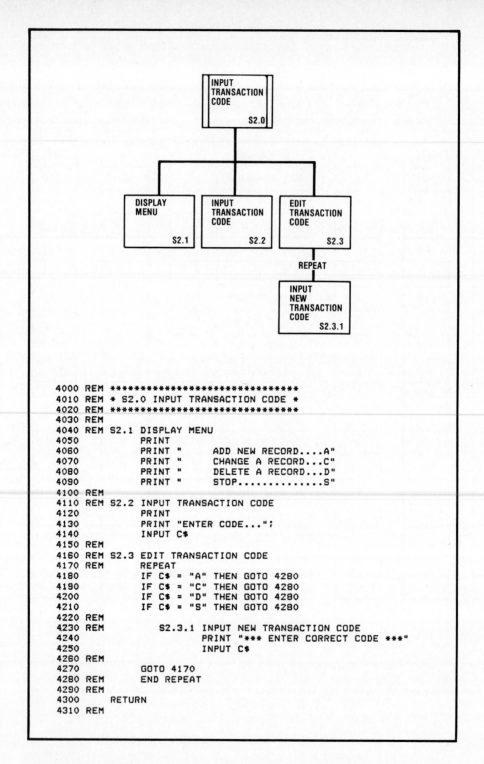

```
4000 REM ********************************
4010 REM * S2.0 INPUT TRANSACTION CODE *
4020 REM ********************************
4030 REM
4040 REM S2.1 DISPLAY MENU
4050         PRINT
4060         PRINT "      ADD NEW RECORD....A"
4070         PRINT "      CHANGE A RECORD...C"
4080         PRINT "      DELETE A RECORD...D"
4090         PRINT "      STOP.............S"
4100 REM
4110 REM S2.2 INPUT TRANSACTION CODE
4120         PRINT
4130         PRINT "ENTER CODE...";
4140         INPUT C$
4150 REM
4160 REM S2.3 EDIT TRANSACTION CODE
4170 REM      REPEAT
4180         IF C$ = "A" THEN GOTO 4280
4190         IF C$ = "C" THEN GOTO 4280
4200         IF C$ = "D" THEN GOTO 4280
4210         IF C$ = "S" THEN GOTO 4280
4220 REM
4230 REM         S2.3.1 INPUT NEW TRANSACTION CODE
4240                 PRINT "*** ENTER CORRECT CODE ***"
4250                 INPUT C$
4260 REM
4270         GOTO 4170
4280 REM      END REPEAT
4290 REM
4300     RETURN
4310 REM
```

Figure 8-8. Structure chart and code for Input Transaction Code subroutine.

Adding Records to Files

The design for the add routine is given in Figure 8-9. This structure chart identifies the four major functions required to add a new record to the master file. First, a heading is displayed to verify that the add function has been activated. Next, the operator is requested to key in the data fields. The design for this function corresponds with the input function design for the previous master and transaction creation programs. Then, the attraction number table is searched to locate the position within the file at which the record should be added. The program will maintain the

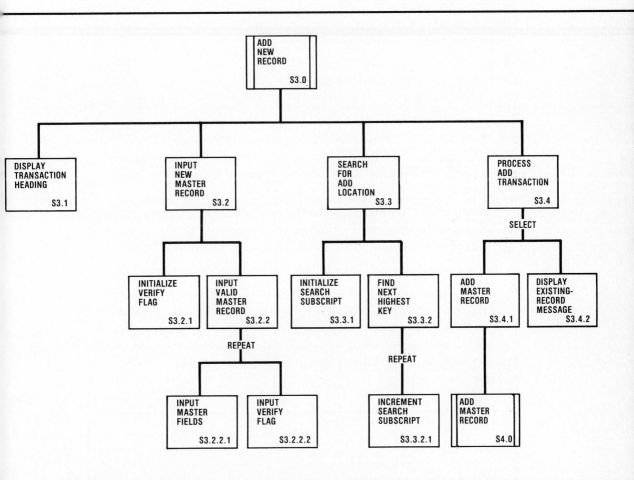

Figure 8-9. Structure chart for Add New Record subroutine.

order provided by the sequence of attraction numbers. All records containing a higher attraction number key are moved down one position when a new record is to be inserted. Finally, the record is placed in the tables.

Code for the S3.0 ADD NEW RECORD subroutine appears in Figure 8-10. Note that the S3.2 INPUT NEW MASTER RECORD module and the input module used in the earlier master file creation program are coded identically.

Module S3.3 SEARCH FOR ADD LOCATION searches the attraction number table, beginning with the first position, for the appropriate table position in which to insert the new record. The search is halted when one of these three conditions occurs:

- An attraction number larger than the attraction number of the new record is encountered (N9(S) > N1). To maintain the sequence of attraction numbers, the position of this table record is the position at which the new record should be added.

- The logical end of the table is encountered (S > Z). This situation indicates that no record with a larger attraction number appears in the table. Therefore, the new record should be added to the end of the file.

- An attraction number equal to the new attraction number is found. This situation indicates that the addition is invalid. The record already exists in the file and, therefore, should not be added.

Figure 8-11 diagrams this search loop and the conditions for terminating the loop.

Subroutine S4.0 ADD MASTER RECORD is called when either the first or second condition is identified. If, on the other hand, a duplicate record is found in the file, a record-already-exists message is displayed, and control returns to the mainline program for input of the next transaction.

```
5000 REM *************************
5010 REM * S3.0 ADD NEW RECORD *
5020 REM *************************
5030 REM
5040 REM S3.1 DISPLAY TRANSACTION HEADING
5050          PRINT
5060          PRINT "*** ADD NEW RECORD ***"
5070 REM
```

```
5080 REM S3.2 INPUT NEW MASTER RECORD
5090 REM
5100 REM      S3.2.1 INITIALIZE VERIFY FLAG
5110                 LET V$ = " "
5120 REM
5130 REM      S3.2.2 INPUT VALID MASTER RECORD
5140 REM             REPEAT
5150                 IF V$ = "Y" THEN GOTO 5370
5160 REM
5170 REM             S3.2.2.1 INPUT MASTER FIELDS
5180                      PRINT
5190                      PRINT "LOCATION CODE........";
5200                      INPUT L1
5210                      PRINT "ATTRACTION NUMBER....";
5220                      INPUT N1
5230                      PRINT "ATTRACTION TYPE......";
5240                      INPUT T1$
5250                      PRINT "ATTRACTION NAME......";
5260                      INPUT N1$
5270                      PRINT "DAYS IN OPERATION....";
5280                      INPUT D1
5290                      PRINT "ATTENDANCE TO DATE...";
5300                      INPUT A1
5310 REM
5320 REM             S3.2.2.2 INPUT VERIFY FLAG
5330                      PRINT "   VERIFY (Y/N)......";
5340                      INPUT V$
5350 REM
5360                 GOTO 5140
5370 REM             END REPEAT
5380 REM
5390 REM S3.3 SEARCH FOR ADD LOCATION
5400 REM
5410 REM      S3.3.1 INITIALIZE SEARCH SUBSCRIPT
5420                 LET S = 1
5430 REM
5440 REM      S3.3.2 FIND NEXT HIGHEST KEY
5450 REM             REPEAT
5460                 IF S > Z      THEN GOTO 5540
5470                 IF N9(S) > N1 THEN GOTO 5540
5480                 IF N9(S) = N1 THEN GOTO 5540
5490 REM
5500 REM             S3.3.2.1 INCREMENT SEARCH SUBSCRIPT
5510                      LET S = S + 1
5520 REM
5530                 GOTO 5450
5540 REM             END REPEAT
5550 REM
5560 REM S3.4 PROCESS ADD TRANSACTION
5570 REM      SELECT
5580          IF S > Z      THEN GOTO 5620
5590          IF N9(S) > N1 THEN GOTO 5620
5600          IF N9(S) = N1 THEN GOTO 5660
5610 REM
5620 REM      S3.4.1 ADD MASTER RECORD
5630                 GOSUB 6000
5640                 GOTO  5690
5650 REM
5660 REM      S3.4.2 DISPLAY EXISTING-RECORD MESSAGE
5670                 PRINT "*** RECORD ALREADY EXISTS ***"
5680 REM
5690 REM      END SELECT
5700 REM
5710      RETURN
5720 REM
```

Figure 8-10. Code for Add New Record subroutine.

Design and code for the S4.0 ADD MASTER RECORD subroutine appear in Figures 8-12 and 8-13. One of two techniques is followed, depending on whether the new record is to be added to the end of the file or between existing records.

The first condition occurs when the search subscript (S) is larger than the table length (Z). In this case, the search ended with the subscript pointing to the table element immediately following the last record in the table. Therefore, the subscript is used to assign the new fields to the corresponding table positions. The tables simply are extended with the addition of the new record. Module S4.2 INSERT NEW MASTER RECORD accomplishes this addition.

For a case in which the new record is to be added among the existing records, the record is placed in the position of the first record with a larger attraction number. This table record and all subsequent records are moved down one position to create a space for the new record. See Figure 8-14.

Module S4.1.1 MOVE TABLE RECORDS DOWN handles the rearrangement of table records. The search subscript (S) indicates the point at which the record will be added. Therefore, all records beyond this position will be moved. A move subscript (S1) is set initially to the table size value (Z). Then, the S4.1.1.2 MOVE A RECORD DOWN module is repeated until the insertion position is reached. Beginning with the last record in the tables, each record is moved down one position. When the move subscript (S1) is less than the insertion subscript value (S), the new record is assigned to the tables using the S4.2 INSERT NEW MASTER RECORD module.

After the new record has been added to the file, the table length variable (Z) is increased by 1. The variable then reflects the increased size of the tables in subsequent processing.

Changing Records in a File

Subroutine S5.0 CHANGE A RECORD is used to modify an existing record. In this case, the operator enters the attraction number of the record to be changed. The program then searches the attraction number table to locate the corresponding record. If a matching number is found, subroutine S6.0 CHANGE MASTER RECORD is called, allowing the operator to alter the fields. If no matching record is found, an error message is displayed and control is returned to the mainline program.

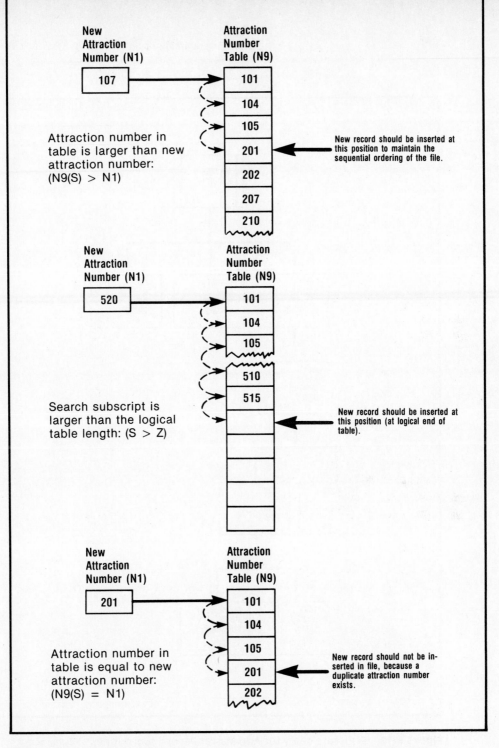

Figure 8-11. Search logic to locate the position at which a new master record should be inserted to the master file or to determine that the record should not be added.

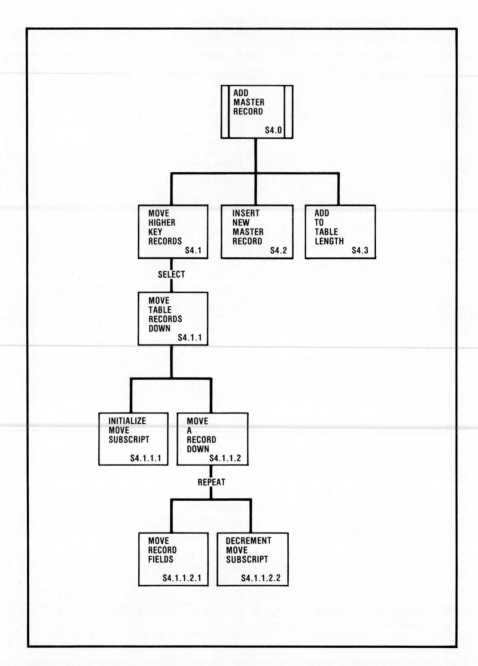

Figure 8-12. Structure chart for Add Master Record subroutine.

```
6000 REM ****************************
6010 REM * S4.0 ADD MASTER RECORD *
6020 REM ****************************
6030 REM
6040 REM S4.1 MOVE HIGHER KEY RECORDS
6050 REM      SELECT
6060           IF S <= Z THEN GOTO 6090
6070                        GOTO 6320
6080 REM
6090 REM      S4.1.1 MOVE TABLE RECORDS DOWN
6100 REM
6110 REM           S4.1.1.1 INITIALIZE MOVE SUBSCRIPT
6120                    LET S1 = Z
6130 REM
6140 REM           S4.1.1.2 MOVE A RECORD DOWN
6150 REM                    REPEAT
6160                        IF S1 < S THEN GOTO 6300
6170 REM
6180 REM                    S4.1.1.2.1 MOVE RECORD FIELDS
6190                             LET L9(S1+1)  = L9(S1)
6200                             LET N9(S1+1)  = N9(S1)
6210                             LET T9$(S1+1) = T9$(S1)
6220                             LET N9$(S1+1) = N9$(S1)
6230                             LET D9(S1+1)  = D9(S1)
6240                             LET A9(S1+1)  = A9(S1)
6250 REM
6260 REM                    S4.1.1.2.2 DECREMENT MOVE SUBSCRIPT
6270                             LET S1 = S1 - 1
6280 REM
6290                         GOTO 6150
6300 REM                     END REPEAT
6310 REM
6320 REM      END SELECT
6330 REM
6340 REM S4.2 INSERT NEW MASTER RECORD
6350           LET L9(S)  = L1
6360           LET N9(S)  = N1
6370           LET T9$(S) = T1$
6380           LET N9$(S) = N1$
6390           LET D9(S)  = D1
6400           LET A9(S)  = A1
6410 REM
6420 REM S4.3 ADD TO TABLE LENGTH
6430           LET Z = Z + 1
6440 REM
6450      RETURN
6460 REM
```

Figure 8-13. Code for Add Master Record subroutine.

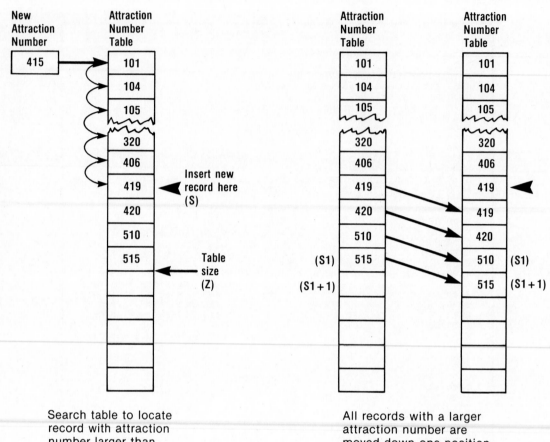

Search table to locate record with attraction number larger than number of record to be added. Subscript S indicates table position at which new record will be added.

All records with a larger attraction number are moved down one position in the table, starting with the last record. Initially, subscript S1 is set to point to the last position in the table (Z). Within a program loop, the record at position S1 is assigned to position S1 + 1 and the subscript is decreased by 1. Reassignment of record positions continues until the move subscript S1 is less than the insert subscript S.

Figure 8-14. Procedure for adding records to a table file.

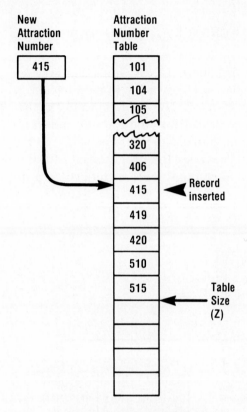

New record is added to table at position indicated by subscript S. The table size (Z) is adjusted to account for the inserted record.

NOTE: All fields in all the moved records are repositioned in the tables. This example illustrates only reassignment of attraction numbers.

Design and code for subroutine S5.0 CHANGE A RECORD are presented in Figures 8-15 and 8-16.

The structure chart for subroutine S6.0 CHANGE MASTER RECORD is shown in Figure 8-17. Code is given in Figure 8-18. In module S6.2.1 INPUT RECORD CHANGES, the program displays the field values of the record to be changed. Following each display line, the operator indicates whether the field is to be changed or is to retain the same value. If the response (R$) is N (no change is to be made), the program skips to the next field and displays its value. A Y response causes the program to

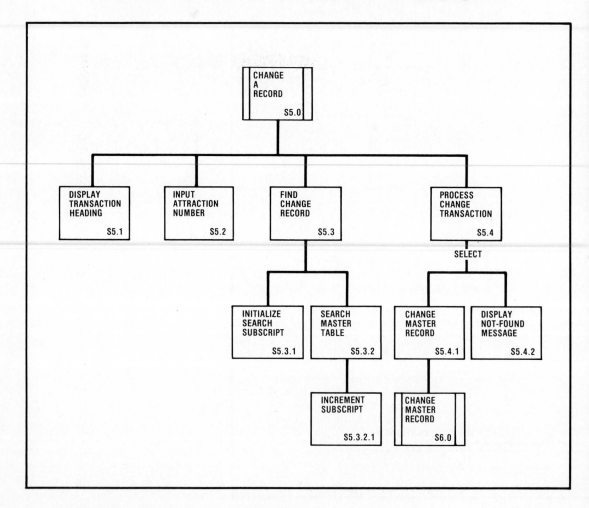

Figure 8-15. Structure chart for Change a Record subroutine.

prompt for an input value on the line beneath the current displayed value. The operator keys in the data value, which then replaces the old value in the table. After all changes or skipped fields have been processed, the operator verifies the changes. If the changes are correct, control returns to the mainline program. Otherwise, the input routine is repeated until all errors are corrected.

```
7000 REM ************************
7010 REM * S5.0 CHANGE A RECORD *
7020 REM ************************
7030 REM
7040 REM S5.1 DISPLAY TRANSACTION HEADING
7050          PRINT
7060          PRINT "*** CHANGE A RECORD ***"
7070 REM
7080 REM S5.2 INPUT ATTRACTION NUMBER.
7090          PRINT
7100          PRINT "ATTRACTION NUMBER...";
7110          INPUT N2
7120 REM
7130 REM S5.3 FIND CHANGE RECORD
7140 REM
7150 REM      S5.3.1 INITIALIZE SEARCH SUBSCRIPT
7160             LET S = 1
7170 REM
7180 REM      S5.3.2 SEARCH MASTER TABLE
7190 REM         REPEAT
7200                IF S > Z       THEN GOTO 7270
7210                IF N9(S) = N2 THEN GOTO 7270
7220 REM
7230 REM            S5.3.2.1 INCREMENT SUBSCRIPT
7240                   LET S = S + 1
7250 REM
7260                GOTO 7190
7270 REM         END REPEAT
7280 REM
7290 REM S5.4 PROCESS CHANGE TRANSACTION
7300 REM      SELECT
7310             IF S > Z       THEN GOTO 7380
7320             IF N9(S) = N2 THEN GOTO 7340
7330 REM
7340 REM         S5.4.1 CHANGE MASTER RECORD
7350                GOSUB 8000
7360                GOTO  7410
7370 REM
7380 REM         S5.4.2 DISPLAY NOT-FOUND MESSAGE
7390                PRINT "*** RECORD NOT FOUND ***"
7400 REM
7410 REM      END SELECT
7420 REM
7430       RETURN
7440 REM
```

Figure 8-16. Code for Change a Record subroutine.

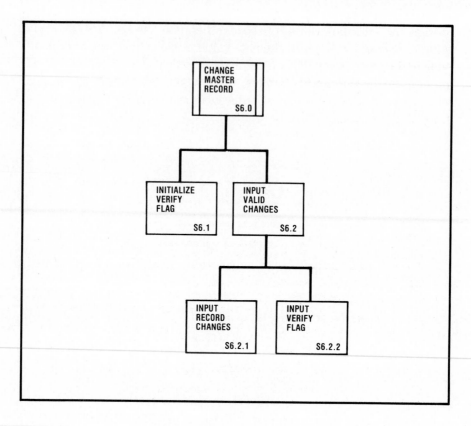

Figure 8-17. Structure chart for Change Master Record subroutine.

Deleting Records in a File

Figure 8-19 provides the design for the DELETE A RECORD subroutine and Figure 8-20 shows the code. First, the attraction number of the designated record is entered by the operator. Then, the attraction number table is searched for the corresponding number. If the record is found, subroutine S8.0 DELETE MASTER RECORD is called. Otherwise, a record-not-found message is displayed and control returns to the mainline program.

To delete a record, it is necessary to move all records below the specified record up one position in the tables. This upward movement writes over the current record. Therefore, a move subscript (S1) is set initially to the value of the search subscript (S), which points to the record

```
8000 REM *****************************
8010 REM * S6.0 CHANGE MASTER RECORD *
8020 REM *****************************
8030 REM
8040 REM S6.1 INITIALIZE VERIFY FLAG
8050          LET V$ = " "
8060 REM
8070 REM S6.2 INPUT VALID CHANGES
8080 REM      REPEAT
8090          IF V$ = "Y" THEN GOTO 8580
8100 REM
8110 REM      S6.2.1 INPUT RECORD CHANGES
8120                 PRINT
8130                 PRINT TAB(32); "CHANGE?"
8140                 PRINT TAB(32); " (Y/N) "
8150                 PRINT TAB(32); "-------"
8160 REM
8170                 PRINT "LOCATION CODE  :"; L9(S); TAB(33);
8180                     INPUT R$
8190                     IF R$ <> "Y" THEN GOTO 8230
8200                         PRINT TAB(15);
8210                         INPUT L9(S)
8220 REM
8230                 PRINT "ATTRACTION NO. :"; N9(S); TAB(33);
8240                     INPUT R$
8250                     IF R$ <> "Y" THEN GOTO 8290
8260                         PRINT TAB(15);
8270                         INPUT N9(S)
8280 REM
8290                 PRINT "ATTRACTION TYPE: "; T9$(S); TAB(33);
8300                     INPUT R$
8310                     IF R$ <> "Y" THEN GOTO 8350
8320                         PRINT TAB(15);
8330                         INPUT T9$(S)
8340 REM
8350                 PRINT "ATTRACTION NAME: "; N9$(S); TAB(33);
8360                     INPUT R$
8370                     IF R$ <> "Y" THEN GOTO 8410
8380                         PRINT TAB(15);
8390                         INPUT N9$(S)
8400 REM
8410                 PRINT "DAYS IN OPER.  :"; D9(S); TAB(33);
8420                     INPUT R$
8430                     IF R$ <> "Y" THEN GOTO 8470
8440                         PRINT TAB(15);
8450                         INPUT D9(S)
8460 REM
8470                 PRINT "ATTN. TO DATE  :"; A9(S); TAB(33);
8480                     INPUT R$
8490                     IF R$ <> "Y" THEN GOTO 8530
8500                         PRINT TAB(15);
8510                         INPUT A9(S)
8520 REM
8530 REM      S6.2.2 INPUT VERIFY FLAG
8540                 PRINT "  VERIFY (Y/N)";
8550                 INPUT V$
8560 REM
8570          GOTO 8080
8580 REM      END REPEAT
8590 REM
8600     RETURN
8610 REM
```

Figure 8-18. Code for Change Master Record subroutine.

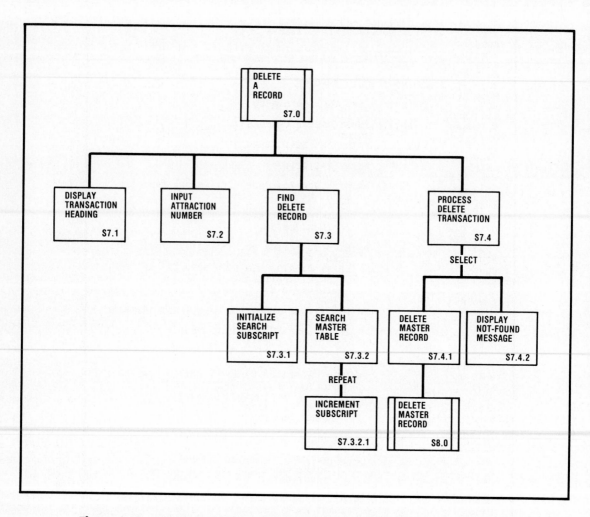

Figure 8-19. Structure chart for Delete a Record subroutine.

```
9000 REM *************************
9010 REM * S7.0 DELETE A RECORD *
9020 REM *************************
9030 REM
9040 REM S7.1 DISPLAY TRANSACTION HEADING
9050          PRINT
9060          PRINT "*** DELETE A RECORD ***"
9070 REM
9080 REM S7.2 INPUT ATTRACTION NUMBER
9090          PRINT
9100          PRINT "ATTRACTION NUMBER...";
9110          INPUT N3
9120 REM
9130 REM S7.3 FIND DELETE RECORD
9140 REM
9150 REM      S7.3.1 INITIALIZE SEARCH SUBSCRIPT
9160               LET S = 1
9170 REM
9180 REM      S7.3.2 SEARCH MASTER TABLE
9190 REM           REPEAT
9200               IF S > Z      THEN GOTO 9270
9210               IF N9(S) = N3 THEN GOTO 9270
9220 REM
9230 REM           S7.3.2.1 INCREMENT SUBSCRIPT
9240                    LET S = S + 1
9250 REM
9260               GOTO 9190
9270 REM           END REPEAT
9280 REM
9290 REM S7.4 PROCESS DELETE TRANSACTION
9300 REM      SELECT
9310          IF S > Z      THEN GOTO 9380
9320          IF N9(S) = N3 THEN GOTO 9340
9330 REM
9340 REM      S7.4.1 DELETE MASTER RECORD
9350               GOSUB 9500
9360               GOTO  9410
9370 REM
9380 REM      S7.4.2 DISPLAY NOT-FOUND MESSAGE
9390               PRINT "*** RECORD NOT FOUND ***"
9400 REM
9410 REM      END SELECT
9420 REM
9430     RETURN
9440 REM
```

Figure 8-20. Code for Delete a Record subroutine.

to be deleted. The next record in the table, identified by subscript S1 + 1, is assigned to the deleted record's position, identified by subscript S1. The move subscript is incremented by 1 and the next record is moved up. This processing continues until the end of the table is reached. Finally, the table length variable (Z) is decreased by 1 to account for the deleted record. Design and code for this subroutine, S8.0 DELETE MASTER RECORD, are given in Figures 8-21 and 8-22. An illustration of the deletion steps is shown in Figure 8-23.

Writing the New File

After all additions, changes, and deletions have been made within the program tables, a new master file is written. In subroutine S9.0 WRITE NEW MASTER FILE, all of the records represented in the tables are written to file FUNUP. The table size variable (Z) is used as an end-of-table

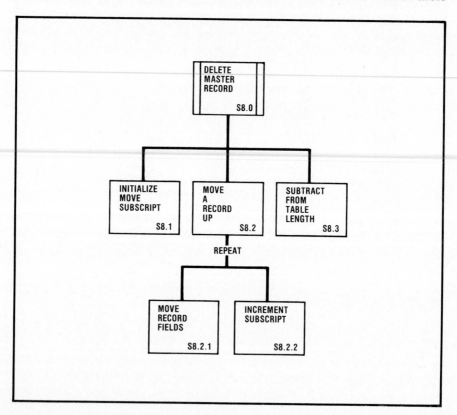

Figure 8-21. Structure chart for Delete Master Record subroutine.

```
9500 REM *****************************
9510 REM * S8.0 DELETE MASTER RECORD *
9520 REM *****************************
9530 REM
9540 REM S8.1 INITIALIZE MOVE SUBSCRIPT
9550         LET S1 = S
9560 REM
9570 REM S8.2 MOVE A RECORD UP
9580 REM      REPEAT
9590         IF S1 = Z THEN GOTO 9730
9600 REM
9610 REM      S8.2.1 MOVE RECORD FIELDS
9620              LET L9(S1)  = L9(S1+1)
9630              LET N9(S1)  = N9(S1+1)
9640              LET T9$(S1) = T9$(S1+1)
9650              LET N9$(S1) = N9$(S1+1)
9660              LET D9(S1)  = D9(S1+1)
9670              LET A9(S1)  = A9(S1+1)
9680 REM
9690 REM      S8.2.2 INCREMENT SUBSCRIPT
9700              LET S1 = S1 + 1
9710 REM
9720             GOTO 9580
9730 REM      END REPEAT
9740 REM
9750 REM S8.3 SUBTRACT FROM TABLE LENGTH
9760              LET Z = Z - 1
9770 REM
9780     RETURN
9790 REM
```

Figure 8-22. Code for Delete Master Record subroutine.

---

indicator to signal all records have been written. Finally, an EOF record is placed in the new file and the file is closed. Control returns to the mainline program, an end-of-program message is displayed, and execution is halted. See Figures 8-24 and 8-25.

At this point, two versions of the master file exist—FUNMF is the original version and FUNUP contains the changes. Therefore, to become the current version of the master file, the new file must be renamed FUNMF. First, FUNMF is deleted by using system commands such as DELETE FUNMF, KILL FUNMF, or the command that is appropriate to your system. Then, the updated file is given the new name by using a command such as the following: RENAME FUNUP, FUNMF or NAME "FUNUP" AS "FUNMF". Now, the updated file can replace the old master file within the system.

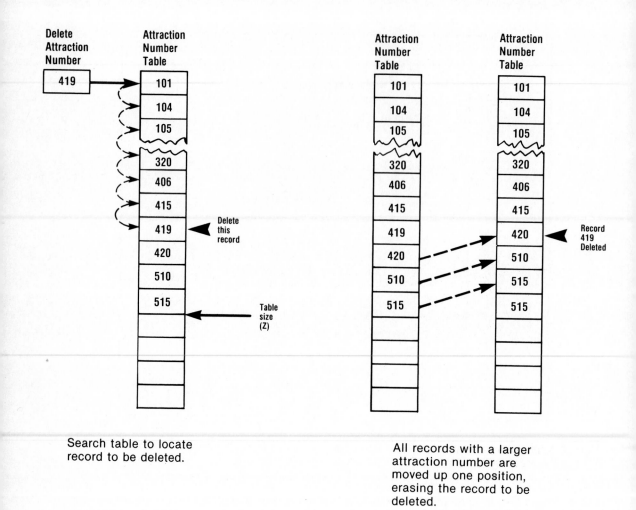

Search table to locate record to be deleted.

All records with a larger attraction number are moved up one position, erasing the record to be deleted.

Figure 8-23. Procedure for deleting records from table files.

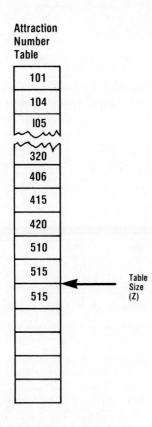

Attraction Number Table

101
104
l05
320
406
415
420
510
515
515

Table Size (Z)

Table size (Z) adjusted to account for the deleted record. Although the last record in the file remains duplicated, processing will not be affected because the logical table size does not include the duplicate.

NOTE: All fields in all the records are repositioned in the tables.

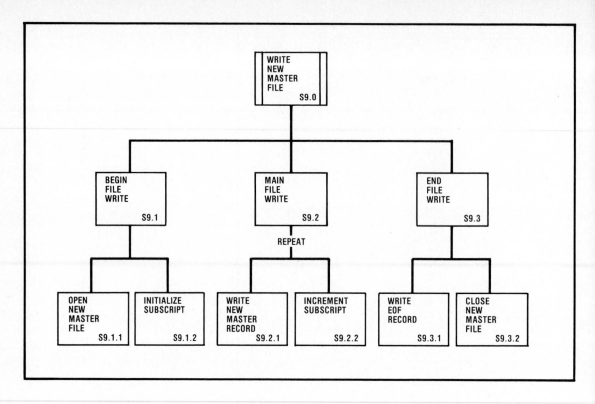

Figure 8-24. Structure chart for Write New Master File subroutine.

LOGGING TRANSACTIONS

Consider that the most recent transaction file, FUNTF, and the master file against which those transactions were posted, FUNBK, were saved. Now, however, interactive changes may be made to the master file individually and directly, without creation of a transaction file. Thus, additions, changes, and deletions are not recorded on storage media for backup and recovery. This means, in turn, that separate procedures are needed for backup and recovery.

As part of file maintenance procedures, magnetic *log files* normally are maintained within interactive update systems. That is, all additions, changes, and deletions are written in chronological order to a disk file. These log records usually include the date of updating, an identification of the affected master record, and an indication of the changes that were made. Routines to write log records are included within the maintenance programs.

Log files, then, can be used to rebuild master files for which batch transaction files are not used. Log files also provide an *audit trail* from

```
10000 REM ******************************
10010 REM * S9.0 WRITE NEW MASTER FILE *
10020 REM ******************************
10030 REM
10040 REM S9.1 BEGIN FILE WRITE
10050 REM
10060 REM      S9.1.1 OPEN NEW MASTER FILE
10070             OPEN "FUNUP" FOR OUTPUT AS FILE #2
10080 REM
10090 REM      S9.1.2 INITIALIZE SUBSCRIPT
10100             LET S = 1
10110 REM
10120 REM S9.2 MAIN FILE WRITE
10130 REM      REPEAT
10140             IF S > Z THEN GOTO 10250
10150 REM
10160 REM      S9.2.1 WRITE NEW MASTER RECORD
10170             PRINT #2, L9(S); ","; N9(S); ",";
10180             PRINT #2, T9$(S); ","; N9$(S); ",";
10190             PRINT #2, D9(S); ","; A9(S)
10200 REM
10210 REM      S9.2.2 INCREMENT SUBSCRIPT
10220             LET S = S + 1
10230 REM
10240             GOTO 10130
10250 REM      END REPEAT
10260 REM
10270 REM S9.3 END FILE WRITE
10280 REM
10290 REM      S9.3.1 WRITE EOF RECORD
10300             PRINT #2, "0, 0, 0, END OF FILE, 0, 0"
10310 REM
10320 REM      S9.3.2 CLOSE NEW MASTER FILE
10330             CLOSE #2
10340 REM
10350      RETURN
10360 END
```

Figure 8-25. Code for Write New Master File subroutine.

which original transactions can be traced from point of origin to the appearance of the transactions within master files. An audit trail represents one of many accounting or security measures that insure the integrity of file data.

Magnetic log files have not been used in the amusement park system. In this case, though, the printed listing of the maintenance program run must be used as the log file. All changes to the master file are documented on the printout, and the printed log should be retained within a manual file. If the master file is destroyed, the hard-copy log can be retrieved and used to re-enter changes to the file. Thus, an audit trail is provided for retracing transactions, even though no transaction file is created.

Figure 8-26 illustrates this printed log. An addition, change, and deletion have been made to the park attraction master file. Figure 8-27 shows a processing run in which transaction errors occur.

ZERO-BALANCE PROGRAM

The Amusement Park Information System will be fully operational with the addition of a zero-balance program. This simple program resets the days-in-operation and attendance-to-date fields of the master records to zero. At the beginning of each month, this program will be run so that monthly balances can be accumulated. A new master file (FUNNM) is created, which will be renamed as FUNMF at the start of the monthly cycle. Specifications for this program are given in Figure 8-28. The design and code appear in Figures 8-29 and 8-30.

Figure 8-31 shows the output from program FUN02, the master file detail report program. The list represents the attraction master file contents following an illustrative run of the maintenance program and the zero-balance program. New records were added and old records changed and deleted. Then, all balances were reset to zero.

SYSTEM OPERATING CYCLES

A CIS functions on an ongoing, daily basis within specified operating cycles and is reinitialized periodically for the next cycle. These operating cycles include daily activities repeated each day for one month. Monthly functions are repeated each month for one quarter. Quarterly activities are repeated every three months for one year.

Some systems process within shorter cycles and/or longer cycles. The point remains, however, that, once created, the computer information system operates within a hierarchy of cycles. Figure 8-32 presents the repetitive functions and reinitialization functions used within processing cycles.

The tasks of designing and programming a computer information system can be anticipated by identifying the processing cycles, the output of those cycles, and, hence, the programs required to implement the system. These programs probably will be drawn from file creation, file updating, report writing, and inquiry programs similar to those developed in the previous chapters.

```
****************************
* MASTER FILE MAINTENANCE *
****************************

        ADD NEW RECORD....A
        CHANGE A RECORD...C
        DELETE A RECORD...D
        STOP..............S

ENTER CODE...? A

*** ADD NEW RECORD ***

LOCATION CODE........? 10
ATTRACTION NUMBER....? 100
ATTRACTION TYPE......? C
ATTRACTION NAME......? FANTASY
DAYS IN OPERATION....? 0
ATTENDANCE TO DATE...? 0
   VERIFY (Y/N)......? Y

        ADD NEW RECORD....A
        CHANGE A RECORD...C
        DELETE A RECORD...D
        STOP..............S

ENTER CODE...? C

*** CHANGE A RECORD ***

ATTRACTION NUMBER...? 510

                             CHANGE?
                             (Y/N)
                             -------
LOCATION CODE  : 50          ? N
ATTRACTION NO. : 510         ? N
ATTRACTION TYPE: F           ? N
ATTRACTION NAME: FRONTIER DAYS  ? N
DAYS IN OPER.  : 4           ? N
ATTN. TO DATE  : 166         ? Y
                 ? 195
   VERIFY (Y/N)? Y

        ADD NEW RECORD....A
        CHANGE A RECORD...C
        DELETE A RECORD...D
        STOP..............S

ENTER CODE...? D

*** DELETE A RECORD ***

ATTRACTION NUMBER...? 310

        ADD NEW RECORD....A
        CHANGE A RECORD...C
        DELETE A RECORD...D
        STOP..............S

ENTER CODE...? S

*** END OF PROCESSING ***
```

Figure 8-26. Printed display of run of maintenance program retained as transaction log.

```
****************************
* MASTER FILE MAINTENANCE *
****************************

        ADD NEW RECORD....A
        CHANGE A RECORD...C
        DELETE A RECORD...D
        STOP..............S

ENTER CODE...? X
*** ENTER CORRECT CODE ***
? A

*** ADD NEW RECORD ***

LOCATION CODE........? 50
ATTRACTION NUMBER....? 510
ATTRACTION TYPE......? F
ATTRACTION NAME......? FRONTIER DAYS
DAYS IN OPERATION....? 4
ATTENDANCE TO DATE...? 166
   VERIFY (Y/N)......? Y
*** RECORD ALREADY EXISTS ***

        ADD NEW RECORD....A
        CHANGE A RECORD...C
        DELETE A RECORD...D
        STOP..............S

ENTER CODE...? C

*** CHANGE A RECORD ***

ATTRACTION NUMBER...? 50
*** RECORD NOT FOUND ***

        ADD NEW RECORD....A
        CHANGE A RECORD...C
        DELETE A RECORD...D
        STOP..............S

ENTER CODE...? D

*** DELETE A RECORD ***

ATTRACTION NUMBER...? 50
*** RECORD NOT FOUND ***

        ADD NEW RECORD....A
        CHANGE A RECORD...C
        DELETE A RECORD...D
        STOP..............S

ENTER CODE...? S

*** END OF PROCESSING ***
```

Figure 8-27. Run of maintenance program showing error in processing.

<u>PROGRAMMING SPECIFICATIONS</u>

System: AMUSEMENT PARK   Date: 05/12/XX
Program: ZERO BALANCES   Program I.D.: FUN11   Analyst: B. LEIGH

Design and write a program to initialize the days-in-operation and attendance-
to-date fields of the attraction master file (FUNMF). Output will be a new
master file (FUNNM) with these two fields set to zero. The program will be
written in BASIC. Figure 8-28.1 shows the system flowchart for this
application.

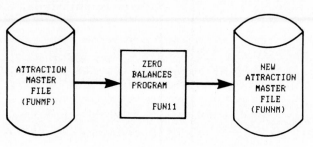

Figure 8-28.1

<u>INPUT</u>

The attraction master file (FUNMF) is the program input. The format of records
is as follows:

Field Name	Data Type
Location Code	Numeric
Attraction Number	Numeric
Attraction Type	Alphanumeric
Attraction Name	Alphanumeric
Days in Operation	Numeric
Attendance to Date	Numeric

<u>PROCESSING</u>

The days-in-operation and attendance-to-date fields are initialized to zero. A
record counter is incremented for each record in the file.

<u>OUTPUT</u>

Output will be a new attraction master file (FUNNM) in the same format as the
current file. A final EOF record will be written to the file.

Figure 8-28.   Programming specifications for zero balances program.

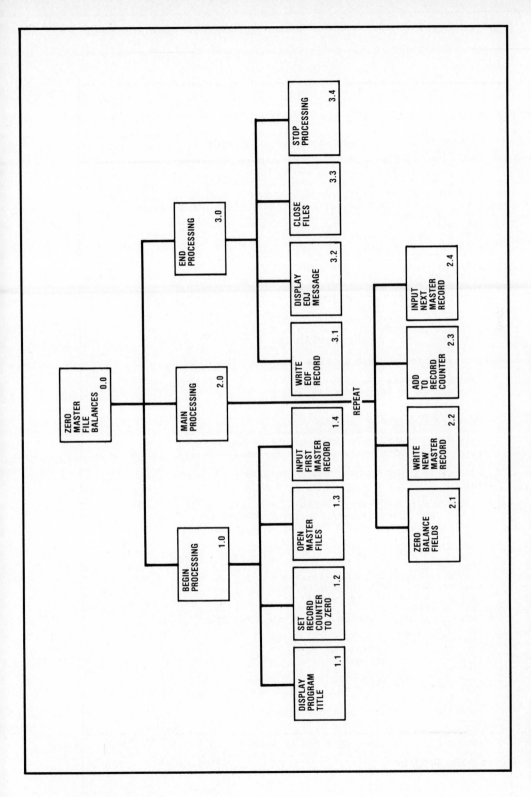

Figure 8-29. Structure chart for zero master file balances program (FUN11).

```
1000 REM FUN11                                          WEL/DRA
1010 REM               ZERO MASTER FILE BALANCES
1020 REM
1030 REM THIS PROGRAM RESETS THE DAYS IN OPERATION AND
1040 REM ATTENDANCE TO DATE FIELDS OF THE AMUSEMENT PARK
1050 REM MASTER FILE (FUNMF) TO ZERO.  A NEW FILE (FUNNM) IS
1060 REM CREATED.  THIS PROGRAM IS RUN AT THE END OF EACH
1070 REM MONTH TO ZERO OUT BALANCES TO BEGIN ACCUMULATING
1080 REM TOTALS FOR THE FOLLOWING MONTH.
1090 REM
1100 REM VARIABLE NAMES
1110 REM
1120 REM INPUT/OUTPUT RECORD:
1130 REM     L....LOCATION CODE
1140 REM     N....ATTRACTION NUMBER
1150 REM     T$...ATTRACTION TYPE
1160 REM     N$...ATTRACTION NAME
1170 REM     D....DAYS IN OPERATION
1180 REM     A....ATTENDANCE TO DATE
1190 REM COUNTERS:
1200 REM     C....RECORD COUNTER
1210 REM
1220 REM 0.0 ZERO MASTER FILE BALANCES
1230 REM
1240 REM ************************
1250 REM * 1.0 BEGIN PROCESSING *
1260 REM ************************
1270 REM
1280 REM 1.1 DISPLAY PROGRAM TITLE
1290          PRINT "*****************************"
1300          PRINT "* ZERO MASTER FILE BALANCES *"
1310          PRINT "*****************************"
1320 REM
1330 REM 1.2 SET RECORD COUNTER TO ZERO
1340          LET C = 0
1350 REM
1360 REM 1.3 OPEN MASTER FILES
1370          OPEN "FUNMF" FOR INPUT AS FILE #1
1380          OPEN "FUNNM" FOR OUTPUT AS FILE #2
1390 REM
1400 REM 1.4 INPUT FIRST MASTER RECORD
1410          INPUT #1, L, N, T$, N$, D, A
1420 REM
1430 REM ************************
1440 REM * 2.0 MAIN PROCESSING  *
1450 REM ************************
1460 REM REPEAT
1470     IF N$ = "END OF FILE" THEN GOTO 1630
1480 REM
1490 REM   2.1 ZERO BALANCE FIELDS
1500            LET D = 0
1510            LET A = 0
1520 REM
1530 REM   2.2 WRITE NEW MASTER RECORD
1540            PRINT #2, L;",";N;",";T$;",";N$;",";D;",";A
1550 REM
1560 REM   2.3 ADD TO RECORD COUNTER
1570            LET C = C + 1
1580 REM
1590 REM   2.4 INPUT NEXT MASTER RECORD
1600            INPUT #1, L, N, T$, N$, D, A
1610 REM
```

```
1620      GOTO 1460
1630 REM END REPEAT
1640 REM
1650 REM ************************
1660 REM * 3.0 END PROCESSING    *
1670 REM ************************
1680 REM
1690 REM 3.1 WRITE EOF RECORD
1700      PRINT #2, "0, 0, 0, END OF FILE, 0, 0"
1710 REM
1720 REM 3.2 DISPLAY EOJ MESSAGE
1730      PRINT
1740      PRINT "MASTER FILE ZEROED"
1750      PRINT C; "RECORDS PROCESSED"
1760 REM
1770 REM 3.3 CLOSE FILES
1780      CLOSE #1
1790      CLOSE #2
1800 REM
1810 REM 3.4 STOP PROCESSING
1820      STOP
1830 END
```

Figure 8-30. Code for zero master file balances program (FUN11).

LISTING OF MASTER FILE FUNMF

LOC. CODE	ATTR. NO.	ATTR. TYPE	ATTRACTION NAME	DAYS IN OPER.	ATTENDANCE TO DATE
10	100	C	FANTASY	0	0
10	101	A	THE BLAZER	0	0
10	105	F	KREEPY KASTLE	0	0
20	201	C	KIDDIE KAR	0	0
20	202	F	PIRATE'S COVE	0	0
20	207	F	JUNGLE SAFARI	0	0
20	210	A	DEVIL'S PIT	0	0
30	312	C	MERRY MOUSE	0	0
30	315	F	GUNGA DIN'S	0	0
30	320	F	WILD CHICKEN	0	0
40	406	A	CRASHIN' CARS	0	0
40	419	F	MUSIC SHOW	0	0
40	420	A	THE CORKSCREW	0	0
50	510	F	FRONTIER DAYS	0	0
50	515	F	SPACE PROBE	0	0
50	520	A	THE SHRIEK	0	0
470	4,863			0	0

TOTAL RECORDS: 16

Figure 8-31. Listing of attraction master file (using program FUN02) following run of zero-balance program (FUN11).

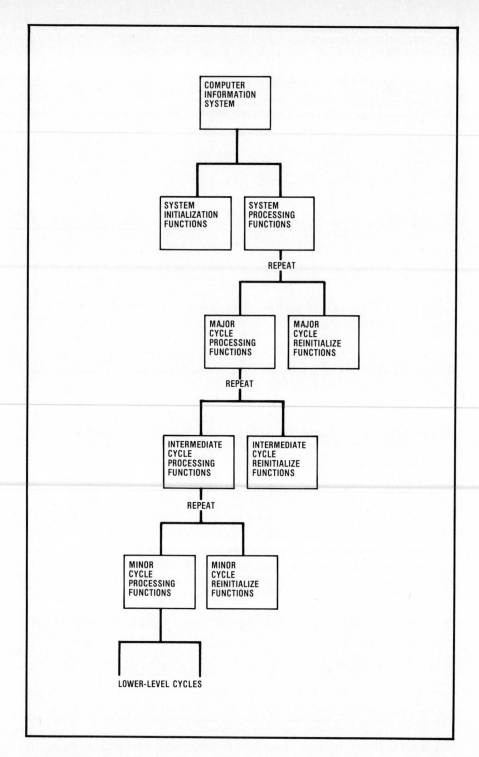

Figure 8-32. General model of computer information systems processing cycles.

Figure 8-33 presents an organized, cyclical hierarchy of the programs used in the Amusement Park Information System. The illustration indicates the point in the course of operations at which each program is to be run. This system, like most information systems, makes no provision for terminating system processing. It is expected that this system, including any additions to be made, will be in production indefinitely, or at least until the business functions that the system supports are no longer needed.

Figure 8-34 presents the Amusement Park Information System flowchart, which indicates the relationships between the system's hardware and software resources. In its current form, the system provides features common to most data processing and management information systems. Although simplified in terms of the amount of data maintained and the amount of information produced, the Amusement Park Information System serves as a realistic model for countless other systems. The system model demonstrates how programs, data files, and manual procedures are integrated within systems to perform common business computing functions.

THE COMPLETE PROGRAMMER

It is important to realize that most of the programs you will write as a professional programmer will be components of systems. A particular program will not exist in isolation, unrelated to other programs you might write. Rather, the programs you write will affect, and will be affected by, programs written by others. Extensive systems of programs are needed to handle business applications. An understanding of the system of programs with which you are involved should make you a better programmer.

A systems viewpoint also can help to increase the value of your programming skills. The main purpose of any program or any system of programs is to contribute to an organization's growth, development, and success. Although technical programming skills are important, your contributions to a business will be measured largely by your ability to use these skills in pursuit of organizational goals. The perspective used in this book is designed to promote an understanding of the business system that underlies the technical hardware/software system. Thus, the systems perspective encourages you to consider the impact of your technical efforts upon the company's overall information needs.

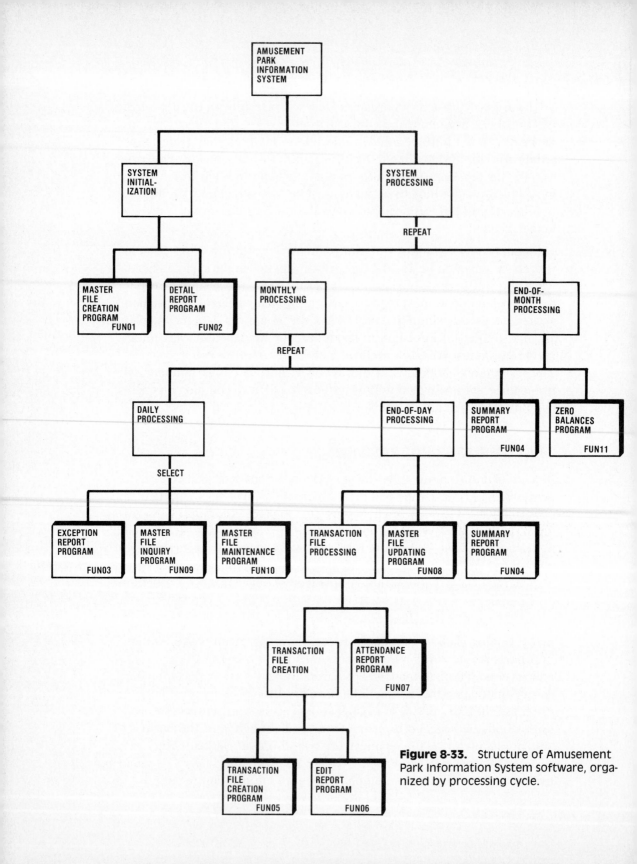

Figure 8-33. Structure of Amusement Park Information System software, organized by processing cycle.

Figure 8-34. System flowchart for Amusement Park Information System.

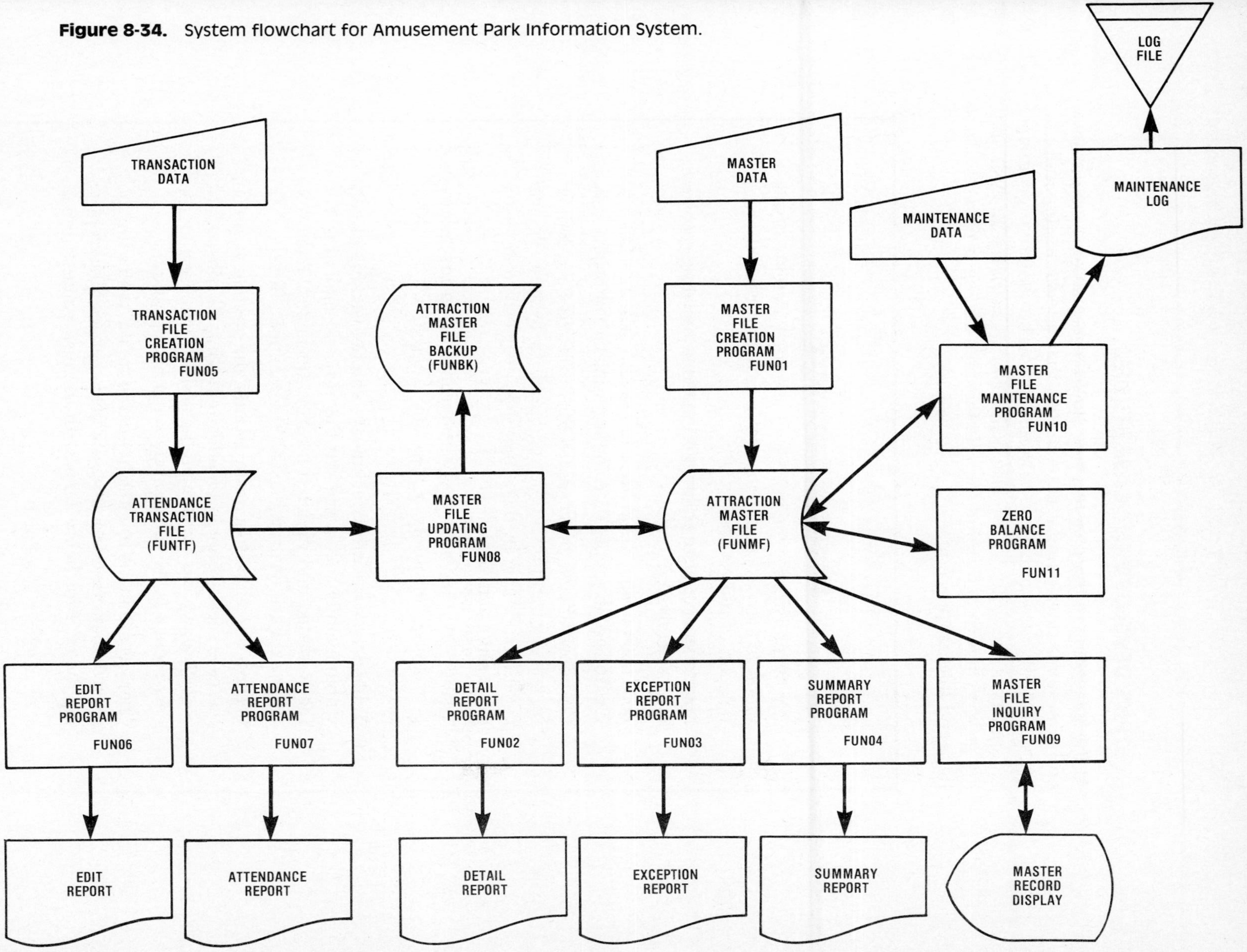

SYSTEMS DEVELOPMENT CASE STUDIES

At the completion of this chapter, you should be prepared to begin work on the systems development case studies that appear in Appendix B. These assignments require you to design and write computer programs to implement the systems. You also will perform necessary analysis and design activities to determine the relationships among programs, data files, and manual procedures.

Chapter Summary

1. File maintenance is the process of altering files with the addition of new records, changes in existing records, and deletion of old records.

2. Maintenance, unlike posting, is limited to updating records with selective changes.

3. Zero balancing is the process of resetting amount fields in files to zero in preparation for accumulation of cycle totals.

4. CIS information is processed within cycles that are defined by key events in the operating life of the system. Typical cycles are defined by daily, monthly, quarterly, and yearly processing activities.

5. Posting, maintenance, and zero-balance programs assure processing continuity across any number of operating cycles.

6. Table-driven updating techniques can be used effectively within maintenance programs that process small files. The file is loaded and updated in program tables. Then, the table data are written back to the magnetic file.

7. Records are added to a file by locating the position at which the new record should be added, moving all subsequent records down one position in the tables, then inserting the new record in its appropriate sequential position.

8. Changes are made to a file by searching the tables for the record of interest, inputting the field changes, then replacing the current field values with the new values.

9. Deletions from a file require that the tables first be searched for the appropriate record. Then, all subsequent records are moved up one position in the tables to overwrite the deleted record.

10. During file additions and deletions, the variable representing the logical size of the tables must be adjusted to reflect the file modifications.

11. Some type of transaction logging procedure must be established for keeping track of maintenance changes. In most interactive systems, a log file of transactions is kept. Transaction information is written to this file as the updates occur. In other systems, the printed output from the terminal session can be used. Regardless of the procedure used, the intent is to record file updates so that an inadvertently destroyed file can be recovered.

12. Transaction logs also provide an audit trail. An audit trail is a continuous record of transaction processing from the point of a transaction's origin to its appearance as a file update.

13. The tasks of designing and programming a computer information system can be anticipated by identifying the processing cycles, the output from those cycles, and, hence, the programs required to implement the system.

14. Programmers typically are involved in writing systems of programs. Gaining a systems perspective contributes to the effectiveness and value of a programmer. This perspective entails a joint understanding of the technical system of programs and the business system that underlies the programs.

Review Questions

1. What is file maintenance and what general processing activities are performed by maintenance procedures?

2. What is a processing cycle and how does this term relate to CIS operations?

3. What is zero balancing?

4. Why are magnetic log files maintained within interactive update systems?

5. Considering that a CIS operates within a hierarchy of cycles, how can a programmer anticipate the tasks of designing and programming a CIS?

6. Why is a systems perspective helpful to a computer programmer?

Programming Assignments

Programming practice assignments for Chapter 8 are located in Appendix A, CASE STUDY ONE and CASE STUDY TWO.

Key Terms

1. maintenance
2. processing cycle
3. zero balancing
4. log files
5. audit trail

III
FILE PROCESSING

Parts I and II of the text explain the development of programs that, together, are integrated to implement a business system. However, computer files for businesses frequently reach sizes that cannot be managed using the processing techniques provided in Chapters 1 through 8.

Part III, therefore, explains techniques for processing large-scale files that exceed the capacities of memory and/or require special, more efficient methods of organization and access. Chapter 9 explains methods of accessing records one at a time, in any order, within a system that maintains thousands, or even millions, of records. Chapter 10 describes the principles and processes used to handle and maintain sequential files that are too large to fit into main memory in their entirety. Chapter 11 discusses advanced BASIC techniques for organizing files and accessing records. These processing concepts are really problem-solving methods that can be used for systems in which the type of business dictates, or at least suggests, the need for tailor-made file processing techniques.

9
PROCESSING DIRECT-ACCESS FILES

OVERVIEW AND OBJECTIVES

This chapter marks a transition in the building of your programming skills. In working through Chapters 1 through 8, you have gained experience in creating and using simple files and in applying the data to a hypothetical business system. Also, you have gained a foundation-level knowledge of computer-based information systems. At this point, you are aware of the types of programs included in typical business information systems, and you have gained experience in designing and writing systems of programs to implement business applications on computers.

So far, your work has involved systems that have been simplified purposely as a basis for learning. Actual business applications are more complex. This chapter and the two that follow are designed to build your understanding and skills in the development of realistic business systems.

Specifically, the files you have encountered thus far have been relatively trivial in size by normal business standards. These files were scaled down to fit into computer memory in their entirety. Such small files allowed you to concentrate on basic computer processing techniques. Thus, you could avoid the complications of large file processing systems. As the memory capacity of microcomputers increases, such approaches can be workable and realistic for personal systems or for systems that support small businesses. However, in the overall business programming environment, it becomes necessary to build files that exceed the capacities of main memory. Thus, the computer must search external, or secondary, storage devices to retrieve and process an individual record only. After the record has been updated, it is written back to secondary storage, and other records are retrieved one at a time.

This chapter discusses direct-access files. Chapter 10 covers sequential files. Chapter 11 discusses transaction processing systems that use combinations of file processing techniques. When you complete your work in this chapter, you should be able to:

☐ Describe direct-access file processing techniques.

☐ Describe and explain how disk files function as direct-access media.

☐ Describe the organization of direct-access files housed on disk devices.

☐ Design and code programs to create direct-access files.

☐ Design and code programs to access direct-access files.

☐ Design and code programs to maintain direct-access files.

HANDLING SMALL FILES

Consider the schematic drawing in Figure 9-1. As shown in this diagram, entire files used for programs described in earlier chapters have been copied into memory. Enough capacity existed in memory to handle all of the programs and files to be used. Techniques for processing files have, in effect, been transparent to the programs you have written. The formats of files have been the same, logically, whether the files existed in memory or on disk.

Think back to the file organization description in Chapter 3. In that chapter, files are introduced and conceptualized as two-dimensional tables. That is, each file is viewed as a series of rows that represent records. The records, in turn, fit into a series of columns, representing fields. All processing is accomplished within the file (table) residing in memory. At the conclusion of processing, the entire updated table is written back to disk.

Both computer memory and disk devices store data in comparable logical units—fields make up records, which make up files. A file built in memory can be written directly onto the surface of a disk in the order in which the records appear in memory. Thus, file handling between disk and memory is accomplished through a straightforward transfer of equal, correspondingly organized units of data.

As long as an entire file is processed as a unit, it makes no difference where or how the data are written on disk or where data are placed in memory when they are recalled. The computer's operating system

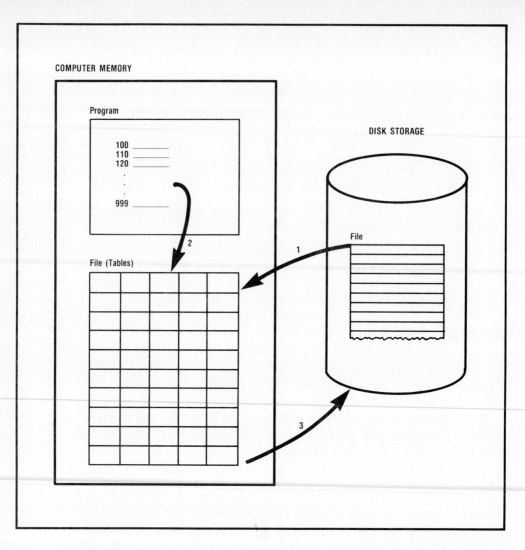

Figure 9-1. Up to this point, files have been processed by (1) copying the entire file into memory and holding it within tables, (2) performing all processing within the tables, and then (3) writing the entire file back onto the storage disk.

handles the transfers. The software builds and maintains directories that relate file names to disk addresses. When a file is processed, its name is passed to the operating system by the program. Then, the system looks in the directory, finds the location of the file, and delivers the entire set of data to the program. The software determines the location in which the file will fit into memory. Also, the software manages data transfers.

All of these processing steps remain simple as long as the system is handling complete files that can be retrieved and processed as complete units within memory. However, many job situations require locating, accessing, and processing individual records one at a time. In these cases, program logic becomes slightly more complex. As a programmer, you must know the organizational approach used to maintain records on the storage device. Also, you must devise methods for accessing and writing records one at a time.

DIRECT-ACCESS FILE PROCESSING

Magnetic disk devices are referred to as *direct-access* media. This term indicates that disk devices present a capability for accessing any one record within a file without the need to search sequentially through the file. Again, recall the processing technique used in previous programs. A file is loaded into tables within memory. To locate a particular record within the file, the tables are searched sequentially, beginning with the first record, until the desired record is found. Fields within the corresponding table elements then are processed individually.

For files stored on disk, however, sequential searching is unnecessary. Any single record can be located within the disk file, accessed and delivered into memory, and then returned to the same disk location following updating. This capability is a necessity for processing certain types of large files.

Figure 9-2 illustrates direct-access file processing. This diagram shows a large file stored on disk. During processing, the program issues a call for a particular record within the file. The system locates the record and makes it available to the program. Following processing, the updated record is written back to the file at the same location from which the original record was retrieved. Direct-access file techniques are most appropriate when:

- Only a few records within the file will be accessed at any one time.
- It is impossible to anticipate the order in which the records will be accessed.

Direct access meets a requirement for *random,* or unpredictable, use of a limited number of records. Examples of the types of systems that require direct access might include inventory management systems, hotel and airline reservation systems, or systems that allow banking transactions through automatic teller machines.

The automatic banking system is a commonplace example. A bank may have records for a million or more accounts maintained on multiple

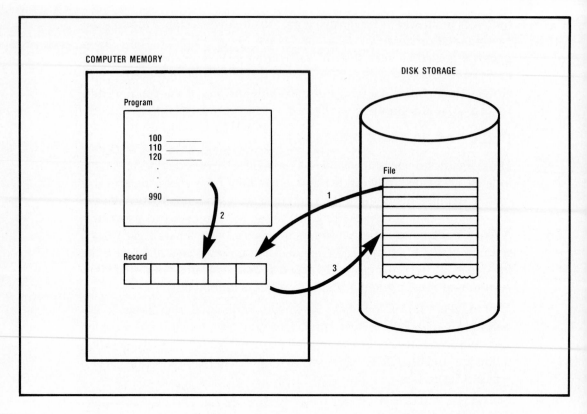

Figure 9-2. For large files, only a single record at a time is processed. Within direct-access files: (1) one record is brought into memory, (2) the record is processed, and then (3) it is written back to the storage disk to replace the original record.

disks. A customer cannot be expected to stand patiently in front of the teller machine while the computer searches sequentially for a single record. Direct-access file processing techniques are necessary for the bank to serve waiting customers quickly. To implement direct-access capabilities, records require the following characteristics:

- Records in a direct-access file must be uniform in length, or *fixed-length files.* That is, the same number of characters must be allocated for each record in the file. Further, records must contain fields that are consistent in sequence and length.

- A logical key must be used to identify the physical location of the record in the file. Usually, a record's location is given by its position relative to the first record in the file. Therefore, the key is used as the relative record number, or is used to derive the relative position of the record in the file. For this reason, a direct-access file is often referred to as a *relative file*.

• Each record in a direct-access file requires a *status code* field. The value in this field indicates whether the record area contains a data record or is unoccupied. Normally, before the file is created, the disk area is initialized, or preformatted. A *null*, or *dummy*, record is written to each record position in the file. A null record contains only spaces and/or zeros in its fields. This technique sets aside sufficient disk space to hold the entire file—plus space for expansion. Initially, each null record normally is assigned a status code of 0 (zero) to indicate that the space is available for adding a record at that location. When the actual data file is created, each added record is given a status code of 1 to indicate that the record position is occupied by an actual data record.

INITIALIZING DIRECT-ACCESS FILES

To implement a direct-access file in BASIC, it usually is necessary to set aside and format the disk area. In effect, an initialized file is a set of electronic "pigeonholes" in which data records will be placed. Thus, initializing a file creates the entire file structure.

The following situation provides an example of direct-access file initialization. A hotel wishes to develop a computerized registration system. The focal point of this system will be a master file of room occupancy. Each record in this file will contain information on the daily room charge, the name of the guest registered in the room, the guest's date of arrival, and the expected departure date. The file will be used for registering guests and for determining room charges based on the daily rate and the length of occupancy. The hotel has rooms numbered from 01 to 99.

The master file will be named HOTEL. Direct access is necessary for this file because rooms are not assigned, nor are room records processed, in any predetermined sequence. Guests reserve rooms in no particular order, and room charges are processed whenever guests check out.

A schematic of the initialized hotel room file is shown in Figure 9-3. Note that the file can be visualized as a table with rows representing the records, and columns representing the record fields. All records and all

Status Code	Room No.	Room Rate	Occupant Name	Arrival Date	Departure Date
0	01	0	ƀ	ƀ	ƀ
0	02	0	ƀ	ƀ	ƀ
0	03	0	ƀ	ƀ	ƀ
0	04	0	ƀ	ƀ	ƀ
0	05	0	ƀ	ƀ	ƀ
0	06	0	ƀ	ƀ	ƀ
0	07	0	ƀ	ƀ	ƀ
.	.	.	.	.	.
.	.	.	.	.	.
.	.	.	.	.	.
0	99	0	ƀ	ƀ	ƀ

Figure 9-3. HOTEL direct-access file following initialization. All status codes are set to zero to indicate the presence of null records. Room number keys also refer to the relative positions of the records in the file.

fields are of fixed length. The room number is used as the record key. Because the room numbers range from 01 to 99, they can be used also as *pointers* to the relative positions of the records in the file. That is, the record for room number 01 is positioned first in the file; the record for room number 02 is positioned second, and so on. Therefore, the room number also relates the location of a record to the first record in the file.

The initialized file, apart from the room number fields, contains zero values in all numeric fields, and blank spaces in all alphanumeric fields. A total of 99 initialized record positions is formatted to accept data records. The status code field appended to each record is set initially to 0.

Once the master file has been formatted on disk, the file is available for adding data records within the record positions. Figure 9-4 shows the effect of placing records within the file. As room reservations are made,

Status Code	Room No.	Room Rate	Occupant Name	Arrival Date	Departure Date
0	01	0	ƀ	ƀ	ƀ
1	02	24.00	ALICE COOK	83/09/12	83/09/13
1	03	55.00	JASON SMALL	83/09/15	83/09/20
0	04	0	ƀ	ƀ	ƀ
1	05	24.00	BART BRANDON	83/10/06	83/10/08
0	06	0	ƀ	ƀ	ƀ
1	07	65.00	MARY JAMES	83/11/10	83/11/15
.	.	.	.	.	.
.	.	.	.	.	.
0	99	0	ƀ	ƀ	ƀ

Figure 9-4. HOTEL direct-access file following addition of original records. Status codes for all record positions containing data are set to 1.

the null records for the associated rooms are retrieved from the file. The appropriate information is added to the fields. Then, the records are written back to the file and replace the initialized records at the same locations. During this updating, the status code fields are assigned the value 1. These particular rooms are not available for assignment.

To initialize a direct-access file, a program is needed to write a null record for each data record anticipated for the file. This program is relatively straightforward, as shown in the structure chart in Figure 9-5. The structure chart provides a general model for direct-access file initialization programs. Pseudocode for this generalized program appears in Figure 9-6.

Figure 9-7 is an example of BASIC code for a file initialization program. This program is based on the general model and establishes the

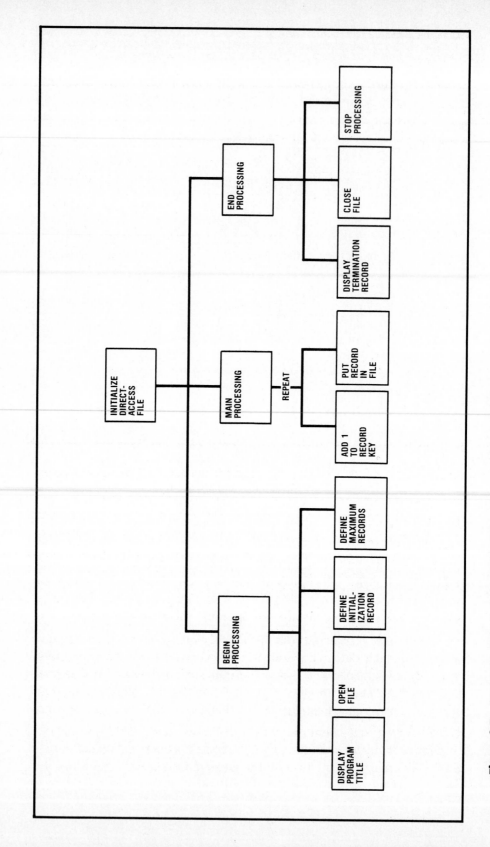

Figure 9-5. Structure chart for generalized direct-access file initialization program.

```
INITIALIZE DIRECT-ACCESS FILE
   BEGIN PROCESSING
        DISPLAY PROGRAM TITLE
             Print program title lines
             Print program initiation message
        OPEN FILE
             Open Master File as Relative File
             Map record format
        DEFINE INITIALIZATION RECORD
             Set Status Code = 0
             Set Record Key = 0
             Set numeric fields = 0
             Set alphanumeric fields = " "
        SET MAXIMUM RECORDS
             Set Maximum Records = file size constant
   MAIN PROCESSING
   REPEAT: until Record Key = Maximum Records
        ADD 1 TO RECORD KEY
             Set Record key = Record Key + 1
        PUT RECORD IN FILE
             Put Master Record, location Record Key
   END REPEAT
   END PROCESSING
        DISPLAY TERMINATION MESSAGE
             Print program termination message
        CLOSE FILE
             Close Master File
        STOP PROCESSING
             Stop
```

Figure 9-6. Pseudocode for generalized direct-access file initialization program.

direct-access file used in the hotel reservation system. The version of BASIC illustrated here is designed to run on a VAX computer. Language differences for other types of computers are presented later. New statements introduced within this program involve variations on the OPEN, MAP, and PUT statements.

Opening Direct-Access Files—The OPEN Statement

The OPEN statement for a direct-access file must contain a parameter to indicate that the file is a direct-access, or relative, file. This parameter is created by including the RELATIVE specification within the statement. This keyword indicates that each record will be located by its position relative to the beginning record of the file.

The OPEN statement includes a MAP parameter. This specification provides the name of the accompanying MAP statement that defines the field formats for the records to be placed in the file.

```
1000! HOTEL91                                                    DRA/WEL
1010!                      INITIALIZE HOTEL FILE
1020!
1030! THIS PROGRAM INITIALIZES A DIRECT-ACCESS FILE NAMED
1040! "HOTEL" THAT IS USED TO MAINTAIN OCCUPANCY RECORDS.
1050! ALL FIELDS ARE SET TO ZERO OR BLANKS TO PREFORMAT THE
1060! FILE.  A TOTAL OF 99 RECORD POSITIONS ARE INITIALIZED.
1070!
1080! VARIABLE NAMES
1090!
1100! MASTER RECORD:
1110!     S.....STATUS CODE      (VALUE 0)
1120!     N.....ROOM NUMBER      (KEY, VALUE 01 TO 99)
1130!     R.....ROOM RATE        (VALUE 0)
1140!     N$....OCCUPANT NAME    (VALUE " ")
1150!     A$....ARRIVAL DATE     (VALUE " ")
1160!     D$....DEPARTURE DATE   (VALUE " ")
1170! COUNTERS:
1180!     M.....MAXIMUM NUMBER OF RECORDS  (VALUE 99)
1190!
2000! 0.0 INITIALIZE HOTEL FILE
2010!
2020! *************************
2030! * 1.0 BEGIN PROCESSING *
2040! *************************
2050!
2060   PRINT "*****************************"
2070   PRINT "* HOTEL FILE INITIALIZATION *"
2080   PRINT "*****************************"
2090   PRINT
2100   PRINT "INITIALIZATION IN PROGRESS..."
2110!
2120   OPEN "HOTEL" AS FILE #1, RELATIVE, MAP FORMAT
2130   MAP (FORMAT) S, N, R, N$=20, A$=8, D$=8
2140!
2150   LET S   = 0
2160   LET N   = 0
2170   LET R   = 0
2180   LET N$  = " "
2190   LET A$  = " "
2200   LET D$  = " "
2210!
2220   LET M = 99
2230!
2240! ***********************
2250! * 2.0 MAIN PROCESSING *
2260! ***********************
2270! REPEAT
2280   IF N = M THEN GOTO 2350
2290!
2300      LET N = N + 1
2310!
2320      PUT #1, RECORD N
2330!
2340   GOTO 2270
2350! END REPEAT
2360!
2370! ***********************
2380! * 3.0 END PROCESSING  *
2390! ***********************
2400!
2410   PRINT
2420   PRINT "INITIALIZATION COMPLETED"
2430   PRINT M; "RECORDS WRITTEN TO FILE"
2440!
2450   CLOSE #1
2460!
2470   STOP
2480   END
```

Figure 9-7. BASIC code for example direct-access file initialization program.

The general format for the OPEN statement used with direct-access files is shown in Figure 9-8. In the example program in Figure 9-7, the OPEN statement appears in line 2120.

Describing Record Formats—The MAP Statement

The MAP statement indicates the format of individual records within a direct-access file. The MAP command includes the map name that appears in the associated OPEN statement. Then, variable names are assigned to the fields that make up a record. Standard naming conventions apply to numeric and string data. A default length of 16 characters is used for strings, with blank spaces used as padding if fewer than 16 characters appear in the field. This default length can be overridden as shown in line 2130 of the example program. Normally, the length of a string will be based on the longest string value expected for any given field. The general format for the MAP statement is shown in Figure 9-9.

Writing Records to Direct-Access Files—The PUT Statement

Records are written to direct-access files with the PUT statement. This statement specifies the file number that appears in the associated OPEN statement. Then, the parameter RECORD indicates the relative position at which the record is to be written within the file.

General Format:
    line # OPEN "filename" AS FILE #file number, [ORGANIZATION] RELATIVE,
        MAP mapname

Example:

```
100 OPEN "DAFILE" AS FILE #1, ORGANIZATION RELATIVE, MAP FORMAT1
```

The file name is the name assigned to the disk file. File number refers to the number that is referenced by subsequent GET, PUT, or UPDATE statements that are used for a particular disk record. Mapname is the name assigned to the associated MAP statement that presents the format for the direct-access record.

Figure 9-8. General format for the OPEN statement to open a direct-access file.

General Format:

   line # MAP (mapname) variable name [= length] [variable name
      [= length]] . . .

Example:

```
100 MAP (FORMAT1) A$, B$=5, C, D, E$=20
```

The keyword MAP is followed by a name, enclosed in parentheses, assigned to the MAP statement. The name distinguishes
the statement from other MAP statements that might appear in
the program. Standard naming conventions apply. Then, one or
more variable names appear, separated by commas. These are
the field names assigned to string and numeric data. A default
length of 16 characters is used for strings. Blank spaces are
added as padding if fewer than 16 characters appear in the
field. The amount of space needed to store string variables can
be set by specifying the exact length of the field. This length
will usually be the length of the longest string expected for any
given field.

Figure 9-9. General format for the MAP statement used to define record formats
for direct-access records.

In the example program, the room-number field serves as the record
key and indicates also the relative position of the record within the file.
This value is incremented from 1 through to the end of the file, with each
succeeding record written in the next available position. Line 2320 of the
example program illustrates how the PUT statement is used. The general
format for this command is shown in Figure 9-10.

Think back to the file creation program developed in Chapter 3. In that
example, a sequential file was created. In setting up sequential files, it
is possible both to initialize a file and to place values into the record areas
in a single operation. In a direct-access file, it is appropriate to create a
series of record positions first. This series is created with a file initialization program. Next, a program is written to add, or insert, actual data
records into the file. Some, but not all, systems require this preformat-
ting operation. However, as a safeguard against error, it is best to pre-
format for all versions of BASIC.

General Format:

line number PUT #file number, RECORD record number

Example:

```
100 PUT #1, RECORD N
```

This statement is used to write a record at the relative location given by the record number (N) in a direct-access file. The file number is the number assigned in the associated OPEN statement.

Figure 9-10. General format for the PUT statement used to write a record to a direct-access file.

CREATING DIRECT-ACCESS FILES

Once a direct-access file has been initialized, it can be loaded with data records. First, the null record in the position at which a record is to be added is accessed from the file. The record is brought into memory, and the zero and blank fields are replaced with actual data values. The status code field is changed from 0 to 1 to indicate the presence of a data record. Then, the updated record is written back to the file and replaces the null record.

This processing continues for all the records added to the file. Also, records are added in random sequence because only the record key controls file access and writing operations.

A structure chart for a generalized direct-access file creation program is shown in Figure 9-11. Structure charts for the subroutines called from this mainline program appear in Figures 9-12 through 9-14. This program is similar to file creation programs presented earlier in the book. The computer prompts the operator through a series of data entry operations. These operations input the fields that build a record. Following verification, the new record is added to the file.

This program includes editing procedures that are more involved than those described in earlier programs. In particular, the program must verify that the record key entered by the operator is within the range

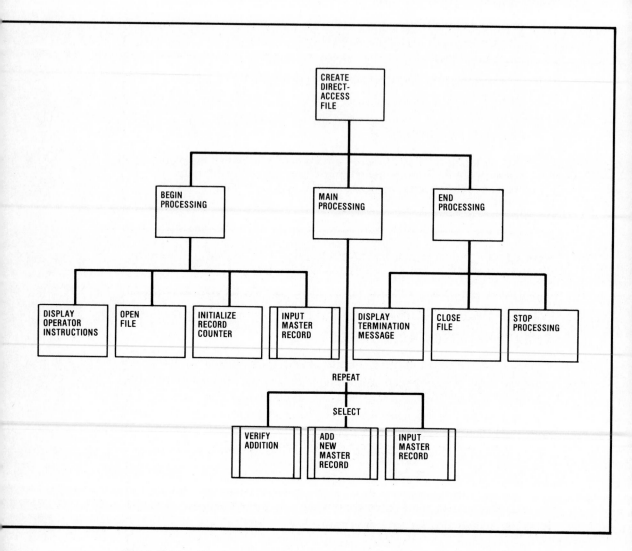

Figure 9-11. Structure chart for generalized mainline program to create a direct-access file.

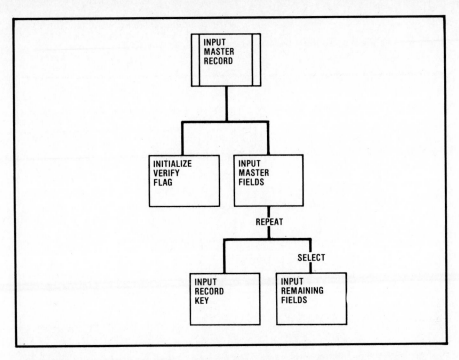

Figure 9-12. Structure chart for input subroutine of program to create a direct-access file.

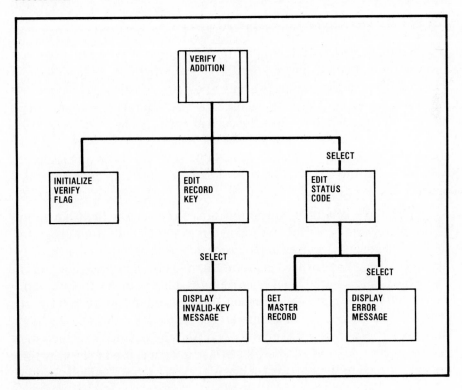

Figure 9-13. Structure chart for verification subroutine of program to create a direct-access file.

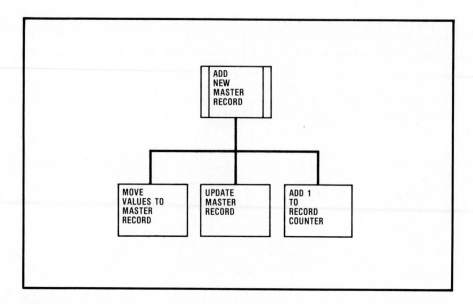

Figure 9-14. Structure chart for add subroutine of program to create a direct-access file.

of values that represents the size of the direct-access file. In other words, a record should not be written to a file location that has not been initialized. Another editing routine prevents the new record from being written over an existing record. Therefore, the program must make sure that the status code of each retrieved record is 0. The record key range test is made in the subroutine named VERIFY ADDITION; the status code is checked in subroutine INPUT MASTER RECORD. The generalized pseudocode shown in Figure 9-15 illustrates the test logic for this program.

An example of a program to create a direct-access file is given in Figure 9-16. This program is a follow-up to the initialization program shown in Figure 9-7. The example program adds records to the HOTEL file initialized in the earlier program. The file creation program builds a data file to support the hotel registration system. Code for the program includes the OPEN and MAP statements that were introduced in the first program. In addition, two other special statements are required. The GET statement is used to access the null record in the position at which the new record is to be added. The UPDATE statement is used to rewrite the updated record to the file. Explanations of these two statements follow.

Figure 9-15. Pseudocode for generalized program to create a direct-access file.

```
CREATE DIRECT-ACCESS FILE
     BEGIN PROCESSING
          DISPLAY OPERATOR INSTRUCTIONS
               Print operator instruction lines
          OPEN FILE
               Open Master File as Relative file
               Map record format
          INITIALIZE RECORD COUNTER
               Set Record Counter = 0
          INPUT MASTER RECORD
               Perform INPUT MASTER RECORD
     MAIN PROCESSING
     REPEAT: until Record Key = 0
          VERIFY ADDITION
               Perform VERIFY ADDITION
          SELECT: on Verify Flag = "Y"
               ADD NEW MASTER RECORD
                    Perform ADD NEW MASTER RECORD
          END SELECT


          INPUT MASTER RECORD
               Perform INPUT MASTER RECORD
          END REPEAT
          END PROCESSING
               DISPLAY TERMINATION RECORD
                    Print program termination line.
               CLOSE FILE
                    Close Master File
               STOP PROCESSING
                    Stop




     INPUT MASTER RECORD
          INITIALIZE VERIFY FLAG
               Set Verify Flag = "N"
          INPUT MASTER FIELDS
          REPEAT: until Verify Flag = "Y"
               INPUT RECORD KEY
                    Print record key prompt
                    Input Record Key
               SELECT: on Record Key () 0
                    INPUT REMAINING FIELDS
                         Print Field 1 prompt
                         Input Field 1
                         Print Field 2 prompt
                         Input Field 2
                              .
                              .
                              .
                         Print verify flag prompt
                         Input Verify Flag
               END SELECT
          END REPEAT
     RETURN
```

```
VERIFY ADDITION
     INITIALIZE VERIFY FLAG
          Set Verify Flag = "Y"
     EDIT RECORD KEY
          SELECT: on Record Key < 0 and > Maximum Records
               DISPLAY INVALID-KEY MESSAGE
                    Print Key-out-of-range message
                    Set Verify Flag = "N"
          END SELECT
     SELECT: on Verify Flag = "Y"
          EDIT STATUS CODE
               GET MASTER RECORD
                    Get Master Record, location Record Key
               SELECT: on Status Code = 1
                    DISPLAY ERROR MESSAGE
                         Print key-already-exists message
                         Set Verify Flag = "N"
               END SELECT
     END SELECT
RETURN




ADD NEW MASTER RECORD
     MOVE VALUES TO MASTER RECORD
          Set Status Code = 1
          Set Master Field 1 = Field 1
          Set Master Field 2 = Field 2
               .
               .
               .
     UPDATE MASTER RECORD
          Update Master Record, location Record Key
     ADD 1 TO RECORD COUNTER
          Set Record Counter = Record Counter + 1
RETURN
```

Figure 9-15. Concluded.

Inputting Direct-Access Records—The GET Statement

The GET command functions much like the INPUT command, except that
GET operates on direct-access files. In Figure 9-16, line 4210 of the program shows that the GET command is associated with the file number
appearing in the OPEN statement. Within the GET statement, the term
RECORD is a keyword accompanied by a variable name. The variable
name represents the key of the record to be accessed. This record is read
under the format specified in the MAP statement. Once in memory, the
record fields are processed in the same manner as records accessed with
INPUT statements. The general format for the GET statement is given
in Figure 9-17.

Figure 9-16. BASIC code for example program to create a direct-access file.

```
1000! HOTEL92                                       DRA/WEL
1010!                  CREATE DIRECT-ACCESS FILE
1020!
1030! THIS PROGRAM CREATES A FILE OF DIRECT-ACCESS RECORDS
1040! FOR THE "HOTEL" FILE.  THE OPERATOR IS PROMPTED FOR
1050! THE DATA FIELDS AND ENTERS THEM THROUGH THE KEYBOARD.
1060! THE PROGRAM CHECKS FOR VALID ROOM NUMBERS (01-99) AND
1070! FOR NONDUPLICATE NUMBERS AND THEN ADDS THE RECORDS TO
1080! THE FILE, REPLACING THE INITIALIZED RECORD. THE STATUS
1090! CODE IS SET TO 1 IN EACH ADDED RECORD.
1100!
1110! VARIABLE NAMES
1120!
1130! MASTER RECORD:
1140!     S.....STATUS CODE        (VALUE 1)
1150!     N.....ROOM NUMBER        (VALUE 01-99)
1160!     R.....ROOM RATE          (FORMAT ##.##)
1170!     N$....OCCUPANT NAME      (FORMAT 20 CHARACTERS)
1180!     A$....ARRIVAL DATE       (FORMAT YY/MM/DD)
1190!     D$....DEPARTURE DATE     (FORMAT YY/MM/DD)
1200! INPUT RECORD:
1210!     N1....ROOM NUMBER
1220!     R1....ROOM RATE
1230!     N1$...OCCUPANT NAME
1240!     A1$...ARRIVAL DATE
1250!     D1$...DEPARTURE DATE
1260! COUNTERS:
1270!     K.....RECORD COUNTER
1280!
2000! 0.0 CREATE DIRECT-ACCESS FILE
2010!
2020! *************************
2030! * 1.0 BEGIN PROCESSING *
2040! *************************
2050!
2060   PRINT "*****************************"
2070   PRINT "* CREATE DIRECT-ACCESS FILE *"
2080   PRINT "*****************************"
2090   PRINT
2100   PRINT "ENTER THE FIELDS INDICATED.  TO"
2110   PRINT "END THE PROGRAM, TYPE "00" FOR"
2120   PRINT "THE ROOM NUMBER."
2130!
2140   OPEN "HOTEL" AS FILE #1, RELATIVE, MAP FORMAT
2150   MAP (FORMAT) S, N, R, N$=20, A$=8, D$=8
2160!
2170   LET K = 0
2180!
2190   GOSUB 3000    !INPUT FIRST MASTER RECORD
2200!
2210! *************************
2220! * 2.0 MAIN PROCESSING   *
2230! *************************
2240! REPEAT
2250   IF N1 = 00 THEN GOTO 2400
2260!
2270     GOSUB 4000    !VERIFY ADDITION
2280!
```

```
2290!    SELECT
2300     IF V$ = "Y" THEN GOTO 2330
2310                        GOTO 2350
2320!
2330        GOSUB 5000    !ADD NEW MASTER RECORD
2340!
2350!    END SELECT
2360!
2370     GOSUB 3000    !INPUT NEXT MASTER RECORD
2380!
2390  GOTO 2240
2400! END REPEAT
2410!
2420! **************************
2430! * 3.0 END PROCESSING    *
2440! **************************
2450!
2460  PRINT
2470  PRINT K; "RECORDS ADDED TO FILE"
2480!
2490  CLOSE #1
2500!
2510  STOP
2520!
3000! *****************************
3010! * S1.0 INPUT MASTER RECORD *
3020! *****************************
3030!
3040  LET V$ = "N"
3050!
3060! REPEAT
3070  IF V$ = "Y" THEN GOTO 3310
3080!
3090     PRINT
3100     PRINT "ROOM NUMBER...........";
3110     INPUT N1
3120!
3130     SELECT
3140     IF N1 <> 00 THEN GOTO 3170
3150                      GOTO 3280
3160!
3170        PRINT "ROOM RATE.............";
3180        INPUT R1
3190        PRINT "OCCUPANT NAME.........";
3200        INPUT N1$
3210        PRINT "ARRIVAL DATE..........";
3220        INPUT A1$
3230        PRINT "DEPARTURE DATE........";
3240        INPUT D1$
3250        PRINT "   VERIFY (Y/N).......";
3260        INPUT V$
3270!
3280!    END SELECT
3290!
3300  GOTO 3060
3310! END REPEAT
3320!
3330  RETURN
3340!
4000! ************************
4010! * S2.0 VERIFY ADDITION *
4020! ************************
4030!
4040  LET V$ = "Y"
4050!
4060! SELECT
4070  IF N1 < 01 AND N1 > 99 THEN GOTO 4100
4080                              GOTO 4140
4090!
4100     PRINT
4110     PRINT "*** ROOM NUMBER OUT OF RANGE ***"
```

```
4120      LET V$ = "N"
4130!
4140! END SELECT
4150!
4160! SELECT
4170   IF V$ = "Y" THEN GOTO 4200
4180                  GOTO 4330
4190!
4200      LET N = N1
4210      GET #1, RECORD N
4220!
4230!     SELECT
4240      IF S = 1 THEN GOTO 4270
4250                  GOTO 4310
4260!
4270         PRINT
4280         PRINT "*** ROOM ALREADY OCCUPIED ***"
4290         LET V$ = "N"
4300!
4310!     END SELECT
4320!
4330! END SELECT
4340!
4350  RETURN
4360!
5000! ******************************
5010! * S3.0 ADD NEW MASTER RECORD *
5020! ******************************
5030!
5040  LET S  = 1
5050  LET R  = R1
5060  LET N$ = N1$
5070  LET A$ = A1$
5080  LET D$ = D1$
5090!
5100  UPDATE #1
5110!
5120  LET K = K + 1
5130!
5140  RETURN
5150!
9990  END
```

Figure 9-16. Concluded.

General Format:

   line number GET #file number, RECORD record number

Example:

```
100 GET #1, RECORD N
```

This statement inputs the record at the relative location given
by the record number (N) from a direct-access file. The file
number is the number used in the associated OPEN statement.

Figure 9-17. General format for the GET statement used to input a record from
a direct-access file.

Rewriting Direct-Access Records— The UPDATE Statement

The UPDATE command performs a function similar to the PUT instruction described in the previous program. However, the UPDATE statement does not require the location of the record that is to be written to the file. Instead, the position of the record most recently accessed with the GET statement becomes the location for the write function. For example, in line 5100 of the program shown in Figure 9-16, a null record within the HOTEL file is replaced with a record containing actual data values. These new values are assigned to the data fields in lines 5040 through 5080.

The general format for the UPDATE statement is given in Figure 9-18. Of course, records can be rewritten to a direct-access file by using the PUT statement. However, the UPDATE command is more convenient because records are rewritten automatically to the locations from which the records were accessed.

REPORTS FROM DIRECT-ACCESS FILES

Once data have been placed in a direct-access file, reports are printed in much the same manner as reports printed from sequential files, as described in Chapter 4. The major difference is that the reading of records from direct-access files must contain a select mechanism. This comparison is performed against the status code. Records with a status code of zero are not printed; only record areas that have data content are output.

Figure 9-19 provides a generalized structure chart for a program that lists the output from a direct-access file. Pseudocode for this program appears in Figure 9-20. BASIC code for a report writing program that uses a direct-access file is given in Figure 9-21. This particular program prints a detail report of records in the HOTEL file. No new BASIC statements are introduced in this program.

MAINTAINING DIRECT-ACCESS FILES

Recall from earlier discussions that file maintenance programs support the addition of new records to a file, the changing of fields within existing records, and the deletion of records that are no longer needed.

General Format:

line number UPDATE #file number

Example:

100 UPDATE #1

This statement is used to rewrite to a direct-access file the previous record accessed by a GET statement. The file number is the number that was assigned in the associated OPEN statement. The statement overwrites the record in the file with the current record in memory.

Figure 9-18. General format for the UPDATE statement used to rewrite a direct-access record to a file.

Direct-access files improve the efficiency of processing for most file maintenance operations because maintenance usually involves the processing of only a few records during any one updating run. Further, it is virtually impossible to anticipate the order in which records will be updated. For these reasons, direct-access files are suited ideally to file maintenance.

Figure 9-22 presents a generalized structure chart for direct-access file maintenance programs. This mainline program is similar in structure to the maintenance program illustrated in Chapter 8. That is, a transaction processing model is followed. A transaction code is input, and program control is dispatched to subroutines that process in detail each maintenance function selected. In the current example, the program can place a new record directly within the file without having to rearrange existing records. Also, changes to records can be made in place and existing records can be deleted without having to close up the vacated positions in the file.

The structure charts in Figures 9-23 through 9-26 present the designs for the subroutines called from the mainline program, which is diagrammed in Figure 9-22. The pseudocode in Figure 9-27 illustrates the overall logic for the program. This general model can be followed in writing maintenance programs from virtually any direct-access file.

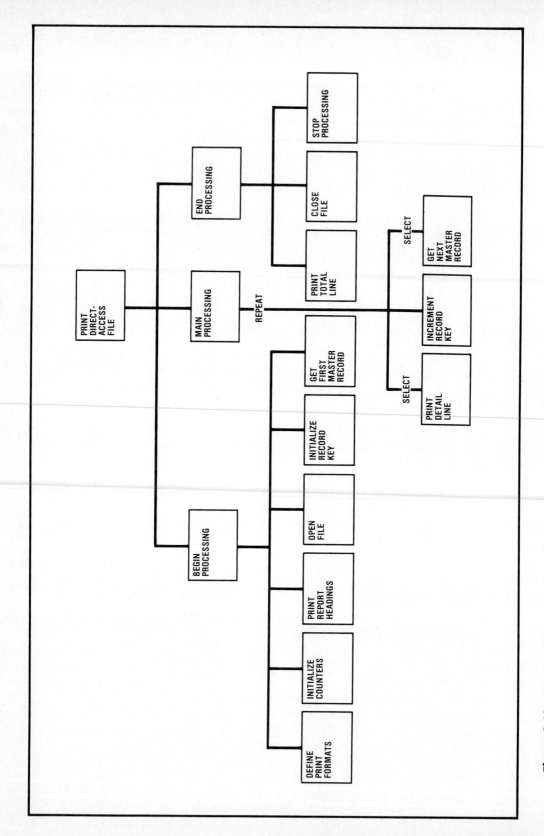

Figure 9-19. Structure chart for generalized program to print a direct-access file.

```
PRINT DIRECT-ACCESS FILE
    BEGIN PROCESSING
        DEFINE PRINT FORMATS
            Define heading lines
            Define detail line
            Define total line
        INITIALIZE COUNTERS
            Set Maximum Records = file size constant
            Set Record Counter = 0
        PRINT REPORT HEADINGS
            Print report title line
            Print blank line
            Print column heading lines
            Print blank line
        OPEN FILE
            Open Master File as Relative file
            Map record format
        INITIALIZE RECORD KEY
            Set Record Key = 1
        GET FIRST MASTER RECORD
            Get Master Record, location Record Key
    MAIN PROCESSING
    REPEAT: until Record Key > Maximum Records
        SELECT: on Status Code = 1
            PRINT DETAIL LINE
                Print detail line
                Set Record Counter = Record Counter = 1
        END SELECT
        INCREMENT RECORD KEY
            Set Record Key = Record Key + 1
        SELECT: on Record Key <= Maximum records
            GET NEXT MASTER RECORD
                Get Master Record, location Record Key
        END SELECT
    END REPEAT

    END PROCESSING
        PRINT TOTAL LINE
            Print total line
        CLOSE FILE
            Close Master File
        STOP PROCESSING
            Stop
```

Figure 9-20. Pseudocode for generalized program to print a direct-access file.

```
1000! HOTEL93                                            DRA/WEL
1010!                    PRINT GUEST REGISTER
1020!
1030! THIS PROGRAM PRINTS A LISTING OF THE ROOM NUMBERS,
1040! GUEST NAMES, AND DATES OF DEPARTURE OF ALL GUESTS
1050! IN THE "HOTEL" FILE.   THE FILE IS SEARCHED IN SEQUENCE
1060! AND ALL RECORDS WITH A STATUS CODE OF 1 ARE PRINTED.
1070!
1080! VARIABLE NAMES
1090!
1100! MASTER RECORD:
1110!    S.....STATUS CODE
1120!    N.....ROOM NUMBER
1130!    R.....ROOM RATE
1140!    N$....OCCUPANT NAME
1150!    A$....ARRIVAL DATE
1160!    D$....DEPARTURE DATE
1170! CONSTANTS:
1180!    M.....MAXIMUM NUMBER OF RECORDS
1190! COUNTERS:
1200!    K.....OCCUPIED ROOM COUNTER
1210! PRINTING FORMATS:
1220!    F1$...MAIN HEADING LINE
1230!    F2$...COLUMN HEADING LINE 1
1240!    F3$...COLUMN HEADING LINE 2
1250!    F4$...DETAIL LINE
1250!    F5$...TOTAL LINE
1260!
2000! *************************
2010! * 1.0 BEGIN PROCESSING *
2020! *************************
2030!
2040  LET F1$ = "                  GUEST REGISTER                   "
2050  LET F2$ = "ROOM                                       DEPARTURE"
2060  LET F3$ = " NO.          GUEST NAME               DATE   "
2070  LET F4$ = " ##          \                    \       \      \"
2080  LET F5$ = "TOTAL ROOMS OCCUPIED:   ##"
2090!
2100  LET M = 99
2110  LET K = 0
2120!
2130  PRINT F1$
2140  PRINT
2150  PRINT F2$
2160  PRINT F3$
2170  PRINT
2180!
2190  OPEN "HOTEL" AS FILE #1, RELATIVE, MAP FORMAT
2200  MAP (FORMAT) S, N, R, N$=20, A$=8, D$=8
2210!
2220  LET N = 1
2230!
2240  GET #1, RECORD N
2250!
2260! *************************
2270! * 2.0 MAIN PROCESSING   *
2280! *************************
2290! REPEAT
2300  IF N > M THEN GOTO 2520
2310!
2320!     SELECT
2330       IF S = 1 THEN GOTO 2360
2340                    GOTO 2390
```

```
2350!
2360        PRINT USING F4$, N, N$, D$
2370        LET K = K + 1
2380!
2390!    END SELECT
2400!
2410     LET N = N + 1
2420!
2430!    SELECT
2440     IF N <= M THEN GOTO 2470
2450                     GOTO 2490
2460!
2470        GET #1, RECORD N
2480!
2490!    END SELECT
2500!
2510  GOTO 2290
2520! END REPEAT
2530!
2540! ************************
2550! * 3.0 END PROCESSING    *
2560! ************************
2570!
2580  PRINT
2590  PRINT USING F5$, K
2600!
2610  CLOSE #1
2620!
2630  STOP
2640!
9990  END
```

Figure 9-21. BASIC code for example program to print a direct-access file.

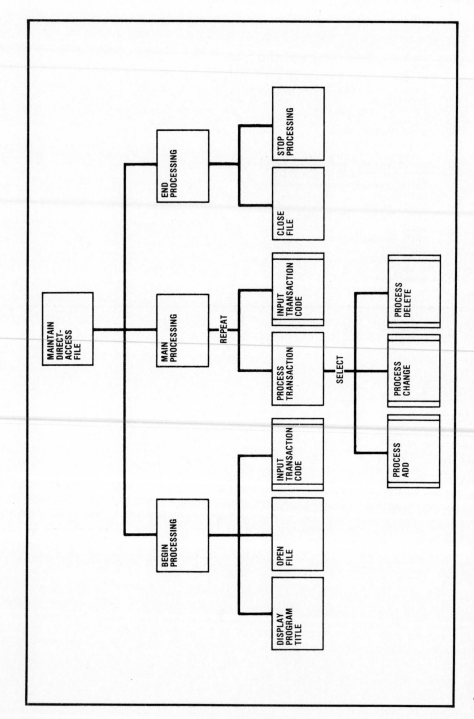

Figure 9-22. Structure chart for generalized direct-access file maintenance program.

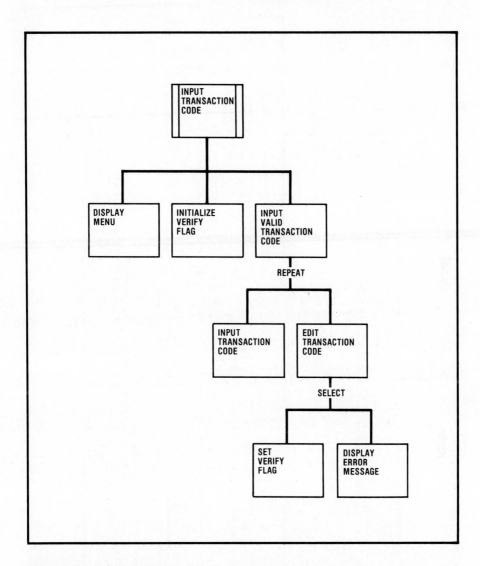

Figure 9-23. Structure chart for transaction code input subroutine of direct-access file maintenance program.

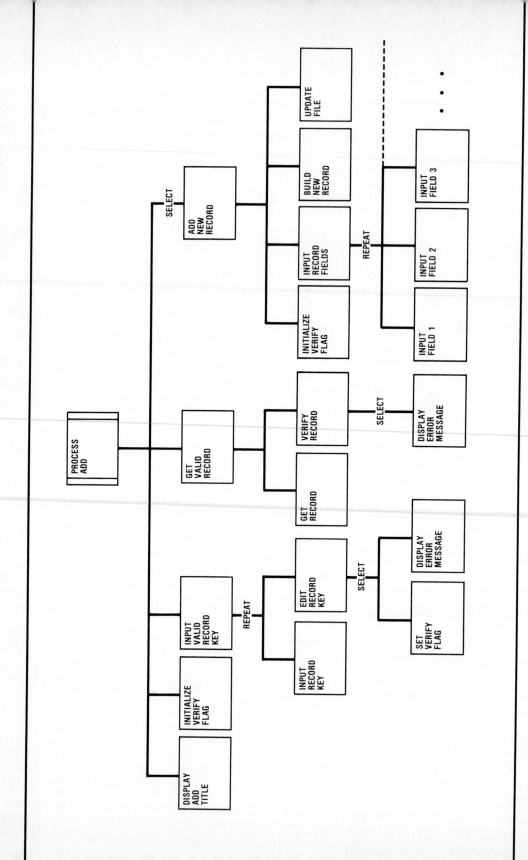

Figure 9-24. Structure chart for add subroutine of direct-access file maintenance program.

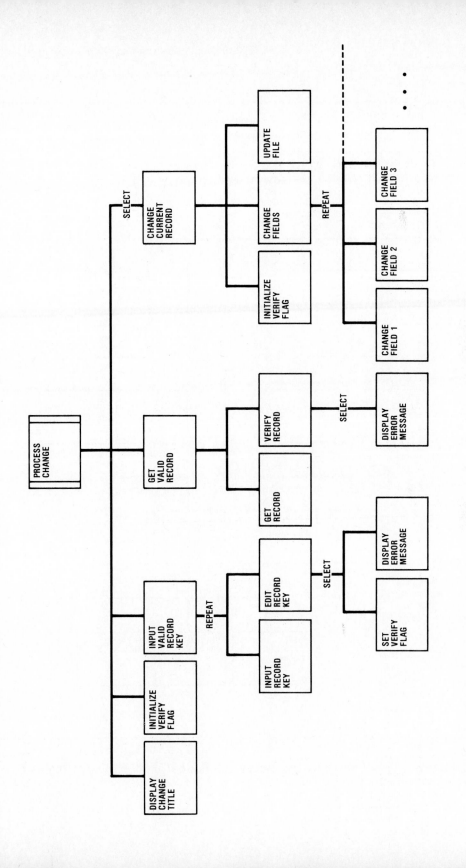

Figure 9-25. Structure chart for change subroutine of direct-access file maintenance program.

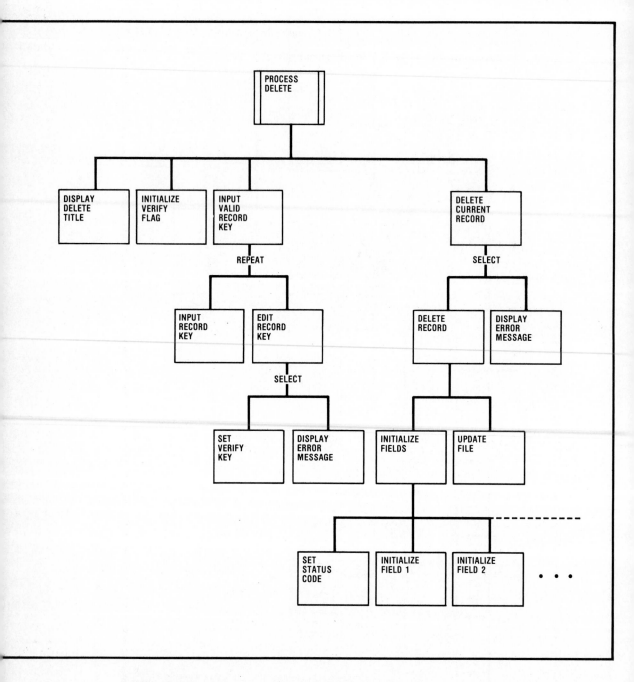

Figure 9-26. Structure chart for delete subroutine of direct-access file maintenance program.

Figure 9-27. Pseudocode for generalized direct-access file maintenance program.

```
MAINTAIN DIRECT-ACCESS FILE
     BEGIN PROCESSING
           DISPLAY PROGRAM TITLE
                Print program title lines
           OPEN FILE
                Open Master File as Relative file
                Map record format
           INPUT TRANSACTION CODE
                Perform INPUT TRANSACTION CODE
     MAIN PROCESSING
     REPEAT: until Trans Code = "S"
           PROCESS TRANSACTION
                SELECT: on Trans Code
                     PROCESS ADD
                          Perform PROCESS ADD
                     PROCESS CHANGE
                          Perform PROCESS CHANGE
                     PROCESS DELETE
                          Perform PROCESS DELETE
                END SELECT
           INPUT TRANSACTION CODE
                Perform INPUT TRANSACTION CODE
     END REPEAT
     END PROCESSING
           CLOSE FILE
                Close Master File
           STOP PROCESSING
                Stop



  INPUT TRANSACTION CODE
       DISPLAY MENU
            Print menu lines
       INITIALIZE VERIFY FLAG
            Set Verify Flag = "N"
       INPUT VALID TRANS CODE
            REPEAT: until Verify Flag = "Y"
                 INPUT TRANS CODE
                      Print transaction code prompt
                      Input Trans Code
                 EDIT TRANS CODE
                      SELECT: on Trans Code
                           SET VERIFY FLAG
                                Set Verify Flag = "Y"
                           DISPLAY ERROR MESSAGE

                                Print invalid-code message
                      END SELECT
            END REPEAT
  RETURN



  PROCESS ADD
       DISPLAY ADD TITLE
            Print add-a-record header
       INITIALIZE VERIFY FLAG
            Set Verify Flag = "N"
```

```
INPUT VALID RECORD KEY
     REPEAT: until Verify Flag = "Y"
          INPUT RECORD KEY
               Print record key prompt
               Input Record Key
          EDIT RECORD KEY
               SELECT: on Record Key
                    SET VERIFY FLAG
                         Set Verify Flag = "Y"
                    DISPLAY ERROR MESSAGE
                         Print invalid-key message
               END SELECT
     END REPEAT
GET VALID RECORD
     GET RECORD
          Get Master Record, location Record Key
     VERIFY RECORD
          SELECT: on Status Code = 1
               DISPLAY ERROR MESSAGE
                    Print record-already-exists message
          END SELECT
SELECT: on Status Code = 0
     ADD NEW RECORD
          INITIALIZE VERIFY FLAG
               Set Verify Flag = "N"
          INPUT RECORD FIELDS
               REPEAT: until Verify Flag = "Y"
                    INPUT FIELD 1
                         Print Field 1 prompt
                         Input Field 1
                    INPUT FIELD 2
                         Print Field 2 prompt
                         Input Field 2
                              .
                              .
                              .
                    INPUT VERIFY FLAG
                         Print verify flag prompt
                         Input Verify Flag
               END REPEAT
          BUILD NEW RECORD
               Set Status Code = 1
               Set Master Record fields = input fields
          UPDATE FILE
               Update Master Record, location Record Key


     END SELECT
RETURN


PROCESS CHANGE
     DISPLAY CHANGE TITLE
          Print change-a-record header
     INITIALIZE VERIFY FLAG
          Set Verify Flag = "N"
     INPUT VALID RECORD KEY
          REPEAT: until Verify Flag = "Y"
               INPUT RECORD KEY
                    Print record key prompt
                    Input Record Key
               EDIT RECORD KEY
                    SELECT: on Record Key
                         SET VERIFY FLAG
                              Set Verify Flag = "Y"
                         DISPLAY ERROR MESSAGE
                              Print invalid-key message
                    END SELECT
          END REPEAT
     GET VALID RECORD
          GET RECORD
               Get Master Record, location Record Key
```

```
                VERIFY RECORD
                    SELECT: on Status Code = 0
                            DISPLAY ERROR MESSAGE
                                Print record-doesn't-exist message
                    END SELECT
            SELECT: on Staus Code = 1
                INITIALIZE VERIFY FLAG
                    Set Verify Flag = "N"
                CHANGE FIELDS
                    REPEAT: until Verify Flag = "Y"
                            CHANGE FIELD 1
                                Print change field 1 prompt
                                Input Field 1
                            CHANGE FIELD 2
                                Print change field 2 prompt
                                Input Field 2
                                  .
                                  .
                                  .
                                  .

                            INPUT VERIFY FLAG
                                Print verify flag prompt
                                Input Verify Flag
        END SELECT
        UPDATE FILE
            Update Master Record, location Record Key
    RETURN



    PROCESS DELETE
        DISPLAY DELETE TITLE

            Print delete-a-record header
        INITIALIZE VERIFY FLAG
            Set Verify Flag = "N"
        INPUT VALID RECORD KEY
            REPEAT: until Verify Flag = "Y"
                    INPUT RECORD KEY
                        Print record key prompt
                        Input Record Key
                    EDIT RECORD KEY
                        SELECT: on Record Key
                            SET VERIFY FLAG
                                Set Verify Flag = "Y"
                            DISPLAY ERROR MESSAGE
                                Print invalid-key message
                        END SELECT
            END REPEAT
        DELETE CURRENT RECORD
            SELECT: on Status Code
                DELETE RECORD
                    INITIALIZE FIELDS
                        SET STATUS CODE
                            Set Status Code = 0
                        INITIALIZE FIELD 1
                            Set Field 1 = 0 (" ")
                        INITIALIZE FIELD 2
                            Set Field 2 = 0 (" ")
                              .
                              .
                              .
                              .

                    UPDATE FILE
                        Update Master Record, location Record Key
                DISPLAY ERROR MESSAGE
                    Print record-doesn't-exist message
            END SELECT
    RETURN
```

Figure 9-27. Concluded.

An example program is coded in Figure 9-28. This program permits on-line maintenance of the HOTEL file used in previous illustrations. The general program model for direct-access file maintenance is followed.

DIRECT-ACCESS FACILITIES ON OTHER SYSTEMS

Computer systems often differ significantly in their handling of direct-access, or relative, files. Although the principles of relative files remain much the same across all systems, the BASIC commands used to implement the processing techniques can vary widely. These differences can be seen in Figures 9-29 through 9-31, which present the BASIC statements

Figure 9-28. BASIC code for example direct-access file maintenance program.

```
1000! HOTEL94                                              DRA/WEL
1010!                    MAINTAIN DIRECT-ACCESS FILE
1020!
1030! THIS PROGRAM PERFORMS MAINTAINANCE ON THE "HOTEL" FILE.
1040! IT ALLOWS NEW RECORDS TO BE ADDED TO THE FILE, CURRENT
1050! RECORDS TO BE CHANGED WITHIN THE FILE, AND OLD RECORDS
1060! TO BE DELETED FROM THE FILE.
1070!
1080! VARIABLE NAMES
1090!
1100! MASTER RECORD:
1110!    S.....STATUS CODE
1120!    N.....ROOM NUMBER (KEY)
1130!    R.....ROOM RATE
1140!    N$....OCCUPANT NAME
1150!    A$....ARRIVAL DATE
1160!    D$....DEPARTURE DATE
1170! NEW MASTER RECORD:
1180!    R1....ROOM RATE
1190!    N1$...OCCUPANT NAME
1200!    A1$...ARRIVAL DATE
1210!    D1$...DEPARTURE DATE
1220! MENU INPUT:
1230!    C$....TRANSACTION CODE
1240! PROGRAM FLAGS:
1250!    V$....VERIFY FLAG
1260!
2000! 0.0 MAINTAIN DIRECT-ACCESS FILE
2010!
2020! ************************
2030! * 1.0 BEGIN PROCESSING *
2040! ************************
2050!
2060    PRINT "***********************"
2070    PRINT "* MAINTAIN HOTEL FILE *"
2080    PRINT "***********************"
2090    PRINT
2100!
2110    OPEN "HOTEL" AS FILE #1, RELATIVE, MAP FORMAT
2120    MAP (FORMAT) S, N, R, N$=20, A$=8, D$=8
2130!
2140    GOSUB 3000    !INPUT TRANSACTION CODE
2150!
```

```
2160! **************************
2170! * 2.0 MAIN PROCESSING  *
2180! **************************
2190! REPEAT
2200   IF C$ = "S" THEN GOTO 2330
2210!
2220!    SELECT
2230!
2240        IF C$ = "A" THEN GOSUB 4000    !ADD NEW RECORD
2250        IF C$ = "C" THEN GOSUB 5000    !CHANGE A RECORD
2260        IF C$ = "D" THEN GOSUB 6000    !DELETE A RECORD
2270!
2280!    END SELECT
2290!
2300     GOSUB 3000    !INPUT TRANSACTION CODE
2310!
2320   GOTO 2190
2330! END REPEAT
2340!
2350! **************************
2360! * 3.0 END PROCESSING    *
2370! **************************
2380!
2390   CLOSE #1
2400!
2410   STOP
2420!
3000! *******************************
3010! * S1.0 INPUT TRANSACTION CODE *
3020! *******************************
3030!
3040   PRINT
3050   PRINT "ADD A NEW RECORD......A"
3060   PRINT "CHANGE A RECORD.......C"
3070   PRINT "DELETE A RECORD.......D"
3080   PRINT "STOP..................S"
3090!
3100   LET V$ = "N"
3110!
3120! REPEAT
3130   IF V$ = "Y" THEN GOTO 3340
3140!
3150     PRINT
3160     PRINT "ENTER TRANSACTION CODE...";
3170     INPUT C$
3180!
3190     SELECT
3200     IF C$ = "A" THEN GOTO 3260
3210     IF C$ = "C" THEN GOTO 3260
3220     IF C$ = "D" THEN GOTO 3260
3230     IF C$ = "S" THEN GOTO 3260
3240                   GOTO 3290
3250!
3260        LET V$ = "Y"
3270        GOTO 3310
3280!
3290        PRINT "*** ENTER A, C, D, OR S ***"
3300!
3310!    END SELECT
3320!
3330   GOTO 3120
3340! END REPEAT
3350!
3360   RETURN
3370!
4000! *******************
4010! * S2.0 PROCESS ADD *
4020! *******************
4030!
4040   PRINT
4050   PRINT "--- ADD A NEW RECORD ---"
4060!
4070   LET V$ = "N"
```

```
4080!
4090! REPEAT
4100   IF V$ = "Y" THEN GOTO 4280
4110!
4120      PRINT
4130      PRINT "ENTER ROOM NUMBER...";
4140      INPUT N
4150!
4160!     SELECT
4170      IF N > 0 AND <= 99 THEN GOTO 4200
4180                           GOTO 4230
4190!
4200         LET V$ = "Y"
4210         GOTO 4250
4220!
4230         PRINT "*** ENTER A NUMBER BETWEEN 1 AND 99 ***"
4240!
4250!     END SELECT
4260!
4270   GOTO 4090
4280! END REPEAT
4290!
4300   GET #1, RECORD N
4310!
4320! SELECT
4330   IF S = 1 THEN GOTO 4360
4340                 GOTO 4380
4350!
4360      PRINT "*** ROOM ALREADY OCCUPIED ***"
4370!
4380! END SELECT
4390!
4400! SELECT
4410   IF S = 0 THEN GOTO 4440
4420                 GOTO 4720
4430!
4440      LET V$ = "N"
4450!
4460!     REPEAT
4470      IF V$ = "Y" THEN GOTO 4620
4480!
4490         PRINT
4500         PRINT "ROOM RATE.............";
4510         INPUT R1
4520         PRINT "OCCUPANT NAME.........";
4530         INPUT N1$
4540         PRINT "ARRIVAL DATE..........";
4550         INPUT A1$
4560         PRINT "DEPARTURE DATE........";
4570         INPUT D1$
4580         PRINT "   VERIFY (Y/N).......";
4590         INPUT V$
4600!
4610      GOTO 4460
4620!     END REPEAT
4630!
4640      LET S  = 1
4650      LET R  = R1
4660      LET N$ = N1$
4670      LET A$ = A1$
4680      LET D$ = D1$
4690!
4700      UPDATE #1
4710!
4720! END SELECT
4730!
4740   RETURN
4750!
```

```
5000! ***********************
5010! * S3.0 PROCESS CHANGE *
5020! ***********************
5030!
5040  PRINT
5050  PRINT "--- CHANGE A RECORD ---"
5060!
5070  LET V$ = "N"
5080!
5090! REPEAT
5100  IF V$ = "Y" THEN GOTO 5280
5110!
5120     PRINT
5130     PRINT "ENTER ROOM NUMBER...";
5140     INPUT N
5150!
5160!    SELECT
5170     IF N > 0 AND <= 99 THEN GOTO 5200
5180                           GOTO 5230
5190!
5200        LET V$ = "Y"
5210        GOTO 5250
5220!
5230        PRINT "*** ENTER A NUMBER BETWEEN 1 AND 99 ***"
5240!
5250!    END SELECT
5260!
5270  GOTO 5090
5280! END REPEAT
5290!
5300  GET #1, RECORD N
5310!
5320! SELECT
5330  IF S = 0 THEN GOTO 5360
5340                 GOTO 5380
5350!
5360     PRINT "*** ROOM NOT OCCUPIED ***"
5370!
5380! END SELECT
5390!
5400! SELECT
5410  IF S = 1 THEN GOTO 5440
5420                 GOTO 5840
5430!
5440     LET V$ = "N"
5450!
5460!    REPEAT
5470     IF V$ = "Y" THEN GOTO 5820
5480!
5490        PRINT
5500        PRINT TAB(32); "CHANGE?"
5510        PRINT TAB(32); "  Y/N  "
5520        PRINT TAB(32); "-------"
5530!
5540        PRINT "ROOM RATE        :"; R; TAB(33);
5550        INPUT R$
5560        IF R$ <> "Y" THEN GOTO 5600
5570           PRINT TAB(15);
5580           INPUT R
5590!
5600        PRINT "OCCUPANT NAME :"; N$; TAB(33);
5610        INPUT R$
5620        IF R$ <> "Y" THEN GOTO 5660
5630           PRINT TAB(15);
5640           INPUT N$
5650!
5660        PRINT "ARRIVAL DATE   :"; A$; TAB(33);
5670        INPUT R$
5680        IF R$ <> "Y" THEN GOTO 5720
5690           PRINT TAB(15);
5700           INPUT A$
5710!
```

```
5720        PRINT "DEPARTURE DATE :"; D$; TAB(33);
5730        INPUT R$
5740        IF R$ <> "Y" THEN GOTO 5780
5750           PRINT TAB(15);
5760           INPUT D$
5770!
5780        PRINT "   VERIFY (Y/N)";
5790        INPUT V$
5800!
5810     GOTO 5460
5820!     END REPEAT
5830!
5840! END SELECT
5850!
5860  UPDATE #1
5870!
5880  RETURN
5890!
6000! ***********************
6010! * S4.0 PROCESS DELETE *
6020! ***********************
6030!
6040  PRINT
6050  PRINT "--- DELETE A RECORD ---"
6060!
6070  LET V$ = "N"
6080!
6090! REPEAT
6100  IF V$ = "Y" THEN GOTO 6280
6110!
6120     PRINT
6130     PRINT "ENTER ROOM NUMBER...";
6140     INPUT N
6150!
6160!    SELECT
6170     IF N > 0 AND <= 99 THEN GOTO 6200
6180                                GOTO 6230
6190!
6200        LET V$ = "Y"
6210        GOTO 6250
6220!
6230        PRINT "***ENTER A NUMBER BETWEEN 1 AND 99 ***"
6240!
6250!    END SELECT
6260!
6270  GOTO 6090
6280! END REPEAT
6290!
6300  GET #1, RECORD N
6310!
6320! SELECT
6330  IF S = 1 THEN GOTO 6360
6340                GOTO 6440
6350!
6360     LET S  = 0
6370     LET R  = 0
6380     LET N$ = " "
6390     LET A$ = " "
6400     LET D$ = " "
6410     UPDATE #1
6420     GOTO 6460
6430!
6440     PRINT "*** ROOM NOT OCCUPIED ***"
6450!
6460! END SELECT
6470!
6480  RETURN
6490!
9990  END
```

Figure 9-28. Concluded.

Figure 9-29. Statements for direct-access processing in BASIC with IBM/Microsoft and TRS-80 systems.

DIRECT ACCESS STATEMENT—IBM/Microsoft
    OPEN "filename" AS #file number LEN = record length

DIRECT ACCESS STATEMENT—TRS-80
    OPEN "R", #file number, "filename", record length

This statement opens a file as a direct-access (relative) file. The file name is the name assigned to the disk file. The file number is the integer value that will be referenced by subsequent GET or PUT statements to input or output a record in the file. The LEN = specification provides the integer value of the total length, in characters (bytes), of each fixed-length record.

    FIELD #FILE number, width AS string variable [, width AS string variable] . . .

This statement describes the format of a data record. Each field is specified by its length and name. The entry "width" is an integer value that provides the size, in characters, of the field. Width is set to equal the largest value expected in any given field. The entry "string variable" is the name of the field. Standard naming conventions apply. All fields within direct-access records must carry string variable names, even though numeric values will be placed there.

    GET #file number [, record number]

This statement reads a record from a direct-access file. The record number is the relative location of the record in the file. If the record number is omitted, the next record (after the GET) is read.

    PUT #file number [, record number]

This statement writes a record to a direct-access file. The record number is the relative location of the record in the file. If the record number is omitted, the record has the next available record number (after the last PUT).

    MKI$, MKS$, MKD$

Any numeric value written to a direct-access file must be converted into a string. These functions are used to make the following conversions: MKI$ converts an integer value to a two-character (two-byte) string; MKS$ converts a single-precision number (up to seven digits) to a four-character string; and MKD$ converts a double-precision number (up to 17 digits) to an eight-character string. The formats of these functions are:

$$\text{string variable} = \left\{ \begin{array}{l} \text{MKI\$(integer expression)} \\ \text{MKS\$(single-precision expression)} \\ \text{MKD\$(double-precision expression)} \end{array} \right\}$$

L SET string variable = converted numeric variable

This statement moves a string formed with an MKI$, MKS$, or MKD$ function to a field within a direct-access record. This movement prepares the string to be written (PUT) to a file. The statement left-margin justifies the value in the field.

CVI, CVS, CVD

These functions convert a numeric string value of a field in a direct-access record to a number. The function CVI converts a two-character string to an integer; the function CVS converts a four-character string to a single-precision number; and the func tion CVD converts an eight-character string to a double-precision number. The formats of these functions are:

$$\text{numeric variable} = \left\{ \begin{array}{l} \text{CVI(2-character string)} \\ \text{CVS(4-character string)} \\ \text{CVD(8-character string)} \end{array} \right\}$$

CLOSE #file number

This statement closes a direct-access file. The format is the same as those used for CLOSE statements for sequential files.

The following program segments show how these statements and functions are used:

```
100 OPEN "DAFILE" AS #1 LEN=36
110 FIELD #1, 2 AS S$, 2 AS N$, 20 AS A$, 4 AS B$, 8 AS C$
120 '
130 GET #1, 10
140 '
150 LSET S1$ = S$
160 LSET N1  = CVI(N$)
170 LSET A1$ = A$
180 LSET B1  = CVS(B$)
190 LSET C1  = CVD(C$)
    .
    .
    .
300 LSET S$ = S1$
310 LSET N$ = MKI$(N1)
320 LSET A$ = A1$
330 LSET B$ = MKS$(B1)
340 LSET C$ = MKD$(C1)
350 '
360 PUT #1, 10
370 '
380 CLOSE #1
390 '
```

Figure 9-29. Concluded.

DIRECT-ACCESS STATEMENTS
Apple II

PRINT CHR$(4); "OPEN filename", Lrecord length

This statement opens a file as a direct-access file. The L specification provides the total length of each fixed-length record. To determine this length, count the number of characters in the longest alphanumeric field and count each digit and decimal point that make up the largest value within a numeric field. Also, count the commas that separate the fields and the carriage return character that appears at the end of the record.

PRINT CHR$(4); "READ filename,R"; record number
INPUT variable name [, variable name] . . .

These statements input a record from a direct-access file. The record number refers to the location of the record, relative to the position of the first file record. The variable names are those of the fields that make up the record.

PRINT CHR$(4); "WRITE filename,R"; record number
PRINT variable name [; "," variable name] . . .

These statements write a record to a direct-access file. The record number refers to the location of the record, relative to the position of the first file record. The variable names are those of the fields that make up the record.

PRINT CHR$(4); "CLOSE filename"

This statement is used to close the direct-access file.

Remember to use a PRINT CHR$(4) statement without additional parameters to remove the file reference. Then, any subsequent INPUT and PRINT statements can be used to input from a keyboard or print to a screen.

Figure 9-30. Statements for direct-access processing in BASIC with Apple II system.

DIRECT ACCESS STATEMENT—PDP-11

OPEN "filename" as FILE #file number

The filename is the name assigned to the disk file. A file number is assigned for use in the associated GET and PUT statements.

FIELD #file number, width AS string variable [, width AS string variable] . . .

This statement describes the format of a data record. Each field is specified by its length and name. The file number is the same number as in the associated OPEN statement. The width entry is an integer value that provides the size, in number of characters, of the field. Width is set to equal the largest value expected in any given field. The string variable entry is the name of the field. Standard naming conventions apply. All fields within direct-access records must have string variable names, even though numeric values will be stored in the fields. The total number of characters in a record cannot exceed 512.

GET #file number [, RECORD record number]

This statement reads a record from a direct-access file. The file number is the number in the associated OPEN statement. The record number is the relative location of the record in the file. If the record number is omitted, the next record (after the GET) is read.

PUT #file number [, RECORD record number]

This statement writes a record to a direct-access file. The file number is the number in the associated OPEN statement. The record number is the relative location of the record in the file. If the record number is omitted, the record uses the next available record number (after the PUT). When the PUT statement is used for updating, it writes over the existing record in the file.

CVT%$, CVTF$

Numeric values written to direct-access files must be converted into character strings. The above functions are used to make the following conversions: CVT%$ converts an integer to a two-character string, and CVTF$ converts a decimal number to a four- or eight-character string. The size of the string depends on whether a two-word or four-word math package has been installed in the system. The current math package is determined by printing the function LEN(CVTF$(0)). These string lengths then become the widths specified in the FIELD statement. The formats of these functions are:

$$\text{string variable} = \begin{cases} \text{CVT\%\$(integer expression)} \\ \text{CVTF\$(decimal expression)} \end{cases}$$

    LSET string variable = converted numeric variable

This statement moves a string that was converted with a CVT%$ or CVTF$ function to a field within a direct-access record. This movement prepares the string to be written (PUT) to a file. The statement left-margin justifies the value in the field.

    CVT$%, CVT$F

These functions perform the processing of the CVT%$ and CVTF$ functions in reverse. That is, the functions convert strings that appear within a direct-access record to their numeric equivalents. The function CVT$% converts a two-character string to an integer and the function CVT$F converts a four- or eight-character string to a decimal number, depending on the math package installed in the system. The formats of these functions are:

$$\text{numeric variable} = \begin{cases} \text{CVT\$\%(two-character string)} \\ \text{CVT\$F(four- or eight-character string)} \end{cases}$$

    CLOSE #file number

This statement closes a direct-access file. The file number is the same number that appears in the corresponding OPEN statement.

Note that these statements are similar in function to those used for the IBM/Microsoft and TRS-80 systems. The use of these statements is indicated in the program segment shown in Figure 9-19.

Figure 9-31. Statements for direct-access processing in BASIC with the PDP-11.

381

and functions for processing direct-access files on the IBM, TRS-80, Apple II, and PDP-11 computers. The commands shown in these figures substitute for the OPEN, MAP, GET, PUT, and UPDATE statements explained in this chapter.

In converting from one version of BASIC to another, peculiarities are encountered in each version. In most cases, however, there is direct correspondence among the statement types.

This chapter presents only the rudiments of large-file processing. In Chapter 11, these concepts are expanded considerably. Before adding to this base of understanding, however, it is necessary to consider some of the principles and techniques used to process sequential files that are too large to fit completely into memory. With this added knowledge and skill, you will be ready to consider the integration of sequential and direct-access file processing within large, on-line computer systems.

Chapter Summary

1. Within most business information systems, file sizes exceed the capacities of computer memory. In these cases, special file processing techniques must be used. These techniques involve accessing and processing a single record at a time from an external storage device.

2. One of the most common methods for processing large files involves use of direct-access devices. Files are stored on disk and allow direct and immediate program access to any particular record in the file.

3. Direct-access files are appropriate under two conditions—when only a few of the records in the file will be processed at any one time, and when it is impossible or impractical to anticipate the order in which records will be processed.

4. Direct-access files also are known as relative files. Each record is located based on its position relative to the first record in the file.

5. A record key serves as a pointer to the relative position of a record in a file. Thus, if the key is known, the corresponding record can be accessed from the file without the need for a sequential search.

6. To create a direct-access file, it often is necessary to initialize the file. A null, or dummy, record contains zero values or blank spaces in the fields where actual data values eventually will appear. In addition, a status code field is defined and initially valued to zero to indicate that the record position is available for adding an actual data record.

7. Once a file has been preformatted with null records, it can receive actual data records. The file is built by accessing the null record at the position in which a data record is to be added, updating the zero and blank fields with data values, and then writing the new record back to the file at the location of the null record. The status code field is set to 1, indicating that the record position is in use.

8. Direct-access files can be accessed sequentially as well as randomly. Sequential access is used for report writing programs. These programs must contain a select mechanism so that null records are bypassed and only those records that have a status code of 1 are printed.

9. File maintenance involves adding records to, changing records within, and deleting records from files. To add records to a direct-access file, the null record at the position to be added is accessed and brought into memory, the new field values are placed in the record, and the updated record, with a status code of 1, is rewritten to the file. Record changes are handled in the same manner, except that actual data fields are updated. The status code remains the same. To delete a record, the status code is changed to 0, and, optionally, the data fields can be assigned null values. However, the record is not removed physically from the file. In all cases, records are updated in place.

10. Computer systems differ in their handling of direct-access files. However, processing principles remain fairly consistent for different systems and versions of BASIC.

Review Questions

1. What is direct access?

2. Why is direct access a necessity for large-scale information processing systems?

3. What are three characteristics required of records that are to be accessed directly?

4. To implement a direct-access file through use of the BASIC language, what must be created on the disk itself?

5. How is the BASIC option RELATIVE used to implement direct-access capability?

6. How is the MAP command used within a program designed to implement direct-access capability?

7. What characteristic must the reading of records from direct-access files possess that is not shared by the reading of records from sequential files?

Practice Exercises

1. Design and write programs that create and process a direct-access file to support an airline reservation system. The master file will contain flight records made up of the following fields:

Status code	(0/1)
Flight number (key)	(# # #)
Origination code	(LAX, CVG, STL, DFW, etc.)
Destination code	(LAX, CVG, STL, DFW, etc.)
Departure time	(XX:XX am/pm)
Arrival time	(XX:XX am/pm)
First-class seats	(# # #)
Coach-class seats	(# # #)

    Four programs are to be written. First, write a file initialization program to format 100 record positions for the 100 potential flight numbers (001 – 100) that will appear in the file. Then, write a file creation program to add the original flight records to the initialized file. Develop data sufficient to load at least 20 records in the file. Next, write a detail report program that lists the content of the file. Finally, write a file maintenance program that allows for additions, changes, and deletions to be made to the file. Develop sufficient test data to check the functioning of this program. The maintenance program will be used for adding new flights, for booking passengers on particular flights, for changing flight information, and for deleting cancelled routes from the file.

2. Modify programs within the amusement park information system that was developed in Chapters 1 through 8. The master file will be implemented as a direct-access file. Therefore, write a file initialization program to allocate space for the file. Then, rewrite the file creation program so that the file can be loaded as a relative file. Enter the original file data into this new file. Next, rewrite the detail report program so that it accesses the new file and prints the same type of report. Finally, revise or rewrite the file maintenance program so that it allows on-line updates to the direct-access file. Use the same maintenance data that appeared in the original program description.

3. Write programs to create, edit, and post a transaction file to the master file illustrated in this chapter. Develop sufficient test data to verify the operations of these programs.

4. Use the systems development projects that appear in Appendix B as the framework for developing a system of programs that implement direct-access file processing methods.

Key Terms

1. direct access
2. random
3. relative file
4. status code

5. null record
6. dummy record
7. pointers

BASIC Library

1. MAP
2. PUT
3. RELATIVE

4. GET
5. UPDATE

10
LARGE
SEQUENTIAL
FILES

OVERVIEW AND OBJECTIVES

Sequential files, like direct access files, usually expand to volumes of records that are beyond the capacities of main memories. Thus, in many applications it is not practical to think about reading an entire file into memory for processing. Rather, the files themselves must exist on secondary storage devices and must be processed at the record level for updating and maintenance.

When sequential files are stored on external devices, processing requirements are altered markedly. As long as a file fits within the bounds of main memory, records can be processed in any order of transactions. Even if an update transaction requires a complete search through the file for the corresponding master record, this can be done without a significant degradation in service. The processing speed of the computer compensates for any inefficiencies that result when transaction keys and master keys do not correspond. However, when files are stored on external devices and records are accessed and processed one after another, the order of records in the transaction file and those in the master file must correspond. With large files, it is impractical and inefficient to perform a complete file search to locate and update each master record. In such cases, then, transaction records that will impact master records must be in the same order as the master records before processing can begin.

Most of the programming challenges associated with large sequential files lie in the sequencing and handling of transactions prior to processing. This chapter describes the principles and processes needed for

386

handling and maintaining these files. When you have completed your work in this chapter, you should be able to:

☐ Describe and implement basic sort procedures.

☐ Describe and implement basic file merging procedures.

☐ Describe and implement basic transaction file edit procedures.

☐ Describe and implement programs for the posting of master files to reflect content of transaction files.

☐ Describe and implement maintenance programs that add records to, delete records from, and change records within master files.

SEQUENTIAL PROCESSING PRINCIPLES

Previous examples involved files that were loaded into memory in their entirety. In those situations, there was no concern about the order in which transactions were presented for processing. Given the speed of main memory and the small sizes of the files, the time required to search through the files to find the records to be processed was not a factor.

There are applications, however, in which there is much to be concerned about in considering the order in which transactions are presented for master file processing. Consider a typical, everyday example. A major bank may have a million or more accounts represented in its master files. Hundreds of thousands of checks may be written against these accounts every day. Most of these transactions arrive at bank computer centers and require processing in relatively compressed, overnight cycles, because checks and deposit slips tend to be accumulated throughout the business day, then carried to a computer center at night.

It would be impossible to load such massive files into computer memory and store them as tables. Even if the bank had computers large enough to accommodate this procedure, the time required to process the hundreds of thousands of deposits and withdrawals would be prohibitive. For each transaction, the computer would have to search sequentially through the file tables to locate the matching master record against which the transaction would be applied.

To overcome these kinds of difficulties, it is necessary to maintain the master and transaction files on secondary storage devices. The files must be processed in memory one record at a time. To support this processing, both master and transaction records must be sequenced correspondingly, according to their keys. In this way, file processing can be completed with a single pass through the master file, maximizing processing speed.

The application of transaction files against master files through single-pass processing is the basis of sequential file processing systems. To implement systems of this type, a series of file processing techniques is required. These techniques include:

- Sort
- Merge
- Sequential edit
- Sequential posting
- Sequential maintenance.

SORTING PROCEDURES

A computer *sort* is a procedure for processing *serial* files and creating sequential files. In this context, a serial file is one in which records are written in chronological order, as the data are captured, without regard for the key values of the records. Serial files are often the result of data entry procedures. At the time of data entry, the records have no logical order—they are placed in the file as transactions occur.

The banking scenario can continue here. Throughout the day, bank tellers process customer transactions. Deposits and withdrawals are made and occur randomly. At the end of the day, the deposit slips and checks are gathered from the teller windows and forwarded to the data processing department. Here, checks and deposit slips are processed through machines which read the magnetically encoded forms and produce transaction records that are written to magnetic tape files. These records are still in the random order in which they were gathered from tellers.

These banking transactions then are used to update the customer master file. The deposit and withdrawal amounts are posted to the corresponding master records. However, before processing can occur, the transaction file must be ordered to correspond with the master file. The order, or sequence, usually is determined by account number.

Sort routines are used to sequence the transaction files. These programs arrange records in ascending or descending order, according to one or more key fields embedded within the records. Sort routines often are provided as one of the *utility programs* of a computer's *operating system.* The operating system is the set of programs that is usually purchased with the computer hardware. These programs control hardware functions and, in general, facilitate use of the system. Although most computer installations will have utility sort programs available, in some cases original routines will have to be written as part of applications programs. Therefore, sorting techniques are described below.

In-Memory Sort

The fastest way to sort a limited number of records is in memory. The routine that controls this function establishes a table of records. The size of the table is accommodated either to the size of the file or to the capacity of memory. For small files that can be held in their entirety in memory, the table size may be equal to the file size. For large files, only a portion of the file will be sorted at one time. In this case, the table size depends on available memory space, because it is preferable to hold as many records as is possible at a time.

It should be noted that sorting is done according to record keys; it is not necessary to sort the records themselves. Therefore, it is common practice to copy keys into a table that is separate from the records. Then, the keys are sorted and used to reorder the records as they are written from the table to the output file.

An in-memory sort procedure for a table of keys is illustrated graphically in Figure 10-1. First, an end-of-table pointer is established to indicate the last element in the table. This element is the location at which the largest key will be placed. Next, a search subscript is defined to point to the next-to-last table element. This is the point at which the search will begin to find a key value higher than the current last value in the table. The subscript is decreased by one following each processing loop to point successively to the table elements from bottom to top. During this indexing, a value may be found that is larger than the value in the last table element. If so, the two values are exchanged: the end-of-table value is copied into an exchange area; the higher key value is copied to the end-of-table element; and the value in the exchange area is copied into the table element vacated by the higher value.

After the initial search through the table has located the highest key value and placed it in the last table element, the search is repeated to find the next-to-highest value. The end-of-table pointer is decreased by one to point to the next-to-last table element. This element is the point at

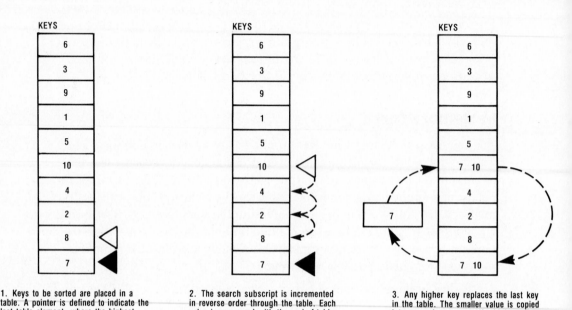

1. Keys to be sorted are placed in a table. A pointer is defined to indicate the last table element, where the highest value will appear. A search subscript is initialized to point to the next-to-last element.

2. The search subscript is incremented in reverse order through the table. Each value is compared with the end-of-table value in search of a higher key.

3. Any higher key replaces the last key in the table. The smaller value is copied into an exchange area; the higher value is copied into the last table position; and the value in the exchange area is copied into the position vacated by the higher key.

Figure 10-1. Table processing procedure for a sort.

which the largest of the remaining keys will be placed. Again, the subscript is indexed from the bottom to the top of the table. Any higher keys are swapped with the key in the next-to-last table position. At the completion of this second pass through the table, then, the last two positions will be occupied by the two highest keys in the file.

Resetting of the end-of-table pointer successively up through the table and searching for the highest of the remaining key values continues until all table positions have been checked and necessary swaps made. The sort is completed when the end-of-table pointer reaches the first table element.

Figure 10-2 presents a generalized structure chart for a replacement sort routine. Figure 10-3 shows the pseudocode. Figure 10-4 gives the

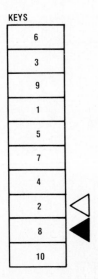

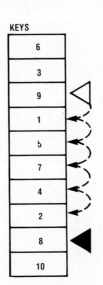

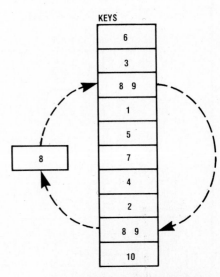

4. After the first pass through the table, the end-of-table pointer is set to point to the next-to-last position. The search subscript is set to point to the preceding table element.

5. The search continues for the highest of the remaining table values.

6. Any higher key is swapped with the next-to-last table value. After the second pass through the table, the pointers are moved up and search and replacement continue across the remaining table values.

BASIC code for an example sort program based on this general model. This program processes a file of customer sales transactions. Each record contains a customer account number, customer name, sales order number, amount of purchase, and order date. These transaction records are used to update a customer accounts receivable file. The customer master records are assumed to be ordered by account number. Therefore, the transaction file will require sequencing in this same order.

Within the begin processing section of the program, a subroutine is called to load the transaction file (named CUSTIF) into a table (named R9$). Within the subroutine, the table is dimensioned to handle up to 50 records. However, only 15 of those positions are used in this program run. Therefore, the subscript used to increment through the table during loading serves as a record counter which, on end of file, is assigned as the table length (Z). Also, the end-of-table pointer (E) is set to the value of the subscript to prepare for sorting.

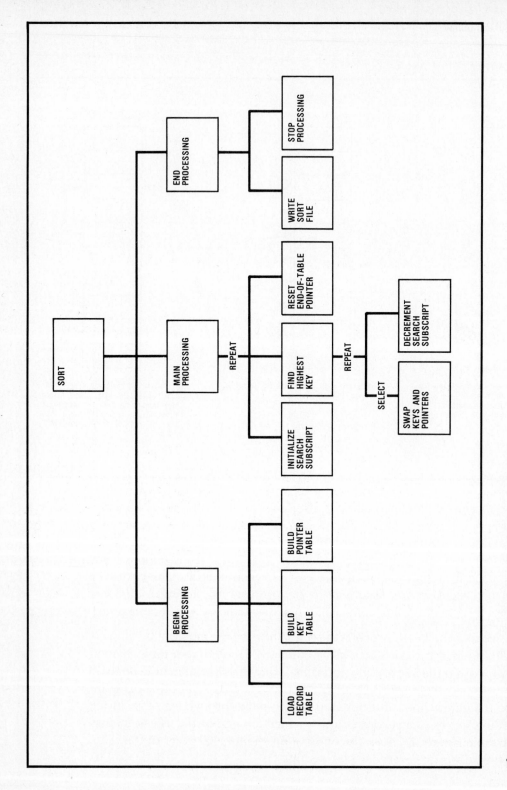

Figure 10-2. General structure chart for replacement sort.

```
SORT
    BEGIN PROCESSING
        LOAD RECORD TABLE
            Dimension Record Table
            Open Unsorted File for input
            Input first Record String
            Set Table Subscript [Sub] = 0
            REPEAT: until EOF Unsorted File
                Set Sub = Sub 1
                Set Record Table (Sub) = Record String
                Input next Record String
            END REPEAT
            Close Unsorted File
            Set Table Length = Sub
            Set End Pointer [End] = Sub
        BUILD KEY TABLE
            Dimension Key Table
            Set Sub = 1
            REPEAT: until Sub > Table Length
                Set Key Table (Sub) = Substring (Record Table (Sub))
                Set Sub = Sub + 1
            END REPEAT
        BUILD POINTER TABLE
            Dimension Pointer Table
            Set Sub = 1
            REPEAT: until Sub > Table Length
                Set Pointer Table (Sub) = Sub
                Set Sub = Sub + 1
            END REPEAT
    MAIN PROCESSING
    REPEAT: until End = 1
        INITIALIZE SEARCH SUBSCRIPT
            Set Sub = End - 1
        FIND HIGHEST KEY
            REPEAT: until Sub = 0
                SELECT: on Key Table (Sub) > Key Table (End)
                    SWAP KEYS AND POINTERS
                        Set Key Exchange     = Key Table (End)
                        Set Key Table (End) = Key Table (Sub)
                        Set Key Table (Sub) = Key Exchange
                        Set Pointer Exchange     = Pointer Table (Sub)
                        Set Pointer Table (End) = Pointer Table (Sub)
                        Set Pointer Table (Sub) = Pointer Exchange
                END SELECT
                DECREMENT SEARCH SUBSCRIPT
                    Set Sub = Sub - 1
            END REPEAT
        RESET END-OF-TABLE POINTER
            Set End = End - 1
    END REPEAT
    END PROCESSING
        WRITE SORT FILE
            Open Sort File for output
            Set Sub = 1
            REPEAT: until Sub > Table Length
                Write Record Table (Pointer Table (Sub))
                Set Sub = Sub + 1
            END REPEAT
            Write end-of-file record
            Close Sort File
        STOP PROCESSING
            Stop
```

Figure 10-3. Pseudocode for generalized sort routine.

Figure 10-4. BASIC code for sort program.

```
1000! SORTDEMO                                          DRA/WEL
1010!                 SORT CUSTOMER TRANS FILE
1020!
1030! THIS PROGRAM DEMONSTRATES A SORT ROUTINE.  THE
1040! INPUT FILE, NAMED "CUSTTF" CONTAINS CUSTOMER SALES
1050! RECORDS.   THIS IS A SERIAL FILE IN WHICH RECORDS
1060! ARE COMPRISED OF THE FOLLOWING FIELDS:
1070!
1080!    ACCOUNT NUMBER (1ST THREE POSITIONS)
1090!    CUSTOMER NAME
1100!    ORDER NUMBER
1110!    ORDER AMOUNT
1120!    ORDER DATE
1130!
1140! THE PROGRAM ARRANGES THE RECORDS IN ASCENDING ORDER BY
1150! ACCOUNT NUMBER AND WRITES THEM TO AN OUTPUT FILE NAMED
1160! "SORTFL".
1170!
1180! VARIABLE NAMES
1190!
1200! INPUT RECORD:
1210!    R$....CUSTOMER SALES RECORD
1220! PROGRAM TABLES:
1230!    R9$...SALES RECORD TABLE
1240!    K9$...ACCOUNT NUMBER KEY TABLE
1250!    P9....POINTER TABLE
1260! SUBSCRIPTS AND POINTERS:
1270!    S.....TABLE SUBSCRIPT
1280!    E.....TABLE END POINTER
1290!    Z.....TABLE LENGTH
1300! WORK AREAS:
1310!    X$....KEY EXCHANGE AREA
1320!    X.....POINTER EXCHANGE AREA
1330!
1350! ************************
1360! * 1.0 BEGIN PROCESSING *
1370! ************************
1380!
1390  GOSUB 2000   ! LOAD ORDER RECORD TABLE
1400  GOSUB 3000   ! BUILD KEY TABLE
1410  GOSUB 4000   ! BUILD POINTER TABLE
1420!
1430! ************************
1440! * 2.0 MAIN PROCESSING  *
1450! ************************
1460! REPEAT
1470  IF E = 1 THEN GOTO 1730
1480!
1490     LET S = E - 1
1500!
1510     REPEAT
1520     IF S = 0 THEN GOTO 1680
1530!
1540        SELECT
1550        IF K9$(S) > K9$(E) THEN GOTO 1570
1560                                GOTO 1630
1570           LET X$      = K9$(E)
1580           LET K9$(E) = K9$(S)
1590           LET K9$(S) = X$
1600           LET X       = P9(E)
1610           LET P9(E)  = P9(S)
1620           LET P9(S)  = X
1630!        END SELECT
```

```
1640!
1650         LET S = S - 1
1660!
1670     GOTO 1510
1680!    END REPEAT
1690!
1700     LET E = E - 1
1710!
1720   GOTO 1460
1730! END REPEAT
1740!
1750! *************************
1760! * 3.0 END PROCESSING    *
1770! *************************
1780!
1790   GOSUB 5000   ! WRITE SORT FILE
1800   STOP
1810!
2000! *******************************
2010! * S1.0 LOAD ORDER RECORD TABLE *
2020! *******************************
2030!
2040   DIM R9$(50)
2050   OPEN "CUSTTF" FOR INPUT AS #1
2060   INPUT LINE #1, R$
2070   LET S = 0
2080!
2090! REPEAT
2100   IF MID$(R$,1,3) = "000" THEN GOTO 2170
2110!
2120     LET S = S + 1
2130     LET R9$(S) = R$
2140     INPUT LINE #1, R$
2150!
2160   GOTO 2100
2170! END REPEAT
2180!
2190   CLOSE #1
2200   LET Z = S
2210   LET E = S
2220   RETURN
2230!
3000! **************************
3010! * S2.0 BUILD KEY TABLE *
3020! **************************
3030!
3040   DIM K9$(50)
3050   LET S = 1
3060!
3070! REPEAT
3080   IF S > Z THEN GOTO 3140
3090!
3100     LET K9$(S) = MID$(R9$(S),1,3)
3110     LET S = S + 1
3120!
3130   GOTO 3070
3140! END REPEAT
3150!
3160   RETURN
3170!
4000! ****************************
4010! * S3.0 BUILD POINTER TABLE *
4020! ****************************
4030!
4040   DIM P9(50)
4050   LET S = 1
4060!
4070! REPEAT
4080   IF S > Z THEN GOTO 4140
4090!
4100     LET P9(S) = S
4110     LET S = S + 1
```

```
4120!
4130  GOTO 4070
4140! END REPEAT
4150!
4160  RETURN
4170!
5000! ************************
5010! * S4.0 WRITE SORT FILE *
5020! ************************
5030!
5040  OPEN "SORTFL" FOR OUTPUT AS #2
5050  LET S = 1
5060!
5070! REPEAT
5080  IF S > Z THEN GOTO 5120
5090     PRINT #2, R9$(P9(S))
5100     LET S = S + 1
5110  GOTO 5070
5120! END REPEAT
5130!
5140  PRINT #2, "000,END OF FILE,000,000.00,00/00"
5150  CLOSE #2
5160  RETURN
5170!
5180  END
```

Figure 10-4. Concluded.

This program differs from earlier examples in that an entire record is treated as a character string. Thus, the fields are not defined in separate tables. Instead, all fields in a single record, along with their separating commas, are written as a single string into the table element. Records are written this way because it is not necessary to have access to individual fields. The entire record is to be sorted. Figure 10-5A shows how the records appear within the table.

Reading of records as character strings is accomplished by using the INPUT LINE (or, in some versions of BASIC, the LINE INPUT) statement. This statement accesses from a file all characters up to (and sometimes including) the line feed and carriage return characters. Then, this character string is made available to the program. In the current program, this string (R$), which represents a complete customer transaction record, is placed in table R9$. The general format for the INPUT LINE statement is given in Figure 10-6.

Note the way in which the subroutine checks for an end of file. Because an entire character string is input for each record, it is not possible to check the fields directly for an end-of-file value. Instead, a portion, or *substring*, of the string must be tested. In this example, the first three characters of the record (the location in the string of the account number) are tested for the value "000" as an indication of the EOF record.

This substring is identified with the MID$ function. The function, MID$(R$,1,3), references the first three positions of string R$, beginning with the first character. Figure 10-7 presents the general format for this function and for other useful string functions. (Note that, in some versions of BASIC, the function names do not end with a $.)

After the table of records is loaded, another table (named K9$) is defined to hold the record table keys. This table will be sorted to place the keys in ascending sequence. See Figure 10-5A. To build this table, the subroutine copies the keys from table R9$, one-to-one, into table K9$. This table is built also by using the string function MID$.

A third table, named P9, is defined. This pointer table initially contains the values 1 through 15, in sequence, to represent the positions of the data records which correspond with the associated keys. As the keys are sorted, the corresponding position values in table P9 are rearranged. At the end of the sort, therefore, each key in table K9$ will still be associated with its corresponding record in table R9$. When it comes time to write the customer records to the sort file, they will be written in the order given in table P9. See Figure 10-5B.

Some versions of BASIC do not support these string functions. In such cases, each field from the input record will have to be retained in a separate table. Still, key and pointer tables are used for sorting and for identifying the order in which records should be output.

Strictly speaking, it is not necessary to use a pointer table when records are sorted. However, if a pointer table is not used, the record table will require searching each of the keys in the key table to locate the record to be written to the output file. With a pointer table, the location of the record to be written is given in the table. This value becomes the subscript of the corresponding record. Searching the record table is not necessary. Therefore, it is good practice to use a pointer table, even though it may not be required.

Having described this method, a qualification is in order. In-memory sort is only one way to sort records. There are many others, some of them more efficient in their use of computer time. However, the purpose here is to establish an understanding of why and how records are sequenced. In practice, as discussed above, most sorting functions are

CUSTOMER TRANSACTION FILE

K9$	P9	R9$
627	1	627,JIM COLE,107,10.47,10/17
154	2	154,ALICE COOKE,129,195.45,10/17
395	3	395,BILL SEREY,132,16.18,10/15
467	4	467,GLORIA GREEN,115,98.45,10/16
829	5	829,MARY TYSON,109,25.00,10/16
175	6	175,LYLE GRAY,130,62.75,10/16
167	7	167,ART KAPLAN,124,140.50,10/17
242	8	242,LINDA DOLIVE,110,38.43,10/14
318	9	318,GARY JOHNSTON,114,295.95,10/13
396	10	396,CARL SLATER,131,3.75,10/17
705	11	705,CONNIE WIDMER,128,107.66,10/14
318	12	318,GARY JOHNSTON,117,12.95,10/17
449	13	449,JUDY TERRELL,122,6.25,10/14
282	14	282,BETH HOWELL,108,114.68,10/15
294	15	294,DICK THOMAS,135,50.00,10/17

A. Records from input file are loaded as character strings into table R9$. Keys are copied into table K9$ and pointer table P9 is established.

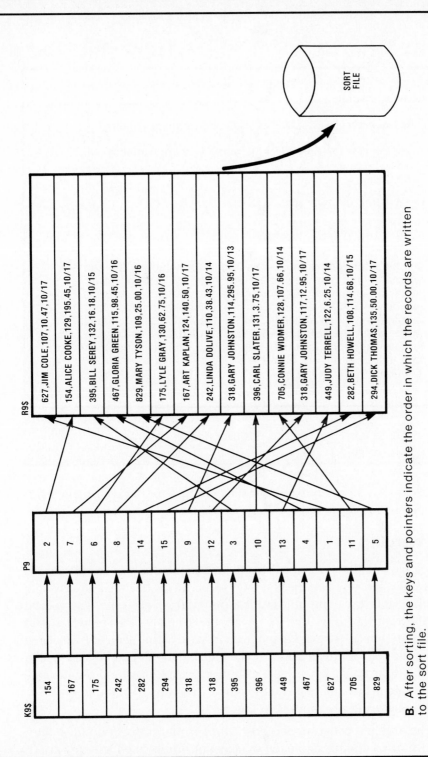

B. After sorting, the keys and pointers indicate the order in which the records are written to the sort file.

Figure 10-5. During sorting (A), only record keys and position pointers need to be kept in order. Following sorting (B), the pointers indicate the location in the record table from which records will be written to the output file.

General Format:

  line number INPUT LINE #file number, string variable

  line number LINE INPUT #file number, string variable

Examples:

1250 INPUT LINE #1, A$

1250 LINE INPUT #1, A$

All characters preceding (and sometimes including) the carriage
return and line feed characters are input as a string. Field
delimiters (commas) are input as part of the string. In some
versions of BASIC, an extra set of carriage return/line feed
characters may be appended to the set that is input. In such
cases, when the string is rewritten to a file, an extra line will be
written. Therefore, before the string is written, it is necessary to
strip these characters from the string by using the MID$
function.

Figure 10-6. Formats for the INPUT LINE (or LINE INPUT) statement.

---

handled under control of packaged utility programs that are usually made
available within systems software.

File Merging

The *merge* function combines two files of sequentially ordered records
into a single file in which the common sequence of the initial files is maintained. That is, the computer reads a record from each file. The record
with the lower key is written to the output file and another record is read
from that source file. Comparing continues with records from each
source file written to the output file alternately, depending on which
record has the lower key. A generalized structure chart and pseudocode
for a merge program are given in Figures 10-8 and 10-9. BASIC code for
an example program appears in Figure 10-10.

     The example program demonstrates the merging of two files. Both
files are in ascending sequence by account number, which appears in

Function Code	Meaning

LEFT$(A$,N) or LEFT(A$,N)	Indicates a substring of string A$ from the first character through the Nth character.
	
	`A$ = "ABCDEFG"`
	`LEFT$(A$,3) = "ABC"`

MID$(A$,N1,N2) or MID(A$,N1,N2)	Indicates a substring of string A$ starting with character N1 and continuing for N2 characters.
	
	`A$ = "ABCDEF"`
	`MID$(A$,2,5) = "BCDE"`

RIGHT$(A$,N) or RIGHT(A$,N)	Indicates a substring of string A$ from the Nth character through the farthest-right character.
	
	`A$ = "ABCDEF"`
	`RIGHT$(A$,3) = "DEF"`

LEN(A$)	Returns the number of characters in string A$, including blank spaces.
	
	`A$ = "ABCDEF   "`
	`LEN(A$) = 9`

+	Indicates a concatenation operation on two strings.
	
	`A$ = "ABC"`
	`B$ = "DEF"`
	`A$ + B$ = "ABCDEF"`

Figure 10-7. BASIC string functions.

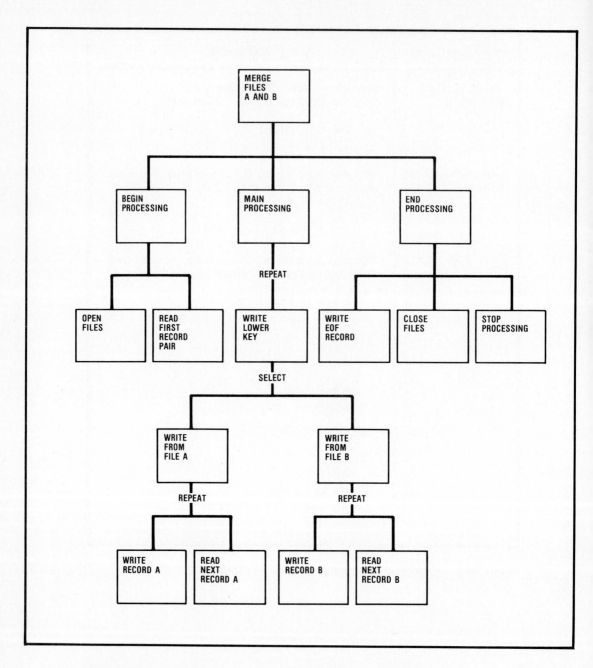

Figure 10-8.   Structure chart for generalized merge program.

```
MERGE FILES A AND B
     BEGIN PROCESSING
          OPEN FILES
               Open File-A for input
               Open File-B for input
               Open Merge File for output
          READ FIRST RECORD PAIR
                    Read first Record-A
                    Read first Record-B
          MAIN PROCESSING
          REPEAT: until EOF File-A and EOF File-B
               WRITE LOWER KEY
                    SELECT: on Key-B > Key-A
                            or EOF File-B
                         WRITE FROM FILE A
                              REPEAT: until Key-A > Key-B
                                          or EOF File-A
                                   WRITE RECORD A
                                        Write Record-A to Merge File
                                   READ NEXT RECORD A
                                        Read Record-A
                              END REPEAT
                    END SELECT
                    SELECT: on Key-A > Key-B
                            or EOF File-A
                         WRITE FROM FILE B
                              REPEAT: until Key-B > Key-A
                                          or EOF File-B
                                   WRITE RECORD B
                                        Write Record-B to Merge File
                                   READ NEXT RECORD B
                                        Read Record-B
                              END REPEAT
                    END SELECT
          END REPEAT
          END PROCESSING
               WRITE EOF RECORD
                    Write end-of-file record to Merge File
               CLOSE FILES
                    Close File-A
                    Close File-B
                    Close Merge File
               STOP PROCESSING
                    Stop
```

Figure 10-9. Pseudocode for generalized merge program.

```
1000! MERGEDEMO                                        DRA/WEL
1010!                 MERGE CUSTOMER TRANS FILES
1020!
1030! THIS PROGRAM DEMONSTRATES THE MERGING OF TWO FILES.
1040! BOTH FILES, NAMED "CUSTTF1" AND "CUSTTF2", CONTAIN
1050! CUSTOMER SALES RECORDS COMPRISED OF THE FOLLOWING
1060! FIELDS:
1070!
1080!     ACCOUNT NUMBER (1ST THREE POSITIONS)
1090!     CUSTOMER NAME
1100!     ORDER NUMBER
1110!     ORDER AMOUNT
1120!     ORDER DATE
1130!
1140! BOTH FILES ARE SEQUENCED ACCORDING TO ACCOUNT
1150! NUMBERS.
1160!
1170! VARIABLE NAMES
1180!
1190! INPUT RECORDS:
1200!     R1$...CUSTTF1 RECORD
1210!     R2$...CUSTTF2 RECORD
1220!
1230! 0.0 MERGE CUSTOMER TRANS FILES
1240!
1250! ************************
1260! * 1.0 BEGIN PROCESSING *
1270! ************************
1280!
1290  OPEN "CUSTTF1" FOR INPUT AS #1
1300  OPEN "CUSTTF2" FOR INPUT AS #2
1310  OPEN "MERGEFL" FOR OUTPUT AS #3
1320!
1330  INPUT LINE #1, R1$
1340  INPUT LINE #2, R2$
1350!
1360! ************************
1370! * 2.0 MAIN PROCESSING  *
1380! ************************
1390! REPEAT
1400  IF MID$(R1$,1,3)="000" AND MID$(R2$,1,3)="000" THEN GOTO 1750
1410!
1420!     SELECT
1430      IF MID$(R2$,1,3) > MID$(R1$,1,3) THEN GOTO 1460
1440      IF MID$(R2$,1,3) = "000"          THEN GOTO 1460
1450                                                GOTO 1560
1460!        REPEAT
1470         IF MID$(R1$,1,3)>MID$(R2$,1,3) AND MID$(R2$,1,3)<>"000" THEN 1540
1480         IF MID$(R1$,1,3) = "000"                                THEN 1540
1490!
1500            PRINT #3, R1$
1510            INPUT LINE #1, R1$
1520!
1530         GOTO 1460
1540         END REPEAT
1550!
1560!     END SELECT
1570!
1580!     SELECT
1590      IF MID$(R1$,1,3) > MID$(R2$,1,3) THEN GOTO 1620
1600      IF MID$(R1$,1,3) = "000"          THEN GOTO 1620
1610                                                GOTO 1720
```

```
1620!        REPEAT
1630           IF MID$(R2$,1,3)>MID$(R1$,1,3)  AND  MID$(R2$,1,3)<>"000"  THEN  1700
1640           IF MID$(R2$,1,3) = "000"                               THEN  1700
1650!
1660             PRINT #3, R2$
1670             INPUT LINE #2, R2$
1680!
1690           GOTO 1620
1700!          END REPEAT
1710!
1720!     END SELECT
1730!
1740   GOTO 1390
1750! END REPEAT
1760!
1770! ************************
1780! * 3.0 END PROCESSING    *
1790! ************************
1800!
1810   PRINT #3, "000,END OF FILE,000,000.00,00/00"
1820!
1830   CLOSE #1
1840   CLOSE #2
1850   CLOSE #3
1860   STOP
1870!
1880   END
```

Figure 10-10. BASIC code for merge program.

the first three character positions in each record. As in the sort example, records to be merged are accessed from the files as strings. The MID$ function is used to locate the account numbers for comparison. These numbers are compared and the record with the lowest value is written to the merge file.

Special tests are set up in this program to handle end-of-file conditions. The end-of-file record in both files contains the value "000" in the account number position. When either of the files is exhausted, this value becomes the comparison value. However, in this case, the record with the lower "account number" should not be written to the merge file. So, a test for the value of "000" bypasses the normal writing of this low record.

The merge function is used also to sort a large file that will not fit within memory in its entirety. A portion of the file must be sorted and merged with previously sorted portions of the file. In such a circumstance, the programming logic involved becomes complicated and exceeds the scope of this book. However, in principle, the sort/merge process works as shown in Figure 10-11. Here, a large source file is broken into three parts, labeled A, B, and C. First, the sort routine sorts portion A within memory and writes it to an output file. Next, portion B is

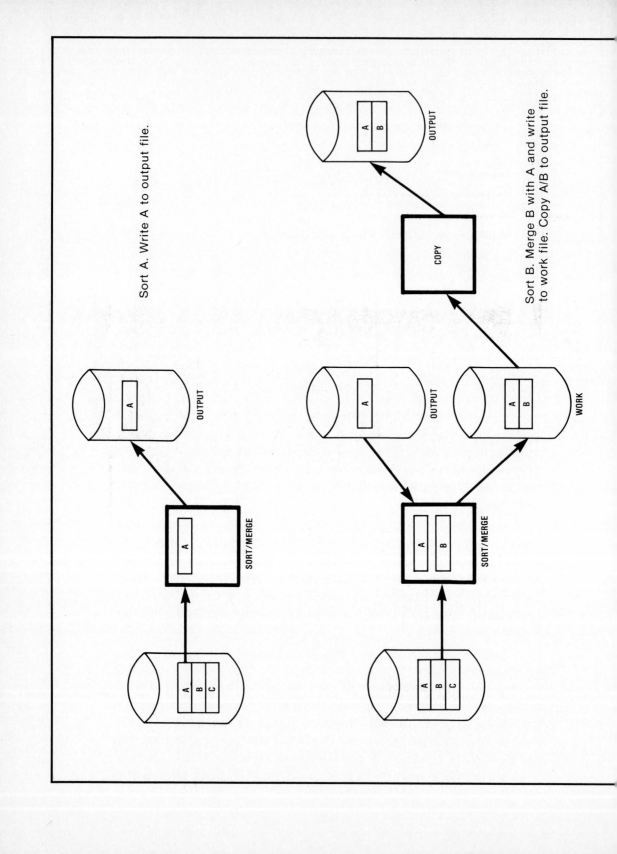

Sort A. Write A to output file.

Sort B. Merge B with A and write
to work file. Copy A/B to output file.

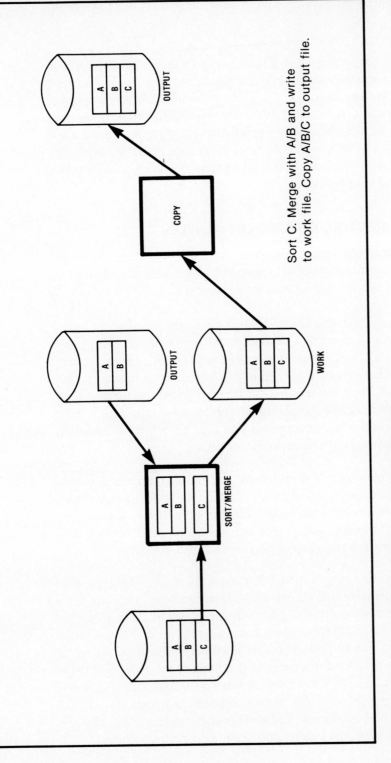

Sort C. Merge with A/B and write to work file. Copy A/B/C to output file.

Figure 10-11. Sort/merge procedure for multiple input files.

brought into memory and sorted. Then, portion B is combined with portion A through a merge routine and the combined sections are written to a work file. At this point, the work file is copied back to the output file. Finally, portion C is brought into memory and sorted. C is merged with the combined A/B output file to produce the completely sorted work file. Then, the work file is copied back to the output file. The output file continues to grow with each additional section of sorted records taken from the original source file.

EDITING AND POSTING OF SEQUENTIAL FILES

Business records are dynamic. In the course of doing business, transactions occur that must be reflected in master files. Periodically, therefore, transactions are posted against master accounts.

Before master files are updated, however, there must be some assurance that transaction files contain valid information. Also, there should be verification that a matching master record exists for each transaction record. Otherwise, a transaction record could be presented for processing against a non-existent master record. To protect against such a situation as well as against updating with erroneous transaction data, it is standard practice to perform an *edit run*, in which transaction records are compared with master file records.

Earlier examples in this book show editing accomplished within memory. That is, the entire master file is loaded into tables against which edits take place. However, with large files, this technique is impractical, if not impossible. Therefore, other techniques must be used to bring both a single master record and transaction record into memory.

This type of processing is straightforward. As shown in the general program model presented in Figure 10-12, transaction records are read one at a time and compared with succeeding records in the master file. If no master record exists for a given transaction record, an error condition is noted on an edit report so that necessary adjustments can be made. If there is a matching master record, editing of the individual fields of the transaction record takes place. Errors in transaction fields are noted on the edit report also. The general logic of the program is shown in Figure 10-13. This pseudocode includes several condition tests that are required to implement the repeat and select control structures.

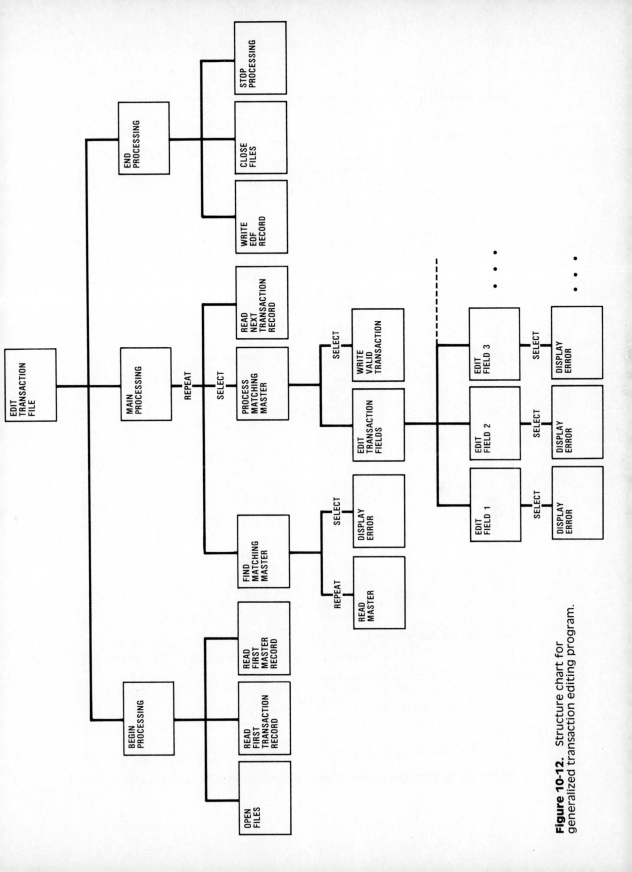

Figure 10-12. Structure chart for generalized transaction editing program.

```
EDIT TRANSACTION FILE
    BEGIN PROCESSING
        OPEN FILES
                Open Master File for input
                Open Trans File for input
                Open Valid Trans File for output
        READ FIRST TRANSACTION RECORD
                Read Trans Record
        READ FIRST MASTER RECORD
                Read Master Record
    MAIN PROCESSING
    REPEAT: until EOF Trans File
        FIND MATCHING MASTER
                REPEAT: until Mstr-Key = Trans-Key
                            or Mstr-Key > Trans-Key
                            or EOF Master File
                    READ MASTER
                            Read Master Record
                END REPEAT
                SELECT: on Mstr-Key > Trans-Key
                        or EOF Master File
                    DISPLAY ERROR
                            Print "master not found" message
                END SELECT
        .SELECT: on Mstr-Key = Trans-Key
                PROCESS MATCHING MASTER
                    Set Valid Flag = "Yes"
                    EDIT TRANSACTION FIELDS
                        EDIT FIELD 1
                            .
                            (Edit procedure)
                            .
                            SELECT: on Valid Flag = "No"
                                    DISPLAY ERROR
                                            Print error message
                            END SELECT
                        EDIT FIELD 2
                            .
                            .
                            .
                        SELECT: on Valid Flag = "Yes"
                            WRITE VALID TRANSACTION
                                    Write Trans Record to Valid Trans File
                        END SELECT
        END SELECT
        READ NEXT TRANSACTION RECORD
                Read Trans Record
    END REPEAT
    END PROCESSING
        WRITE EOF RECORD
            Write end-of-file record to Valid Trans File
        CLOSE FILES
            Close Master File
            Close Trans File
            Close Valid Trans File
        STOP PROCESSING
            Stop
```

Figure 10-13. Pseudocode for generalized transaction file edit program.

Once the results of the edit run have been used to validate the transaction file and erroneous records have been corrected, the transaction file can be posted to the master file. Figure 10-14 is a model structure chart for the processing required to post transaction amounts to master records. Provision is made, however, for the possibility that transaction records will be found that do not have corresponding master records. Pseudocode for this posting program is shown in Figure 10-15.

SEQUENTIAL FILE MAINTENANCE

Recall that maintenance is the process of changing master files to reflect additions of new records, deletions of old records, and changes to existing records to correct erroneous or out-of-date information. Whereas posting changes only the data content of existing master records, maintenance may change the number of records in the file. For this reason, and because maintenance activities must protect the sequential integrity of the master file, sequential file maintenance is one of the most difficult logical challenges faced by business applications programmers.

In Chapter 8, master file maintenance is handled easily by reading the entire file into memory for updating. Because of this internal handling of the master file, transactions need not be in the same sequential order as the master records. The internal processing speed of the computer makes it possible to update by conducting multiple passes through the table file. With large files, however, this technique is impractical. Multiple passes through the file—once for each transaction record—are time consuming and require multiple openings and closings of the master file. So, large master files are updated sequentially on a single pass through both the transaction file and the master file. A new master file is created in the process.

Sequential file maintenance involves three files:

- A *transaction file* is an input file containing (1) records to be added to the master file, (2) records containing changes to be made to the master file, and (3) records containing keys that signify records to be deleted from the master file.
- An *old master file* is an input file representing the file to be updated with the additions, changes, and deletions.
- A *new master file* is the output of file maintenance.

Thus, transaction records are applied against the old master records to create a new master file. The programming challenge lies in matching

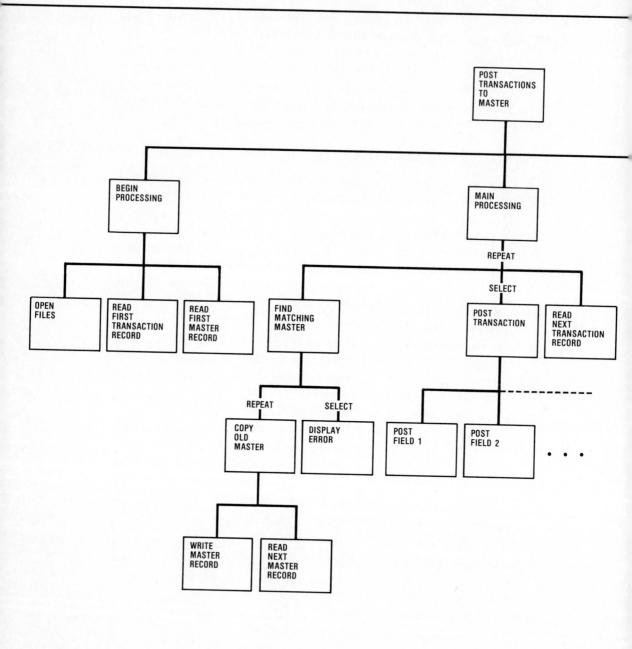

Figure 10-14. Structure chart for generalized master file posting program.

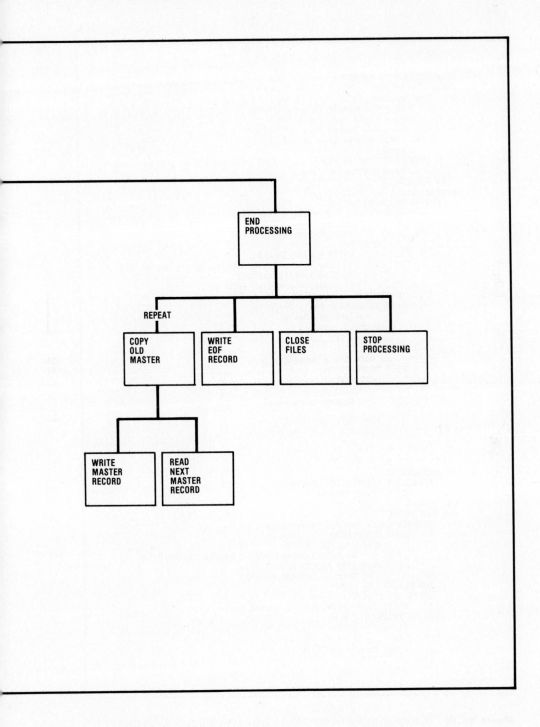

```
POST TRANSACTIONS TO MASTER
     BEGIN PROCESSING
          OPEN FILES
                Open Old Master File for input
                Open Trans File for input
                Open New Master File for output
          READ FIRST TRANSACTION RECORD
                Read Trans Record
          READ FIRST MASTER RECORD
                Read Old Master Record
     MAIN PROCESSING
     REPEAT: until EOF Trans File
          FIND MATCHING MASTER
                REPEAT: until Mstr-Key = Trans-Key
                        or Mstr-Key > Trans-Key
                        or EOF Old Master File
                     COPY OLD MASTER
                          WRITE MASTER RECORD
                                Write Old Master Record to New Master File
                          READ NEXT MASTER RECORD
                                Read Old Master Record
                END REPEAT
                SELECT: on Mstr-Key > Trans-Key
                        or EOF Old Master
                     DISPLAY ERROR
                          Print "master not found" message
                END SELECT
          SELECT: on Mstr-Key = Trans-Key
                POST TRANSACTION
                     POST FIELD 1
                            .
                          (Updating routine)
                            .
                     POST FIELD 2
                            .
                            .
                            .
                            .
          END SELECT
          READ NEXT TRANSACTION RECORD
                Read Trans Record
     END REPEAT
     END PROCESSING
          REPEAT: until EOF Old Master File
                COPY OLD MASTER
                     WRITE MASTER RECORD
                          Write Old Master Record to New Master File
                     READ NEXT MASTER RECORD
                          Read Old Master Record
          END REPEAT
          WRITE EOF RECORD
                Write end-of-file record to New Master File
          CLOSE FILES
                Close Old Master File
                Close Trans File
                Close New Master File
          STOP PROCESSING
                Stop
```

Figure 10-15. Pseudocode for generalized master file posting program.

multiple transactions against individual master records, creating an entirely new master file, and, at the same time, maintaining the key sequence of the output file.

The structure chart in Figure 10-16 presents a general model for a sequential file maintenance program. The design is based upon what is referred to often as a *transaction processing* model. That is, a transaction record is accessed from the file. Then, depending on whether a transaction code signifies an addition, change, or deletion, program control is dispatched to a section of the program that carries out the processing in total.

As can be seen in Figure 10-16, processing begins with the reading of the first transaction record and the first master record from their respective files. Within the main processing section of the program, the transaction request is evaluated and control branches to one of the three primary processing routines—add, change, or delete. Following processing, the next transaction record is read and processing continues until the end of the transaction file. At this point, any remaining old master records are copied to the new master file and the program is halted.

To process an add transaction, two steps are required. First, the position within the old master file at which the new record should be added must be established. This involves reading through the old master file, at the same time copying the records to a new file, until one of three things happens. Either (1) a master record with the same key as the transaction record is encountered, (2) a master record with a key value higher than the transaction record is read, or (3) the end of the master file is signaled.

In the first instance, an error condition exists, since a record with that same key should not be created and added to the file. In this case, an error message is written or displayed, and processing continues with the next transaction. If a higher master key is read or the end of the old master file is encountered, this becomes the position at which the new record should be added. So, a new master record is built within a work area in memory to await writing to the new master file during subsequent processing. The record is not written immediately, since subsequent transaction records may require changes to or deletion of this new record.

A change transaction involves copying the old master file to the new master file until, again, either (1) a matching record is found, (2) a record

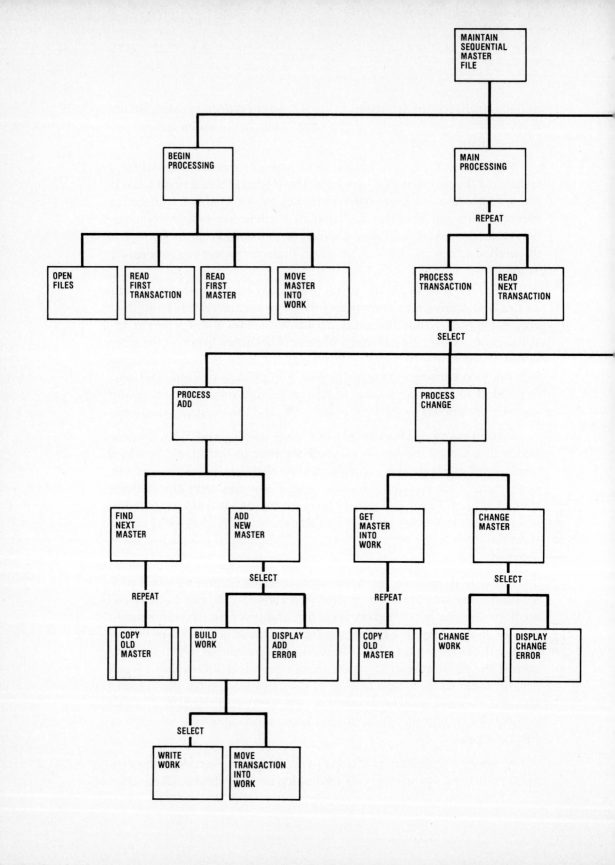

Figure 10-16. Structure chart for generalized master file maintenance program.

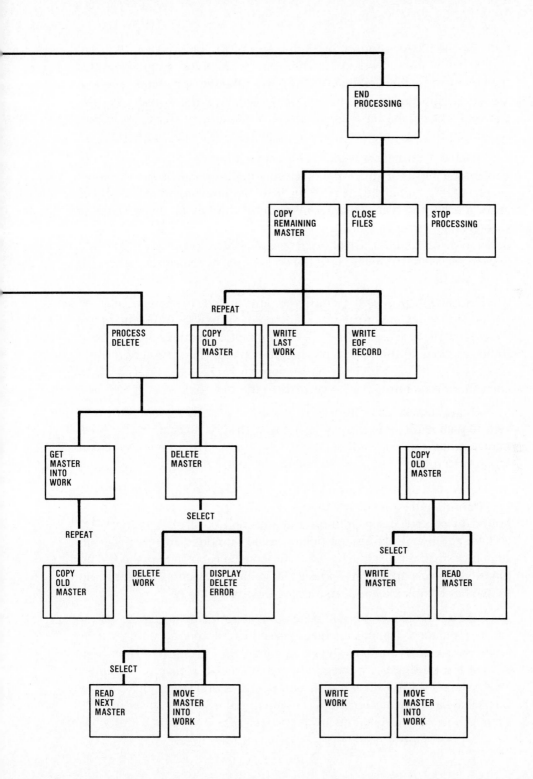

with a higher key is found, or (3) the end of the old master file is encountered. In the second and third instances, an error is signaled, since the record to be changed does not appear in the file. If a match is found, however, the old master record is copied into the work area and changed. The old master record remains in this area to await subsequent writing to the new master file during the next file copy activity.

A delete transaction begins with copying the old master file to the new master file until one of the three conditions occurs. If an old master record with a higher key is read, or if the end of the old master file is encountered, the transaction is in error. If the key of the old master record matches the key of the transaction record, the deletion transaction can be carried out. Deletion occurs simply by reading the next old master record and copying it to the work area, overwriting the record to be deleted.

Transaction processing continues until either the end of the old master file or the end of the transaction file is signaled. If the end of the old master file is signaled first, all remaining transactions are assumed to be additions to the file. If, on the other hand, the transaction file is processed completely and old master records remain, the final step is to copy these remaining master records to the new file.

When processing is completed, the new master file becomes the current file while the old master file, along with the transaction file, is retained as backup. Thus, if the new file is destroyed inadvertently, it can be recreated by rerunning the maintenance program.

Figure 10-17 contains a skeletal outline of pseudocode for the model program. Included are descriptions of the condition tests that are required to control the repetition and selection control structures. Of course, additional processing details could be added to this program structure to adapt it to particular maintenance requirements and data fields. However, this overall design is valuable in understanding the somewhat complex logic of sequential file maintenance.

Figure 10-18 shows a BASIC program that performs sequential master file maintenance. The master file represents customer account records keyed to account number. The customer's name, account balance, and date of last purchase are included in each record. Figure 10-19 shows the format of this file. The transaction file, given in Figure 10-20, will be applied against the master file. Transaction records can represent additions, changes, and deletions to the master file.

Figure 10-17. Pseudocode for generalized master file maintenance program.

```
MAINTAIN SEQUENTIAL MASTER FILE
    BEGIN PROCESSING
        OPEN FILES
            Open Old Master File for input
            Open Trans File for input
            Open new Master File for output
        READ FIRST TRANSACTION
            Read Trans Record
        READ FIRST MASTER
            Read Old Master Record
        MOVE MASTER INTO WORK
            Set Work Record = Old Master Record
    MAIN PROCESSING
    REPEAT: until EOF Trans File
        PROCESS TRANSACTION
            SELECT: on Trans Code
            PROCESS ADD
                FIND NEXT MASTER
                    REPEAT: until Old-Mstr-Key > Trans-Key
                            or Old-Mstr-Key = Trans-Key
                            or EOF Old Master File
                        Perform COPY OLD MASTER
                    END REPEAT
                ADD NEW MASTER
                    SELECT: on Old-Mstr-Key > Trans-Key
                            or EOF Old Master File
                        BUILD WORK
                            SELECT: on Old-Mstr-Key <> Work-Key
                                WRITE WORK
                                    Write Work Record to
                                            New Master File
                            END SELECT
                            MOVE TRANSACTION INTO WORK
                                Set Work Record = Trans Record
                    END SELECT
                    SELECT: on Old-Mstr-Key = Trans-Key
                        DISPLAY ADD ERROR
                            Print "Record already exists" message
                    END SELECT
            PROCESS CHANGE
                GET MASTER INTO WORK
                    REPEAT: until Work-Key = Trans-Key
                            or Work-Key > Trans-Key
                            or EOF Old Master File
                        Perform COPY OLD MASTER
                    END REPEAT
                CHANGE MASTER
                    SELECT: on Work-Key = Trans-Key
                        CHANGE WORK
                            Set Work Fields = Trans-Fields
                    END SELECT
                    SELECT: on Work-Key > Trans-Key
                            or EOF Old Master File
                        DISPLAY CHANGE ERROR
                            Print "Record doesn't exist" message
                    END SELECT
```

```
PROCESS DELETE
    GET MASTER INTO WORK
        REPEAT: until Work-Key = Trans-Key
                or Work-Key > Trans-Key
                or EOF Old Master File

                        Perform COPY OLD MASTER
            END REPEAT
        DELETE MASTER
            SELECT: on Work-Key = Trans-Key
                DELETE WORK
                    SELECT: on Old-Mstr-Key = Work-Key
                        READ NEXT MASTER
                            Read Old Master Record
                    END SELECT
                    MOVE MASTER INTO WORK
                            Set Work Record = Old Master Record
            END SELECT
            SELECT: on Work-Key > Trans-Key
                    or EOF Old Master File
                DISPLAY DELETE ERROR
                        Print "Record doesn't exist" message
            END SELECT
        END SELECT
        READ NEXT TRANSACTION
            Read Trans Record
    END REPEAT
END PROCESSING
    COPY REMAINING MASTER
        REPEAT: until EOF Old Master File
            Perform COPY OLD MASTER
        END REPEAT
        WRITE LAST WORK
            Write Work Record to New Master File
        WRITE EOF RECORD
            Write Old Master Record to New Master File
    CLOSE FILES
        Close Old Master File
        Close Trans File
        Close New Master File
    STOP PROCESSING
        Stop


COPY OLD MASTER
    SELECT: on Old-Mstr-Key <> Work-Key
        WRITE MASTER
            WRITE WORK
                Write Work Record to New Master File
            MOVE MASTER INTO WORK
                Set Work Record = Old Master Record
    END SELECT
    READ MASTER
        Read Old Master Record
RETURN
```

Figure 10-17. Concluded.

Figure 10-18. Code for sequential master file maintenance program.

```
1000! MAINTAINDEMO                                        DRA/WEL
1010!                      MASTER FILE MAINTENANCE
1020!
1030! THIS PROGRAM DEMONSTRATES A SEQUENTIAL MASTER FILE
1040! MAINTENANCE ROUTINE.  TRANSACTION RECORDS REPRESENT
1050! RECORDS TO BE ADDED TO A MASTER FILE, RECORDS TO BE
1060! DELETED FROM THE MASTER FILE, AND CHANGES TO BE MADE
1070! TO RECORDS WITHIN THE MASTER FILE.  THE FOLLOWING
1080! RECORD FORMATS APPLY:
1090!
1100! MASTER RECORD:
1110!    A1$...CUSTOMER ACCOUNT NUMBER
1120!    N1$...CUSTOMER NAME
1130!    B1$...ACCOUNT BALANCE
1140!    D1$...DATE OF LAST PURCHASE
1150! ADD-TRANSACTION RECORD:
1160!    C$.....TRANSACTION CODE           ("A")
1170!    A2$...CUSTOMER ACCOUNT NUMBER
1180!    N2$...CUSTOMER NAME
1190!    B2$...ACCOUNT BALANCE
1200!    D2$...DATE OF LAST PURCHASE
1210! CHANGE-TRANSACTION RECORD:
1220!    C$.....TRANSACTION CODE           ("C")
1230!    A2$...CUSTOMER ACCOUNT NUMBER
1240!    N2$...CUSTOMER NAME
1250!    B2$...ACCOUNT BALANCE
1260!    D2$...DATE OF LAST PURCHASE
1270! DELETE-TRANSACTION RECORD:
1280!    C$.....TRANSACTION CODE           ("D")
1290!    A2$...CUSTOMER ACCOUNT NUMBER
1300!    N2$...CUSTOMER NAME
1310!    B2$...ACCOUNT BALANCE
1320!    D2$...DATE OF LAST PURCHASE
1330! WORK AREA:
1340!    A9$...CUSTOMER ACCOUNT NUMBER
1350!    N9$...CUSTOMER NAME
1360!    B9$...ACCOUNT BALANCE
1370!    D9$...DATE OF LAST PURCHASE
1380!
1390! 0.0 MAINTAIN SEQUENTIAL MASTER FILE
1400!
1410! ************************
1420! * 1.0 BEGIN PROCESSING *
1430! ************************
1440!
1450  OPEN "CUSTMF" FOR INPUT   AS #1
1460  OPEN "CUSTTF" FOR INPUT   AS #2
1470  OPEN "CUSTNM" FOR OUTPUT AS #3
1480!
1490  INPUT #2, C$, A2$, N2$, B2$, D2$
1500  INPUT #1,     A1$, N1$, B1$, D1$
1510!
1520  LET A9$ = A1$
1530  LET N9$ = N1$
1540  LET B9$ = B1$
1550  LET D9$ = D1$
1560!
1570! ************************
1580! * 2.0 MAIN PROCESSING  *
1590! ************************
1600! REPEAT
1610  IF N2$ = "END OF FILE" THEN GOTO 1720
1620!
```

```
1630!     SELECT
1640           IF C$ = "A" THEN GOSUB 2000     ! ADD
1650           IF C$ = "C" THEN GOSUB 3000     ! CHANGE
1660           IF C$ = "D" THEN GOSUB 4000     ! DELETE
1670!     END SELECT
1680!
1690      INPUT #2, C$, A2$, N2$, B2$, D2$
1700!
1710  GOTO 1600
1720! END REPEAT
1730!
1740! **************************
1750! * 3.0 END PROCESSING     *
1760! **************************
1770!
1780! REPEAT
1790  IF N1$ = "END OF FILE" THEN GOTO 1840
1800!
1810      GOSUB 5000   ! COPY OLD MASTER
1820!
1830  GOTO 1780
1840! END REPEAT
1850!
1860  PRINT #3, A9$; ","; N9$; ","; B9$; ","; D9$
1870  PRINT #3, A1$; ","; N1$; ","; B1$; ","; D1$
1880!
1890  CLOSE #1
1900  CLOSE #2
1910  CLOSE #3
1920!
1930  STOP
1940!
2000! ******************************
2010! * S1.0 ADD NEW MASTER RECORD *
2020! ******************************
2030!
2040! REPEAT
2050  IF A1$  > A2$             THEN GOTO 2120
2060  IF A1$  = A2$             THEN GOTO 2120
2070  IF N1$ = "END OF FILE" THEN GOTO 2120
2080!
2090      GOSUB 5000    ! COPY OLD MASTER
2100!
2110  GOTO 2040
2120! END REPEAT
2130!
2140! SELECT
2150  IF A1$ > A2$              THEN GOTO 2190
2160  IF N1$ = "END OF FILE" THEN GOTO 2190
2170  IF A1$ = A2$              THEN GOTO 2340
2180!
2190!     SELECT
2200      IF A1$ <> A9$ THEN GOTO 2230
2210                           GOTO 2250
2220!
2230          PRINT #3, A9$; ","; N9$; ","; B9$; ","; D9$
2240!
2250!     END SELECT
2260!
2270      LET A9$ = A2$
2280      LET N9$ = N2$
2290      LET B9$ = B2$
2300      LET D9$ = D2$
2310!
2320          GOTO 2360
2330!
2340      PRINT "==>RECORD "; A2$; " ALREADY EXISTS"
2350!
2360! END SELECT
2370  RETURN
2380!
```

```
3000! *****************************
3010! * S2.0 CHANGE MASTER RECORD *
3020! *****************************
3030!
3040! REPEAT
3050   IF A9$ = A2$              THEN GOTO 3120
3060   IF A9$ > A2$              THEN GOTO 3120
3070   IF N1$ = "END OF FILE" THEN GOTO 3120
3080!
3090      GOSUB 5000   ! COPY OLD MASTER
3100!
3110   GOTO 3040
3120! END REPEAT
3130!
3140! SELECT
3150   IF A9$ = A2$              THEN GOTO 3190
3160   IF A9$ > A2$              THEN GOTO 3360
3170   IF N1$ = "END OF FILE" THEN GOTO 3360
3180!
3190!     SELECT
3200     IF N2$ = "" THEN GOTO 3220
3210        LET N9$ = N2$
3220!     END SELECT
3230!
3240!     SELECT
3250     IF B2$ = "" THEN GOTO 3270
3260        LET B9$ = B2$
3270!     END SELECT
3280!
3290!     SELECT
3300     IF D2$ = "" THEN GOTO 3320
3310        LET D9$ = D2$
3320!     END SELECT
3330!
3340        GOTO 3380
3350!
3360      PRINT "==>RECORD "; A2$; " DOESN'T EXIST"
3370!
3380! END SELECT
3390   RETURN
3400!
4000! *****************************
4010! * S3.0 DELETE MASTER RECORD *
4020! *****************************
4030!
4040! REPEAT
4050   IF A9$ = A2$              THEN GOTO 4120
4060   IF A9$ > A2$              THEN GOTO 4120
4070   IF N1$ = "END OF FILE" THEN GOTO 4120
4080!
4090      GOSUB 5000   ! COPY OLD MASTER
4100!
4110   GOTO 4040
4120! END REPEAT
4130!
4140! SELECT
4150   IF A9$ = A2$              THEN GOTO 4190
4160   IF A9$ > A2$              THEN GOTO 4310
4170   IF N1$ = "END OF FILE" THEN GOTO 4310
4180!
4190!     SELECT
4200     IF A1$ <> A9$ THEN GOTO 4220
4210        INPUT #1, A1$, N1$, B1$, D1$
4220!     END SELECT
4230!
4240     LET A9$ = A1$
4250     LET N9$ = N1$
4260     LET B9$ = B1$
4270     LET D9$ = D1$
4280!
4290        GOTO 4330
4300!
```

```
4310      PRINT "==>RECORD "; A2$; " DOESN'T EXIST"
4320!
4330! END SELECT
4340  RETURN
4350!
5000! ************************
5010! * S4.0 COPY OLD MASTER *
5020! ************************
5030!
5040! SELECT
5050  IF A1$ = A9$ THEN GOTO 5140
5060!
5070      PRINT #3, A9$; ","; N9$; ","; B9$; ","; D9$
5080!
5090      LET A9$ = A1$
5100      LET N9$ = N1$
5110      LET B9$ = B1$
5120      LET D9$ = D1$
5130!
5140! END SELECT
5150!
5160  INPUT #1, A1$, N1$, B1$, D1$
5170!
5180  RETURN
5190!
5200  END
```

Figure 10-18. Concluded.

```
154,ALICE COOKE,100.00,09/21
157,JOHN JONES,0.00,09/15
160,DICK SLATER,27.95,09/12
167,ART KAPLAN,133.65,09/18
172,CRIS LANGFORD,10.17,09/08
175,LYLE GRAY,247.93,08/22
240,BETTY KRUSE,6.43,07/17
242,LINDA DOLIVE,29.12,09/25
282,BETH HOWELL,0.00,09/17
294,DICK THOMAS,0.00,05/30
318,GARY JOHNSTON,118.36,07/01
320,ANN RUSTIN,14.45,09/30
337,CARRIE BROWN,122.98,09/27
395,BILL SEREY,0.00,03/15
396,CARL SLATER,10.50,09/24
449,JUDY TERRELL,0.00,09/17
467,GLORIA GREEN,12.67,09/28
627,JIM COLE,13.45,09/05
705,CONNIE WIDMER,6.12,08/30
775,BRET JORDAN,0.00,01/01
829,MARY TYSON,25.00,09/15
000,END OF FILE,000.00,00/00
```

Figure 10-19. Format of records in master file.

```
A,100,JEAN CARSON,0.00,00/00
C,100,GENE CARSON,,
D,157,,,
A,160,ART KAPLAN,0.00,00/00
C,170,,0.00,
A,180,BARRY JAMES,0.00,00/00
D,325,,,
C,467,,,09/30
A,500,JUDY SNYDER,0.00,00/00
C,500,,50.00,
C,500,,,10/15
A,627,JIM COLE,0.00,00/00
D,627,,,
C,705,CONNIE WIDMIR,6.25,09/01
C,800,JOHN KARNES,,
D,825,,,
A,850,DON ALLYN,0.00,00/00
C,850,,125.00,10/17
C,850,DON ALLEN,,
D,850,,,
E,000,END OF FILE,000.00,00/00
```

Figure 10-20. Transaction file records to be applied against master file.

For an add transaction, signified with the character A in the transaction code field, a new master record is created from the transaction fields. The new record is built within a work area and then is written to the new master file.

For a change transaction, identified with the code C, corresponding old master fields are replaced with the new values given in the transaction record. Only those fields that have data values trigger a change. Otherwise, a missing, or *null*, transaction field signals to the program that the master field should not be updated.

A deletion transaction, identified with the code D, provides the account number of the old master record that should be eliminated from the file. Deletion is accomplished by not writing the record to the new file.

The program is designed to allow multiple valid transactions against a single master record. That is, the addition of a new master record could be followed by one or more changes to that record—or even by a deletion. It is assumed, however, that additions must precede changes, which must precede deletions for any one master record. For changes and deletions, the program displays error messages in response to missing master

```
100,GENE CARSON,0.00,00/00
154,ALICE COOKE,100.00,09/21
160,DICK SLATER,27.95,09/12
167,ART KAPLAN,133.65,09/18
172,CRIS LANGFORD,10.17,09/08
175,LYLE GRAY,247.93,08/22
180,BARRY JAMES,0.00,00/00
240,BETTY KRUSE,6.43,07/15
242,LINDA DOLIVE,29.12,09/25
282,BETH HOWELL,0.00,09/17
294,DICK THOMAS,0.00,05/30
318,GARY JOHNSTON,118.36,07/01
320,ANN RUSTIN,14.45,09/30
337,CARRIE BROWN,122.98,09/27
395,BILL SEREY,0.00,03/15
396,CARL SLATER,10.50,09/24
449,JUDY TERRELL,0.00,09/17
467,GLORIA GREEN,12.67,09/30
500,JUDY SNYDER,50.00,10/15
705,CONNIE WIDMIR,6.25,09/01
775,BRET JORDAN,0.00,01/01
829,MARY TYSON,25.00,09/15
000,END OF FILE,000.00,00/00
```

Figure 10-21. New master file following run of maintenance program.

records. During additions, error messages are displayed for already existing master records. Figure 10-21 shows the resulting new master file following the program run.

It should be noted in the example program all data fields are processed as character strings, because arithmetic operations are not applied to the data. Even during change transactions, old master fields are being replaced by new fields. Such processing is typical in master file maintenance. Therefore, the convenience of manipulating character strings warrants their use for representing all data within the program.

The main purpose of this chapter is to build your understanding of the techniques for processing large sequential files. Although direct-access methods often are favored because of their flexibility, many systems still exist that depend on sequential files supported by sequential processing. In some cases, sequential methods still may be the best choice, even though direct-access methods are available.

Chapter Summary

1. In processing large sequential files, it is impractical to consider reading an entire file into memory. Rather, the files must remain on external storage devices and records must be brought into and processed within memory, one record at a time.

2. In updating sequential files, both the master file and the transaction file must be in the same key order.

3. A serial file is one in which records are written in chronological order, as data are captured.

4. A computer sort is a procedure for processing serial files and creating sequential files.

5. The fastest way to sort a limited number of records is to bring a batch into memory and sort the records there. The program that controls in-memory sorts establishes a table of records. Record keys are copied from this table and are set up in a separate table. The keys, rather than the records themselves, are sorted. The relationships among

sorted keys and data records are maintained in a table of pointers.

6. In sorting large files, only a portion of the file is sorted internally at one time. Each sorted portion is combined with previously sorted portions through use of merge routines.

7. For most computer systems, general-purpose, utility sort routines are provided as part of the operating system.

8. A computer merge function is used to combine two sequential files into one, maintaining the record key sequence of both. During merging, the program compares the keys of a record from each file and writes the one with the lower key to a new file.

9. Prior to master file updating, it is standard practice to use an edit run to verify the content of transaction records before the records are processed against the master file.

10. Posting is the process of adding to the data content of master records to reflect ongoing business activity. Posting often involves accumulating totals and establishing current balances.

11. File maintenance is the practice of changing the content of files. Maintenance transactions involve adding new records to a file, changing the content of selected records in the file, and deleting records from the file.

12. Sequential file maintenance requires three files: a transaction file, which is the input of additions, changes, and deletions to be applied against the master file; the old master file, to which maintenance transactions are applied; and the new master file, which is the output of the maintenance run.

13. After master file maintenance is completed, the transaction file and the old master file are retained for backup in case the new file is destroyed inadvertently.

Review Questions

1. What is the sequencing requirement for records that are to be accessed from large files and processed sequentially?

2. Under what circumstances is sequential processing used?

3. What is a computer sort?

4. How are record fields written into the table element when an entire record is to be sorted?

5. For what purpose is the merge function used?

6. What are the two basic processing stages of a transaction processing model?

Practice Assignments

1. Design, write, and test a BASIC program to perform a sort on a file of payroll transaction records. This file will require sequencing in the same order as the payroll master file so that weekly payroll processing can be accomplished. The following data file should be used to test the program:

Dept. No.	Employee Number	Employee Name	Regular Hours	Overtime Hours
14	187	JOHN MARKS	40	0.0
16	245	CYNTHIA CARLSON	38	0.0
15	142	BRENDA SMITH	40	5.0
14	125	CARL NOYD	40	0.0
17	206	BILL JONES	35	0.0
18	287	JIM CARPENTER	40	9.0
14	193	JANICE SHOWMER	40	0.5
15	194	MINDY JOHNSON	38	0.0
17	133	LOUIS BINGHAM	40	1.5
16	219	ALICIA DIRKSOME	40	0.0

You will need to create this file either by writing a file creation program similar to the ones used in the earlier chapters or by using the text editor that is on your computer system. Also, you will need a listing program to display the resulting sort file. You may either write this program or use the utility list routine that comes with your system. This file is to be sorted in ascending sequence by employee number. Program a sort technique that makes use of both key and pointer tables.

2. Design, write, and test a BASIC program to merge two files. The two files, which have been sorted on employee number, are shown below:

FILE 1			FILE 2		
Dept. No.	Employee Number	Position Code	Dept. No.	Employee Number	Position Code
13	125	10	15	120	20
14	127	30	17	130	50
17	131	20	14	142	20
16	154	50	18	149	30
18	216	30	15	178	30
11	217	80	13	190	10
14	233	40	14	220	50
13	304	10	14	231	40
14	313	30	15	287	20
16	359	70	12	340	30

Either write the programs to create the files and print the resulting merged file, or use the text editor and utility listing routines that are on your computer system.

3. Design and write a program to perform a sequential master file update. Create the necessary master and transaction files for testing the program, making sure that the transactions represent additions to, changes in, and deletions from the master file. Code the program in BASIC and run it to verify its correctness.

Key Terms

1. sort
2. serial
3. utility program
4. operating system
5. substring
6. merge
7. edit run
8. transaction file
9. old master file
10. new master file
11. transaction processing
12. null

11
FILE ORGANIZATION AND ACCESS METHODS

OVERVIEW AND OBJECTIVES

This chapter covers several advanced techniques that can be incorporated within BASIC programs to organize files and access records. Up to this point, standard sequential and direct-access methods have been discussed. Sequential file organization has been described as an appropriate method for supporting batch processing programs that update most of the records in a master file during each processing run. Sequential processing is used when it is practical and efficient to organize transactions in an order that matches the physical sequence of records within a master file. By contrast, direct-access, or relative, file organization is generally used whenever on-line processing is deemed necessary. In these cases, systems users require immediate and direct retrieval of records. Also, the order in which transactions are presented for processing cannot be determined in advance.

Consider again: If you are standing in front of a bank late at night and want to withdraw money from an automatic teller machine, you are not interested in waiting until a batch of transactions is assembled from several customers for efficient processing. You want to get on with whatever else you have to do, with your money in hand. Similarly, if you are making an airline or hotel reservation, you would expect an agent to provide prompt responses to your questions. Most large airlines and hotels know that delaying customers means a reduction in business.

On the other hand, it is not critical that a company enter and record the hours worked for each employee at the end of every hour or even at the end of each day. Rather, it is sufficient to wait until the end of the work week to enter this data into the payroll system and to generate paychecks. All employee pay information can be processed effectively at one time, at the close of the work week, rather than as the work is performed. Thus, the nature of the service performed, of the business that renders the service, and of the transactions themselves usually dictates whether sequential (batch), direct-access (on-line), or some combination of the two methods is appropriate.

Many systems integrate batch and on-line methods. Usually, the sequential file processing techniques described in Chapter 10 can be applied to both small- and large-scale systems. On-line processing, however, requires that the programmer know how to convert record keys into disk addresses, how to provide both sequential and random access to records within a file, and how to integrate sequential and direct-access files within a system. These programming concerns are the topics of this chapter.

When you complete your work in this chapter, you should be able to:

☐ Define hashing functions and describe their use in converting record keys into disk addresses.

☐ Design and write hashing algorithms for programs that create and retrieve direct-access records.

☐ Define indexed file organization and access methods and describe their uses.

☐ Design and write program routines to create and access indexed files.

☐ Discuss the relationships among file organization structures, access methods, and on-line transaction processing systems.

ON-LINE TRANSACTION PROCESSING

On-line systems have overlapping elements of simplicity and complexity. From the standpoint of the user, these systems appear fairly simple to operate when compared with batch-oriented systems. Figure 11-1 is a diagram of a typical batch system. Separate procedures and programs are used for creating a transaction file, editing the file, sorting transaction records into key sequence, and posting the transactions against the master file. Individual programs within the system may be relatively simple; however, the sequencing, timing, and operation of the programs introduce potential scheduling, monitoring, and rerun complications.

Logically and functionally, on-line systems are less complex in some ways than batch systems. From the standpoint of the user, on-line systems are relatively simple to operate, as indicated in the diagram in

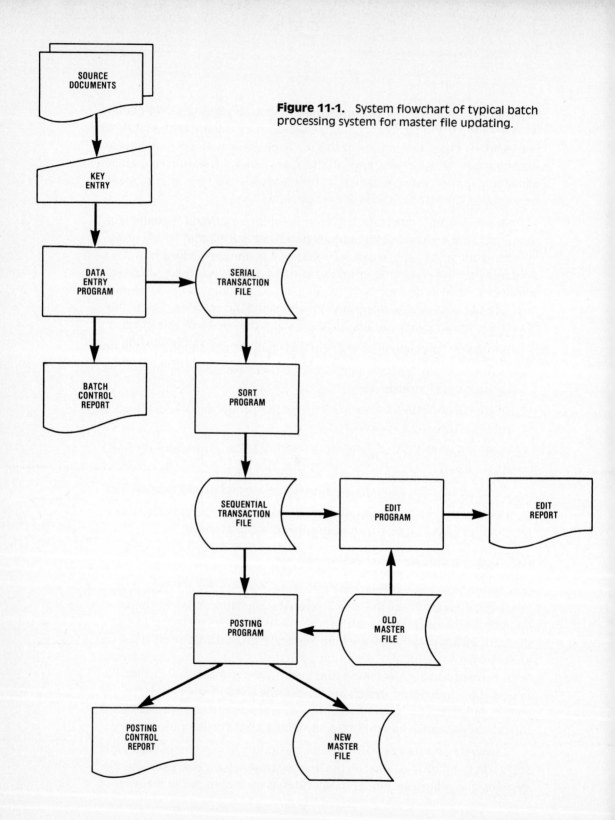

Figure 11-1. System flowchart of typical batch processing system for master file updating.

Figure 11-2. Transactions are processed individually as each transaction is received. All needed editing takes place at the time the transaction is entered. Transactions need not be sorted in key sequence. Thus, processing is completed, or the transaction is perfected, in a single sequence of events. Within a matter of seconds, the needed master record is found, updating takes place, and the record is rewritten to the file.

On-line systems, however, may require more time and effort to develop than batch systems because the program that drives the on-line system must be comprehensive in its processing features. The on-line program is required to perform all of the editing functions associated with transaction processing. Within a batch environment, the data entry function usually is performed by trained professionals. These persons are hired because of their relatively high levels of clerical skills. Data entry personnel are trained to anticipate, check for, and correct data transcription errors. In addition, trained computer operators provide job setups, initiate processing, monitor the run continually, and initiate recovery procedures if errors are introduced. Thus, skilled operations personnel are in charge of processing, from the moment a transaction enters the system until the transaction is reflected within master files and reports. By contrast, in an on-line environment, data entry responsibilities often lie

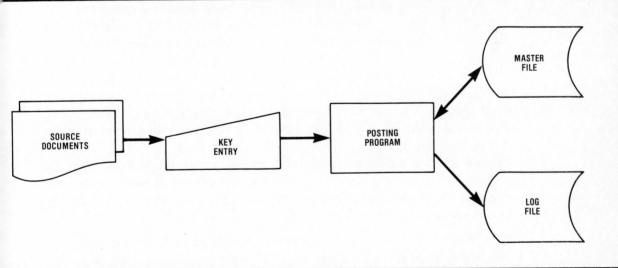

Figure 11-2. System flowchart of typical on-line processing system for master file updating.

with the end users. These users might be managers, production line employees, customers, or other persons who are not trained to perform in the exacting environment of computers. Consequently, extensive checking of processing commands and transactions must be written into the programs. Otherwise, incorrect data can enter the system or invalid commands can abort processing.

Also, on-line systems rewrite records in place as the records are updated. Thus, existing, or old, master records are wiped out following processing. An audit trail of transactions will not exist. In other words, an on-line system does not contain a built-in method to trace the transaction from its entry point into the system to the point at which the transaction affects the values stored within the master file.

In a batch environment, an audit trail of transactions is established easily. Information on original source documents is written to serial transaction files. The same information also appears within sorted transaction files and on edit reports. Finally, the effects of the information are reflected in differences among the old and new versions of the master file and the posting control report. A transaction processed in batch mode leaves a clear trail from the time it enters the system until it becomes part of the data base maintained by the company.

Since on-line processing does not produce audit trails, it is necessary to build the trails into such systems. As shown in Figure 11-2, a *log file* is maintained as output. In effect, a log file is an electronic journal that documents the existence, the content, and the impact of a transaction. Typically, the following information is included within a log entry: a copy of the master record before updating, a copy of the transaction record itself, and a copy of the master record after updating. Date and time entries establish the chronology of master file processing activities. Thus, it is possible to reconstruct the sequence of events that brought about changes in the master file, even though source documents, transaction reports, and separate generations of master files are not available. With availability of this electronic journal, the system can be audited easily and can be rebuilt if the master file is destroyed inadvertently.

Unlike batch processing, new generations of master files are not produced automatically during updating of on-line files. Therefore, one feature of on-line systems is the scheduled copying of master files. The copied file can be thought of as a picture showing the status of a system at any given time. Cumulatively, this duplicated master and the log file (the portion created between the start-up of service and the copying of the next generation of the master file) represent the potential for rebuilding the system if the existing master file is destroyed. In such a case, the copy of the master file would be activated, the log file would be entered, and the records would be processed as though they were live transactions. The master file would be updated in the same order, with the same transactions that were processed by on-line users.

Although a flowchart showing an on-line system is relatively simple in structure, the processing that takes place within the software portion of the system can become rather complex. A single on-line program integrates functions that would have separate programs in batch systems. These functions include data entry, editing, updating, and reporting. Also, software for on-line systems must include many of the scheduling and monitoring responsibilities that would be performed by trained operators in a batch environment.

Figure 11-3 presents a generalized structure chart of the processing modules that are often a part of on-line updating programs. This structure chart enlarges upon the single processing box in the flowchart of Figure 11-2. Note that the first module in the begin-processing portion of the structure chart copies the existing master file. Then, modules within the main processing portion of the program establish the sequence for editing and posting of transactions. In this example, an invalid transaction record would trigger a message back to the terminal, and corrections or other decisions would be entered immediately, before the transaction is released for updating. Following updating, a record of the transaction and its effect are written to a log file.

The program shown in Figure 11-3 may be part of a much larger program that performs other on-line functions. For example, a large on-line system may include processing routines to allow inquiry into files, to produce reports, to generate transaction documents, and to allow other common processing activities—all in addition to single file updating. Such expanded systems would include several programs under control of a single master control program. Menus would allow users to call up processing routines and would provide interactive guidance through the processing steps. Also, the program could involve processing that uses multiple master files. Although a complete discussion of design and programming techniques for such comprehensive systems is beyond the scope of this book, you should be aware of the potential for building multiple layers of processing within a single software structure. In effect,

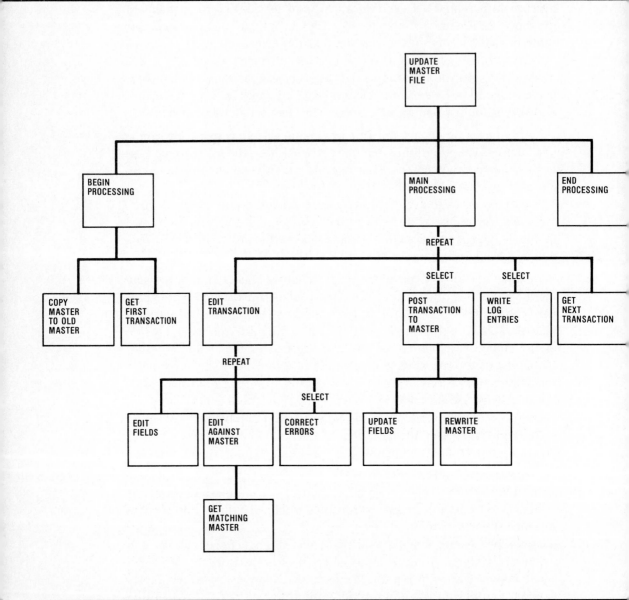

Figure 11-3. Structure chart for generalized on-line processing system for master file updating.

a single program can support an entire system of on-line routines. Such a developmental task should not be viewed as intimidating. Complex systems are still collections of simple routines.

FILE ORGANIZATION APPROACHES

File organization is the arrangement of records on a storage medium to facilitate a certain type of *file access*. File access refers to the method used to retrieve files from storage media. As shown in Figure 11-4, file organization can be approached in several fundamental ways. First, the programmer must determine whether direct-access capabilities are required. If direct access is not required, simple serial or sequential files may be suitable. Within the direct-access category, alternative file organization methods are possible. The appropriate method is determined primarily by noting the characteristics of the keys that are used to identify and access the records.

Thus, the designer or programmer of a direct-access file system does not choose freely or randomly. Rather, determining the best file organization approach is a matter of matching techniques to circumstances. Each of the alternatives has associated prerequisites or conditions. The challenge lies in studying the needs and conditions of a system, then matching file capabilities to meet those needs. For example, as noted previously, sequential files fit best into an environment in which transactions can be processed in batches, with a comparatively large number of master files updated, in key order, during a single processing run.

In choosing the most appropriate direct-access method, the following additional criteria are applied:

- If the key field for all records in a file consists of unique, closely sequenced numbers, a direct, or relative, access file organization can be used. This type of file organization is described in Chapter 9. In a relative file, the keys can be used as the relative positions of the associated records. The record with a key value of 1 appears in the first position in the file, the record with a key value of 2 appears in the second position in the file, and so on. If there are gaps in the numbering sequence of keys, corresponding blank areas are left in the file. Thus, relative file organization is appropriate and practical if keys can be related directly to storage positions within the file and if there are no large gaps within the key numbering sequence.

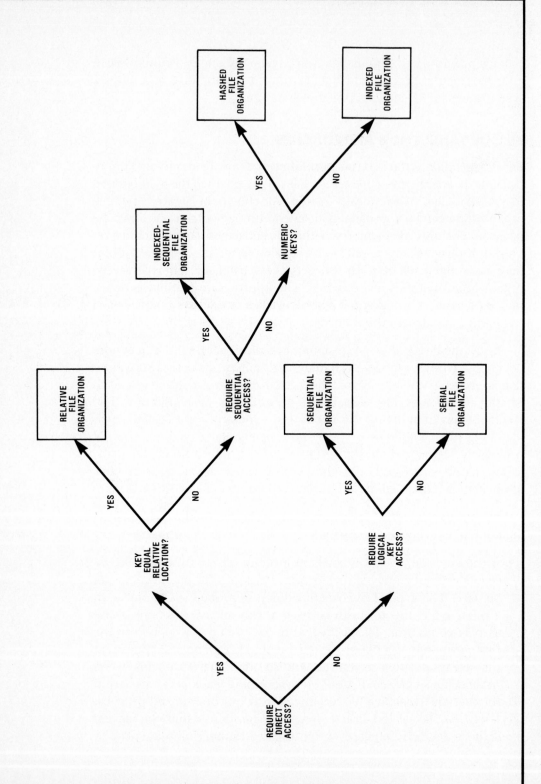

Figure 11-4. Relationships among file organization methods.

- Other file organization schemes are necessary if record keys cannot be equated directly to file locations. For example, a distribution business may reference items according to part numbers set up by several different manufacturers. In addition, a particular manufacturer might follow an identification plan that is different from another manufacturer's plan. The keys may not represent straight numeric sequences and may include nonnumeric identification codes. Key values, for instance, may be sequenced from 10000 to 99999 in increments of 100. A relative file using these values as keys would have to provide for 99,999 record positions, even though only 900 of those positions would be used. In some cases, alphanumeric keys, such as 12J34T, XT100-M, or other such combinations, may be required. In other instances, such keys as persons' names might be used. Obviously, it is impossible to use these types of values as record locations. Thus, if the record key cannot be used as a locator, files must be organized through one of two other approaches.

- The use of calculated addresses is achieved through a *hashing function.* A program routine performs arithmetic calculations on numeric keys, converting those keys to a range of values that directly equate to relative file locations. Hashing, or *randomizing,* algorithms also can be applied to nonnumeric keys by first converting the alphabetic or special characters into numeric equivalents and then into file addresses that fall within a given range of values.

- Instead of using hashing algorithms, a program may use tables to equate keys with file locations. In effect, directories are used to establish relative addresses. Files that use directories, or indexes, are known as *indexed* files.

- In some cases, records within an indexed file might need to be accessed in key sequence as well as randomly. In such a case, a special indexed organization method called *indexed-sequential* is used. Within this organization scheme, records are maintained in key sequence, and indexes are used to allow random access.

This chapter discusses programming techniques for building and accessing hashed files and indexed files. A discussion of indexed-sequential files is beyond the scope of this book. However, the indexed-sequential file organization method is based on the use of the sequential and indexed methods that are discussed here. The chapter closes with a look at database management systems and how the hashed and indexed access methods are integrated within comprehensive file management and access systems.

HASHED FILES

Suppose you are setting up an inventory management system for an auto parts store. The store buys parts from manufacturers and sells them to garages or car owners for use in repairs or replacement. Assume that the store has a system for deriving a five-digit part number key for all items in stock. This key is derived by adapting the manufacturers' numbers so that the store's own system is uniform. Assume that the file should be large enough to handle a total of 1,000 parts.

The system needs a direct-access inventory file. Sales personnel can view this file from terminals at the counter. When a customer places a request, either by phone or in person, the salesperson can call up the record for the desired part number, determine whether the item is in stock, and provide the customer with supply and pricing information. If the customer chooses to purchase or order the item (or any number of items), the terminal can be used to create an invoice to complete the transaction. Item description and pricing information read from the file are imprinted on the invoice.

In creating a direct-access file to support these inventory applications, however, a fundamental problem must be solved: Somehow, the five-digit part numbers must be used as pointers to the locations of the records within the file. The numbers themselves are poor candidates for direct use because such a method would require a file of up to 99,999 available positions to ensure a sufficient number of potential locations. Actually, though, only 1,000 positions are necessary. Far too much disk space would be wasted if the part numbers themselves were used. Therefore, a method is needed for converting the five-digit numbers into file addresses that fall within the range of 1 through 1000.

Hashing Functions

The procedure for setting up a direct-access file and for equating record keys with storage locations is as follows:

1. First, determine the number of storage positions required for the file. This value usually is found by noting the current number of records to be stored and then adding 20 percent for expansion. Thus, in the

parts inventory file, the total number of positions to be allocated to the file is 1,200 (1,000 × .20 = 200 + 1,000 = 1,200.)

2. Next, choose a hashing algorithm to convert the keys to file location values that are within the range of required storage addresses. For the parts file, an algorithm is required to convert the five-digit key to a file position between 1 and 1200.

3. Code the algorithm for use within all programs that either create or access the file. Thus, each time a particular key value is presented for processing, it is converted into the same location value.

Several hashing functions can be used. In all cases, a key value must be converted to a file location that is within a range of addresses. The use of hashing functions is illustrated in Figure 11-5. Here, a logical record key (12014) is presented to a program for processing. The program includes a hashing routine to convert the key to a physical file location (11). Then, the program issues a GET to that file location to retrieve the record with the associated key.

One variety of hashing function divides the value of the key by the number of positions required in the file. Then, the value 1 is added to the integer value of the quotient to produce the file location. This method is illustrated in Figure 11-6, which presents the BASIC statement used to perform the hashing function. Also shown is a set of 25 logical keys that could represent part numbers within the auto parts inventory file described above, along with the relative record numbers that were derived with the hashing function.

Once a relative address is derived, processing proceeds as described in Chapter 9. The only difference between a system in which the key is equal to the relative address and the method shown in Figure 11-6 is the insertion of the hashing function between the entering of the key and the file access operation.

Another method of equating key values with relative file positions is known as the *division/remainder method.* Under this method, the storage location is determined by first dividing the numeric key by the number of positions required for the file. Then, the value 1 is added to the remainder to derive the location value. For example, for part number 12345, the number is first divided by 1200 (the number of actual positions required for the inventory file). Then, the value 1 is added to the remainder (345) to derive the relative file location (346). The section of

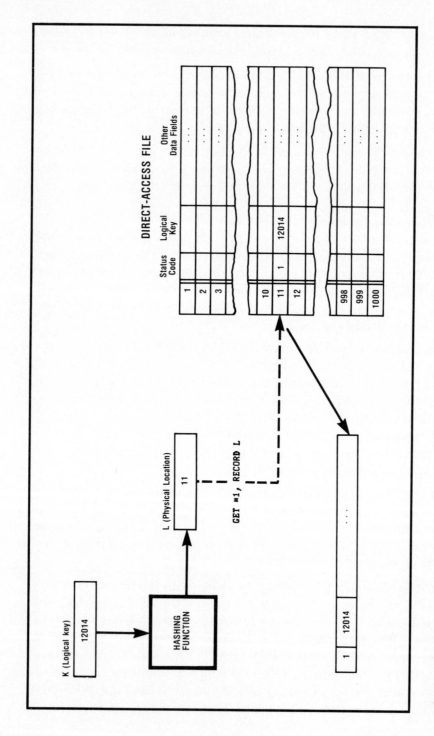

Figure 11-5. Use of hashing function to locate and retrieve record from direct-access file.

HASHING FUNCTION:

Physical Location = Integer(Logical Key / Total Positions) + 1

```
LET L = INT(K / 1200) + 1
```

Logical Key (K)	Physical Location (L)
12014	11
15618	14
18003	16
21607	19
25211	22
28815	25
31200	27
32419	28
34804	30
38408	33
42012	36
45616	39
48001	41
51605	44
55209	47
58813	50
62417	53
64802	55
68406	58
72010	61
75614	64
79218	67
81603	69
85207	72
88811	75

Figure 11-6. Application of hashing function to determine location of record based on logical key.

BASIC code shown in Figure 11-7 illustrates this hashing algorithm. Also shown in this figure are representative key values and the file locations that have been calculated to correspond with the values.

There is an inherent problem with hashing functions, however. When hashing functions are applied, duplications of file address values

HASHING FUNCTION:

Quotient = Integer(Logical Key / Total Positions)
Remainder = Logical Key − (Quotient * Total Positions)
Physical Location = Remainder + 1

```
LET Q = INT(K / 1200)
LET R = K - (Q * 1200)
LET L = R + 1
```

Logical Key (K)	Physical Location (L)
12014	15
15618	19
18003	4
21607	8
25211	12
28815	16
31200	1
32419	20
34804	5
38408	9
42012	13
45616	17
48001	2
51605	6
55209	10
58813	14
62417	18
64802	3
68406	7
72010	11
75614	15 ⎫
79218	19 ⎬ Synonyms
81603	4
85207	8
88811	12 ⎭

Figure 11-7. Application of alternative hashing function to determine location of record based on logical key.

result. This situation is inevitable, because a constant is used as a divisor and applied to a random set of dividends. For example, note in Figure 11-7 that a set of 25 keys is shown. Five of these keys hash to identical relative file locations (4, 8, 12, 15, and 19). Such identical locator values are called *synonyms.* Of course, it is impossible to place two or more records in the same file location. Therefore, techniques must be used to find alternative addresses for values that hash to the same positions.

Figure 11-8 illustrates one of the several methods for handling synonyms. Under the straightforward approach shown here, a record that hashes to a location already occupied is written to the next available position in the file. For example, the record with key 75614 hashes to file location 15. However, this record cannot be written at location 15, because that space already is occupied by record 12014. Therefore, record 75614 is placed in the next unused position in the file—location 21. This procedure is the *consecutive-spill* method for handling synonyms. In building and updating files, therefore, programs must contain both a hashing algorithm and a procedure for locating the next available position if the *home position,* or hashed position, is occupied.

The BASIC code shown in Figure 11-9 illustrates this method of locating available space to add a record to a hashed file. First, the physical location (L) is calculated in the hashing function. Then, the location is used to retrieve the record at that home position. A test is made to determine if the accessed record is null (S = 0). If not, the location value is incremented by 1—to point to the next position in the file—and another record is retrieved. The program continues to access records from the file until either a null record is encountered or the end of the file is reached. When an open location is found, the new record is added to the file.

To reduce the occurrence of synonyms, a *prime number* can be used as the divisor in the hashing algorithm. A prime number is evenly divisible only by itself and the value 1. Tables of prime numbers can be used to determine the number closest in value to the number of positions required for the file. Then, this prime number is divided into the key value to calculate the file address. Refer again to the example in Figure 11-7. Instead of dividing the part number key by 1200 (the total number of storage positions required for the file), the number key is divided by the number 1199 (the prime number closest in value to the file size).

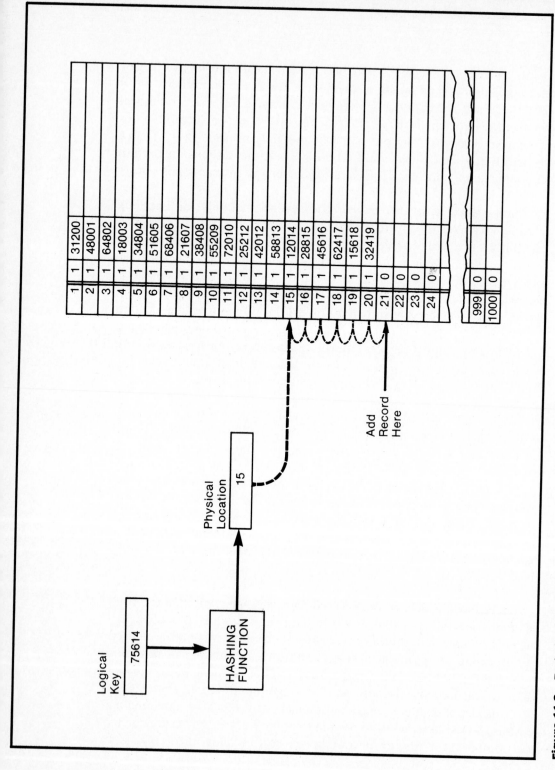

Figure 11-8. Technique for handling synonyms within direct-access file.

```
9000! ***************************************
9010! * S9.0 WRITE RECORD TO HASHED FILE *
9020! ***************************************
9030!
9040! THIS SUBROUTINE WRITES A NEW RECORD TO A HASHED FILE.
9050! IT CALCULATES THE HOME POSITION OF THE NEW RECORD AND
9060! RETRIEVES THE NULL (OR ACTUAL) RECORD AT THAT LOCATION.
9070! IF THE POSITION IS ALREADY OCCUPIED, AS INDICATED BY A
9080! STATUS CODE OF 1, THEN THE NEW RECORD IS WRITTEN IN
9090! THE FIRST AVAILABLE POSITION BEYOND THE HOME ADDRESS.
9100!
9110! VARIABLE NAMES:
9120!     L....RECORD LOCATION
9130!     K....RECORD KEY
9140!     M....MAXIMUM RECORDS IN FILE
9150!     S....STATUS CODE
9160!     D$...DATA WITHIN FILE RECORD
9170!     D1$..DATA TO BE WRITTEN TO FILE RECORD
9180!
9190  LET L = INT(K / M) + 1
9200!
9210  GET #1, RECORD L
9220!
9230! REPEAT
9240  IF S = 0 OR L > M THEN GOTO 9310
9250!
9260      LET L = L + 1
9270!
9280      GET #1, RECORD L
9290!
9300  GOTO 9230
9310! END REPEAT
9320!
9330! SELECT
9340  IF S = 0 THEN GOTO 9360
9350                GOTO 9410
9360      LET S  = 1
9370      LET D$ = D1$
9380      UPDATE #1
9390        GOTO 9430
9400!
9410      PRINT "*** FILE FULL ***"
9420!
9430! END SELECT
9440!
9450  RETURN
```

Figure 11-9. BASIC code illustrating the consecutive-spill method of locating space to add a record within a hashed file.

Figure 11-10 shows the same key values that appear in Figure 11-7, along with the position numbers derived by using the prime number 1199 as the divisor in the hashing algorithm. Notice that none of the keys in Figure 11-10 resulted in synonyms. Although the use of prime numbers as divisors will reduce the number of synonyms, it is still necessary to include procedures within file creation and access programs to check for synonym occurrence and to employ consecutive-spill techniques.

Hashing on Nonnumeric Keys

Relative files and hashed files are convenient organization methods for records with numeric key values. Occasionally, however, the keys will contain nonnumeric characters. In many cases, part numbers in inventory files are combinations of numeric, alphabetic, and special characters. For instance, the key value AX-21953-R is perfectly legitimate for use in an inventory system. In other cases, customer files may be keyed to the customer name, in which case the key is alphabetic. Thus, a direct-access file organization method must be able to handle these nonnumeric keys.

One method of deriving numeric file locations for nonnumeric keys is to establish a table of values that equates particular alphabetic and special characters with particular numeric values. The numbers are extracted from the table and used in the hashing function. For example, under a system in which the letters are equated so that $A = 1, B = 2, C = 3$, and so forth, the key AC214F would be converted to the number 132146 for use in the hashing function. The same principle would apply to all-alphabetic keys or keys made up of alphabetic and special characters.

Another possible method for converting alphanumeric keys into numeric keys is to use only the numeric portions of the keys. For example, from the key AX-21953-R, the numeric value 21953 would be extracted and used in the hashing function. The string function MID$ can be used to locate and extract the numeric substring. Then, the VAL function can be applied to convert the substring into a number. The VAL function is used to convert strings of numbers into numeric equivalents. For the example key shown above, the statement LET K = VAL(MID$(K$,4,5,)) extracts the substring "21953" from the string "AX-21953-R" and converts it into the number 21953. Then, this number can be used in a hashing function to calculate a file storage position.

HASHING FUNCTION:

Quotient = Integer(Logical Key / Prime Number)
Remainder = Logical Key − (Quotient * Prime Number)
Physical Location = Remainder + 1

```
LET Q = INT(K / 1199)
LET R = K - (Q * 1199)
LET L = R + 1
```

Logical Key (K)	Physical Location (L)
12014	25
15618	32
18003	19
21607	26
25211	33
28815	40
31200	27
32419	47
34804	34
38408	41
42012	48
45616	55
48001	42
51605	49
55209	56
58813	63
62417	70
64802	57
68406	64
72010	71
75614	78
79218	85
81603	72
85207	79
88811	86

Figure 11-10. Application of alternate hashing function using prime number as the divisor.

INDEXED FILES

Often, an indexed file is used for records with nonnumeric keys. With this organization method, it is not necessary to convert nonnumeric characters to numeric values. Also, indexed files allow for two or more keys per file.

An indexed file has two parts, or subfiles. As illustrated in Figure 11-11, one of these file areas is for data, and the other is for an *index*. The data area uses a relative organization plan. As each new record is created, it is assigned the next available position in the file. Thus, records are written in sequence from the beginning of the file to the end. Whenever a record is loaded into the file, the relative position of the record is entered into the index, in correspondence with the key of that record. The index entries are maintained in the same key sequence as in the data file.

To control the organization and access functions for an indexed file, the index must reside in memory. Thus, the index is used in the same general manner as the sequential file structures you encountered in the first eight chapters. When an access function is applied to the file, the index is searched sequentially for the record key. This search leads the program to the location value that is the relative address of the record in the data file. This location value is used to access the record from the file in the same manner as in relative organization methods.

Maintaining the index in memory speeds up the search for keys and provides processing efficiencies. When not in use, the index is stored on disk, along with the data file. Thus, whenever a direct-access program uses an indexed file, one of the program's first functions is to load the index into tables.

When a new record is added to the data file, the record key is entered into the next available position in the index. The location value that corresponds with the key then becomes the target position for adding the new record to the data file. The data record, therefore, also is placed in the next available position in the data file.

To delete a record from an indexed file, the program searches the index to locate the key of the specified record. Then, the location value that corresponds with the key is used to access the record from the data file. Deletion involves changing the status code of the record to 0. In other words, the record itself is not removed physically from the file. Rather, a flag is used to indicate that the position is available. Optionally, the data

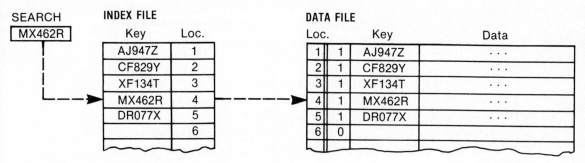

A. To access a record within an indexed file, the program searches the index sequentially to locate the key of the specified record.

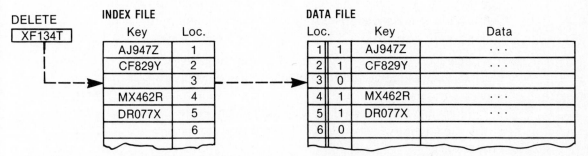

B. To delete a record from an indexed file, the program first performs the search function shown above (A). When the specified record is accessed, the status code of the record is changed to 0, which indicates that the position is available.

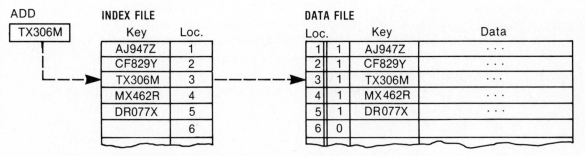

C. To add a record into an indexed file, the record key is entered into the next available position in the index. The data record also is placed in the next available position.

Figure 11-11. Organization and operation of an indexed file.

fields within the record area can be set to zero and blank values. In any case, the index entry is removed. This removal is accomplished by overwriting the key with blank spaces to indicate that the space and its associated location value are eligible for use in adding a new record to the file.

Indexed file organization methods work for numeric, alphabetic, and alphanumeric keys. In fact, it is possible to have multiple keys by using multiple indexes to refer to the same file. For example, the kind of indexing system shown in Figure 11-12 would be used by a company that wanted to access customer records either by account number or by customer name. One index would be set up according to the account number, and the other by name. The program would search the appropriate index depending upon which key was specified by the user. In either case, the index would be searched sequentially to locate the key value, and the associated file location value would be used to access the corresponding record.

Certain applications of indexed files may require records to be processed in key sequence, either alphabetically or numerically. Sequential access is possible if the index is sorted in key sequence. Then, records in the data file are accessed by location values, in the order presented in the sorted index. Figure 11-13 shows how indexed files are accessed sequentially.

In other types of applications, an index may be applied to a sequentially organized data file. Random access is conducted by searching the index and retrieving records according to locations. Sequential access does not use the index. Data records, which are maintained in key sequence, are accessed serially. This organization scheme, known as indexed-sequential, is used widely for files that require both random and sequential processing. Customer files for organizations such as banks or public utilities often are established as indexed-sequential files. Although beyond the scope of this book, indexed-sequential organization is a popular and convenient method of providing flexible access to data records.

FILE ACCESS AND ORGANIZATION

File management operations have two dimensions. One dimension is the file access technique, illustrated in Figure 11-14. This technique includes serial, sequential, and random approaches. The other dimension is file

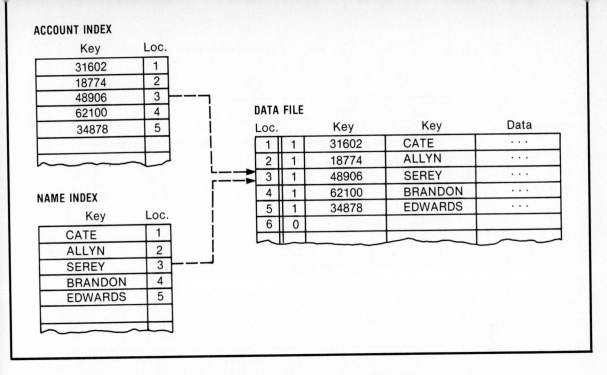

Figure 11-12. Organization of indexed file with multiple indexes.

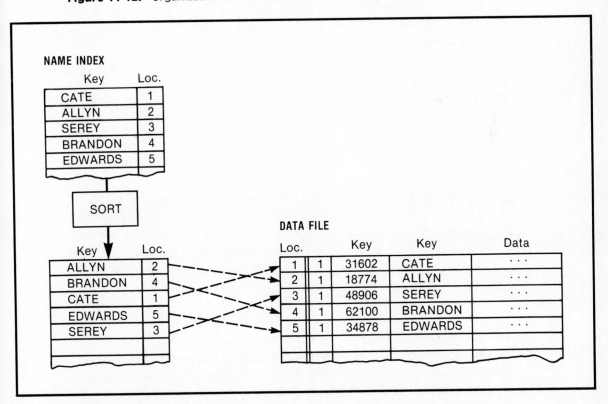

Figure 11-13. Sequential access to an indexed file is provided by first sorting the index. Then, records are accessed from the data file in the serial order of location values in the resulting index.

		Organization				
		SEQUENTIAL	RELATIVE	HASHED	INDEXED	INDEXED-SEQUENTIAL
Access	SERIAL	X	X	X	X	X
	SEQUENTIAL	X			X[1]	X
	RANDOM		X	X	X	X

[1]Requires sorting of index in key sequence

Figure 11-14. Relationships between file organization and access.

organization plan. With this plan, sequential, relative, hashed, or indexed organization approaches are available.

File Access

The term file access refers to the user's view of the data maintained within a file. In other words, a user application requires that data be made available for processing in one of the following three ways:

- Records may be processed serially. Serial processing refers to records that will be accessed in the physical order in which the records appear in the file. The key sequence of the records is ignored, or is unimportant to the application.

- Records may be accessed and processed in key sequence. For this type of processing, it is plausible and convenient to anticipate the logical order of processing. Transactions are arranged in a key sequence before being submitted for processing.

- When the processing sequence cannot be anticipated in advance, a random-access method is appropriate.

In some cases, combinations of access methods are required for the same file. For example, it may be necessary to support both serial and random access or sequential and random access. Selection of an access method is not considered to be a technical decision. It is a business decision, predicated on the types of processing services to be rendered.

File Organization

The term file organization refers to the computer's view of the data maintained within a file. The organization scheme determines the physical arrangement and maintenance of data on secondary storage devices. The choice of an organization method is a technical decision. The appropriate organization plan is selected for its ability to support a given file access need.

Figure 11-14 presents the types of access supported by sequential, relative, hashed, indexed, and indexed-sequential organization schemes. As indicated, sequential file organization can support both serial and sequential access (which, in this case, happen to be the same). However, if it is impractical or impossible to anticipate the processing sequence of records within a file, sequential organization is not a viable choice. On the other hand, if most of the records in a file will be accessed during a processing run, and if it is convenient to arrange transactions in a key order that matches the order of records in the file, sequential organization is probably the best choice. If random access is a necessary requirement for a file, either relative, hashed, or indexed organization should be chosen. The choice of random access alternatives depends, in turn, upon other criteria, such as the types of keys that are used and whether sequential access must be possible also.

ACCESS METHODS

Access methods are software routines that allow use of file organization schemes. These software packages are usually vendor-supplied and come with or are purchased for particular computer systems. Access methods allow programmers and other users to perform record creation, access, deletion, and modification functions without detailed knowledge of the physical device requirements for maintaining files. That is, access methods effectively disguise, or make transparent to their users, the hardware characteristics and physical access requirements of secondary storage devices.

Virtually all microcomputers, for example, are equipped with access-method routines to allow creation and maintenance of sequential and relative files. These access methods are part of a computer's operating system. As a programmer, you call upon these routines by including special BASIC commands within your programs. To use the sequential access method, for instance, the OPEN, INPUT, PRINT, and CLOSE commands are coded. These statements do not actually read and write to files. Rather, the statements call upon particular access-method routines that perform the actual transfers of data to and from specified devices. For relative files, the commands GET, PUT, and UPDATE, along with variations on the OPEN and CLOSE statements, call up routines from the relative access method. These routines do not require the programmer to possess technical knowledge about hardware devices.

Most microcomputers do not come equipped with indexed access methods. The programmer must provide this access method by using the sequential and relative access capabilities that come with the system. Thus, sequential techniques are used to build and maintain indexes, and relative techniques are employed for maintaining associated data files. Also, computer operating systems normally do not provide hashing routines. Therefore, the programmer must devise and implement any needed hashing method.

As the programmer moves to larger computer systems, additional access methods become available. Minicomputers and mainframe computers usually provide some form of indexed-sequential access method. Commands designed to maintain indexed files are part of the programming language. The user is not required to adapt other access methods that allow indexed organization. Indexed access methods are available for some types of microcomputers that use certain programming languages. In general, however, these software tools are not available to support the BASIC language.

The most comprehensive type of access method is a *database management system (DBMS)*. A DBMS uses sequential, relative, and indexed file organization techniques to integrate and manage multiple files related to a particular application or set of applications. A DBMS represents an additional layer of software placed between the user and the actual access methods. Thus, the user has no control over which file organization method to use or the access technique to be supported. In effect, any and all access requirements can be supported. Therefore, a DBMS is a high-level access method that makes even the traditional access methods transparent to the user. Database management systems are available for most computer systems, from microcomputers to mainframe computers, although this software usually is not provided as part of the standard operating system. The programmer calls upon DBMS routines through special commands that are provided in the programming languages supported by the database management system.

Chapter Summary

1. In batch processing systems, file creation, updating, maintenance, and reporting functions are provided in separate programs. By contrast, an on-line system may encompass many or all of these functions within a single software product.

2. On-line systems usually are easy to operate, because it is not necessary to run and monitor separate programs within a continuous job stream. However, the provision for ease of operation compromises the ease with which such systems can be developed. On-line systems require programs that are more complex, because these systems handle many of the functions that are performed by trained operations personnel in batch systems.

3. In on-line systems, records are updated in place. Because this processing activity wipes out existing master records, on-line systems require logging of all entries to maintain a history, or audit trail, of transaction and master file activity.

4. Periodically, it is necessary to create and store remotely copies of on-line files. The copied file, in effect, portrays the status of a system at a given time. This duplicated master and the corresponding log file can be used to rebuild the system if the existing files are destroyed.

5. Support of on-line transaction processing systems requires direct access to master files. This requirement can be met through a number of different file organization schemes. The challenge lies in studying the needs and conditions of a system, then matching file capabilities to those needs.

6. A relative file organization scheme can be used if the key field for all of the records in a file consists of unique, closely sequenced numbers that parallel the range of disk storage locations required for the file.

7. If the record key cannot be used directly as a locator, files must be organized through other schemes—hashed or indexed.

8. For a hashed file, calculations are applied to record keys to convert key values to locator values within the range of addresses needed for the file. If the key contains non-numeric characters, techniques must be used to convert the characters to numbers before applying the hashing function.

9. The application of hashing functions results in a duplication of file address numbers. These identical locator values are called synonyms. Whenever a key hashes to an address that already is occupied by a data record, the synonym is written to the next available position in the file.

10. An indexed file has two subfiles. One of these files is a relative file that holds the data records. The other file is an index that associates record keys with file positions.

11. To support the organization and access functions for an indexed file, the index must reside in memory during processing. When not in use, the index may be kept on a secondary storage device.

12. In an indexed file, records are written randomly to the data file. They are accessed by searching the index first for the matching key and then using the associated position value to retrieve the record.

13. Although they appear in random order, records in an indexed file can be processed sequentially. This processing involves sorting the index in key order and then retrieving the records in the serial order of locator values.

14. It is possible to have multiple indexes that refer to a single data file. In effect, the file has multiple keys, any of which can be used to search for records.

15. An index may be applied to a data file that is set up sequentially. This technique allows a file to be accessed sequentially, either by reading serially through the file, or randomly, by looking up the position value of a record within the index. This file organization method is called indexed-sequential.

16. The term file access refers to the user's view of the file. The access plan represents the way in which records must be provided for processing in support of a business function. The three types of file access are serial, sequential, and random.

17. The term file organization refers to the computer's view of a file and represents the way in which records appear physically on secondary storage devices. The types of file organizations available include sequential, relative, hashed, and indexed. Different organization schemes provide different access capabilities.

18. The term *access method* refers to a set of software routines that support a variety of file organizations and access potentials. An access method provides language commands that programmers use to call upon system routines to perform actual read and write operations to a file.

19. A database is a collection of files that can be accessed and processed on a coordinated, integrated basis. Typically, a database contains files organized through combinations of sequential, relative, and indexed methods. A database management system is a software product that provides an interface between the user and the access methods used for storing data within files. A DBMS helps make the hardware environment of the computer system transparent to the user.

Review Questions

1. In terms of the processing of transactions, how do the methods used by an on-line system differ from batch methods?

2. What is a log file and why are such files maintained for on-line systems?

3. What general criteria should a programmer use to determine which direct-access file organization method is the most appropriate for a particular system?

4. What does a hashing function locate?

5. What is the major characteristic of an indexed file?

6. For what purpose is each of the two subfile areas within an indexed file used?

Key Terms

1. log file
2. file access
3. file organization
4. hashing function
5. randomizing
6. indexed
7. indexed-sequential
8. division/remainder method
9. synonym
10. consecutive-spill
11. home position
12. prime number
13. index
14. file access technique
15. file organization plan
16. access method
17. database management system (DBMS)

BASIC Library

1. MID$
2. VAL

A
PROGRAMMING
CASE STUDIES

CASE STUDY ONE

The following case study presents a business situation that calls for the BASIC programming methods and techniques that are described in Chapters 1 through 8. The development of this particular system progresses in stages that parallel the reading material in each chapter. Thus, the first practice assignment allows you to test your understanding of the concepts discussed in Chapters 1 through 3. When you complete the final practice assignment in the Chapter 8 section, you will have worked through the programming phases that result in an operational computer information system.

A PROGRAMMING SCENARIO: UNDERWOOD'S DISCOUNT HARDWARE STORE

Imagine a situation in which a retail outlet might benefit from a computerized accounts receivable system. Underwood's Discount Hardware store sells consumer goods within three main departments: general hardware, small appliances, and garden supplies. Although primarily a cash-and-carry business, the store does sell merchandise on account to its preferred-credit customers.

At present, all of the store's record keeping is done by hand. The clerical staff spends much of its time managing the bookkeeping for the store's accounts receivable (A/R) system. This system is used to record and report on accounts for credit customers. Staff duties include recording purchases and payments made on accounts, maintaining account balances, and reporting account activity to store managers. Present procedures require that several ledger books and journals be used by office clerks to keep track of credit purchases and payments, and that hand-written status reports be prepared from these books of account for store and department managers.

Underwood's Discount Hardware recently purchased a microcom-puter. Eventually, most of the store's record-keeping procedures will be automated. However, store management feels that it is necessary to im-prove control over credit accounts and to receive more timely informa-tion regarding account activity. Thus, applications priority is given to the accounts receivable system.

You have been hired to write the programs for this system. You will be working with store managers and the office staff to define the pro-grams and procedures that will computerize the application. However, you will have sole responsibility for implementing the A/R system.

CASE STUDY ONE—CHAPTERS 1–3

Practice assignments are based on the preceding narrative for Under-wood's Discount Hardware. These assignments should be undertaken after reading Chapters 1 through 3 of the text.

Practice Assignment 1: Creating the Master File

The first order of business in implementing the A/R system is to create the customer master file. This file will be the main storehouse for infor-mation about credit-customer accounts. The customer master file, or Accounts Receivable Master File, will be kept on magnetic disk and will be the focal point for most of the accounts receivable applications. The programming specifications for this master file creation program appear in Figure A-1.

After this program is written and tested, use it to build the accounts receivable master file. Remember that this file will be used in several subsequent programs that you write. Therefore, be certain that the file is correct before you attempt further programming.

CASE STUDY ONE—CHAPTER 4

With creation of the customer master file (ARMF) for Underwood's Dis-count Hardware, the primary support file for the accounts receivable system is in place. The ARMF will be used to record credit purchases and payments and to maintain continuing account balances. Over time, new

Figure A-1. Programming specifications for master file creation.

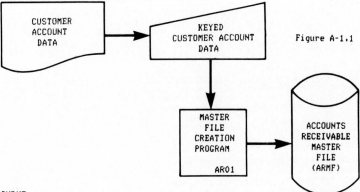

PROGRAMMING SPECIFICATIONS

System: ACCOUNTS RECEIVABLE   Date: 07/05/XX
Program: MASTER FILE CREATION   Program I.D.: AR01   Analyst: D. ADAMS

Design and write a program to create the accounts receivable master file (ARMF)
for Underwood's Discount Hardware. Data for this file are entered interactively through a computer terminal. Records are written to a disk file and
ordered sequentially by customer account number. The program will be coded in
BASIC. Figure A-1.1 shows the system flowchart for this application.

Figure A-1.1

INPUT

The credit customer account data taken from accounts receivable ledgers are the
program input. The following 20 records are written to the disk file in the
order shown:

Credit Category	Customer Account Number	Customer Name	Month-to-Date Purchases	Account Balance	Days Since Last Payment
A	100	JIM ADAMS	200.50	200.50	10
A	101	MORRIS BEAM	1,980.75	50.00	5
A	105	DON ROBERTS	450.00	25.00	22
A	110	MARY DUNN	62.87	178.49	30
A	112	JAY HILL	0.00	0.00	1
A	120	JUDY FORSCH	940.35	575.00	43
B	207	NANCY BLAKE	0.00	38.55	17
B	210	BOB WOODS	1,127.05	1,127.05	12
B	212	DAN HOYT	1,878.00	0.00	5
B	219	FRAN LYONS	0.00	2,500.00	47
B	224	GARY CLAYTON	12.50	12.50	23
B	228	MARK TRUSTY	625.00	840.40	33
B	230	SALLY MANN	947.32	0.00	8
B	235	JACK WILLIS	87.49	1,087.49	21
C	300	DAVE ROBERT	0.00	1.98	157
C	306	DICK THOMAS	9.86	205.49	16
C	310	SARA CASIO	14.75	620.75	10
C	318	DONNA COLE	288.84	25.00	2⁵
C	320	TIM SMART	1,200.00	350.98	62
C	327	CHUCK GANTZ	431.10	0.00	7

The records will contain the following fields of data:

Credit Category: The credit rating for this customer as determined by the credit manager. The codes assigned are:

        A = Credit limit of $200.00 on any
           one purchase.
        B = Credit limit of $500.00 on any
           one purchase.
        C = Credit limit of $1000.00 on any
           one purchase.

Customer
Account Number: This number is assigned by the account clerk as individual account identification.

Customer Name: The name includes first and last names of customers who apply for credit and are approved by the credit manager.

Month-to-Date
Purchases: This field is a total of all credit purchases made during the current month. The field is reset to zero at the beginning of each month.

Account Balance: This field is a total of purchases and payments made on account. The figure is the current balance.

Days Since
Last Payment: This field is the number of days elapsed since a payment was made on the account. The field is reset to zero whenever a payment is made.

PROCESSING

For each record to be written to the master file, the following processing steps take place:

1. The program prompts for each field, which is entered by the operator. As the data are keyed, they are echoed by the system and displayed next to the prompt.

2. After all fields for a single record have been entered, they are verified visually by the operator. The operator then indicates whether the record is correct. If all fields have been keyed correctly, the record is written to the disk file. Incorrect records are rekeyed.

3. After all account records have been written to the file, an EOF record is created. This record contains zeros in all fields except the customer-name field, which contains the string "END OF FILE".

OUTPUT

Figure A-1.2 illustrates the file creation session as it will appear to the operator on the terminal screen or printer.

```
    00000000011111111112222222222333333
    12345678901234567890123456789012345  6
01      MASTER FILE CREATION
02      *********************
03
04 ENTER THE DATA FIELDS INDICATED.
05 TO END THE PROGRAM, KEY THE FIELDS:
06 '0,0,END OF FILE,0,0,0' TO PLACE AN
07 END-OF-FILE RECORD IN THE FILE.
```

```
08
09 CREDIT CATEGORY....? X
10 ACCOUNT NUMBER.....? ###
11 CUSTOMER NAME......? XXXXXXXXXXXX
12 MTD PURCHASES......? #######
13 ACCOUNT BALANCE....? #######
14 LAST PAYMENT DAY...? ###
15    VERIFY (Y/N)....? X
16  .
17  .
18  .
19 CREDIT CATEGORY....? 0
20 ACCOUNT NUMBER.....? 0
21 CUSTOMER NAME......? END OF FILE
22 MTD PURCHASES......? 0
23 ACCOUNT BALANCE....? 0
24 LAST PAYMENT DAY...? 0
25    VERIFY (Y/N)....? Y
26
27 *** END OF SESSION ***
28
29                              Figure A-1.2
```

Figure A-1. Concluded.

customer accounts will be added to this file, accounts will be removed from the file, and changes will be made in the data fields. Therefore, programs must be developed that allow users of the system to check on the status of this file. In particular, there is a need for detail reporting capabilities.

Practice Assignment 2: Detail Report Program

A detail report program must be written for the A/R system. This program is especially useful because it can be run at any time to assist in verifying file content. Figure A-2 provides the programming specifications for the detail report program.

Practice Assignment 3: Exception Report Program

It is important to any company to have an efficient method of collecting on overdue accounts. Underwood's Discount Hardware is faced constantly with this type of cash flow problem. Although the situation is not serious at present, the store wants to improve its ability to collect on overdue accounts. Thus, the store's credit manager needs a past-due accounts report. This report lists customers with past-due accounts.

Bills are sent to customers at the end of each month. Customers are expected to pay a minimum of 10 percent of their outstanding balances

System: ACCOUNTS RECEIVABLE   Date: 07/07/XX
Program: MASTER FILE LISTING   Program I.D.: AR02   Analyst: D. ADAMS

Design and write a program to produce a detail report listing the content of
the accounts receivable master file (ARMF). The report will list all the
fields in all the records and will provide control totals for the following
fields: account number, month-to-date purchases, account balance, and number of
days since last payment. The total number of records in the file also will be
printed. The program will be coded in BASIC. The system flowchart for this
application is shown in Figure A-2.1 below.

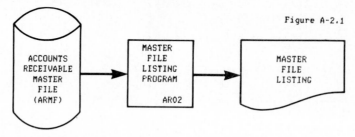

Figure A-2.1

INPUT

The accounts receivable master file (ARMF) is the program input. The following
table provides the format of records in this file:

Field Name	Data Type
Credit Category	Alphanumeric
Account Number	Numeric
Customer Name	Alphanumeric
Month-to-Date Purchases	Numeric
Account Balance	Numeric
Days Since Last Payment	Numeric

PROCESSING

Totals are to be accumulated for these fields: account number, month-to-date
purchases, account balance, and days since last payment. Also, the total
number of records in the file is to be accumulated.

OUTPUT

Program output will be a detail report in the format shown in Figure A-2.2.

```
    00000000011111111112222222222333333333344444444445555555555
    12345678901234567890123456789012345678901234567890123456789
01                    LISTING OF MASTER FILE ARMF
02
03  CREDIT  ACCT.    CUSTOMER      MTD       ACCOUNT    LAST
04  CAT.    NO.        NAME      PURCHASES   BALANCE   PAY DAY
05
06    X     ###   XXXXXXXXXXXX   #,###.##   #,###.##     ###
07    X     ###   XXXXXXXXXXXX   #,###.##   #,###.##     ###
08
09
10
11
12          #,###                ##,###.##  ##,###.##   #,###
13
14  TOTAL RECORDS: ##
15
```

Figure A-2.2

Figure A-2. Programming specifications for master file listing.

each month. Consequently, the credit manager needs to know which customers have not made payments within the past 30 days and the balances due on these accounts. Once this information is available, special collection procedures can be initiated.

The third program for the A/R system, then, will produce an exception report for the credit manager. The program will scan the accounts receivable master file and list the customers who have not made payments on their accounts within the last month. The programming specifications for this program are provided in Figure A-3.

CASE STUDY ONE—CHAPTER 5

The following assignment is a continuation of the accounts receivable system being built for Underwood's Discount Hardware. This assignment should be attempted only after reading Chapter 5 of the text.

Practice Assignment 4: Summary Report Program

Management of Underwood's Discount Hardware requires a summary of monthly purchases and account balances for all credit customers. This report will be produced monthly and at other times as determined by management's needs for account information. Figure A-4 illustrates the structure of processing functions within the A/R system after the summary report program has been added.

So far, this system provides for file creation and report writing. The master file contains the customer account information, which the current programs access and use to produce the various management reports. Subsequent practice assignments add features that keep the master file up to date with ongoing purchase and payment transactions. Such features will make possible the production of reports that present the current status of accounts.

At present, however, the account balance program, identified as bubble 5.0 on the data flow diagram (Figure A-4), will be implemented. The programming specifications for this program are presented in Figure A-5.

CASE STUDY ONE—CHAPTER 6

The ARMF for Underwood's Discount Hardware is designed to maintain customer credit account information. Each day, credit purchases and payments made against account balances will be posted to the file. Thus,

System: ACCOUNTS RECEIVABLE   Date: 07/10/XX
Program: OVERDUE ACCOUNTS   Program I.D.: AR03   Analyst: D. ADAMS

Design and write a program to produce an overdue accounts report. Input to
this program is the accounts receivable master file (ARMF). Output will be a
printed exception report listing those customers who have not made payment on
their accounts within the past 30 days. The program will be written in BASIC.
Figure A-3.1 shows the system flowchart for this application.

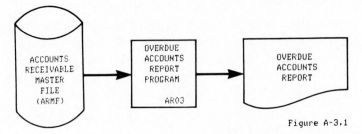

Figure A-3.1

INPUT

The accounts receivable master file (ARMF) is the program input. The format of
records in this file is as follows:

Field Name	Data Type
Credit Category	Alphanumeric
Account Number	Numeric
Customer Name	Alphanumeric
Month-to-Date Purchases	Numeric
Account Balance	Numeric
Days Since Last Payment	Numeric

PROCESSING

The program selects those customer records for which the days-since-last-
payment field is greater than 30. Then, the number of days past due is
calculated by subtracting 30 from the value in the field. The account balance
for this record is added into an accumulator to determine the total amount of
past-due accounts.

OUTPUT

The exception report produced by this program will be in the format shown in
Figure A-3.2

```
     00000000011111111112222222222333333333344444444445555
     12345678901234567890123456789012345678901234567890123
01                   OVERDUE ACCOUNTS
02              (MORE THAN 30 DAYS PAST DUE)
03
04  ACCT.      CUSTOMER      CREDIT    ACCOUNT      DAYS
05   NO.         NAME         CAT.     BALANCE    PAST DUE
06
07  ###    #############      X       #,###.##      ###
08  ###    #############      X       #,###.##      ###
09
10
11
12
13  TOTAL AMOUNT PAST DUE: $###,###.##
14
```

Figure A-3.2

Figure A-3.   Programming specifications for overdue accounts report.

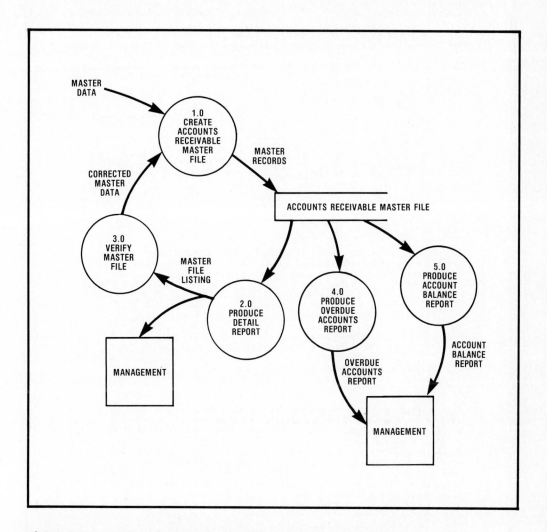

Figure A-4. Data flow diagram for A/R system with summary report.

the posting of account transactions will maintain file currency. Each month, account summaries are used to prepare payment requests for billing customers.

Two separate transaction files will be used within the system. The first transaction file (ARPRCH) will contain information on credit customer purchases. Purchase receipts, issued whenever merchandise is sold on credit, will provide the data for this file. Figure A-6 is an example of a credit purchase receipt.

System: ACCOUNTS RECEIVABLE   Date: 07/12/XX
Program: ACCOUNT BALANCES   Program I.D.: AR04   Analyst: D. ADAMS

Design and write a program to summarize monthly purchases and account balance
for customers in the accounts receivable master file (ARMF). The output report
will list each customer record, amount totals for each credit category, and a
final total for all customers. The report requires multiple pages, and the
program will be written in BASIC. Figure A-5.1 shows the system flowchart for
this application.

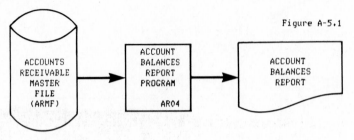

Figure A-5.1

INPUT

The accounts receivable master file (ARMF) is the program input. Master
records are organized in sequence by account number within credit category.
The format of records in this file is as follows:

Field Name	Data Type
Credit Category	Alphanumeric
Account Number	Numeric
Customer Name	Alphanumeric
Month-to-Date Purchases	Numeric
Account Balance	Numeric
Days Since Last Payment	Numeric

PROCESSING

Totals are accumulated and printed for the month-to-date-purchases and account-
balance fields. Group subtotals for these fields are printed whenever the
credit category changes. Final totals are printed at the bottom of the report.

Each page should have no more than 20 lines. After each group of 20 lines,
which includes heading and detail lines, a page break should occur and a new
set of heading lines printed. Following a page break, there should be at least
one detail line printed after the headings. In other words, a subtotal or
final total line should not appear as the first line of printing on any page.
The assumed physical page size is 25 lines.

OUTPUT

Figure A-5.2 shows the format of this summary report with control breaks.

```
      00000000011111111111222222222233333333334444444444455555555
      12345678901234567890123456789012345678901234567890123456
   01            CUSTOMER ACCOUNT BALANCES           PAGE 33
   02               BY CREDIT CATEGORY
   03
   04 CREDIT    ACCT.     CUSTOMER        MTD          ACCOUNT
   05 CAT.      NO.        NAME        PURCHASES       BALANCE
   06
   07   X       ###     XXXXXXXXXXXX    #,###.##       #,###.##
   08   X       ###     XXXXXXXXXXXX    #,###.##       #,###.##
   09
   10
   11   TOTALS FOR CREDIT CATEGORY X    ##,###.##     ##,###.##
   12
   13   X       ###     XXXXXXXXXXXX    #,###.##      ##,###.##
   14   X       ###     XXXXXXXXXXXX    #,###.##      ##,###.##
```

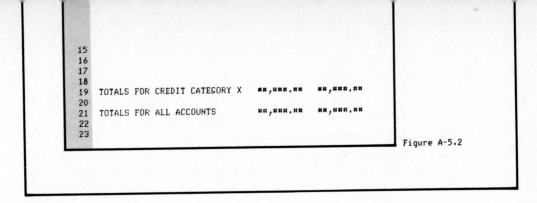

Figure A-5. Programming specifications for account balances report.

PURCHASE RECEIPT	**UNDERWOOD'S DISCOUNT HARDWARE** Muncie, Indiana			DEPT. _10_

ACCT. NO. _100_
NAME _JIM ADAMS_

MDSE. CODE	QTY.	DESCRIPTION	PRICE	AMOUNT
_110_	_1_	_HAMMER_	_6 95_	_6 95_
_130_	_2_	_HINGES_	_1 25_	_2 50_
_160_	_1_	_SCREWS_	_79_	_79_
				_10 24_

SALES CLERK _B.A.V._
CUSTOMER _JIM ADAMS_

Figure A-6. Credit purchase receipt from which data are compiled.

Each day, these receipts are collected from the departments. An office clerk then transcribes the information to a special transmittal form that is used to enter the data into the computer. The receipts are arranged in department number order and an office clerk then transcribes the purchase data to a special transmittal form, in order, by merchandise code. An example of this transmittal form is shown in Figure A-7.

A total of all daily purchases is calculated and entered on the transmittal form. This figure will provide a control total for checking the accuracy of data entry.

The payments file (ARPYMT) is the second transaction file to be prepared daily. This file contains the amounts paid by customers against their credit balances. Data for the payments file are taken from checks received from customers. A special transmittal form is prepared to assist in data entry. This form is illustrated in Figure A-8.

The purchases and payments files require editing before the files can be used to update the accounts receivable master file. Therefore, the system will require two editing programs. The purchases file editing program will validate codes and account numbers, verify sequencing of codes, and test for purchase amounts within credit limits established for the credit categories. This program will produce an edit report indicating the records containing errors so that corrections can be made to the file. A similar program will be required to edit and report on the validity of the payments file.

After the purchases file has been built, a daily sales report will be prepared. This report will list the sales totals for each merchandise type, within each department, and will be a multiple control break report.

The sales report also will list the names of the merchandise categories that correspond with the codes appearing on the purchases file transmittal form and in the file itself. A table of the codes and corresponding merchandise types is presented in Figure A-9.

The information in Figure A-9 will be used to build program tables that can be accessed by the purchases file edit program and the sales report program. A merchandise file (ARMDSE) will be created containing these codes and descriptions. The merchandise file will be used to load merchandise tables within the two programs. Therefore, another program will be required to create the merchandise file.

DATA ENTRY FORM
Purchases File

Date: 07/15/84

DEPT. CODE	MDSE. CODE	ACCOUNT NUMBER	PURCHASE AMOUNT
10	110	100	35 00
10	110	228	10 95
10	110	327	125 25
10	130	212	7 95
10	130	105	16 40
10	140	207	8 95
10	140	310	67 00
10	140	318	25 00
10	160	224	56 79
20	210	235	349 95
20	210	327	6 75
20	220	230	28 00
20	230	228	289 00
20	230	212	98 45
20	230	300	175 50
20	240	306	9 95
20	240	112	18 75
20	240	207	349 80
20	240	318	67 49
30	320	300	12 98
30	320	110	14 55
30	320	100	3 95
30	330	207	5 00
30	330	310	25 65
30	350	230	195 95
			2005 01

Figure A-7. Transmittal form for purchases transaction file.

DATA ENTRY FORM
Payments File

Date: 07/15/84

ACCOUNT NUMBER	PAYMENT AMOUNT
210	400 00
100	200 50
320	350 98
235	1087 49
219	250 00
105	25 00
300	1 98
120	575 00
110	178 49
224	12 50
	3081 94

Figure A-8. Transmittal form for payments transaction file.

MERCHANDISE CODE	MERCHANDISE TYPE*
110	HAND TOOLS
120	AUTOMOTIVE
130	GENERAL HARDWARE
140	HOUSEHOLD
150	PAINT
160	NUTS & BOLTS
170	POWER TOOLS
210	KITCHEN APPLIANCES
220	ELECTRICAL SUPPLY
230	AIR CONDITIONING
240	RADIO/TV
310	LAWNMOWERS
320	GARDEN TOOLS
330	SEEDS/PLANTS
340	INSECTICIDES
350	TILLERS

*NOTE: These merchandise types are general categories within which to fit the merchandise descriptions listed on the purchase receipts.

Figure A-9. Table of merchandise data.

In summary, six programs will be added to the accounts receivable system. Three file creation programs will be written—for merchandise, purchases, and payments files. Two editing programs will be written—one for the purchases file and one for the payments file. Finally, a daily sales report program will be written. After these programs are added (along with the supporting manual procedures), the system will function as shown in the data flow diagram in Figure A-10. The highlighted areas are system programs. The lighter areas refer to manual procedures.

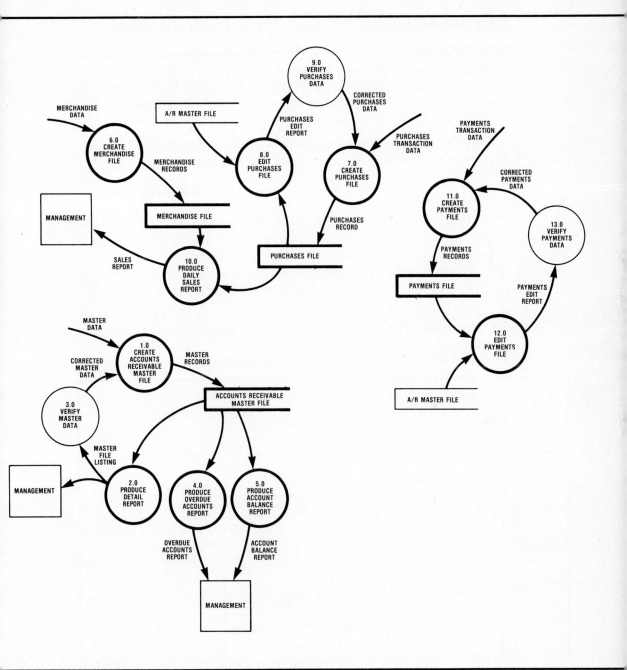

Figure A-10. Data flow diagram of first six programs of A/R system.

Practice Assignment 5: Creating the Merchandise File

Write the program to create a file of merchandise codes and descriptions. This file will provide input for subsequent programs that will build reference tables. The tables will be used to locate valid codes and to access merchandise descriptions to be printed on reports. The specifications for the file creation program are provided in Figure A-11.

Use the written file creation program to build the merchandise file. The program input data are given in the merchandise table in Figure A-9.

Practice Assignment 6: Creating the Purchases File

Write the program to create the purchases file, which contains records pertaining to credit purchases. The program will be run daily to prepare a transaction file of purchases. The purchases transaction file, in turn, will be used to update the accounts receivable master file. Programming specifications for this program are given in Figure A-12.

After you have written the merchandise file creation program, use it to create the purchases file. Input data for this program are provided on the purchases transmittal form (Figure A-7).

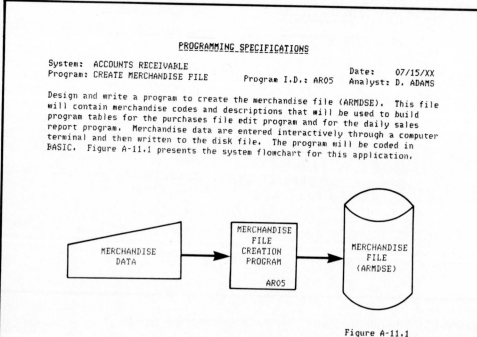

PROGRAMMING SPECIFICATIONS

System: ACCOUNTS RECEIVABLE   Date: 07/15/XX
Program: CREATE MERCHANDISE FILE   Program I.D.: AR05   Analyst: D. ADAMS

Design and write a program to create the merchandise file (ARMDSE). This file
will contain merchandise codes and descriptions that will be used to build
program tables for the purchases file edit program and for the daily sales
report program. Merchandise data are entered interactively through a computer
terminal and then written to the disk file. The program will be coded in
BASIC. Figure A-11.1 presents the system flowchart for this application.

Figure A-11.1

INPUT

The merchandise codes and descriptions, entered in sequence by merchandise code, are the program input. The merchandise records shown in Figure A-9 are used to build the file.

PROCESSING

For each record written to the file, the following processing steps take place:

1. The program prompts for a data field, which is keyed by the operator.

2. After both the code and description fields are entered, they are visually verified by the operator and rekeyed if in error. If the record is correct, it is written to the disk file.

3. After all records have been written to the file, an EOF record is created. This record contains the value zero in the merchandise code field and the string "END OF FILE" in the merchandise description field.

This program should follow the general data entry program design presented in the text. Also, the design should be similar to that used for the master file creation program written in Practice Assignment 1.

OUTPUT

Figure A-11.2 presents the file creation program as it will appear to the operator on the terminal screen or printer.

```
      00000000011111111112222222222333333333
      12345678901234567890123456789012345 6
01       MERCHANDISE FILE CREATION
02       ***************************
03
04  KEY THE CODES AND DESCRIPTIONS
05  FOR EACH MERCHANDISE CATEGORY.
06  END THE PROGRAM BY KEYING THE
07  FIELDS '0' AND 'END OF FILE'.
08
09  MDSE. CODE..........? ###
10  MDSE. DESCRIPTION...? XXXXXXXXXXXX
11     VERIFY (Y/N).....? X
12     .
13     .
14     .
15  MDSE. CODE..........? 0
16  MDSE. DESCRIPTION...? END OF FILE
17     VERIFY (Y/N).....Y
18
19  *** END OF SESSION ***
20
21
```

Figure A-11.2

Figure A-11. Programming specifications for merchandise file creation.

PROGRAMMING SPECIFICATIONS

System: ACCOUNTS RECEIVABLE   Date: 07/18/XX
Program: CREATE PURCHASES FILE   Program I.D.: AR06   Analyst: D. ADAMS

Design and write a program to create the purchases file. This file will contain customer credit purchase records and will be used to update the accounts
receivable master file. Purchase data are entered interactively through
computer terminals and then written to disk. The program will be coded in
BASIC. The system flowchart for this application is given in Figure A-12.1.

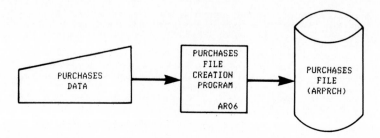

Figure A-12.1

INPUT

The purchase data taken from the purchases transmittal form (Figure A-7) are
the program input. Four fields of data are contained in each purchase record:
department code, merchandise code, account number, and purchase amount. The
data are entered in sequence by merchandise code within department code values.
These values are provided on the transmittal form.

PROCESSING

The program prompts for each of the four fields within each input record. The
terminal operator keys in the data and verifies each record before writing it
to the file. A control total of all purchase amounts for all records is
developed and displayed at the end of the program. After all records are
written, an EOF record, containing zeros in all fields, is placed in the file.

OUTPUT

Output from this program will be the accounts receivable purchases file
(ARPRCH). Each record in this file will contain the four data fields entered
by the terminal operator. The chart presented in Figure A-12.2 shows the data
entry session as it will appear on the terminal screen or printer.

```
      00000000011111111112222222
      12345678901234567890123467
01       FILE CREATION
02       PURCHASE FILE
03       *************
04 TYPE THE DATA FIELDS FOR
05 EACH PURCHASE ON ACCOUNT.
06 END THE SESSION BY TYPING
07 '0' (ZERO) FOR ALL FIELDS.
08
09 DEPT. CODE.....? ##
```

```
10 MDSE. CODE......? ###
11 ACCOUNT NO......? ###
12 PURCHASE AMT...? ####.##
13 VERIFY (Y/N)...? X
14     .
15     .
16     .
17 DEPT. CODE......? 0
18 MDSE. CODE......? 0
19 ACCOUNT NO......? 0
20 PURCHASE AMT...? 0
21 VERIFY (Y/N)...? Y
22
23 TOTAL PURCHASES: $##,###.##
24
25
```

Figure A-12.2

Figure A-12. Programming specifications for purchases file creation.

Practice Assignment 7: Creating the Payments File

Write a program to build the payments transaction file. This file, like the purchases transaction file, will be used to update the ARMF so that the master file reflects ongoing daily payments and purchases on account. This payments file creation program is similar in design to the purchases file creation program. The programming specifications for building the payments transaction file are provided in Figure A-13.

After this program is written, use it to create the payments file. Input data for this program are given on the payments transmittal form illustrated in Figure A-8.

Practice Assignment 8: Edit Report Program

Prepare an edit report program for the purchases file. The edit program will check the data in each record and indicate any fields that are in error. The report will be used to correct the purchases file to ensure that purchases are posted to the customer master file accurately. Programming specifications for the edit report program are given in Figure A-14.

This editing program should be run with test data to make certain the program functions correctly. A test file can be created by modifying the purchases file creation program (AR06). Assign a different file name than ARPRCH so that you will not overwrite the file that was created in Practice Assignment 6. Then, the test file, containing errors to be checked by the edit program, can be input to the edit program. The

System: ACCOUNTS RECEIVABLE   Date: 07/20/XX
Program: CREATE PAYMENTS FILE   Program I.D.: AR07   Analyst: D. ADAMS

Design and write a program to create the payments file (ARPYMT). This file
will contain information on customer payments made against accounts in the
accounts receivable file. Payment data are entered interactively through
computer terminals and written to a disk file. The program will be coded in
BASIC. The system flowchart for this application is shown in Figure A-13.1
below.

Figure A-13.1

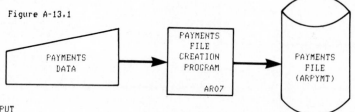

INPUT

The payment data taken from payment transmittal forms are the program input.
Two fields of data are included in each record: account number and payment
amount. These data are entered by the terminal operator and then written to
the file.

PROCESSING

The program prompts the operator for each of the two fields of each record.
The operator keys in and verifies the data before they are placed in the file.
A control total of all payment amounts for all records is developed and displayed at the end of the program. After all records are written, an EOF
record, containing zeros in both fields, is placed in the file.

OUTPUT

Output from this program will be the payments file (ARPYMT). Each record will
contain the two data fields entered by the operator. The chart in Figure
A-13.2 shows the data entry session as it will appear on the terminal screen
or printer.

```
   0000000001111111111222222222233
   12345678901234567890123456789012
01      FILE CREATION
02      PAYMENT  FILE
03      *************
04
05 KEY THE DATA FIELDS FOR
06 EACH PAYMENT ON ACCOUNT.
07 END THE PROGRAM BY KEYING
08 '0' (ZERO) FOR ALL FIELDS.
09
10 ACCOUNT NUMBER...? ###
11 PAYMENT AMOUNT...? ####.##
12 VERIFY (Y/N).....? X
13      .
14      .
15      .
16 ACCOUNT NUMBER...? 0
17 PAYMENT AMOUNT...? 0
18 VERIFY (Y/N).....? Y
19
20 TOTAL PAYMENTS:  $##,###.##
21
```

Figure A-13.2

Figure A-13. Programming specifications for payments file creation.

Figure A-14.　Programming specifications for purchases file editing.

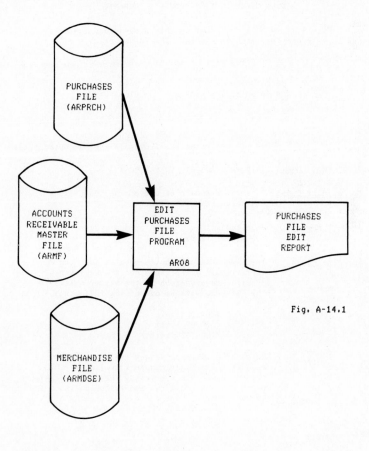

PROGRAMMING SPECIFICATIONS

System: ACCOUNTS RECEIVABLE   Date: 07/22/XX
Program: EDIT PURCHASES FILE   Program I.D.: AR08   Analyst: D. ADAMS

Design and write a program to edit the accounts receivable purchases file. The
program will produce a report that lists the records and describes the fields
in error. The accounts receivable master file (ARMF) and the merchandise file
(ARMDSE) also are used to build program tables of account and merchandise
information. Then, purchase records can be checked against this information.
The program will be coded in BASIC. Figure A-14.1 presents the system flowchart for this application.

PURCHASES
FILE
(ARPRCH)

ACCOUNTS
RECEIVABLE
MASTER
FILE
(ARMF)

EDIT
PURCHASES
FILE
PROGRAM

AR08

PURCHASES
FILE
EDIT
REPORT

Fig. A-14.1

MERCHANDISE
FILE
(ARMDSE)

<u>INPUT</u>

The accounts receivable purchases file (ARPRCH) is the primary program input. This file contains the records to be edited. Record fields and formats for the purchases file are:

Field Name	Data Type
Department Code	Numeric
Merchandise Code	Numeric
Account Number	Numeric
Purchase Amount	Numeric

The accounts receivable master file (ARMF) also is used in this program. Data from the ARMF are loaded into program tables and are accessed during editing. Record formats for the master file are as follows:

Field Name	Data Type
Credit Category	Alphanumeric
Account Number	Numeric
Customer Name	Alphanumeric
Month-to-Date Purchases	Numeric
Account Balance	Numeric
Days Since Last Payment	Numeric

The merchandise file (ARMDSE) is input by this program and loaded into tables that can be searched for matching values. The format of this file is:

Field Name	Data Type
Merchandise Code	Numeric
Merchandise Description	Alphanumeric

<u>PROCESSING</u>

The following edits should take place on the fields in the purchases file:

<u>Department Code</u>: This value should be either 10, 20, or 30.

<u>Merchandise Code</u>: This field should be one of the code values in the merchandise file.

<u>Account Number</u>: This field should be an account number in the master file.

<u>Purchase Amount</u>: This amount should be no greater than the credit limit established for the customer's credit category given in the master file. The category will be one of the following:

        A = $200.00 limit
        B = $500.00 limit
        C = $1000.00 limit

Note: The purchase amount field can be edited only if the account number is valid; if the account number is not valid, the field is skipped during this program run and tested during a subsequent run.

<u>OUTPUT</u>

Output from this program will be an edit report in the format shown in Figure A-14.2. You will not need to write the program used to produce a multiple-page report.

```
0000000000111111111122222222223333333333344444444
12345678901234567890123456789012345678901234567
01                    EDIT REPORT
02                   PURCHASES FILE
03
04 DEPT MDSE ACCT PURCHASE
05 CODE CODE  NO   AMOUNT    ERROR MESSAGE
06 ----  ----  ----  --------     --------------------
07
08 ##   ###   ###   #,###.##
09                            INVALID DEPT. CODE
10                            INVALID MDSE. CODE
11                            INVALID ACCT. NO.
12                            AMOUNT OVER LIMIT
13 ##   ###   ###   #,###.##
14                            XXXXXXXXXXXXXXXXX
15
```

Figure A-14.2

Figure A-14. Concluded.

---

edit program initially is written to edit the test file and then is modified for the purchases file. This program modification takes place after the purchases file has been verified. Use the name TESTPR to create and edit the test file. Include the records shown in Figure A-15.

After running the edit program with the test file, run the program with the purchases file (ARPRCH) to verify that all records are correct. Make all changes that are necessary to remove file errors.

DEPT. CODE	MDSE. CODE	ACCOUNT NUMBER	PURCHASE AMOUNT
10	100	100	50.00
11	110	105	200.00
20	230	212	600.00
20	270	300	1,475.75
30	310	110	250.95
40	420	102	360.89
30	330	306	120.50

Figure A-15. Records used to edit test file.

Practice Assignment 9: Edit Report Program 2

Prepare an edit report for the payments file (ARPYMT). This report is similar to the one produced for the purchases file. Then, write a program to perform the file edits. The specifications for this program are presented in Figure A-16.

Run the editing program with test data. Modify program AR07 to allow creation of a test file named TESTPY. Then, enter the data shown in Figure A-17 into the file.

Run the editing program using the test file. If the program works correctly, modify and run it with the payments file (ARPYMT). Make sure that the payments file is correct before proceeding with Practice Assignment 10.

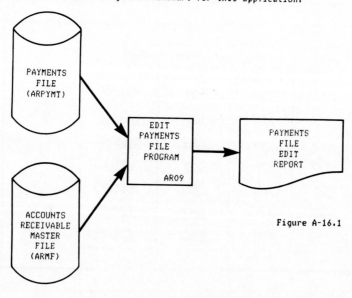

PROGRAMMING SPECIFICATIONS

System: ACCOUNTS RECEIVABLE   Date: 07/23/XX
Program: EDIT PAYMENTS FILE   Program I.D.: AR09   Analyst: D. ADAMS

Design and write a program to edit the accounts receivable payments file
(ARPYMT). The program will produce a report that lists fields in error. The
accounts receivable master file (ARMF) also is used to build program tables
against which payment data can be checked. The program will be coded in BASIC.
Figure A-16.1 shows the system flowchart for this application.

PAYMENTS
FILE
(ARPYMT)

EDIT
PAYMENTS
FILE
PROGRAM

AR09

PAYMENTS
FILE
EDIT
REPORT

ACCOUNTS
RECEIVABLE
MASTER
FILE
(ARMF)

Figure A-16.1

INPUT

The accounts receivable payments file (ARPYMT) is the primary program input. Records in this file are edited for correctness. The format and fields for records in this file are:

Field Name	Data Type
Account Number	Numeric
Payment Amount	Numeric

The ARMF also is used for this program. Data in this file are loaded into program tables and accessed during editing. The format of records in this file is:

Field Name	Data Type
Credit Category	Alphanumeric
Account Number	Numeric
Customer Name	Alphanumeric
Month-to-Date Purchases	Numeric
Account Balance	Numeric
Days Since Last Payment	Numeric

Build tables only for those fields needed for editing.

PROCESSING

The following edits should take place on the fields in the payments file:

Account Number: This field should be one of the account numbers represented in the master file.

Payment Amount: This amount should not be greater than the account balance or less than the minimum payment, which is 10% of the account balance. This field cannot be edited if the account number is incorrect.

OUTPUT

Program output will be an edit report in the format shown in Figure A-16.2 below. You will not need to write the program to produce a multiple-page report.

```
   0000000001111111111222222222233333333334444444
   12345678901234567890123456789012345678901234567
01                EDIT REPORT
02               PAYMENTS FILE
03
04 ACCOUNT      PAYMENT
05   NO.        AMOUNT          ERROR MESSAGE
06 -------     --------      -------------------
07
08   ###       #,###.##
09                           INVALID ACCOUNT NO.
10                           AMOUNT > BALANCE
11                           AMOUNT < MINIMUM
12   ###       #,###.##
13                           XXXXXXXXXXXXXXXXXXX
14
15
```

Figure A-16.2

Figure A-16. Programming specifications for payments file editing.

ACCOUNT NUMBER	PAYMENT AMOUNT
100	25.00
105	20.00
113	150.00
219	25.00
300	10.00

Figure A-17. Data used to edit test file.

Practice Assignment 10: Producing the Sales Report

Use the verified purchases transaction file to produce a daily sales report. This report will list the amounts of credit purchases for each merchandise category within each department. The report will be provided daily to store managers, who will use the report to evaluate purchase trends within the various departments. This will be a multiple control-break program. Figure A-18 provides the program specifications.

CASE STUDY ONE—CHAPTER 7

All of the files necessary to support ongoing processing for Underwood's Discount Hardware A/R system have now been established. The next requirement, then, is to create programs that allow the ARMF to be updated with transactions contained in the purchases file (ARPRCH) and the payments file (ARPYMT). A master file inquiry program also is needed so that store managers and clerks can inquire interactively into the status of customer accounts. The data flow diagram presented in Figure A-19 includes these three programs.

Practice Assignment 11: Updating the Master File—Program 1

Write a program so that the ARMF can be updated daily with purchase transactions in the purchases file. Purchase amounts are to be added to the month-to-date purchases fields and the account balance fields of the master records. This program is one of the two update programs that

Figure A-18. Programming specifications for credit sales report.

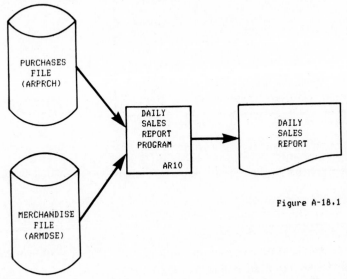

PROGRAMMING SPECIFICATIONS

System: ACCOUNTS RECEIVABLE   Date: 07/25/XX
Program: SALES REPORT   Program I.D.: AR10   Analyst: D. Adams

Design and write a program to produce a daily credit sales report. The input
will be the accounts receivable purchases file (ARPRCH) and the merchandise
file (ARMDSE). Output will be a multiple-page report showing the total purchases by merchandise type within department. The program will be coded in
BASIC. Figure A-18.1 shows the system flowchart for this application.

Figure A-18.1

INPUT

The purchases file (ARPRCH) is the primary program input. The format of this
file is as follows:

Field Name	Data Type
Department Code	Numeric
Merchandise Code	Numeric
Account Number	Numeric
Purchase Amount	Numeric

The merchandise file (ARMDSE) also is input to this program. Records in this
file are loaded into program tables from which merchandise descriptions can be
extracted based on matching codes in the purchases file. The format of the
merchandise file is:

Field Name	Data Type
Merchandise Code	Numeric
Merchandise Description	Alphanumeric

PROCESSING

Totals are developed for each merchandise category represented in the file, for
each department, and for all purchases. Control breaks are taken whenever the
merchandise code or department code changes. When a merchandise total line is
printed, the merchandise description is extracted from the table and printed on
the line. A maximum of 20 lines is to be printed on each page. The assumed
physical page size is 25 lines.

The sales report will be printed in the format shown in Figure A-18.2 below.

```
         0000000001111111111222222222233333333334444444444
         1234567890123456789012345678901234567890123456789012345678
01                     DAILY SALES REPORT        PAGE ##
02                  CREDIT SALES BY DEPARTMENT
03
04 DEPT      MDSE       MERCHANDISE           PURCHASE
05 CODE      CODE          TYPE               AMOUNT
06
07  ##        ###      XXXXXXXXXXXXX          X,XXX.XX
08  ##        ###      XXXXXXXXXXXXX          X,XXX.XX
09
10
11              TOTAL FOR DEPARTMENT ##    $##,###.##
12
13              TOTAL FOR ALL DEPARTMENTS  $##,###.##
14
15
```

Figure A-18.2

Figure A-18. Concluded.

will be used to keep the master file current. The specifications for this program are provided in Figure A-20.

Practice Assignment 12: Updating the Master File—Program 2

Write a program for updating the ARMF daily with payments against account balances. Payment amounts are to be subtracted from account balances. Then, the corresponding days-since-last-payment fields are reset to zero. This program is the second of the two updating programs used to keep the master file current. To simplify programming, use two separate posting programs instead of combining the processing into a single program. The specifications for this program appear in Figure A-21. Note that the specifications are similar to those presented for the purchases posting program.

Practice Assignment 13: Master File Inquiry

With master record updating capabilities now built into the A/R system, it becomes practical to add inquiry capability into the master file. Write a program that will allow store managers and clerks to inquire into the

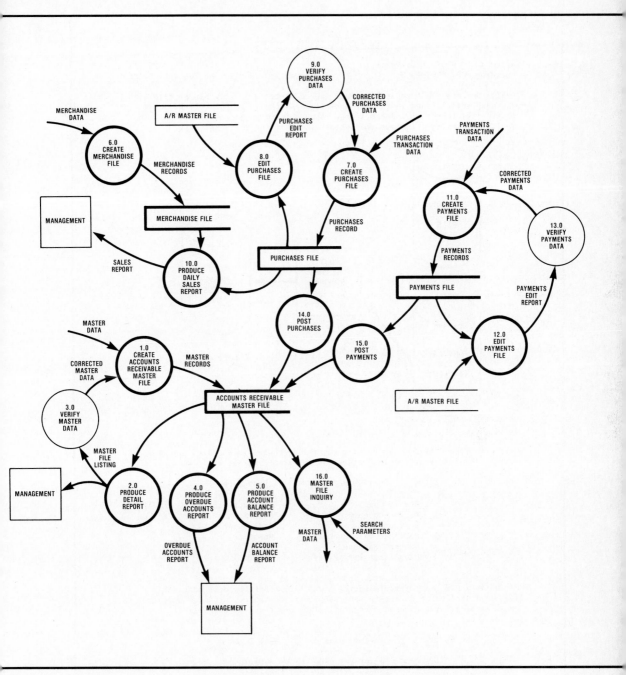

Figure A-19. Data flow diagram with updating and inquiry programs added.

PROGRAMMING SPECIFICATIONS

System: ACCOUNTS RECEIVABLE   Date: 07/26/XX
Program: POST PURCHASES   Program I.D.: AR11   Analyst: D. ADAMS

Design and write a program to update the accounts receivable master file with
purchase transactions in the purchase file (ARPRCH). Output will be a new
master file (ARNM) of updated master records. The program will be coded in
BASIC. Figure A-20.1 shows the system flowchart for this application.

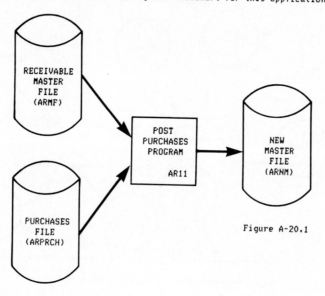

Figure A-20.1

INPUT

The accounts receivable master file and the purchases file are the program
input. The following table provides the format of the master file:

Field Name	Data Type
Credit Code	Alphanumeric
Account Number	Numeric
Customer Name	Alphanumeric
Month-to-Date Purchases	Numeric
Account Balance	Numeric
Days Since Last Payment	Numeric

The master file is loaded into program tables at the beginning of processing.
Purchases are posted within these tables. Provision should be made for
loading a maximum of 25 master records within the tables, although only 20
table elements will be used currently. The format of the purchases file is
as follows:

Field Name	Data Type
Department Code	Numeric
Merchandise Code	Numeric
Account Number	Numeric
Purchase Amount	Numeric

PROCESSING

PROCESSING

The purchase amount in the purchase record is added to the month-to-date purchases and account-balance fields of the corresponding master record. Records
are updated within the program tables created from the master file. A tally
will be maintained of the number of purchase records processed.

OUTPUT

Following all updates, a new master file will be written from the master file
tables. The program will write an appropriate EOF record to the new file.
Figure A-20.2 shows the messages that will be displayed on the terminal while
the program is executing.

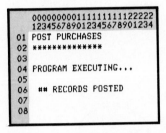

Figure A-20.2

After this posting program has been run, the two master files should be renamed
as follows:

    1. File ARMF renamed ARMFBK, which will be maintained as a backup.

    2. ARNM renamed ARMF, which will be the new version.

Following updating, program AR02 should be run to list the master file for
verification of posting.

The purchases file (ARPRCH) should be renamed ARPRBK to provide backup for the
transaction file.

Figure A-20. Programming specifications for purchases posting.

---

status of customer accounts. The program will operate interactively and
permit retrieval and display of records based on account numbers,
customer names, account balances, and number of days since last payment on accounts. The specifications for this program are presented in
Figure A-22.

CASE STUDY ONE—CHAPTER 8

Two final programs are needed to make the A/R System for Underwood's
Discount Hardware fully operational. A master file maintenance program
is required to allow for the addition of new customer records to the file,
to permit changes in the field values within existing records, and to allow
records to be deleted from the file. Also, a program is needed to initialize

<u>PROGRAMMING SPECIFICATIONS</u>

System: ACCOUNTS RECEIVABLE   Date: 07/28/XX
Program: POST PAYMENTS   Program I.D.: AR12   Analyst: D. ADAMS

Design and write a program to update the accounts receivable master file (ARMF)
with payment transactions in the payments file (ARPYMT). Output will be a new
master file (ARNM) of updated master records. The program will be coded in
BASIC. The system flowchart for this application is given in Figure A-21.1.

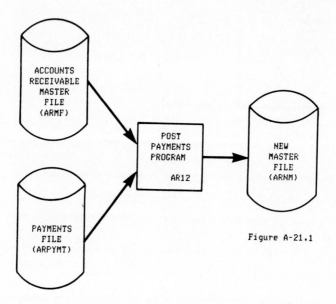

Figure A-21.1

INPUT

The accounts receivable master file and the payments file are the program
input. The format of the master file is:

Field Name	Data Type
Credit Code	Alphanumeric
Account Number	Numeric
Customer Name	Alphanumeric
Month-to-Date Purchases	Numeric
Account Balance	Numeric
Days Since Last Payment	Numeric

The master file is loaded into program tables at the beginning of processing.
Payments will be posted within these tables. Provision should be made for
loading a maximum of 25 master records. The format of the purchases file is:

Field Name	Data Type
Account Number	Numeric
Payment Amount	Numeric

The payment amount in the payment record is subtracted from the account-balance field of the corresponding master record. Also, the days-since-last-payment field of the master field is reset to zero. Records are updated within the program tables created from the master file. A count is to be maintained of the number of payment records processed.

OUTPUT

Following all updates, a new master file will be written from the master file tables. This posting program will write an appropriate EOF record to the new file. Figure A-21.2 shows the messages that will be displayed while the program is executing.

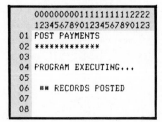

```
    00000000011111111112222
    12345678901234567890123
 01 POST PAYMENTS
 02 *************
 03
 04 PROGRAM EXECUTING...
 05
 06   ** RECORDS POSTED
 07
 08
```
Figure A-21.2

After the program has been run, the two master files should be renamed as follows:

1. File ARMF renamed ARMFBK, which will be maintained as a backup.

2. ARNM renamed as ARMF, which will be the new version.

Following updating, program AR02 should be run to list the master file for verification of posting.

The payments file (ARPYMT) also should be renamed ARPYBK to provide backup for the transaction file.

Figure A-21. Programming specifications for payments posting.

---

master record fields at the beginning of daily and monthly operating cycles. Each day, it will be necessary to increment the days-since-last-payment field in all the records. At the beginning of each month, the month-to-date purchases field must be reset to zero so that the month's totals can be accumulated. This complete system is documented in the data flow diagram presented in Figure A-23.

Practice Assignment 14: Master File Maintenance

Write a master file maintenance program that will allow records to be added to, deleted from, and changed within the ARMF. This program will be used to create new master records for new customers, to delete

493

Figure A-22. Programming specifications for master file inquiry.

PROGRAMMING SPECIFICATIONS

System: ACCOUNTS RECEIVABLE   Date: 07/30/XX
Program: MASTER FILE INQUIRY   Program I.D.: AR13 Analyst: D. ADAMS

Design and write a program to allow selective inquiry into and display of
records from the accounts receivable master file (ARMF). This program is
interactive and menu-driven. The terminal operator provides account numbers,
customer names, account balances, and days since last payment on accounts for
records to be selected from the file and displayed. Any number of inquiries
can be made. Figure A-22.1 provides the system flowchart for this application.

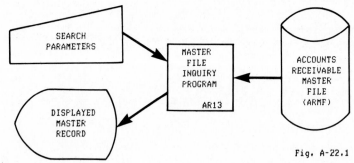

Fig. A-22.1

INPUT

The accounts receivable master file is the program input. Records are loaded
into program tables from which selected records are displayed. Provision
should be made for storing a maximum of 25 records within the tables. The
formats of master records are shown in the following table:

Field Name	Data Type
Credit Code	Alphanumeric
Account Number	Numeric
Customer Name	Alphanumeric
Month to Date Purchases	Numeric
Account Balance	Numeric
Days Since Last Payment	Numeric

PROCESSING AND OUTPUT

The operator enters any of the following four search parameters: an account
number, a customer name, a range of account balances, or a range of days-since-
last-payment on account.

The program then searches the program tables to locate and display records that
correspond with the values of these four search parameters. Any number of
inquiries can be made.

For each inquiry, the program displays a menu of searches. The operator keys
the number that indicates the type of search parameter to be supplied. Then,
the program asks for search values for an account number, a customer name, a
range of account balances, or a range of days since last payment. The program
searches the tables for the corresponding value or values and displays the

record or records. Following the display, the menu is recalled and processing
continues with the next inquiry. Figures A-22.2 through A-22.6 show the
display formats for the inquiry session.

```
     00000000011111111112222222222333333333334
     12345678901234567890123456789012345678901234567890
01   I------------------------I
02   I        INQUIRY MENU        I
03   I                            I
04   I   ACCOUNT NUMBER.....1     I
05   I   CUSTOMER NAME......2     I
06   I   ACCOUNT BALANCE....3     I
07   I   LAST PAYMENT DAY...4     I
08   I   STOP...............5     I
09   I                            I
10   I------------------------I
11
12   ENTER CODE...? #
13
14
```

Format for menu display. This
format should appear following
each inquiry performed by the
program. The code should be
verified. The program should
allow the operator to reenter
invalid codes.

Figure A-22.2

```
     00000000011111111112222222222333333333334
     12345678901234567890123456789012345678901234567890
01   ENTER ACCOUNT NUMBER...? ###
02
03   CREDIT CATEGORY:              X
04   ACCOUNT NUMBER:               ###
05   CUSTOMER NAME:                XXXXXXXXXXX
06   MONTH-TO-DATE PURCHASES:      #######
07   ACCOUNT BALANCE:              #######
08   DAYS SINCE LAST PAYMENT:      ###
09
10
```

Format for account number inquiry. If no matching number
is found in the master file,
the result should be indicated
by the program.

Figure A-22.3

```
     00000000011111111112222222222333333333334
     12345678901234567890123456789012345678901234567890
01   ENTER CUSTOMER NAME...? XXXXXXXXXXX
02
03   CREDIT CATEGORY:              X
04   ACCOUNT NUMBER:               ###
05   CUSTOMER NAME:                XXXXXXXXXXX
06   MONTH-TO-DATE PURCHASES:      #######
07   ACCOUNT BALANCE:              #######
08   DAYS SINCE LAST PAYMENT:      ###
09
10
```

Format for customer name inquiry. If a matching name is
not found, the result should
be indicated by the program.

Figure A-22.4

```
     00000000011111111112222222222333333333334
     12345678901234567890123456789012345678901234567890
01   ENTER RANGE OF ACCOUNT BALANCES
02      LOWER LIMIT...? #######
03      UPPER LIMIT...? #######
04
05   ACCOUNT NUMBER:               ###
06   CUSTOMER NAME:                XXXXXXXXXXX
07   ACCOUNT BALANCE:              #######
08   DAYS SINCE LAST PAYMENT:      ###
09
10   HIT (CR) TO CONTINUE...?
11
```

Format for range-of-account-
balance inquiry. The program
locates and displays records
with balances that are within
range. The lower and upper
limits are the same on inquiries for a specific,
single balance value.
Note that it is possible to
display more than one record
or even no record.

Figure A-22.5

```
         00000000011111111112222222222233333333334
         12345678901234567890123456789012345678901234567890
      01 ENTER RANGE OF LAST PAYMENT DAYS:
      02    LOWER LIMIT...? ###
      03    UPPER LIMIT...? ###
      04
      05 ACCOUNT NUMBER:            ###
      06 CUSTOMER NAME:             XXXXXXXXXXX
      07 ACCOUNT BALANCE:           #######
      08 DAYS SINCE LAST PAYMENT:   ###
      09
      10 HIT (CR) TO CONTINUE...?
      11
      12
```

Format for range-of-last-payment-days inquiry. The program locates and displays records with days that are within the selected range. The lower and upper limits are the same on inquiries for a specific, single day value. Note that it is possible to display more than one record or even no record.

Figure A-22.6

Figure A-22. Concluded.

records for customers who no longer have credit accounts with the store, and to change field values within customer records so that the records reflect customer status accurately. Figure A-24 provides the specifications for the file maintenance program.

After this program has been written and tested, it will be used to make the following changes to the ARMF:

```
   1. ADD record      A, 125, BARBARA COLE, 0, 0, 0

   2. CHANGE record:   A, 100, JIM ADAMS, 239.45, 38.95, 0
               to:     A, 100, JAMES ADAMS, 239.45, 38.95, 0

   3. CHANGE record:   C, 320, TIM SMART, 1200.00, 0.00, 0
               to:     C, 320, TIM SMART, 1250.00, 50.00, 2

   4. DELETE record:   A, 120, JUDY FORSCH, 940.35, 0.00, 0

   5. DELETE record:   B, 228, MARK TRUSTY, 924.95, 1140.35, 33

   6. ADD record:      C, 328, MARK TROSTY, 924.95, 1140.35, 33

   7. ADD record:      C, 330, JUDY SNYDER, 50.25, 50.25, 0
```

Next, run program AR02 (Master File Listing) to verify that the changes are correct.

Practice Assignment 15: Cycle Initialization Program

Now, write the final cycle initialization program. This program will be run daily to increment the days-since-last-payment fields of the master records by one to account for the passage of another calendar day. It also will be run at the end of each month to reset the month-to-date purchases field to zero. Specifications for this program appear in Figure A-25.

496

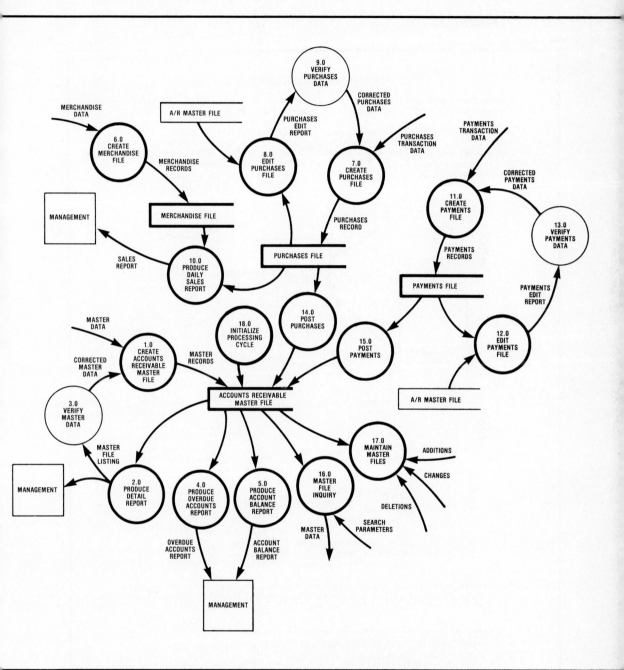

Figure A-23. Data flow diagram showing completed A/R system.

Figure A-24. Programming specifications for master file maintenance.

PROGRAMMING SPECIFICATIONS

System: ACCOUNTS RECEIVABLE   Date: 08/01/XX
Program: MASTER FILE MAINTENANCE   Program I.D.: AR14   Analyst: D. ADAMS

Design and write a program to maintain the accounts receivable master file
(ARMF). The program allows interactive updates in the form of additions and
changes to, and deletions from, the file. The master file (ARMF) is rewritten
following updating. Figure A-24.1 presents the system flowchart for this
application.

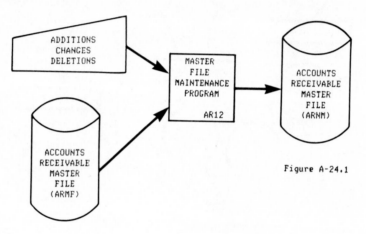

Figure A-24.1

INPUT

The accounts receivable master file and the file updates keyed through computer
terminals are the file input. The following table provides the master file
record format:

Field Name	Data Type
Credit Code	Alphanumeric
Account Number	Numeric
Customer Name	Alphanumeric
Month-to-Date Purchases	Numeric
Account Balance	Numeric
Days Since Last Payment	Numeric

Maintenance transactions are entered interactively through a terminal keyboard.
The program is menu-driven and requests data from the operator. Figure A-24.2
shows the formats of interactions between the computer and the operator.

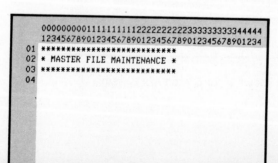

```
05      ADD NEW RECORD....A
06      CHANGE A RECORD...C
07      DELETE A RECORD...D
08      STOP..............S
09
10 ENTER CODE...? X
11
12 *** ADD NEW RECORD ***
13
14 CREDIT CATEGORY............? X
15 ACCOUNT NUMBER.............? ###
16 CUSTOMER NAME..............? XXXXXXXXXXX
17 MTD PURCHASES..............? #######
18 ACCOUNT BALANCE............? #######
19 DAYS SINCE LAST PAYMENT...? ###
20     VERIFY (Y/N)...........? X
21
22 *** CHANGE A RECORD ***
23
24 ACCOUNT NUMBER...? ###
25                                     CHANGE?
26                                      (Y/N)
27                                     -------
28 CREDIT CATEGORY        : X          ? X
29 ACCOUNT NUMBER         : ###        ? X
30 CUSTOMER NAME          : XXXXXXXXXXX ? X
31 MTD PURCHASES          : #######    ? X
32 ACCOUNT BALANCE        : #######    ? X
33 DAYS SINCE LAST PAYMENT: ###        ? Y
34                        ? ###
35     VERIFY (Y/N)........? X
36
37 *** DELETE A RECORD ***
38
39 ACCOUNT NUMBER...? ###
40
41
```

Figure A-24.2

PROCESSING

The master file is loaded into program tables within which all updates take place. The tables should be dimensioned large enough so that records can be added as needed in the future.

Adding Records: The computer promts the operator for the sequence of fields contained in a master record. After all fields are entered, the operator visually verifies the entries before the record is added to the tables. If all entries are correct, the new record is added to the appropriate file position, based on the account number. The account number table is searched to locate the first record with a larger account number than that of the record to be added. This location is the position at which the new record will appear in the file. To make room for the new record, all records with a larger account number are moved down one position in the tables. After insertion of the record, the table length is increased to signify the new logical table length.

Changing Records: The operator enters the account number of the record to be changed. Then, the account number table is searched to locate the matching record. The fields of the current record are displayed one at a time. The operator indicates whether the displayed field is to be changed. If no change is indicated, the computer displays the next field. If the field value is to be replaced, a prompt is displayed on the next line below the current value and the new value is keyed on this

line. After all changes are made, the entries are verified. If an error is found, all fields are displayed
again. As each new field value is keyed, the change is
made to the table record.

Deleting Records: The operator keys the account number of the record to
be deleted. Then, the program searches the table to locate the matching number. All records below the record
to be deleted are moved up one position in the tables.
Following deletion, the table length is decreased to
indicate the new logical table length.

Error Processing: The display formats in Figure A-24.3 show the kinds of
errors to be anticipated as well as the system responses.

```
     00000000011111111112222222222333333333344444
     12345678901234567890123456789012345678901234
01   ****************************
02   * MASTER FILE MAINTENANCE *
03   ****************************
04
05      ADD NEW RECORD....A
06      CHANGE A RECORD...C
07      DELETE A RECORD...D
08      STOP..............S
09
10   ENTER CODE...? X
11   *** ENTER CORRECT CODE ***
12   ? X
13
14   *** ADD NEW RECORD ***
15
16   CREDIT CATEGORY...........? X
17   ACCOUNT NUMBER............? ###
18   CUSTOMER NAME.............? XXXXXXXXXXX
19   MTD PURCHASES.............? #######
20   ACCOUNT BALANCE...........? #######
21   DAYS SINCE LAST PAYMENT...? ###
22      VERIFY (Y/N)...........? X
23   *** RECORD ALREADY EXISTS ***
24
25   *** CHANGE A RECORD ***
26
27   ACCOUNT NUMBER...? ###
28   *** RECORD NOT FOUND ***
29
30   *** DELETE A RECORD ***
31
32   ACCOUNT NUMBER...? ###
33   *** RECORD NOT FOUND ***
34
35
```

Figure A-24.3

OUTPUT

After all maintenance activities are completed, the table data are written back
to the file named ARMF. The new version of the master file will replace the
old version. An appropriate EOF record should be written to the file.

Figure A-24. Concluded.

Figure A-25. Programming specifications for cycle initialization.

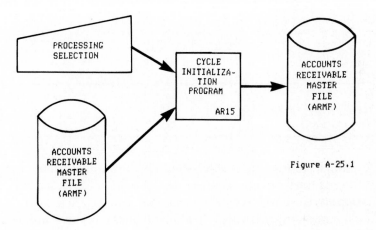

PROGRAMMING SPECIFICATIONS

System: ACCOUNTS RECEIVABLE   Date: 08/03/XX
Program: CYCLE INITIALIZATION   Program I.D.: AR15   Analyst: D. ADAMS

Design and write a program to increment the days-since-last-payment fields of
the accounts receivable master file (ARMF) by one and to revalue the month-to-
date-purchases field to zero. Output will be a rewritten version of the master
file (ARMF). Figure A-25.1 shows the system flowchart for this application.

```
 _____
|  PROCESSING    |
|  SELECTION     |          ┌──────────────┐          ⎛ ACCOUNTS  ⎞
|_____|          │   CYCLE      │          │ RECEIVABLE │
          \                 │ INITIALIZA-  │   ───▶   │  MASTER    │
           \                │    TION      │          │   FILE     │
            \               │  PROGRAM     │          │  (ARMF)    │
   ⎛ ACCOUNTS  ⎞            │              │          ⎝           ⎠
   │ RECEIVABLE │   ───▶    │    AR15      │
   │  MASTER    │           └──────────────┘
   │   FILE     │
   │  (ARMF)    │                                     Figure A-25.1
   ⎝           ⎠
```

INPUT

The accounts receivable master file (ARMF) is input to this program in the
following format:

Field Name	Data Type
Credit Code	Alphanumeric
Account Number	Numeric
Customer Name	Alphanumeric
Month-to-Date Purchases	Numeric
Account Balance	Numeric
Days Since Last Payment	Numeric

The master file is loaded into tables within which all updates take place.

PROCESSING

The program prompts the operator for the type of processing desired. Either or
both of the field initialization activities can be performed. This selection
is shown in Figure A-25.2.

```
0000000001111111111222222222233333333334444444
1234567890123456789012345678901234567890123456
01 **************************
02 * CYCLE INITIALIZATION *
03 **************************
04
05 INCREMENT DAYS SINCE LAST PAYMENT (Y/N)...? X
06    VERIFY (Y/N)...? X
07
08 ZERO MONTH-TO-DATE PURCHASES (Y/N)...? X
09    VERIFY (Y/N)...? X
10
11 *** END OF PROCESSING ***
12
13
```

Figure A-25.2

For the situation shown in line 5 of Figure A-25.2, the value in the days-since-last-payment field is incremented by 1 within all records. In line 8, the month-to-date purchases field is set to zero within all records.

OUTPUT

Following all updates, the data in the tables will be rewritten to the master file (ARMF). Then, program AR02 should be run to verify file content.

Figure A-25. Concluded.

The accounts receivable system is now fully operational. As added testing of the software package, data should be generated to exercise the programs in simulation of several processing cycles. Also, as additional documentation, software structure charts and/or systems flowcharts describing the complete system might be prepared. Finally, it might be worthwhile practice to prepare *operations manuals* that describe the use of the programs and their relationship in a timing, or chronological sequence. Such manuals would be provided to users to familiarize them with the operation of the system.

CASE STUDY TWO

The following case study presents a business situation that calls for the BASIC programming methods and techniques that are described in Chapters 1 through 8. The development of this particular system progresses in stages that parallel the reading material given in each chapter. Thus, the first practice assignment allows you to test your understanding of the concepts discussed in Chapters 1 through 3. When you complete the final practice assignment in the Chapter 8 section, you will have worked through the programming phases that result in an operational computer information system.

A PROGRAMMING SCENARIO: THE UNIVERSAL BOOK COMPANY

The Universal Book Company (UBCO), located in Reseda, California, is a small, privately-owned producer of high school and college textbooks. The company is responsible for producing book manuscripts under contract to publishing companies, which, in turn, print the books for marketing to schools and school bookstores. UBCO employs a total of 15 persons within three main departments: contracting, editing, and production. All employees are wage earners, paid on the basis of hourly wages and number of hours worked per week.

The current, manually maintained payroll system for the company records employee work histories, produces weekly paychecks, and generates periodic management reports that indicate the amounts of wages paid and withheld in taxes. In the past, this manual payroll system has performed adequately. However, UBCO now is experiencing rapid growth and anticipates that this trend will continue for several years. Thus, the company president, along with the departmental managers, has determined that a computerized payroll system is necessary to maintain current and accurate management reports on personnel costs. The company already uses a small business computer on which other job-cost, accounts receivable, accounts payable, and inventory control systems run.

All of the software running on the computer system has been acquired through vendors. So far, these standardized packages have been flexible enough to meet the specialized needs of the company. After surveying the market in payroll packages, however, the president has determined that none of the available products will meet requirements. A tailor-made payroll system is necessary. Thus, you have been hired as an independent consultant to design and write this system.

After meeting with the president and reviewing payroll processing requirements, you agree to undertake the project. The following assignments represent your decisions on the structure of software, data files, manual procedures required, and sequence of programming activities needed to implement the system.

CASE STUDY TWO—CHAPTERS 1–3

Practice assignments are based on the preceding narrative for the Universal Book Company. These assignments should be undertaken only after reading Chapters 1 through 3 of the text.

Practice Assignment 1: Create Payroll Master File

The first order of business is to establish the payroll master file, which will serve as the focal point for most of the processing activities. Therefore, a program is needed to transfer master data from the payroll books of account into this file. To accomplish this conversion, you requested one of the office clerks to transcribe the current payroll information to a special form that identifies the data fields to be maintained within the master file. This manual form will be used to build the master file through the interactive data entry program. The completed form is shown in Figure A-26.

Programming specifications for the master file creation program are provided in Figure A-27. This program will be interactive. In response to program prompts, the terminal operator enters the payroll data contained on the form shown in Figure A-26. Each line of data on the form will become a master record within the file, organized in the given sequence. This program will be used one time only—to create the payroll master file.

After this program has been written, it is used to create the master file. The employee records provided in the table in Figure A-27 are entered in the order given.

CASE STUDY TWO—CHAPTER 4

The following practice assignments continue development of the Universal Book Company payroll system begun in the Chapters 1 through 3 section of this case study. These assignments should be undertaken only after completing Chapter 4 of the text.

Practice Assignment 2: List Payroll Master File

Write a program that will list the content of the payroll master file. This program will be used to verify the correctness of the file built with program PAY01. The current program will be run at different times during system development to check the results of processing performed on the master file. Besides listing the complete content of the file, the program will produce check totals for all of the numeric fields. Further, this detail listing can be used to reconstruct the file in case the file is destroyed inadvertently. The programming specifications are given in Figure A-28.

DEPT. NO.	JOB CODE	EMP. NO.	EMPLOYEE NAME	PAY RATE	NO. OF EXEMPTIONS	YTD GROSS PAY	YTD FED. TAX	YTD FICA TAX
10	A	101	J. EWING	7.25	2	12,820.60	3,846.19	897.44
10	A	103	W. COYOTE	6.00	1	6,841.25	2,257.59	479.31
10	A	104	J. CLAMPETT	6.40	3	7,800.50	2,184.14	546.04
10	B	107	B. DUKE	4.50	2	4,680.92	1,404.28	327.66
10	B	108	E. PRESLEY	3.75	2	3,500.60	1,050.18	245.04
20	C	110	B. KRUSE	5.00	4	5,300.00	1,325.00	371.00
20	C	111	O. OGLEBY	7.00	2	7,580.45	2,274.14	530.63
20	D	113	S. WHITMAN	5.00	3	3,100.00	868.00	217.00
20	D	114	J. DANIELS	8.00	1	10,525.75	3,473.50	736.80
20	D	118	M. MOUSE	5.25	1	5,200.00	1,716.00	364.00
30	E	120	M. PIGGY	7.00	2	7,620.90	2,216.27	533.46
30	E	121	F. SANFORD	6.45	6	5,640.30	1,297.27	394.82
30	E	123	P. ROSE	6.10	3	6,900.00	1,932.00	483.00
30	F	124	B. LAGOSI	5.75	2	8,475.50	2,542.65	593.28
30	F	127	E. SCRUGGS	6.00	4	4,960.35	1,240.09	347.22
CHECK TOTALS 300		1704		89.45	37	100,953.12	29,677.29	7,066.70

Figure A-26. Data entry form for master file creation program.

PROGRAMMING SPECIFICATIONS

System: PAYROLL
Program: CREATE MASTER FILE   Program I.D.: PAY01   Date: 10/07/XX
                                                            Analyst: D. ADAMS

Design and write a program to create the payroll master file (PAYMF). Payroll
data are entered interactively through a terminal keyboard in response to
program prompts for each of the data fields. After operator verification, the
collection of fields is written as a master record to a disk file. The program
will be coded in BASIC. Figure A-27.1 shows the system flowchart for this
application.

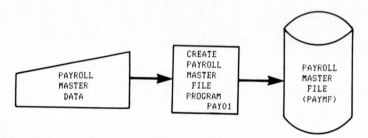

Figure A-27.1

INPUT

The master file data, entered interactively through a computer terminal, are
the program input. The program prompts for the data fields individually, after
which the terminal operator keys in the field values. After all fields are
entered, the operator verifies them visually. If all fields are correct, they
are written as a master record to the file. If any field has been entered in
error, the operator indicates this fact and the prompts are repeated for that
record. The data entry session is terminated with the keying of an EOF record,
which becomes the last record in the file. Figure A-27.2 shows the general
format for the data entry session.

```
   00000000011111111112222222222333333333344444444444
   12345678901234567890123456789012345678901234567890
01 **************************
02 * MASTER FILE CREATION *
03 **************************
04
05 KEY THE FILES FOR THE DATA
06 ITEMS INDICATED. TO END THE
07 PROGRAM, KEY THE VALUES:
08 '0,0,0,END OF FILE,0,0,0,0,0'.
09
10 DEPT. NUMBER........? ##
11 JOB CODE............? X
12 EMPLOYEE NUMBER.....? ###
13 EMPLOYEE NAME.......? XXXXXXXXXXX
14 PAY RATE............? #.##
15 NO. OF EXEMPTIONS...? #
16 YTD GROSS PAY.......? #####.##
17 YTD FEDERAL TAX.....? ####.##
18 YTD FICA TAX........? ###.##
19    VERIFY (Y/N).....? X
20
21    .
22    .
23    .
```

```
24
25  DEPT. NUMBER.........?  0
26  JOB CODE............?  0
27  EMPLOYEE NUMBER......?  0
28  EMPLOYEE NAME........?  END OF FILE
29  PAY RATE............?  0
30  NO. OF EXEMPTIONS...?  0
31  YTD GROSS PAY.......?  0
32  YTD FEDERAL TAX.....?  0
33  YTD FICA TAX........?  0
34     VERIFY (Y/N).....?  Y
35
36  *** END OF SESSION ***
38
39
```

Figure A-27.2

OUTPUT

This program will output the payroll master file (PAYMF). Each record in this file should correspond with the set of nine data fields entered for each employee during input. The format of fields contained in each master record is as follows:

Field Name	Data Type
Department Number	Numeric
Job Code	Alphanumeric
Employee Number	Numeric
Employee Name	Alphanumeric
Pay Rate	Numeric
No. of Exemptions	Numeric
Year-to-Date Gross Pay	Numeric
Year-to-Date Federal Tax	Numeric
Year-to-Date FICA Tax	Numeric

A total of 16 records should be written to the file--the 15 employee master records plus the EOF record. Records should be entered in employee number sequence.

Figure A-27. Programming specifications for master file creation.

After this program is written, it should be run to verify the content of the master file. Errors in the file must be corrected before continuing with additional assignments.

Practice Assignment 3: Employee Pay Report

Department managers often ask for reports that detail payroll information for employees within a particular job classification. For example, a manager may wish to know the various pay rates of the editorial staff. Or, the manager may request gross pay figures for artists in the production department. Therefore, write a program to produce reports that respond to these requests. The program will allow the manager to request

PROGRAMMING SPECIFICATIONS

System: PAYROLL
Program: LIST MASTER FILE   Date: 10/09/XX
                        Program I.D.: PAY02   Analyst: D. ADAMS

Design and write a program to produce a detail listing of the payroll master
file (PAYMF). The output report will identify and list all data fields in the
records and will produce check totals for all numeric fields. The program will
be coded in BASIC. Figure A-28.1 presents the system flowchart for this
application.

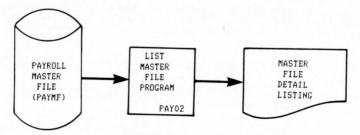

Figure A-28.1

INPUT

The payroll master file is the program input. The format of records in this
file is as follows:

Field Name	Data Type
Department Number	Numeric
Job Code	Alphanumeric
Employee Number	Numeric
Employee Name	Alphanumeric
Pay Rate	Numeric
No. of Exemptions	Numeric
Year-to-Date Gross Pay	Numeric
Year-to-Date Federal Tax	Numeric
Year-to-Date FICA Tax	Numeric

An EOF record completes the file. This record contains zeros in all but the
employee name field, which contains the value "END OF FILE".

PROCESSING

The program inputs and prints all of the field values for all employee records.
In addition, totals will be developed and printed at the end of the report for
the following fields: department number, employee number, pay rate, number of
exemptions, year-to-date gross pay, year-to-date federal tax, and year-to-date
FICA tax. Although only the last three totals provide meaningful information,
all totals are processed to check the accuracy of data entry performed in
program PAY01.

OUTPUT

The program will output a detail report in the format shown in Figure A-28.2.

```
00000000011111111112222222222333333333344444444445555555555566666666667777
12345678901234567890123456789012345678901234567890123456789012345678901234567890012
01                              FILE LISTING
02                          PAYROLL MASTER FILE
03
04  DEPT  JOB  EMPL   EMPLOYEE       PAY    NO      YTD         YTD        YTD
05   NO   CODE  NO      NAME         RATE   EXMP  GROSS PAY   FED TAX    FICA TAX
06
07   ##    X    ###  XXXXXXXXXXX    #,##    #    ##,###.##   #,###.##   #,###.##
08   ##    X    ###  XXXXXXXXXXX    #,##    #    ##,###.##   #,###.##   #,###.##
09
10
11
12  ###         ####               ###.##  ##   ###,###.##  ##,###.##  ##,###.##
13
14
```

Figure A-28.2

Figure A-28. Programming specifications for master file listing.

payroll information through a terminal. First, a job code will be entered. Then, the program will select master file information pertaining to employees who fit that job code. This information, in turn, is to be printed on the report, which will list the employee's name, pay rate, gross pay, net pay, and the average hourly rate for all employees in the job classification. Programming specifications for this program are presented in Figure A-29.

CASE STUDY TWO—CHAPTER 5

The following practice assignment is a continuation of the payroll system under development for the Universal Book Company. This assignment should be attempted only after reading Chapter 5 of the text.

Practice Assignment 4: Payroll Summary Report

The management of UBCO has asked you to write a payroll summary report to be produced periodically. This summary report will list year-to-date gross pay and net pay amounts. Usually, this report is prepared monthly so that management can compare year-to-date personnel expenses with expense totals indicated on previous reports produced for the current year. Also, management will compare current totals with expenses incurred in previous years. Therefore, write a program to produce this report based on the information accumulated in the payroll master file. The report will list year-to-date totals for each employee, for each department, and for the company as a whole. The specifications for this program appear in Figure A-30.

PROGRAMMING SPECIFICATIONS

System: PAYROLL   Date: 10/13/XX
Program: EMPLOYEE PAY REPORT   Program I.D.: PAY03   Analyst: D. ADAMS

Design and write a program that selects employee names (by job code) from the
payroll master file (PAYMF). The program will produce a report listing payroll
information for the selected employees. The job code is entered through a
computer terminal, and the output will be a printed report. The program will
be coded in BASIC. Figure A-29.1 shows the system flowchart for this
application.

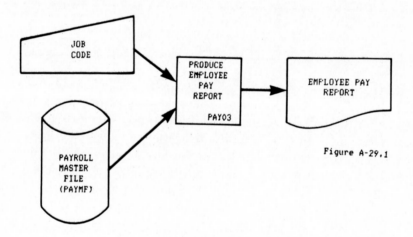

Figure A-29.1

INPUT

The initial input to this program is a job code (A-F) used in searching the
master file for employee records that fall within the corresponding job
category. The job code is entered through a computer terminal as shown in
Figure A-29.2.

```
     0000000001111111111222222222
     123456789012345678901234567 89
01  *** EMPLOYEE PAY REPORT ***
02
03  ENTER JOB CODE...? X
04
05
```
                                   Figure A-29.2

The payroll master file (PAYMF) also is input to the program. The format of records is as follows:

Field Name	Data Type
Department Number	Numeric
Job Code	Alphanumeric
Employee Number	Numeric
Employee Name	Alphanumeric
Pay Rate	Numeric
No. of Exemptions	Numeric
Year-to-Date Gross Pay	Numeric
Year-to-Date Federal Tax	Numeric
Year-to-Date FICA Tax	Numeric

The last record in this file contains the value "END OF FILE" in the employee-name field.

PROCESSING

The program must perform the following processing phases:

1. The computer checks the job code for each record in the file. If the code in the record matches the code that was input through the terminal, additional processing is required as outlined in steps 2 and 3 below.

2. For each matching employee record, the computer calculates the employee's net pay. Year-to-date net pay is derived by subtracting year-to-date federal taxes and year-to-date FICA taxes from the year-to-date gross pay.

3. The average pay rate is calculated for all matching records. The pay rate is derived by dividing the total of pay rates for all employees within the job category by the total number of employees in the category. These two totals are accumulated for all matching employee records. Then, at the completion of processing, the average rate is calculated.

OUTPUT

Program output is a detail report in the format shown in Figure A-29.3. Note that the job code entered through the terminal is printed as part of the report heading.

```
          0000000001111111111222222222233333333334444444444 5
          1234567890123456789012345678901234567890123456789 0
01                   EMPLOYEE PAY REPORT
02                    FOR JOB CLASS X
03
04        EMPLOYEE    PAY       YTD           YTD
05          NAME      RATE    GROSS PAY     NET PAY
06
07        XXXXXXXXXXX  #.##    ##,###.##    ##,###.##
08        XXXXXXXXXXX  #.##    ##,###.##    ##,###.##
09
10
11
12        AVERAGE PAY RATE:  $#.##
13
14
```

Figure A-29.3

Figure A-29. Programming specifications for employee pay report.

511

PROGRAMMING SPECIFICATIONS

System: PAYROLL   Date: 10/14/XX
Program: PRODUCE PAYROLL SUMMARY   Program I.D.: PAY04   Analyst: D. ADAMS

Design and write a program to produce a payroll summary report. The input is
the payroll master file (PAYMF). Output will be a multiple-page report listing
year-to-date gross pay and net pay totals for each employee, for each department, and for the entire company. The program will be coded in BASIC. Figure
A-30.1 presents the system flowchart for this application.

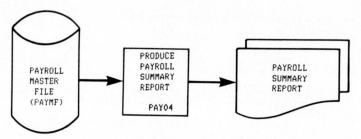

Figure A-30.1

INPUT

The payroll master file (PAYMF) is the program input. The format of records is
as follows:

Field Name	Data Type
Department Number	Numeric
Job Code	Alphanumeric
Employee Number	Numeric
Employee Name	Alphanumeric
Pay Rate	Numeric
No. of Exemptions	Numeric
Year-to-Date Gross Pay	Numeric
Year-to-Date Federal Tax	Numeric
Year-to-Date FICA Tax	Numeric

An EOF record completes the file. This record contains the value "END OF FILE"
in the employee name field. Records in the file are organized in department
number sequence.

PROCESSING

1. Totals will be accumulated and printed for year-to-date gross
   pay and year-to-date net pay. Year-to-date net pay is calculated
   by subtracting year-to-date federal tax and year-to-date FICA
   tax from year-to-date gross pay. Subtotals are printed whenever
   the department number changes. Final totals are printed at the
   bottom of the report.

2. A maximum of 20 lines are to be printed per page. After each
   group of 20 lines, a page break should occur and a new set of
   headings written. Assume a physical page size of 27 lines.
   The pages should be numbered.

The payroll summary report should appear in the general format shown in Figure A-30.2. All total lines are preceded and followed by a single blank line.

```
00000000011111111112222222222233333333333444444444445555555555
12345678901234567890123456789012345678901234567890123456789
01              YEAR-TO-DATE PAYROLL SUMMARY          ## ←
02                     BY DEPARTMENT              (Page No.)
03
04 DEPT    EMPL     EMPLOYEE          YTD          YTD
05  NO      NO        NAME         GROSS PAY     NET PAY
06
07  ##     ###    XXXXXXXXXXXX    ##,###.##     ##,###.##
08  ##     ###    XXXXXXXXXXXX    ##,###.##     ##,###.##
09
10
11
12         TOTALS FOR DEPT. ##    ##,###.##     ##,###.##
13
14             COMPANY TOTALS    ###,###.##    ###,###.##
15
```

Figure A-30.2

Figure A-30. Programming specifications for payroll summary report.

The data flow diagram in Figure A-31 describes the payroll information system produced so far. Remember that the payroll master file is at the heart of the system and is the focal point of all processing activities. Current programs place information into the master file and provide reports of file content. Subsequent programs will expand the system so that master file information can be kept up to date. Additional reporting features also will be included. As new facilities are added to the system, expanded data flow diagrams will be provided to bring an overall perspective to each practice assignment.

CASE STUDY TWO—CHAPTER 6

The payroll master file for UBCO's payroll system will require weekly updates to accumulate year-to-date totals for the gross pay, federal tax, and FICA tax fields. These totals are maintained for year-end tax reports. Therefore, the payroll information system must include features that will permit weekly payroll data to be captured and recorded for subsequent updating of the master file. The following procedures will be used to create the payroll transaction file that will become input for the updating program:

Time cards. The number of hours worked by employees is recorded daily on manual time cards. These cards require the employee to enter

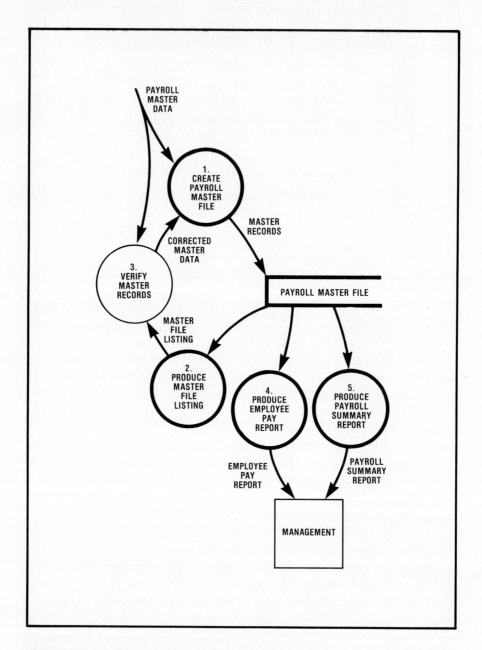

Figure A-31. Data flow diagram of first four programs.

the number of regular and overtime hours worked per week. An example of a time card is shown in Figure A-32.

Data entry. At the end of each week, time cards are collected from all employees, checked for accuracy, and approved by the appropriate supervisor. All of the cards are arranged in sequence by employee number. The information then is transcribed to a data entry form for input to the computer. An example of this data entry form is shown in Figure A-33.

Updating. Information from the form shown in Figure A-33 is used to build the payroll transaction file. This file, in turn, is used to update the master file and also to produce a weekly payroll report.

Three new programs will be written for the payroll information system. First, a transaction file creation program is required to build the transaction file from information included on the data entry form. Then, a

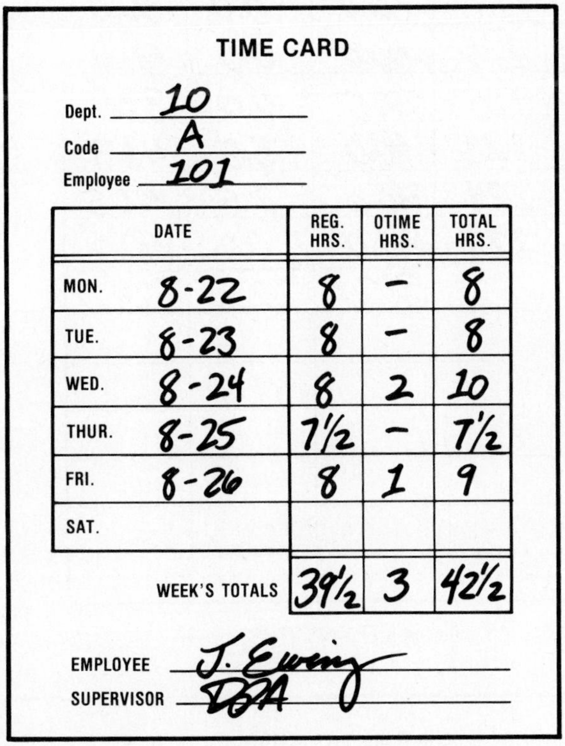

TIME CARD

Dept. __10__
Code __A__
Employee __101__

DATE		REG. HRS.	OTIME HRS.	TOTAL HRS.
MON.	8-22	8	—	8
TUE.	8-23	8	—	8
WED.	8-24	8	2	10
THUR.	8-25	7½	—	7½
FRI.	8-26	8	1	9
SAT.				
WEEK'S TOTALS		39½	3	42½

EMPLOYEE __J. Ewing__
SUPERVISOR __DSA__

Figure A-32. Time card from which payroll data are taken.

PAYROLL TRANSACTIONS
DATA ENTRY FORM

FOR WEEK OF **8-22** TO **8-27**

DEPT. NO.	JOB CODE	EMPL. NO.	REG. HRS.	OTIME HRS.	TOTAL HRS.
10	A	101	39.5	3.0	42.5
10	A	103	40.0	0.0	40.0
10	A	104	38.0	0.0	38.0
10	B	107	40.0	0.0	40.0
10	B	108	40.0	2.0	42.0
20	C	110	40.0	1.5	41.5
20	C	111	40.0	0.5	40.5
20	D	114	36.0	0.0	36.0
20	D	118	40.0	0.0	40.0
30	E	120	38.5	0.0	38.5
30	E	123	40.0	3.5	43.5
30	F	124	40.0	1.5	41.5
30	F	127	40.0	0.0	40.0
			512.0	12.0	524.0

Prepared by _SMD_

Figure A-33. Data entry form for payroll transactions file.

transaction file edit program is needed to validate all records and to ensure that the data are correct. Finally, a program will be written to produce a gross pay report. This report will summarize employee earnings for the week and report total payroll expenses by job class and department.

With the addition of these three programs, the system can activate all procedures necessary for master file updating and operation of the system across weekly payroll processing cycles. The data flow diagram presented in Figure A-34 shows how these programs are integrated within the system.

Practice Assignment 5: Create Payroll Transaction File

A program is required to create the payroll transaction file from the information provided on the payroll data entry form. This program will operate interactively; the operator will key the information in response to program prompts. After the operator verifies the entered data visually, the records are written in sequence to the transaction file. Specifications for this program are given in Figure A-35.

After this program is written, the data shown in Figure A-33 should be used to build the transaction file. After this file has been created, check the totals produced by the program against those on the data entry form to verify processing accuracy.

Practice Assignment 6: Edit Payroll Transaction File

A program is required to edit and check all of the fields within the payroll transaction file before the file is used for further processing. The program will produce an edit report. Programming specifications are provided in Figure A-36.

Before the edit report program is placed in production, it should be tested thoroughly. A special file of test data should be created and input into this program to make sure all edits are performed correctly. Program PAY05 (transaction file creation) should be modified to create a test file named TESTF. Rerun the modified program using the data shown in Figure A-37.

Next, modify program PAY06 (edit report) so that the test file is input and an edit report is produced. The report should display all possible error messages. When you are certain that the tested edit program

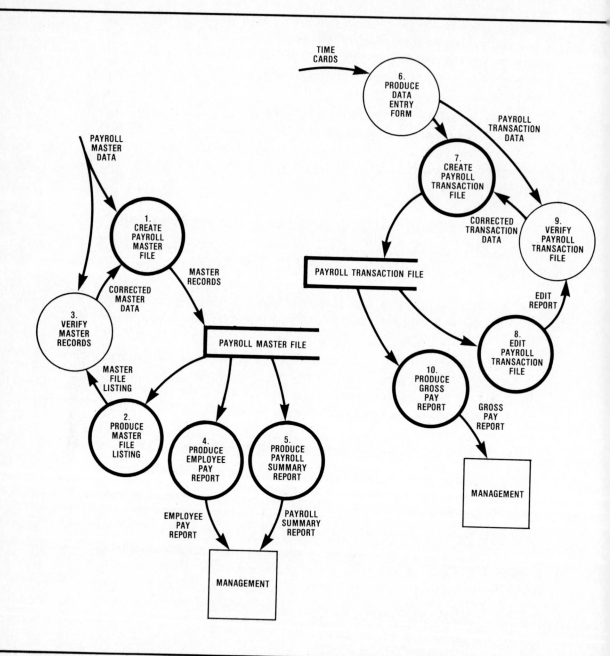

Figure A-34. Data flow diagram with transaction file creation and editing and gross pay report programs added.

Figure A-35. Programming specifications for transaction file creation.

<u>PROGRAMMING SPECIFICATIONS</u>

System: PAYROLL   Date: 10/16/XX
Program: CREATE TRANSACTION FILE   Program I.D.: PAY05   Analyst: D. ADAMS

Design and write a program to create the payroll transaction file (PAYTF). The
data entry form is used as input for the payroll transaction records, which are
organized sequentially and written to a disk file. Data are entered interactively through a terminal keyboard. The program will be coded in BASIC.
Figure A-35.1 shows the system flowchart for this application.

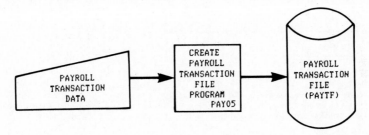

Fig. A-35.1

<u>INPUT</u>

Employee identification and weekly hours worked data are the primary program
input. The following fields are entered:

Field Name	Data Type
Department Number	Numeric
Job Code	Alphanumeric
Employee Number	Numeric
Regular Hours	Numeric
Overtime Hours	Numeric

Following verification by the operator, the fields are written to the file as
an employee transaction record to the file.

Before any data records are input, however, a date record must be entered into
the file. This header record identifies the pay period that applies to
subsequent transaction records. The operator enters the week-ending date in
the format MM/DD. The final EOF record contains zeros in all fields.

The format of the data entry session is illustrated in Figure A-35.2.

```
      0000000001111111111222222222233333333
      12345678901234567890123456789012234567
01    ******************************
02    * TRANSACTION FILE CREATION *
03    ******************************
04
05    ENTER ENDING DATE (MM/DD)...? XX/XX
06
07    KEY THE VALUES FOR THE DATA
08    ITEMS INDICATED.  TO END THE
09    SESSION, KEY THE VALUES:
10    '0,0,0,0,0'.
```

```
11
12 DEPT, NUMBER......? ##
13 JOB CODE..........? X
14 EMPLOYEE NUMBER...? ###
15 REGULAR HOURS.....? ##.#
16 OVERTIME HOURS....? ##.#
17    VERIFY (Y/N)...? X
18   .
19   .
20   .
21 DEPT, NUMBER......? 0
22 JOB CODE..........? 0
23 EMPLOYEE NUMBER...? 0
24 REGULAR HOURS.....? 0
25 OVERTIME HOURS....? 0
26    VERIFY (Y/N)...? Y
27
28 *** END OF SESSION ***
29
30 TOTAL RECORDS     ###.#
31 TOTAL REG. HRS.   ###.#
32 TOTAL OTIME. HRS. ###.#
33
34
```

Figure A-35.2

PROCESSING

For all valid records, totals are developed for the number of records, total regular hours, and total overtime hours. These totals are compared with those developed on the data entry form to provide initial validation of the file.

OUTPUT

Output from this program will be the payroll transaction file (PAYTF). The date record is written to the file first. Subsequent records are employees' weekly work records. The last record contains zeros in all fields to indicate an end-of-file condition.

Figure A-35. Concluded.

Figure A-36.   Programming specifications for edit report.

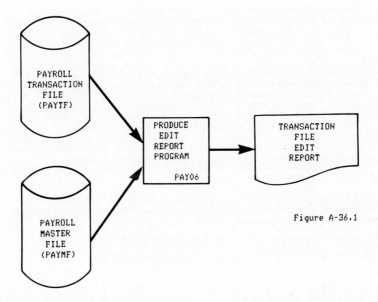

PROGRAMMING SPECIFICATIONS

System: PAYROLL   Date: 10/17/XX
Program: PRODUCE EDIT REPORT   Program I.D.: PAY06   Analyst: D. ADAMS

Design and write a program in BASIC to edit the payroll transaction file
(PAYTF). Output will be an edit report that lists all fields for all records
and displays an error message for fields in error. Figure A-36.1 shows the
system flowchart for this application.

PAYROLL
TRANSACTION
FILE
(PAYTF)

PRODUCE
EDIT
REPORT
PROGRAM

PAY06

TRANSACTION
FILE
EDIT
REPORT

PAYROLL
MASTER
FILE
(PAYMF)

Figure A-36.1

INPUT

The payroll transaction file (PAYTF) produced in program PAY05 is the primary
program input. This transaction file contains weekly work records in the
following format:

Field Name	Data Type
Department Number	Numeric
Job Code	Alphanumeric
Employee Number	Numeric
Regular Hours	Numeric
Overtime Hours	Numeric

A date record in the format MM/DD appears first in the file. The date appears
in the first heading line of the edit report. An EOF record with zero values
in all fields appears last.

The second input file is the payroll master file (PAYMF), which is loaded into program tables at the beginning of the program run and used during editing to verify transaction values. The file format is as follows:

Field Name	Data Type
Department Number	Numeric
Job Code	Alphanumeric
Employee Number	Numeric
Employee Name	Alphanumeric
Pay Rate	Numeric
No. of Exemptions	Numeric
Year-to-Date Gross Pay	Numeric
Year-to-Date Federal Tax	Numeric
Year-to-Date FICA Tax	Numeric

PROCESSING

The following edits will be made:

1. The employee number in the transaction record is verified against the numbers in the master file. If no matching number is found, the following two edits should be skipped.

2. The department number in the transaction record is verified against the corresponding employee's department number, as indicated in the master file. This edit is not made if the master file does not show a matching department number for an employee.

3. The job code in the transaction record is verified against the corresponding master record. This edit is skipped if a matching employee record does not exist.

4. The regular-hours value in the transaction record should be less than or equal to 40 hours, but not less than 0 hours.

5. The overtime-hours value in the transaction record should be less than or equal to 10 hours, but not less than 0 hours.

OUTPUT

Program output will be an edit report in the format shown in Figure A-36.2. The report will consist of multiple pages with a maximum of 24 lines per page. The physical page size will be 30 lines.

```
      000000000111111111122222222223333333333344444444445555
      1234567890123456789012345678901234567890123456789012345678901234567890123
01 XX/XX              EDIT REPORT              PAGE ##
02              PAYROLL TRANSACTION FILE
03
04 DEPT JOB  EMPL REG  OTIME
05  NO  CODE  NO  HRS   HRS          ERROR
06 ---- ---- ---- ---- ----- ------------------------
07
08  ##   X   ###  ##.#  ##.#
09  ##   X   ###  ##.#  ##.#
10                       INVALID EMPL NO.
11                       INVALID DEPT. NO.
12                       INVALID JOB CODE
13                       REG. HRS. OUT OF RANGE
14                       OTIME. HRS. OUT OF RANGE
15
16
```

Figure A-36.2

Figure A-36. Concluded.

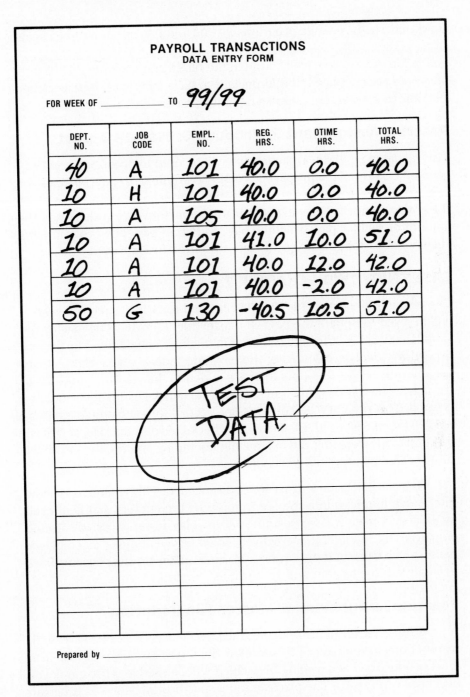

Figure A-37. Test data used for transaction file editing.

works correctly, change programs PAY05 and PAY06 so that they again process the regular transaction file. Run program PAY06 with the transaction file. If any errors are found in the file, rerun program PAY05 until all errors are corrected. It is important to have an error-free transaction file before subsequent processing takes place.

Practice Assignment 7: Produce Gross Pay Report

The validated payroll transaction file will be used to produce a gross pay report. This report is prepared weekly to summarize payroll costs for each employee, for each job classification, for each department, and for the entire company. Preparation of this report involves calculating the amount of regular pay, overtime pay, and gross pay. The programming specifications for this program are presented in Figure A-38.

CASE STUDY TWO—CHAPTER 7

The payroll transaction file (PAYTF) created for UBCO's payroll system will be used to update the payroll master file (PAYMF). The master file is updated weekly, after the transaction file has been edited. The posting procedure involves calculating the pay, and federal and social security tax amounts. These amounts then are added to the year-to-date fields in the master file. At the same time, a separate check-writing file should be created. This file (PAYCK) contains one record for each employee to be paid. The file is used to write paychecks. Programs are required, therefore, for updating the master file (including writing the paycheck file) and for printing the paychecks.

A master file inquiry program also is needed. This routine will allow interactive inquiries into the file to monitor the current status of each employee. A user will be permitted to display the records of selected employees by submitting interactively an employee number, an employee name, a department number, or a job code. After these programs have been added, the system will perform as shown in Figure A-39.

Practice Assignment 8: Master File Updating

A program is required for updating the payroll master file (PAYMF) with transactions in the payroll transaction file (PAYTF). This program also must produce a check-writing file, which will be used to write employee paychecks and stubs. The programming specifications for this program are given in Figure A-40.

Figure A-38. Programming specifications for gross pay report.

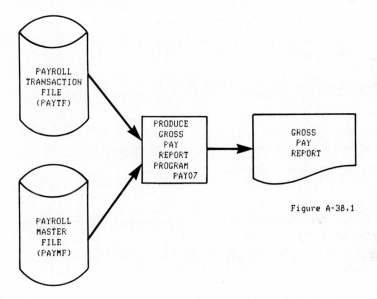

PROGRAMMING SPECIFICATIONS

System: PAYROLL   Date: 10/20/XX
Program: PRODUCE GROSS PAY REPORT   Program I.D.: PAY07   Analyst: D. ADAMS

Design and write a BASIC program to produce a gross pay report. The payroll
transaction file (PAYTF) and the payroll master file (PAYMF) are the input.
Output will be a report summarizing the regular pay, overtime pay, and gross
pay for each employee, job classification, department, and for the company as a
whole. The systems flowchart for this application is shown in Figure A-38.1.

PAYROLL
TRANSACTION
FILE
(PAYTF)

PRODUCE
GROSS
PAY
REPORT
PROGRAM
PAY07

GROSS
PAY
REPORT

Figure A-38.1

PAYROLL
MASTER
FILE
(PAYMF)

INPUT

The payroll transaction file (PAYTF) is the program input. A date record in
the format MM/DD is placed in the first file position. Then, employee work
records are written in the following format:

Field Name	Data Type
Department Number	Numeric
Job Code	Alphanumeric
Employee Number	Numeric
Regular Hours	Numeric
Overtime Hours	Numeric

The file is sequenced by employee number within job code within department. A
final EOF record, identified by zeros in all fields, is written to the file.

The payroll master file (PAYMF) is used to build program tables that can be
searched for employee pay rates contained in the transaction file. The format
of this file is as follows:

```
              Field Name                        Data Type
        --------------------------            ------------
          Department Number                     Numeric
          Job Code                              Alphanumeric
          Employee Number                       Numeric
          Employee Name                         Alphanumeric
          Pay Rate                              Numeric
          No. of Exemptions                     Numeric
          Year-to-Date Gross Pay                Numeric
          Year-to-Date Federal Tax              Numeric
          Year-to-Date FICA Tax                 Numeric
```

PROCESSING

At the beginning of processing, tables are built to hold the employee numbers
represented in the payroll master file and the associated pay rates for the
employees. Only these two fields from the master records are used. It is not
necessary to load all master fields into tables.

The following processing steps are repeated for each employee name in the
transaction file:

1. The employee number table is searched for the value that
   matches the value in the transaction record. Then, the
   corresponding pay rate for that employee is extracted from
   the pay rate table. A match will exist for all numbers.

2. Regular pay is calculated by multiplying the pay rate times
   the regular hours indicated in the transaction record.

3. Overtime pay is calculated by multiplying the pay rate times
   the overtime hours indicated in the transaction record. The
   result is multiplied by 1 1/2 to allow time and a half for
   overtime hours worked.

4. Gross pay is calculated by adding regular pay and overtime pay.

5. Regular pay, overtime pay, and gross pay are added into accumulators established for job code totals, department totals, and
   for the entire company.

OUTPUT

The format for the output report is shown in Figure A-38.2. This will be a
multiple-page report with a maximum of 25 lines per page. Assume a physical
page size of 30 lines.

```
    0000000001111111111222222222233333333334444444444555555555566666
    1234567890123456789012345678901234567890123456789012345678901234567890123
01                        GROSS PAY REPORT                    PAGE ##
02                      FOR WEEK ENDING XX/XX
03
04  DEPT JOB  EMPL   EMPLOYEE      REGULAR    OVERTIME     GROSS
05  NO   CODE NO      NAME          PAY         PAY         PAY
06  ---- ---- ----  ------------  ---------   ---------   ---------
07
08  ##    X   ###   XXXXXXXXXXXX   ###.##      ###.##      ###.##
09  ##    X   ###   XXXXXXXXXXXX   ###.##      ###.##      ###.##
10
11         TOTAL FOR JOB CODE X   #,###.##    #,###.##    #,###.##
12
13  ##    X   ###   XXXXXXXXXXXX   ###.##      ###.##      ###.##
14  ##    X   ###   XXXXXXXXXXXX   ###.##      ###.##      ###.##
15
16         TOTAL FOR JOB CODE X   #,###.##    #,###.##    #,###.##
17
18     TOTAL FOR DEPARTMENT ##   ##,###.##   ##,###.##   ##,###.##
19
20            COMPANY TOTALS    ##,###.##   ##,###.##   ##,###.##
21
22
```

Figure A-38.2

Figure A-38. Concluded.

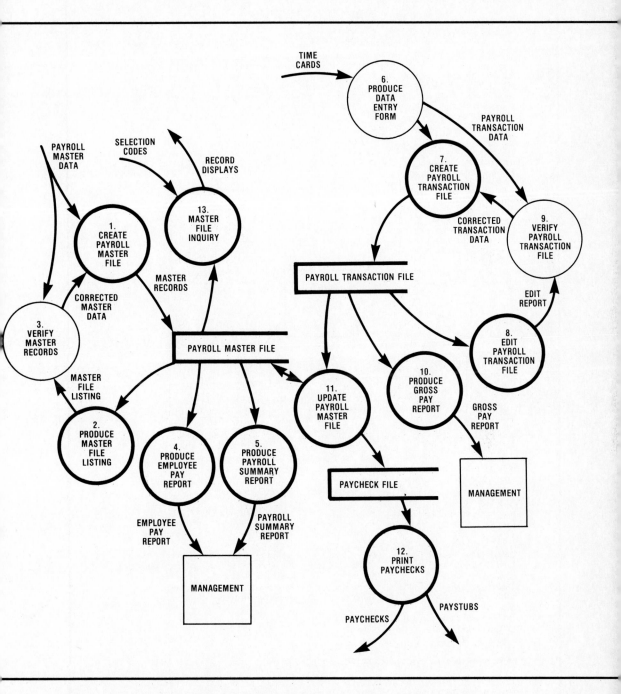

Figure A-39. Data flow diagram with updating and inquiry programs added.

Figure A-40. Programming specifications for payroll master file updating.

System: PAYROLL
Program: UPDATE PAYROLL MASTER FILE   Program I.D.: PAY08

Date: 10/20/XX
Analyst: D. ADAMS

Design and write a program to update the payroll master file (PAYMF) with data
in the payroll transaction file (PAYTF). The program will perform necessary
calculations for weekly gross pay, federal tax, and FICA tax and will update
the master records with these amounts. Then, the current and year-to-date
amounts will be written to a check-writing file (PAYCK) for later printing of
employee paychecks and stubs. The program will be coded in BASIC. Figure
A-40.1 shows the system flowchart for this application.

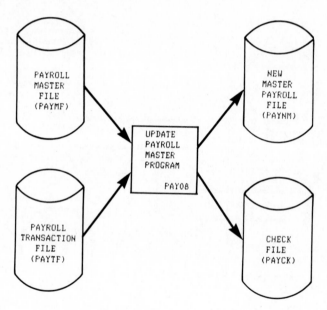

INPUT   Fig. A-40.1

The payroll master file and the payroll transaction file are the program input.
The formats of these files are as follows:

MASTER FILE		TRANSACTION FILE	
Field Name	Data Type	Field Name	Data Type
Department Number	Numeric	Department Number	Numeric
Job Code	Alphanumeric	Job Code	Alphanumeric
Employee Number	Numeric	Employee Number	Numeric
Employee Name	Alphanumeric	Regular Hours	Numeric
Pay Rate	Numeric	Overtime Hours	Numeric
No. of Exemptions	Numeric		
Year-to-Date Gross Pay	Numeric		
Year-to-Date Federal Tax	Numeric		
Year-to-Date FICA Tax	Numeric		

A date record in the format MM/DD is placed first in the transaction file.

The master file is loaded into tables within which all updating takes place.
Tables should be defined to hold a maximum of 30 records. Transaction records
are read individually from the file and processed one at a time.

PROCESSING

For each transaction record, the following processing will take place:

1. Regular pay is calculated by multiplying the pay rate in the master record by the regular hours in the transaction record. Overtime pay is calculated by multiplying the pay rate by overtime hours by 1 1/2 to allow time-and-a-half for overtime hours worked. Then, regular pay is added to overtime pay to determine gross pay for the week.

2. Federal tax is calculated according to the number of exemptions reported in the master record. The following percentages apply:

Exemptions	Tax Rate
1	33%
2	30
3	27
4	24
5	20

   The tax amount is determined by multiplying the gross pay by the applicable percentage.

3. FICA (social security) tax is withheld only on the first $30,000 of gross pay. Therefore, year-to-date gross pay will have to be checked to determine if, and how much, tax should be withheld. If year-to-date gross pay is equal to or greater than $30,000, no tax should be withheld. If the sum of year-to-date gross pay plus the current week's gross pay is less than or equal to $30,000, the tax amount is equal to 7% of gross pay. If the sum of year-to-date gross pay plus the current week's gross pay is greater than $30,000, the 7% tax should be applied against the difference of $30,000 and gross pay.

4. After calculating gross pay, federal tax, and FICA tax, the week's net pay is determined by subtracting the tax amounts from gross pay.

5. All the year-to-date fields in the master record are updated by adding to the fields the gross pay, federal tax, and FICA tax amounts.

6. The program will count the records updated. At the end of the program run, this total will be displayed.

OUTPUT

Following updating, the master records are written from the tables to a new file named PAYNM. The file appears in the same format as the old master file PAYMF. An EOF record should be written to this file.

A second output file will contain information for printing employee paychecks and stubs. One record is produced for each transaction record. The format and data fields for the records are shown below:

Field Name	Data Type
Date	Alphanumeric
Employee Number	Numeric
Employee Name	Alphanumeric
Net Pay	Numeric
Gross Pay	Numeric
Federal Tax	Numeric
FICA Tax	Numeric
Year-to-Date Gross Pay	Numeric
Year-to-Date Federal Tax	Numeric
Year-to-Date FICA Tax	Numeric

An EOF record should be written as the last record in this file.

During the program run, status messages should be displayed to the terminal.
The format of the screen displays is given in Figure A-40.2.

```
     00000000011111111111222222222223
     12345678901234567890123456789 0
01   ***********************
02   * MASTER FILE UPDATE *
03   ***********************
04
05   UPDATING...
06
07   END OF PROCESSING
08   ## RECORDS UPDATED AND
09      WRITTEN TO CHECK FILE
10
11
```

Figure A-40.2

Figure A-40. Concluded.

After the master file updating program has been run, the detail report program should be modified to read the master file and produce a listing of the updated records. Once verified, the new master file should replace the old master file. The old file will be renamed PAYBK to serve as a backup. The new file should be renamed PAYMF to replace the old file as the current master file.

Practice Assignment 9: Print Paychecks

The check file (PAYCK) produced in the previous practice assignment is to be used as the source file for printing the paychecks and stubs for the employees. A program is needed to input this file and to format the data onto preprinted check forms. The specifications for this program appear in Figure A-41.

Practice Assignment 10: Master File Inquiry

The payroll information system now has the mechanisms in place to update the master file with weekly payroll information. The system can operate across multiple cycles and provide processing continuity from week to week. In other words, current data are available continuously on the status of employees.

The payroll system is still incomplete, however. Additions are necessary to provide greater flexibility of access to the information contained in the master file. For example, should a department manager require information about a particular employee or group of employees, the present system would not have the means to provide this information without producing one of the current reports. This report-writing

530

Figure A-41. Programming specifications for printing of paychecks.

PROGRAMMING SPECIFICATIONS

System: PAYROLL   Date: 10/22/XX
Program: PRINT PAYCHECKS   Program I.D.: PAY09   Analyst: D. ADAMS

Design and write a program to input the check file (PAYCK) and produce
paychecks and paystubs. The program will be written in BASIC. Figure A-41.1
shows the system flowchart for this application.

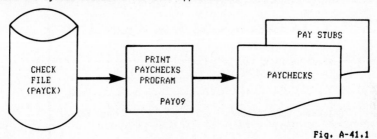

Fig. A-41.1

INPUT

Program input is the check file (PAYCK). This file contains information from
the master file updating run and provides payment and tax amounts for employees
for the current payroll period and for year to date. The format of records in
this file is as follows:

Field Name	Data Type
Date	Alphanumeric
Employee Number	Numeric
Employee Name	Alphanumeric
Net Pay	Numeric
Gross Pay	Numeric
Federal Tax	Numeric
FICA Tax	Numeric
Year-to-Date Gross Pay	Numeric
Year-to-Date Federal Tax	Numeric
Year-to-Date FICA Tax	Numeric

PROCESSING

During the printing of the paychecks and paystubs, two calculations are
required. The year-to-date net pay figure that appears on the checkstub must
be calculated by subtracting year-to-date federal tax and year-to-date FICA tax
from the year-to-date gross pay. Also, the dollars and cents amounts that
appear in written form on the check must be calculated. The net pay amount
must be separated into a dollars amount and a cents amount because these two
amounts are printed in separate locations on the line in the middle of the
paycheck. This separation is accomplished by assigning the integer value of
the net pay amount as the dollars portion, and then subtracting this number
from the net pay to determine the cents portion. The two amounts then are
assigned to different variables so that each amount can be printed in a
separate position on the line.

OUTPUT

The output from this program will appear as shown in the accompanying diagram.
Assume that special, preprinted check forms will be used. Therefore, only the

variables produced by the program require printing. Output should be formatted to appear in the assumed columns on the appropriate lines. Thus, the following fields are printed on the check: date, employee name (PAYEE), net pay (AMOUNT), dollars amount, and cents amount. The stub portion includes the following fields: date, employee number, gross pay, federal tax, FICA tax, net pay, year-to-date gross pay, year-to-date federal tax, year-to-date FICA tax, and year-to-date net pay. (The ambitious programmer also might want to print the forms as well as the data.)

```
00000000011111111112222222222333333333344444444445555555556
12345678901234567890123456789012345678901234567890123456789
01
02      UNIVERSAL BOOK COMPANY                      NO. ###
03      Galley Street
04      Reseda, CA  91324                   DATE XX/XX
05
06
07   PAYEE: XXXXXXXXXXXXXXX              AMOUNT: $##,###.##
08
09
10         PAY EXACTLY ##,### DOLLARS AND ## CENTS
11
12
13      FIRST RATIONAL BANK
14      Los Angeles, CA 91013    _____
15
16  ----------------------------------------------------------
17
18   UNIVERSAL BOOK COMPANY                    DATE XX/XX
19
20
21   Emp.   Gross Pay    Fed. Tax    FICA Tax    Net Pay
22
23   ###     ###.##      ###.##      ###.##      ###.##
24
25
26          YTD          YTD         YTD         YTD
27          Gross Pay    Fed. Tax    FICA Tax    Net Pay
28
29        ##,###.##    ##,###.##   ##,###.##   ##,###.##
30
31
```

Figure A-41.2

Figure A-41. Concluded.

procedure is time consuming and generates more information than would be needed for such a situation. The existing detail report and summary report programs do not provide employee status information in a convenient and concise form. The manager's request requires the system to provide inquiry capability into the master file so that selected employee records can be called up and displayed. This service must be provided in an interactive mode.

The following program adds the necessary inquiry capabilities to the payroll information system. The programming specifications for this routine are given in Figure A-42.

Figure A-42. Programming specifications for master file inquiry.

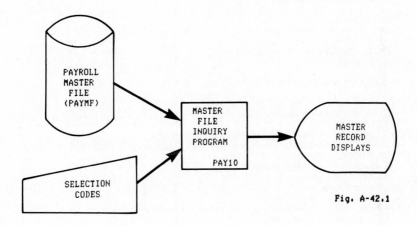

PROGRAMMING SPECIFICATIONS

System: PAYROLL   Date: 10/24/XX
Program: MASTER FILE INQUIRY   Program I.D.: PAY10 Analyst: D. ADAMS

Design and write a program to allow interactive inquiry into the payroll master
file (PAYMF). The program allows the user to present the system with an
employee number, employee name, department number, or job code and has the
system display information relative to that person or group. The program will
be coded in BASIC. Figure A-42.1 presents the system flowchart for this
application.

PAYROLL
MASTER
FILE
(PAYMF)

MASTER
FILE
INQUIRY
PROGRAM

PAY10

MASTER
RECORD
DISPLAYS

SELECTION
CODES

Fig. A-42.1

INPUT

The payroll master file (PAYMF) is the program input. This file is loaded into
program tables within which the search for records is conducted. The following
table presents the format of records in this file:

Field Name	Data Type
Department Number	Numeric
Job Code	Alphanumeric
Employee Number	Numeric
Employee Name	Alphanumeric
Pay Rate	Numeric
No. of Exemptions	Numeric
Year-to-Date Gross Pay	Numeric
Year-to-Date Federal Tax	Numeric
Year-to-Date FICA Tax	Numeric

The tables used for storing the file should be dimensioned to hold a maximum of
30 records, allowing for possible expansion of the master file

PROCESSING

The program is menu driven. The user enters a code signifying the type of search to be conducted within the file. Four types of inquiries are supported. If the user provides an employee number or employee name, the program will look for matches within the file and will display the entire record. If a department number is selected, the program will access and display the employee numbers, employee names, job codes, and pay rates for all employees within the department. If a job code is entered, the program will display the employee numbers, employee names, and pay rates for all employees under that job classification.

OUTPUT

Figure A-42.2 provides the formats in which the accessed information will be displayed. In addition to the normal system responses, provision should be made for handling inquiry errors. A suitable set of system responses should be developed for incorrect entries of numbers, names, and codes.

```
      0000000001111111111222222222233333333
      1234567890123456789012345678901234567 8
01    **************************
02    * MASTER FILE INQUIRY *
03    **************************
04
05       EMPLOYEE NO.      1
06       EMPLOYEE NAME     2
07       DEPARTMENT NO.    3
08       JOB CODE          4
09       STOP              5
10
11    SELECT OPTION...? *
12
13
14    ENTER EMPLOYEE NO....? ***
15
16    DEPT NO.      **
17    JOB CODE      X
18    NUMBER        ***
19    NAME          XXXXXXXXXXXX
20    PAY RATE      *.**
21    EXEMPTIONS    *
22    YTD GROSS     *****.**
23    YTD FED.      *****.**
24    YTD FICA      *****.**
25
26
27    ENTER EMPLOYEE NAME...? XXXXXXXXXXXX
28
29    DEPT. NO.     **
30    JOB CODE      X
31    EMPL NO.      ***
32    EMPL NAME     XXXXXXXXXXXX
33    PAY RATE      *.**
34    EXEMPTIONS    *
35    YTD GROSS     *****.**
36    YTD FED.      *****.**
37    YTD FICA      *****.**
38
39
40    ENTER DEPT NUMBER...? **
41
42    NO.       NAME       CODE    RATE
43    ***    XXXXXXXXXXXX    X     *.**
44    ***    XXXXXXXXXXXX    X     *.**
45    ***    XXXXXXXXXXXX    X     *.**
46     .          .         .       .
47     .          .         .       .
48     .          .         .       .
49    ENTER JOB CODE...? X
```

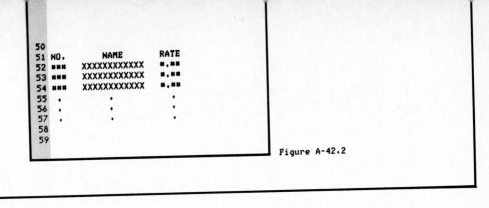

```
50
51 NO.     NAME          RATE
52 ***     XXXXXXXXXXXX   #.##
53 ***     XXXXXXXXXXXX   #.##
54 ***     XXXXXXXXXXXX   #.##
55 .           .           .
56 .           .           .
57 .           .           .
58
59
```

Figure A-42.2

Figure A-42. Concluded.

CASE STUDY TWO—Chapter 8

A final set of three programs is required to make UBCO's payroll information system fully operational. A master file maintenance program must be written to allow new employee records to be added to the file, to permit changes in the values of fields within existing records, and to allow records to be deleted from the file. Second, a program is needed to produce federal W-2 forms. These are end-of-year reports of earnings and withholdings that provide employees with the information required for filing of tax returns. Finally, a cycle initialization program will be written. This program will reset the year-to-date fields within master records to zero so that accumulations can proceed for the next year.

The complete system is documented in the data flow diagram shown in Figure A-43.

Practice Assignment 11: Master File Maintenance

Write a master file maintenance program so that records can be added to, changed within, and deleted from the payroll master file. The program will be used for the following situations:

- Whenever new employees are hired.
- Whenever employee records need to be modified to reflect changed employment status.
- To correct errors in employee records.
- To delete records of former employees.

This maintenance program will be menu-driven and will permit interactive processing. Figure A-44 provides the specifications for this program.

535

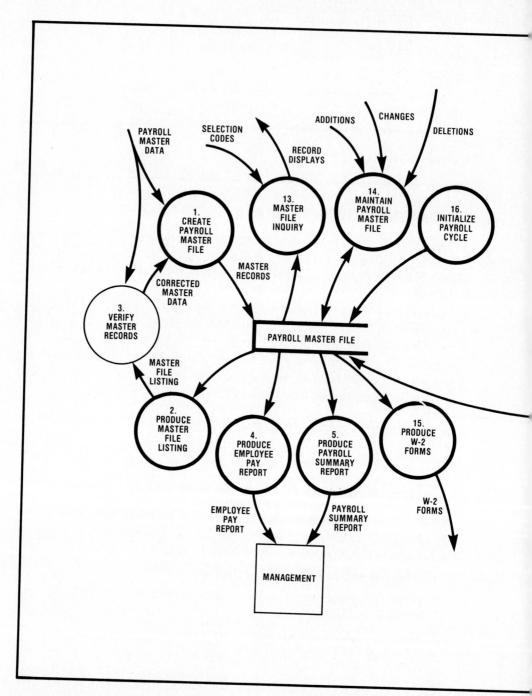

Figure A-43. Data flow diagram showing completed payroll system.

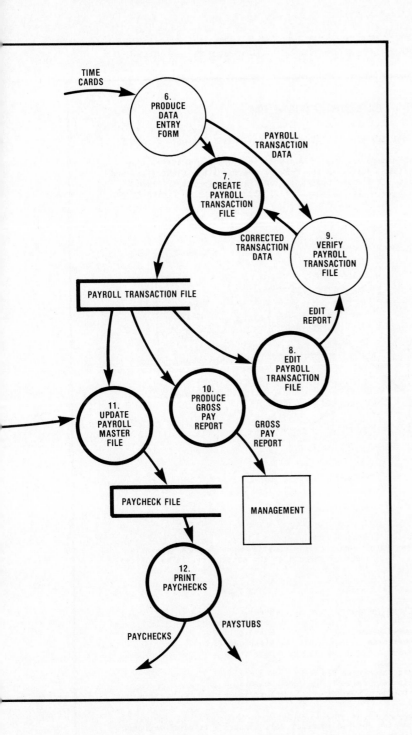

Figure A-44. Programming specifications for master file maintenance.

PROGRAMMING SPECIFICATIONS

System: PAYROLL
Program: MASTER FILE MAINTENANCE   Date: 10/25/XX
                                          Program I.D.: PAY11   Analyst: D. ADAMS

Design and write a program to maintain the payroll master file (PAYMF). The
program allows interactive updates in the form of additions to, changes to, and
deletions from the file. Following updating, the file is rewritten. The
program will be written in BASIC. Figure A-44.1 shows the system flowchart for
this application.

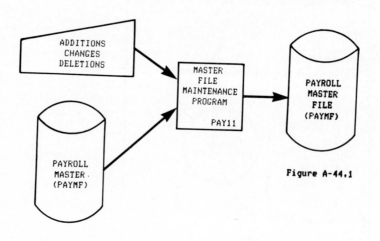

Figure A-44.1

<u>**INPUT**</u>

The payroll master file (PAYMF) and the file updates keyed through terminals
are the program input. The format of records in the master file is as follows:

Field Name	Data Type
Department Number	Numeric
Job Code	Alphanumeric
Employee Number	Numeric
Employee Name	Alphanumeric
Pay Rate	Numeric
No. of Exemptions	Numeric
Year-to-Date Gross Pay	Numeric
Year-to-Date Federal Tax	Numeric
Year-to-Date FICA Tax	Numeric

Maintenance transactions are entered interactively through a terminal keyboard.
The program is menu driven and requests data from the operator. Figure A-44.2
shows the formats of communication between the program and the operator.

```
0000000C011111111111222222222233333333334
1234567890123456789012345678901234567890
01 ***************************
02 * MASTER FILE MAINTENANCE *
03 ***************************
04
05      ADD NEW RECORD....A
06      CHANGE A RECORD...C
07      DELETE A RECORD...D
08      STOP..............S
09
10 ENTER SELECTION...? X
11
12 *** ADD NEW RECORD ***
13
14 DEPT. NUMBER........? ##
15 JOB CODE............? X
16 EMPLOYEE NUMBER.....? ###
17 EMPLOYEE NAME.......? XXXXXXXXXXX
18 PAY RATE............? #.##
19 NO. OF EXEMPTIONS...? #
20 YTD GROSS PAY.......? #####.##
21 YTD FEDERAL TAX.....? ####.##
22 YTD FICA TAX........? ###.##
23    VERIFY (Y/N)......? X
24
25
26 *** CHANGE A RECORD  ***
27
28 EMPLOYEE NUMBER...? ###
29                                CHANGE?
30                                (Y/N)
31                                -------
32 DEPT. NUMBER     : ##          ? X
33 JOB CODE         : X           ? X
34 EMPLOYEE NUMBER  : ###         ? X
35 EMPLOYEE NAME    : XXXXXXXXXXX  ? X
36 PAY RATE         : #.##        ? X
37 NO. OF EXEMPTIONS: #           ? X
38 YTD GROSS PAY    : #####.##     ? X
39 YTD FEDERAL TAX  : ####.##      ? X
40 YTD FICA TAX     : ###.##       ? X
41                  ? ###.##
42    VERIFY (Y/N)..? X
43
44 *** DELETE A RECORD ***
45
46 EMPLOYEE NUMBER...? ###
47
48
```

Figure A-44.2

PROCESSING

The master file is loaded into program tables within which all updates take place. The tables should be dimensioned to allow a maximum of 30 master records to be processed at any one time.

Adding Records: The operator is prompted through the sequence of fields contained in a master record. After all fields are entered, the operator visually verifies the entries before the record is added to the tables. If the fields are correct, the new record is added to the file in its appropriate employee number sequence. The employee number table is searched to locate the first record with a number larger than that of the record to be added. This file position will be the location of the new record. All records with an employee number larger than the number of the new record are moved down one position in the tables. Then, the new record is inserted and the table length pointer is increased by one to account for the added length of the table.

Changing Records: The operator enters the employee number of the record to be changed. Then, the employee number table is searched to locate the matching record. The fields of the current record are displayed one at a time. If the value for a particular field is to be replaced, a prompt is displayed on the line below the value. Then, the new value is keyed on this line. After all changes are made, the entries are visually verified. If an error is found, all fields are again displayed and, as each new field is keyed, the change is made to the table record.

Deleting Records: The operator keys in the employee number of the record to be deleted. The program searches the table to locate the matching record. All records below the record to be deleted are moved up one position in the tables. This operation overwrites the undesired record. Then, the table length is decreased by one.

Error Processing: The program should check for and respond to the following potential processing errors: an incorrect menu code, the addition of a record with an employee number that already exists in the file, the attempted changing of a record with a number that does not appear in the file, and the attempted deletion of a record for which there is no matching employee number.

OUTPUT

After all maintenance activites are completed, the table data are written back to file PAYMF. This new file version will replace the old version. An EOF record should be written to complete the file.

Figure A-44. Concluded.

After you have written and tested the maintenance program, use it to make the following changes to the payroll master file:

1.	ADD record:	10, A, 100, G. SMART, 5.75, 1, 0.00, 0.00, 0.00
2.	CHANGE record 121:	Change Pay Rate = 6.65
		Change No. of Exemptions = 4
3.	DELETE record 101	
4.	CHANGE record 108:	Change Department Number = 20
		Change Job Code = "C"
		Change Pay Rate = 4.25
5.	ADD record:	10, B, 109, A. FURN, 3.75, 3, 0.00, 0.00, 0.00
6.	CHANGE record 127:	Change YTD Gross Pay = 4,962.35
7.	CHANGE record 120:	Change No. of Exemptions = 3
8.	CHANGE record 114:	Change Employee Name = "J. DANIALS"
9.	DELETE record 103	
10.	ADD record:	30, F, 130, D. JUAN, 5.50, 1, 0.00, 0.00, 0.00

After completing the updates, run program PAY02 (master file listing) to verify the correctness of the changes.

Practice Assignment 12: Print W-2 Forms

At the close of a year, companies provide employees with statements of earnings and withholdings for the preceding 12-month period. Employees must file copies of these federal W-2 and other tax forms, along with federal 1040 and state tax forms. The information on the W-2 form is used to summarize an employee's tax earnings and withholdings for the year.

Write a program to extract year-to-date information from the payroll master file and to print the information on W-2 forms. This program will be run one time at the end of the year. Specifications for this program appear in Figure A-45.

Practice Assignment 13: Cycle Initialization

Now, you are ready to write the final program in the payroll information system. This cycle initialization program will be run at the close of the year, following the printing of the W-2 forms. The program resets year-to-date fields in the master record to zero so that year-to-date totals can be accumulated for the upcoming year. Specifications for this program appear in Figure A-46.

The payroll information system is now fully operational. To test the system, data should be provided to run the programs in simulation of several processing cycles. Also, as added documentation, structure charts and/or systems flowcharts describing the complete system might be prepared. Finally, it might be worthwhile to prepare a simple operations manual, which describes the system's operating procedures to users.

<u>PROGRAMMING SPECIFICATIONS</u>

System: PAYROLL
Program: PRINT W-2 FORMS

Date: 10/27/XX
Program I.D.: PAY12   Analyst: D. ADAMS

Design and write a program to access the payroll master file (PAYMF) and
extract year-to-date information to be printed on W-2 tax forms. This program
will be written in BASIC. Figure A-45.2 provides the system flowchart for this
application.

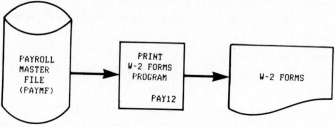

Fig. A-45.1

<u>INPUT</u>

The payroll master file (PAYMF) is the program input. The format of records in
this file is:

Field Name	Data Type
Department Number	Numeric
Job Code	Alphanumeric
Employee Number	Numeric
Employee Name	Alphanumeric
Pay Rate	Numeric
No. of Exemptions	Numeric
Year-to-Date Gross Pay	Numeric
Year-to-Date Federal Tax	Numeric
Year-to-Date FICA Tax	Numeric

<u>OUTPUT</u>

Program output will be a set of W-2 tax forms, as shown in Figure A-45.2. The
information will be printed on special, preprinted forms. Therefore, it is
necessary to print only the variable information shown in the accompanying
format illustration. (For this assignment, it may be interesting to print the
form itself, if preferred.)

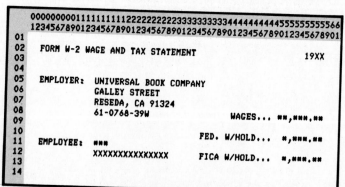

Figure A-45.2

Figure A-45. Programming specifications for printing of W-2 forms.

PROGRAMMING SPECIFICATIONS

System: PAYROLL   Date: 10/28/XX
Program: PAYROLL CYCLE INITIALIZATION Program I.D.: PAY13 Analyst: D. ADAMS

Design and write a program to initialize the payroll master file (PAYMF) for
the upcoming payroll year. Output will be a new master file with year-to-date
fields set to zero. The program will be written in BASIC. Figure A-46.1
presents the system flowchart for this application.

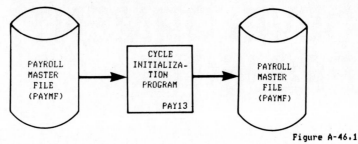

Figure A-46.1

INPUT

The payroll master file (PAYMF) is the program input. Records should appear in
the following format:

Field Name	Data Type
Department Number	Numeric
Job Code	Alphanumeric
Employee Number	Numeric
Employee Name	Alphanumeric
Pay Rate	Numeric
No. of Exemptions	Numeric
Year-to-Date Gross Pay	Numeric
Year-to-Date Federal Tax	Numeric
Year-to-Date FICA Tax	Numeric

Master records are loaded into tables within which all updating takes place.

PROCESSING

Processing involves changing the year-to-date fields to zero. No other
processing is required. While the program is running, screen displays should
indicate processing status as shown in Figure A-46.2.

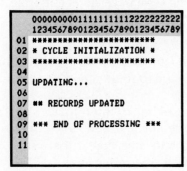

Figure A-46.2

OUTPUT

Following processing, the data in the tables will be rewritten as the payroll
master file (PAYMF). Program PAY02 should be run to verify initialization.

Figure A-46.   Programming specifications for payroll cycle initialization.

B
SYSTEM DEVELOPMENT PROJECTS

INTRODUCTION

The following comprehensive system development projects allow you to work through and integrate the programming techniques described in Chapters 1 through 8. Each project requires you to design and write the computer programs that will implement the system. You also are asked to perform necessary analysis and design activities to determine the relationships among programs, data files, and manual procedures.

Each project is a case scenario in which you are given processing requirements in the form of user-based needs. Thus, the scenarios are expressed in terms that represent the types of major business problems that you, as a BASIC programmer, may be asked to help solve. In addition, suggested program types are presented, along with the file data that are necessary to support processing. The system development projects, then, require you to:

1. Design layouts for the master and transaction files, for the input documents and forms, and for any output reports and displays.

2. Prepare system and program documentation, including structure charts, system flowcharts, pseudocode, and any other types of documentation that would facilitate operation of the system, such as operator instructions for users of the programs.

3. Design, write, code, and test all programs that fulfill system specifications, and develop any other programs that you feel should be included in the system.

Complete documentation for the systems should be submitted on 8½-by-11-inch paper contained in a suitable binder. The project documentation should be subdivided into these four parts:

☐ Part I: System design. This part includes data flow diagrams, system flowcharts, system structure charts, program descriptions, file layouts, record layouts, forms design, and test data.

☐ Part II: Program design. This part encompasses programming specifications, structure charts, and pseudocode.

☐ Part III: Program coding (program listings).

☐ Part IV: System testing. This part includes listings of program runs with test data.

All format conventions for the case projects should follow those used in this book. System testing is to include at least three tests of each processing cycle in the system.

Because these cases are expected to result in complete operational systems, it is recommended that you complete study of Chapters 1 through 8 before starting any projects. A thorough understanding of these chapters should enable you to bring a perspective of integrated systems to the projects.

It should be noted also that both projects closely parallel the designs of the example system presented in the text, as well as in CASE STUDY ONE and CASE STUDY TWO of Appendix A. Thus, familiarity with these systems is a prerequisite for successful design and implementation of the case projects.

For example, each master file in the case projects requires programs for creating, editing, listing, updating, maintaining, and producing reports on file content. Similar types of programs are required for each transaction file. In some cases, specific reports are requested. In other cases, judgment should be exercised to determine whether additional reports, file displays, or inquiry processing are appropriate. As a general guideline, 10 to 15 separate programs can be expected for each system.

Each project should take no more than three to four weeks to complete. During this time, your instructor will serve as the client, or potential user of the system. Any questions you have pertaining to the satisfaction of user requirements will be answered by the instructor. Providing solutions for any problems concerning system design and programming will be your responsibility. However, the project should be submitted to the instructor periodically for review and comment, particularly as each section of documentation is completed.

PROJECT ONE—JOB TIME ACCOUNTING SYSTEM

Your programming department needs a system that will keep track of the personnel and machine hours spent programming the various systems that are under development. The systems are identified by three-character names. The programs in the system are assigned three-digit numbers. For example, the name GLS003 indicates program 003 of the general ledger system (GLS).

Each week, information is collected from the programmers pertaining to the amount of time each spent on particular programs. This information is submitted on a job-time form ruled into four columns: system name, program number, number of working hours on the program, and number of computer hours used in writing or testing the program. At the top of the form, a space is provided for the programmer to write his or her name; at the bottom, a space is provided for the supervisor's signature. Vacation time is identified by the special code VAC001. Sick days are indicated by code SIK001 in the system and program columns. Of course, an entry of zero is made in the machine-time column of the form for these codes. Each job-time sheet should total no more than 40 programming hours per week.

These job-time transactions are to be posted each week to a master file of systems development accounts. This master file will contain the following fields: system name, program number, month-to-date programming hours, month-to-date machine hours, year-to-date programming hours, and year-to-date machine hours. At the end of each month, management wants a report of total programming and machine hours used for each program, and of total hours used for vacation and sick time. Also, a total for each system should be provided.

PROJECT TWO—GENERAL LEDGER SYSTEM

Your company wants a system that will aid in general accounting. This system is to maintain month-to-date and year-to-date totals of additions to and subtractions from each of the company's general ledger accounts. These accounts summarize all monetary effects of business transactions. Each account, therefore, is a summary of the changes in value of one of the assets (things owned), liabilities (amounts owed), or types of company transactions.

Each month, the accountants prepare a sheet of transactions made during the month. This sheet has three columns: account number (three digits), account description (up to 20 characters), and transaction amount (plus or minus value). The total of all positive and negative amounts should be zero.

The information on this sheet is used to update the general ledger file each month. This master file should contain the following fields: account number, account name, account type (B for balance sheet and I for income statement), month-to-date account total, and year-to-date account total.

At the end of the month, the accountants need a report that shows total transactions for each account. The accounts will summarize month-to-date and year-to-date totals. Also, balance sheet and income statement reports are to be provided. The balance sheet report will show account numbers, account names, and year-to-date balances for all accounts (identified as B and I accounts in the master file). The income statement report will list account numbers, account names, and month-to-date and year-to-date amounts for income statement accounts (identified as I accounts in the master file). Both reports will provide final totals.

Also, provision should be made for maintaining and allowing inquiry into the master file. At the end of the month, all month-to-date account balances are to be zeroed. Similarly, at the end of the year, income statement account year-to-date balances are to be zeroed. The year-to-date balance sheet balances, however, never are zeroed. Actually, balances on this sheet are business-to-date summaries to be maintained for the entire life of the company.

C
DESIGN AND CODING CONVENTIONS FOR PROGRAM CONTROL STRUCTURES

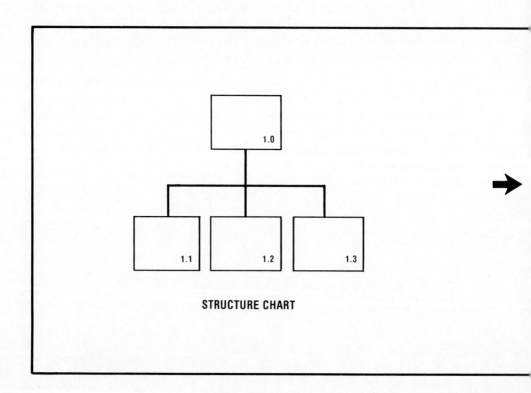

STRUCTURE CHART

```
1.0 MODULE
     1.1 MODULE

          -------------
          -------------
          -------------
          -------------
     1.2 MODULE

          -------------
          -------------
          -------------
          -------------
     1.3 MODULE

          -------------
          -------------
          -------------
          -------------


     PSEUDOCODE
```

Figure C-1. Design convention for sequence control structures.

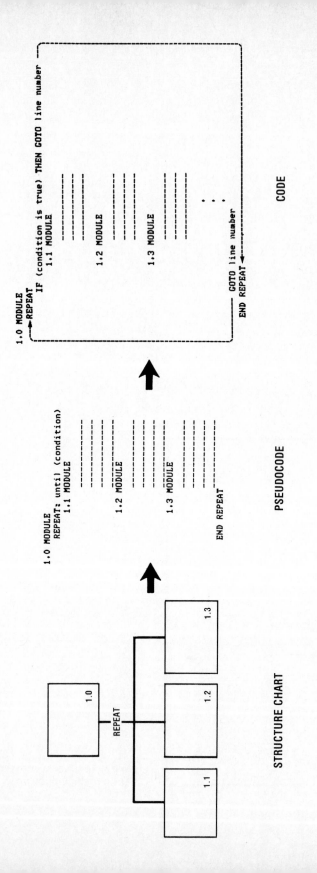

Figure C-2. Design and coding conventions for repetition control structure.

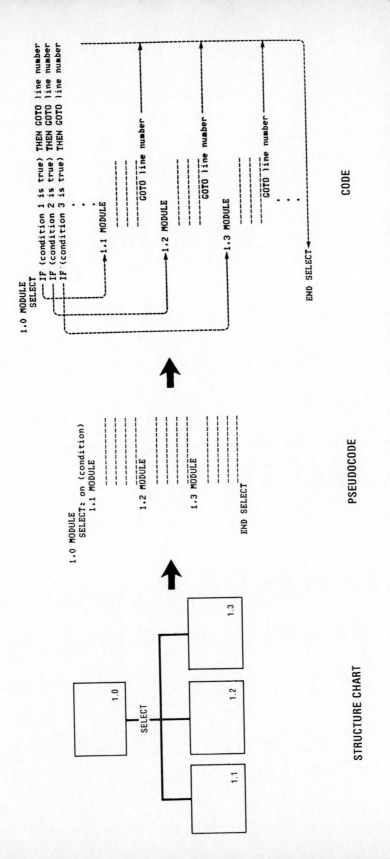

Figure C-3. Design and coding conventions for selection control structure.

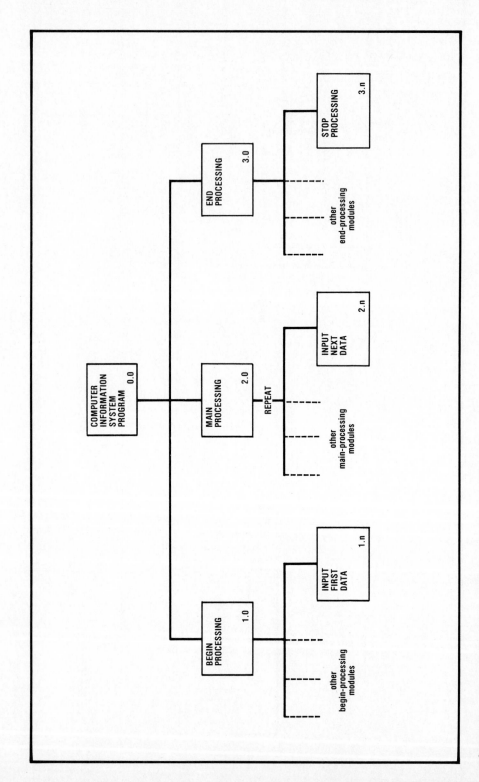

Figure C-4. Computer information systems program model.

D
BASIC LANGUAGE SUMMARY

BASIC STATEMENTS

CLOSE
DIM
END
FIELD
GET
GOSUB-RETURN
IF
INPUT
INPUT LINE
LET
LSET
OPEN
PRINT
PRINT USING
PUT
READ
REM
STOP
UPDATE
WRITE

BASIC FUNCTIONS

ABS
SGN
INT
SQR
RND
LEFT$
LEFT
MID$
MID
RIGHT$
RIGHT
LEN
MKI$
MKS$
MKD$
CVI
CVS
CVD
CVT%$
CVTF$
CVT$%
CVT$F

CLOSE

DEC, TRS-80, IBM/Microsoft Systems

General Format:
   line number CLOSE #file number

Example:

```
1650 CLOSE #1
```

The keyword CLOSE is followed by the file reference number (or buffer number) that appeared in the OPEN statement.

Apple II System

General Format:
   line number PRINT CHRS$(4); "CLOSE file name"

Example:

```
1650 PRINT CHR$(4); "CLOSE FUNMF"
```

The file name that appeared in the OPEN statement is repeated in the CLOSE statement.

DIM

General Format:
   line number DIM variable name(No. of elements) {, variable
      name(no. of elements) . . . }

Example:

```
3070 DIM N2(15), L2(15)
```

The keyword DIM (dimension) precedes one or more variable names to be assigned to program tables. Immediately following each name, the number of storage positions, or elements, of the table is coded within parentheses. The variables are separated by commas. Any number of DIM statements can appear in the program.

END

General Format:
line number END

Example:

9990 END

The keyword END appears by itself, with no other specifications, and always on the last line of the program.

FIELD

IBM, TRS-80, and DEC Systems

FIELD #FILE number, width AS string variable [, width AS string variable] . . .

This statement describes the format of a data record. Each field is specified by its length and name. The entry "width" is an integer value that provides the size, in characters, of the field. Width is set to equal the largest value expected in any given field. The entry "string variable" is the name of the field. Standard naming conventions apply. All fields within direct-access records must carry string variable names, even though numeric values will be placed there.

Functions (1)

ABS(expression)	Returns the absolute value of the expression.

```
ABS(-5.27) = 5.27
ABS(+80.1) = 80.1
```

SGN(expression)	Returns the sign of the expression preceding the value 1 except when the expression is 0.

```
SGN(1.45) = +1
SGN(-2.7) = -1
SGN(0)    = 0
```

INT(expression)	Returns the integer value of the expression.

```
INT(3.75) = 3
INT(-8.06) = -8
INT(16.5 * 2.7) = 44
```

Can be used to round numbers to the nearest integer with the expression INT(expression + .5)

SQR(expression)	Returns the square root of the expression.

```
SQR(144) = 12
```

RND	Returns a random number between 0 and 1. In general, to produce a set of random numbers over the range from A to B, use:

```
(B - A) * RND + A
```

To generate a set of whole numbers between 1 and B, use:

```
INT(B * RND + .5)
```

The same set of random numbers will be generated each time the program is run. To obtain different numbers, the following statement must be included before the RND function is executed the first time:

line number RANDOMIZE

LEFT$(A$,N) or
LEFT(A$,N)
	Indicates a substring of string A$ from the first character through the Nth character.
	
	`A$ = "ABCDEFG"`
	`LEFT$(A$,3) = "ABC"`

MID$(A$,N1,N2) or
MID(A$,N1,N2)
	Indicates a substring of string A$ starting with character N1 and continuing for N2 characters.
	
	`A$ = "ABCDEF"`
	`MID$(A$,2,5) = "BCDE"`

RIGHT$(A$,N) or
RIGHT(A$,N)
	Indicates a substring of string A$ from the Nth character through the farthest-right character.
	
	`A$ = "ABCDEF"`
	`RIGHT$(A$,3) = "DEF"`

LEN(A$)	Returns the number of characters in string A$, including blank spaces.
	
	`A$ = "ABCDEF    "`
	`LEN(A$) = 9`

+	Indicates a concatenation operation on two strings.
	
	`A$ = "ABC"`
	`B$ = "DEF"`
	`A$ + B$ = "ABCDEF"`

Functions (3)

IBM and TRS-80 Systems

MKI$, MKS$, MKD$

Any numeric value written to a direct-access file must be converted into a string. These functions are used to make the following conversions: MKI$ converts an integer value to a two-character (two-byte) string; MKS$ converts a single-precision number (up to seven digits) to a four-character string; and MKD$ converts a double-precision number (up to 17 digits) to an eight-character string. The formats of these functions are:

$$\text{string variable} = \begin{cases} \text{MKI\$(integer expression)} \\ \text{MKS\$(single-precision expression)} \\ \text{MKD\$(double-precision expression)} \end{cases}$$

CVI, CVS, CVD

These functions convert a numeric string value of a field in a direct-access record to a number. The function CVI converts a two-character string to an integer; the function CVS converts a four-character string to a single-precision number; and the function CVD converts an eight-character string to a double-precision number. The formats of these functions are:

$$\text{numeric variable} = \begin{cases} \text{CVI(2-character string)} \\ \text{CVS(4-character string)} \\ \text{CVD(8-character string)} \end{cases}$$

PDP-11 System

CVT%$, CVTF$

Numeric values written to direct-access files must be converted into character strings. The above functions are used to make the following conversions: CVT%$ converts an integer to a two-character string, and CVTF$ converts a decimal number to a four- or eight-character string. The size of the string depends on whether a two-word or four-word math package has been installed in the system. The current math package is determined by printing the function LEN(CVTF$(0)). These string lengths then become the widths specified in the FIELD statement. The formats of these functions are:

$$\text{string variable} = \begin{cases} \text{CVT\%\$(integer expression)} \\ \text{CVTF\$(decimal expression)} \end{cases}$$

CVT$%, CVT$F

These functions perform the processing of the CVT%$ and CVTF$ functions in reverse. That is, the functions convert strings that appear within a direct-access record to their numeric equivalents. The function CVT$% converts a two-character string to an integer and the function CVT$F converts a four- or eight-character string to a decimal number, depending on the math package installed in the system. The formats of these functions are:

$$\text{numeric variable} = \begin{cases} \text{CVT\$\%(two-character string)} \\ \text{CVT\$F(four- or eight-character string)} \end{cases}$$

GET

General Format:

line number GET #file number, RECORD record number

Example:

```
100 GET #1, RECORD N
```

This statement inputs the record at the relative location given by the record number (N) from a direct-access file. The file number is the number used in the associated OPEN statement.

General Formats:
line number GOSUB line number
line number RETURN

Examples:

1400 GOSUB 2000

    ↑

    ↑

    ↑

2330 RETURN

The line number that follows the keyword GOSUB is used for
the first statement of a subroutine. Control branches to that
statement to execute the statements within the subroutine.
When the program reaches the RETURN statement (the last line
of a subroutine), control branches back to the statement immediately following the GOSUB statement to continue the
normal sequential execution of statements. The action of a
subroutine call and return is represented in the following lines
of code:

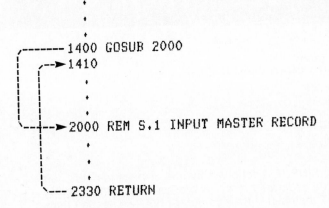

IF

General Format:
line number IF condition test THEN GOTO line number

Example:

```
1660 IF A1 < M THEN GOTO 1690
```

The keyword IF is followed by a condition test. The test compares two values using the relational operators < (less than), = (equal to), > (greater than), < = (less than or equal to), > = (greater than or equal to), or < > (not equal to). If the test is evaluated as true, control branches to the line number that follows the word GOTO. If the test is evaluated as false, processing continues, in sequence, starting with the statement that follows the IF statement.

INPUT
(Keyboard)

General Format:
line number INPUT variable name [, variable name . . .]

Examples:

```
2140 INPUT L
3000 INPUT A, B, C$, N1
```

The keyword INPUT is followed by one or more variable names. Variables are separated from each other by commas. For each INPUT statement, the computer prints a question mark prompt and pauses while the operator enters and transmits the expected number of data values. The transmitted data are retained in memory under the variable names. The values must be keyed in the order implied by the list of names. Also, the expected data type (numeric or alphanumeric) is implied by the names.

DEC, TRS-80, IBM/Microsoft Systems

General Format:
  line number INPUT #file number, variable name {, variable
  name . . . }

Example:

```
1620 INPUT #1, L, N, T$, N$, D, A
```

The keyword INPUT is followed by the file reference number
(buffer number) that appears in the associated OPEN statement.
A comma is coded next, followed by one or more variable
names in the order in which the fields appear in the input
record. The variable names are separated by commas.

Apple II System

General Formats:

  line number PRINT CHR$(4); "READ file name"
  line number INPUT variable name {, variable name . . . }

Examples:

```
1615 PRINT CHR$(4); "READ FUNMF"
1620 INPUT L, N, T$, N$, D, A
```

The PRINT statement identifies the file from which records will
be input and signifies that the subsequent INPUT statement will
read from this file. The INPUT statement lists the variable
names that will be associated with the input fields. The variable
names are listed in the order in which the fields appear.

INPUT LINE

General Format:

line number INPUT LINE #file number, string variable

line number LINE INPUT #file number, string variable

Examples:

```
1250 INPUT LINE #1, A$
```

```
1250 LINE INPUT #1, A$
```

All characters preceding (and sometimes including) the carriage return and line feed characters are input as a string. Field delimiters (commas) are input as part of the string. In some versions of BASIC, an extra set of carriage return/line feed characters may be appended to the set that is input. In such cases, when the string is rewritten to a file, an extra line will be written. Therefore, before the string is written, it is necessary to strip these characters from the string by using the MID$ function.

LET

General Format:

line number LET variable name = $\begin{bmatrix} \text{variable name} \\ \text{constant} \\ \text{expression} \end{bmatrix}$

The keyword LET is followed by the name of an area in memory where a value will be assigned (=). The content of another area in memory, a numeric or string constant, or the results of an arithmetic calculation can be retained in the variable.

Examples:

```
120 LET A = B
130 LET A$ = B$
```
The content of the area in memory named to the right of the equal sign is copied into the area named to the left of the equal sign. Then, both areas contain the same value.

```
210 LET A = 0
220 LET A = 3.5
230 LET A$ = "STRING"
```
The numeric or string constant appearing to the right of the equal sign is retained in the area named to the left of the equal sign.

```
310 LET A = B + C
320 LET A = B - C
330 LET A = B * C
340 LET A = B / C
350 LET A = A + 1
360 LET A = (B + C + D) / E
370 LET A = (B * (C - D)) - 5
```
The result of the arithmetic expression given to the right of the equal sign is assigned to the variable to the left of the equal sign. Arithmetic expressions are formed with variable names and/or numeric constants combined with arithmetic operators. The operators are + (add), − (subtract), * (multiply), and / (divide). Parentheses are used to control the order of computation. The computer clears parentheses from the innermost to the outermost set.

LSET

IBM, TRS-80, and PDP-11 Systems

LSET string variable = converted numeric variable

This statement moves a string that was converted with a CVT%$ or CVTF$ function to a field within a direct-access record. This movement prepares the string to be written (PUT) to a file. The statement left-margin justifies the value in the field.

OPEN (Sequential)

Digital Equipment Corporation (DEC) System

General Format:
line number OPEN "file name" $\begin{Bmatrix} \text{FOR INPUT} \\ \text{FOR OUTPUT} \end{Bmatrix}$ AS FILE #file num.

Example:

```
1280 OPEN "FUNMF" FOR OUTPUT AS FILE #1
```

The file name is supplied by the programmer, who keys from one to six alphabetic and numeric characters. The first character must be alphabetic. The file name must be enclosed in quotation marks. The optional phrases FOR INPUT or FOR OUTPUT may be coded. If neither phrase is used, the system will attempt to open the file for input. However, if the file does not exist yet, the system will open a new file to receive output. The phrase AS FILE # is followed by a file reference number. Any integer from 1 to 12 may be used.

Radio Shack TRS-80 System

General Format:

line number OPEN $\begin{Bmatrix} \text{"I"} \\ \text{"O"} \end{Bmatrix}$, buffer number, "file name"

Example:

```
1280 OPEN "O", 1, "FUNMF"
```

The mode "I", for input, or "O", for output, is used to open the file. The buffer number is used in a manner similar to the file reference number for the DEC system. The file name may contain one to eight characters. The first character must be a letter of the alphabet. The file name must be enclosed in quotation marks.

IBM/Microsoft System

General Format:
    line number OPEN "file name" $\begin{Bmatrix} \text{FOR INPUT} \\ \text{FOR OUTPUT} \end{Bmatrix}$ AS #file number

Example:

```
1280 OPEN "FUNMF" FOR OUTPUT AS #1
```

The file name may contain one to eight characters and must be enclosed in quotation marks. The file reference number associates the named file with a particular input or output statement.

Apple II System

General Format:
    line number PRINT CHR$(4); "OPEN file name"

Example:

```
1280 PRINT CHR$(4); "OPEN FUNMF"
```

This statement is used to open a file for either input or output. If a file does not exist for input, the system will open a new file for output. The file name may contain up to 30 characters. The first character must be alphabetic.

General Format:
    line # OPEN "filename" AS FILE #file number, [ORGANIZATION] RELATIVE,
        MAP mapname

Example:

```
100 OPEN "DAFILE" AS FILE #1, ORGANIZATION RELATIVE, MAP FORMAT1
```

The file name is the name assigned to the disk file. File number refers to the number that is referenced by subsequent GET, PUT, or UPDATE statements that are used for a particular disk record. Mapname is the name assigned to the associated MAP statement that presents the format for the direct-access record.

OPEN (2)
(Direct Access)

General Format:

line # MAP (mapname) variable name [= length] [variable name
  [= length]] . . .

Example:

```
100 MAP (FORMAT1) A$, B$=5, C, D, E$=20
```

The keyword MAP is followed by a name, enclosed in parentheses, assigned to the MAP statement. The name distinguishes
the statement from other MAP statements that might appear in
the program. Standard naming conventions apply. Then, one or
more variable names appear, separated by commas. These are
the field names assigned to string and numeric data. A default
length of 16 characters is used for strings. Blank spaces are
added as padding if fewer than 16 characters appear in the
field. The amount of space needed to store string variables can
be set by specifying the exact length of the field. This length
will usually be the length of the longest string expected for any
given field.

OPEN (3)
(Direct Access)

Apple II System

PRINT CHR$(4); "OPEN filename", Lrecord length

This statement opens a file as a direct-access file. The L
specification provides the total length of each fixed-length
record. To determine this length, count the number of
characters in the longest alphanumeric field and count each
digit and decimal point that make up the largest value within a
numeric field. Also, count the commas that separate the fields
and the carriage return character that appears at the end of the
record.

OPEN (4) (Direct Access)

DIRECT ACCESS STATEMENT—IBM/Microsoft

OPEN "filename" AS #file number LEN = record length

DIRECT ACCESS STATEMENT—TRS-80

OPEN "R", #file number, "filename", record length

This statement opens a file as a direct-access (relative) file. The file name is the name assigned to the disk file. The file number is the integer value that will be referenced by subsequent GET or PUT statements to input or output a record in the file. The LEN = specification provides the integer value of the total length, in characters (bytes), of each fixed-length record.

PRINT (1) (To Printer)

General Formats:
line number PRINT
line number PRINT "string"

Examples:

```
1330 PRINT
1340 PRINT "KEY THE DATA FIELDS INDICATED."
```

The keyword PRINT is followed by either (1) no additional specifications, which causes a blank line to be displayed, or (2) a string of printable characters enclosed in quotation marks. The string represents the literal value to be displayed.

General Format:

$$\text{line number PRINT} \left[\begin{array}{l} \text{string} \\ \text{variable name} \end{array} \right] \left[\left[\begin{array}{l} \text{,} \\ \text{;} \end{array} \right| \left[\begin{array}{l} \text{TAB(column number)} \\ \end{array} \right] \left[\begin{array}{l} \text{string} \\ \text{variable name} \end{array} \right] \right] \ldots \right\}$$

The keyword PRINT is followed by one or more strings and/or variable names, which are separated by the following specifications:

TAB This specification identifies the column number in which to print the variable data or string that follows the TAB.

Comma (,) This specification causes printing to begin in the next print zone.

Semicolon (;) This specification directs printing to continue in the next immediate column. In some versions of BASIC, a semicolon is not required to cause printing in the next column.

The IBM and TRS-80 systems use the LPRINT keyword instead of PRINT to direct output to an attached printer rather than to the CRT screen.

On Apple II computers, if the integer value refers to the printer interface card slot used, output is directed to an attached printer with the following command:

    line number PR #integer

Typically, slot #1 contains the printer interface card. This command must appear in the program prior to the first use of the associated PRINT statement. For example, the following statements will direct output of variables A, B, and C$ to the printer:

    220 PR #1
    230 PRINT A, B, C$

To return output to the CRT screen, the following command precedes a PRINT statement that directs printing to the screen:

    line number PR #0

The PR statement can direct output interchangeably between the CRT screen and printer.

```
                                                    PRINT
                                                  (To File)
```

DEC, TRS-80, IBM/Microsoft Systems

General Format:
line number PRINT #file number, variable name {;",";variable
name . . . }

Example:

```
1490 PRINT #1, L;",";N;",";T$;",";N$;",";D;",";A
```

The keyword PRINT is followed by the file reference number
(buffer number) that appeared in the associated OPEN statement. A comma is coded next. Thereafter, one or more variable
names are keyed in the order in which the fields are to appear
in the record. Field values are separated by commas. The
variable names and commas are separated by semicolons.

Apple II System

General Formats:
line number PRINT CHR$(4); "WRITE file name"
line number PRINT CHR$(4);variable name {;",";" variable
name . . . }
line number PRINT CHR$(4)

Examples:

```
1490 PRINT CHR$(4); "WRITE FUNMF"
1491 PRINT CHR$(4); L;",";N;",";T$;",";N$;",";
     D;",";A
1492 PRINT CHR$(4)
```

Three PRINT statements are required to write a record to a file.
The first statement indicates the file to which the record will be
written. The second provides the variable names that contain
the data for the record fields. The second statement also writes
commas between the fields. The third statement tells the computer to stop writing to the file so that subsequent PRINT
statements, which may be intended to display headings or
prompts, are not activated.

PRINT USING (1)

DEC, TRS-80, IBM/Microsoft Systems

General Format:
   line number PRINT USING variable name$ {, variable name . . . }

Examples:

```
1520 PRINT USING F1$
1760 PRINT USING F4$, L, N, T$, N$, D, A
```

The keywords PRINT USING are followed by the variable name that references the appropriate format string retained with the LET statement. The printing of heading lines does not require any additional specifications because the heading values are defined by the format itself. When data are printed according to the format, the variable name that references the format is followed by a comma and by one or more variable names of the areas in memory that contain the data. These variable names must be listed in the order in which they will be printed across the line.

IBM and TRS-80 Systems (with printers)

General Format:
   line number LPRINT USING variable name$ {, variable name . . . }

With the IBM and TRS-80 computers, the LPRINT USING statement is used to format the output to be printed. All other specifications are the same as those used with the PRINT USING statement that formats output to the CRT screen.

DEC System (alternate format)

General Format:
   line number PRINT USING line number {, variable name . . . . }

When an image statement is used to retain printing formats in memory, the PRINT USING statement includes the line number of the associated image statement (:).

PRINT USING (2)

DEC, TRS-80, IBM/Microsoft Systems

General Format:
line number LET variable name$ = string

Examples:

```
150 LET F1$ = "      MAIN HEADING"
170 LET F2$ = "COL.1       COL.2      COL.3"
210 LET F3$ = "###        !  \              \   ##,###.##"
340 LET F4$ = "TOTAL = $##,###.##"
```

The keyword LET is followed by the name of a string variable, an equal sign (=), and a character string enclosed in quotation marks. The string can include heading values and/or field editing symbols arranged to provide an image of a printed line. The string is assigned to (retained in) the variable and is available for use at any time during program execution.

Apple II System

The LET statement is valid for retaining character strings in memory. However, the strings cannot be used as printing formats because the Apple II does not recognize format images and does not have a PRINT USING statement.

PRINT USING (3)

General Format:
  line number: string

Examples:

```
1370:            LISTING OF MASTER FILE FUNMF
1400: ##     ### 'L    'LLLLLLLLLLLLLL    ###    ##,###
1420: TOTAL RECORDS: ##
```

The line number is followed by a colon (:) and by the character string that describes the image of the printed line. Alphanumeric fields are indicated by one or more L characters. The number of L characters used depends on the size of the field. The L string is preceded by an apostrophe ('). Numeric fields are described the same as in the LET statement.

PUT

General Format:

  line number PUT #file number, RECORD record number

Example:

```
100 PUT #1, RECORD N
```

This statement is used to write a record at the relative location given by the record number (N) in a direct-access file. The file number is the number assigned in the associated OPEN statement.

Apple II System

    PRINT CHR$(4); "READ filename,R"; record number
    INPUT variable name [, variable name] . . .

These statements input a record from a direct-access file. The record number refers to the location of the record, relative to the position of the first file record. The variable names are those of the fields that make up the record.

General Format:
    line number REM comments

Example:

1030 REM THIS PROGRAM CREATES A MASTER FILE

The keyword REM is followed by any combination of printable characters, including the blank (space) character. On some computer systems, an exclamation mark (!) or apostrophe (') can be used in place of the word REM. (See program code used in Chapters 9 through 11.)

General Format:
    line number STOP

Example:

1720 STOP

The keyword STOP appears on a line by itself, with no other specifications.

UPDATE

General Format:

line number UPDATE #file number

Example:

`100 UPDATE #1`

This statement is used to rewrite to a direct-access file the previous record accessed by a GET statement. The file number is the number that was assigned in the associated OPEN statement. The statement overwrites the record in the file with the current record in memory.

WRITE

Apple II System

PRINT CHR$(4); "WRITE filename,R"; record number
PRINT variable name [; "," variable name] . . .

These statements write a record to a direct-access file. The record number refers to the location of the record, relative to the position of the first file record. The variable names are those of the fields that make up the record.

GLOSSARY

A

access method Technique selected for locating data and making them available for processing.

accumulator An area within memory used to develop and retain totals of processing cycles or of amounts being computed.

ad hoc report *See* on-demand report.

alphanumeric data A character set that includes numeric digits, alphabetic characters, and other special symbols.

analysis A method of studying a programming requirement and devising a workable approach, typically by partitioning an overall problem into a series of smaller, solvable parts.

architectural structure In programming, the formal, logical portrayal of the relationships among processing modules within a system of programs.

arithmetic expression In BASIC, a combination of variable names and/or numeric constants with arithmetic operators that presents arithmetic functions for computer execution.

arithmetic operator In programming, a symbol that stands for an arithmetic calculation.

assignment statement An instruction that places a data value into a named area in memory.

audit trail A combination of source documents, files, and electronic logs that facilitates tracing a transaction from its source through all processing steps.

B

backup Alternative systems, procedures, methods, and data files that can be used to restore service in the event of system malfunctions or the loss of data resources.

backup file *See* backup.

batch A group of data records processed together at the same time.

batch balances *See* control totals.

branch To alter the normal sequential execution of program statements.

bubble In a data flow diagram, a circle that represents a processing activity, program, or manual procedure that transforms data.

bug Improperly written program command or logical error that produces an incorrect or unexpected output from the computer.

C

call *See* subroutine call.

carriage return key *See* transmit key.

case construct *See* selection.

central processing unit The part of a computer in which arithmetic and logical operations are performed.

code Instructions that implement a program in a language understandable to and executable by a computer.

coder A person who translates program designs into executable computer instructions.

coding The process of translating a set of computer processing specifications into a formal programming language.

computer information system (CIS) A coordinated collection of hardware, software, people, data, and support resources that performs an integrated series of functions that include input, processing, output, and storage.

computer program A set of detailed instructions establishing the sequence in which processing activities must be performed on data to produce desired results.

computer programmer A person who designs solutions to stated problems and writes sets of detailed instructions to implement the solutions.

computer system The collection of software and hardware integrated to input, process, and store programs and data, and to print or display programs and the results of processing.

condition test In a program, a comparison between two data items to determine whether one value is greater than, equal to, less than, not greater than, not equal to, or not less than the second value.

consecutive-spill A method used to handle synonyms by writing a record that hashes to an occupied position in the next available file position.

constant A value in a computer program that does not change during program execution.

control break Point during program processing at which some special processing event takes place. A control break usually is signalled by a change in the value of a control field within a data record.

control field A field in a data record used to identify and classify the record. *See also* record key.

control group Records in a file that share the same key value.

control statement A program command that establishes the logical sequence of processing operations.

control totals Accumulations of numeric data fields that are used to check on the accuracy of the input, processing, or output data. Also called batch balances.

cursor An indicator on a terminal screen that shows the point at which a keystroke will be displayed.

D

data Raw facts that have meaning and relate to people, things, and events.

data definition statement A statement that identifies data files to be processed.

data flow analysis In programming, the study of the movement of data into, within, and out of computer memory. In systems analysis, the study of the movement of data among processing activities.

data flow diagram (DFD) A graphic tool that portrays the flow of data through a system, identifies the files that are used, and designates the processing that takes place. Can show manual processing.

data processing system (DPS) The collection of hardware, software, data, people, and support resources designed to maintain data within files, report on their content, and facilitate the flow of work through an organization.

data store Files represented by open-ended rectangles in a data flow diagram.

database management system (DBMS) Software to integrate, manage, and control data resources.

debugging The process of finding and correcting improperly written

statements or logical errors in a program.

decision support system (DSS) A type of computer information system that assists managers and executives in formulating policies and plans by projecting the likely consequences of decisions.

delimiter A symbol used to distinguish data items or data fields as separate entities.

detail line A line of information within a detail report that usually corresponds with the data fields contained in a single file record.

detail modules In a top-down program design, the modules that carry out the actual program processing under control of executive modules.

detail report Report that presents one line of output for each record in a file.

dimension Procedure for allocating sufficient table positions to hold the data values to be placed in a program table.

direct access Method of reading and writing specific records without processing all preceding records in a file.

direct-access file A file in which the location of each record is given by its position relative to the first record in the file. Also called a relative file.

distribution of control *See* top-down design.

division/remainder method A method of calculating file storage locations by first dividing the numeric key of a record by the number of positions required for the file and then adding 1 to the remainder to derive the location value.

documentation Written explanations of the development, design, coding, and operation of a program or system.

documentation statement In BASIC, a non-executable statement within a program. Used as a note of explanation to the program reader to facilitate understanding.

dummy record *See* null record.

E

echo Display of characters on a terminal output device as they are being keyed.

edit report A report that lists the content of a file and prints an error message for each field of data that is invalid.

edit run The practice of checking a transaction file, often against master file records, to locate and flag erroneous data.

editing symbols Special characters used to represent field formats for printing of report lines.

end-of-file (EOF) record A record that marks the final item in a file. Created so that programs accessing the file subsequently can determine the point at which all records have been input.

entry key *See* transmit key.

exception An unexpected or irregular development in an organization's operations.

exception report A management report produced to highlight business conditions that are outside the range defined as normal.

executive control module In a top-down program design, a module that provides all or part of the overall control logic for the program.

extended variable name A variable name that allows for the use of up to 30 or more alphabetic and numeric characters.

F

field A single item of data, usually part of a record that is located on an input, output, or storage medium.

file A repository for data and information. A collection of data records organized on a storage medium in compliance with an established access method.

file access technique The method used to retrieve records on storage media.

file creation program A program used to build original master or transaction files.

file inquiry User capability to access records in computer files through entries into terminals.

file maintenance The process of changing, correcting, or deleting information in files. *See also* file updating program.

file organization A method, or scheme, for arranging records for access and file maintenance.

file updating program Program used to post transaction data to master files or to maintain master files through record additions, changes, or deletions.

fixed-length file A file containing records that are uniform in length.

flag In programming, a data item used to signal the occurrence of an expected event or special condition that arises during processing.

footing The final section of an output report, containing accumulated totals for numeric fields or other types of summary information.

format The physical arrangement of data characters, fields, records, and files.

G

generation *See* processing cycle.

H

hard copy Document printed or written on paper. Denotes distinction between paper documents and non-printed displays.

hardware Physical computer equipment. Can include the processor unit, input units, output units, storage units, and other peripherals.

hash total The summation of values within nonsignificant data fields such as key fields and identification number fields. Used as a batch control.

hashing function A program routine that performs arithmetic calculations on numeric keys, converting those keys to a range of values that equate directly to relative file locations. *See also* division/remainder method.

heading Report identification information presented in the topmost lines of an output report. Includes the report title.

hierarchy A top-down, multilevel organizational scheme. In program design, a structure in which components of problems, systems, or programs are layered in a top-to-bottom, general-to-detail fashion.

hierarchy chart *See* structure chart.

home position The file location to which a record hashes.

I

image A formatted pictorial representation used to guide computer printing of reports.

indexed file A file in which tables that equate record keys with file locations are used as references to relative addresses.

indexed-sequential File organization method in which records are maintained in logical sequence and indexes, or tables, are used to reference their storage addresses. This method allows both serial and direct access to records.

information system *See* computer information system.

input unit Equipment used to enter programs and data into a computer.

inquiry program *See* file inquiry.

interactive processing Processing method under which a user intervenes during program execution, providing input as required by the problem. Also called menu-driven.

intermediate control break   An interruption in the normal printing of report lines to list totals that fall between the major and minor levels.

iteration   *See* repetition.

L

line number   In BASIC, a sequential number preceding each statement within program code.

log file   A sequential record of transactions handled by a computer system. Maintained separately from the master files against which transactions are processed.

logical control structure   A construct within a program. Can encompass sequences, repetitions, and selections.

logical end   The point at which program processing ends, which is not necessarily the physical end of the program.

logical error   Programming error that causes the wrong processing to take place even though the program is syntactically correct.

logical operator   A symbol that stands for a comparison operation between two data values.

logical solution   A sequence of processing steps designed to solve a programming problem.

loop   *See* repetition.

M

machine-dependent   In programming, processing operations that are restricted in use to certain computer systems.

mainline program   The section of a program, usually the top-level module, that controls the order of execution of other modules in the program.

maintenance   *See* file maintenance.

maintenance program   A program used to keep master files complete and up-to-date through the processing of transactions. *See also* file updating program.

major control break   An interruption in the normal printing of report lines to list major level totals.

management by exception   Management method that concentrates on correcting out-of-control or undesirable business situations.

management information system (MIS)   Type of computer information system that provides information to support monitoring of business operations by reporting selected conditions on the basis of data content to draw attention to situations requiring corrective action.

master file   A file containing permanent or semipermanent information that reflects the status of a business or business segment at a given time.

memory   Area within a computer in which programs and data reside temporarily during processing.

menu   A list of processing options displayed to the user on a CRT.

menu-driven *See* interactive processing.

merge A function that combines two files of sequentially ordered records into a single file in which the sequence is maintained.

minor control break An interruption in the normal printing of report lines to list the lowest level of report totals.

module A system component representing a processing function that will be carried out by a computer.

N

new master file An updated master file or the output of file maintenance.

null character A special character whose meaning is undefined.

null record A record that contains only spaces and/or zeros in its fields.

numeric data Character set that includes the decimal digits 0–9 and, optionally, a sign symbol and decimal point.

O

old master file An existing file containing records to be updated with additions, changes, and deletions. Retained as backup following updating.

on-demand report A report that is not produced on a regular schedule, but is produced when needed for some special purpose. Also called an ad-hoc report.

on-line processing Data processing accomplished by use of devices attached or wired directly to a computer. On-line processing equipment provides immediate, direct communication between a terminal and the central processing unit.

operating system The sets of programs and other software routines that monitor and operate the computer hardware to facilitate its use. A form of systems software.

operational level The level of management supported by data processing systems.

output unit Unit of equipment used to print or display programs and the results of processing. Also includes devices that present data as communication signals or audio messages.

P

partitioning In programming, the decomposition of a problem into its component parts in a top-down, hierarchical fashion. In processing, the setting up of separate memory areas to hold multiple programs and sets of data records. *See also* analysis.

physical end The actual end of a program as indicated by the END statement in BASIC.

planning level The management level aided by decision support systems.

pointer Record key used to indicate the relative position of a record in a direct-access file. Used in chaining references among records.

posting program A program used to update master files with transactions that result from normal, day-to-day business operations. *See also* file up-dating program.

prime number   A number evenly divisible only by itself and 1.

primitive   Arithmetic or logical opera-tion performed on data by a computer. Refers to the limited specific functions that can be executed by computers.

print zone   A fixed-length area on an output device within which data are aligned in columns.

processing cycle   The length of time between key events in a company's operations. Often used to establish fre-quency of execution of posting and maintenance programs.

processing statement   Statement that instructs a computer to perform data manipulation operations.

processor unit   The hardware unit encompassing memory and the central processing unit.

program structure   The underlying logic of the arrangement of and rela-tionships among modules within a program.

programmer/analyst   Person who analyzes processing requirements, then designs systems and writes programs to implement the systems.

programming language   Language with special syntax and style conven-tions for coding computer programs. BASIC is one of many such languages.

programming specifications   Nar-rative descriptions of input, processing, output, and storage requirements for a program.

prompt   Message displayed by a com-puter to request data or require an operator action.

pseudocode   A detailed specification of a program given in a series of stylized English statements representing the actual instructions that will form a final computer program. Makes possible detailed analysis of processing design before code is written.

R

random access   Disk access tech-nique under which records can be read from and written directly to disk media without regard to the order of their record keys.

randomizing   *See* hashing function.

record   Collection of data fields per-taining to a particular person, entity, or event.

record key   Control field within a record that identifies the record uniquely or classifies it as a member of a category of records within a file.

relational operator   A symbol that stands for a comparison operation be-tween two data values.

relative file   *See* direct-access file.

remarks statement   In BASIC, a line of nonexecutable documentation in program code. Used to describe the program to readers of code.

repetition   Repeated executions of program statements or modules until a signal is presented to cause a halt to the activity. Also called an iteration or loop.

report title Describes the purpose of an output report and/or the type of information the report contains.

report writing program A program that accesses information from files and communicates the information in the form of hard-copy or displayed outputs.

S

scheduled report A report issued at regular, periodic intervals—yearly, monthly, daily, or even more frequently. The reporting period depends on the nature of the report.

selection A program control structure in which one of two alternative processing paths is taken in reaction to a condition test. Also called a case construct.

sequence Program control structure in which statements are executed in the physical order in which they appear in the program.

sequential access A method of access in which records are brought into memory in order of their keys.

sequential file organization The arrangement of records in a physical order that corresponds with their logical (key) values.

serial file A file that contains records written in the physical order in which they are captured.

software Collection of programs that controls computer equipment and directs processing of applications.

sort To arrange data records into ascending or descending numeric or alphabetic sequence.

source document Form used for initial recording of data prior to system input.

statement In programming, a single command that directs the computer to carry out a processing operation.

status code A field value within a record that indicates whether the record area within the file contains data or is unoccupied.

storage unit Device used for long-term retention of programs and data within the computer system.

string One or more literal alphanumeric values defined in a computer program and used, exactly as defined, as a constant during processing or output.

structure chart System and program design tool for documenting the organization of program modules and the control logic that relates them to one another. Also known as a hierarchy chart.

subroutine A block of code that can be called up and executed at any time from any point in a program.

subroutine call In processing, a set of coded instructions that direct the computer to branch from the mainline portion of a program to a portion that can be activated repeatedly as needed.

subscript A value used to reference an item of data stored in a table.

substring A portion of a character string.

summary report A report that minimizes the content of reports by presenting totals for groups, or categories, of data items rather than listing all records in a file.

synonym In processing, a record that has a duplicate file address value.

syntactical error Condition that occurs in a program when a programmer violates the grammatical rules of the programming language.

synthesis The organization of analyzed programming subproblems into an integrated whole that can be implemented on a computer. *See also* analysis.

system flowchart Graphic representation of a system, showing flow of control in computer processing at the individual job level.

system of programs Programs that are organized to work together to implement a major processing job or application.

systems analyst A person who studies information requirements and prepares a set of functional specifications that identify what a new or replacement system should accomplish and that serve as a basis for designing and developing the system.

systems perspective A way of viewing programs as integrated parts of a larger, overall computer information system rather than as pieces of software that function independently.

T

table In programming, an area of memory containing multiple locations, all referenced by the same name, for holding or retaining data.

testing Activity of running a program with test data or operating a system to see if it meets processing specifications.

top-down design Process of designing a system or program through decomposition of functions into successive levels of detail beginning with the top-level module, which represents the general system or program function as a whole, through to lower-level modules that perform actual processing.

transaction An act of doing business.

transaction file File used for recording day-to-day business activity and for updating master files with new information.

transaction processing Procedures that implement the processing of transactions as they occur rather than in batches.

transformation Any function or step that processes data to create information.

transmit key On a terminal keyboard, the key used to execute commands and enter program lines into the computer. Also called the carriage return or entry key.

U

updating File processing activity in which master records are modified through posting of transactions. New or altered master files then reflect current business status.

users People who need and use the information produced by computer systems. Operators of terminals connected to on-line computer systems.

utility program Systems service program that performs a common data processing task, such as sorting a file, merging files, or copying a file from one medium to another.

V

variable In BASIC programming, a name that stands for a memory location at which a data value is retained.

Z

zero balancing The practice of resetting balance fields within master records to zero so that the accumulation of totals for the next processing cycle can begin.

INDEX

Page numbers in *italics* refer to figures in text.